THE ADVENTURE ZONE
The Crystal Kingdom

THE ADVENTURE ZONE

The Crystal Kingdom

Based on the podcast by

Griffin McElroy   Clint McElroy

Travis McElroy   Justin McElroy

Adaptation by

Clint McElroy   Carey Pietsch

Art by

Carey Pietsch

:01

First Second

New York

First Second

Text © 2021 by Clint McElroy, Griffin McElroy, Justin McElroy, Travis McElroy
Illustrations © 2021 by Carey Pietsch

Letterer: Tess Stone
Flatters: Ensley Chau, Leigh Davis, Sara Goetter, Aliza Layne, Natalie Riess, Cassandra Tassoni
Inking Assistants: Hannah Krieger, Liz Fleming, Eric Lide, Niki Smith, Tess Stone
Authenticity Reader: Ryan Douglass
Goldcliff map photo © 2021 by Laura Berry and Lisa Aurigemma
Fan art gallery © 2021 by (respectively):
Alice Valerie
Arkko
Arthur Janecek
Izel Guadalupe Tamayo
Jocelyn James
Virginia Lee
Katarzyna Madej
Kelenia
L. S. Tee
Michael Pounds
Kezia Tubbs
Rachel Geiger
Rebecca Mock
Sara Ford
Shannon Bennion
T Zysk
Miles Lazarus

Published by First Second
First Second is an imprint of Roaring Brook Press,
a division of Holtzbrinck Publishing Holdings Limited Partnership
120 Broadway, New York, NY 10271

Don't miss your next favorite book from First Second!
For the latest updates go to firstsecondnewsletter.com and sign up for our newsletter.

Library of Congress Control Number: 2020919562
Hardcover ISBN: 978-1-250-23266-3
Paperback ISBN: 978-1-250-23265-6
Special Edition ISBN: 978-1-250-81094-6
Special Edition ISBN: 978-1-250-81095-3
Special Edition ISBN: 978-1-250-81096-0

Our books may be purchased in bulk for promotional, educational, or business use.
Please contact your local bookseller or the Macmillan Corporate and Premium Sales Department
at (800) 221-7945 ext. 5442 or by email at MacmillanSpecialMarkets@macmillan.com.

First edition, 2021
Edited by Calista Brill and Alison Wilgus
Cover design by Kirk Benshoff and Carey Pietsch
Series design by Andrew Arnold
Interior book design by Molly Johanson
Printed in China by 1010 Printing International Limited, North Point, Hong Kong

Penciled with a 2B pencil-style tool in Procreate. Inked with a brush-style digital nib
in Clip Studio Paint and colored digitally in Photoshop.

Paperback: 10 9 8 7 6 5 4 3 2 1
Hardcover: 10 9 8 7 6 5 4 3 2 1

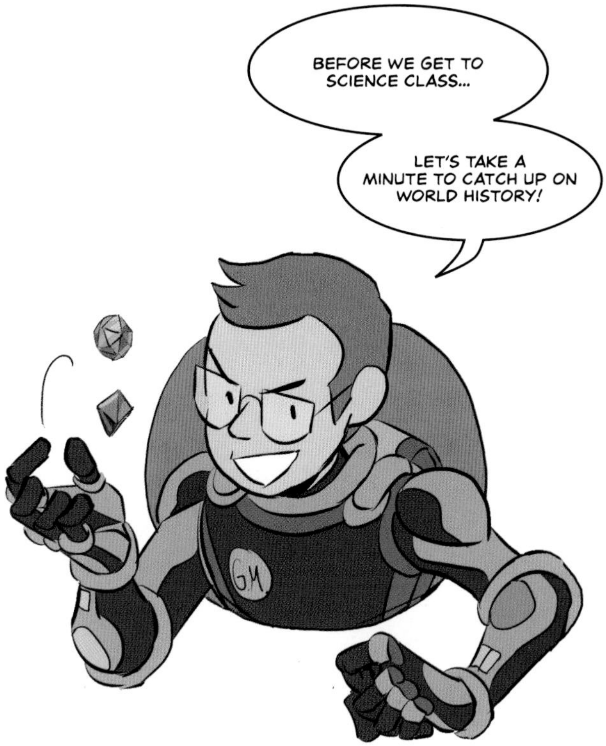
BEFORE WE GET TO SCIENCE CLASS...
LET'S TAKE A MINUTE TO CATCH UP ON WORLD HISTORY!
G.M.

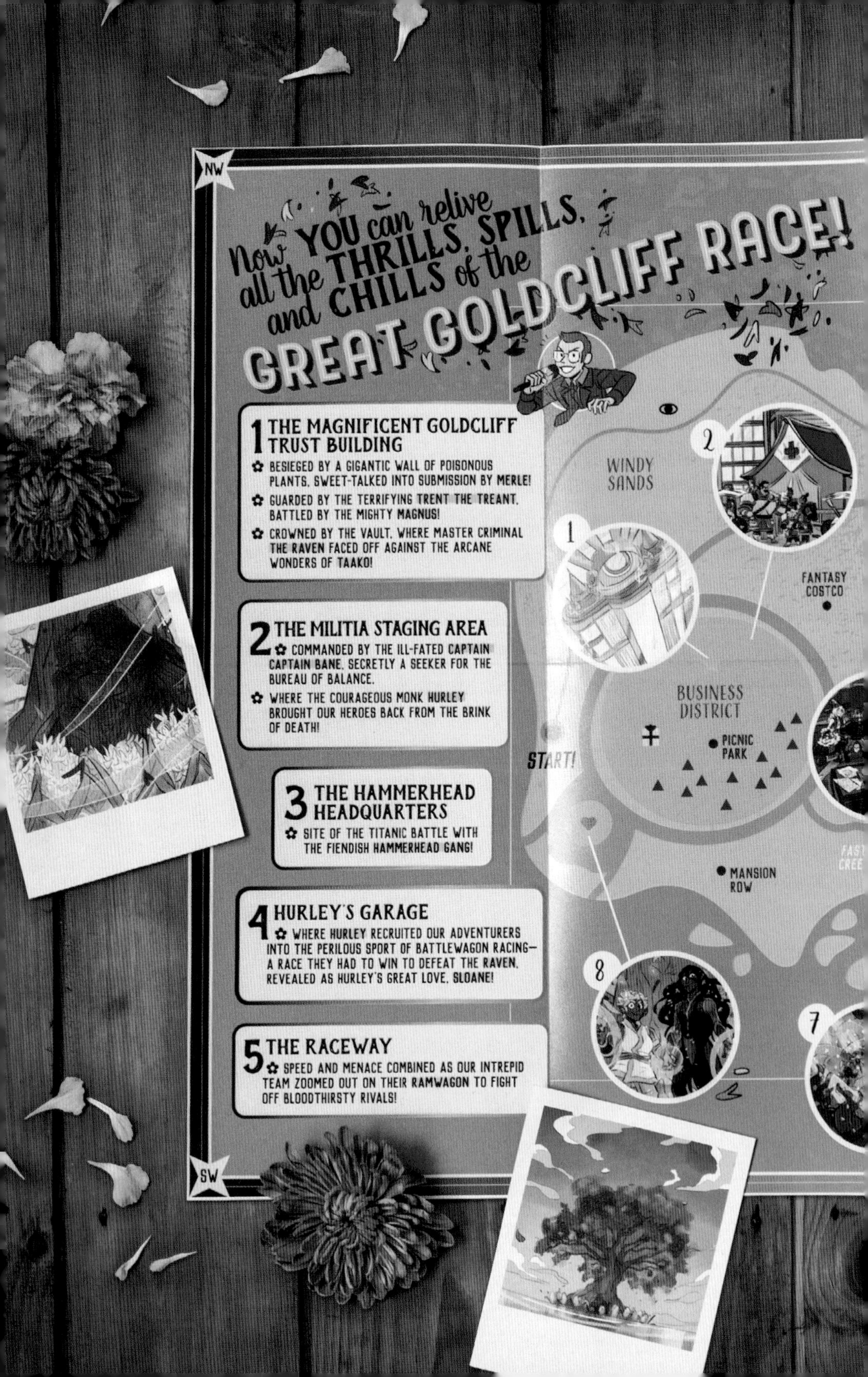
NW
Now YOU can relive all the THRILLS, SPILLS, and CHILLS of the
GREAT GOLDCLIFF RACE!
1 THE MAGNIFICENT GOLDCLIFF TRUST BUILDING
BESIEGED BY A GIGANTIC WALL OF POISONOUS PLANTS, SWEET-TALKED INTO SUBMISSION BY MERLE!
GUARDED BY THE TERRIFYING TRENT THE TREANT, BATTLED BY THE MIGHTY MAGNUS!
CROWNED BY THE VAULT, WHERE MASTER CRIMINAL THE RAVEN FACED OFF AGAINST THE ARCANE WONDERS OF TAAKO!
2 THE MILITIA STAGING AREA
COMMANDED BY THE ILL-FATED CAPTAIN CAPTAIN BANE, SECRETLY A SEEKER FOR THE BUREAU OF BALANCE.
WHERE THE COURAGEOUS MONK HURLEY BROUGHT OUR HEROES BACK FROM THE BRINK OF DEATH!
3 THE HAMMERHEAD HEADQUARTERS
SITE OF THE TITANIC BATTLE WITH THE FIENDISH HAMMERHEAD GANG!
4 HURLEY'S GARAGE
WHERE HURLEY RECRUITED OUR ADVENTURERS INTO THE PERILOUS SPORT OF BATTLEWAGON RACING—A RACE THEY HAD TO WIN TO DEFEAT THE RAVEN, REVEALED AS HURLEY'S GREAT LOVE, SLOANE!
5 THE RACEWAY
SPEED AND MENACE COMBINED AS OUR INTREPID TEAM ZOOMED OUT ON THEIR RAMWAGON TO FIGHT OFF BLOODTHIRSTY RIVALS!
SW
WINDY SANDS
2
1
FANTASY COSTCO
BUSINESS DISTRICT
PICNIC PARK
START!
MANSION ROW
8
7

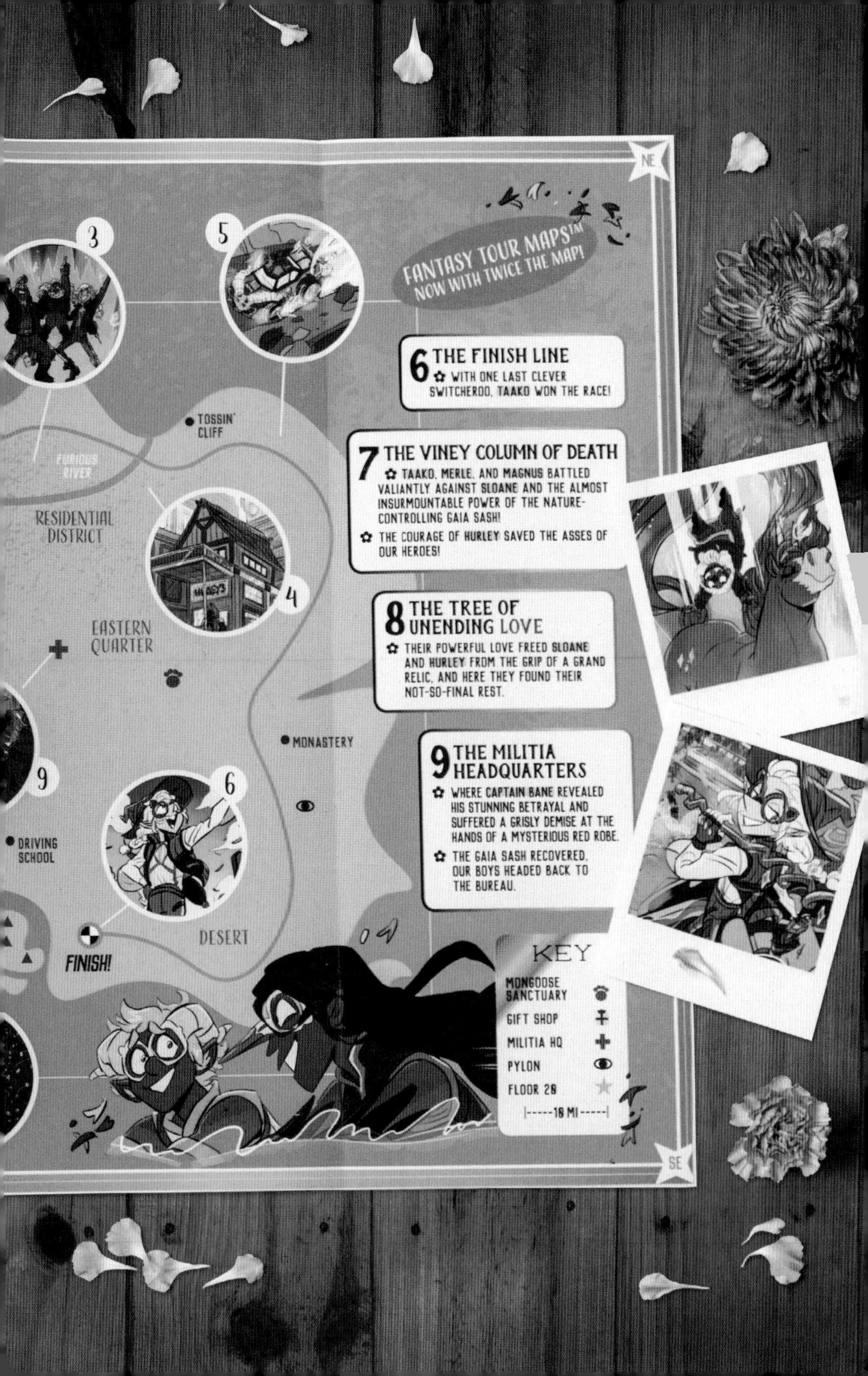

3
5
FANTASY TOUR MAPS™
NOW WITH TWICE THE MAP!
6 THE FINISH LINE
WITH ONE LAST CLEVER SWITCHEROO, TAAKO WON THE RACE!
TOSSIN' CLIFF
FURIOUS RIVER
7 THE VINEY COLUMN OF DEATH
TAAKO, MERLE, AND MAGNUS BATTLED VALIANTLY AGAINST SLOANE AND THE ALMOST INSURMOUNTABLE POWER OF THE NATURE-CONTROLLING GAIA SASH!
THE COURAGE OF HURLEY SAVED THE ASSES OF OUR HEROES!
RESIDENTIAL DISTRICT
4
EASTERN QUARTER
8 THE TREE OF UNENDING LOVE
THEIR POWERFUL LOVE FREED SLOANE AND HURLEY FROM THE GRIP OF A GRAND RELIC, AND HERE THEY FOUND THEIR NOT-SO-FINAL REST.
MONASTERY
9 THE MILITIA HEADQUARTERS
WHERE CAPTAIN BANE REVEALED HIS STUNNING BETRAYAL AND SUFFERED A GRISLY DEMISE AT THE HANDS OF A MYSTERIOUS RED ROBE.
THE GAIA SASH RECOVERED, OUR BOYS HEADED BACK TO THE BUREAU.
9
6
DRIVING SCHOOL
DESERT
FINISH!
KEY
MONGOOSE SANCTUARY
GIFT SHOP
MILITIA HQ
PYLON
FLOOR 28
|-----10 MI-----|
NE
SE

Chapter
1

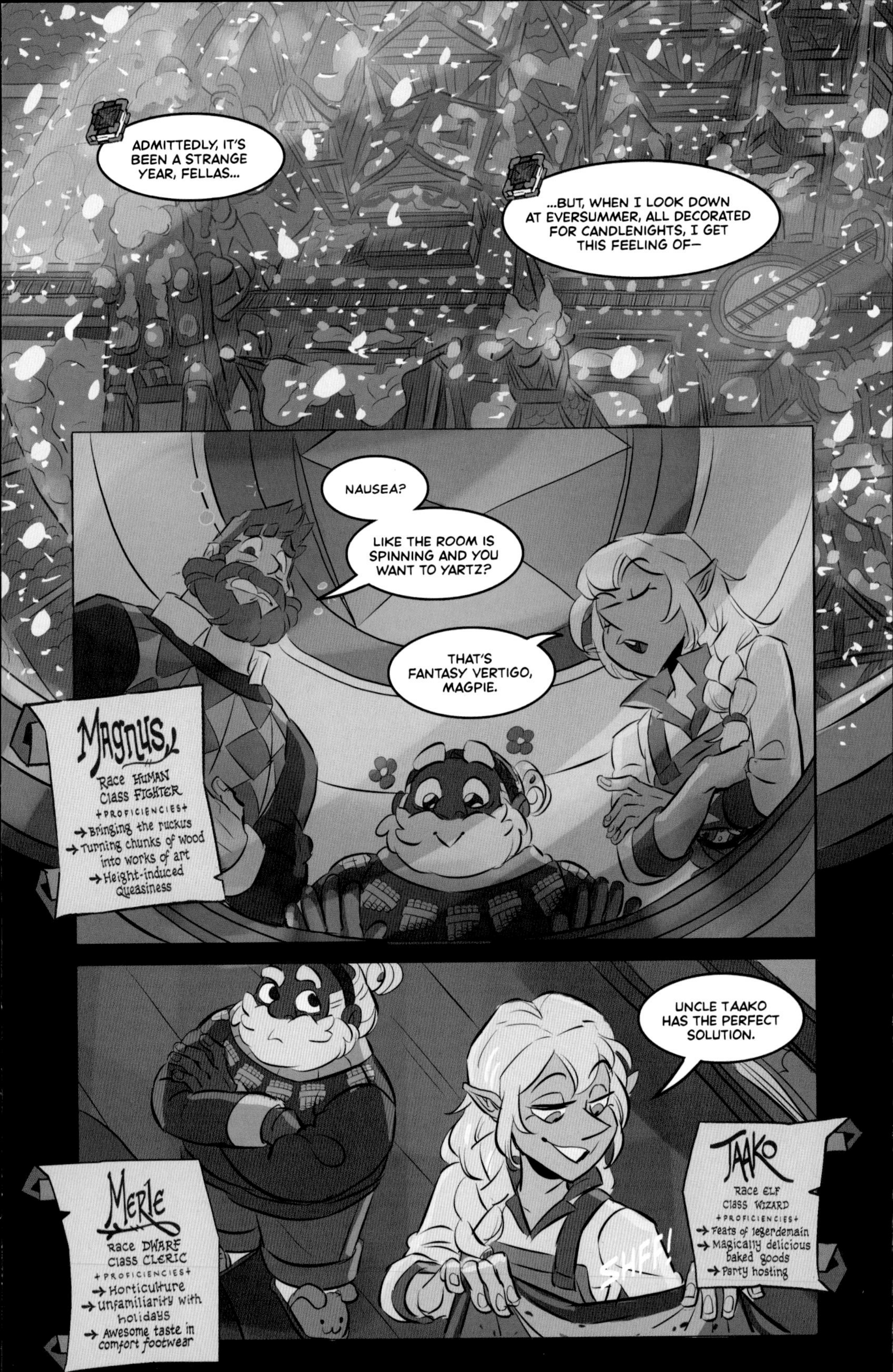
ADMITTEDLY, IT'S BEEN A STRANGE YEAR, FELLAS...
...BUT, WHEN I LOOK DOWN AT EVERSUMMER, ALL DECORATED FOR CANDLENIGHTS, I GET THIS FEELING OF—
NAUSEA?
LIKE THE ROOM IS SPINNING AND YOU WANT TO YARTZ?
THAT'S FANTASY VERTIGO, MAGPIE.
Magnus
Race HUMAN
Class FIGHTER
PROFICIENCIES
→ Bringing the ruckus
→ Turning chunks of wood into works of art
→ Height-induced Queasiness
UNCLE TAAKO HAS THE PERFECT SOLUTION.
Merle
Race DWARF
Class CLERIC
PROFICIENCIES
→ Horticulture
→ Unfamiliarity with holidays
→ Awesome taste in comfort footwear
SHFF!
TAAKO
Race ELF
Class WIZARD
PROFICIENCIES
→ Feats of legerdemain
→ Magically delicious baked goods
→ Party hosting

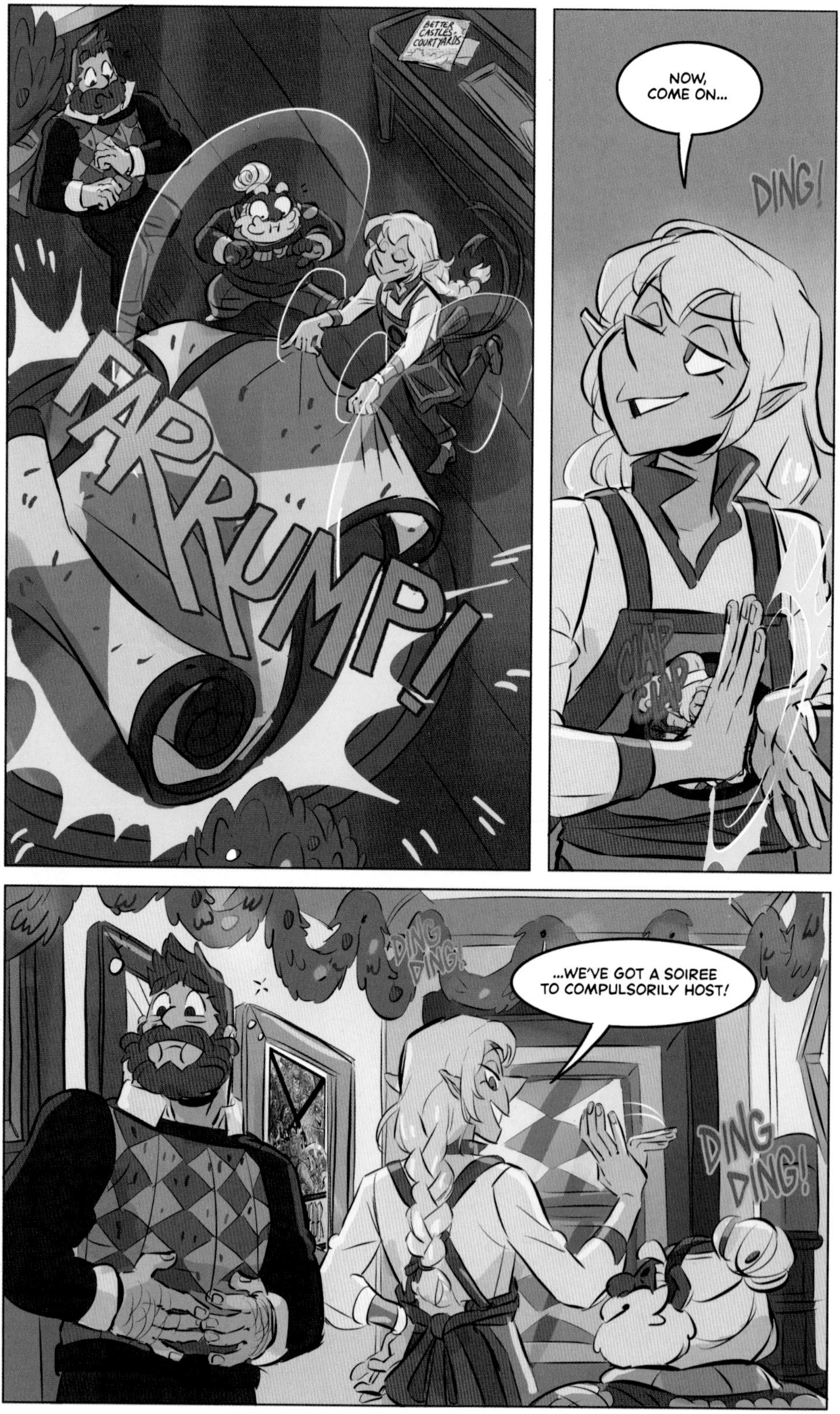
BETTER CASTLES, COURTYARDS
FARRUMP!
NOW, COME ON...
DING!
CLAP CLAP
DING DING!
...WE'VE GOT A SOIREE TO COMPULSORILY HOST!
DING DING!

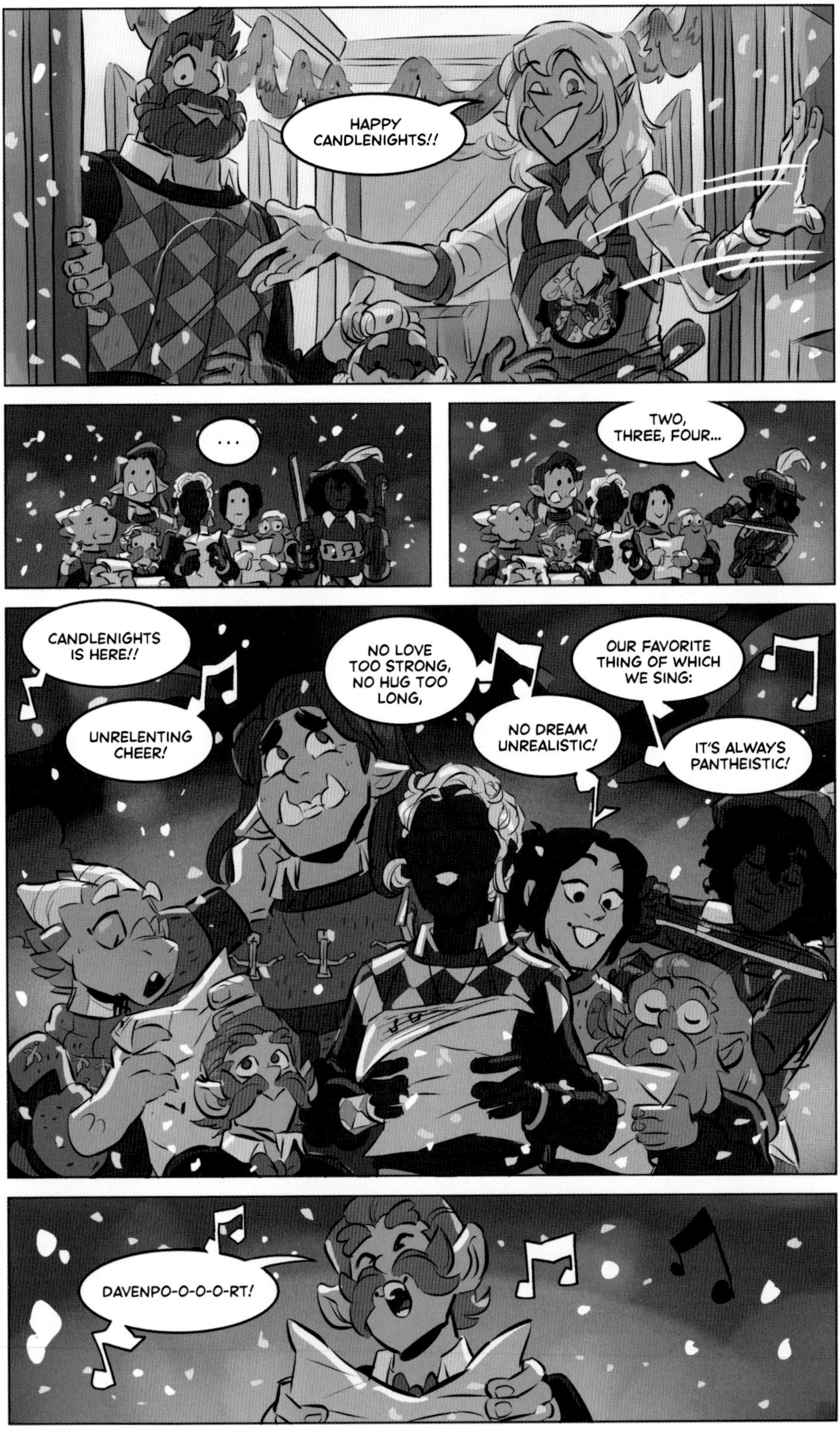
HAPPY CANDLENIGHTS!!
...
TWO, THREE, FOUR...
CANDLENIGHTS IS HERE!!
UNRELENTING CHEER!
NO LOVE TOO STRONG, NO HUG TOO LONG,
NO DREAM UNREALISTIC!
OUR FAVORITE THING OF WHICH WE SING:
IT'S ALWAYS PANTHEISTIC!
DAVENPO-O-O-O-RT!

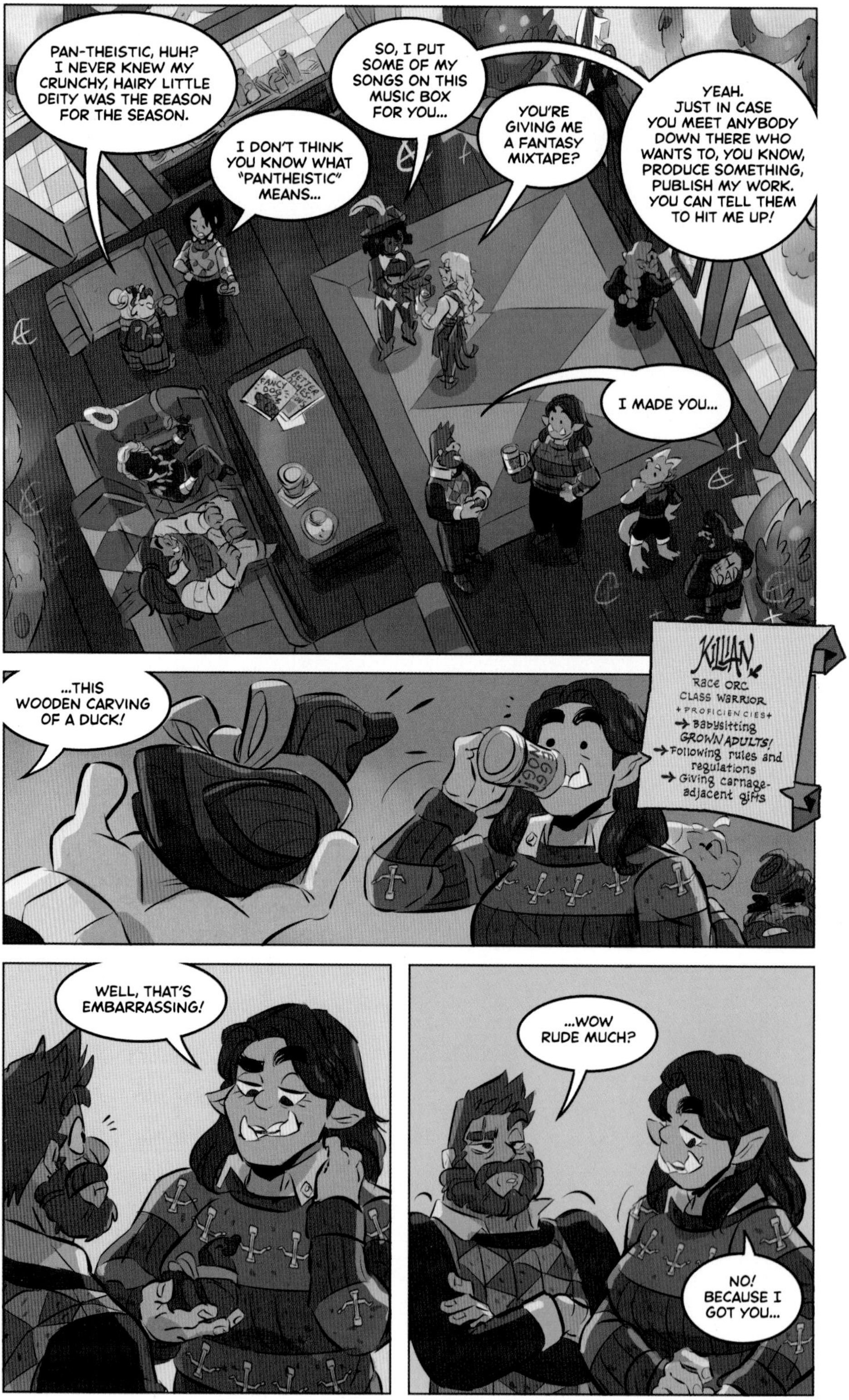
PAN-THEISTIC, HUH? I NEVER KNEW MY CRUNCHY, HAIRY LITTLE DEITY WAS THE REASON FOR THE SEASON.
I DON'T THINK YOU KNOW WHAT "PANTHEISTIC" MEANS...
SO, I PUT SOME OF MY SONGS ON THIS MUSIC BOX FOR YOU...
YOU'RE GIVING ME A FANTASY MIXTAPE?
YEAH. JUST IN CASE YOU MEET ANYBODY DOWN THERE WHO WANTS TO, YOU KNOW, PRODUCE SOMETHING, PUBLISH MY WORK. YOU CAN TELL THEM TO HIT ME UP!
I MADE YOU...
...THIS WOODEN CARVING OF A DUCK!
KILLIAN
Race ORC
CLASS WARRIOR
+PROFICIENCIES+
→ Babysitting GROWN ADULTS!
→ Following rules and regulations
→ Giving carnage-adjacent gifts
WELL, THAT'S EMBARRASSING!
...WOW RUDE MUCH?
NO! BECAUSE I GOT YOU...

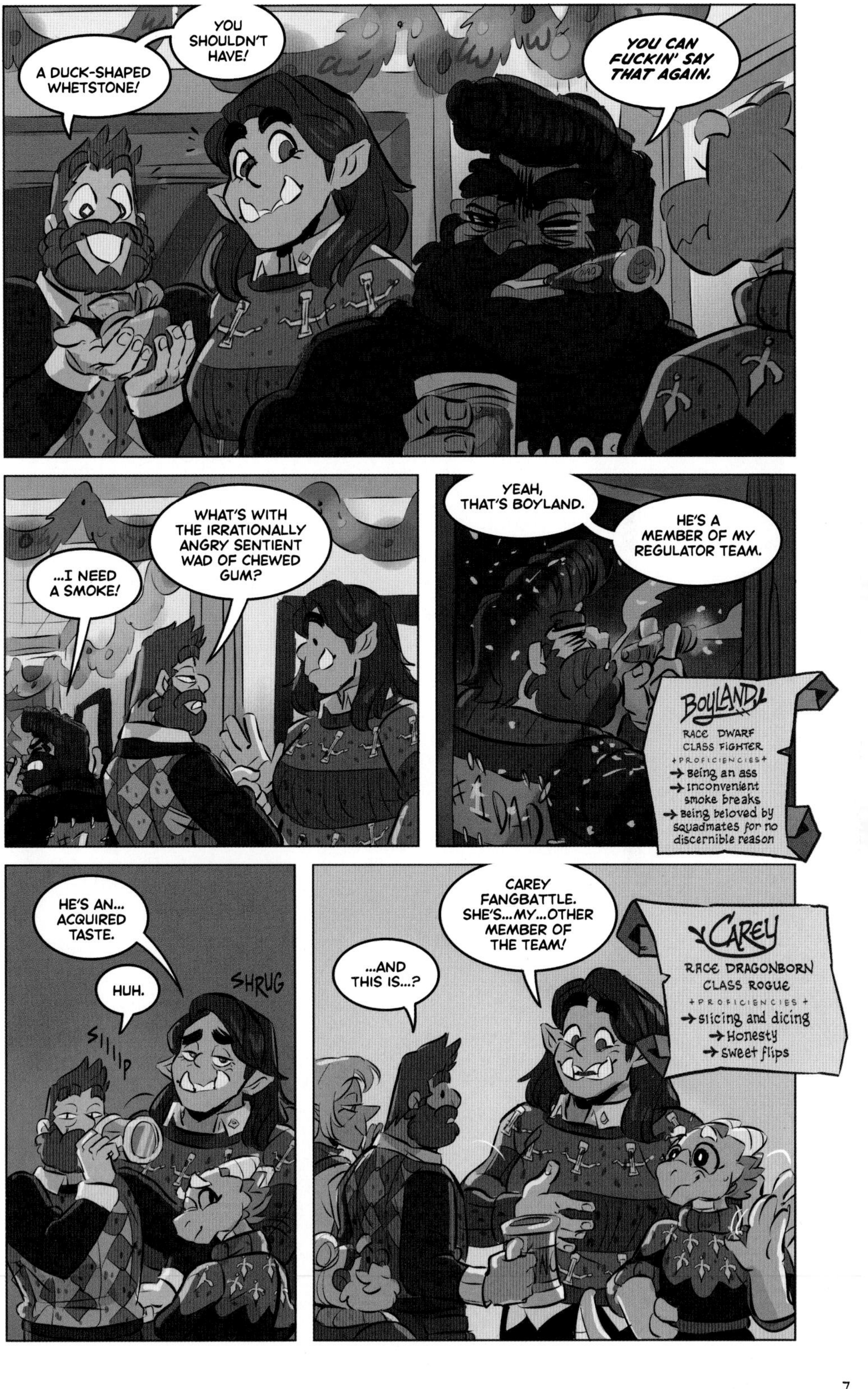

A DUCK-SHAPED WHETSTONE!
YOU SHOULDN'T HAVE!
YOU CAN FUCKIN' SAY THAT AGAIN.
WHAT'S WITH THE IRRATIONALLY ANGRY SENTIENT WAD OF CHEWED GUM?
...I NEED A SMOKE!
YEAH, THAT'S BOYLAND.
HE'S A MEMBER OF MY REGULATOR TEAM.
BOYLAND
RACE DWARF
CLASS FIGHTER
PROFICIENCIES
→ Being an ass
→ inconvenient smoke breaks
→ Being beloved by squadmates for no discernible reason
HE'S AN... ACQUIRED TASTE.
HUH.
SHRUG
SIIIIP
...AND THIS IS...?
CAREY FANGBATTLE. SHE'S...MY...OTHER MEMBER OF THE TEAM!
CAREY
RACE DRAGONBORN
CLASS ROGUE
PROFICIENCIES
→ slicing and dicing
→ Honesty
→ sweet flips

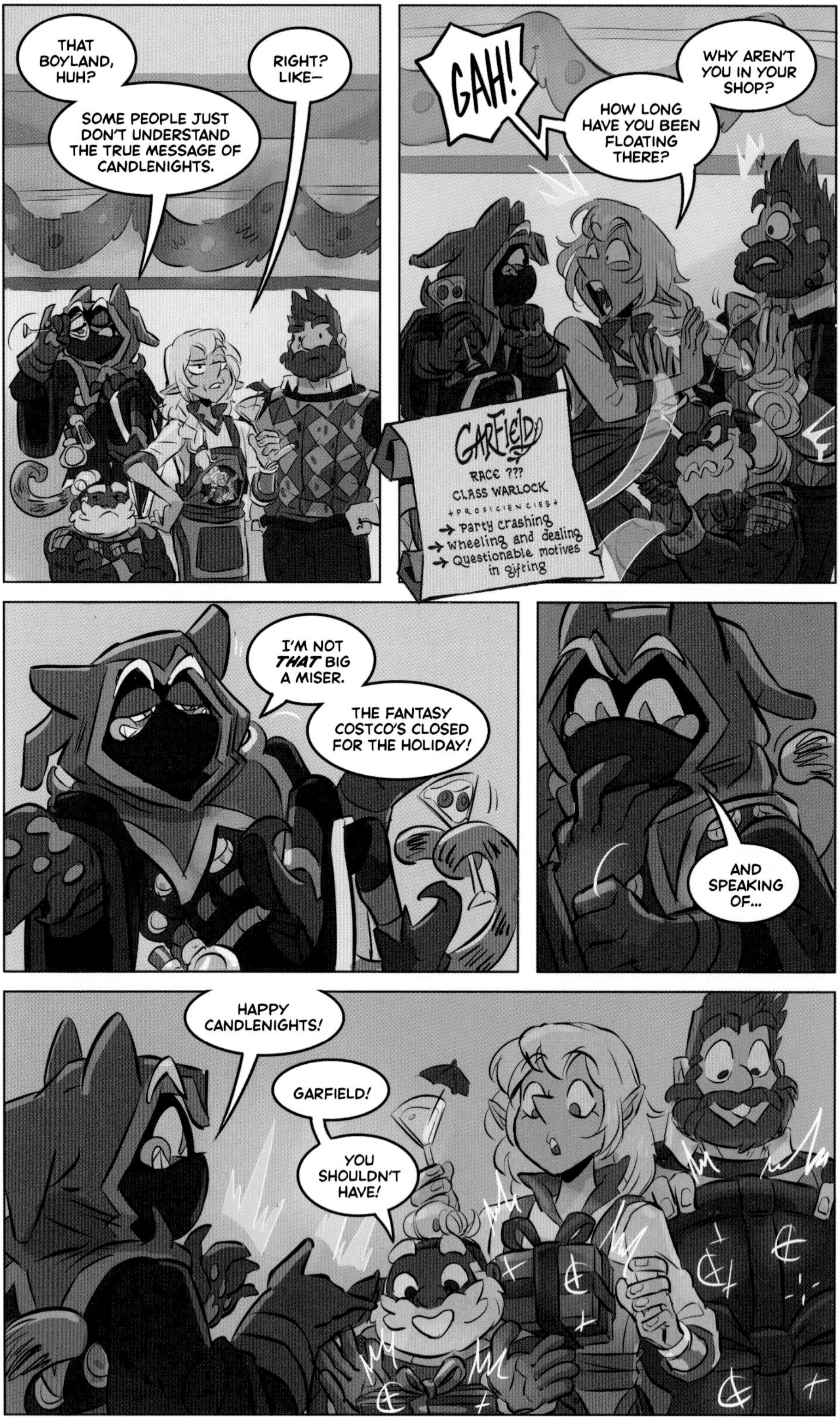
THAT BOYLAND, HUH?
SOME PEOPLE JUST DON'T UNDERSTAND THE TRUE MESSAGE OF CANDLENIGHTS.
RIGHT? LIKE—
GAH!
HOW LONG HAVE YOU BEEN FLOATING THERE?
WHY AREN'T YOU IN YOUR SHOP?
GARFIELD
RACE ???
CLASS WARLOCK
+PROFICIENCIES+
→ Party crashing
→ Wheeling and dealing
→ Questionable motives in gifting
I'M NOT *THAT* BIG A MISER.
THE FANTASY COSTCO'S CLOSED FOR THE HOLIDAY!
AND SPEAKING OF...
HAPPY CANDLENIGHTS!
GARFIELD!
YOU SHOULDN'T HAVE!

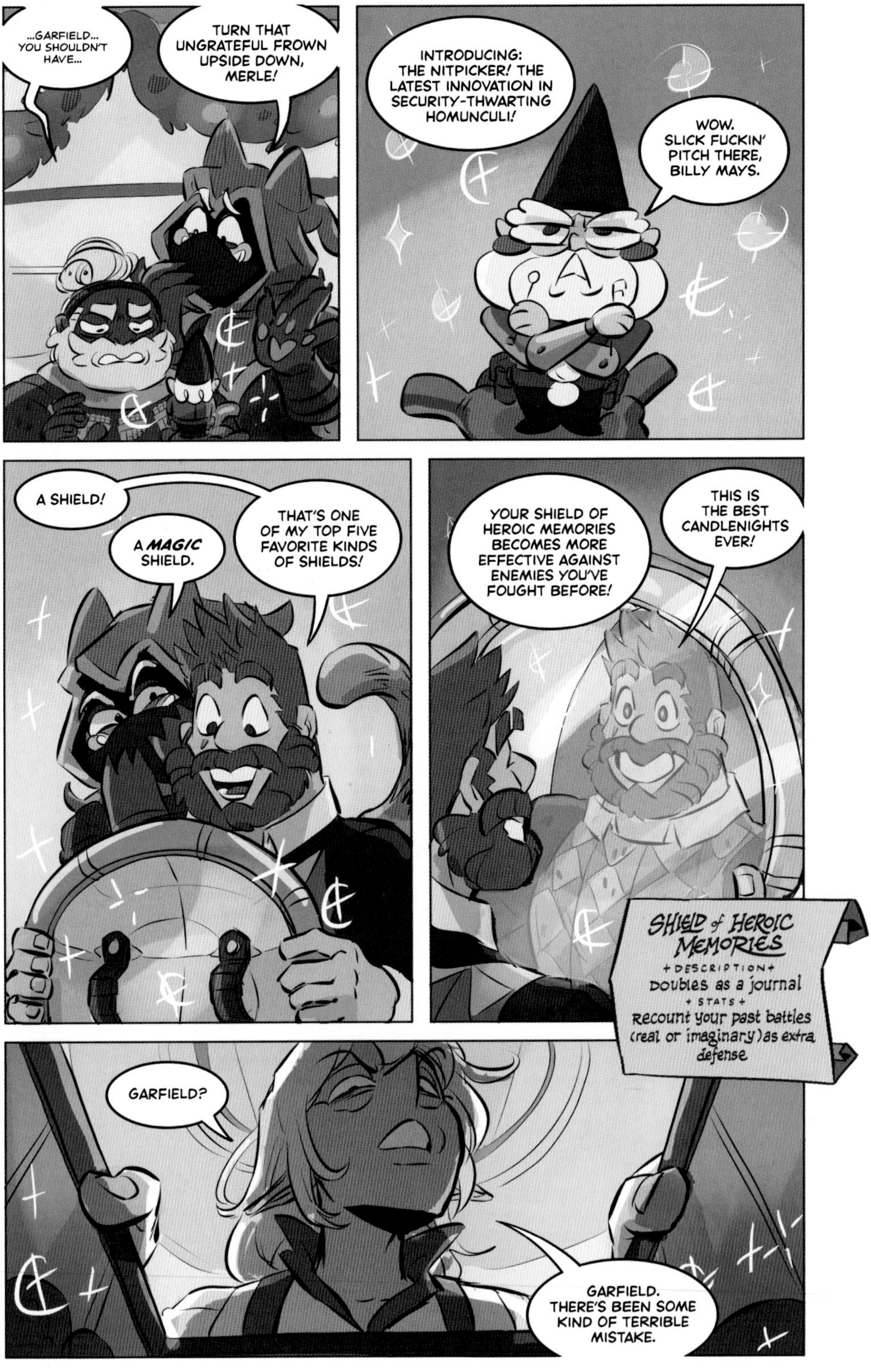
...GARFIELD... YOU SHOULDN'T HAVE...
TURN THAT UNGRATEFUL FROWN UPSIDE DOWN, MERLE!
INTRODUCING: THE NITPICKER! THE LATEST INNOVATION IN SECURITY-THWARTING HOMUNCULI!
WOW. SLICK FUCKIN' PITCH THERE, BILLY MAYS.
A SHIELD!
A MAGIC SHIELD.
THAT'S ONE OF MY TOP FIVE FAVORITE KINDS OF SHIELDS!
YOUR SHIELD OF HEROIC MEMORIES BECOMES MORE EFFECTIVE AGAINST ENEMIES YOU'VE FOUGHT BEFORE!
THIS IS THE BEST CANDLENIGHTS EVER!
SHIELD of HEROIC MEMORIES
+ DESCRIPTION +
Doubles as a journal
+ STATS +
Recount your past battles (real or imaginary) as extra defense
GARFIELD?
GARFIELD. THERE'S BEEN SOME KIND OF TERRIBLE MISTAKE.

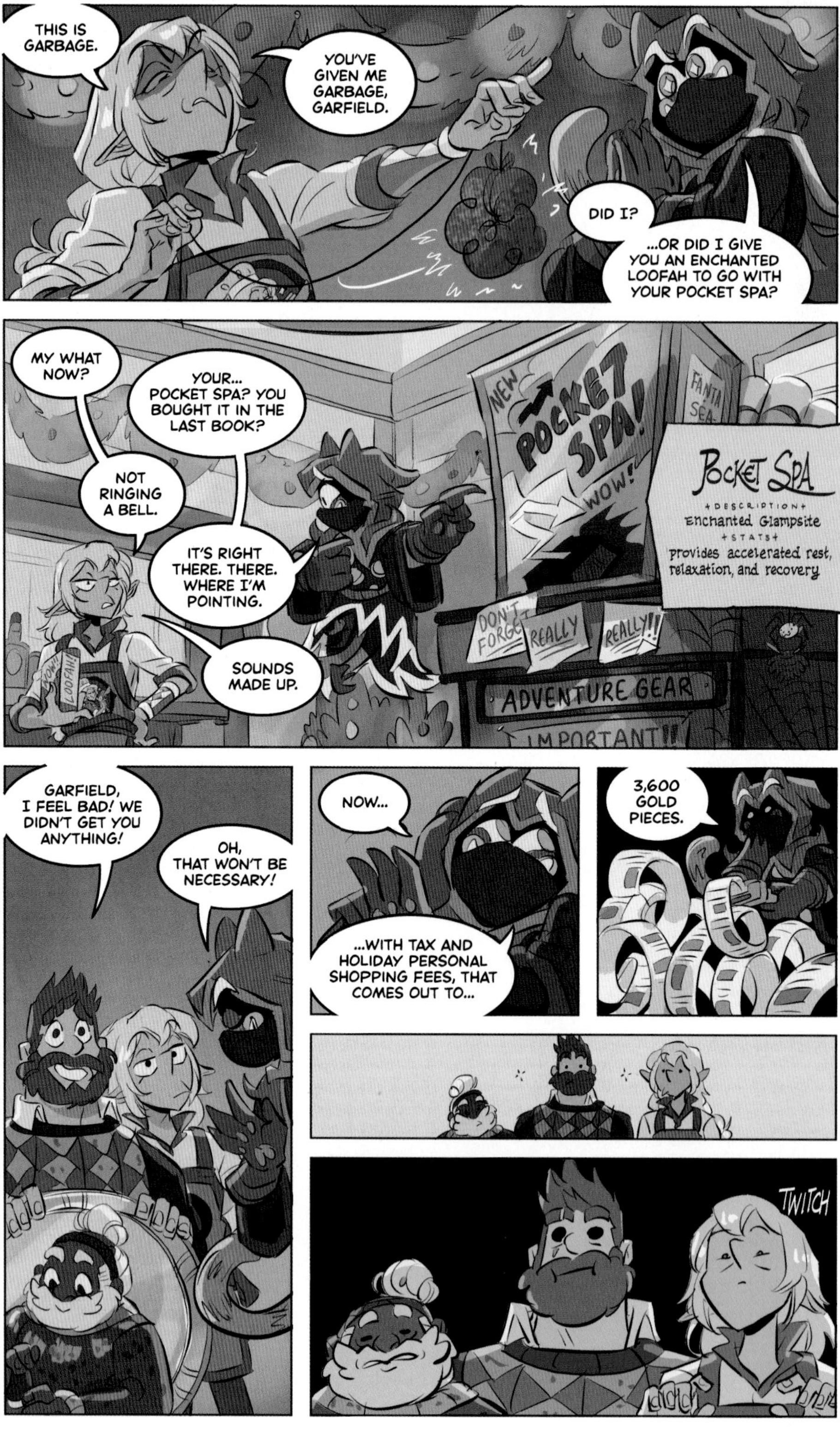

THIS IS GARBAGE.
YOU'VE GIVEN ME GARBAGE, GARFIELD.
DID I?
...OR DID I GIVE YOU AN ENCHANTED LOOFAH TO GO WITH YOUR POCKET SPA?
MY WHAT NOW?
YOUR... POCKET SPA? YOU BOUGHT IT IN THE LAST BOOK?
NEW POCKET SPA! WOW!
Pocket Spa
DESCRIPTION
Enchanted Glampsite
STATS
provides accelerated rest, relaxation, and recovery
NOT RINGING A BELL.
IT'S RIGHT THERE. THERE. WHERE I'M POINTING.
SOUNDS MADE UP.
DON'T FORGET
REALLY
REALLY!!
ADVENTURE GEAR
IMPORTANT!!
GARFIELD, I FEEL BAD! WE DIDN'T GET YOU ANYTHING!
OH, THAT WON'T BE NECESSARY!
NOW...
...WITH TAX AND HOLIDAY PERSONAL SHOPPING FEES, THAT COMES OUT TO...
3,600 GOLD PIECES.
TWITCH

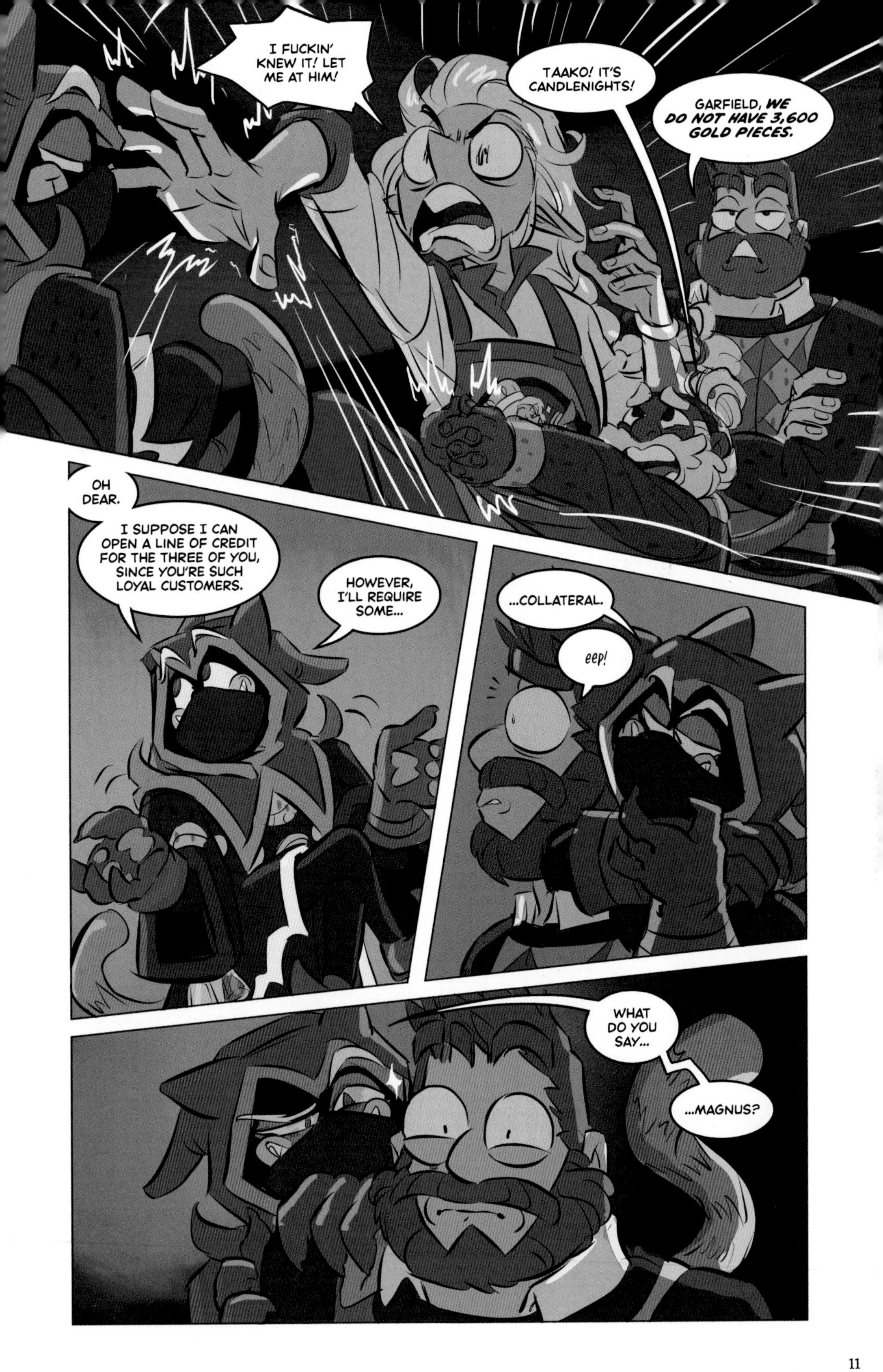
I FUCKIN' KNEW IT! LET ME AT HIM!
TAAKO! IT'S CANDLENIGHTS!
GARFIELD, WE DO NOT HAVE 3,600 GOLD PIECES.
OH DEAR.
I SUPPOSE I CAN OPEN A LINE OF CREDIT FOR THE THREE OF YOU, SINCE YOU'RE SUCH LOYAL CUSTOMERS.
HOWEVER, I'LL REQUIRE SOME...
...COLLATERAL.
eep!
WHAT DO YOU SAY...
...MAGNUS?

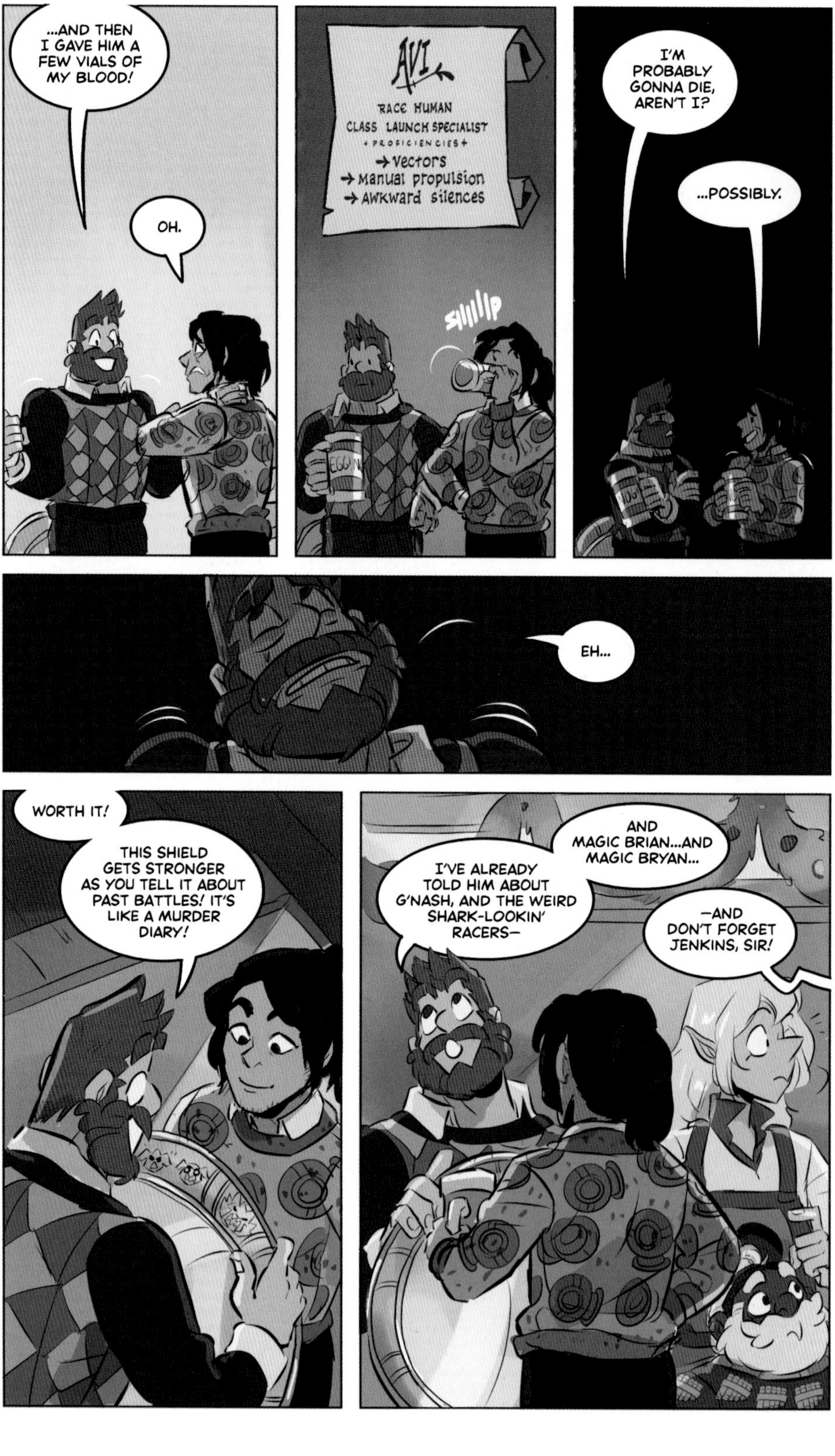
...AND THEN I GAVE HIM A FEW VIALS OF MY BLOOD!
OH.
AVI
RACE HUMAN
CLASS LAUNCH SPECIALIST
PROFICIENCIES
→Vectors
→Manual propulsion
→Awkward silences
SHLLLP
I'M PROBABLY GONNA DIE, AREN'T I?
...POSSIBLY.
EH...
WORTH IT!
THIS SHIELD GETS STRONGER AS YOU TELL IT ABOUT PAST BATTLES! IT'S LIKE A MURDER DIARY!
I'VE ALREADY TOLD HIM ABOUT G'NASH, AND THE WEIRD SHARK-LOOKIN' RACERS—
AND MAGIC BRIAN...AND MAGIC BRYAN...
—AND DON'T FORGET JENKINS, SIR!

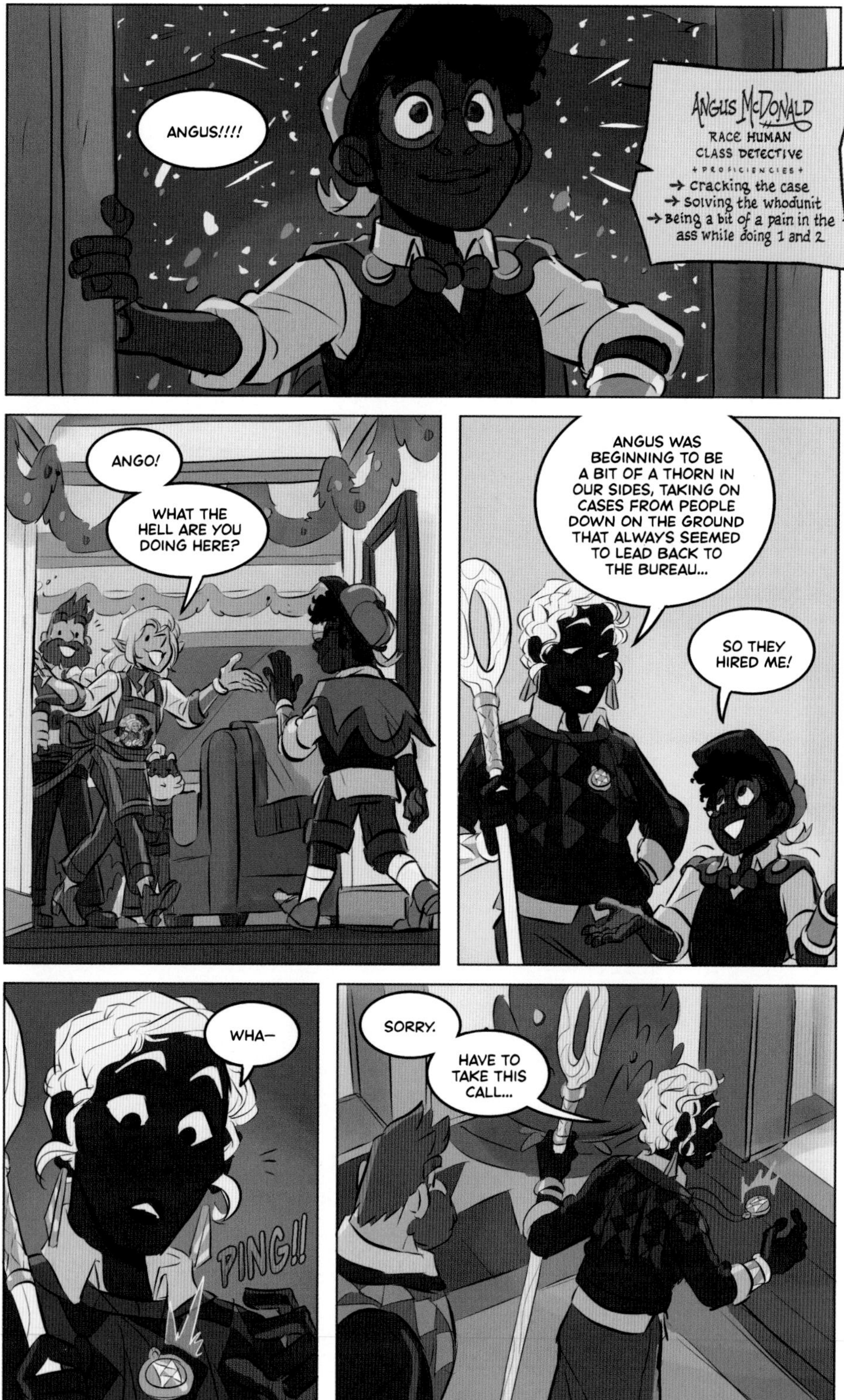
ANGUS!!!!
ANGUS McDONALD
RACE HUMAN
CLASS DETECTIVE
PROFICIENCIES
→ Cracking the case
→ Solving the whodunit
→ Being a bit of a pain in the ass while doing 1 and 2
ANGO!
WHAT THE HELL ARE YOU DOING HERE?
ANGUS WAS BEGINNING TO BE A BIT OF A THORN IN OUR SIDES, TAKING ON CASES FROM PEOPLE DOWN ON THE GROUND THAT ALWAYS SEEMED TO LEAD BACK TO THE BUREAU...
SO THEY HIRED ME!
WHA–
PING!!
SORRY.
HAVE TO TAKE THIS CALL...

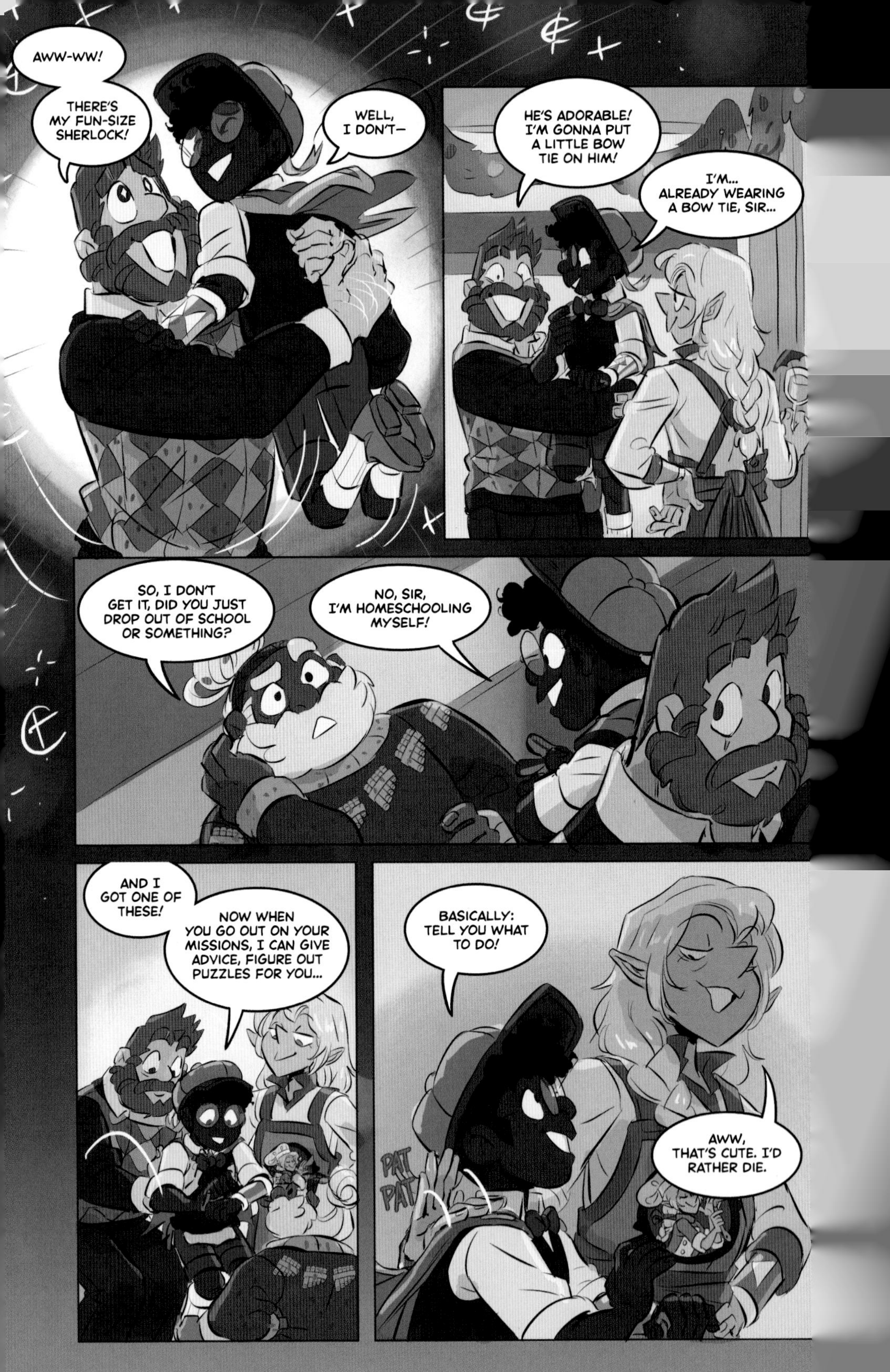
AWW-WW!
THERE'S MY FUN-SIZE SHERLOCK!
WELL, I DON'T—
HE'S ADORABLE! I'M GONNA PUT A LITTLE BOW TIE ON HIM!
I'M... ALREADY WEARING A BOW TIE, SIR...
SO, I DON'T GET IT, DID YOU JUST DROP OUT OF SCHOOL OR SOMETHING?
NO, SIR, I'M HOMESCHOOLING MYSELF!
AND I GOT ONE OF THESE!
NOW WHEN YOU GO OUT ON YOUR MISSIONS, I CAN GIVE ADVICE, FIGURE OUT PUZZLES FOR YOU...
BASICALLY: TELL YOU WHAT TO DO!
PAT PAT
AWW, THAT'S CUTE. I'D RATHER DIE.

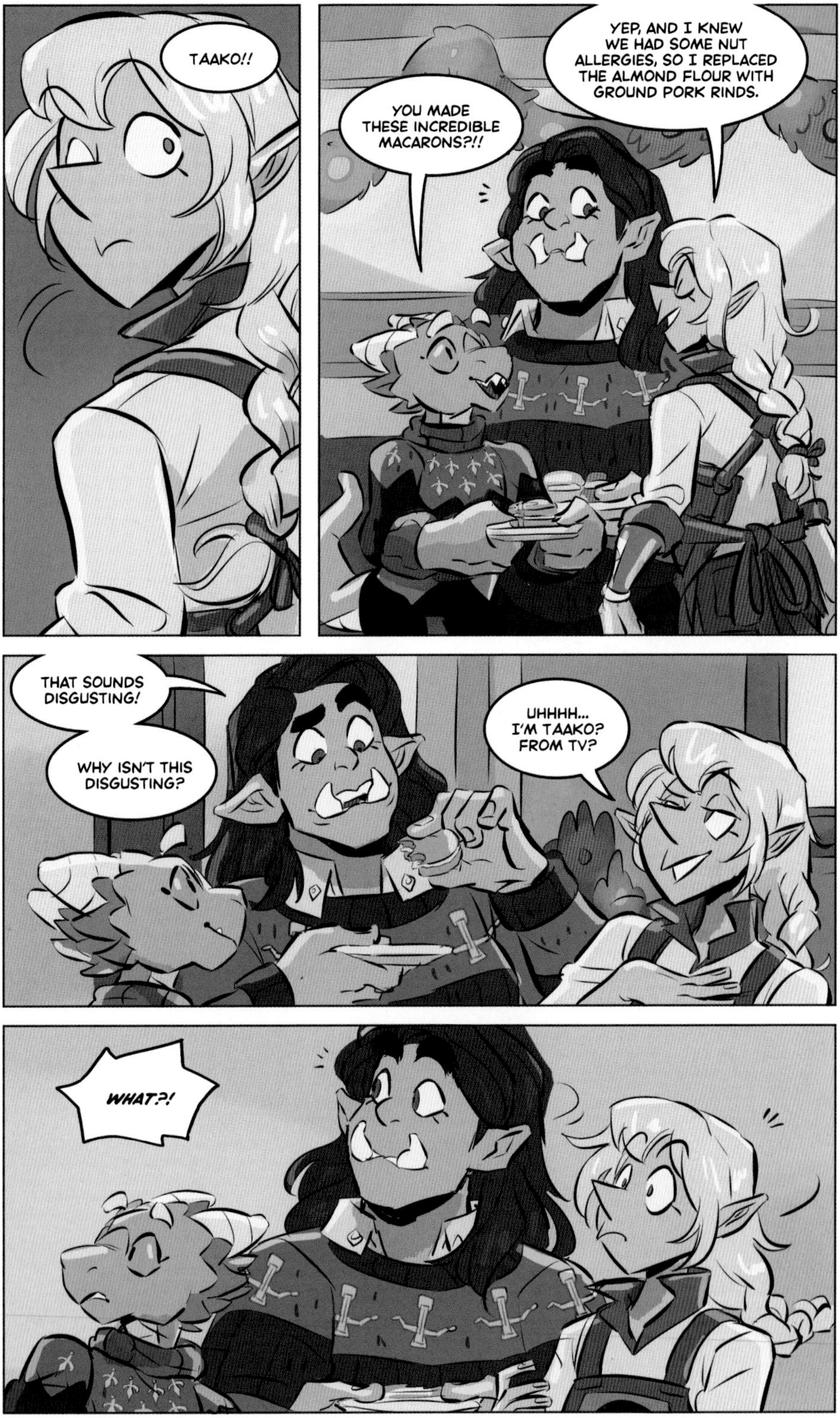
TAAKO!!
YOU MADE THESE INCREDIBLE MACARONS?!!
YEP, AND I KNEW WE HAD SOME NUT ALLERGIES, SO I REPLACED THE ALMOND FLOUR WITH GROUND PORK RINDS.
THAT SOUNDS DISGUSTING!
WHY ISN'T THIS DISGUSTING?
UHHHH... I'M TAAKO? FROM TV?
WHAT?!

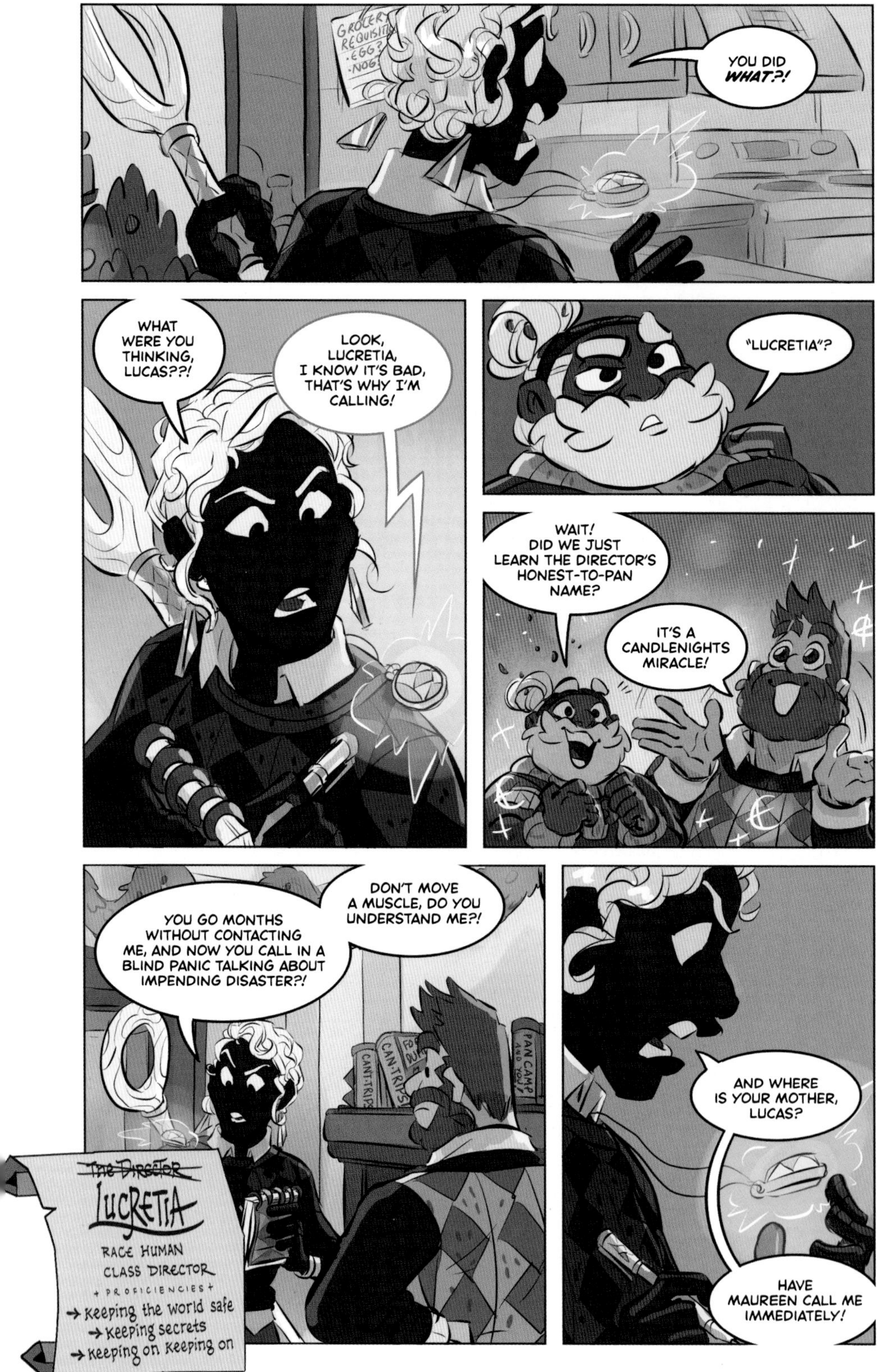
GROCERY REQUISITION
·EGG?
·NOG?
YOU DID *WHAT?!*
WHAT WERE YOU THINKING, LUCAS??!
LOOK, LUCRETIA, I KNOW IT'S BAD, THAT'S WHY I'M CALLING!
"LUCRETIA"?
WAIT! DID WE JUST LEARN THE DIRECTOR'S HONEST-TO-PAN NAME?
IT'S A CANDLENIGHTS MIRACLE!
YOU GO MONTHS WITHOUT CONTACTING ME, AND NOW YOU CALL IN A BLIND PANIC TALKING ABOUT IMPENDING DISASTER?!
DON'T MOVE A MUSCLE, DO YOU UNDERSTAND ME?!
CAN-TRIPS
PAN CAMP AND YOU
AND WHERE IS YOUR MOTHER, LUCAS?
HAVE MAUREEN CALL ME IMMEDIATELY!
~~The Director~~
LUCRETIA
RACE HUMAN
CLASS DIRECTOR
PROFICIENCIES
→ Keeping the World safe
→ Keeping secrets
→ Keeping on Keeping on

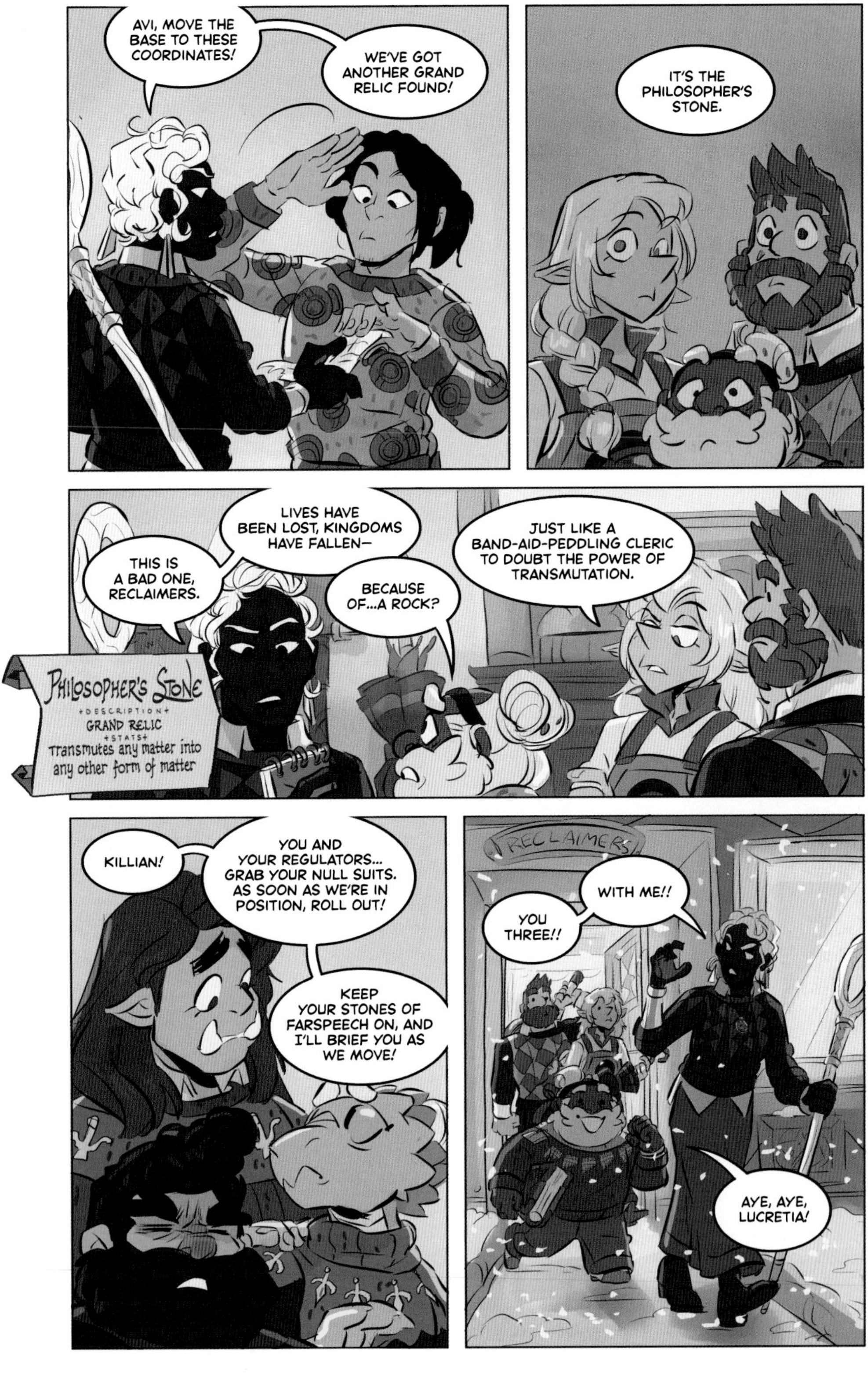
AVI, MOVE THE BASE TO THESE COORDINATES!
WE'VE GOT ANOTHER GRAND RELIC FOUND!
IT'S THE PHILOSOPHER'S STONE.
THIS IS A BAD ONE, RECLAIMERS.
LIVES HAVE BEEN LOST, KINGDOMS HAVE FALLEN—
BECAUSE OF...A ROCK?
JUST LIKE A BAND-AID-PEDDLING CLERIC TO DOUBT THE POWER OF TRANSMUTATION.
PHILOSOPHER'S STONE
DESCRIPTION
GRAND RELIC
STATS
Transmutes any matter into any other form of matter
KILLIAN!
YOU AND YOUR REGULATORS... GRAB YOUR NULL SUITS. AS SOON AS WE'RE IN POSITION, ROLL OUT!
KEEP YOUR STONES OF FARSPEECH ON, AND I'LL BRIEF YOU AS WE MOVE!
RECLAIMERS
YOU THREE!!
WITH ME!!
AYE, AYE, LUCRETIA!

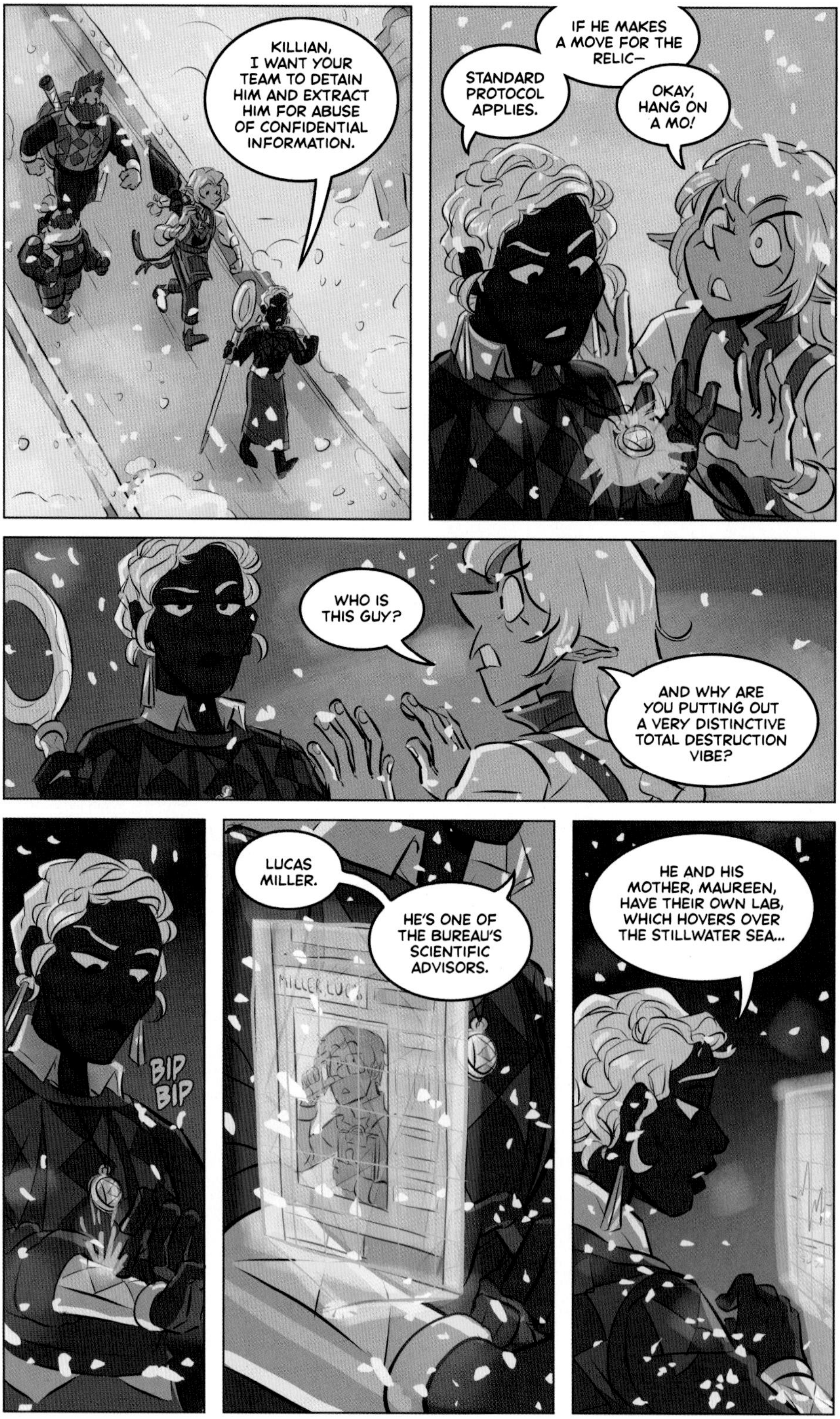
KILLIAN, I WANT YOUR TEAM TO DETAIN HIM AND EXTRACT HIM FOR ABUSE OF CONFIDENTIAL INFORMATION.
STANDARD PROTOCOL APPLIES.
IF HE MAKES A MOVE FOR THE RELIC—
OKAY, HANG ON A MO!
WHO IS THIS GUY?
AND WHY ARE YOU PUTTING OUT A VERY DISTINCTIVE TOTAL DESTRUCTION VIBE?
BIP BIP
LUCAS MILLER.
HE'S ONE OF THE BUREAU'S SCIENTIFIC ADVISORS.
MILLER, LUCAS
HE AND HIS MOTHER, MAUREEN, HAVE THEIR OWN LAB, WHICH HOVERS OVER THE STILLWATER SEA...

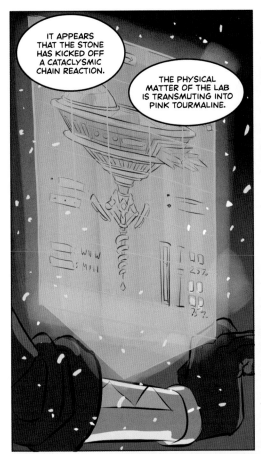

IT APPEARS THAT THE STONE HAS KICKED OFF A CATACLYSMIC CHAIN REACTION.

THE PHYSICAL MATTER OF THE LAB IS TRANSMUTING INTO PINK TOURMALINE.

IF THE TRANSFORMATION ISN'T STOPPED, THE LAB WILL CRASH INTO THE SEA—

WELL, THAT REALLY WOULDN'T BE THE END OF THE WORLD, WOULD IT?

—AT WHICH POINT THE CHAIN REACTION WOULD SPREAD AND TURN THE ENTIRE PLANET TO CRYSTAL.

OH.

SO IT *WOULD.*

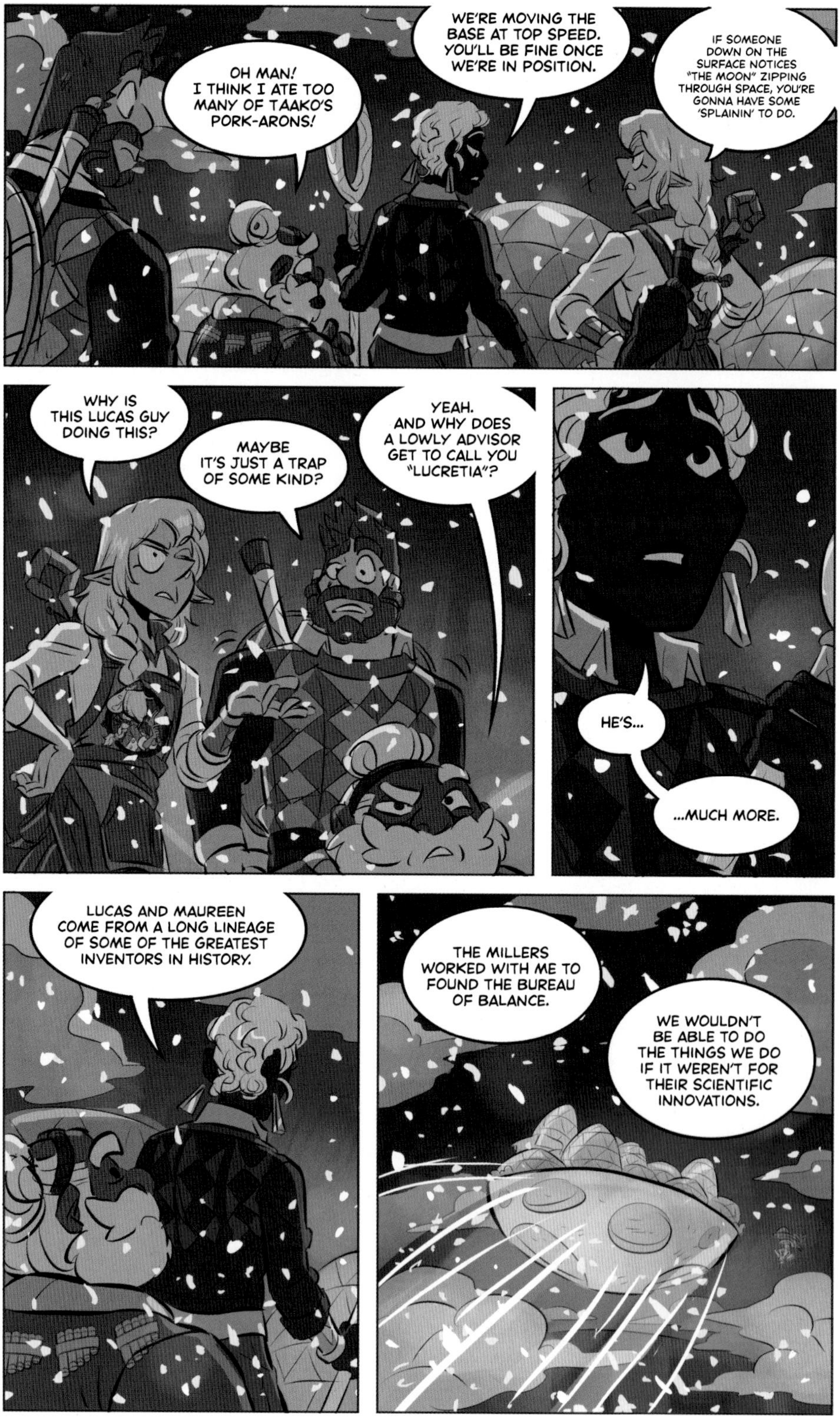
OH MAN! I THINK I ATE TOO MANY OF TAAKO'S PORK-ARONS!
WE'RE MOVING THE BASE AT TOP SPEED. YOU'LL BE FINE ONCE WE'RE IN POSITION.
IF SOMEONE DOWN ON THE SURFACE NOTICES "THE MOON" ZIPPING THROUGH SPACE, YOU'RE GONNA HAVE SOME 'SPLAININ' TO DO.
WHY IS THIS LUCAS GUY DOING THIS?
MAYBE IT'S JUST A TRAP OF SOME KIND?
YEAH. AND WHY DOES A LOWLY ADVISOR GET TO CALL YOU "LUCRETIA"?
HE'S...
...MUCH MORE.
LUCAS AND MAUREEN COME FROM A LONG LINEAGE OF SOME OF THE GREATEST INVENTORS IN HISTORY.
THE MILLERS WORKED WITH ME TO FOUND THE BUREAU OF BALANCE.
WE WOULDN'T BE ABLE TO DO THE THINGS WE DO IF IT WEREN'T FOR THEIR SCIENTIFIC INNOVATIONS.

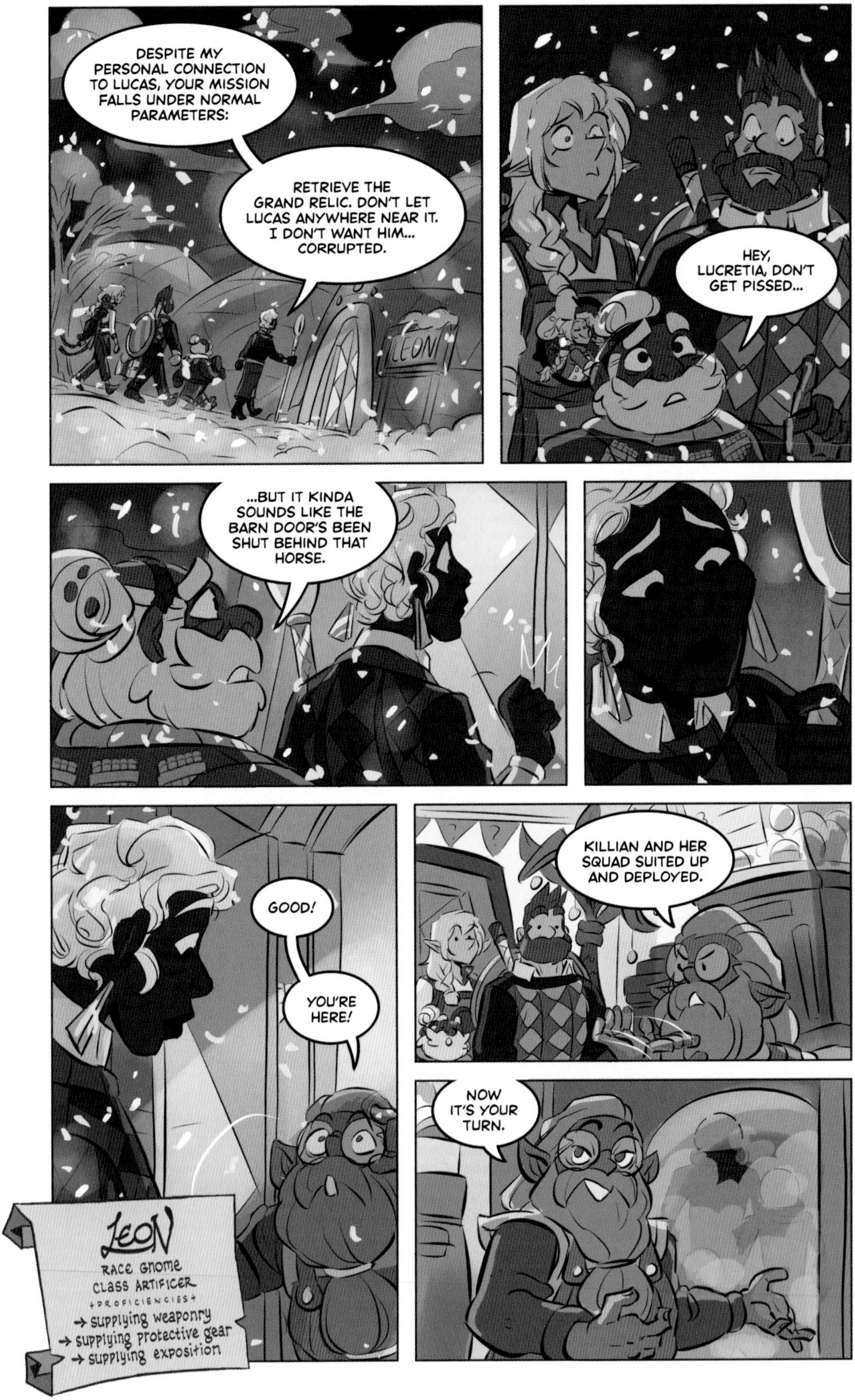
DESPITE MY PERSONAL CONNECTION TO LUCAS, YOUR MISSION FALLS UNDER NORMAL PARAMETERS:
RETRIEVE THE GRAND RELIC. DON'T LET LUCAS ANYWHERE NEAR IT. I DON'T WANT HIM... CORRUPTED.
LEON
HEY, LUCRETIA, DON'T GET PISSED...
...BUT IT KINDA SOUNDS LIKE THE BARN DOOR'S BEEN SHUT BEHIND THAT HORSE.
GOOD!
YOU'RE HERE!
LEON
RACE GNOME
CLASS ARTIFICER
PROFICIENCIES
→ supplying weaponry
→ supplying protective gear
→ supplying exposition
KILLIAN AND HER SQUAD SUITED UP AND DEPLOYED.
NOW IT'S YOUR TURN.

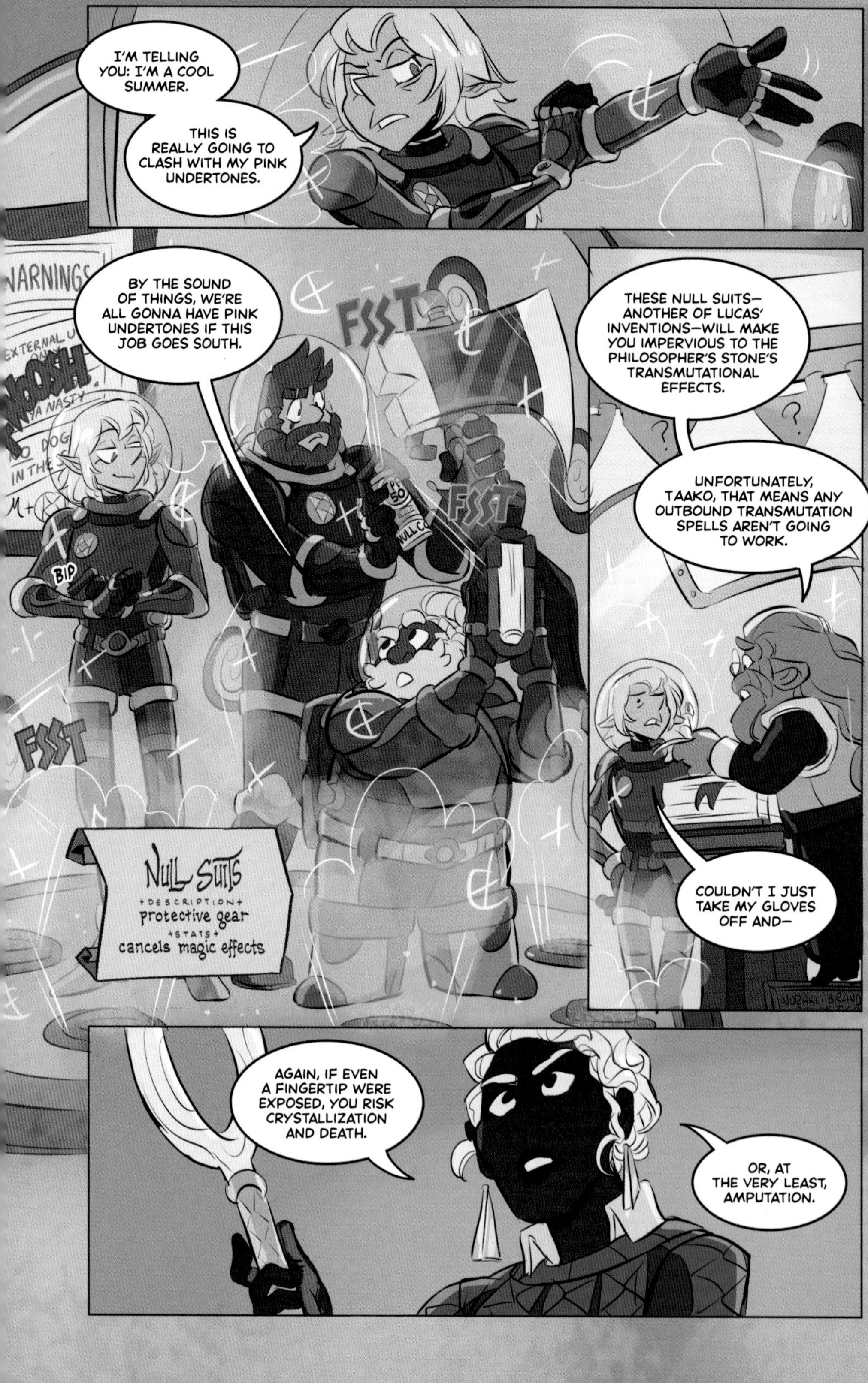
I'M TELLING YOU: I'M A COOL SUMMER.
THIS IS REALLY GOING TO CLASH WITH MY PINK UNDERTONES.
BY THE SOUND OF THINGS, WE'RE ALL GONNA HAVE PINK UNDERTONES IF THIS JOB GOES SOUTH.
FSST
FSST
FSST
BIP
NULL SUITS
DESCRIPTION
protective gear
STATS
cancels magic effects
THESE NULL SUITS—ANOTHER OF LUCAS' INVENTIONS—WILL MAKE YOU IMPERVIOUS TO THE PHILOSOPHER'S STONE'S TRANSMUTATIONAL EFFECTS.
UNFORTUNATELY, TAAKO, THAT MEANS ANY OUTBOUND TRANSMUTATION SPELLS AREN'T GOING TO WORK.
COULDN'T I JUST TAKE MY GLOVES OFF AND—
AGAIN, IF EVEN A FINGERTIP WERE EXPOSED, YOU RISK CRYSTALLIZATION AND DEATH.
OR, AT THE VERY LEAST, AMPUTATION.

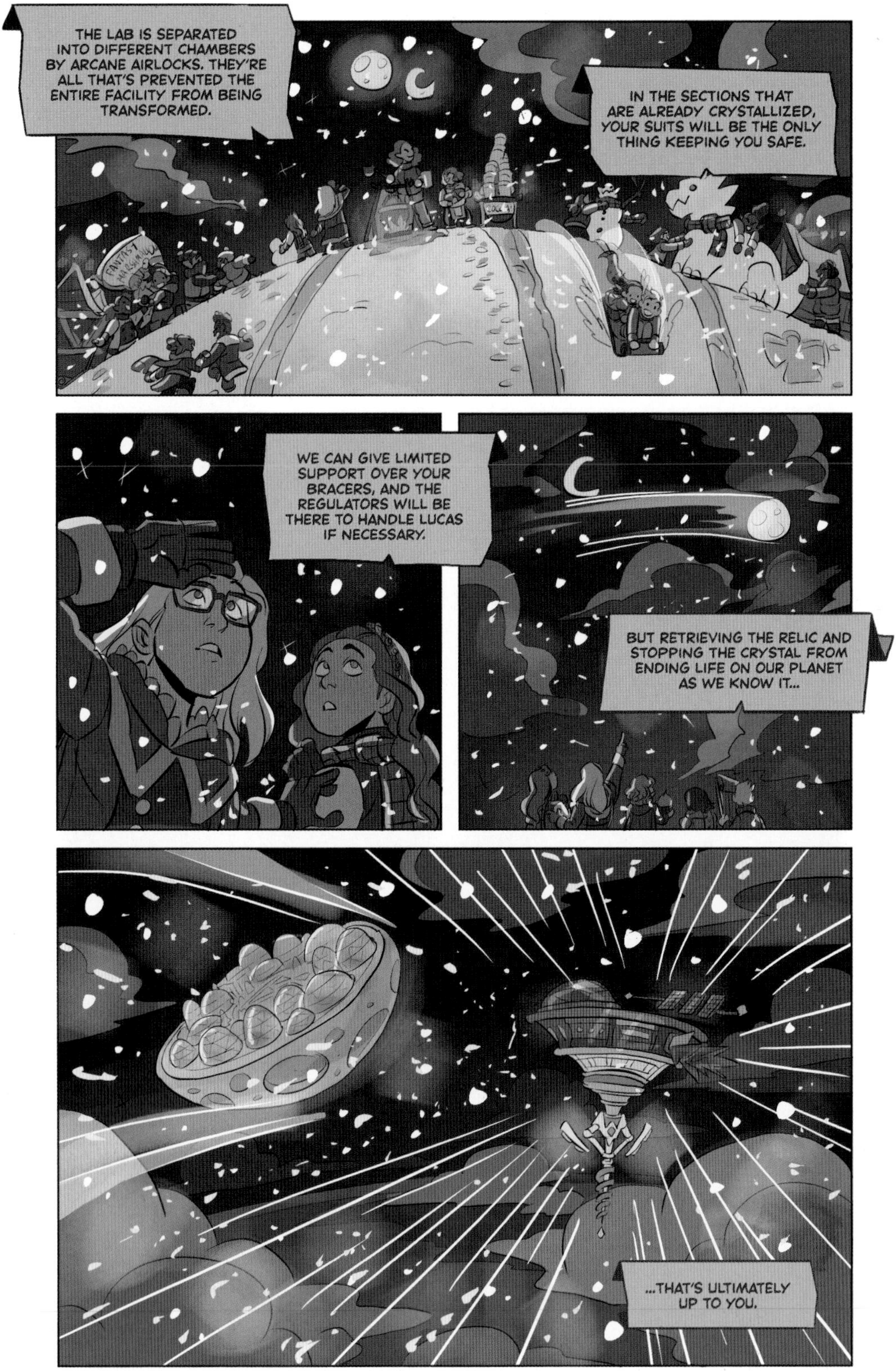
THE LAB IS SEPARATED INTO DIFFERENT CHAMBERS BY ARCANE AIRLOCKS. THEY'RE ALL THAT'S PREVENTED THE ENTIRE FACILITY FROM BEING TRANSFORMED.
IN THE SECTIONS THAT ARE ALREADY CRYSTALLIZED, YOUR SUITS WILL BE THE ONLY THING KEEPING YOU SAFE.
WE CAN GIVE LIMITED SUPPORT OVER YOUR BRACERS, AND THE REGULATORS WILL BE THERE TO HANDLE LUCAS IF NECESSARY.
BUT RETRIEVING THE RELIC AND STOPPING THE CRYSTAL FROM ENDING LIFE ON OUR PLANET AS WE KNOW IT...
...THAT'S ULTIMATELY UP TO YOU.

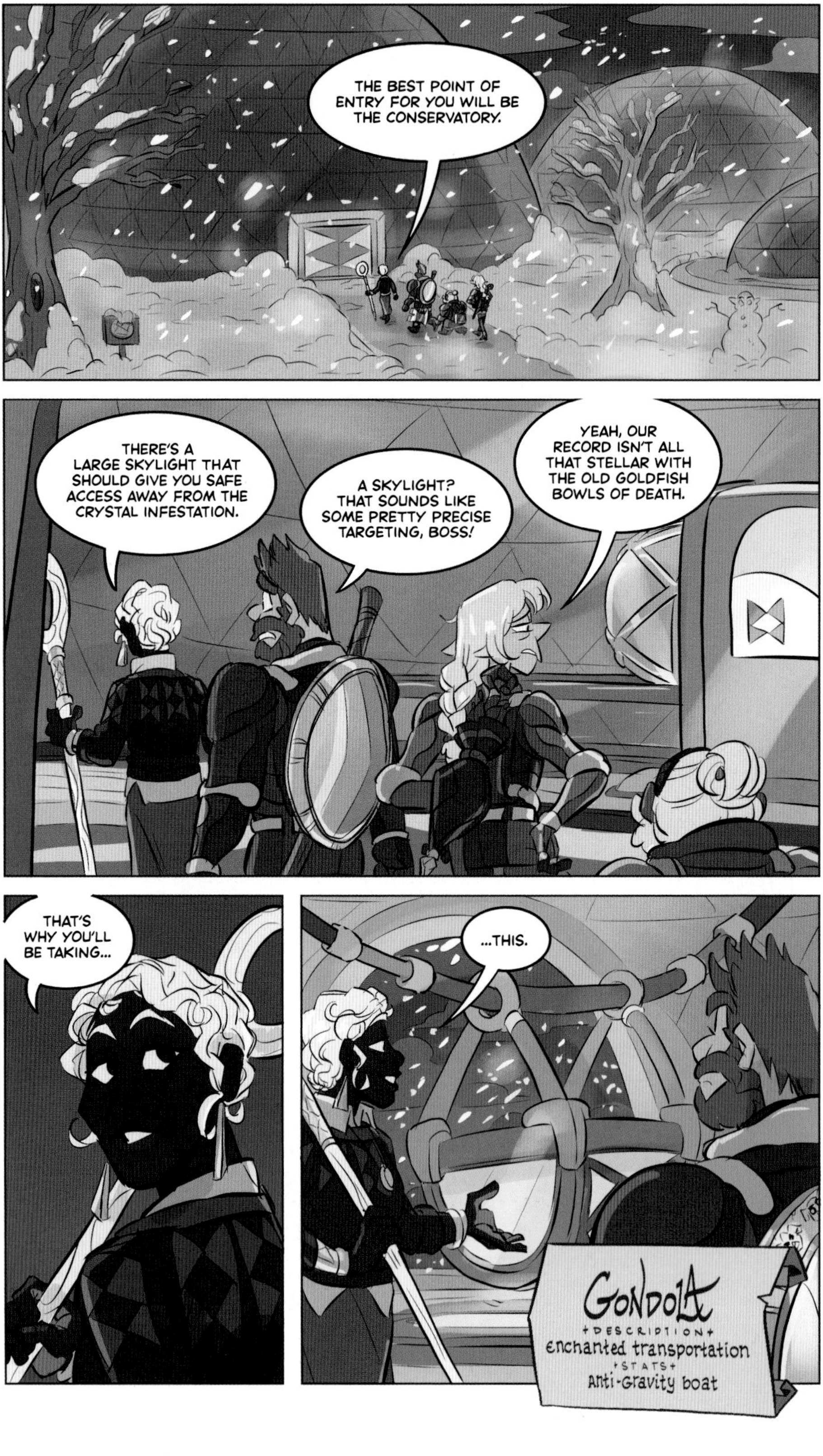
THE BEST POINT OF ENTRY FOR YOU WILL BE THE CONSERVATORY.
THERE'S A LARGE SKYLIGHT THAT SHOULD GIVE YOU SAFE ACCESS AWAY FROM THE CRYSTAL INFESTATION.
A SKYLIGHT? THAT SOUNDS LIKE SOME PRETTY PRECISE TARGETING, BOSS!
YEAH, OUR RECORD ISN'T ALL THAT STELLAR WITH THE OLD GOLDFISH BOWLS OF DEATH.
THAT'S WHY YOU'LL BE TAKING...
...THIS.
GONDOLA
DESCRIPTION
Enchanted transportation
STATS
Anti-Gravity boat

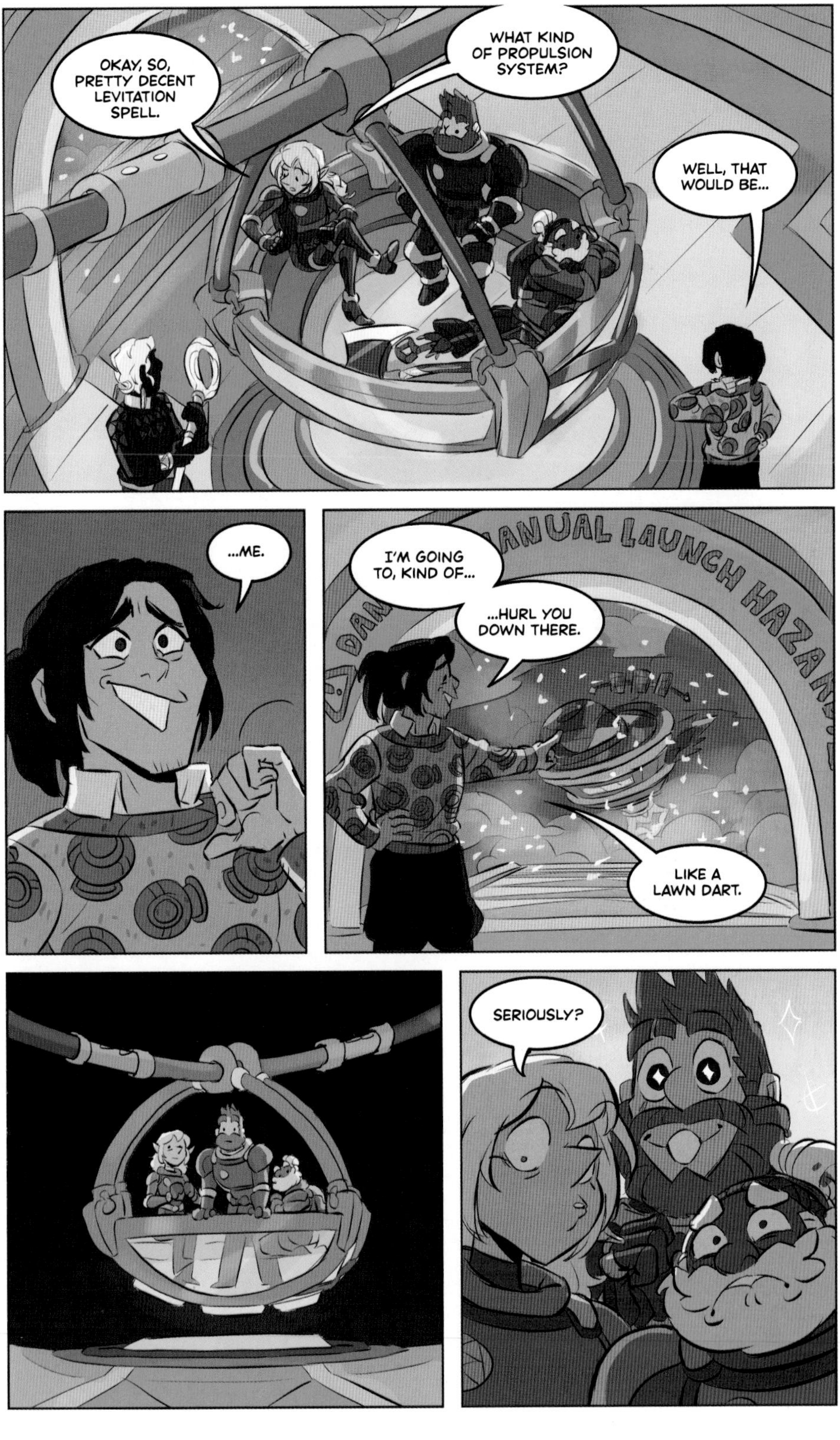
OKAY, SO, PRETTY DECENT LEVITATION SPELL.
WHAT KIND OF PROPULSION SYSTEM?
WELL, THAT WOULD BE...
...ME.
LAUNCH
I'M GOING TO, KIND OF...
...HURL YOU DOWN THERE.
LIKE A LAWN DART.
SERIOUSLY?

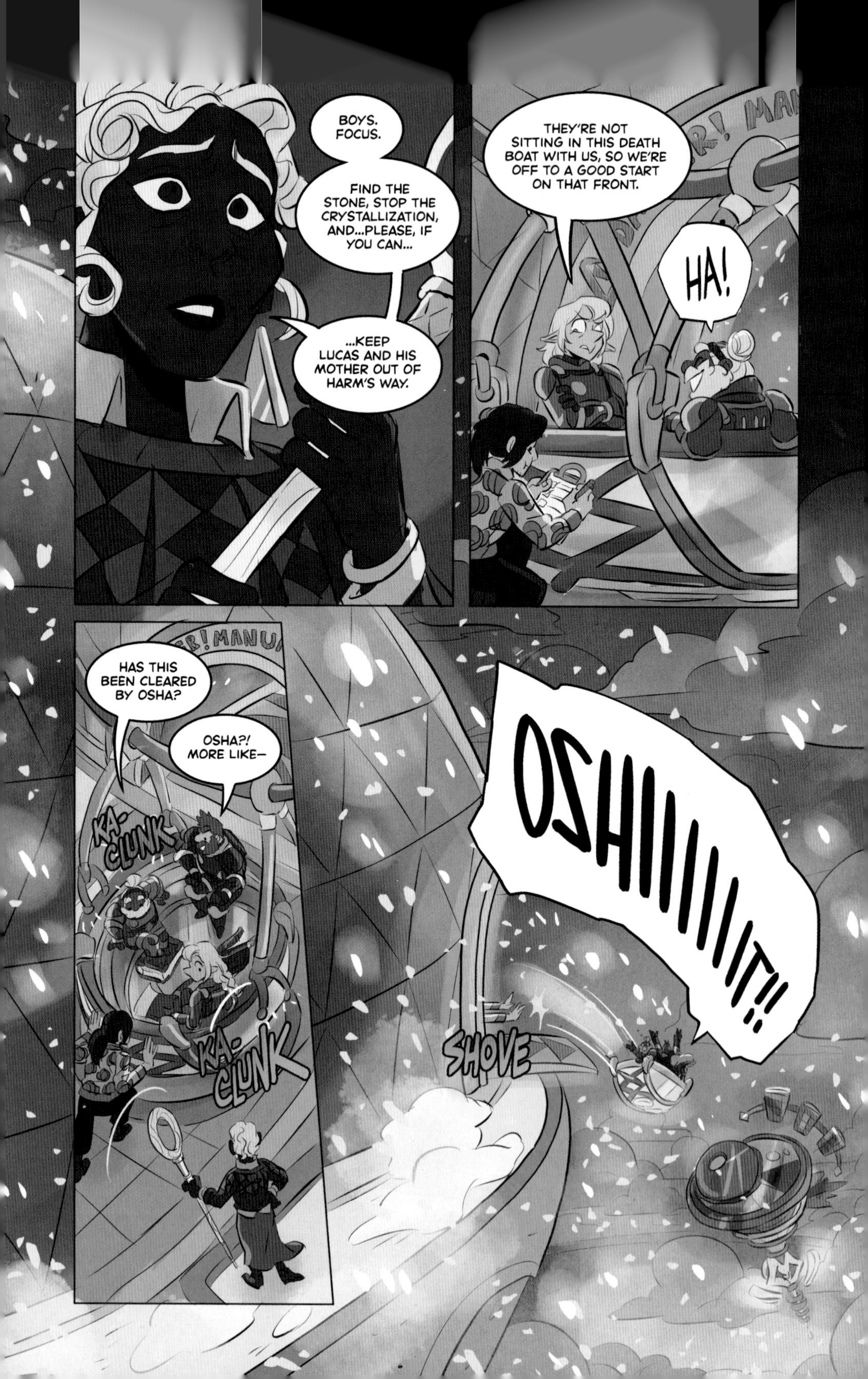
BOYS. FOCUS.
FIND THE STONE, STOP THE CRYSTALLIZATION, AND...PLEASE, IF YOU CAN...
...KEEP LUCAS AND HIS MOTHER OUT OF HARM'S WAY.
THEY'RE NOT SITTING IN THIS DEATH BOAT WITH US, SO WE'RE OFF TO A GOOD START ON THAT FRONT.
HA!
HAS THIS BEEN CLEARED BY OSHA?
OSHA?! MORE LIKE—
KA-CLUNK
KA-CLUNK
OSHIIIIIIT!!
SHOVE

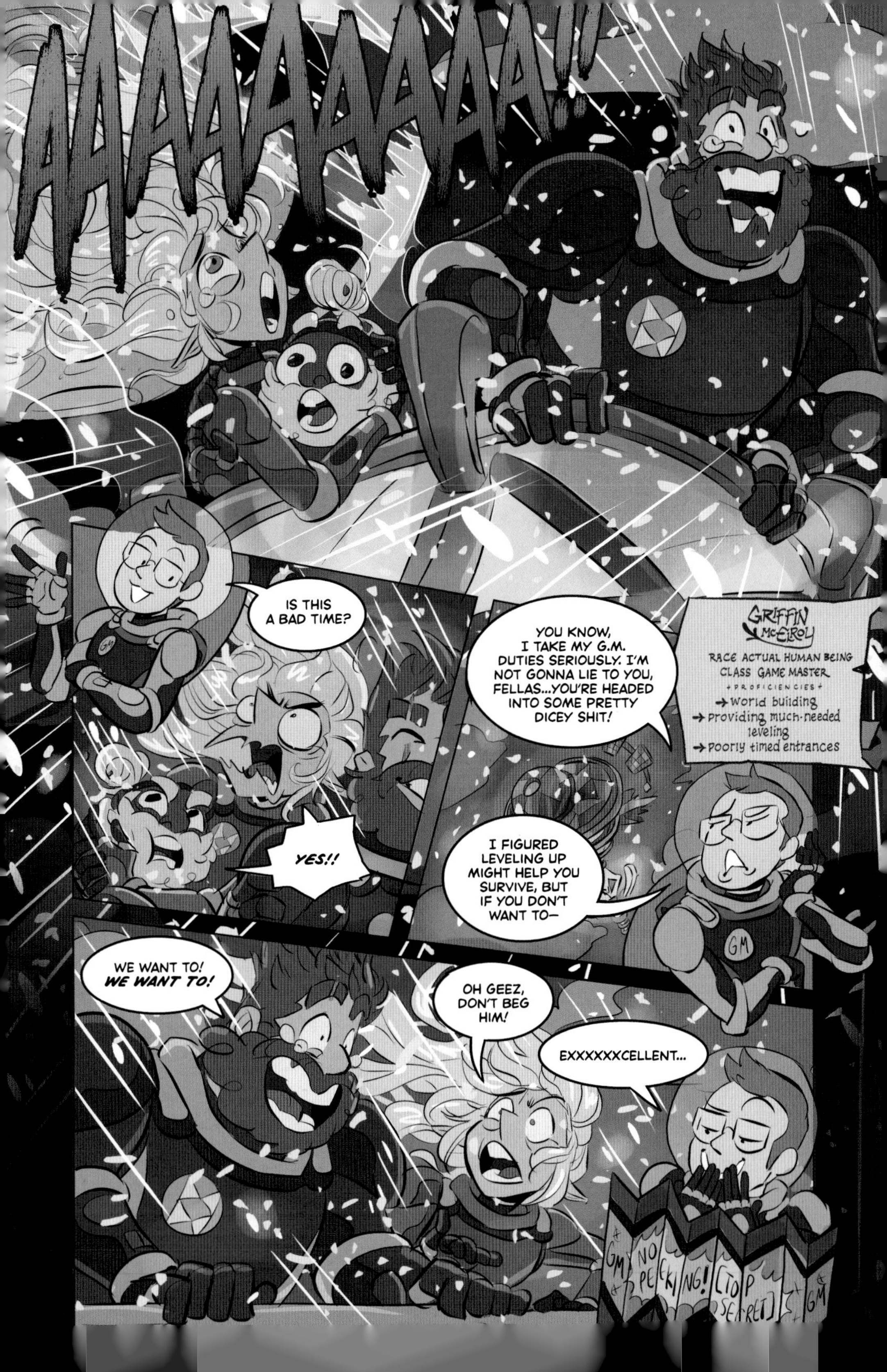
AAAAAAAAA!!!
IS THIS A BAD TIME?
YES!!
YOU KNOW, I TAKE MY G.M. DUTIES SERIOUSLY. I'M NOT GONNA LIE TO YOU, FELLAS...YOU'RE HEADED INTO SOME PRETTY DICEY SHIT!
GRIFFIN McELROY
RACE ACTUAL HUMAN BEING
CLASS GAME MASTER
PROFICIENCIES
→World building
→Providing much-needed leveling
→Poorly timed entrances
I FIGURED LEVELING UP MIGHT HELP YOU SURVIVE, BUT IF YOU DON'T WANT TO—
WE WANT TO! WE WANT TO!
OH GEEZ, DON'T BEG HIM!
EXXXXXXCELLENT...
GM NO PEEKING! [TOP SECRET] GM

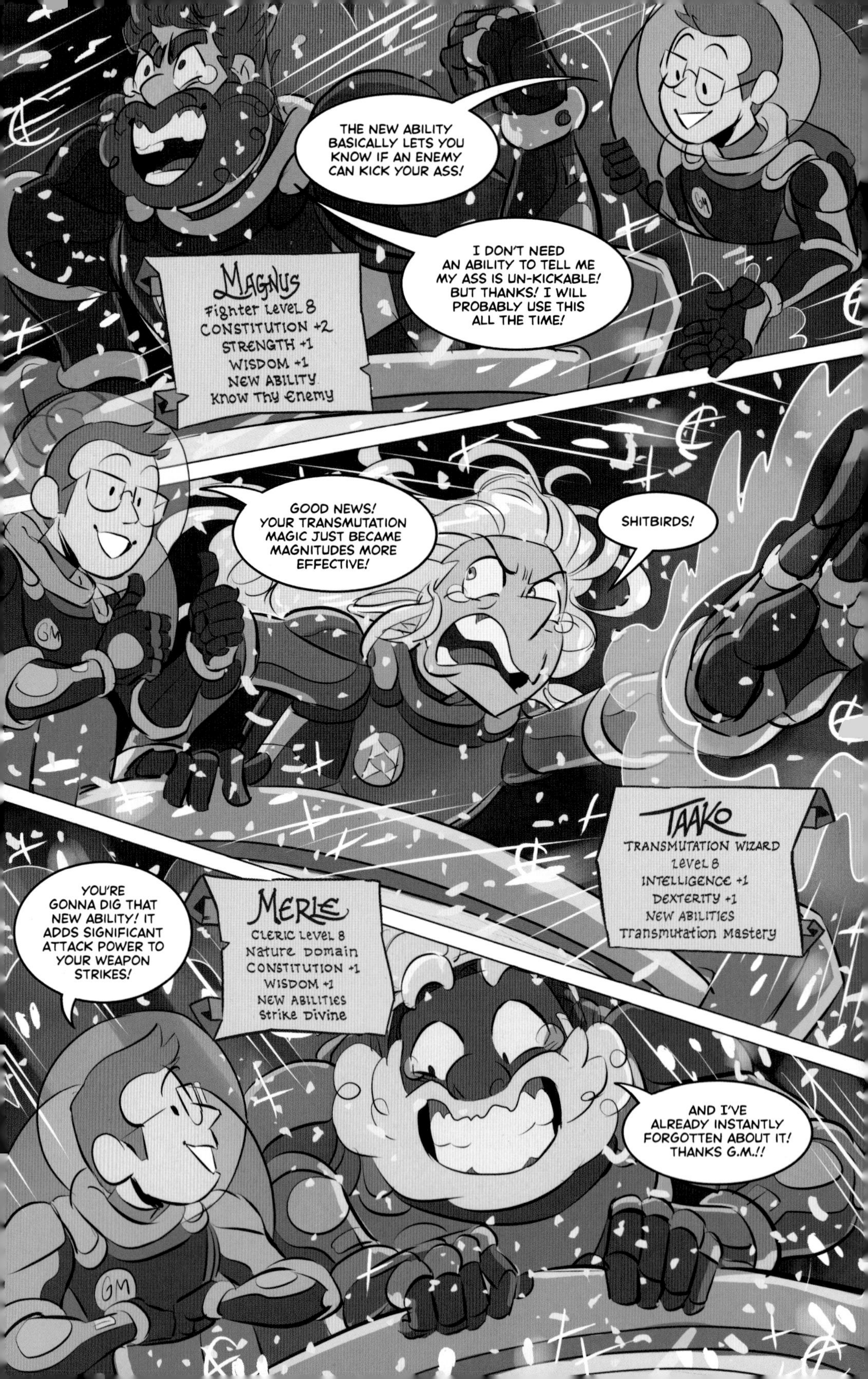

THE NEW ABILITY BASICALLY LETS YOU KNOW IF AN ENEMY CAN KICK YOUR ASS!
I DON'T NEED AN ABILITY TO TELL ME MY ASS IS UN-KICKABLE! BUT THANKS! I WILL PROBABLY USE THIS ALL THE TIME!
MAGNUS
Fighter Level 8
CONSTITUTION +2
STRENGTH +1
WISDOM +1
NEW ABILITY
Know Thy Enemy
GOOD NEWS! YOUR TRANSMUTATION MAGIC JUST BECAME MAGNITUDES MORE EFFECTIVE!
SHITBIRDS!
TAAKO
TRANSMUTATION WIZARD
Level 8
INTELLIGENCE +1
DEXTERITY +1
NEW ABILITIES
Transmutation Mastery
YOU'RE GONNA DIG THAT NEW ABILITY! IT ADDS SIGNIFICANT ATTACK POWER TO YOUR WEAPON STRIKES!
MERLE
Cleric Level 8
Nature Domain
CONSTITUTION +1
WISDOM +1
NEW ABILITIES
Strike Divine
AND I'VE ALREADY INSTANTLY FORGOTTEN ABOUT IT! THANKS G.M.!!

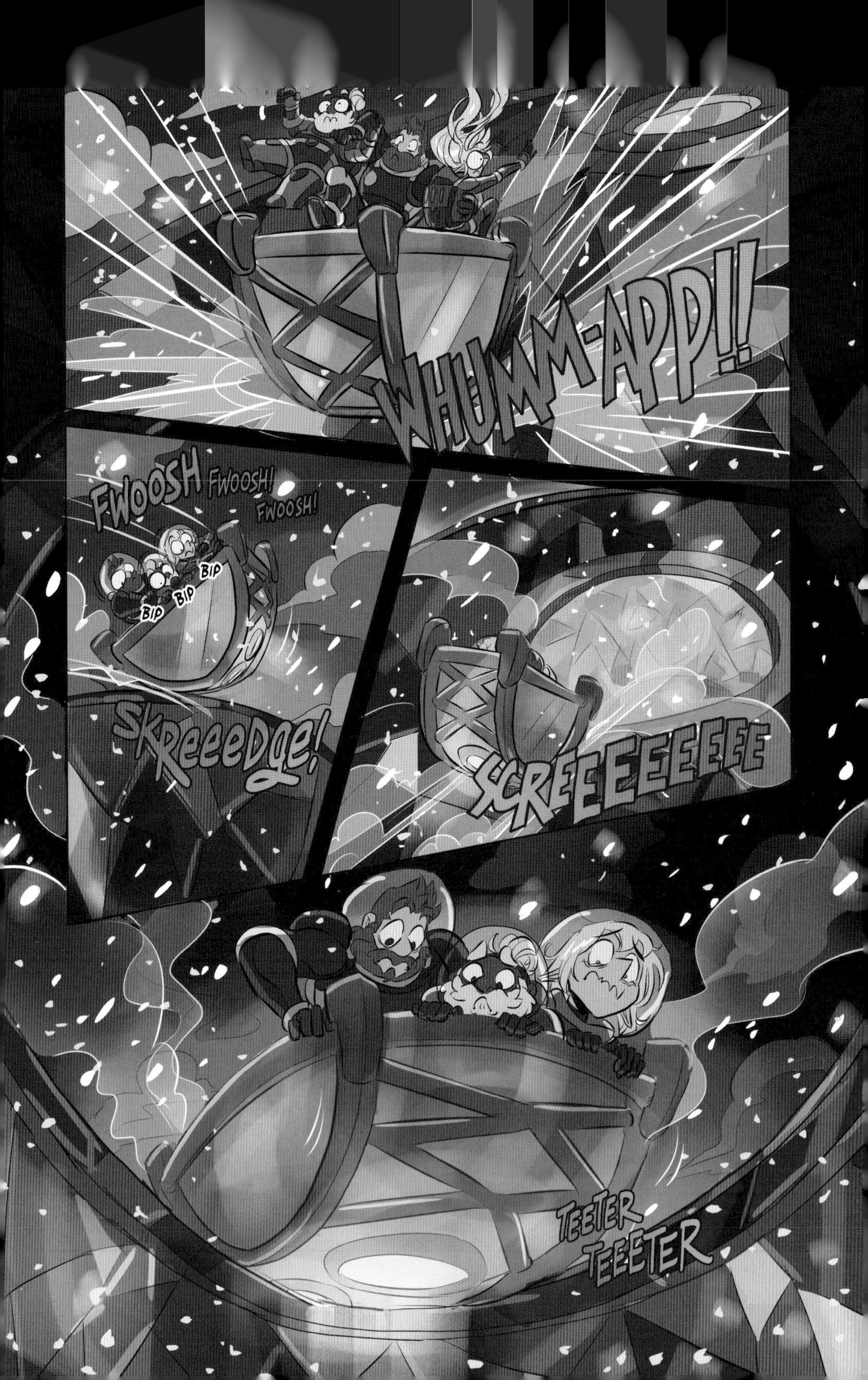
WHUMM-APP!!
FWOOSH FWOOSH! FWOOSH!
BIP
BIP
BIP
SKREEEDGE!
SCREEEEEEEEE
TEETER
TEEETER

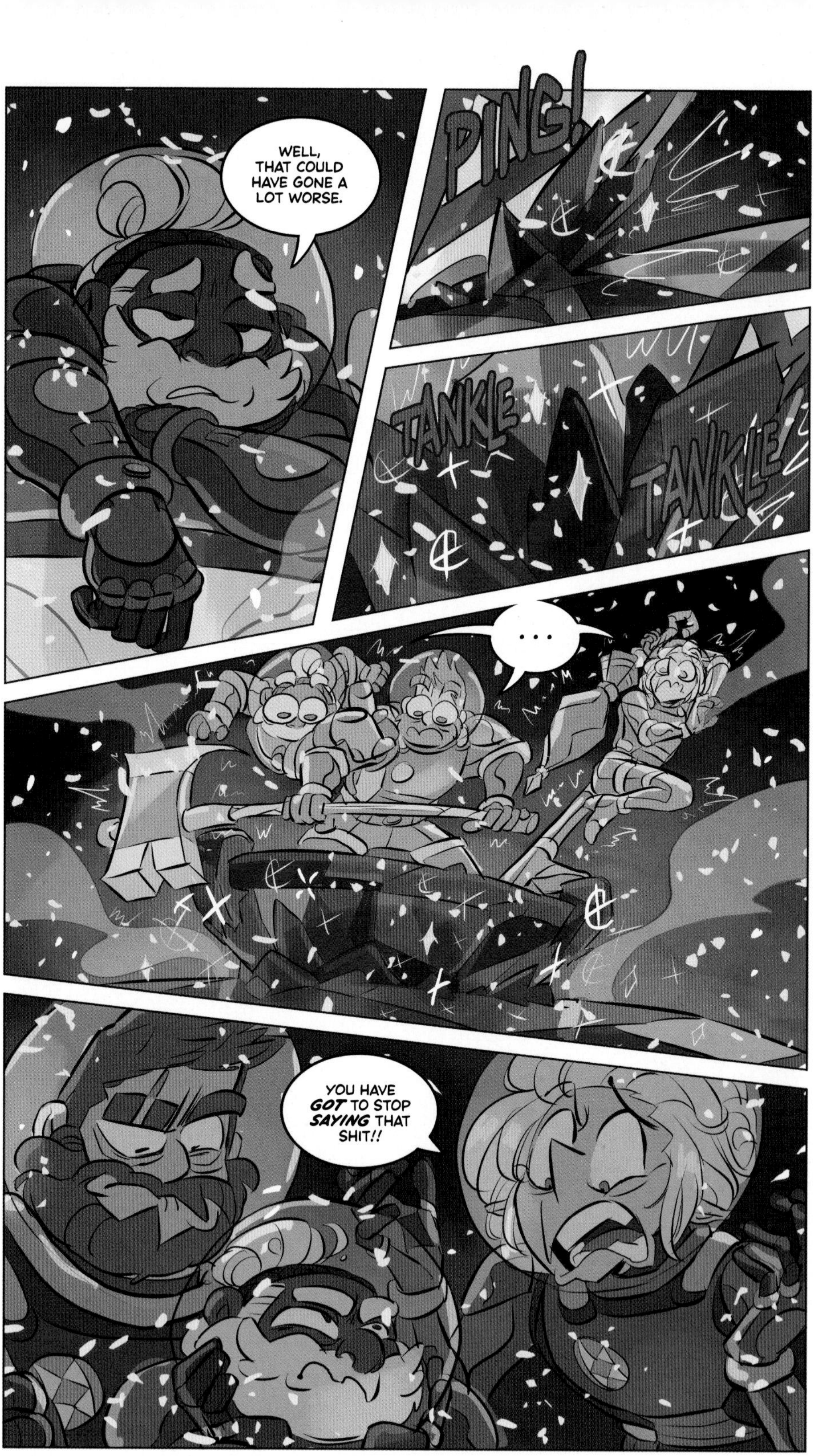
WELL, THAT COULD HAVE GONE A LOT WORSE.
PING!
TANKLE
TANKLE!
...
YOU HAVE **GOT** TO STOP **SAYING** THAT SHIT!!

Chapter
2

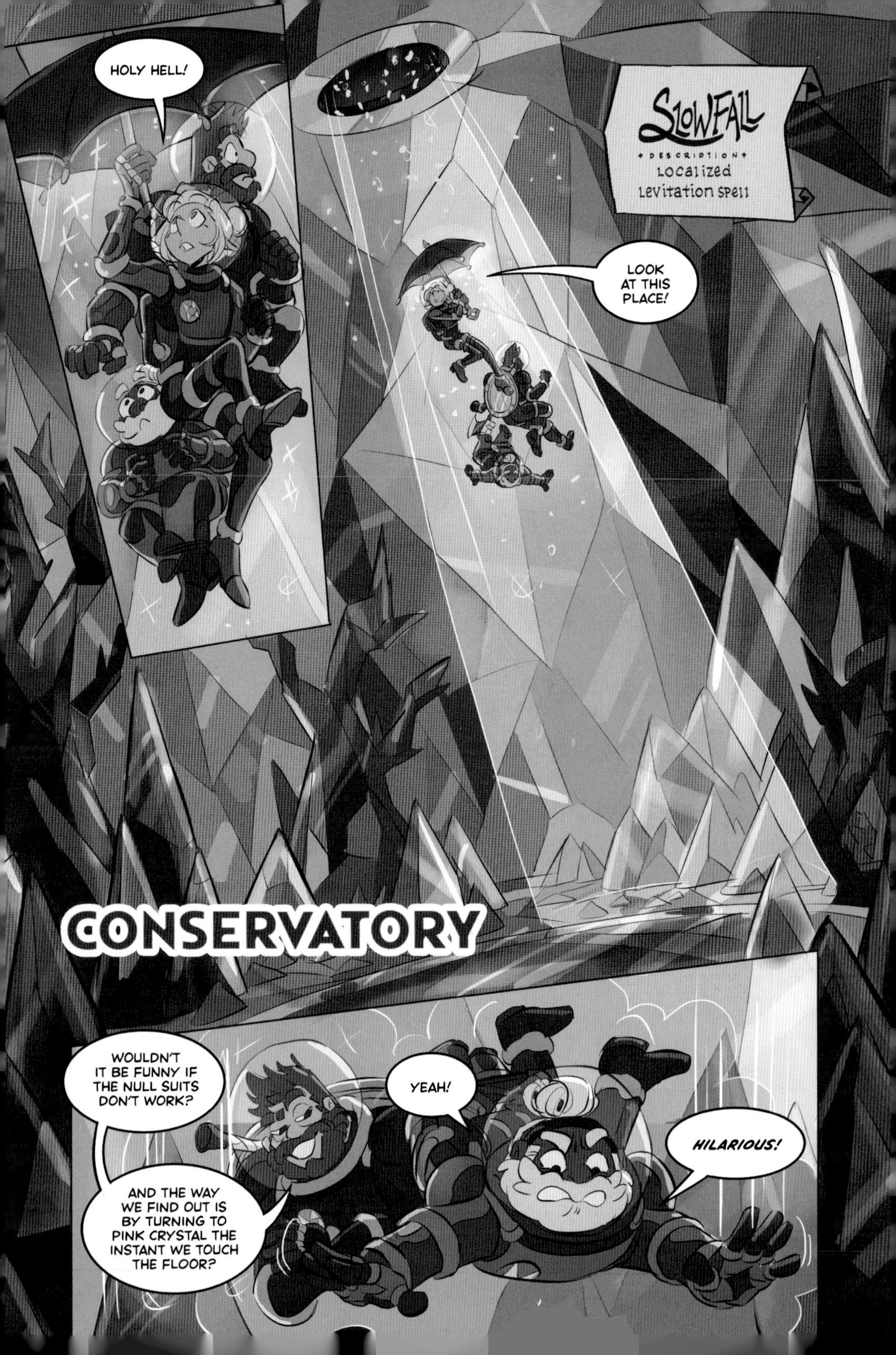
HOLY HELL!
SLOWFALL
DESCRIPTION
Localized Levitation Spell
LOOK AT THIS PLACE!
CONSERVATORY
WOULDN'T IT BE FUNNY IF THE NULL SUITS DON'T WORK?
AND THE WAY WE FIND OUT IS BY TURNING TO PINK CRYSTAL THE INSTANT WE TOUCH THE FLOOR?
YEAH!
HILARIOUS!

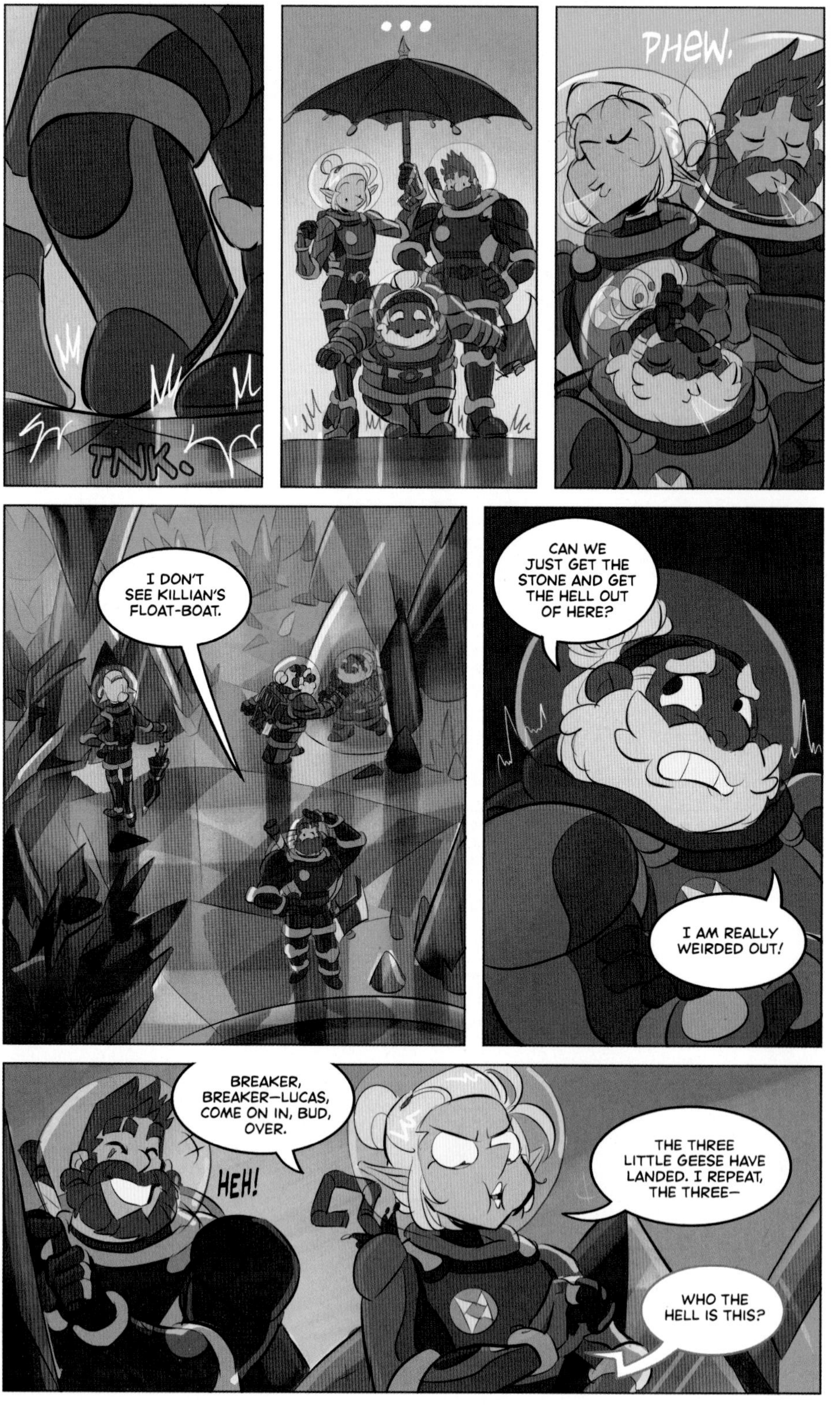
TNK.
• • •
PHEW.
I DON'T SEE KILLIAN'S FLOAT-BOAT.
CAN WE JUST GET THE STONE AND GET THE HELL OUT OF HERE?
I AM REALLY WEIRDED OUT!
BREAKER, BREAKER—LUCAS, COME ON IN, BUD, OVER.
HEH!
THE THREE LITTLE GEESE HAVE LANDED. I REPEAT, THE THREE—
WHO THE HELL IS THIS?

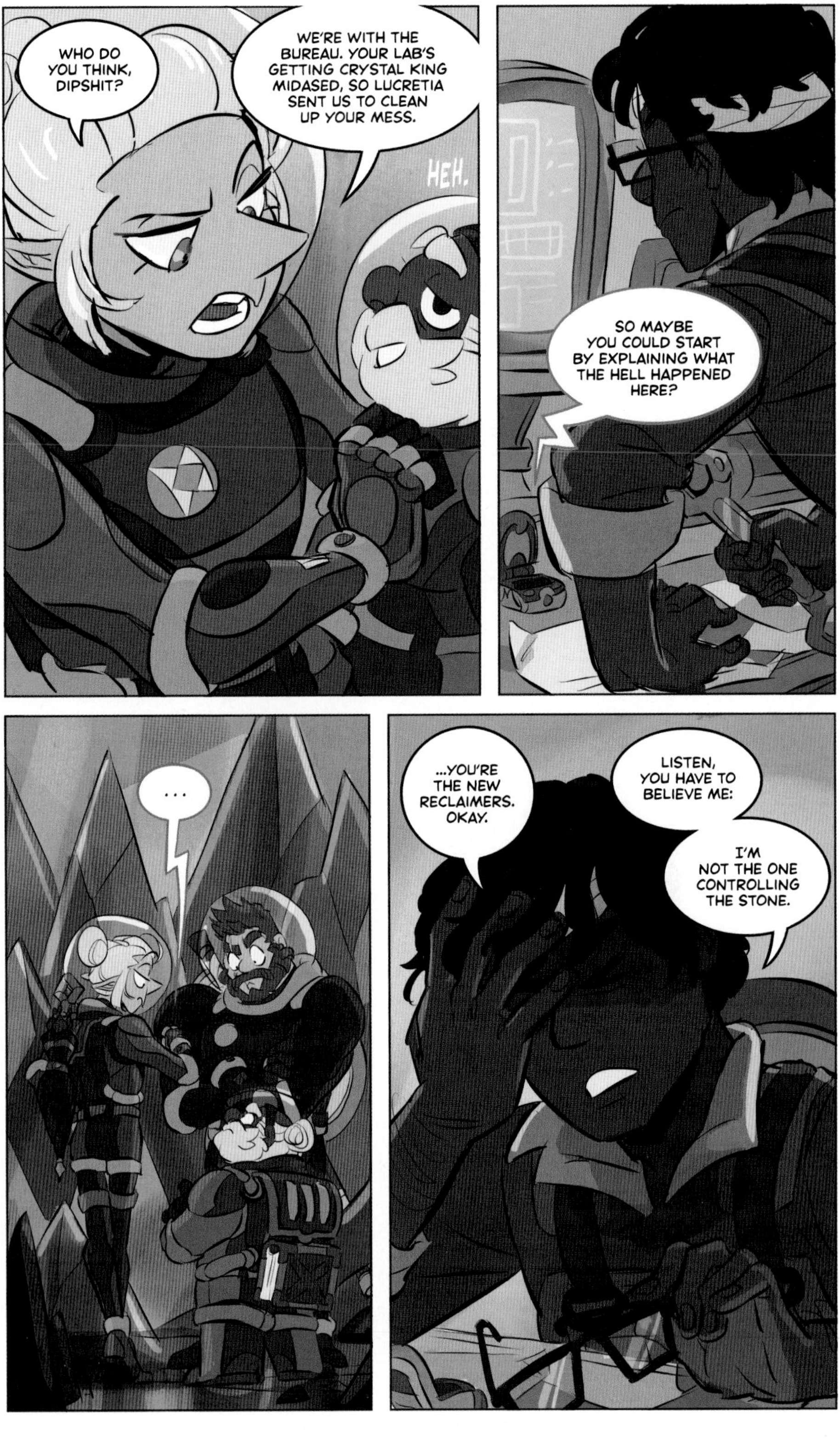
WHO DO YOU THINK, DIPSHIT?
WE'RE WITH THE BUREAU. YOUR LAB'S GETTING CRYSTAL KING MIDASED, SO LUCRETIA SENT US TO CLEAN UP YOUR MESS.
HEH.
SO MAYBE YOU COULD START BY EXPLAINING WHAT THE HELL HAPPENED HERE?
...
...YOU'RE THE NEW RECLAIMERS. OKAY.
LISTEN, YOU HAVE TO BELIEVE ME:
I'M NOT THE ONE CONTROLLING THE STONE.

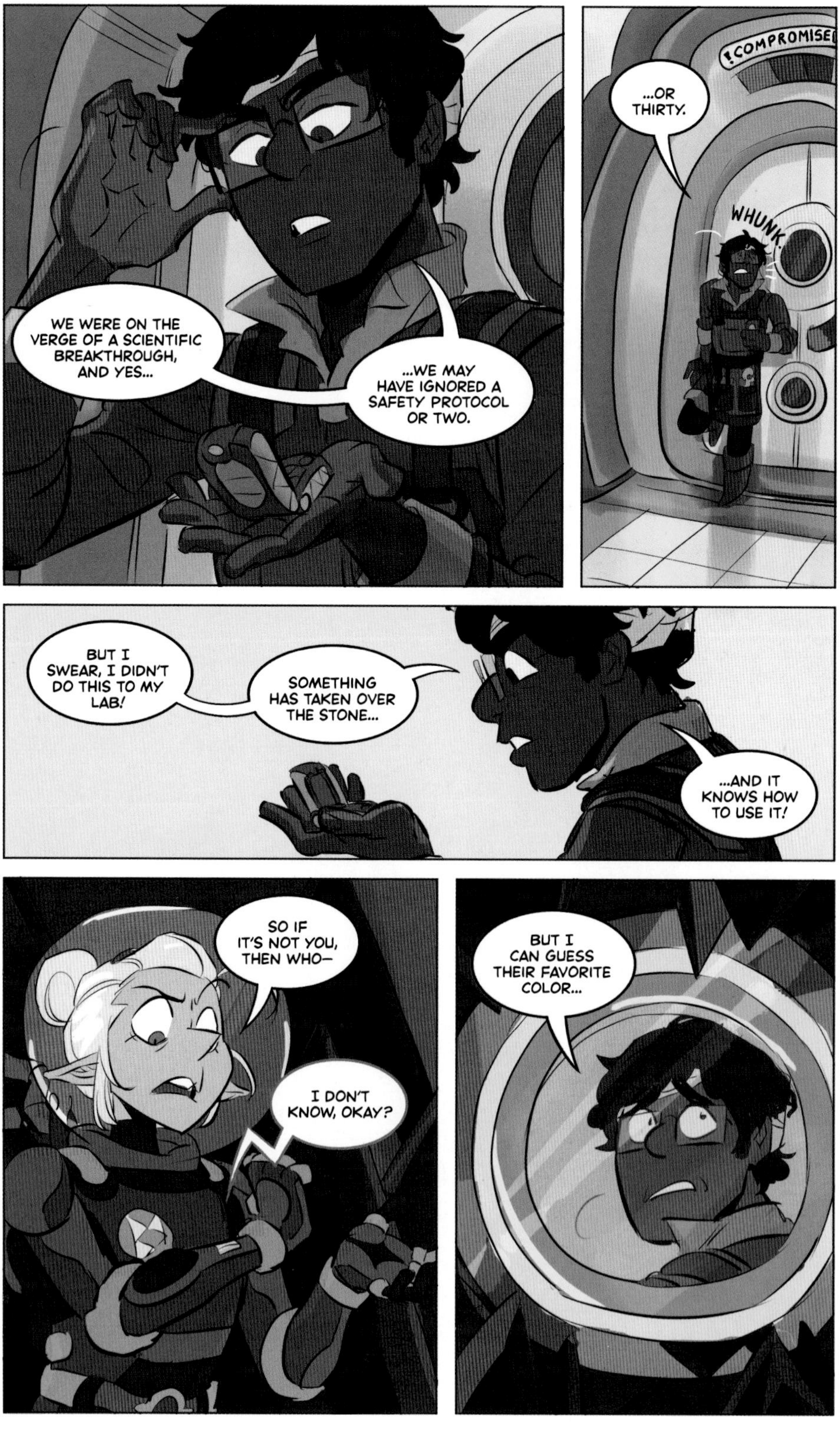
WE WERE ON THE VERGE OF A SCIENTIFIC BREAKTHROUGH, AND YES...
...WE MAY HAVE IGNORED A SAFETY PROTOCOL OR TWO.
COMPROMISED
...OR THIRTY.
WHUNK.
BUT I SWEAR, I DIDN'T DO THIS TO MY LAB!
SOMETHING HAS TAKEN OVER THE STONE...
...AND IT KNOWS HOW TO USE IT!
SO IF IT'S NOT YOU, THEN WHO—
I DON'T KNOW, OKAY?
BUT I CAN GUESS THEIR FAVORITE COLOR...

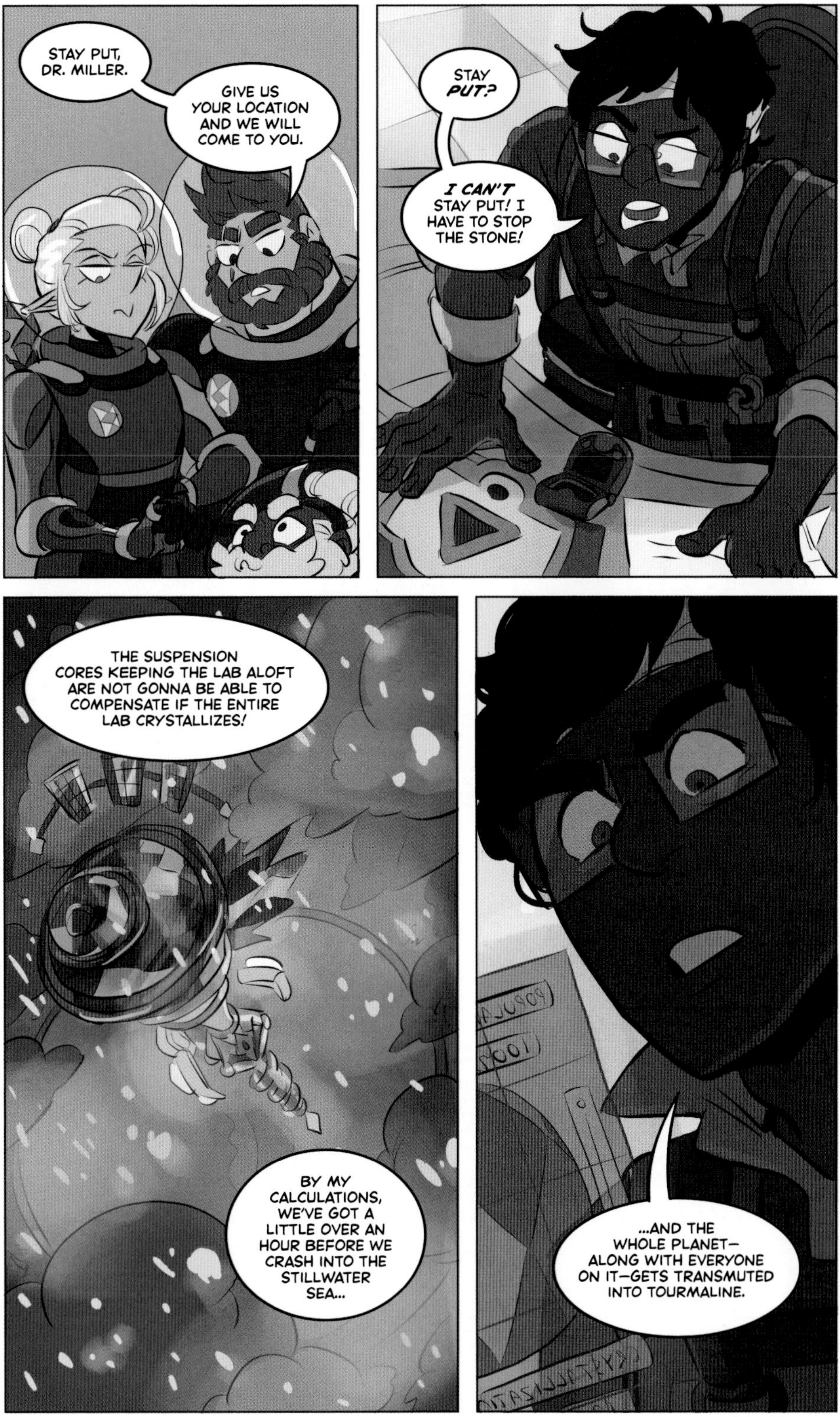
STAY PUT, DR. MILLER.
GIVE US YOUR LOCATION AND WE WILL COME TO YOU.
STAY *PUT?*
I CAN'T STAY PUT! I HAVE TO STOP THE STONE!
THE SUSPENSION CORES KEEPING THE LAB ALOFT ARE NOT GONNA BE ABLE TO COMPENSATE IF THE ENTIRE LAB CRYSTALLIZES!
BY MY CALCULATIONS, WE'VE GOT A LITTLE OVER AN HOUR BEFORE WE CRASH INTO THE STILLWATER SEA...
...AND THE WHOLE PLANET—ALONG WITH EVERYONE ON IT—GETS TRANSMUTED INTO TOURMALINE.

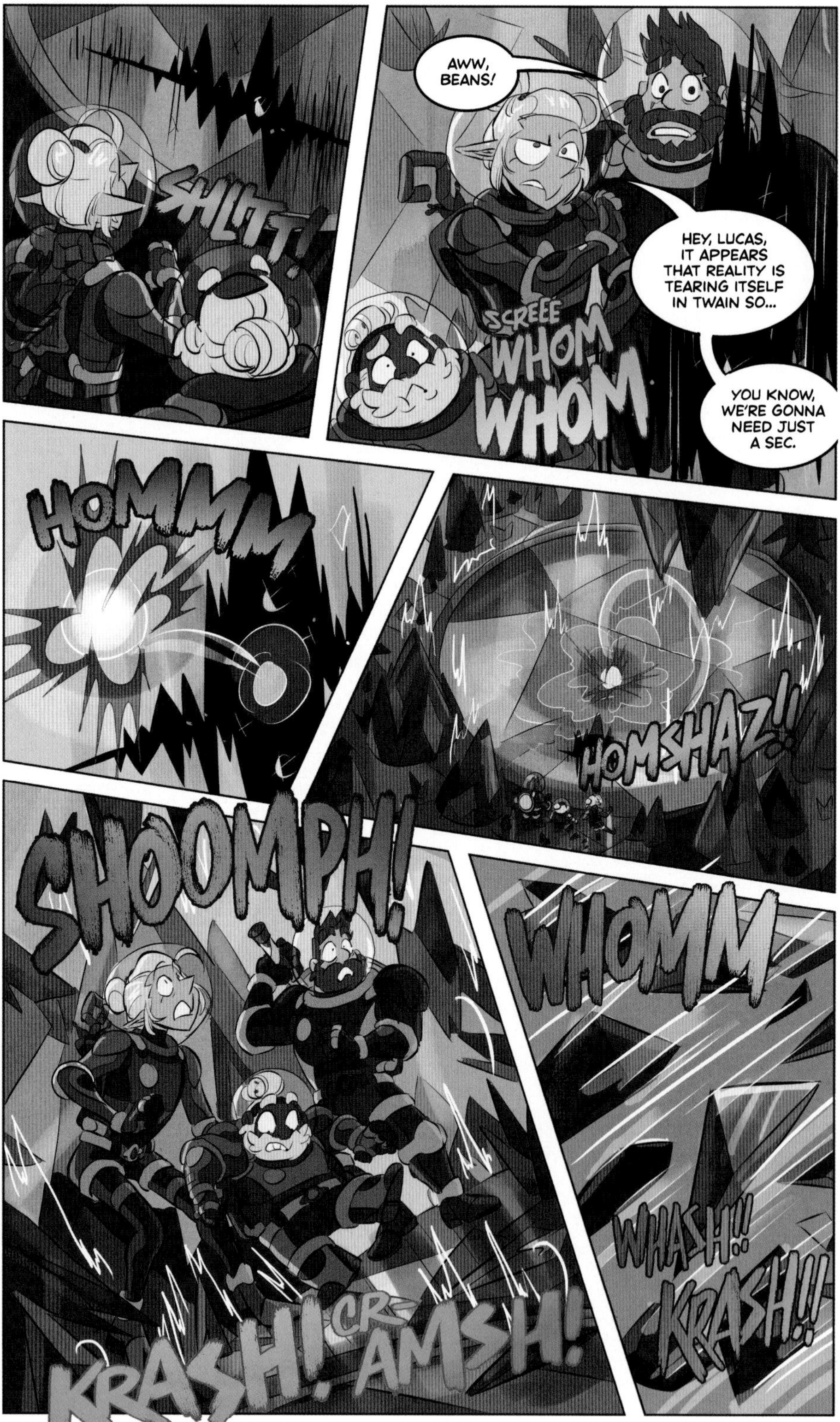
SHLITT!
AWW, BEANS!
HEY, LUCAS, IT APPEARS THAT REALITY IS TEARING ITSELF IN TWAIN SO...
SCREEE
WHOM
WHOM
YOU KNOW, WE'RE GONNA NEED JUST A SEC.
HOMMM
HOMSHAZ!!
SHOOMPH!
KRASH!
CR-AMSH!
WHOMM
WHASH!!
KRASH!!

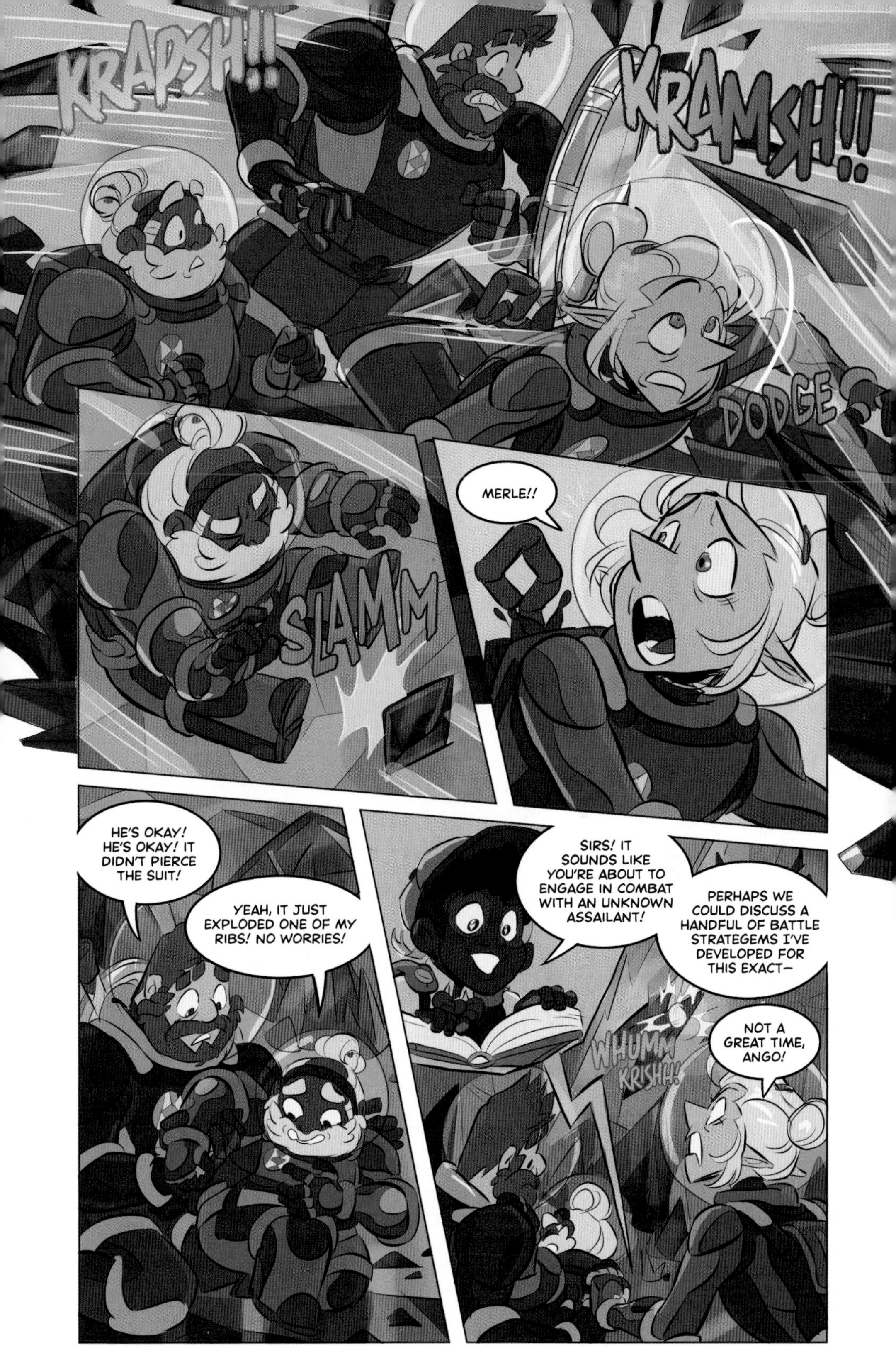
KRADSH!!
KRAMSH!!
DODGE
MERLE!!
SLAMM
HE'S OKAY! HE'S OKAY! IT DIDN'T PIERCE THE SUIT!
YEAH, IT JUST EXPLODED ONE OF MY RIBS! NO WORRIES!
SIRS! IT SOUNDS LIKE YOU'RE ABOUT TO ENGAGE IN COMBAT WITH AN UNKNOWN ASSAILANT!
PERHAPS WE COULD DISCUSS A HANDFUL OF BATTLE STRATEGEMS I'VE DEVELOPED FOR THIS EXACT—
WHUMM
KRISHH!
NOT A GREAT TIME, ANGO!

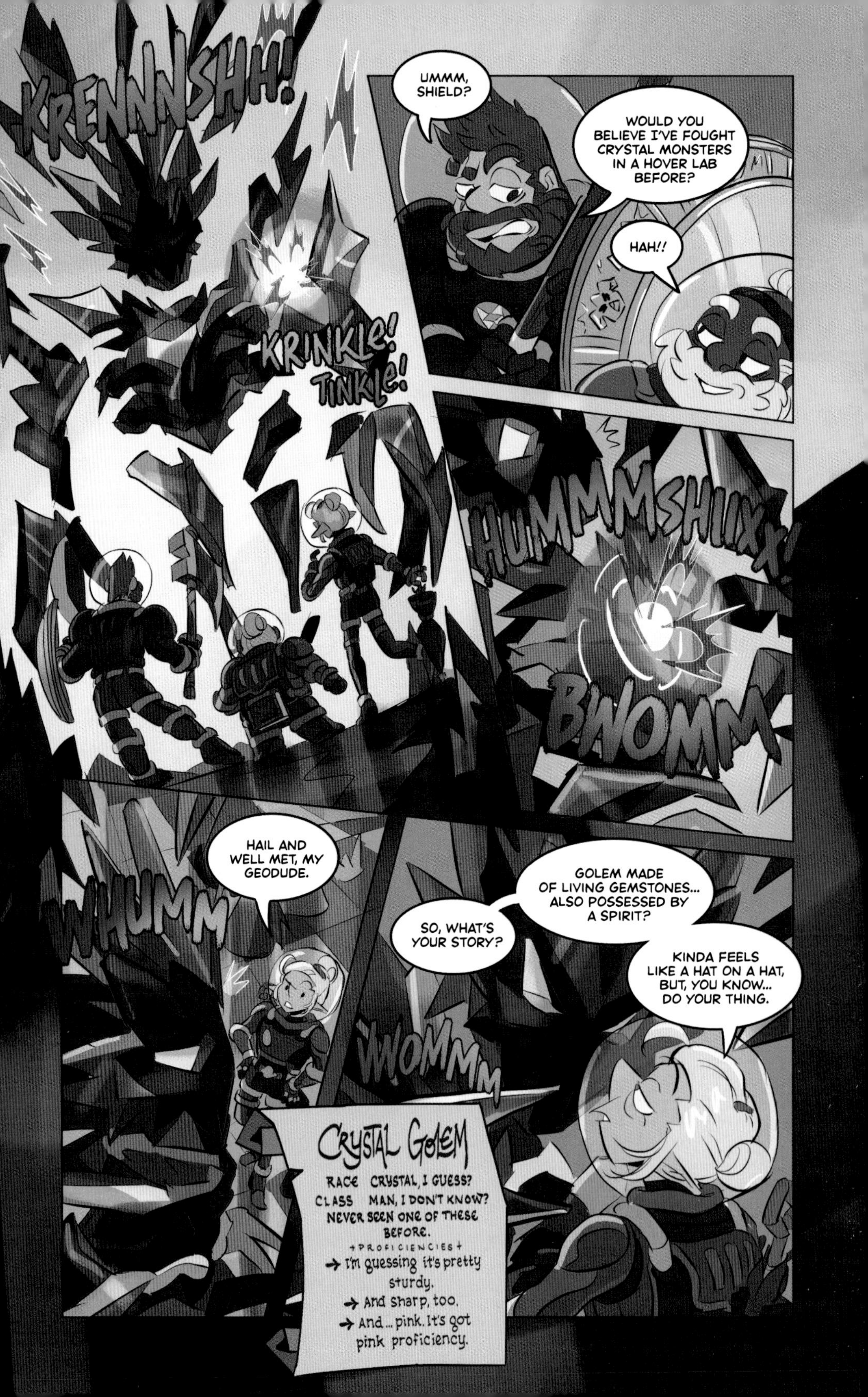
KRENNNSHH!
KRINKLE! TINKLE!
UMMM, SHIELD?
WOULD YOU BELIEVE I'VE FOUGHT CRYSTAL MONSTERS IN A HOVER LAB BEFORE?
HAH!!
HUMMMSHIIXX!
BWOMM
WHUMM
HAIL AND WELL MET, MY GEODUDE.
GOLEM MADE OF LIVING GEMSTONES... ALSO POSSESSED BY A SPIRIT?
SO, WHAT'S YOUR STORY?
KINDA FEELS LIKE A HAT ON A HAT, BUT, YOU KNOW... DO YOUR THING.
WOMMM
CRYSTAL GOLEM
RACE CRYSTAL, I GUESS?
CLASS MAN, I DON'T KNOW? NEVER SEEN ONE OF THESE BEFORE.
+PROFICIENCIES+
→ I'm guessing it's pretty sturdy.
→ And sharp, too.
→ And... pink. It's got pink proficiency.

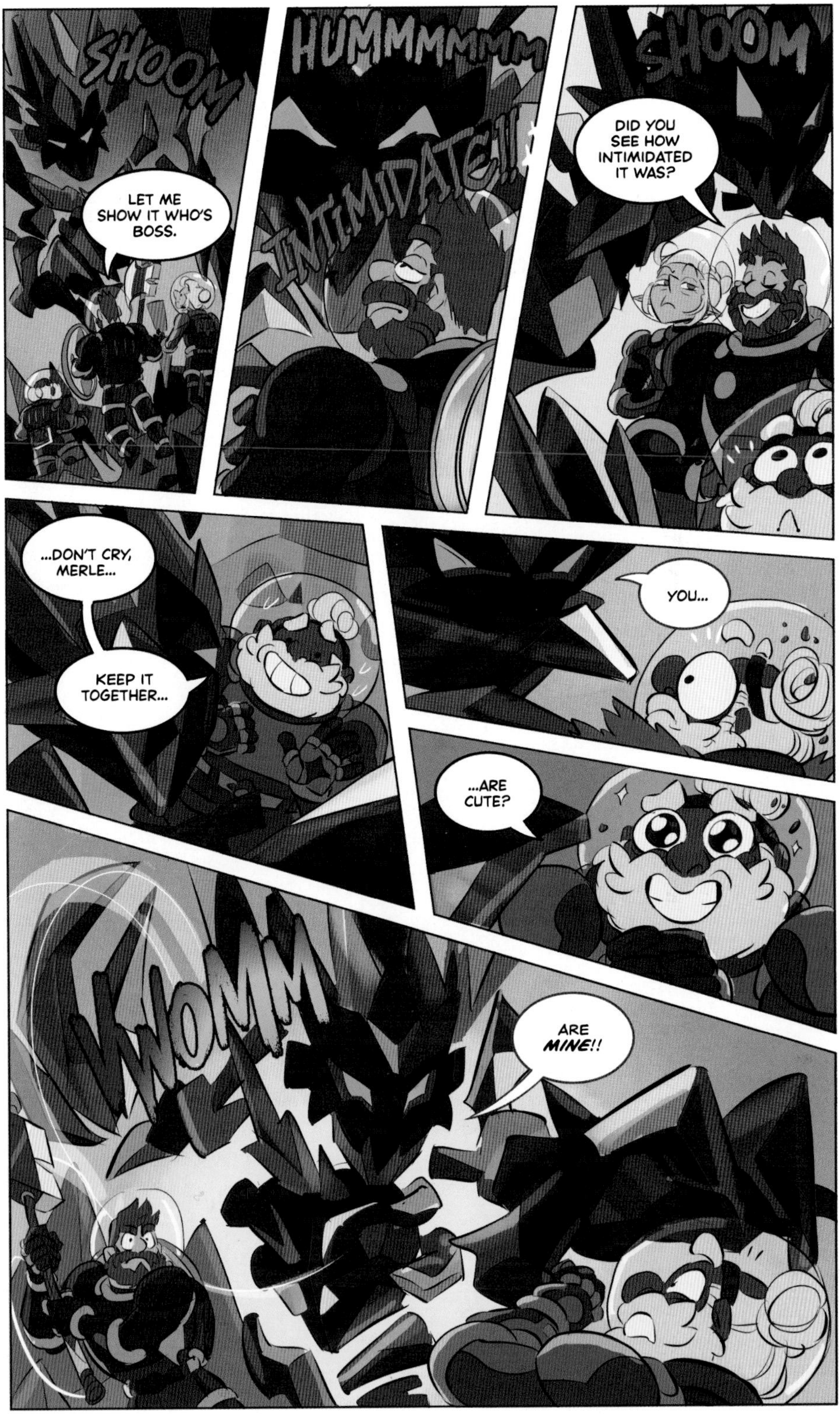
SHOOM
LET ME SHOW IT WHO'S BOSS.
HUMMMMMMM
INTIMIDATE!!
SHOOM
DID YOU SEE HOW INTIMIDATED IT WAS?
...DON'T CRY, MERLE...
KEEP IT TOGETHER...
YOU...
...ARE CUTE?
WOMM
ARE *MINE*!!

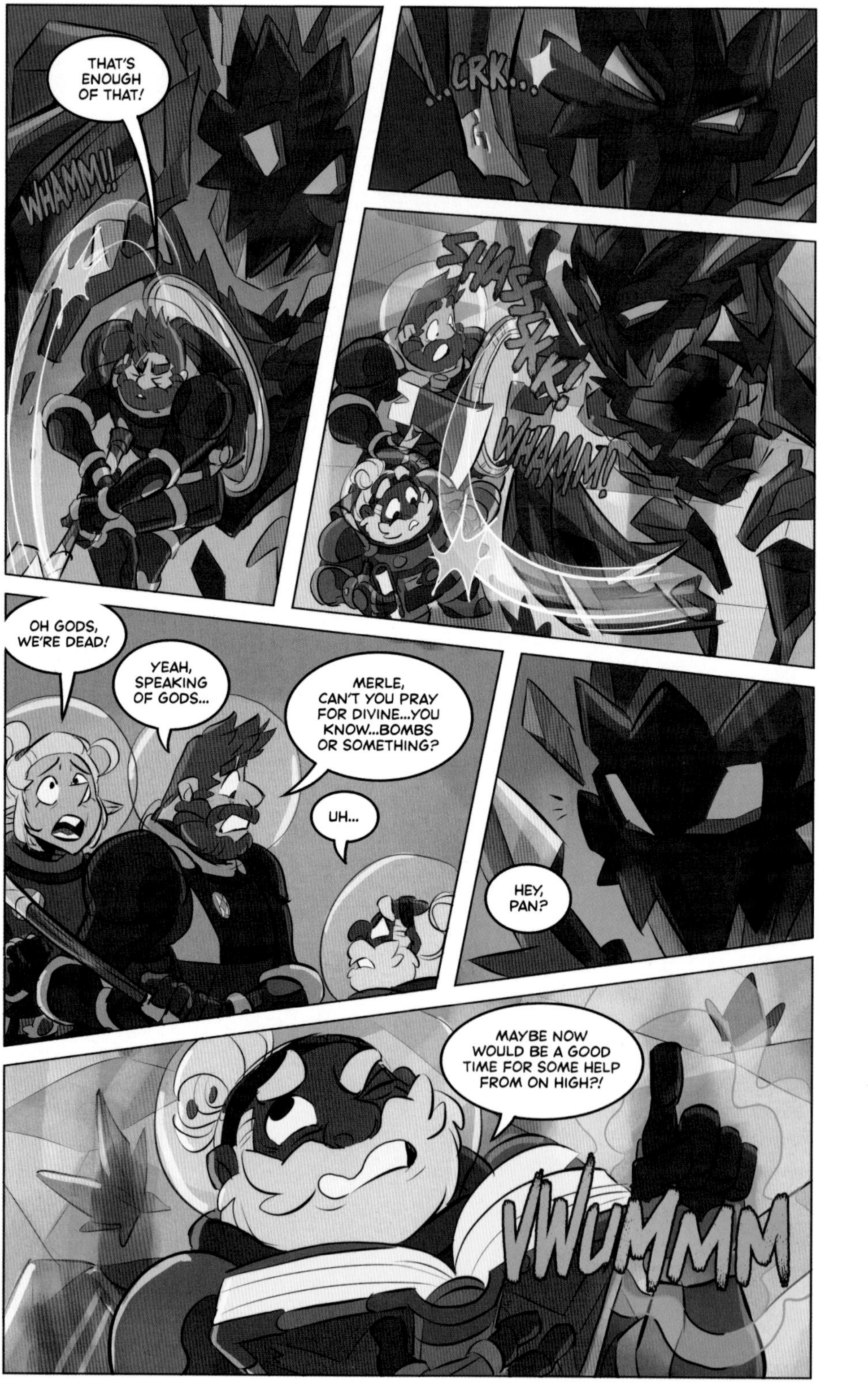
THAT'S ENOUGH OF THAT!
WHAMM!!
...CRK...!
SHASKKK!
WHAMM!
OH GODS, WE'RE DEAD!
YEAH, SPEAKING OF GODS...
MERLE, CAN'T YOU PRAY FOR DIVINE...YOU KNOW...BOMBS OR SOMETHING?
UH...
HEY, PAN?
MAYBE NOW WOULD BE A GOOD TIME FOR SOME HELP FROM ON HIGH?!
VWUMMM

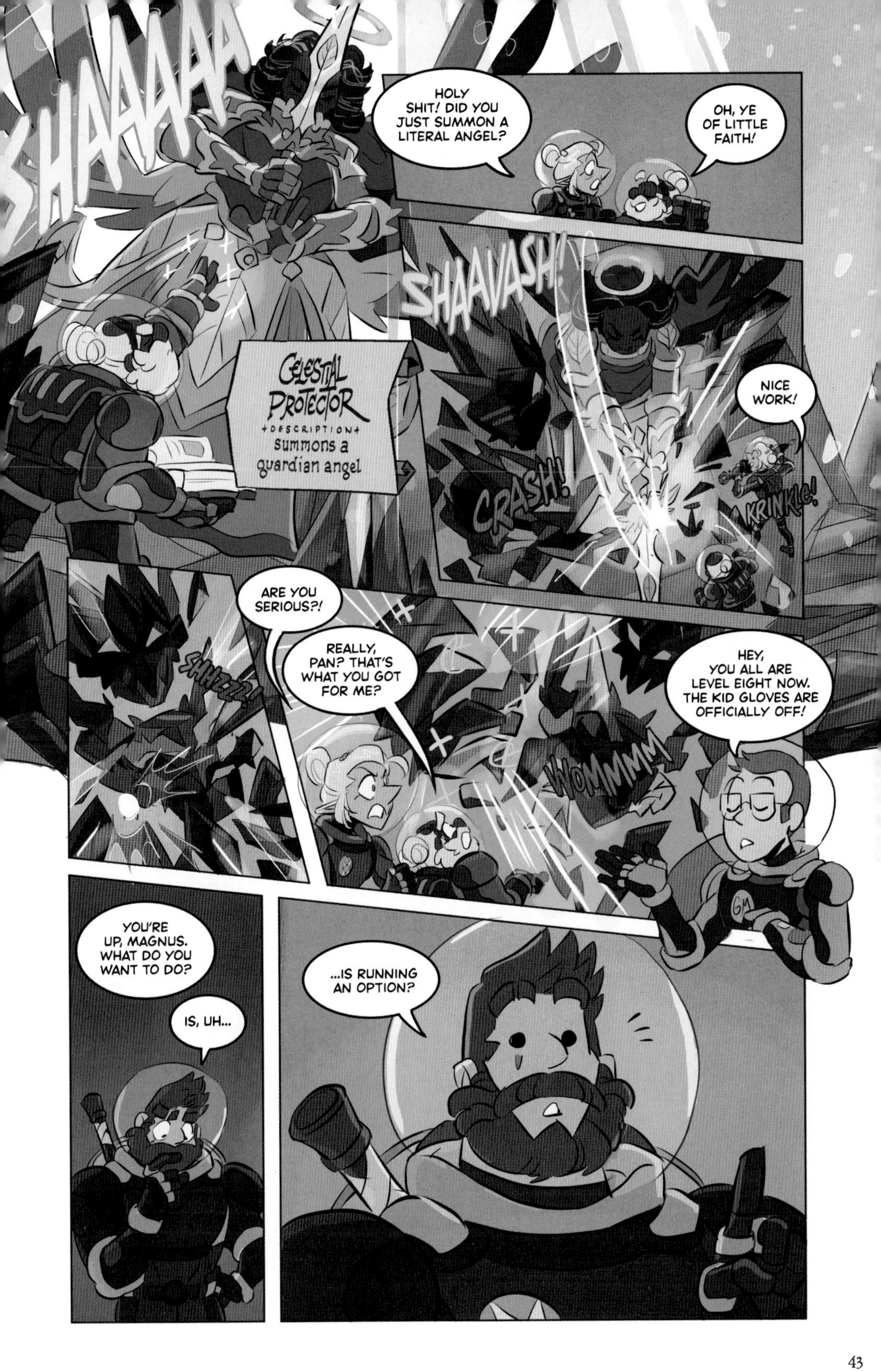
SHAAAAA
HOLY SHIT! DID YOU JUST SUMMON A LITERAL ANGEL?
OH, YE OF LITTLE FAITH!
CELESTIAL PROTECTOR
+DESCRIPTION+
summons a guardian angel
SHAAVASH!
NICE WORK!
CRASH!
KRINKLE!
SHHEZZZ!
ARE YOU SERIOUS?!
REALLY, PAN? THAT'S WHAT YOU GOT FOR ME?
HEY, YOU ALL ARE LEVEL EIGHT NOW. THE KID GLOVES ARE OFFICIALLY OFF!
WOMMMM
GM
YOU'RE UP, MAGNUS. WHAT DO YOU WANT TO DO?
IS, UH...
...IS RUNNING AN OPTION?

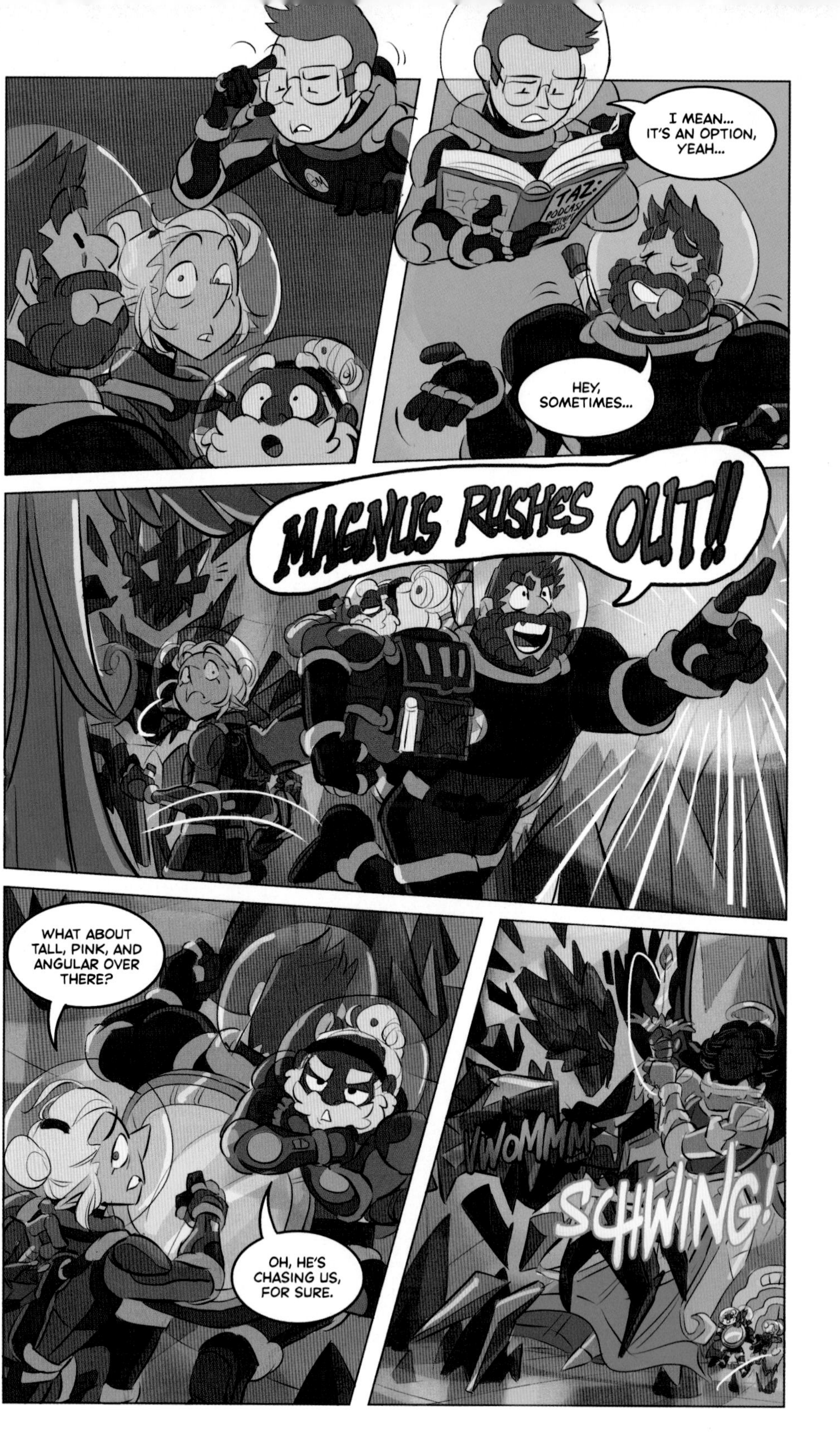
I MEAN... IT'S AN OPTION, YEAH...
HEY, SOMETIMES...
MAGNUS RUSHES OUT!!
WHAT ABOUT TALL, PINK, AND ANGULAR OVER THERE?
OH, HE'S CHASING US, FOR SURE.
VWOMMM
SCHWING!

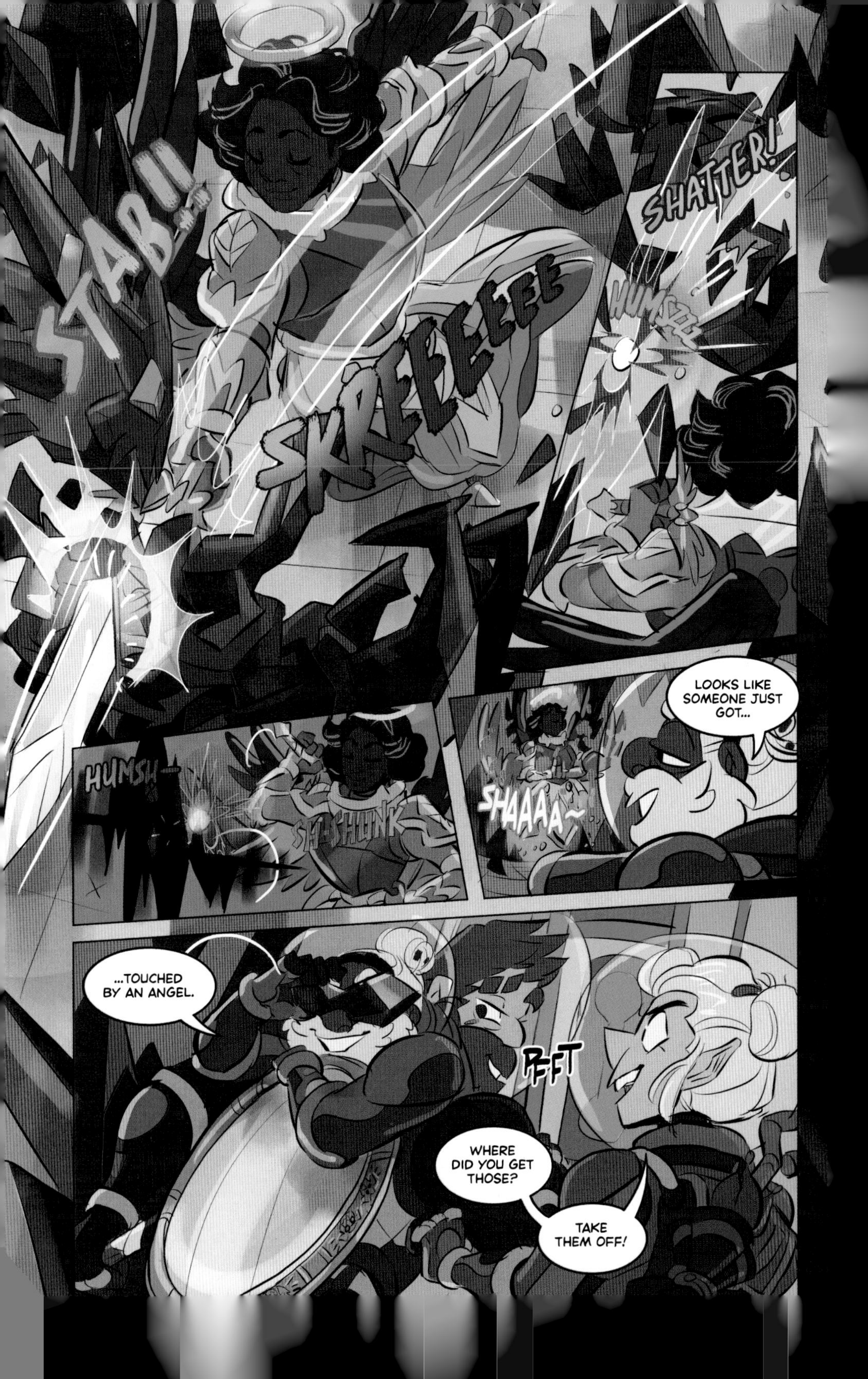
STAB!!
SKREEEEEE
SHATTER!
HUMSZZ
HUMSH
SH-SHUNK
SHAAAA~
LOOKS LIKE SOMEONE JUST GOT...
...TOUCHED BY AN ANGEL.
PFFT
WHERE DID YOU GET THOSE?
TAKE THEM OFF!

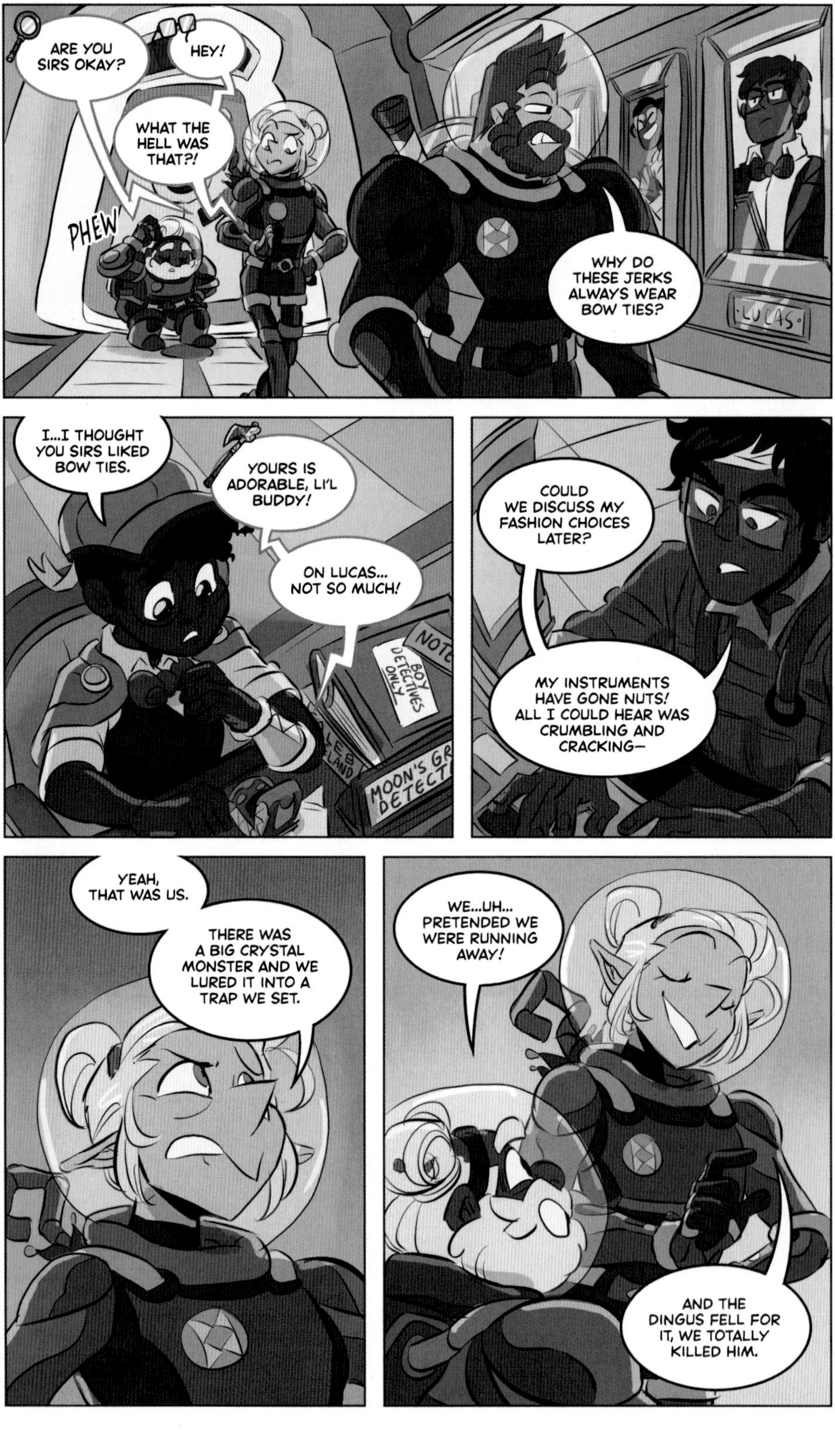
ARE YOU SIRS OKAY?
HEY!
WHAT THE HELL WAS THAT?!
PHEW
WHY DO THESE JERKS ALWAYS WEAR BOW TIES?
LUCAS
I...I THOUGHT YOU SIRS LIKED BOW TIES.
YOURS IS ADORABLE, LI'L BUDDY!
ON LUCAS... NOT SO MUCH!
NOTE
BOY DETECTIVES ONLY
COULD WE DISCUSS MY FASHION CHOICES LATER?
MY INSTRUMENTS HAVE GONE NUTS! ALL I COULD HEAR WAS CRUMBLING AND CRACKING—
YEAH, THAT WAS US.
THERE WAS A BIG CRYSTAL MONSTER AND WE LURED IT INTO A TRAP WE SET.
WE...UH... PRETENDED WE WERE RUNNING AWAY!
AND THE DINGUS FELL FOR IT, WE TOTALLY KILLED HIM.

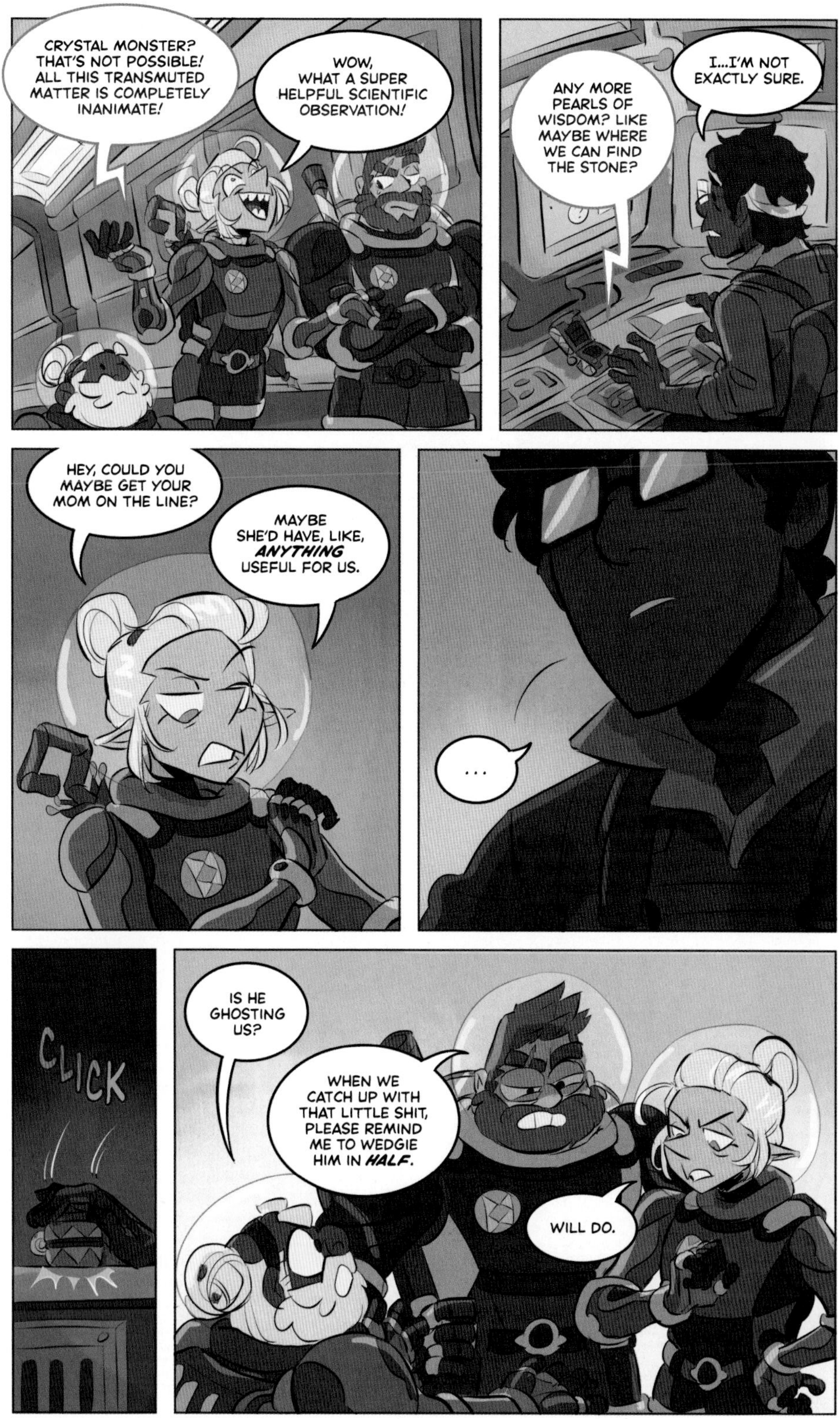
CRYSTAL MONSTER? THAT'S NOT POSSIBLE! ALL THIS TRANSMUTED MATTER IS COMPLETELY INANIMATE!
WOW, WHAT A SUPER HELPFUL SCIENTIFIC OBSERVATION!
ANY MORE PEARLS OF WISDOM? LIKE MAYBE WHERE WE CAN FIND THE STONE?
I...I'M NOT EXACTLY SURE.
HEY, COULD YOU MAYBE GET YOUR MOM ON THE LINE?
MAYBE SHE'D HAVE, LIKE, *ANYTHING* USEFUL FOR US.
...
CLICK
IS HE GHOSTING US?
WHEN WE CATCH UP WITH THAT LITTLE SHIT, PLEASE REMIND ME TO WEDGIE HIM IN *HALF*.
WILL DO.

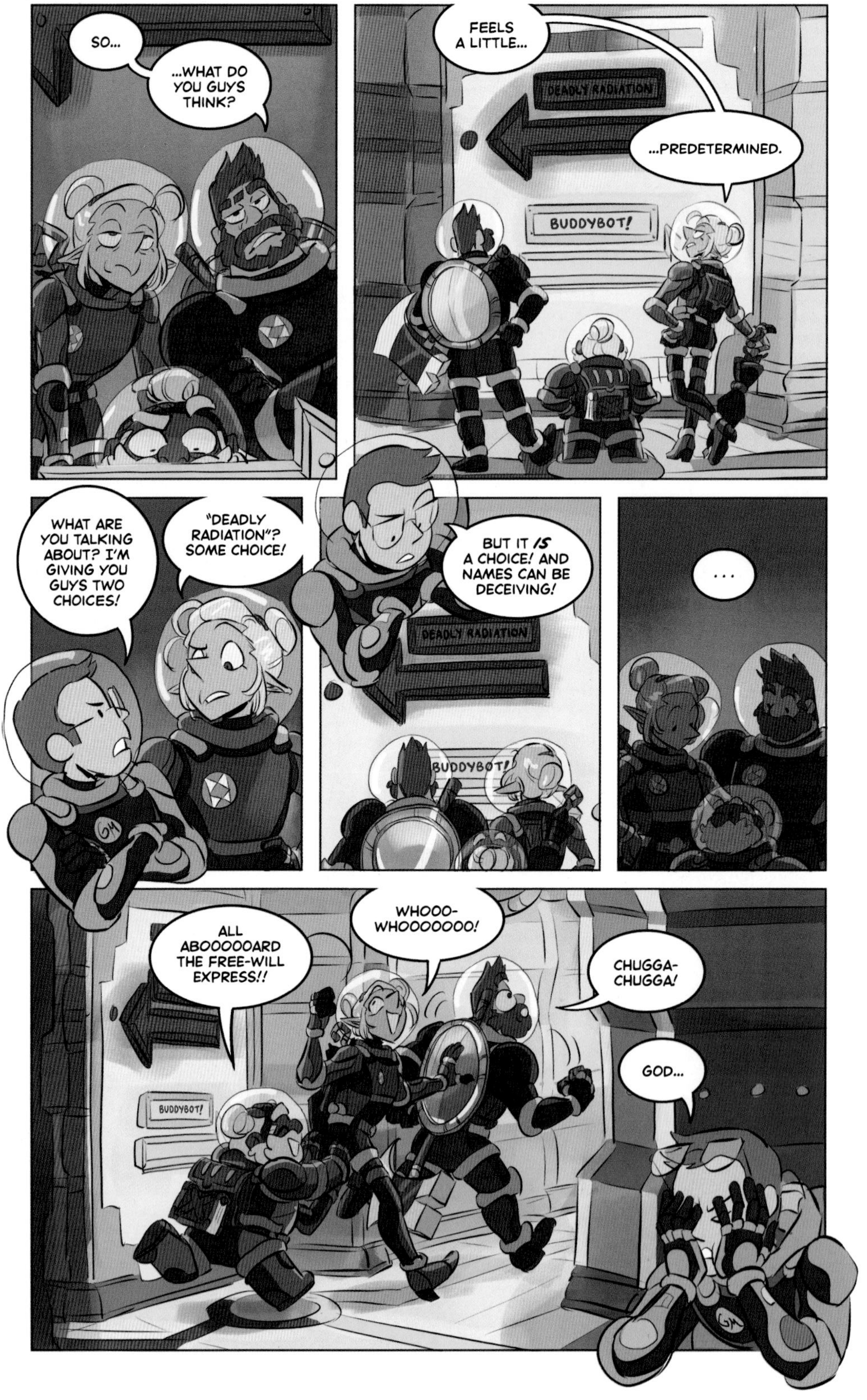
SO...
...WHAT DO YOU GUYS THINK?
FEELS A LITTLE...
DEADLY RADIATION
...PREDETERMINED.
BUDDYBOT!
WHAT ARE YOU TALKING ABOUT? I'M GIVING YOU GUYS TWO CHOICES!
"DEADLY RADIATION"? SOME CHOICE!
BUT IT *IS* A CHOICE! AND NAMES CAN BE DECEIVING!
DEADLY RADIATION
BUDDYBOT!
. . .
ALL ABOOOOOARD THE FREE-WILL EXPRESS!!
WHOOO-WHOOOOOOO!
CHUGGA-CHUGGA!
GOD...
BUDDYBOT!

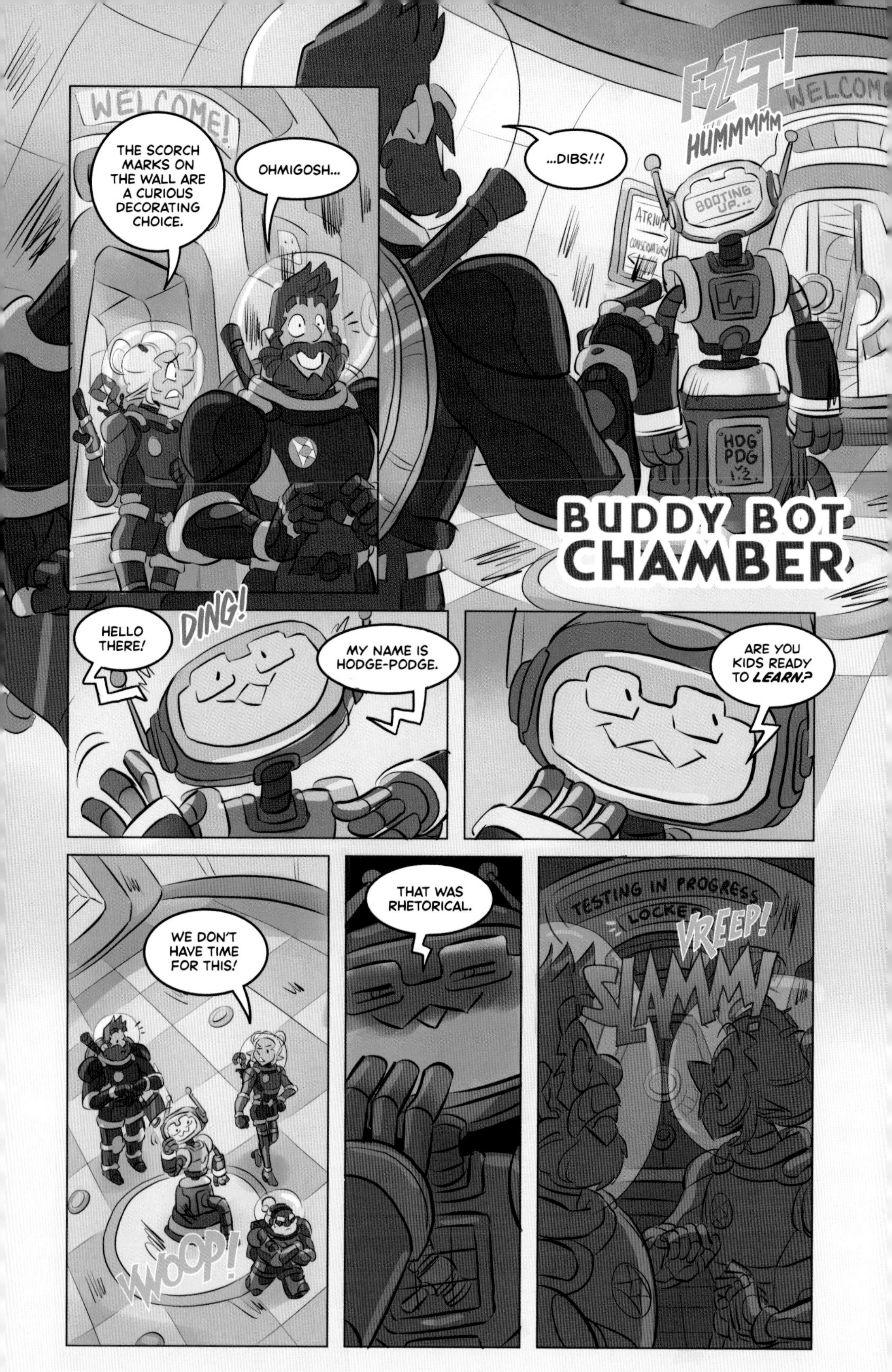
WELCOME!
THE SCORCH MARKS ON THE WALL ARE A CURIOUS DECORATING CHOICE.
OHMIGOSH...
...DIBS!!!
FZZT!
HUMMMMM
WELCOM
BOOTING UP...
ATRIUM
CONSERVATORY
HDG PDG V.2
BUDDY BOT CHAMBER
HELLO THERE!
DING!
MY NAME IS HODGE-PODGE.
ARE YOU KIDS READY TO *LEARN?*
WE DON'T HAVE TIME FOR THIS!
WOOP!
THAT WAS RHETORICAL.
TESTING IN PROGRESS
VREEP!
SLAMM!

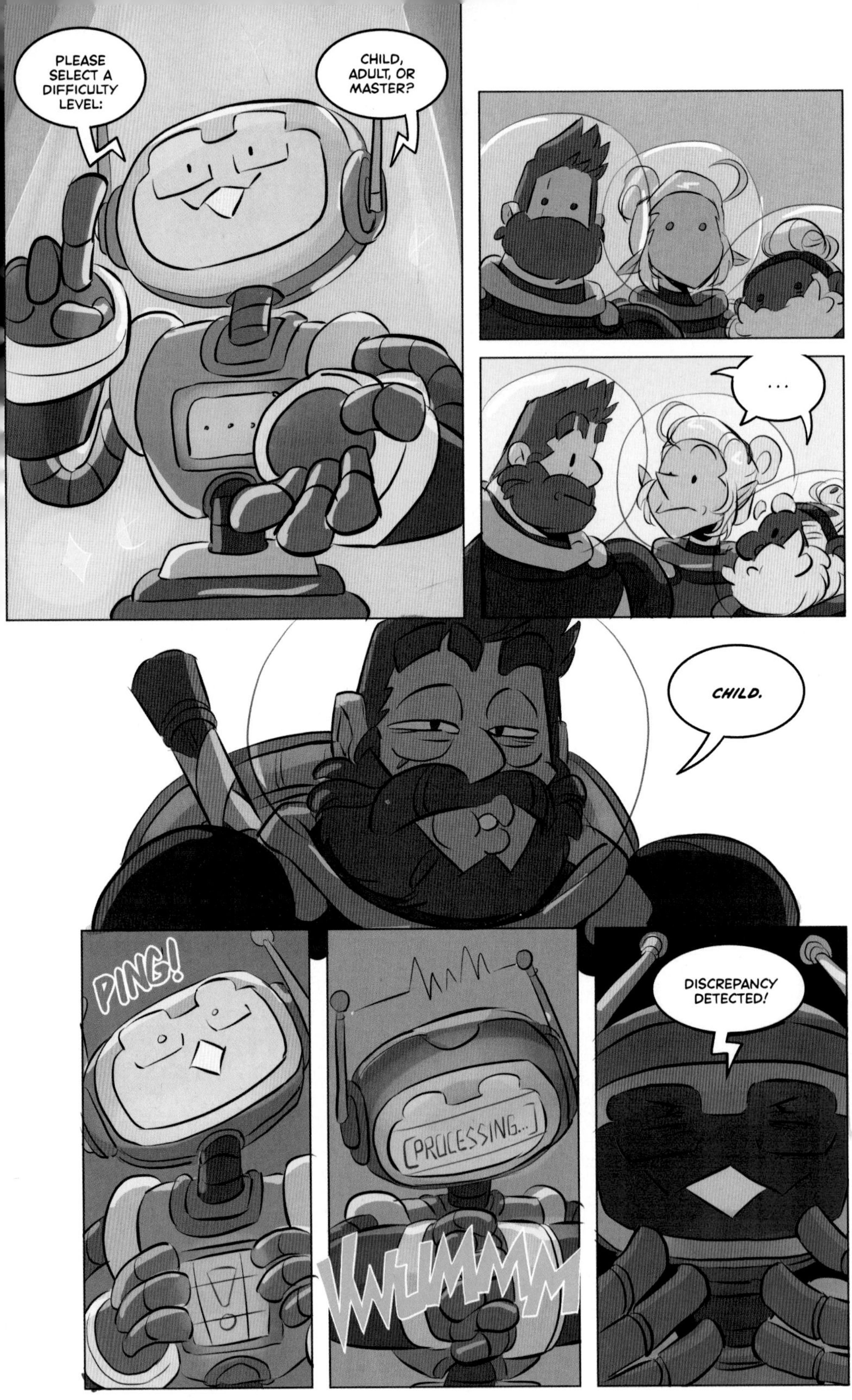
PLEASE SELECT A DIFFICULTY LEVEL:
CHILD, ADULT, OR MASTER?
...
CHILD.
PING!
PROCESSING...
WUMMM
DISCREPANCY DETECTED!

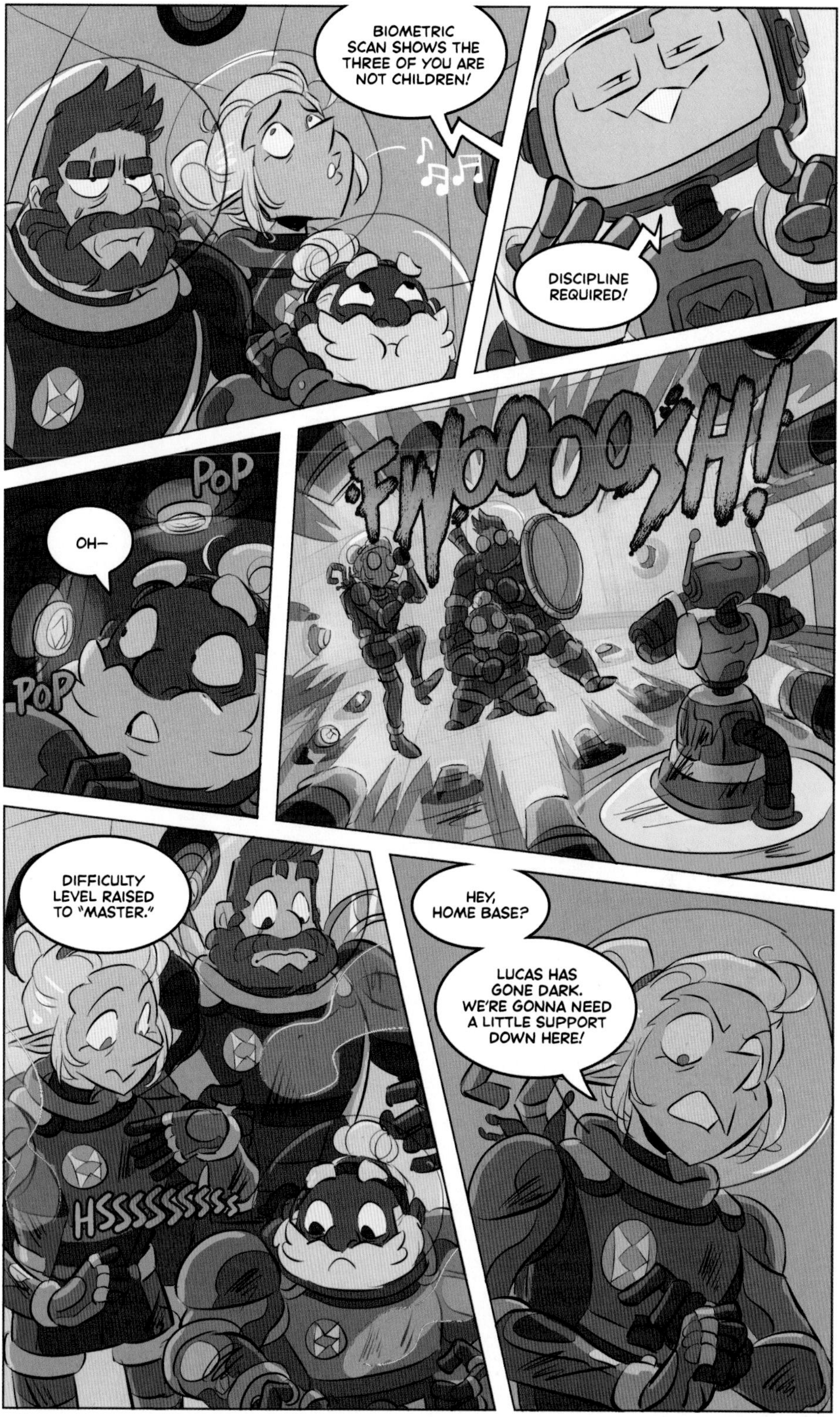
BIOMETRIC SCAN SHOWS THE THREE OF YOU ARE NOT CHILDREN!
DISCIPLINE REQUIRED!
FWOOOOSH!
POP
OH—
POP
DIFFICULTY LEVEL RAISED TO "MASTER."
HSSSSSSSSS
HEY, HOME BASE?
LUCAS HAS GONE DARK. WE'RE GONNA NEED A LITTLE SUPPORT DOWN HERE!

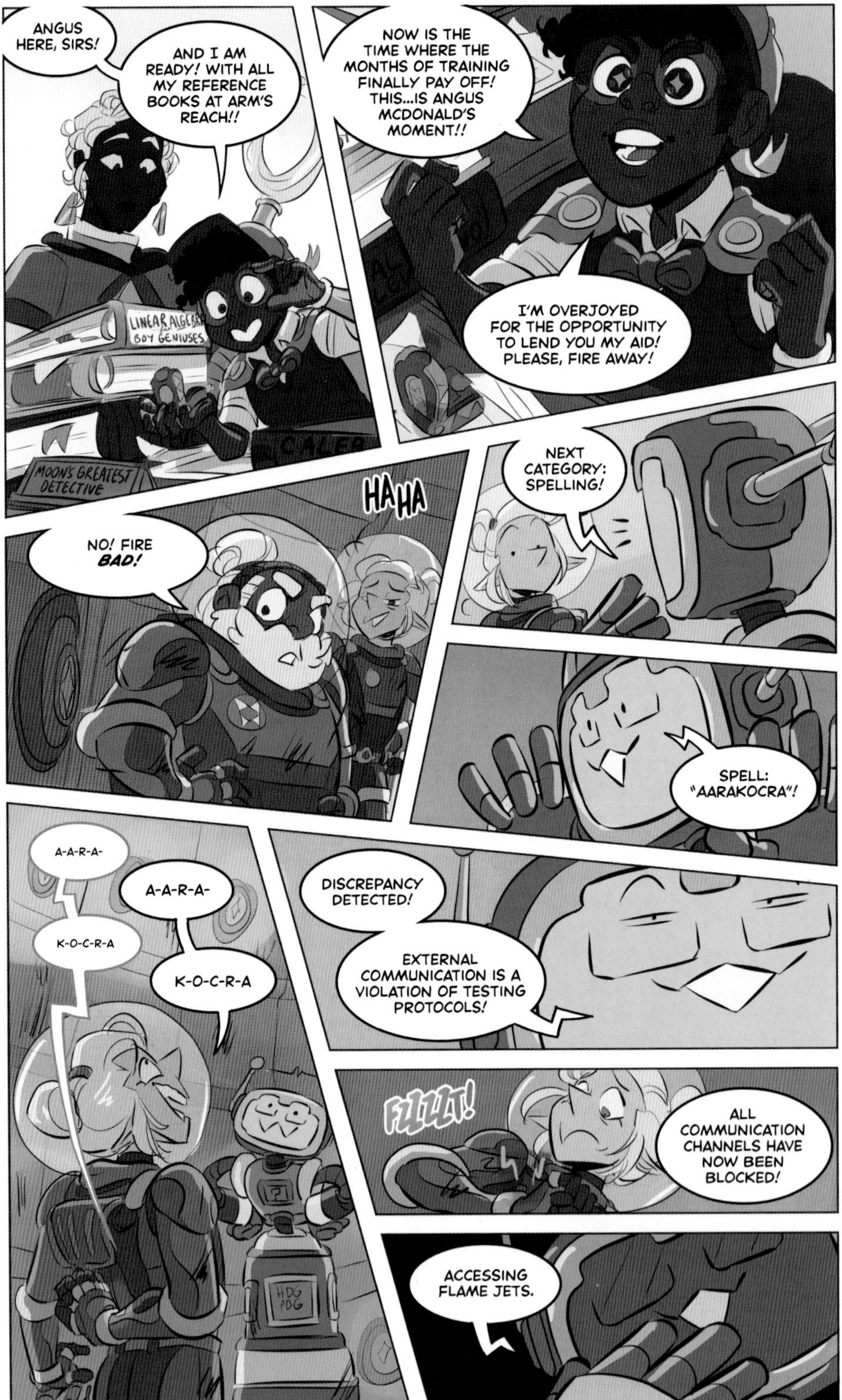
ANGUS HERE, SIRS!
AND I AM READY! WITH ALL MY REFERENCE BOOKS AT ARM'S REACH!!
LINEAR ALGEBRA BOY GENIUSES
MOON'S GREATEST DETECTIVE
NOW IS THE TIME WHERE THE MONTHS OF TRAINING FINALLY PAY OFF! THIS...IS ANGUS MCDONALD'S MOMENT!!
I'M OVERJOYED FOR THE OPPORTUNITY TO LEND YOU MY AID! PLEASE, FIRE AWAY!
NEXT CATEGORY: SPELLING!
HAHA
NO! FIRE BAD!
SPELL: "AARAKOCRA"!
A-A-R-A-
A-A-R-A-
K-O-C-R-A
K-O-C-R-A
DISCREPANCY DETECTED!
EXTERNAL COMMUNICATION IS A VIOLATION OF TESTING PROTOCOLS!
FZZZT!
ALL COMMUNICATION CHANNELS HAVE NOW BEEN BLOCKED!
ACCESSING FLAME JETS.

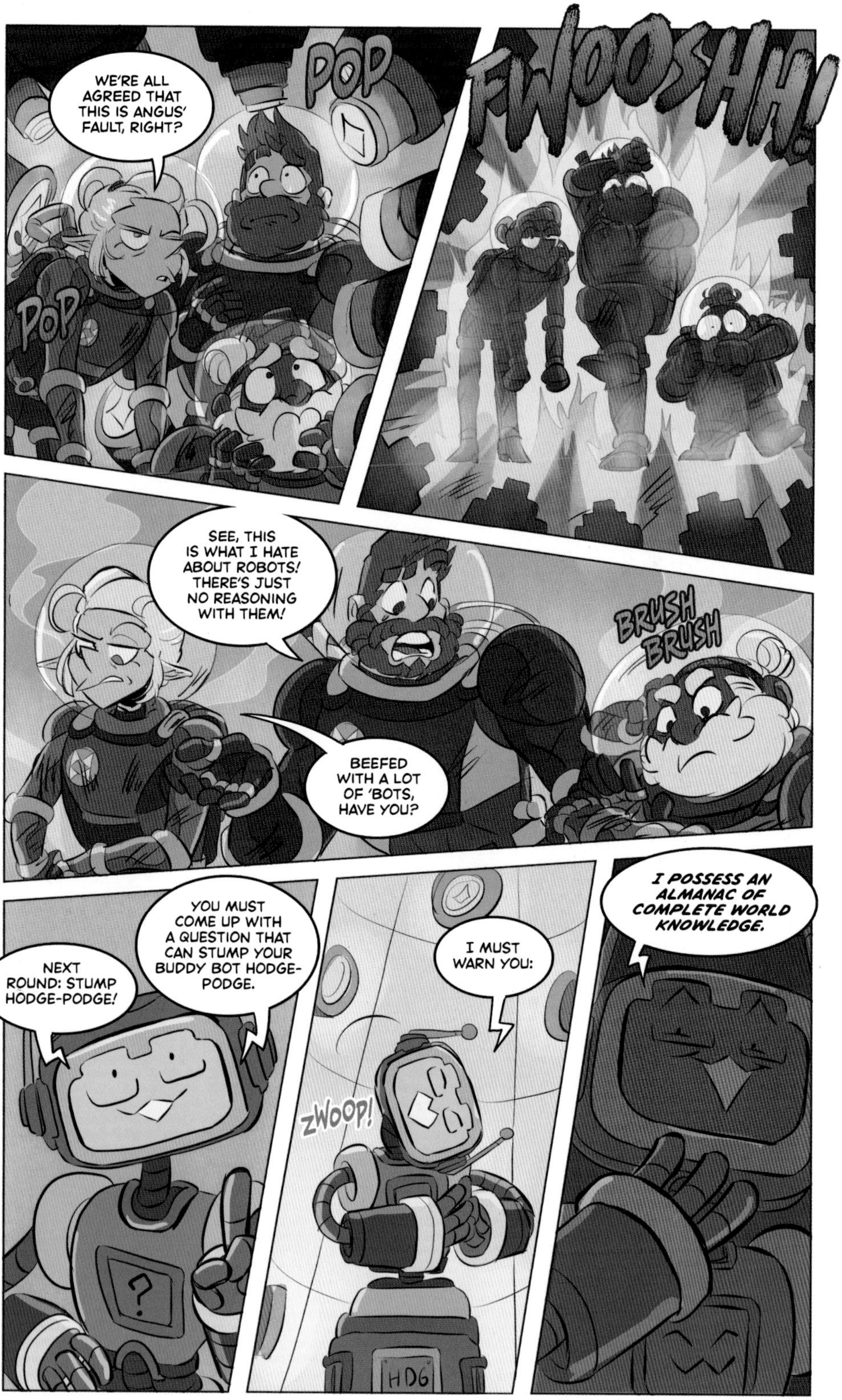
WE'RE ALL AGREED THAT THIS IS ANGUS' FAULT, RIGHT?
POP
POP
FWOOSHH!
SEE, THIS IS WHAT I HATE ABOUT ROBOTS! THERE'S JUST NO REASONING WITH THEM!
BRUSH BRUSH
BEEFED WITH A LOT OF 'BOTS, HAVE YOU?
NEXT ROUND: STUMP HODGE-PODGE!
YOU MUST COME UP WITH A QUESTION THAT CAN STUMP YOUR BUDDY BOT HODGE-PODGE.
I MUST WARN YOU:
ZWOOP!
HDG
I POSSESS AN ALMANAC OF COMPLETE WORLD KNOWLEDGE.

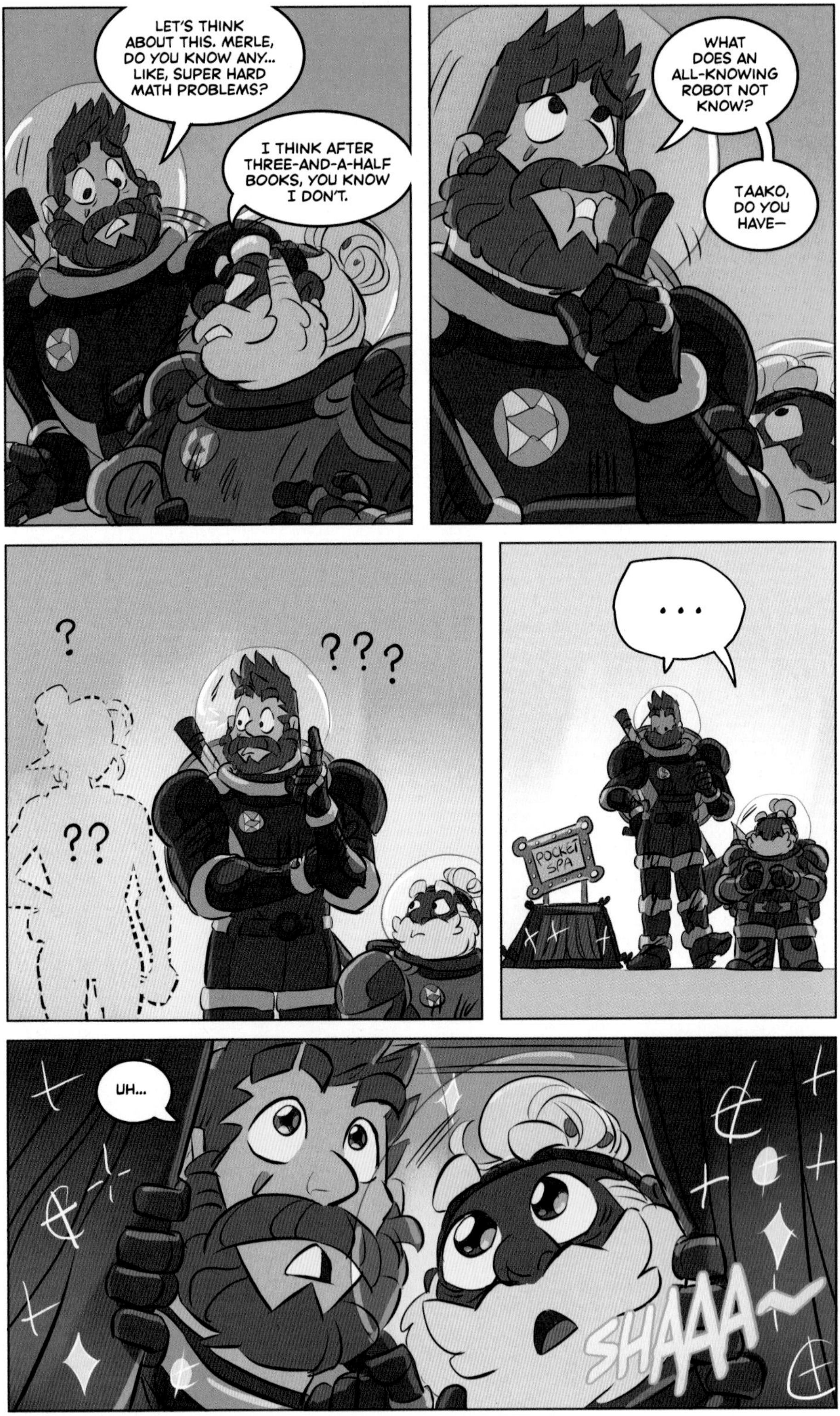
LET'S THINK ABOUT THIS. MERLE, DO YOU KNOW ANY... LIKE, SUPER HARD MATH PROBLEMS?
I THINK AFTER THREE-AND-A-HALF BOOKS, YOU KNOW I DON'T.
WHAT DOES AN ALL-KNOWING ROBOT NOT KNOW?
TAAKO, DO YOU HAVE—
?
???
??
...
POCKET SPA
UH...
SHAAA~

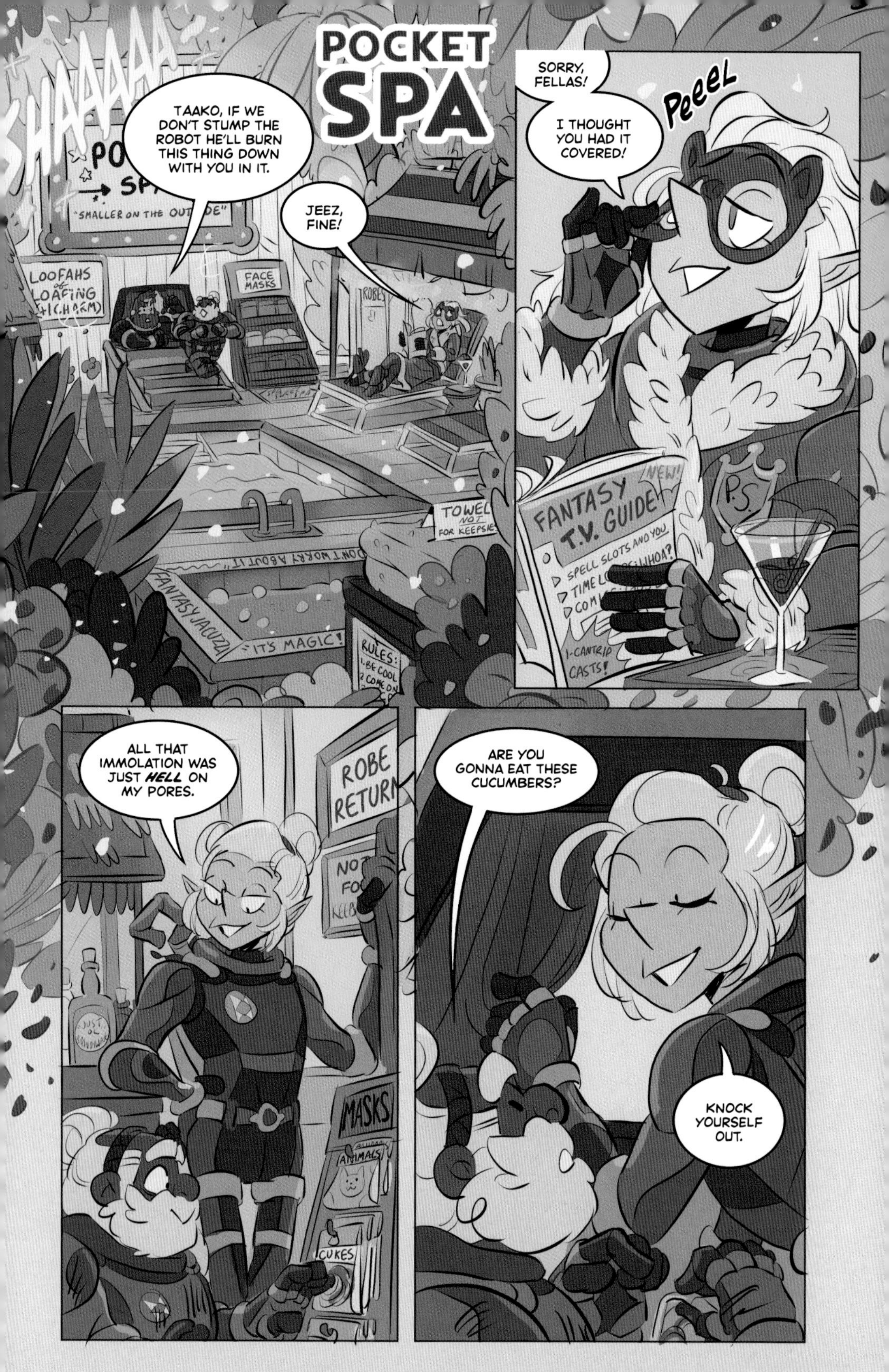
POCKET SPA
SHAAAAA
POCKET SPA
"SMALLER ON THE OUTSIDE"
TAAKO, IF WE DON'T STUMP THE ROBOT HE'LL BURN THIS THING DOWN WITH YOU IN IT.
LOOFAHS of LOAFING
FACE MASKS
ROBES
JEEZ, FINE!
TOWEL NOT FOR KEEPSIES
"DON'T WORRY ABOUT IT"
FANTASY JACUZZI
IT'S MAGIC!
RULES: 1. BE COOL 2. COME ON
SORRY, FELLAS!
I THOUGHT YOU HAD IT COVERED!
Peeel
FANTASY T.V. GUIDE
NEW!
SPELL SLOTS AND YOU
WHOA?
1-CANTRIP CASTS!
P.S.
ALL THAT IMMOLATION WAS JUST ***HELL*** ON MY PORES.
ROBE RETURN
MASKS
ANIMALS
CUKES
ARE YOU GONNA EAT THESE CUCUMBERS?
KNOCK YOURSELF OUT.

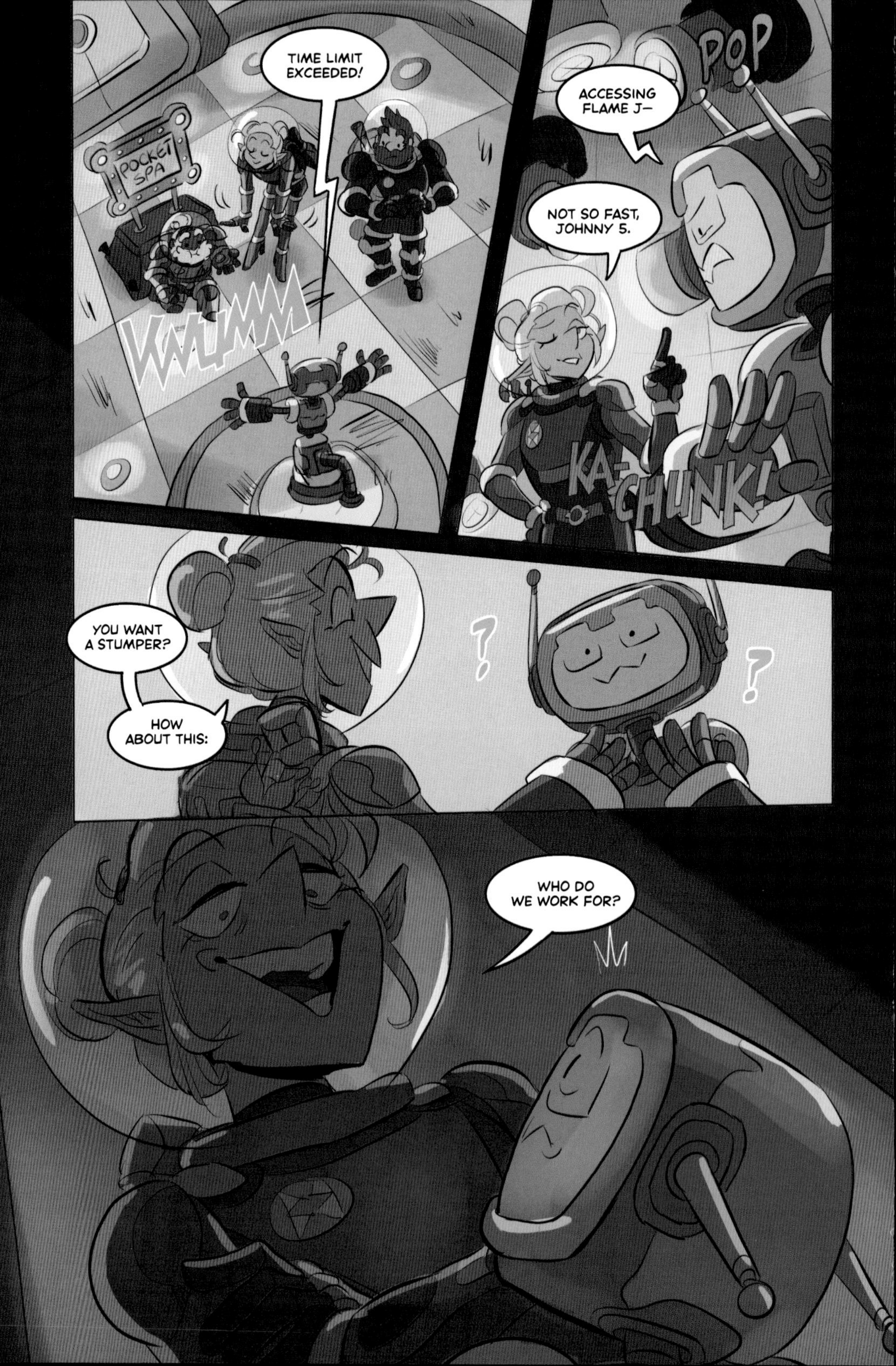
POCKET SPA
TIME LIMIT EXCEEDED!
KWUMM
POP
ACCESSING FLAME J—
NOT SO FAST, JOHNNY 5.
KA-CHUNK!
YOU WANT A STUMPER?
HOW ABOUT THIS:
?
?
WHO DO WE WORK FOR?

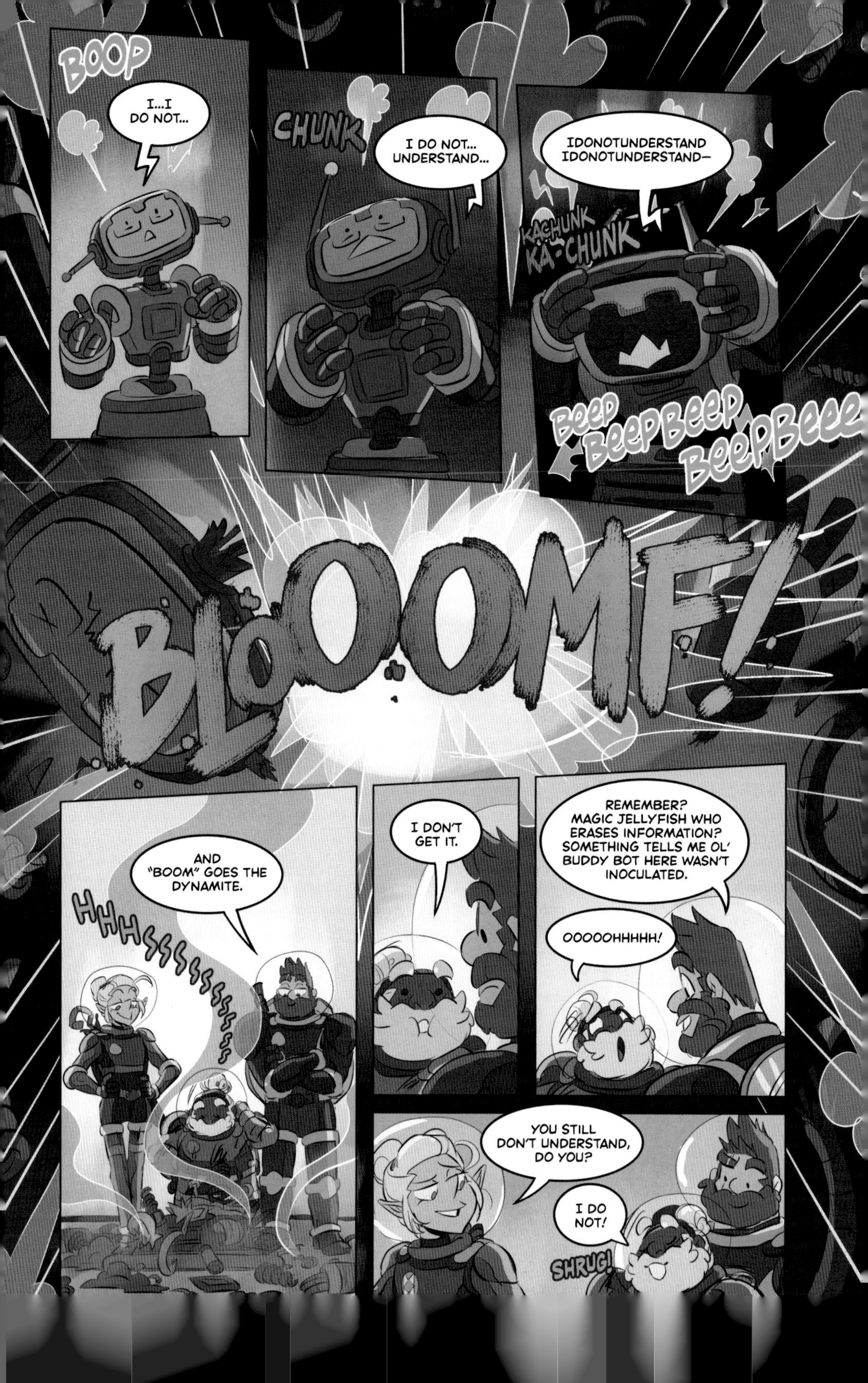
BOOP
I...I DO NOT...
CHUNK
I DO NOT... UNDERSTAND...
IDONOTUNDERSTAND IDONOTUNDERSTAND—
KACHUNK KA-CHUNK
Beep BeepBeep BeepBeee
BLOOOMF!
AND "BOOM" GOES THE DYNAMITE.
HHHSSSSSSSSSS
I DON'T GET IT.
REMEMBER? MAGIC JELLYFISH WHO ERASES INFORMATION? SOMETHING TELLS ME OL' BUDDY BOT HERE WASN'T INOCULATED.
OOOOOHHHHH!
YOU STILL DON'T UNDERSTAND, DO YOU?
I DO NOT!
SHRUG!

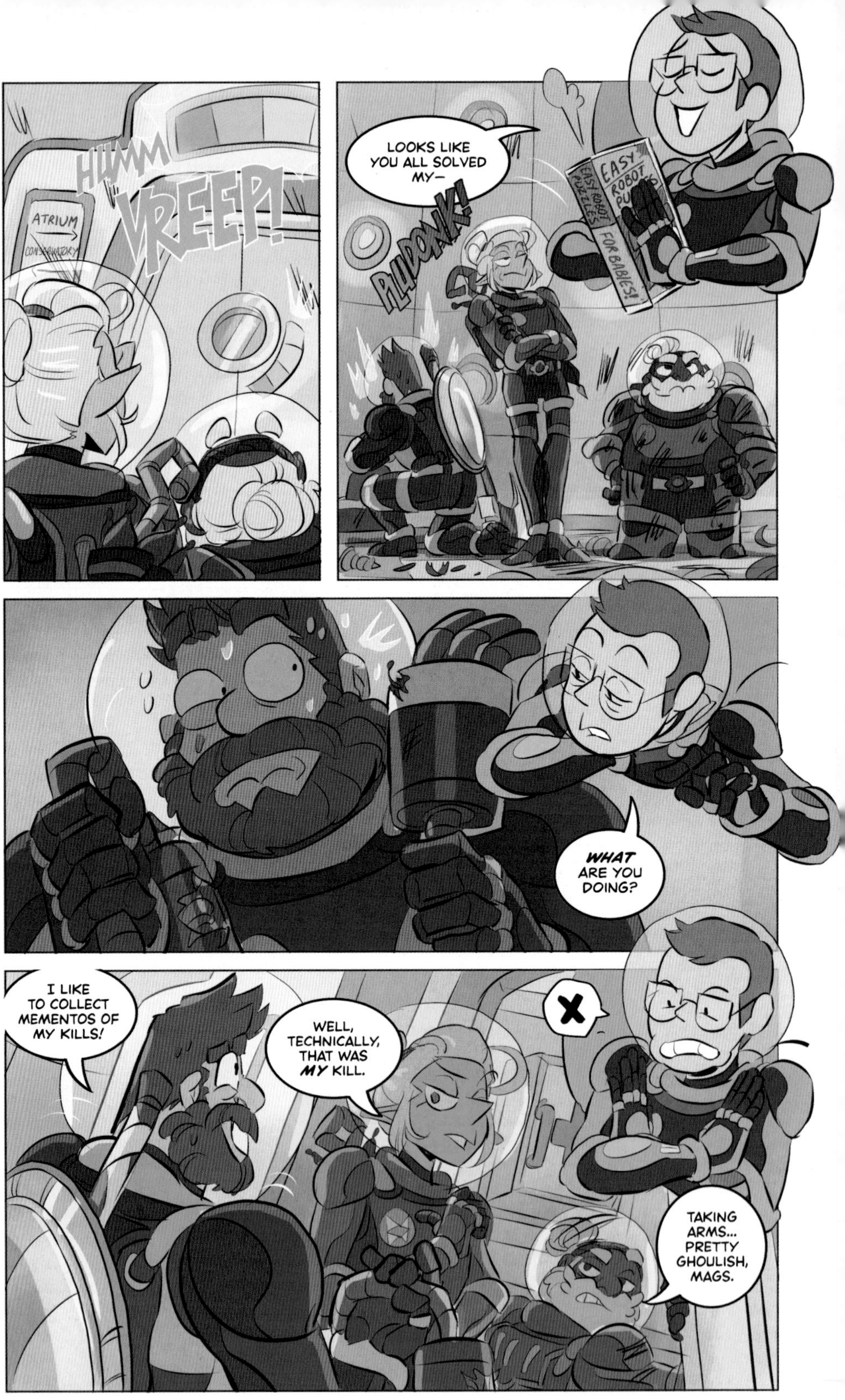
HUMM
VREEP!
ATRIUM
CONSERVATORY
LOOKS LIKE YOU ALL SOLVED MY—
PLDONK!
EASY ROBOT PUZZLES
EASY ROBOT PU...
FOR BABIES!
WHAT ARE YOU DOING?
I LIKE TO COLLECT MEMENTOS OF MY KILLS!
WELL, TECHNICALLY, THAT WAS MY KILL.
X
TAKING ARMS... PRETTY GHOULISH, MAGS.

Chapter
3

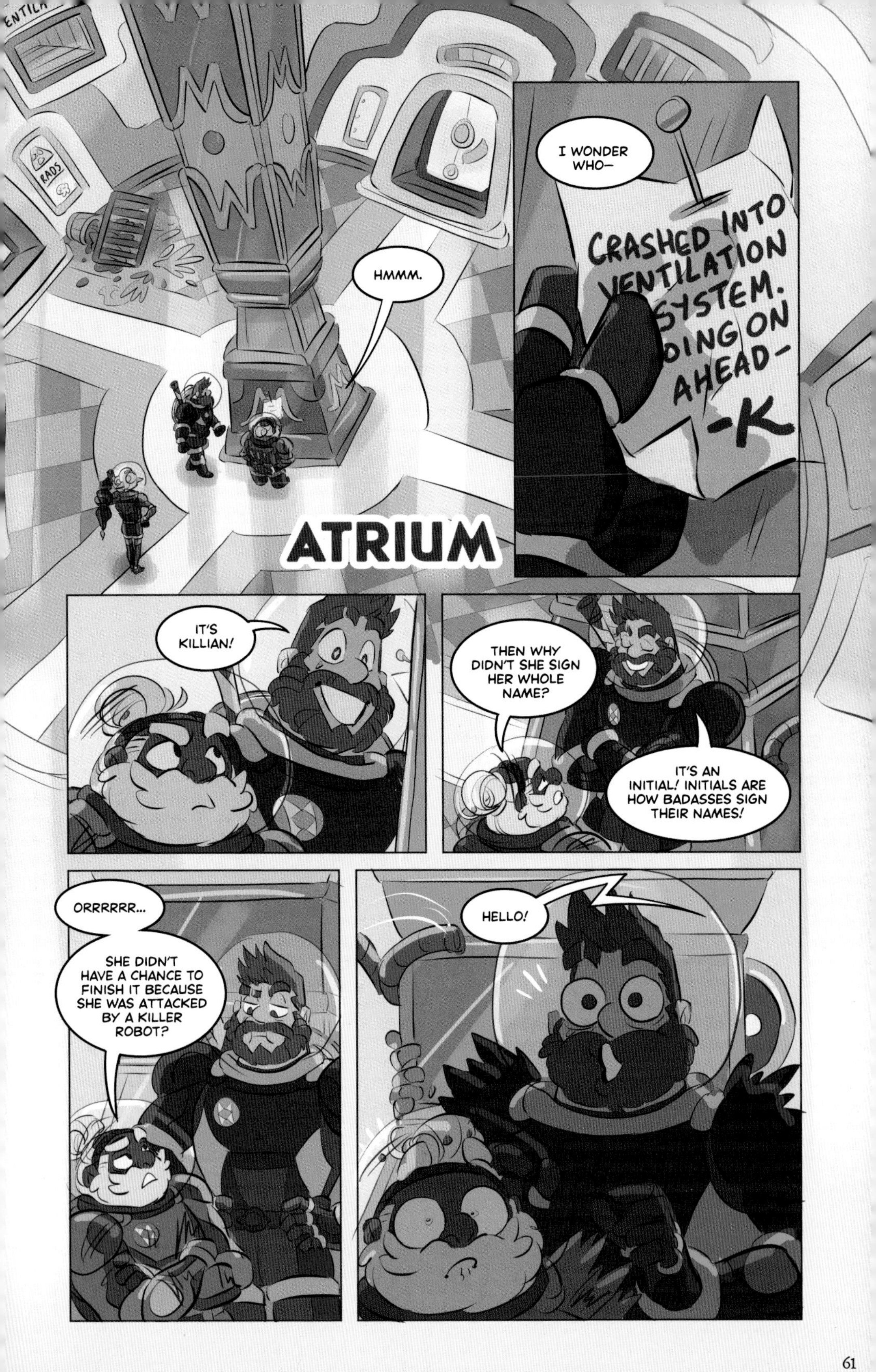
ENTILA
RADS
HMMM.
I WONDER WHO–
CRASHED INTO VENTILATION SYSTEM. GOING ON AHEAD– -K
ATRIUM
IT'S KILLIAN!
THEN WHY DIDN'T SHE SIGN HER WHOLE NAME?
IT'S AN INITIAL! INITIALS ARE HOW BADASSES SIGN THEIR NAMES!
ORRRRRR...
SHE DIDN'T HAVE A CHANCE TO FINISH IT BECAUSE SHE WAS ATTACKED BY A KILLER ROBOT?
HELLO!

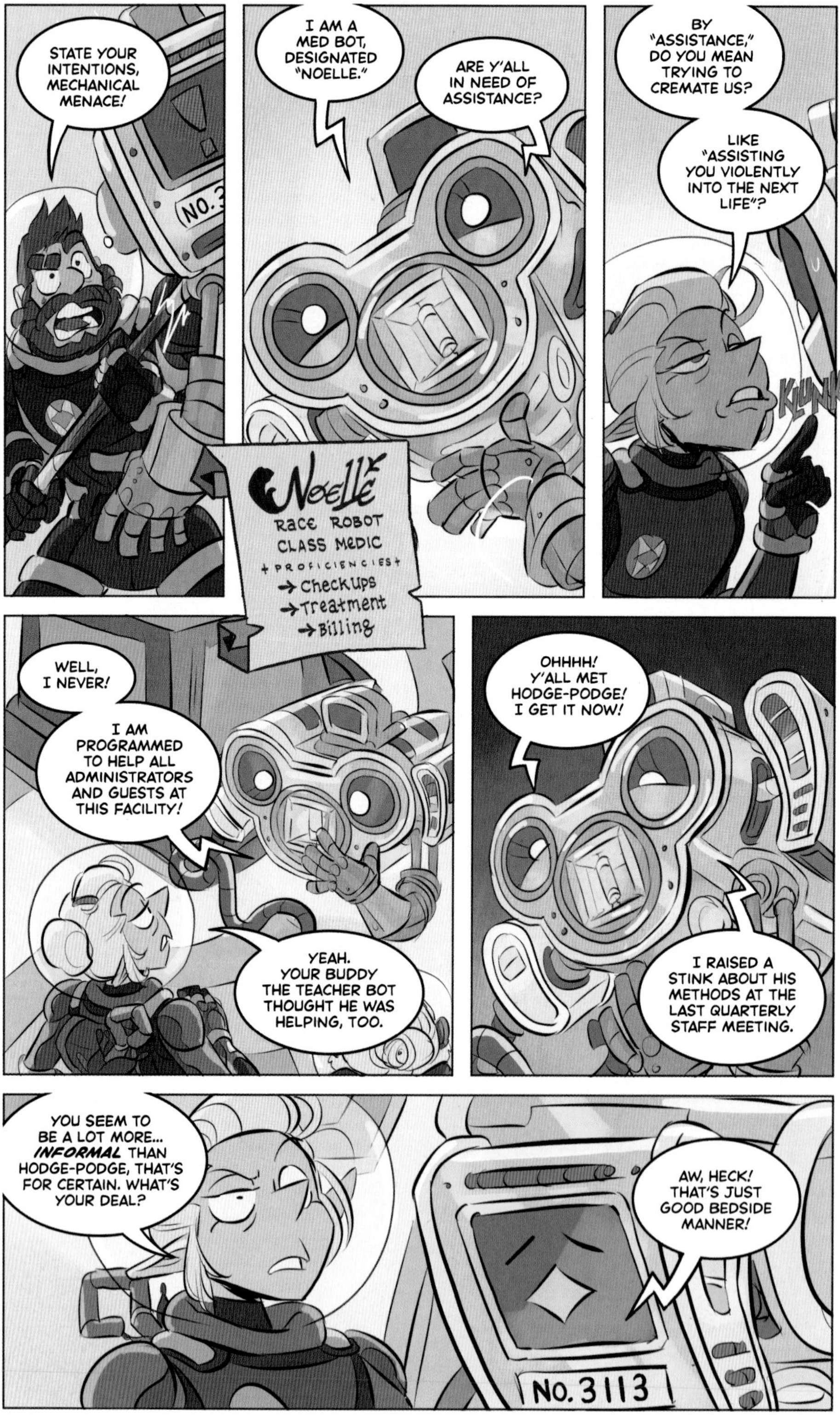
STATE YOUR INTENTIONS, MECHANICAL MENACE!
NO. 3
I AM A MED BOT, DESIGNATED "NOELLE."
ARE Y'ALL IN NEED OF ASSISTANCE?
BY "ASSISTANCE," DO YOU MEAN TRYING TO CREMATE US?
LIKE "ASSISTING YOU VIOLENTLY INTO THE NEXT LIFE"?
KLUNK
Noelle
RACE ROBOT
CLASS MEDIC
+ PROFICIENCIES +
→ Checkups
→ Treatment
→ Billing
WELL, I NEVER!
I AM PROGRAMMED TO HELP ALL ADMINISTRATORS AND GUESTS AT THIS FACILITY!
YEAH. YOUR BUDDY THE TEACHER BOT THOUGHT HE WAS HELPING, TOO.
OHHHH! Y'ALL MET HODGE-PODGE! I GET IT NOW!
I RAISED A STINK ABOUT HIS METHODS AT THE LAST QUARTERLY STAFF MEETING.
YOU SEEM TO BE A LOT MORE... *INFORMAL* THAN HODGE-PODGE, THAT'S FOR CERTAIN. WHAT'S YOUR DEAL?
AW, HECK! THAT'S JUST GOOD BEDSIDE MANNER!
NO. 3113

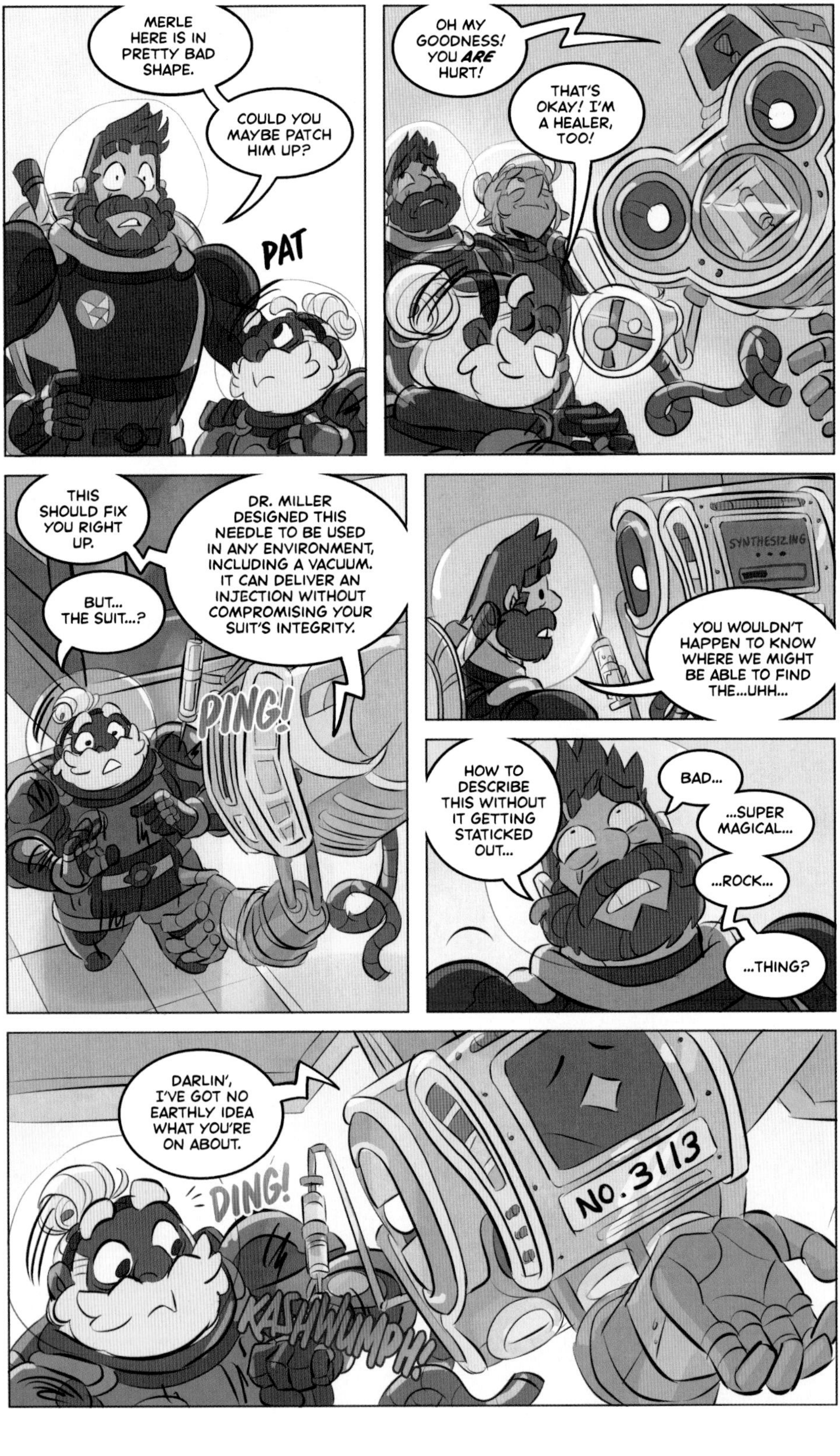
MERLE HERE IS IN PRETTY BAD SHAPE.
COULD YOU MAYBE PATCH HIM UP?
PAT
OH MY GOODNESS! YOU **ARE** HURT!
THAT'S OKAY! I'M A HEALER, TOO!
THIS SHOULD FIX YOU RIGHT UP.
DR. MILLER DESIGNED THIS NEEDLE TO BE USED IN ANY ENVIRONMENT, INCLUDING A VACUUM. IT CAN DELIVER AN INJECTION WITHOUT COMPROMISING YOUR SUIT'S INTEGRITY.
BUT... THE SUIT...?
PING!
SYNTHESIZING
YOU WOULDN'T HAPPEN TO KNOW WHERE WE MIGHT BE ABLE TO FIND THE...UHH...
HOW TO DESCRIBE THIS WITHOUT IT GETTING STATICKED OUT...
BAD...
...SUPER MAGICAL...
...ROCK...
...THING?
DARLIN', I'VE GOT NO EARTHLY IDEA WHAT YOU'RE ON ABOUT.
DING!
NO. 3113
KASHWUMPH!

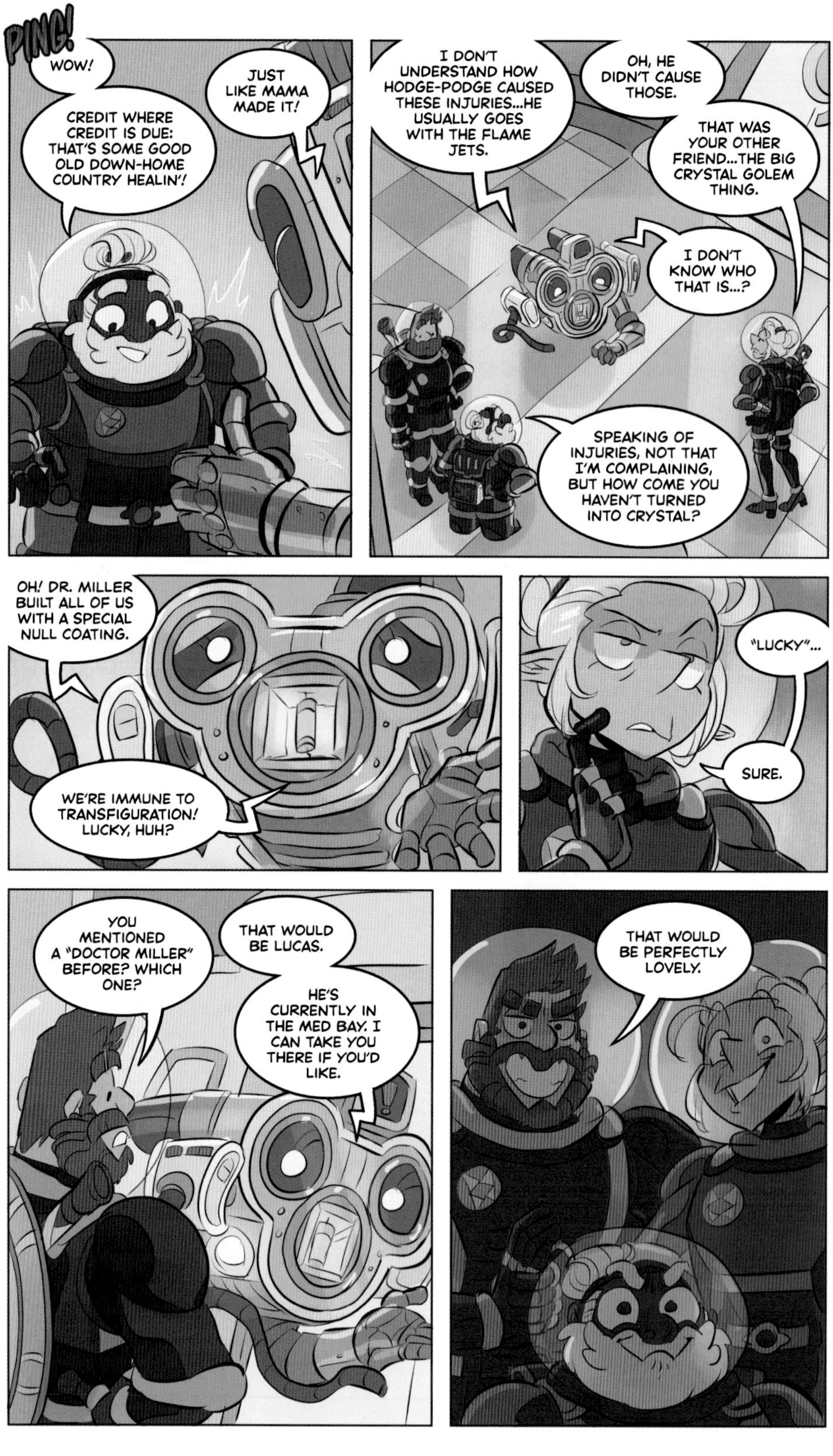
PING!
WOW!
CREDIT WHERE CREDIT IS DUE: THAT'S SOME GOOD OLD DOWN-HOME COUNTRY HEALIN'!
JUST LIKE MAMA MADE IT!
I DON'T UNDERSTAND HOW HODGE-PODGE CAUSED THESE INJURIES...HE USUALLY GOES WITH THE FLAME JETS.
OH, HE DIDN'T CAUSE THOSE.
THAT WAS YOUR OTHER FRIEND...THE BIG CRYSTAL GOLEM THING.
I DON'T KNOW WHO THAT IS...?
SPEAKING OF INJURIES, NOT THAT I'M COMPLAINING, BUT HOW COME YOU HAVEN'T TURNED INTO CRYSTAL?
OH! DR. MILLER BUILT ALL OF US WITH A SPECIAL NULL COATING.
WE'RE IMMUNE TO TRANSFIGURATION! LUCKY, HUH?
"LUCKY"...
SURE.
YOU MENTIONED A "DOCTOR MILLER" BEFORE? WHICH ONE?
THAT WOULD BE LUCAS.
HE'S CURRENTLY IN THE MED BAY. I CAN TAKE YOU THERE IF YOU'D LIKE.
THAT WOULD BE PERFECTLY LOVELY.

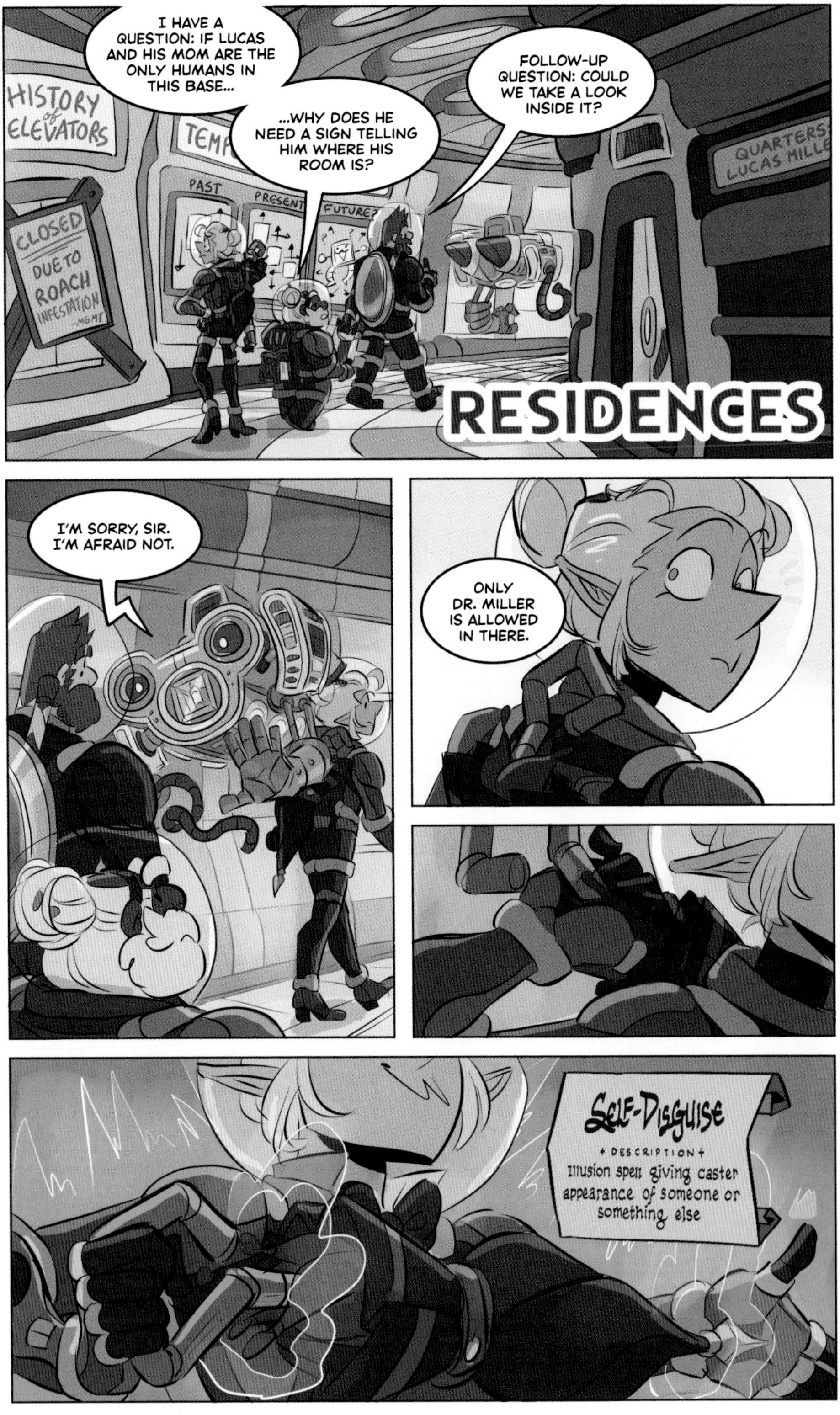

I HAVE A QUESTION: IF LUCAS AND HIS MOM ARE THE ONLY HUMANS IN THIS BASE...
...WHY DOES HE NEED A SIGN TELLING HIM WHERE HIS ROOM IS?
FOLLOW-UP QUESTION: COULD WE TAKE A LOOK INSIDE IT?
HISTORY of ELEVATORS
CLOSED DUE TO ROACH INFESTATION -MGMT
PAST
PRESENT
FUTURE?
RESIDENCES
I'M SORRY, SIR. I'M AFRAID NOT.
ONLY DR. MILLER IS ALLOWED IN THERE.
SELF-DISGUISE
DESCRIPTION
Illusion spell giving caster appearance of someone or something else

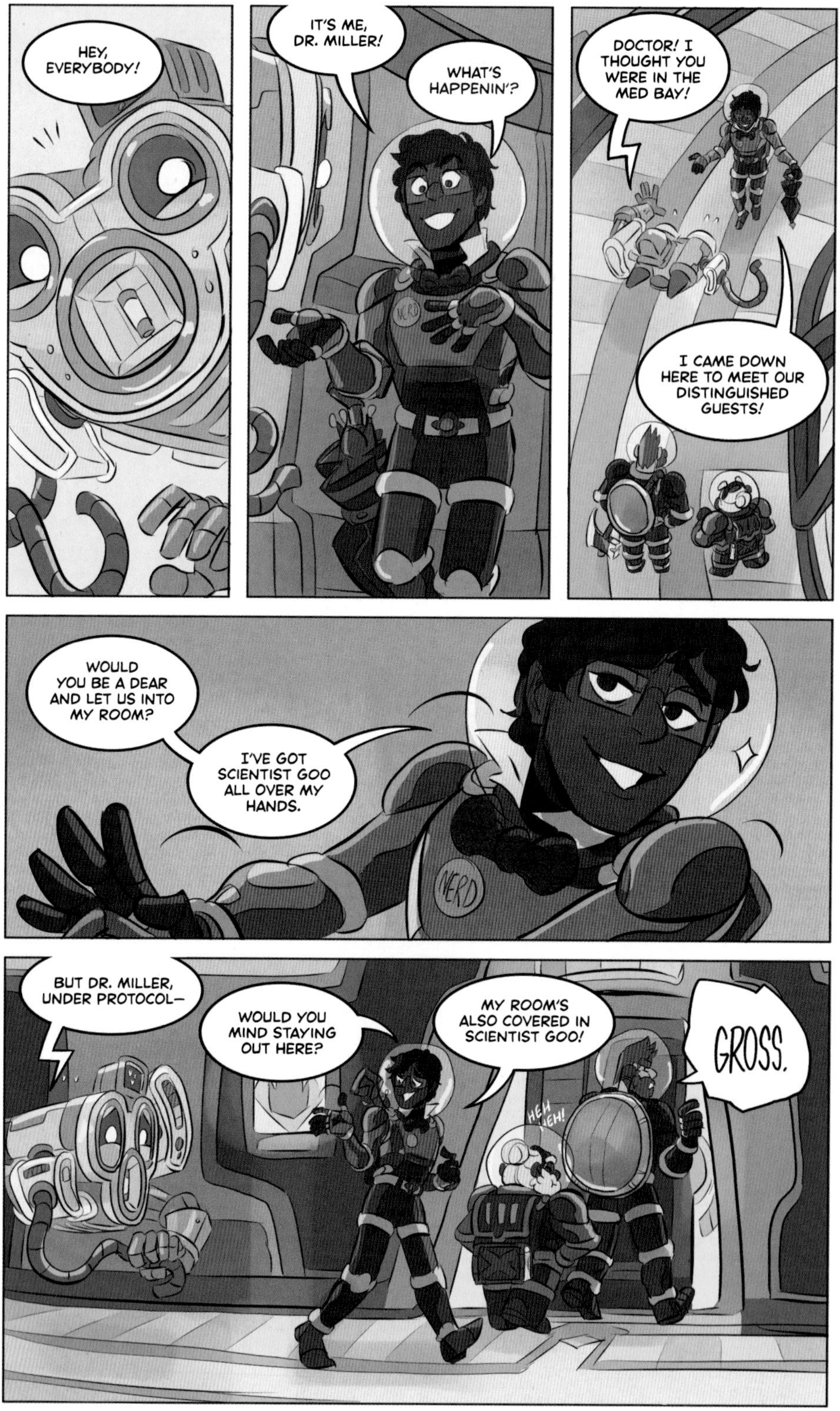
HEY, EVERYBODY!
IT'S ME, DR. MILLER!
WHAT'S HAPPENIN'?
DOCTOR! I THOUGHT YOU WERE IN THE MED BAY!
I CAME DOWN HERE TO MEET OUR DISTINGUISHED GUESTS!
NERD
WOULD YOU BE A DEAR AND LET US INTO MY ROOM?
I'VE GOT SCIENTIST GOO ALL OVER MY HANDS.
NERD
BUT DR. MILLER, UNDER PROTOCOL—
WOULD YOU MIND STAYING OUT HERE?
MY ROOM'S ALSO COVERED IN SCIENTIST GOO!
HEH HEH!
GROSS.

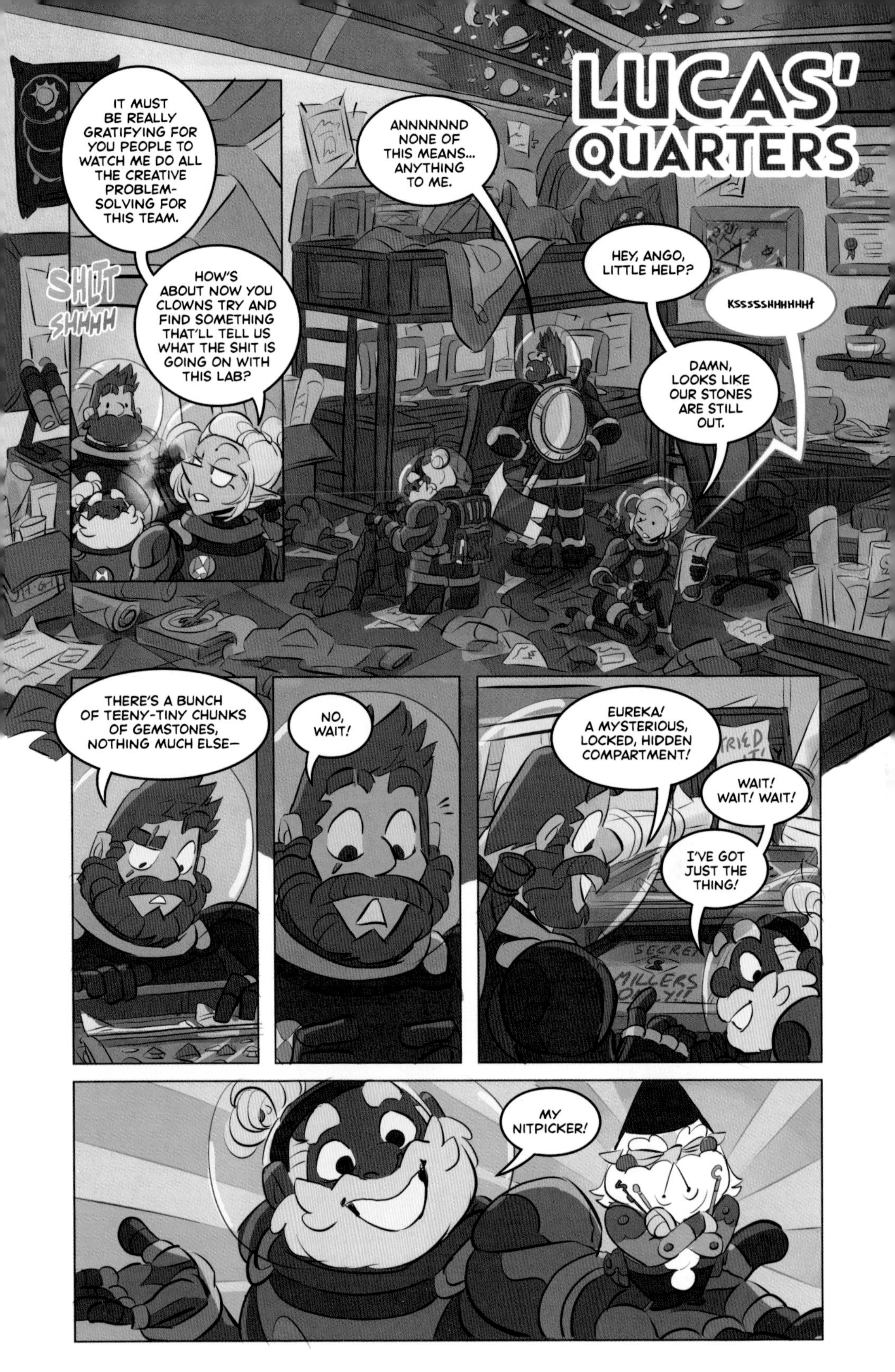
LUCAS' QUARTERS
IT MUST BE REALLY GRATIFYING FOR YOU PEOPLE TO WATCH ME DO ALL THE CREATIVE PROBLEM-SOLVING FOR THIS TEAM.
SHLIT SHHHH
HOW'S ABOUT NOW YOU CLOWNS TRY AND FIND SOMETHING THAT'LL TELL US WHAT THE SHIT IS GOING ON WITH THIS LAB?
ANNNNNND NONE OF THIS MEANS... ANYTHING TO ME.
HEY, ANGO, LITTLE HELP?
KSSSSSHHHHHH
DAMN, LOOKS LIKE OUR STONES ARE STILL OUT.
THERE'S A BUNCH OF TEENY-TINY CHUNKS OF GEMSTONES, NOTHING MUCH ELSE—
NO, WAIT!
EUREKA! A MYSTERIOUS, LOCKED, HIDDEN COMPARTMENT!
WAIT! WAIT! WAIT!
I'VE GOT JUST THE THING!
MY NITPICKER!

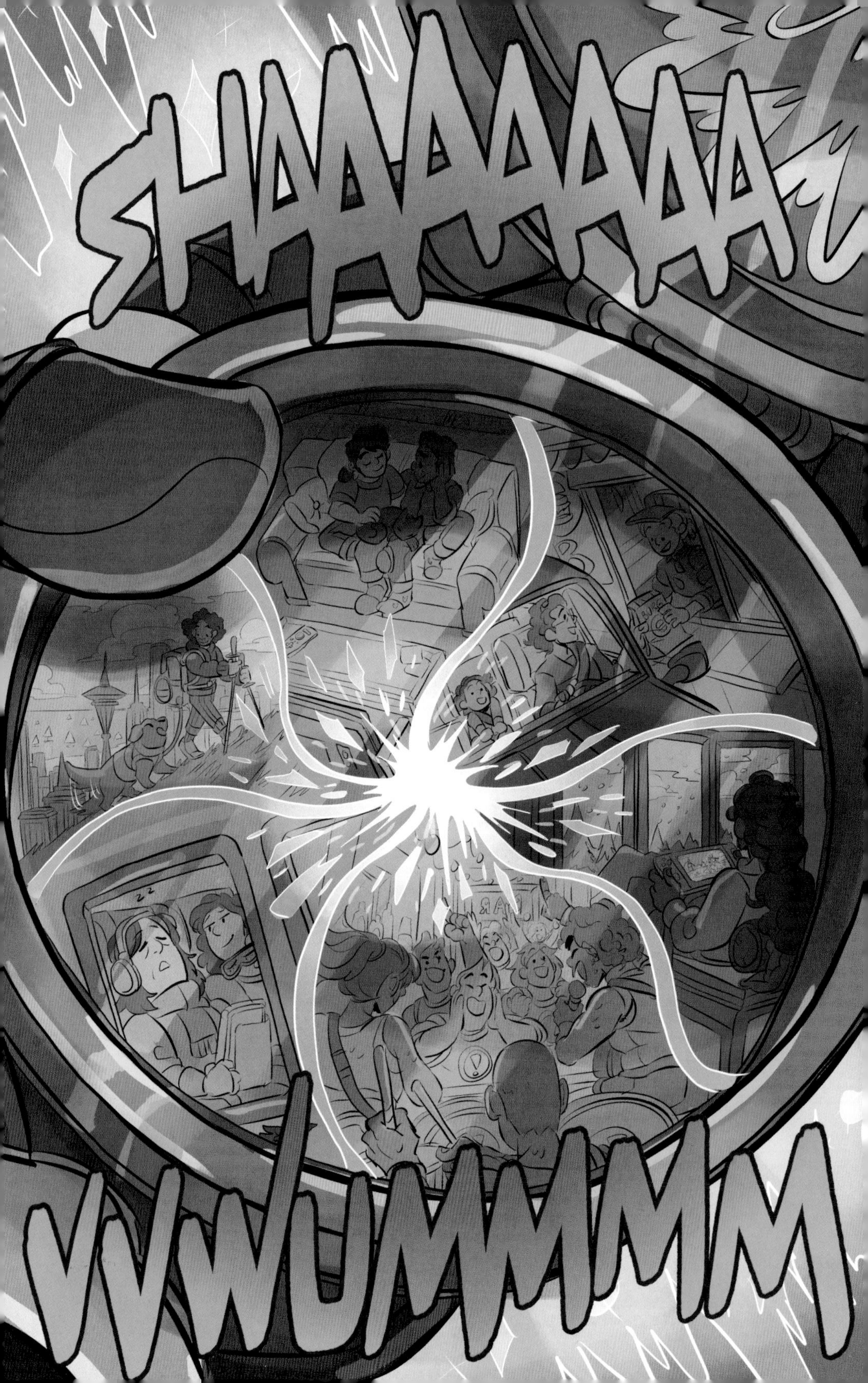
SHAAAAAAA
VWUMMMMM

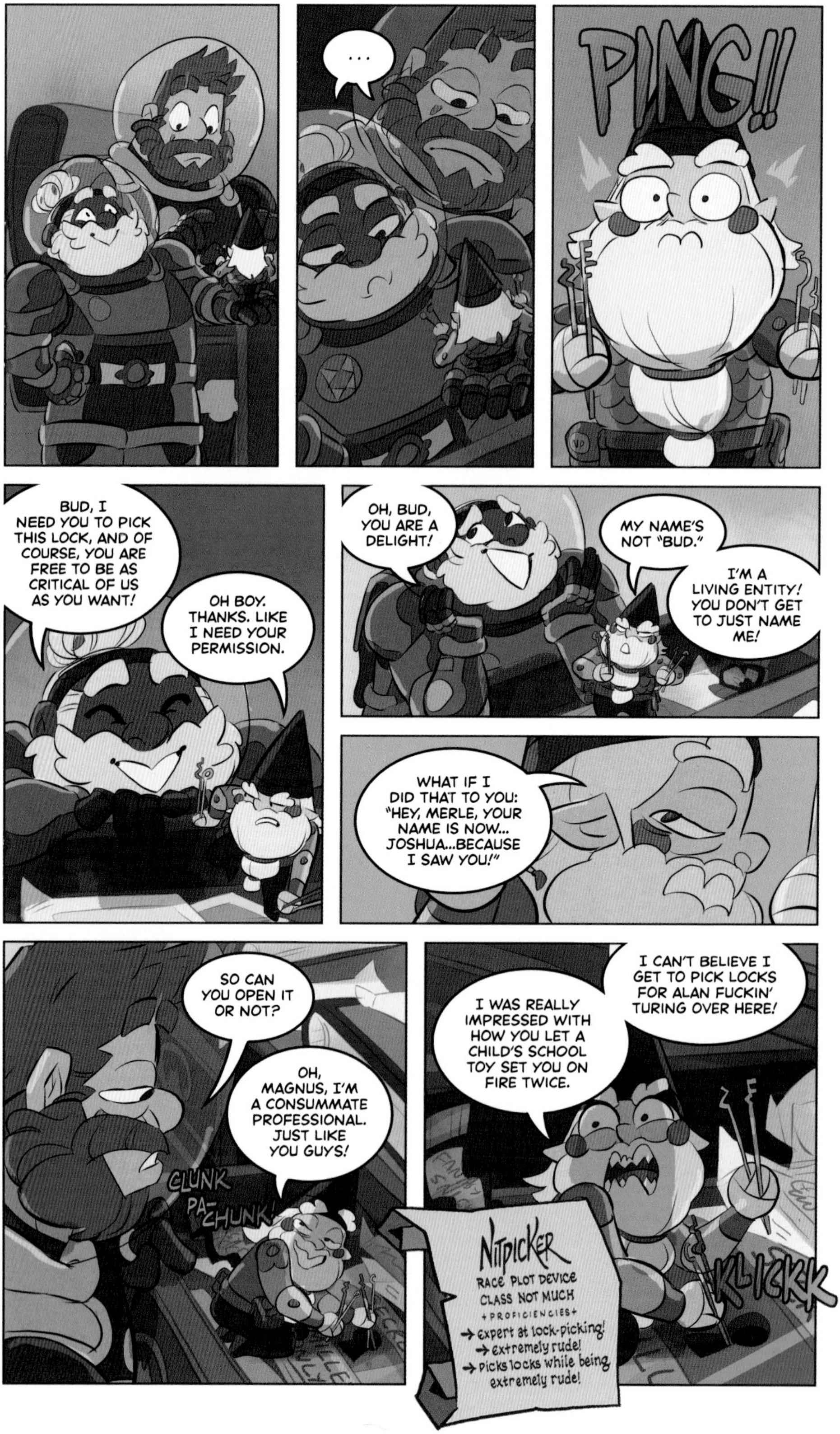
...
PING!!
BUD, I NEED YOU TO PICK THIS LOCK, AND OF COURSE, YOU ARE FREE TO BE AS CRITICAL OF US AS YOU WANT!
OH BOY. THANKS. LIKE I NEED YOUR PERMISSION.
OH, BUD, YOU ARE A DELIGHT!
MY NAME'S NOT "BUD."
I'M A LIVING ENTITY! YOU DON'T GET TO JUST NAME ME!
WHAT IF I DID THAT TO YOU: "HEY, MERLE, YOUR NAME IS NOW... JOSHUA...BECAUSE I SAW YOU!"
SO CAN YOU OPEN IT OR NOT?
OH, MAGNUS, I'M A CONSUMMATE PROFESSIONAL. JUST LIKE YOU GUYS!
CLUNK PA-CHUNK!
I CAN'T BELIEVE I GET TO PICK LOCKS FOR ALAN FUCKIN' TURING OVER HERE!
I WAS REALLY IMPRESSED WITH HOW YOU LET A CHILD'S SCHOOL TOY SET YOU ON FIRE TWICE.
KLICKK
NITPICKER
RACE PLOT DEVICE
CLASS NOT MUCH
+PROFICIENCIES+
→ expert at lock-picking!
→ extremely rude!
→ picks locks while being extremely rude!

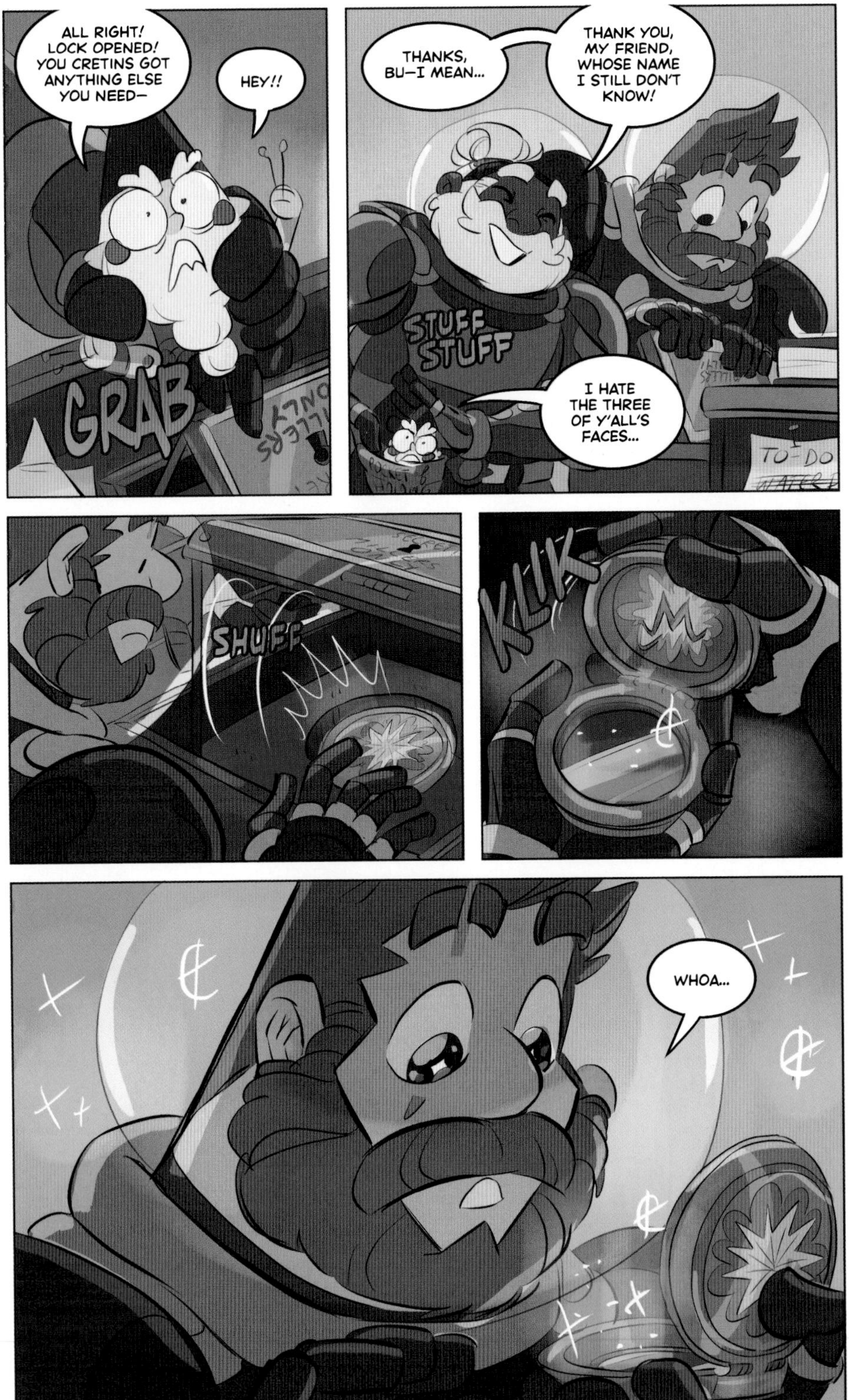
ALL RIGHT! LOCK OPENED! YOU CRETINS GOT ANYTHING ELSE YOU NEED—
HEY!!
GRAB
THANKS, BU—I MEAN...
THANK YOU, MY FRIEND, WHOSE NAME I STILL DON'T KNOW!
STUFF STUFF
I HATE THE THREE OF Y'ALL'S FACES...
TO-DO
SHUFF
KLIK
WHOA...

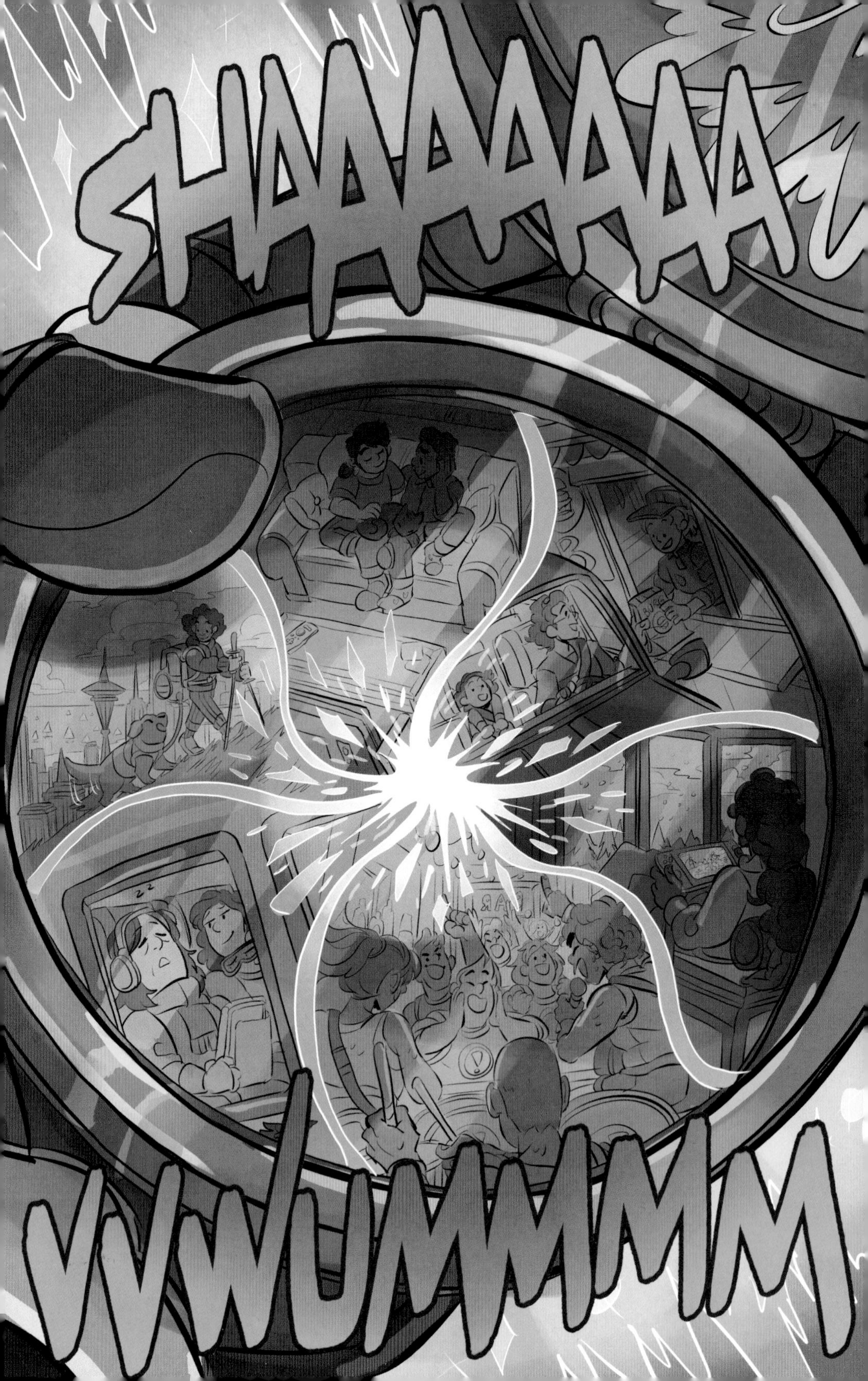
SHAAAAAAA
VWUMMMMM

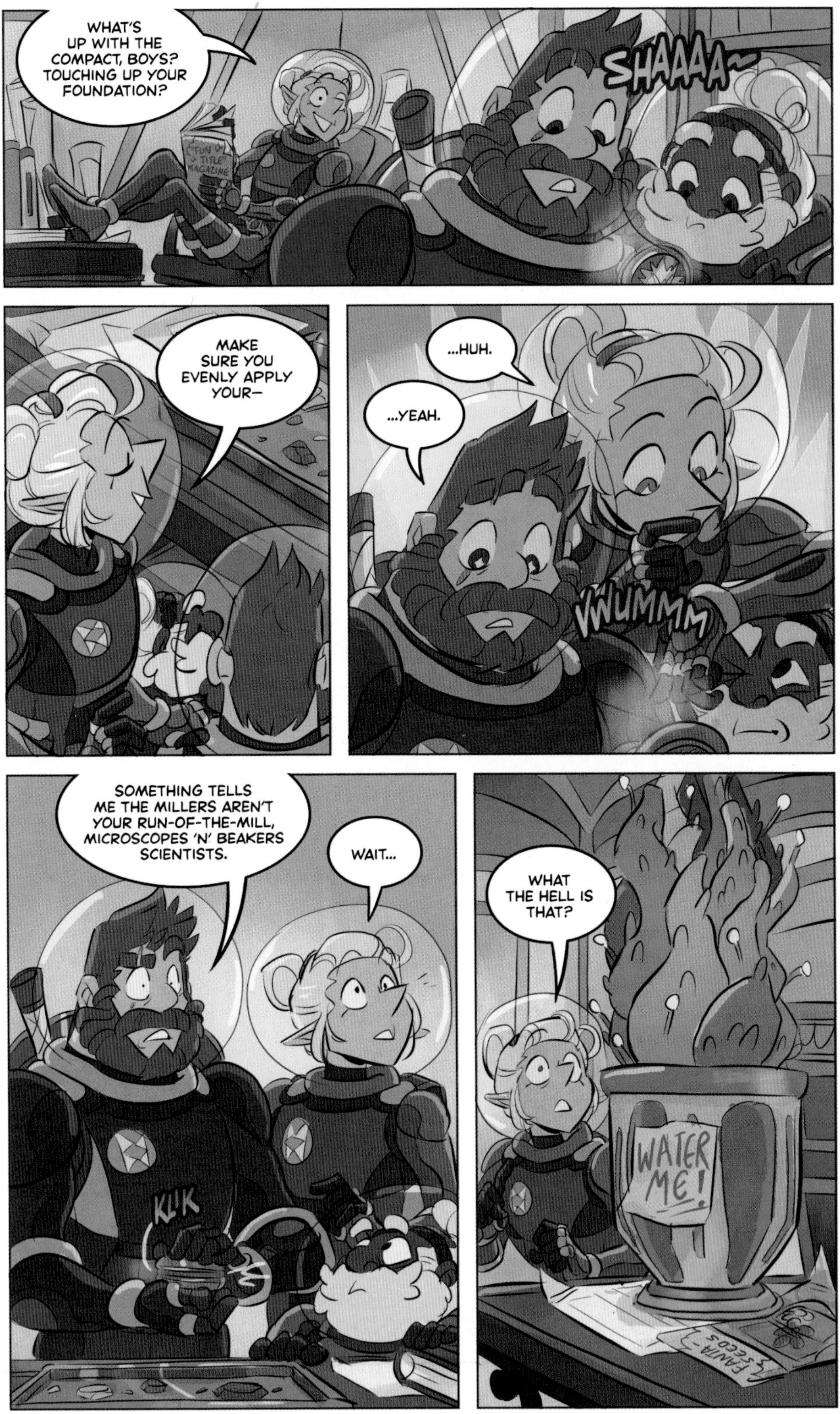
WHAT'S UP WITH THE COMPACT, BOYS? TOUCHING UP YOUR FOUNDATION?
FUN TITLE MAGAZINE
SHAAAA~
MAKE SURE YOU EVENLY APPLY YOUR—
...HUH.
...YEAH.
VWUMMM
SOMETHING TELLS ME THE MILLERS AREN'T YOUR RUN-OF-THE-MILL, MICROSCOPES 'N' BEAKERS SCIENTISTS.
WAIT...
KLIK
WHAT THE HELL IS THAT?
WATER ME!

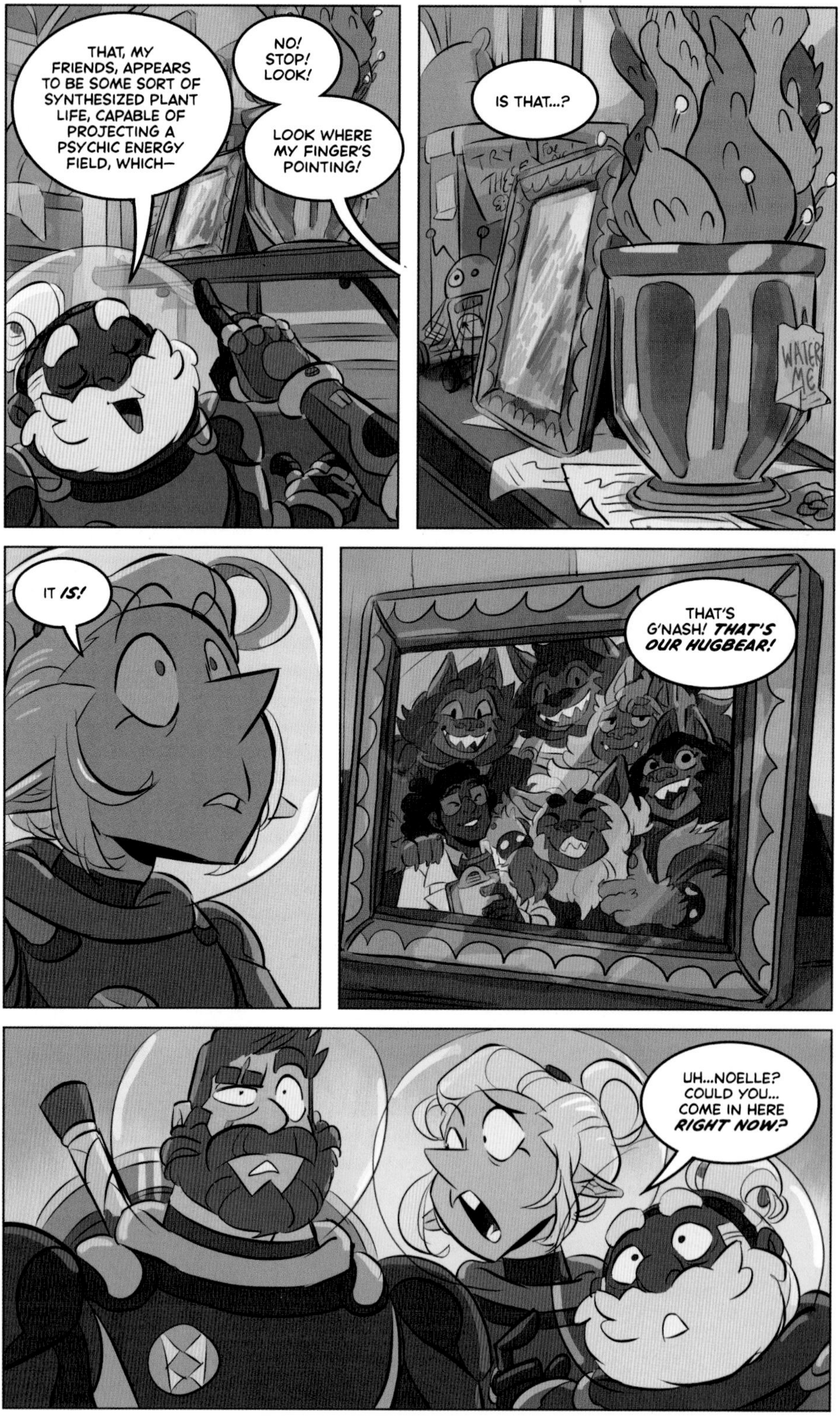
THAT, MY FRIENDS, APPEARS TO BE SOME SORT OF SYNTHESIZED PLANT LIFE, CAPABLE OF PROJECTING A PSYCHIC ENERGY FIELD, WHICH—
NO! STOP! LOOK!
LOOK WHERE MY FINGER'S POINTING!
IS THAT...?
TRY THESE
WATER ME
IT *IS!*
THAT'S G'NASH! ***THAT'S OUR HUGBEAR!***
UH...NOELLE? COULD YOU... COME IN HERE ***RIGHT NOW?***

ABSOLU—

WAIT! WHERE'S DOCTOR MILLER?

HE JUST WALKED PAST YOU! SHEESH! YOU REALLY NEED TO PAY MORE ATTENTION TO YOUR SURROUNDINGS, NOELLE!

WOBBLE

CAN YOU... HOW DID...WHAT THE *SHIT?*

OH!

THOSE'RE THE PILOT MEMBERS OF THE BUGBEAR SCIENCE FELLOWSHIP!

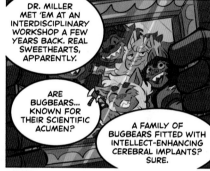

DR. MILLER MET 'EM AT AN INTERDISCIPLINARY WORKSHOP A FEW YEARS BACK. REAL SWEETHEARTS, APPARENTLY.

ARE BUGBEARS... KNOWN FOR THEIR SCIENTIFIC ACUMEN?

A FAMILY OF BUGBEARS FITTED WITH INTELLECT-ENHANCING CEREBRAL IMPLANTS? SURE.

WAIT, HAVE Y'ALL HAD A RUN-IN WITH ONE OF THESE HERE BUGBEARS?

NOPE! NO, MA'AM.

HE JUST SEEMS...

...VAGUELY FAMILIAR...

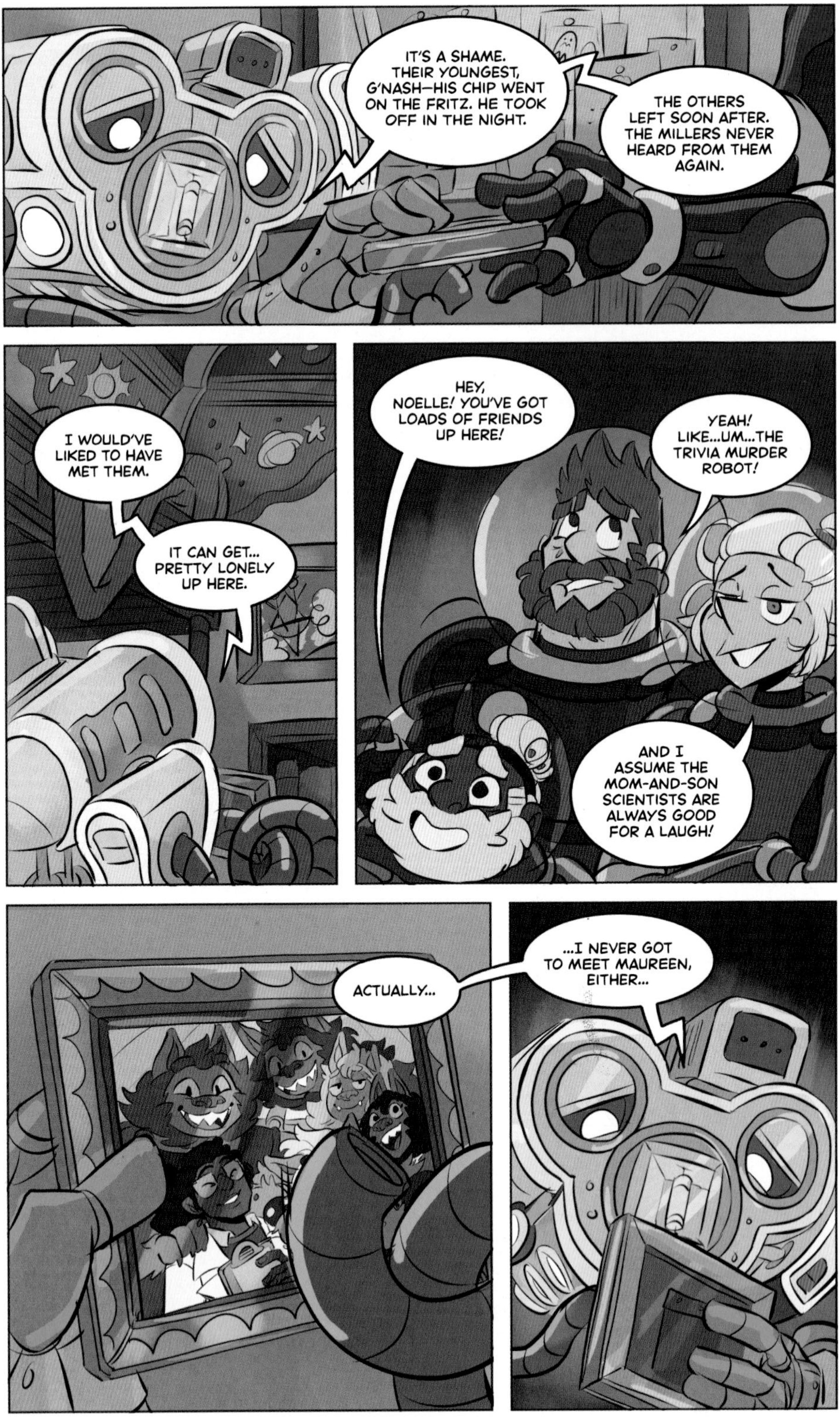
IT'S A SHAME. THEIR YOUNGEST, G'NASH—HIS CHIP WENT ON THE FRITZ. HE TOOK OFF IN THE NIGHT.
THE OTHERS LEFT SOON AFTER. THE MILLERS NEVER HEARD FROM THEM AGAIN.
I WOULD'VE LIKED TO HAVE MET THEM.
IT CAN GET... PRETTY LONELY UP HERE.
HEY, NOELLE! YOU'VE GOT LOADS OF FRIENDS UP HERE!
YEAH! LIKE...UM...THE TRIVIA MURDER ROBOT!
AND I ASSUME THE MOM-AND-SON SCIENTISTS ARE ALWAYS GOOD FOR A LAUGH!
ACTUALLY...
...I NEVER GOT TO MEET MAUREEN, EITHER...

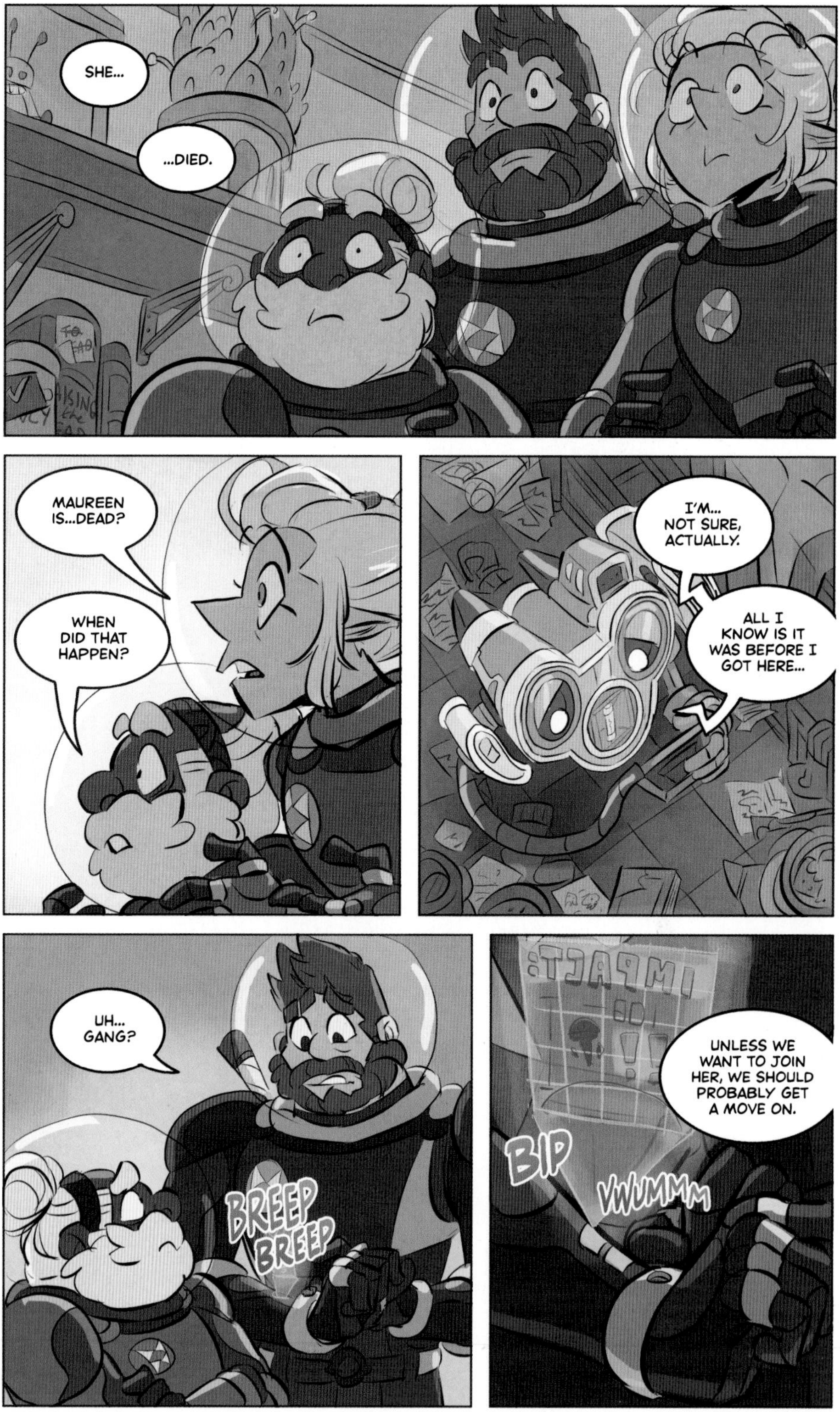
SHE...
...DIED.
MAUREEN IS...DEAD?
WHEN DID THAT HAPPEN?
I'M... NOT SURE, ACTUALLY.
ALL I KNOW IS IT WAS BEFORE I GOT HERE...
UH... GANG?
BREEP BREEP
UNLESS WE WANT TO JOIN HER, WE SHOULD PROBABLY GET A MOVE ON.
BIP
VWUMMM

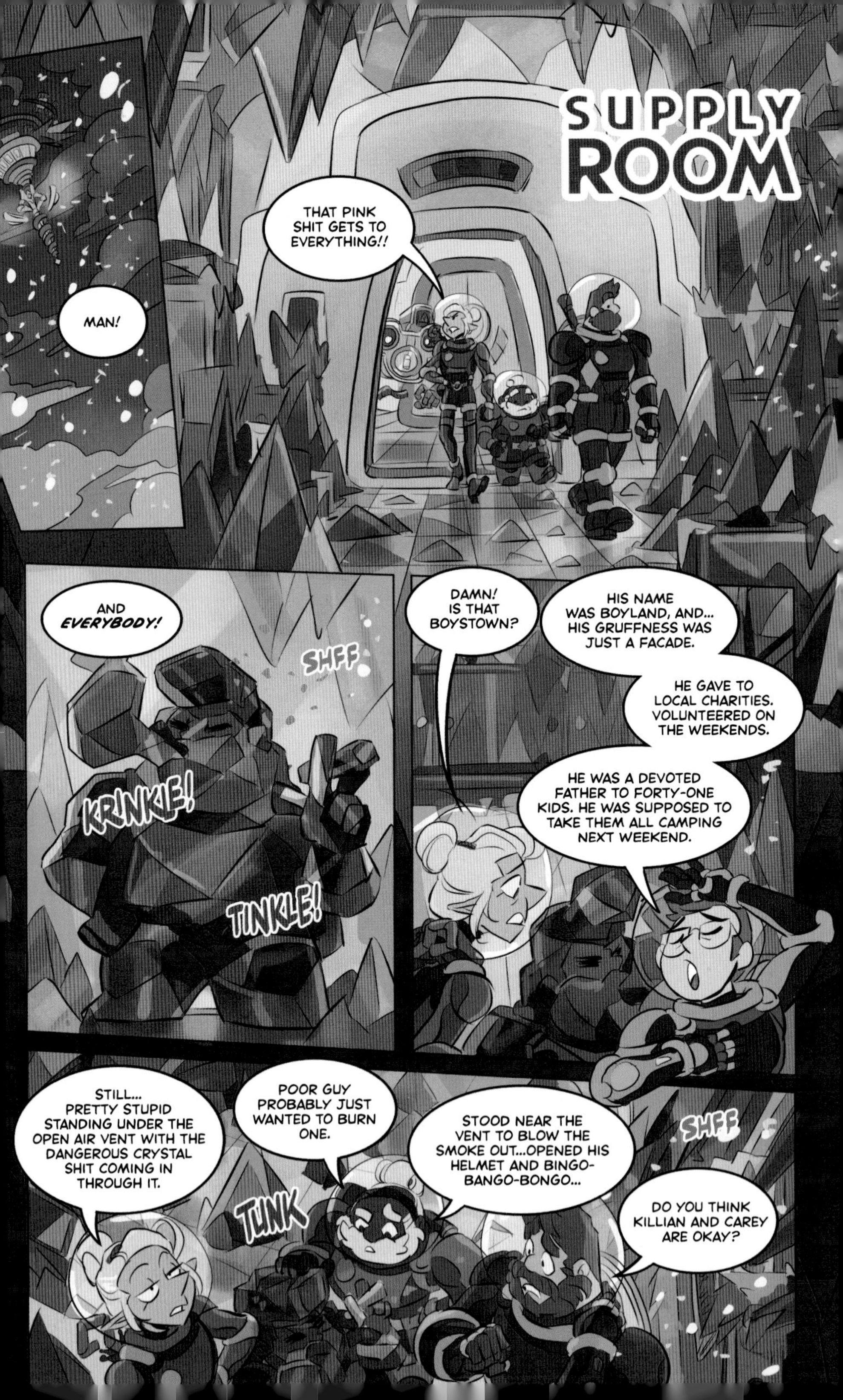
SUPPLY ROOM
MAN!
THAT PINK SHIT GETS TO EVERYTHING!!
AND *EVERYBODY!*
SHFF
KRINKLE!
TINKLE!
DAMN! IS THAT BOYSTOWN?
HIS NAME WAS BOYLAND, AND... HIS GRUFFNESS WAS JUST A FACADE.
HE GAVE TO LOCAL CHARITIES. VOLUNTEERED ON THE WEEKENDS.
HE WAS A DEVOTED FATHER TO FORTY-ONE KIDS. HE WAS SUPPOSED TO TAKE THEM ALL CAMPING NEXT WEEKEND.
STILL... PRETTY STUPID STANDING UNDER THE OPEN AIR VENT WITH THE DANGEROUS CRYSTAL SHIT COMING IN THROUGH IT.
POOR GUY PROBABLY JUST WANTED TO BURN ONE.
STOOD NEAR THE VENT TO BLOW THE SMOKE OUT...OPENED HIS HELMET AND BINGO-BANGO-BONGO...
SHFF
TUNK
DO YOU THINK KILLIAN AND CAREY ARE OKAY?

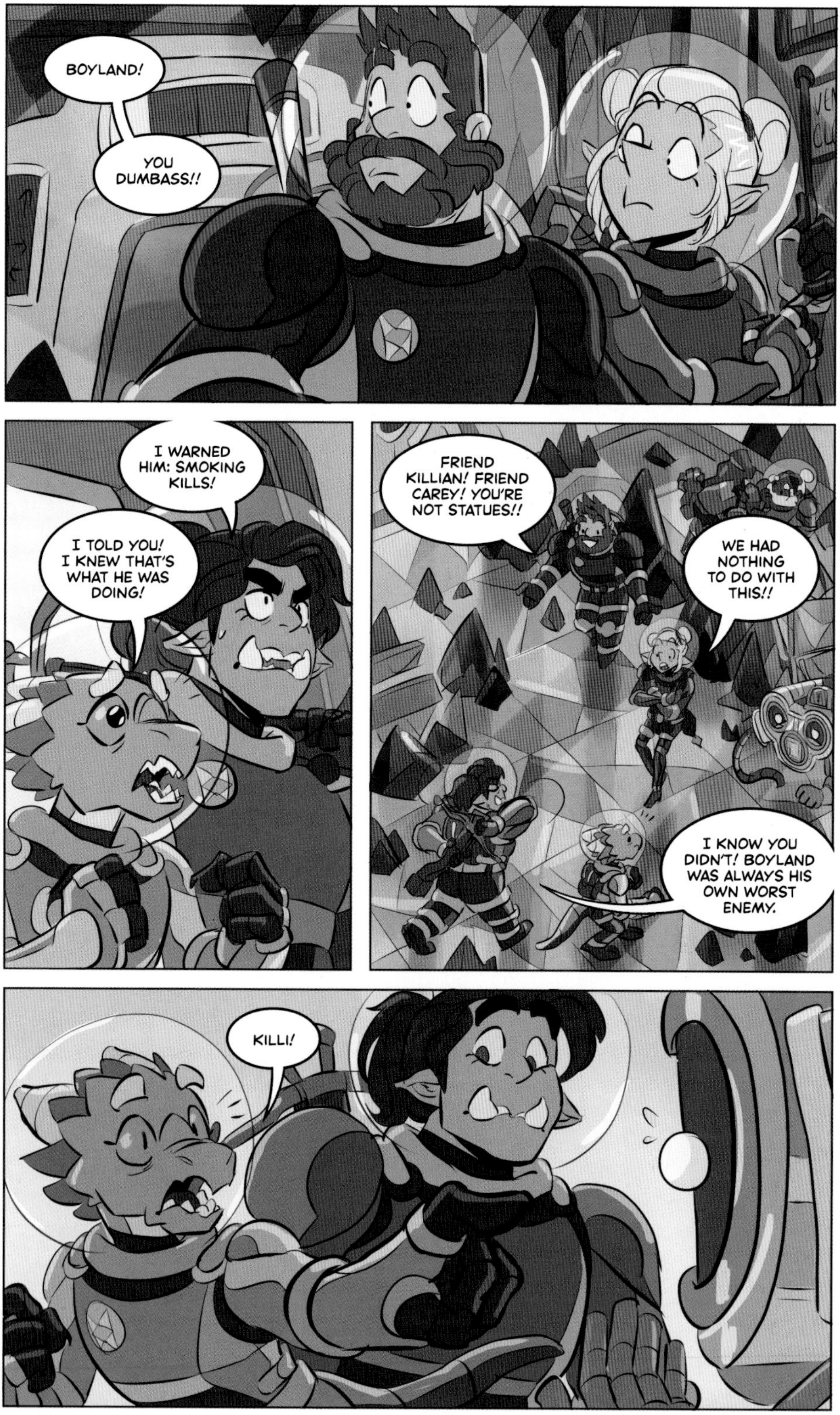
BOYLAND!
YOU DUMBASS!!
I WARNED HIM: SMOKING KILLS!
I TOLD YOU! I KNEW THAT'S WHAT HE WAS DOING!
FRIEND KILLIAN! FRIEND CAREY! YOU'RE NOT STATUES!!
WE HAD NOTHING TO DO WITH THIS!!
I KNOW YOU DIDN'T! BOYLAND WAS ALWAYS HIS OWN WORST ENEMY.
KILLI!

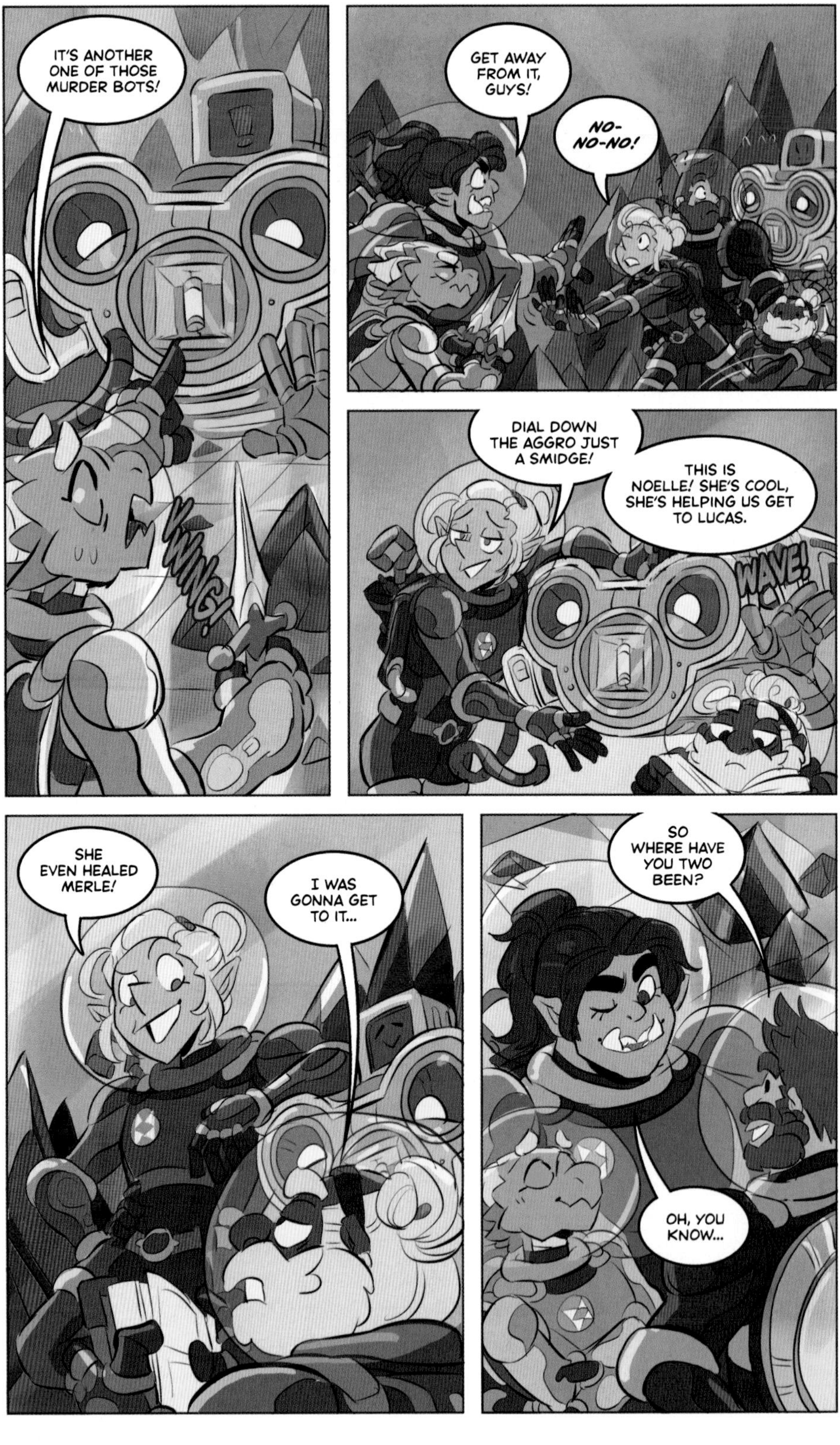
IT'S ANOTHER ONE OF THOSE MURDER BOTS!
VWING!
GET AWAY FROM IT, GUYS!
NO-NO-NO!
DIAL DOWN THE AGGRO JUST A SMIDGE!
THIS IS NOELLE! SHE'S COOL, SHE'S HELPING US GET TO LUCAS.
WAVE!
SHE EVEN HEALED MERLE!
I WAS GONNA GET TO IT...
SO WHERE HAVE YOU TWO BEEN?
OH, YOU KNOW...

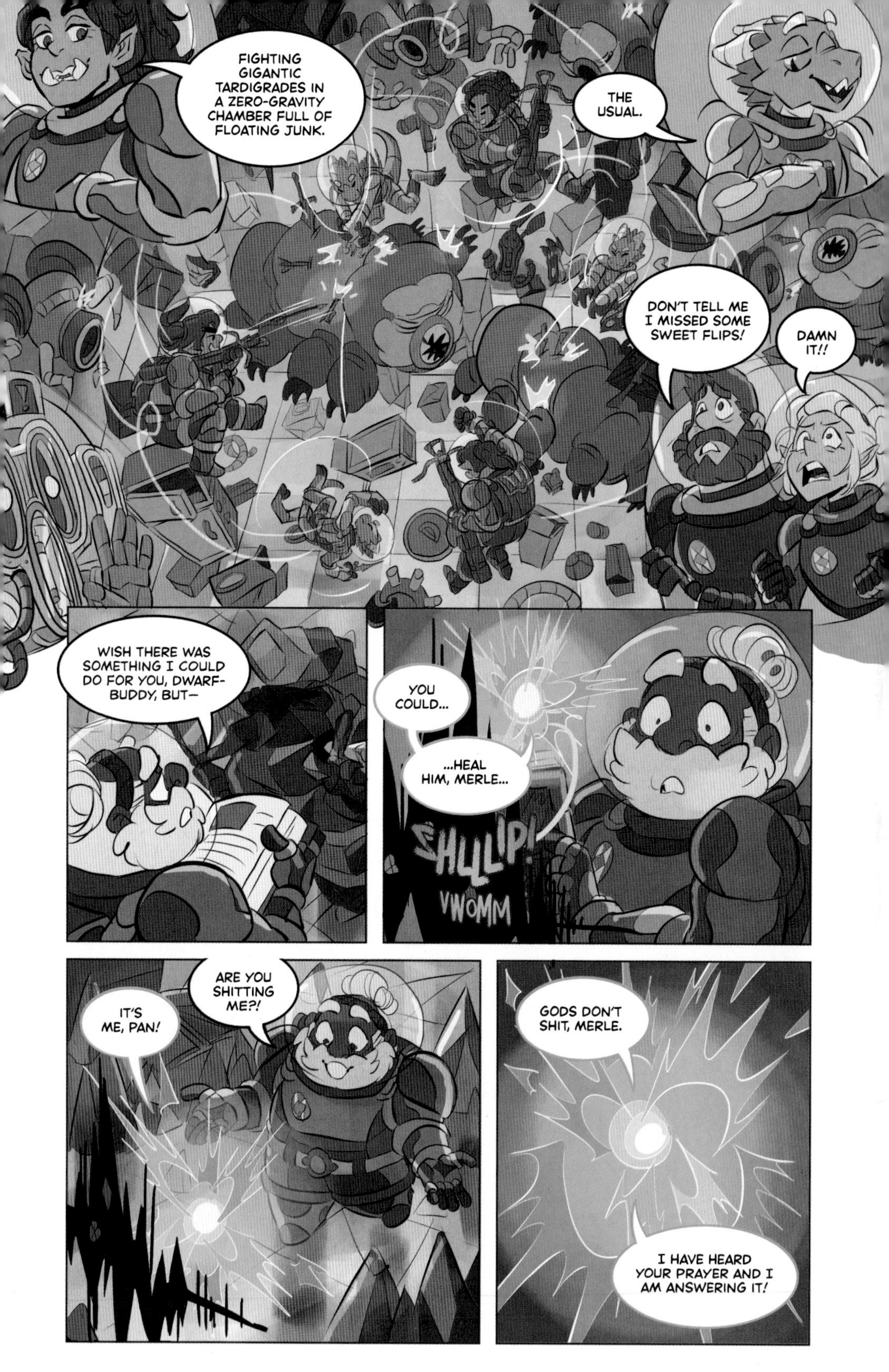
FIGHTING GIGANTIC TARDIGRADES IN A ZERO-GRAVITY CHAMBER FULL OF FLOATING JUNK.
THE USUAL.
DON'T TELL ME I MISSED SOME SWEET FLIPS!
DAMN IT!!
WISH THERE WAS SOMETHING I COULD DO FOR YOU, DWARF-BUDDY, BUT—
YOU COULD...
...HEAL HIM, MERLE...
SHLLIP!
VWOMM
IT'S ME, PAN!
ARE YOU SHITTING ME?!
GODS DON'T SHIT, MERLE.
I HAVE HEARD YOUR PRAYER AND I AM ANSWERING IT!

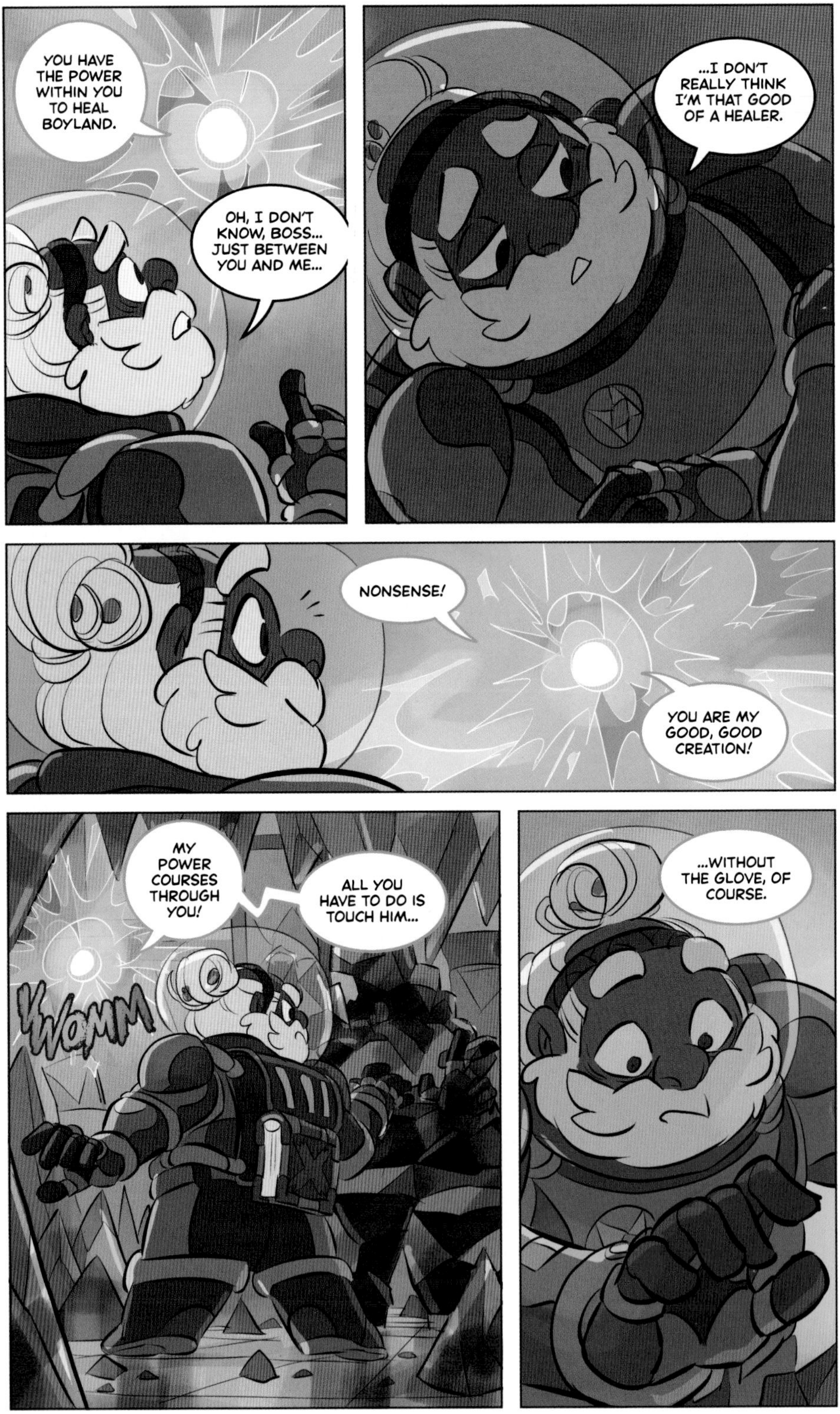
YOU HAVE THE POWER WITHIN YOU TO HEAL BOYLAND.
OH, I DON'T KNOW, BOSS... JUST BETWEEN YOU AND ME...
...I DON'T REALLY THINK I'M THAT GOOD OF A HEALER.
NONSENSE!
YOU ARE MY GOOD, GOOD CREATION!
MY POWER COURSES THROUGH YOU!
ALL YOU HAVE TO DO IS TOUCH HIM...
KWOMM
...WITHOUT THE GLOVE, OF COURSE.

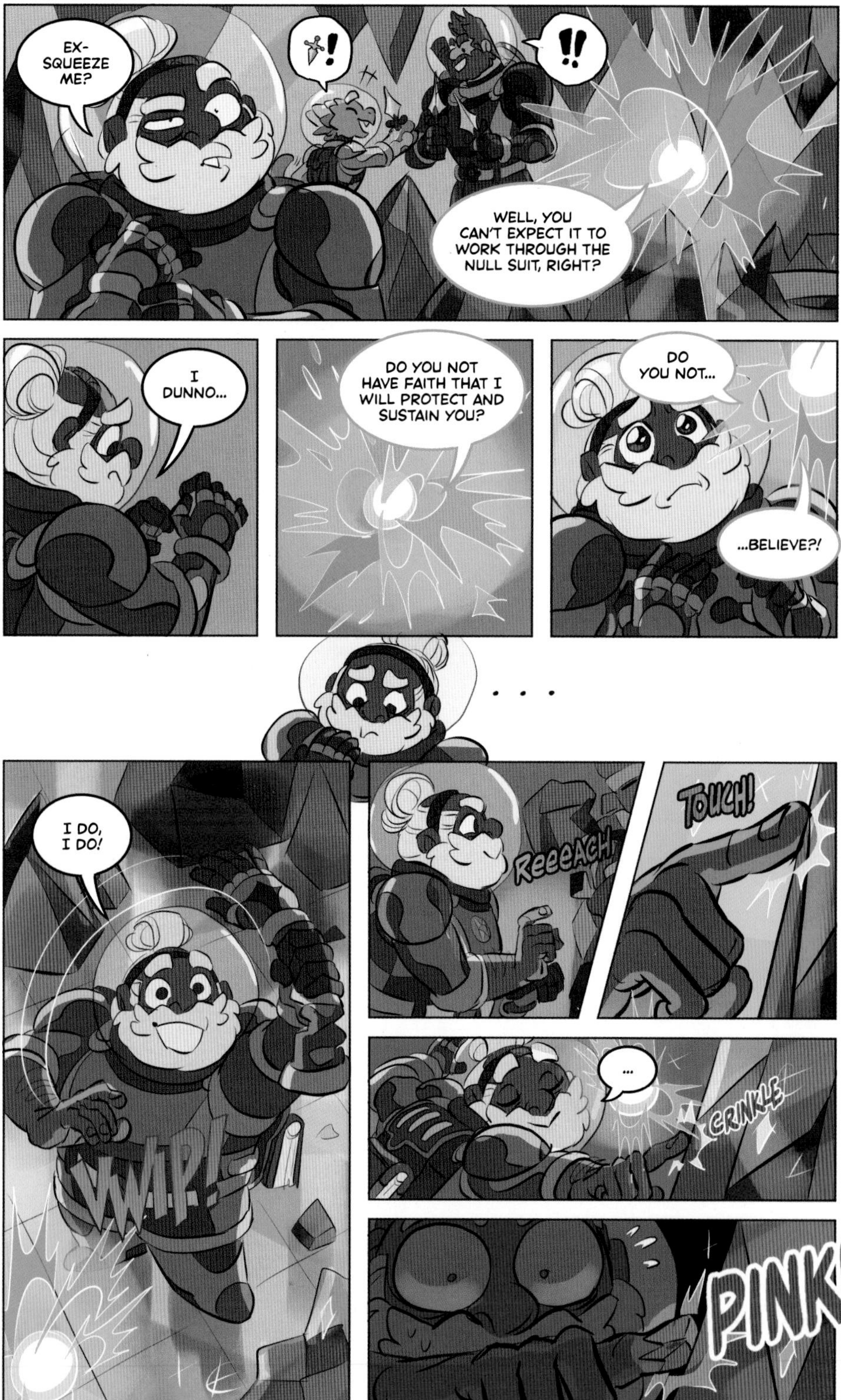
EX-SQUEEZE ME?
!
!!
WELL, YOU CAN'T EXPECT IT TO WORK THROUGH THE NULL SUIT, RIGHT?
I DUNNO...
DO YOU NOT HAVE FAITH THAT I WILL PROTECT AND SUSTAIN YOU?
DO YOU NOT...
...BELIEVE?!
. . .
I DO, I DO!
VWIP!
ReeeACH
TOUCH!
...
CRINKLE
PINK!

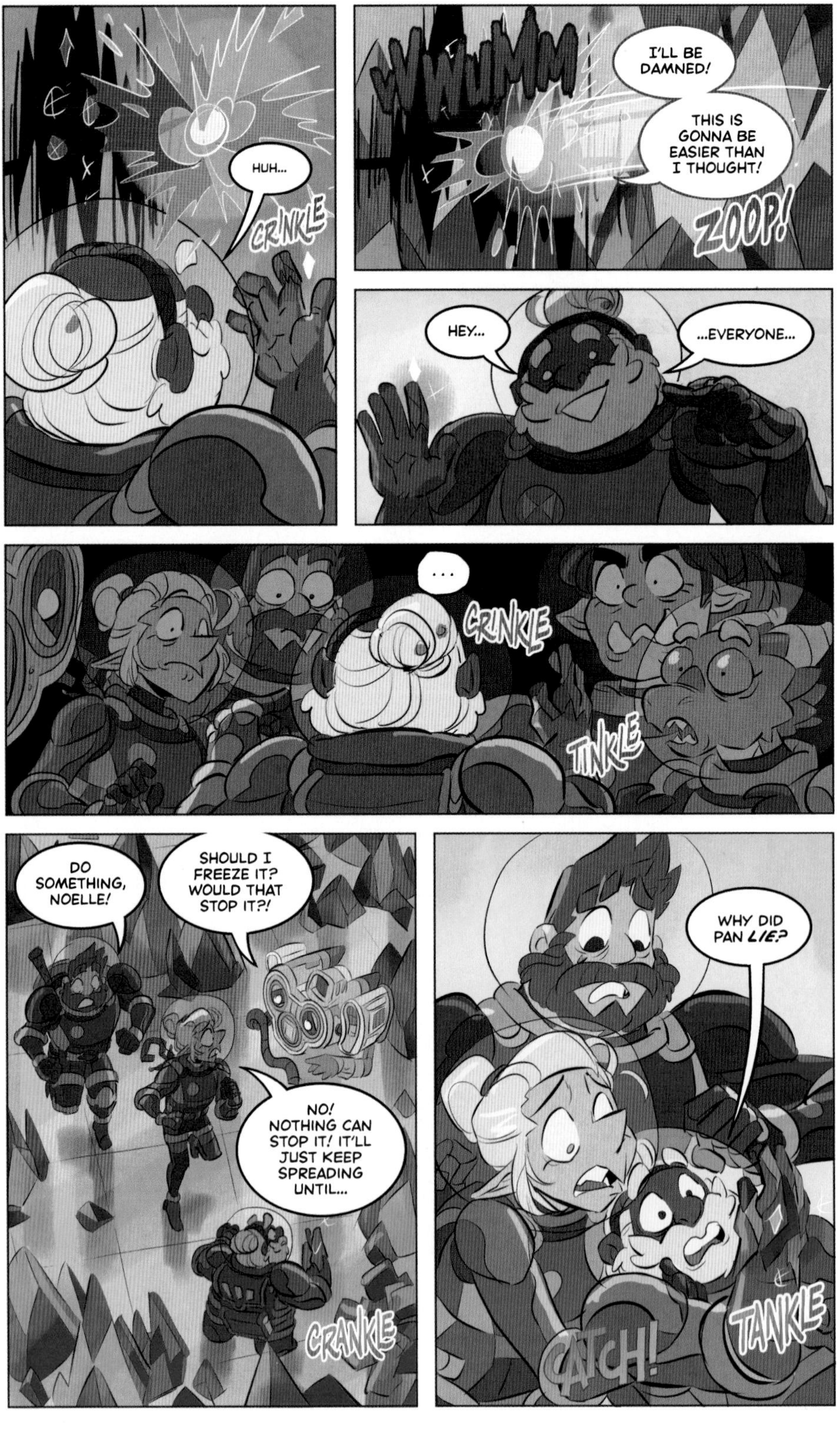
HUH...
CRINKLE
WWUMM
I'LL BE DAMNED!
THIS IS GONNA BE EASIER THAN I THOUGHT!
ZOOP!
HEY...
...EVERYONE...
...
CRINKLE
TINKLE
DO SOMETHING, NOELLE!
SHOULD I FREEZE IT? WOULD THAT STOP IT?!
NO! NOTHING CAN STOP IT! IT'LL JUST KEEP SPREADING UNTIL...
CRANKLE
WHY DID PAN LIE?
CATCH!
TANKLE

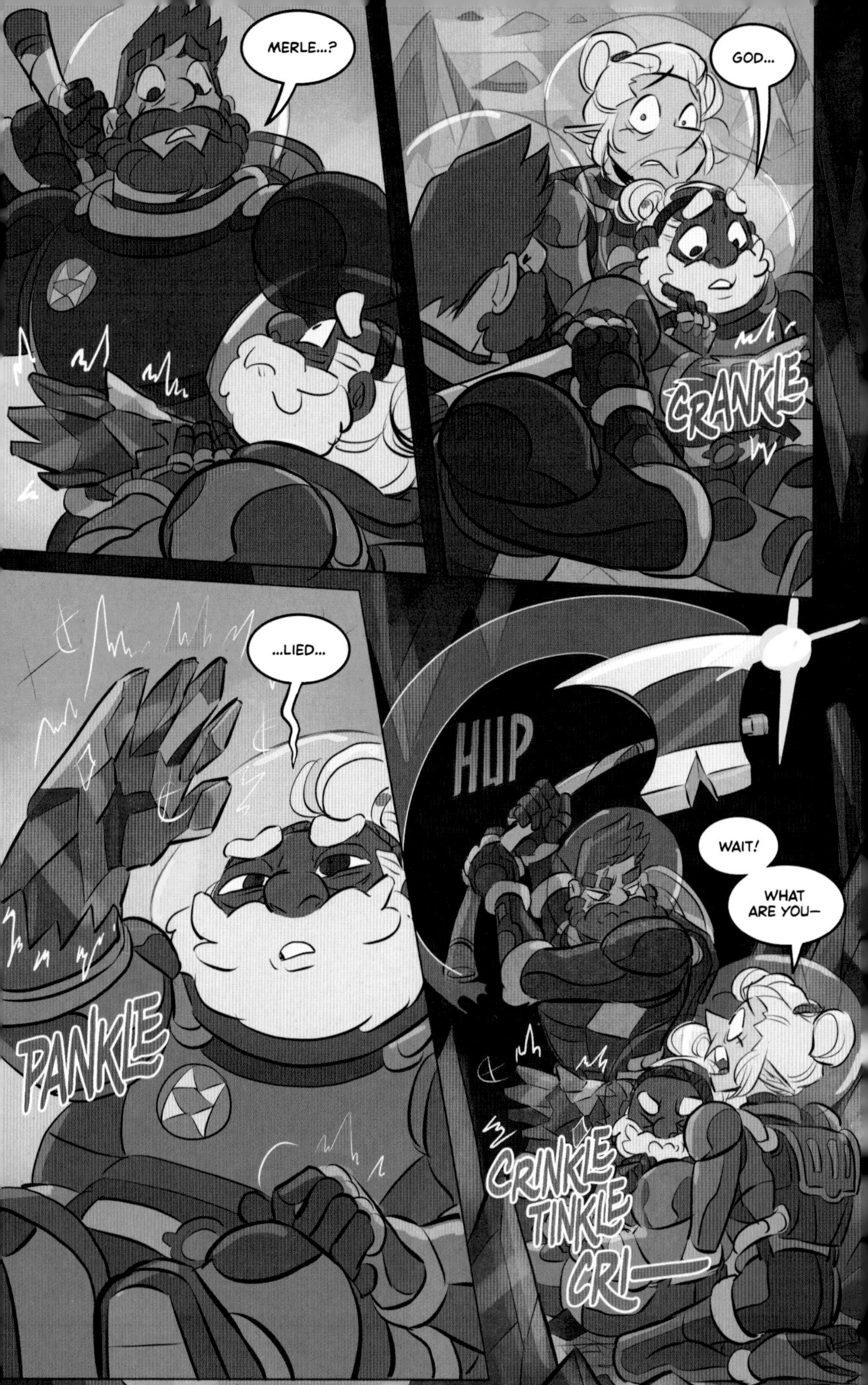
MERLE...?
GOD...
CRANKLE
...LIED...
PANKLE
HUP
WAIT!
WHAT ARE YOU—
CRINKLE
TINKLE
CRI—

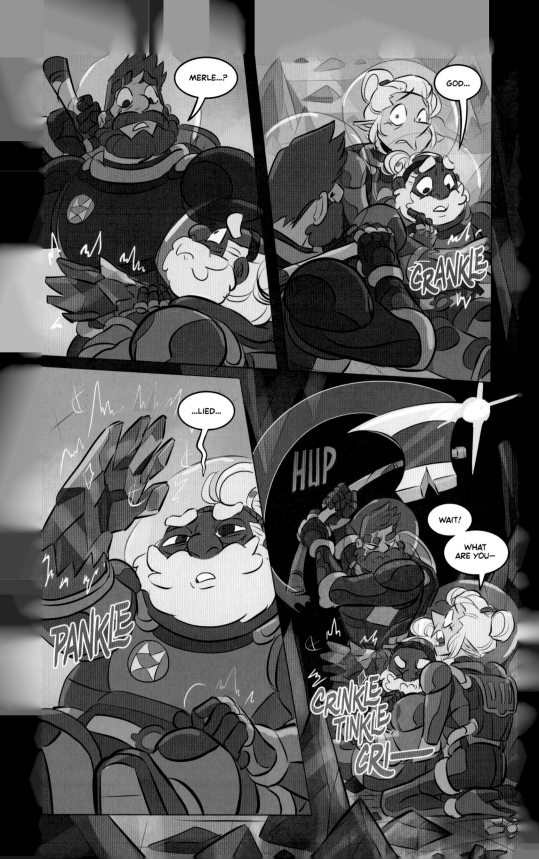

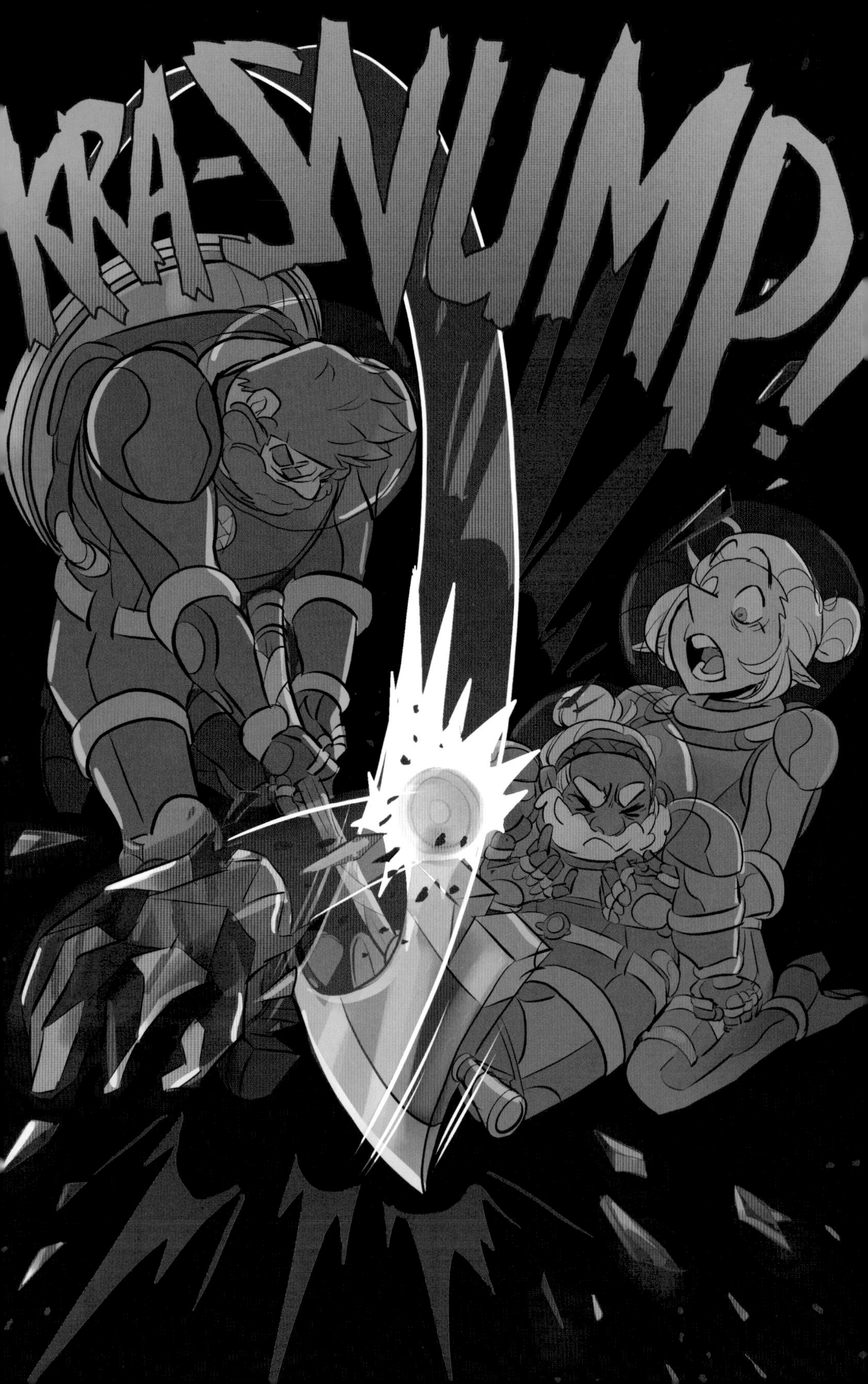
KRA-SWUMP!

Chapter
4

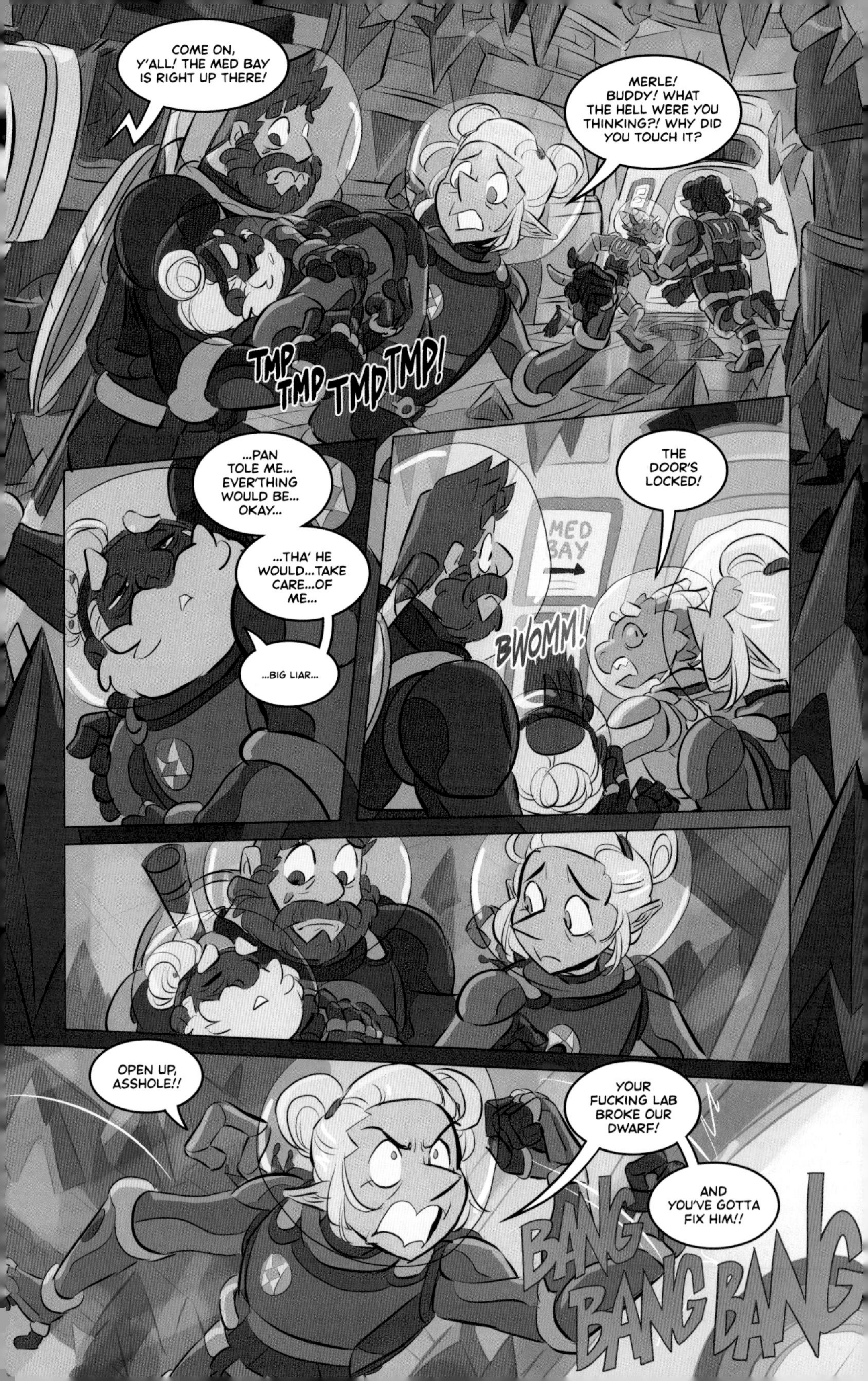
COME ON, Y'ALL! THE MED BAY IS RIGHT UP THERE!
MERLE! BUDDY! WHAT THE HELL WERE YOU THINKING?! WHY DID YOU TOUCH IT?
TMP TMP TMP TMP!
...PAN TOLE ME... EVER'THING WOULD BE... OKAY...
...THA' HE WOULD...TAKE CARE...OF ME...
...BIG LIAR...
THE DOOR'S LOCKED!
MED BAY
BWOMM!
OPEN UP, ASSHOLE!!
YOUR FUCKING LAB BROKE OUR DWARF!
AND YOU'VE GOTTA FIX HIM!!
BANG BANG BANG

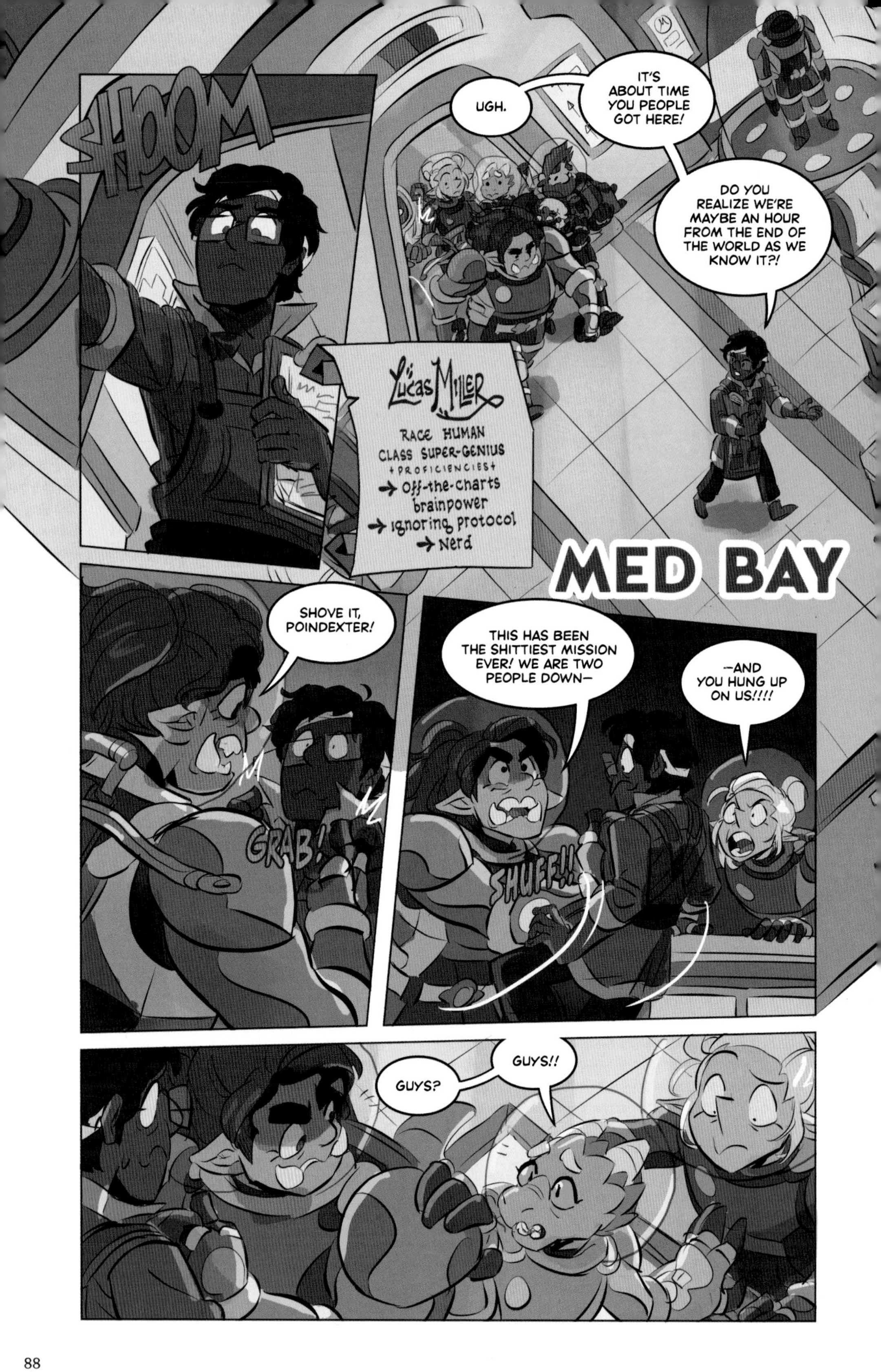
SHOOM
UGH.
IT'S ABOUT TIME YOU PEOPLE GOT HERE!
DO YOU REALIZE WE'RE MAYBE AN HOUR FROM THE END OF THE WORLD AS WE KNOW IT?!
Lucas Miller
RACE HUMAN
CLASS SUPER-GENIUS
+PROFICIENCIES+
→ Off-the-charts brainpower
→ ignoring protocol
→ Nerd
MED BAY
SHOVE IT, POINDEXTER!
GRAB!
THIS HAS BEEN THE SHITTIEST MISSION EVER! WE ARE TWO PEOPLE DOWN—
—AND YOU HUNG UP ON US!!!!
SHUFF!!
GUYS?
GUYS!!

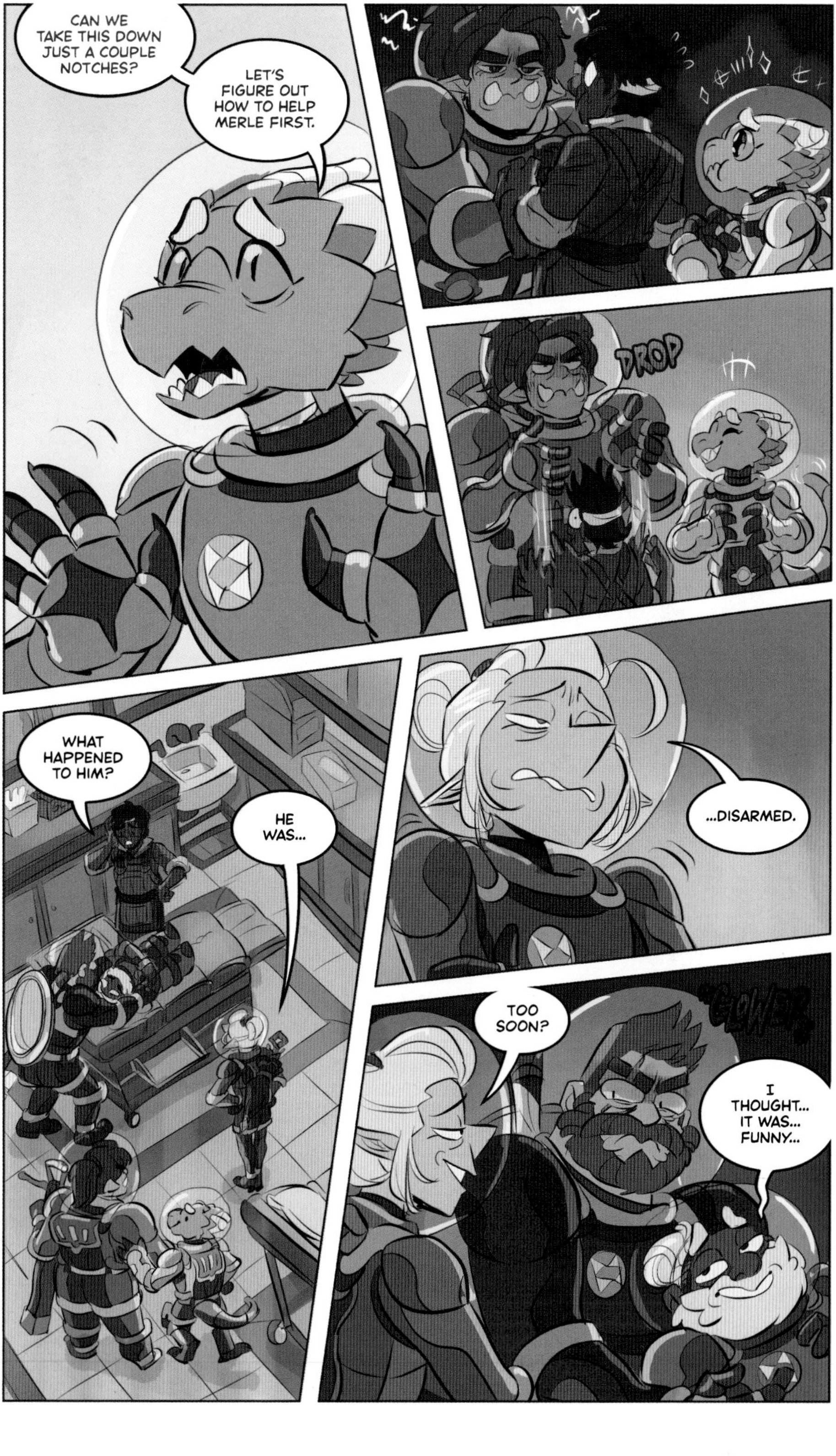
CAN WE TAKE THIS DOWN JUST A COUPLE NOTCHES?
LET'S FIGURE OUT HOW TO HELP MERLE FIRST.
DROP
WHAT HAPPENED TO HIM?
HE WAS...
...DISARMED.
TOO SOON?
GLOWER
I THOUGHT... IT WAS... FUNNY...

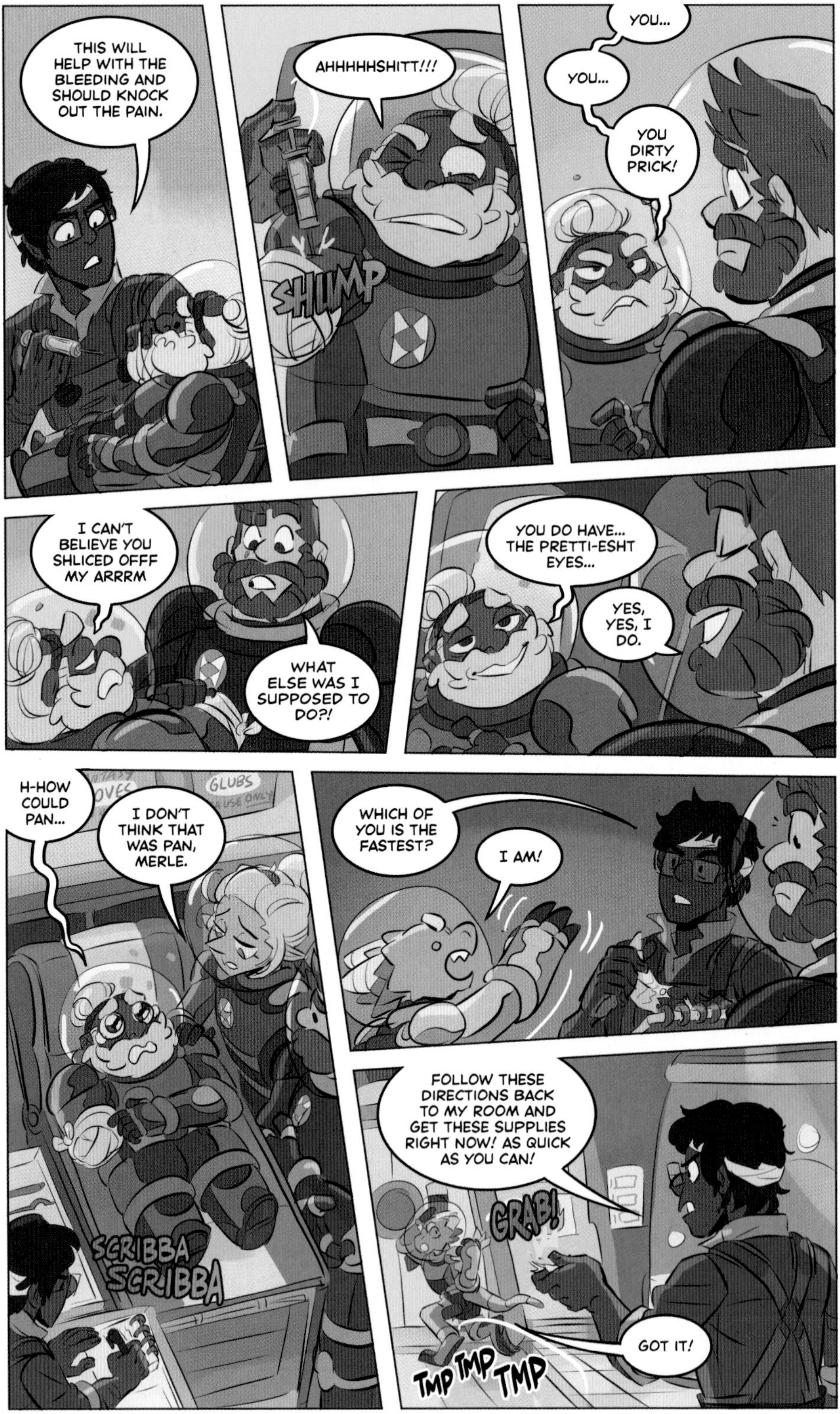
THIS WILL HELP WITH THE BLEEDING AND SHOULD KNOCK OUT THE PAIN.
AHHHHHSHITT!!!
SHUMP
YOU...
YOU...
YOU DIRTY PRICK!
I CAN'T BELIEVE YOU SHLICED OFFF MY ARRRM
WHAT ELSE WAS I SUPPOSED TO DO?!
YOU DO HAVE... THE PRETTI-ESHT EYES...
YES, YES, I DO.
H-HOW COULD PAN...
I DON'T THINK THAT WAS PAN, MERLE.
GLUBS
SCRIBBA SCRIBBA
WHICH OF YOU IS THE FASTEST?
I AM!
FOLLOW THESE DIRECTIONS BACK TO MY ROOM AND GET THESE SUPPLIES RIGHT NOW! AS QUICK AS YOU CAN!
GRAB!
GOT IT!
TMP TMP TMP

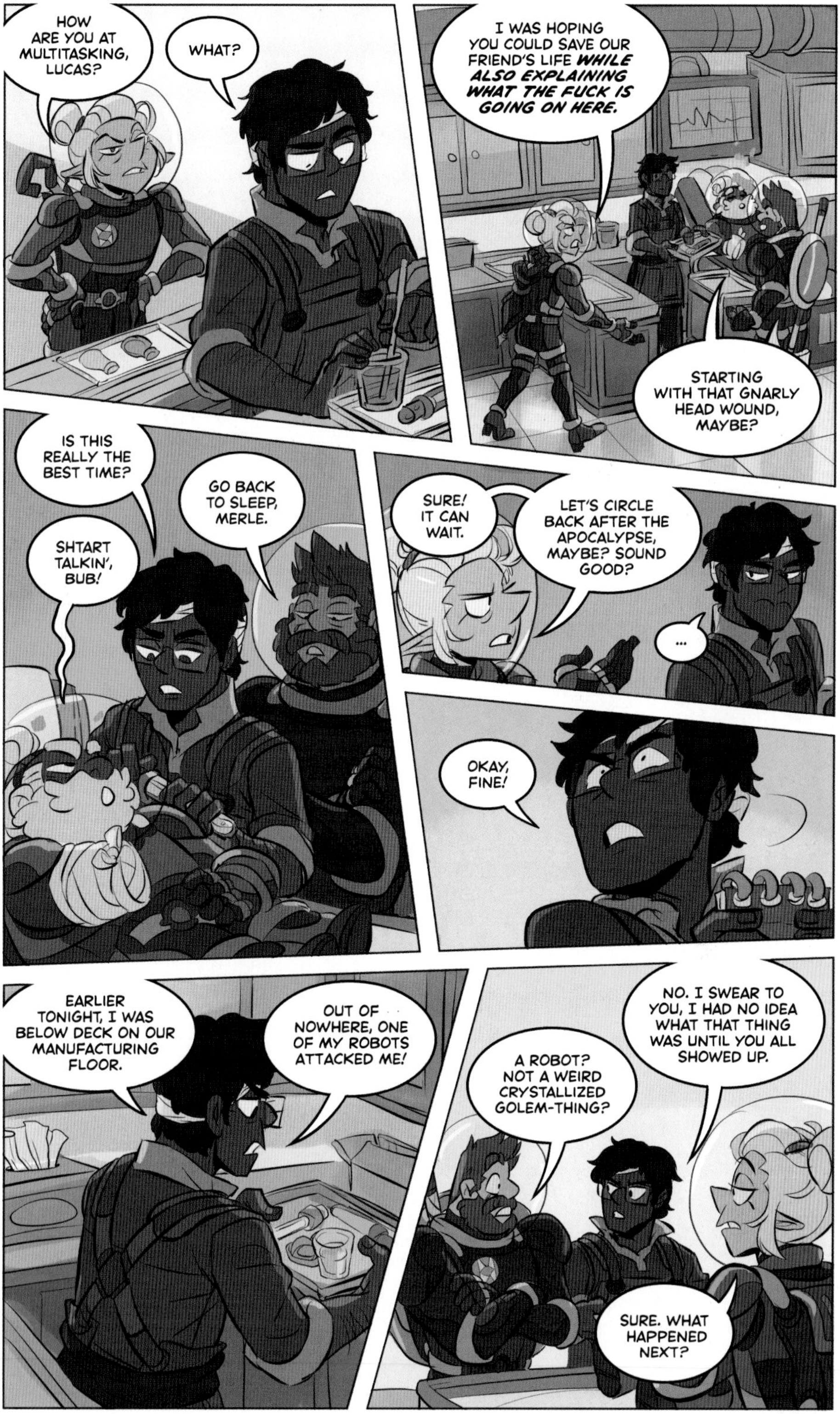
HOW ARE YOU AT MULTITASKING, LUCAS?
WHAT?
I WAS HOPING YOU COULD SAVE OUR FRIEND'S LIFE ***WHILE ALSO EXPLAINING WHAT THE FUCK IS GOING ON HERE.***
STARTING WITH THAT GNARLY HEAD WOUND, MAYBE?
IS THIS REALLY THE BEST TIME?
GO BACK TO SLEEP, MERLE.
SHTART TALKIN', BUB!
SURE! IT CAN WAIT.
LET'S CIRCLE BACK AFTER THE APOCALYPSE, MAYBE? SOUND GOOD?
...
OKAY, FINE!
EARLIER TONIGHT, I WAS BELOW DECK ON OUR MANUFACTURING FLOOR.
OUT OF NOWHERE, ONE OF MY ROBOTS ATTACKED ME!
A ROBOT? NOT A WEIRD CRYSTALLIZED GOLEM-THING?
NO. I SWEAR TO YOU, I HAD NO IDEA WHAT THAT THING WAS UNTIL YOU ALL SHOWED UP.
SURE. WHAT HAPPENED NEXT?

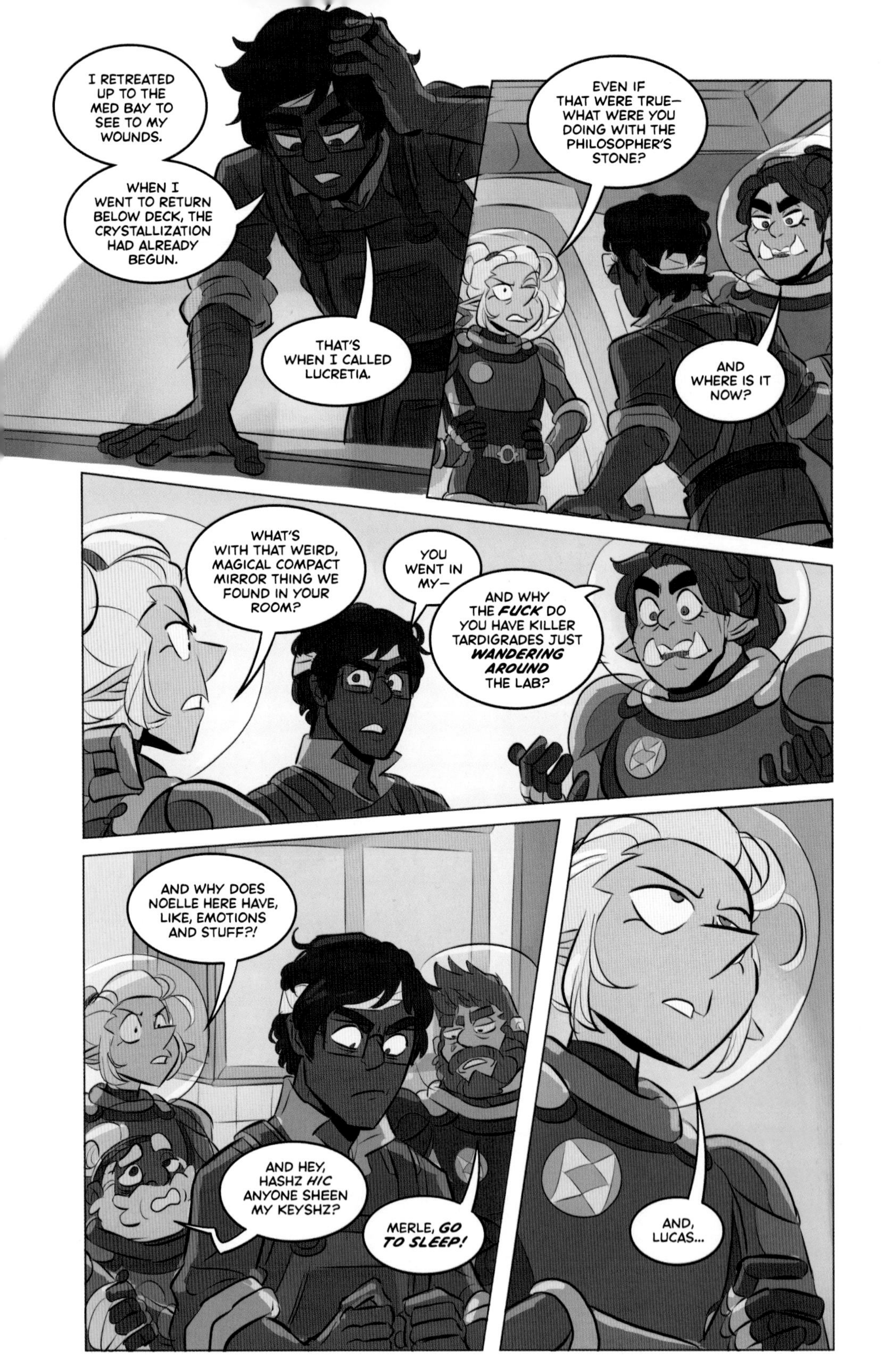
I RETREATED UP TO THE MED BAY TO SEE TO MY WOUNDS.
WHEN I WENT TO RETURN BELOW DECK, THE CRYSTALLIZATION HAD ALREADY BEGUN.
THAT'S WHEN I CALLED LUCRETIA.
EVEN IF THAT WERE TRUE— WHAT WERE YOU DOING WITH THE PHILOSOPHER'S STONE?
AND WHERE IS IT NOW?
WHAT'S WITH THAT WEIRD, MAGICAL COMPACT MIRROR THING WE FOUND IN YOUR ROOM?
YOU WENT IN MY—
AND WHY THE FUCK DO YOU HAVE KILLER TARDIGRADES JUST WANDERING AROUND THE LAB?
AND WHY DOES NOELLE HERE HAVE, LIKE, EMOTIONS AND STUFF?!
AND HEY, HASHZ HIC ANYONE SHEEN MY KEYSHZ?
MERLE, GO TO SLEEP!
AND, LUCAS...

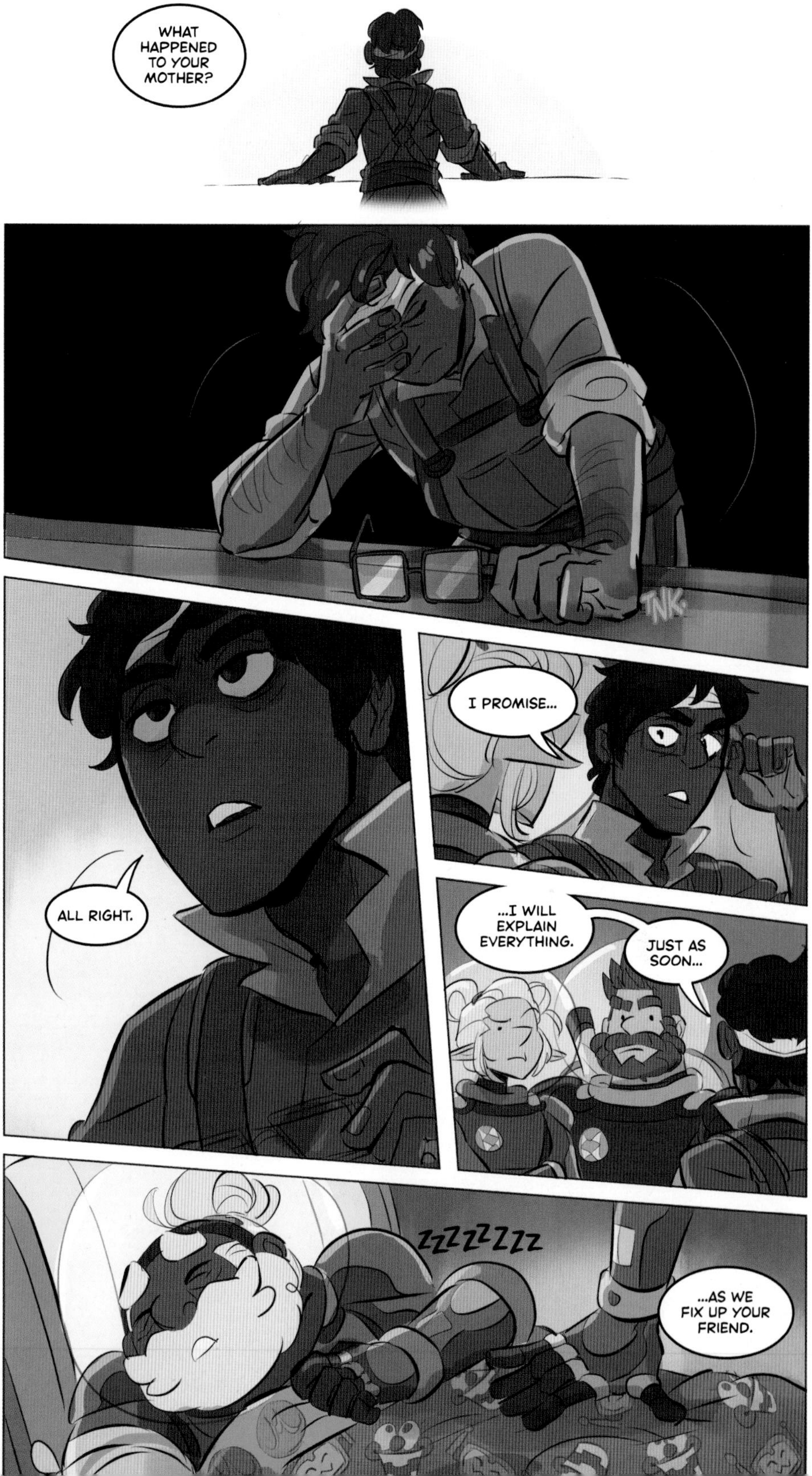
WHAT HAPPENED TO YOUR MOTHER?
TNK
ALL RIGHT.
I PROMISE...
...I WILL EXPLAIN EVERYTHING.
JUST AS SOON...
ZZZZZZZZ
...AS WE FIX UP YOUR FRIEND.

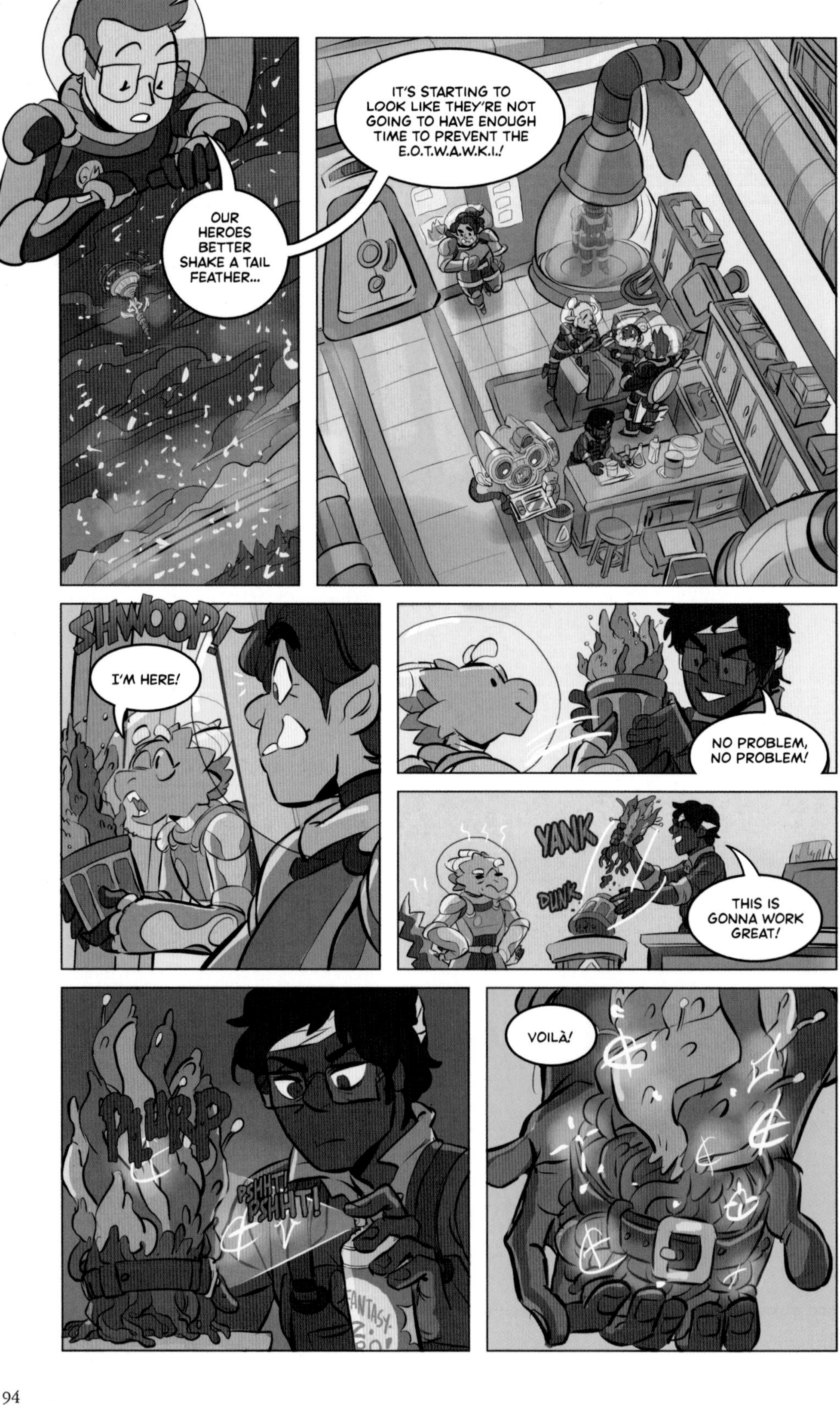
OUR HEROES BETTER SHAKE A TAIL FEATHER...
IT'S STARTING TO LOOK LIKE THEY'RE NOT GOING TO HAVE ENOUGH TIME TO PREVENT THE E.O.T.W.A.W.K.I.!
SHWOOP!
I'M HERE!
NO PROBLEM, NO PROBLEM!
YANK
DUNK
THIS IS GONNA WORK GREAT!
PLURP
PSHHT! PSHHT!
FANTASY-GO!
VOILÀ!

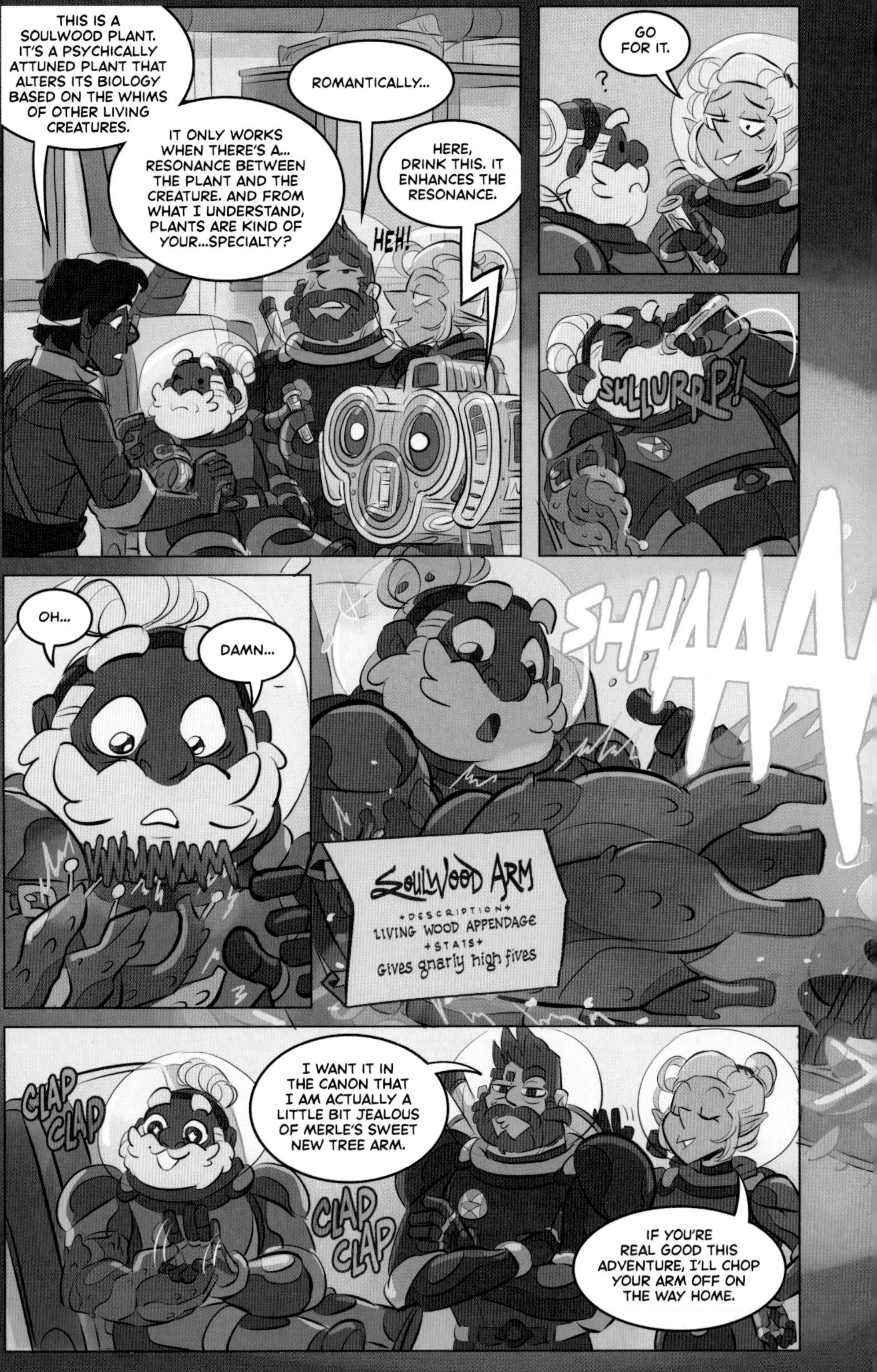
THIS IS A SOULWOOD PLANT. IT'S A PSYCHICALLY ATTUNED PLANT THAT ALTERS ITS BIOLOGY BASED ON THE WHIMS OF OTHER LIVING CREATURES.
IT ONLY WORKS WHEN THERE'S A... RESONANCE BETWEEN THE PLANT AND THE CREATURE. AND FROM WHAT I UNDERSTAND, PLANTS ARE KIND OF YOUR...SPECIALTY?
ROMANTICALLY...
HEH!
HERE, DRINK THIS. IT ENHANCES THE RESONANCE.
?
GO FOR IT.
SHLLURRP!
OH...
DAMN...
SHHAAA
SOULWOOD ARM
DESCRIPTION
LIVING WOOD APPENDAGE
STATS
Gives gnarly high fives
CLAP CLAP
I WANT IT IN THE CANON THAT I AM ACTUALLY A LITTLE BIT JEALOUS OF MERLE'S SWEET NEW TREE ARM.
CLAP CLAP
IF YOU'RE REAL GOOD THIS ADVENTURE, I'LL CHOP YOUR ARM OFF ON THE WAY HOME.

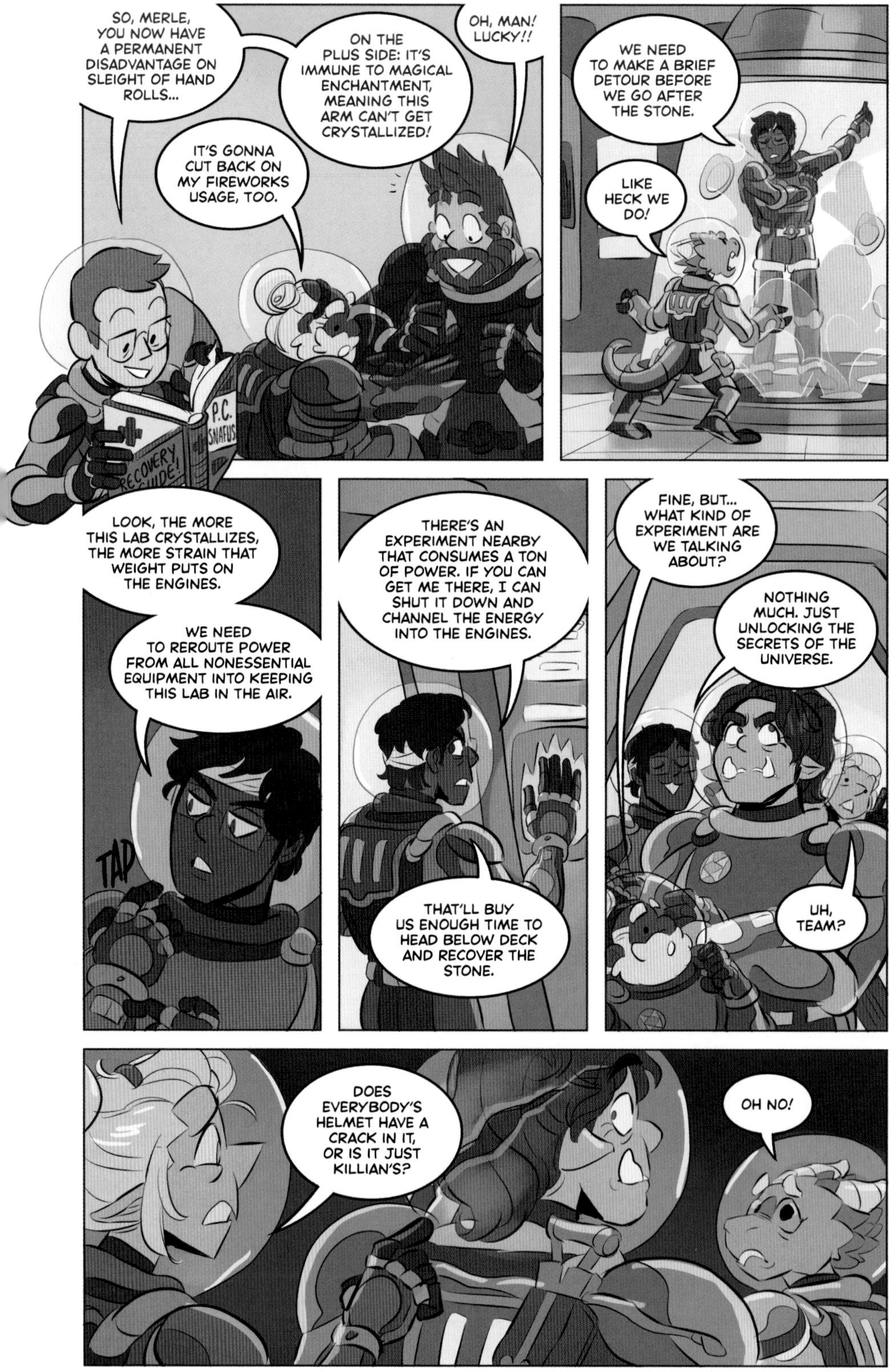
SO, MERLE, YOU NOW HAVE A PERMANENT DISADVANTAGE ON SLEIGHT OF HAND ROLLS...
ON THE PLUS SIDE: IT'S IMMUNE TO MAGICAL ENCHANTMENT, MEANING THIS ARM CAN'T GET CRYSTALLIZED!
OH, MAN! LUCKY!!
IT'S GONNA CUT BACK ON MY FIREWORKS USAGE, TOO.
P.C. SNAFUS
RECOVERY GUIDE!
WE NEED TO MAKE A BRIEF DETOUR BEFORE WE GO AFTER THE STONE.
LIKE HECK WE DO!
LOOK, THE MORE THIS LAB CRYSTALLIZES, THE MORE STRAIN THAT WEIGHT PUTS ON THE ENGINES.
WE NEED TO REROUTE POWER FROM ALL NONESSENTIAL EQUIPMENT INTO KEEPING THIS LAB IN THE AIR.
TAP
THERE'S AN EXPERIMENT NEARBY THAT CONSUMES A TON OF POWER. IF YOU CAN GET ME THERE, I CAN SHUT IT DOWN AND CHANNEL THE ENERGY INTO THE ENGINES.
THAT'LL BUY US ENOUGH TIME TO HEAD BELOW DECK AND RECOVER THE STONE.
FINE, BUT... WHAT KIND OF EXPERIMENT ARE WE TALKING ABOUT?
NOTHING MUCH. JUST UNLOCKING THE SECRETS OF THE UNIVERSE.
UH, TEAM?
DOES EVERYBODY'S HELMET HAVE A CRACK IN IT, OR IS IT JUST KILLIAN'S?
OH NO!

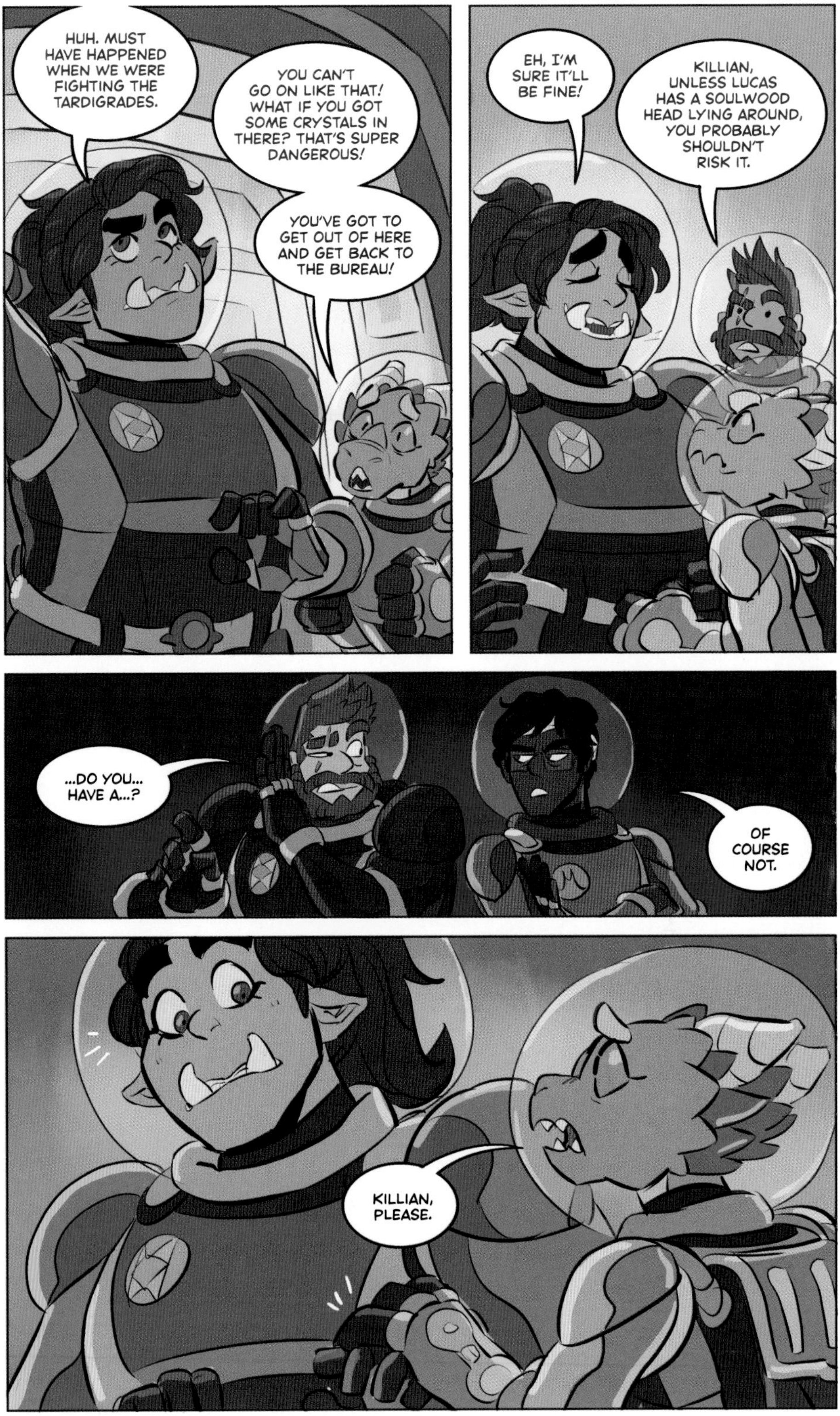
HUH. MUST HAVE HAPPENED WHEN WE WERE FIGHTING THE TARDIGRADES.
YOU CAN'T GO ON LIKE THAT! WHAT IF YOU GOT SOME CRYSTALS IN THERE? THAT'S SUPER DANGEROUS!
YOU'VE GOT TO GET OUT OF HERE AND GET BACK TO THE BUREAU!
EH, I'M SURE IT'LL BE FINE!
KILLIAN, UNLESS LUCAS HAS A SOULWOOD HEAD LYING AROUND, YOU PROBABLY SHOULDN'T RISK IT.
...DO YOU... HAVE A...?
OF COURSE NOT.
KILLIAN, PLEASE.

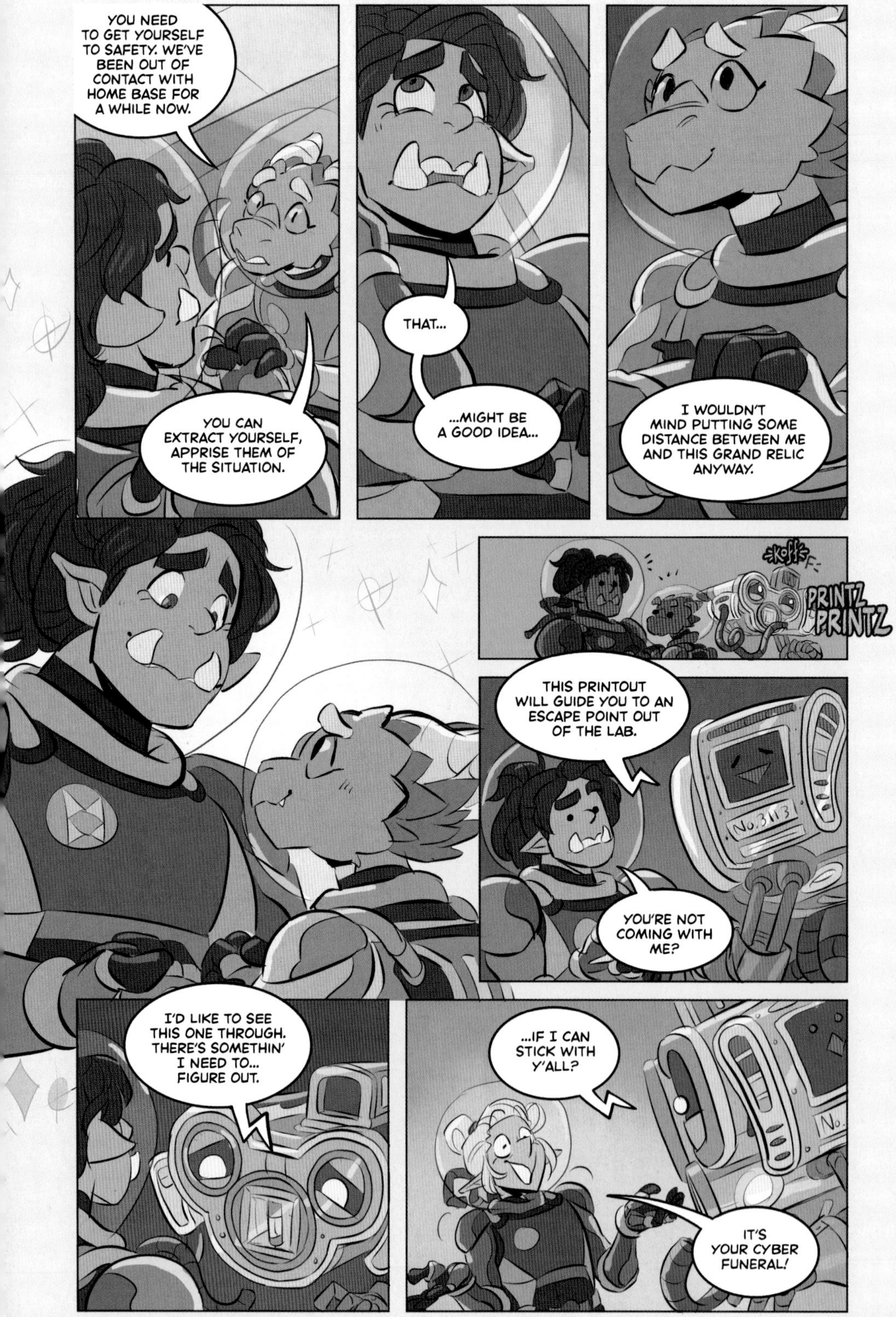
YOU NEED TO GET YOURSELF TO SAFETY. WE'VE BEEN OUT OF CONTACT WITH HOME BASE FOR A WHILE NOW.
YOU CAN EXTRACT YOURSELF, APPRISE THEM OF THE SITUATION.
THAT...
...MIGHT BE A GOOD IDEA...
I WOULDN'T MIND PUTTING SOME DISTANCE BETWEEN ME AND THIS GRAND RELIC ANYWAY.
PRINTZ PRINTZ
THIS PRINTOUT WILL GUIDE YOU TO AN ESCAPE POINT OUT OF THE LAB.
No.3113
YOU'RE NOT COMING WITH ME?
I'D LIKE TO SEE THIS ONE THROUGH. THERE'S SOMETHIN' I NEED TO... FIGURE OUT.
...IF I CAN STICK WITH Y'ALL?
IT'S YOUR CYBER FUNERAL!

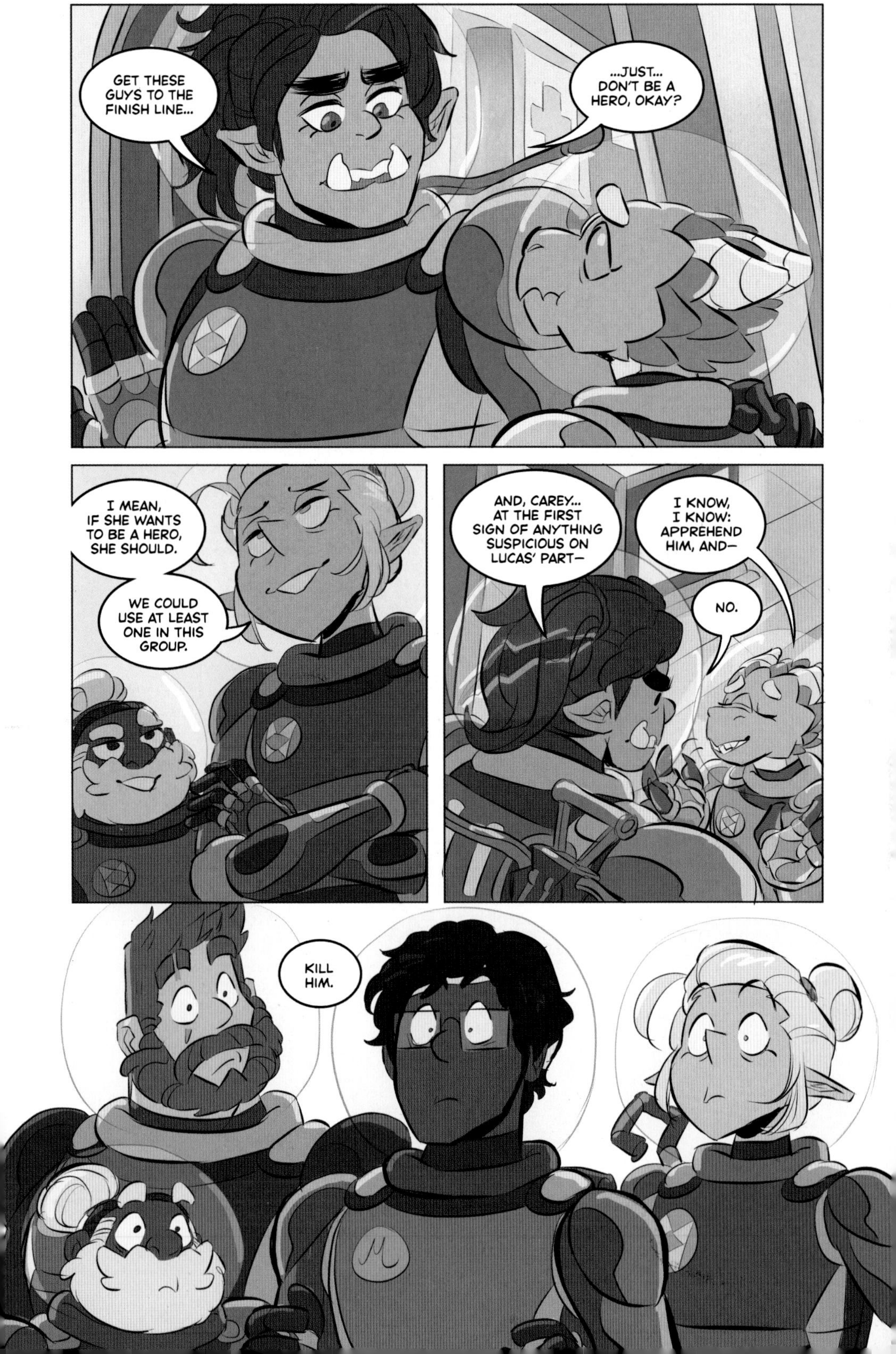
GET THESE GUYS TO THE FINISH LINE...
...JUST... DON'T BE A HERO, OKAY?
I MEAN, IF SHE WANTS TO BE A HERO, SHE SHOULD.
WE COULD USE AT LEAST ONE IN THIS GROUP.
AND, CAREY... AT THE FIRST SIGN OF ANYTHING SUSPICIOUS ON LUCAS' PART—
I KNOW, I KNOW: APPREHEND HIM, AND—
NO.
KILL HIM.

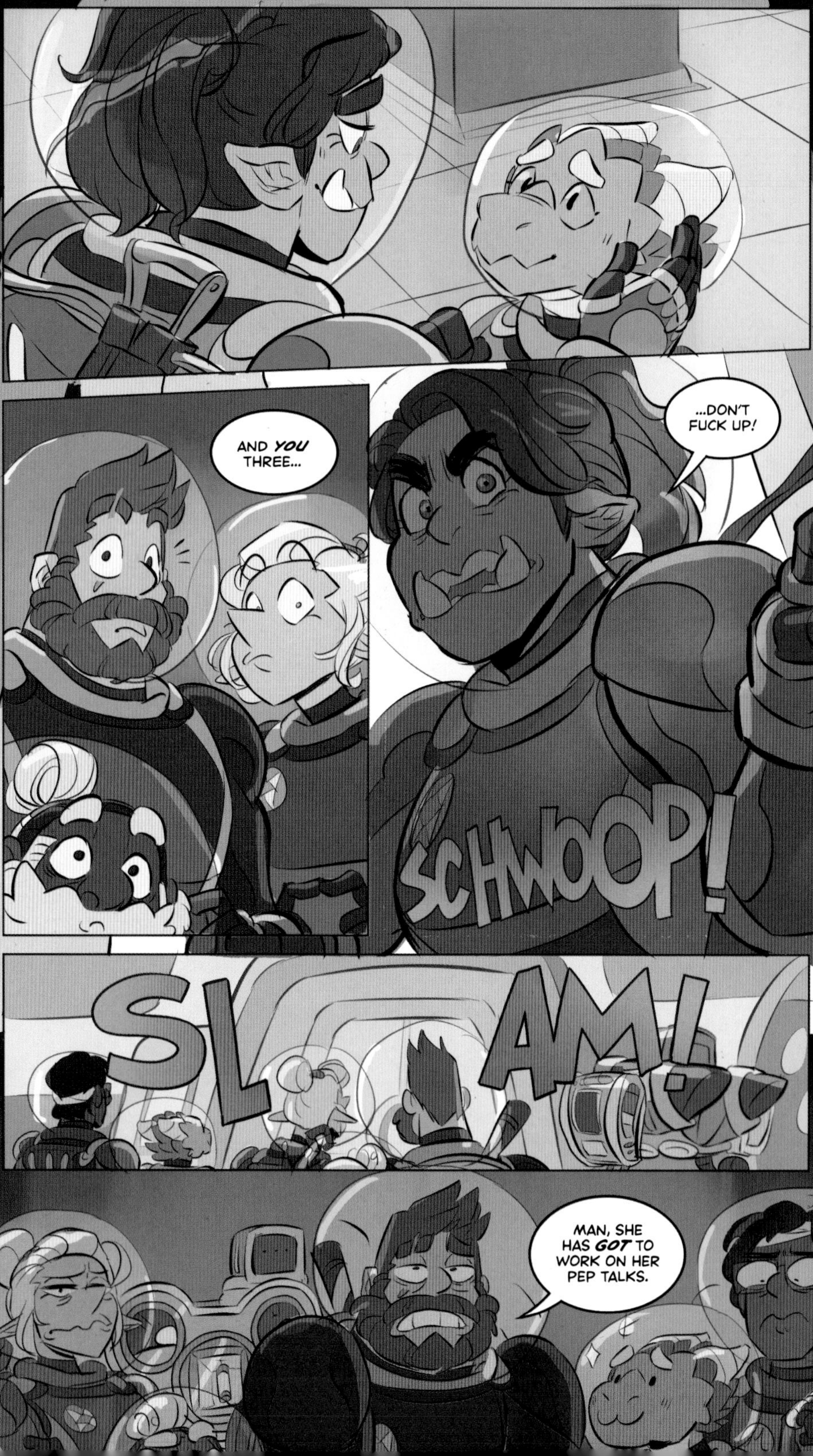
AND YOU THREE...
...DON'T FUCK UP!
SCHWOOP!
SLAM!
MAN, SHE HAS GOT TO WORK ON HER PEP TALKS.

Chapter
5

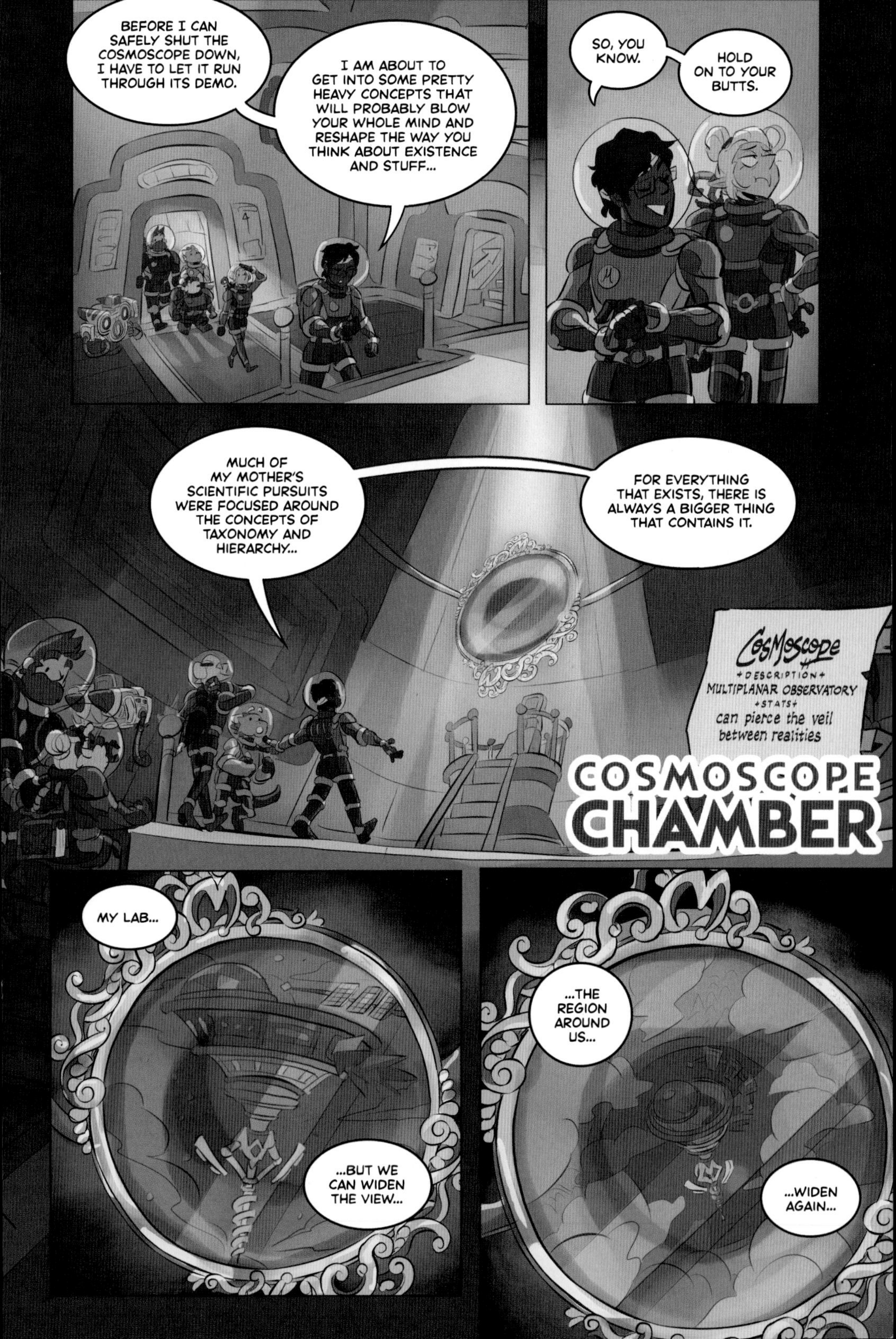
BEFORE I CAN SAFELY SHUT THE COSMOSCOPE DOWN, I HAVE TO LET IT RUN THROUGH ITS DEMO.
I AM ABOUT TO GET INTO SOME PRETTY HEAVY CONCEPTS THAT WILL PROBABLY BLOW YOUR WHOLE MIND AND RESHAPE THE WAY YOU THINK ABOUT EXISTENCE AND STUFF...
SO, YOU KNOW.
HOLD ON TO YOUR BUTTS.
MUCH OF MY MOTHER'S SCIENTIFIC PURSUITS WERE FOCUSED AROUND THE CONCEPTS OF TAXONOMY AND HIERARCHY...
FOR EVERYTHING THAT EXISTS, THERE IS ALWAYS A BIGGER THING THAT CONTAINS IT.
CosMoscope
DESCRIPTION
MULTIPLANAR OBSERVATORY
STATS
can pierce the veil between realities
COSMOSCOPE CHAMBER
MY LAB...
...BUT WE CAN WIDEN THE VIEW...
...THE REGION AROUND US...
...WIDEN AGAIN...

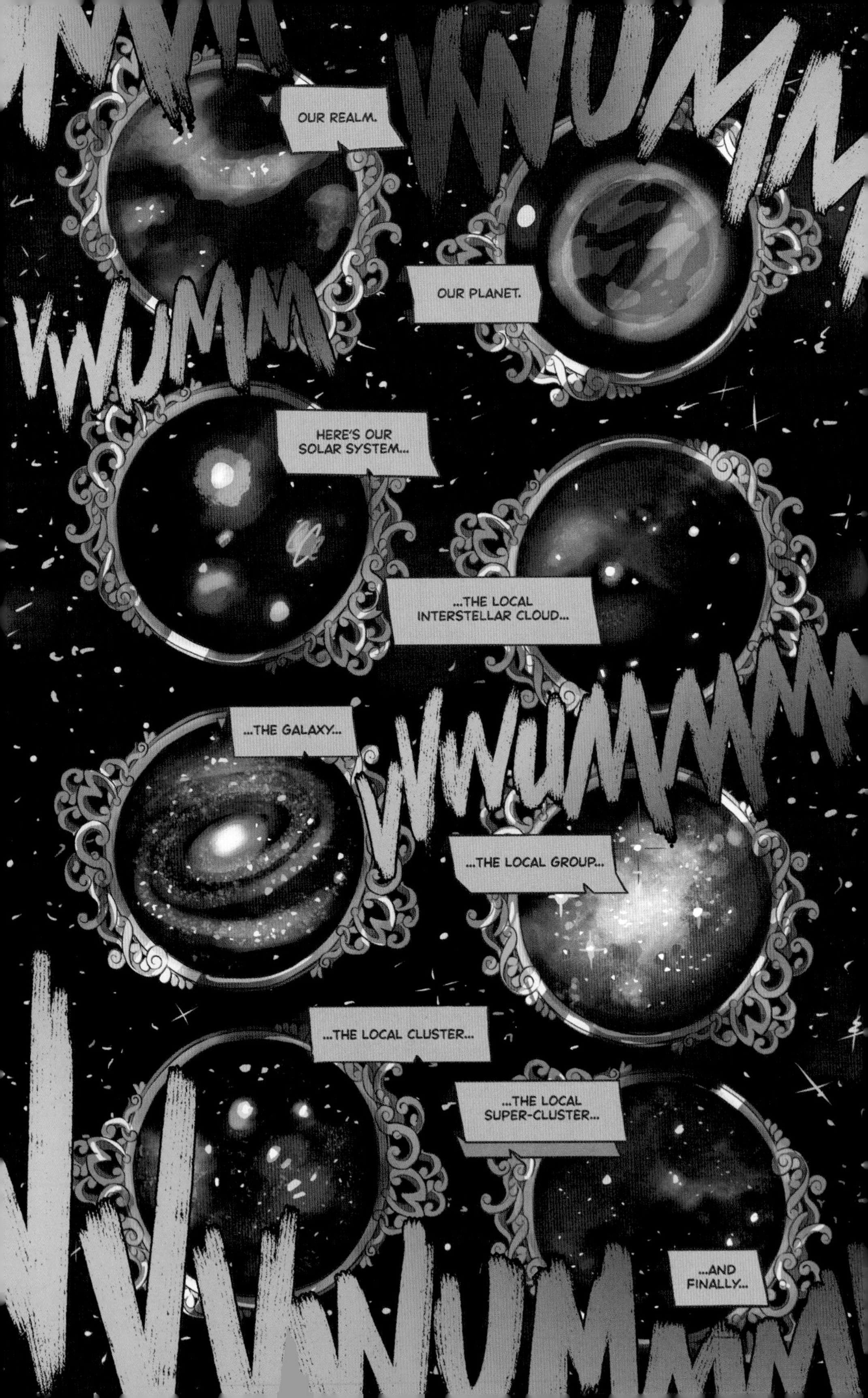

WUMM
OUR REALM.
OUR PLANET.
WUMM
HERE'S OUR SOLAR SYSTEM...
...THE LOCAL INTERSTELLAR CLOUD...
...THE GALAXY...
WUMMM
...THE LOCAL GROUP...
...THE LOCAL CLUSTER...
...THE LOCAL SUPER-CLUSTER...
...AND FINALLY...

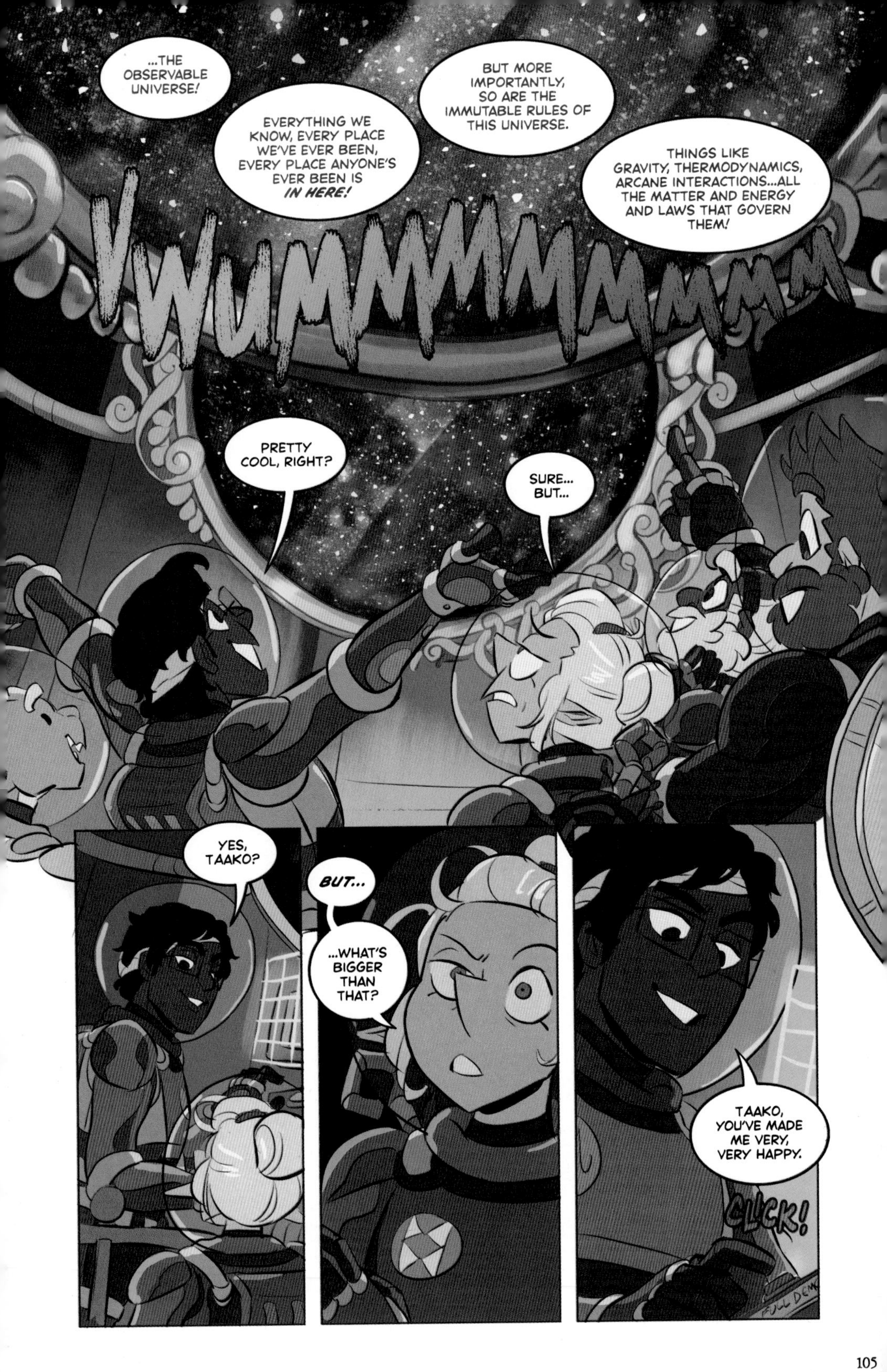

...THE OBSERVABLE UNIVERSE!
EVERYTHING WE KNOW, EVERY PLACE WE'VE EVER BEEN, EVERY PLACE ANYONE'S EVER BEEN IS *IN HERE!*
BUT MORE IMPORTANTLY, SO ARE THE IMMUTABLE RULES OF THIS UNIVERSE.
THINGS LIKE GRAVITY, THERMODYNAMICS, ARCANE INTERACTIONS...ALL THE MATTER AND ENERGY AND LAWS THAT GOVERN THEM!
VWUMMMMMMMMMM
PRETTY COOL, RIGHT?
SURE... BUT...
YES, TAAKO?
BUT...
...WHAT'S BIGGER THAN THAT?
TAAKO, YOU'VE MADE ME VERY, VERY HAPPY.
CLICK!

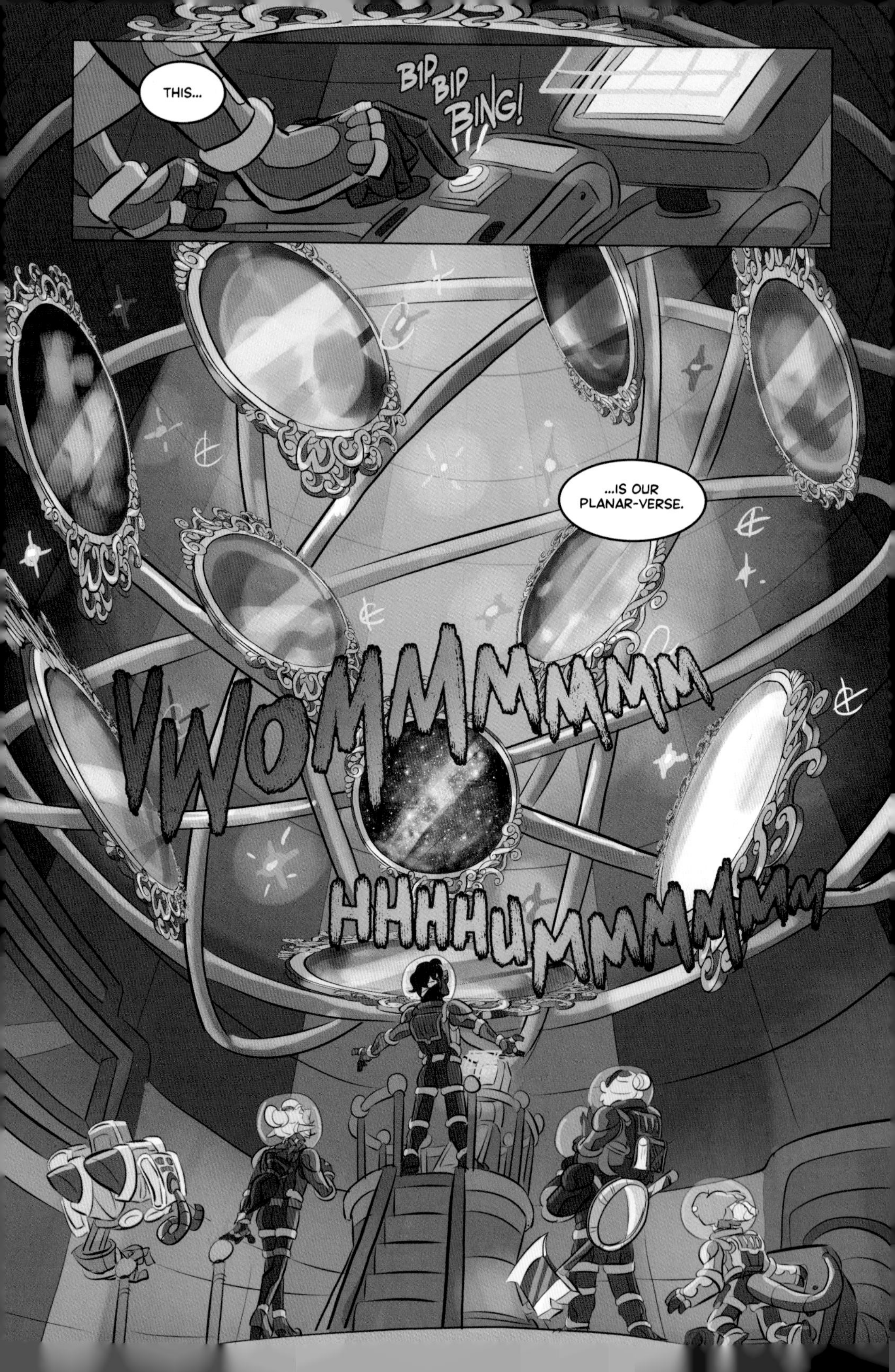
THIS...
BIP BIP BING!
...IS OUR PLANAR-VERSE.
VWOMMMMMMM
HHHHUMMMMMMM

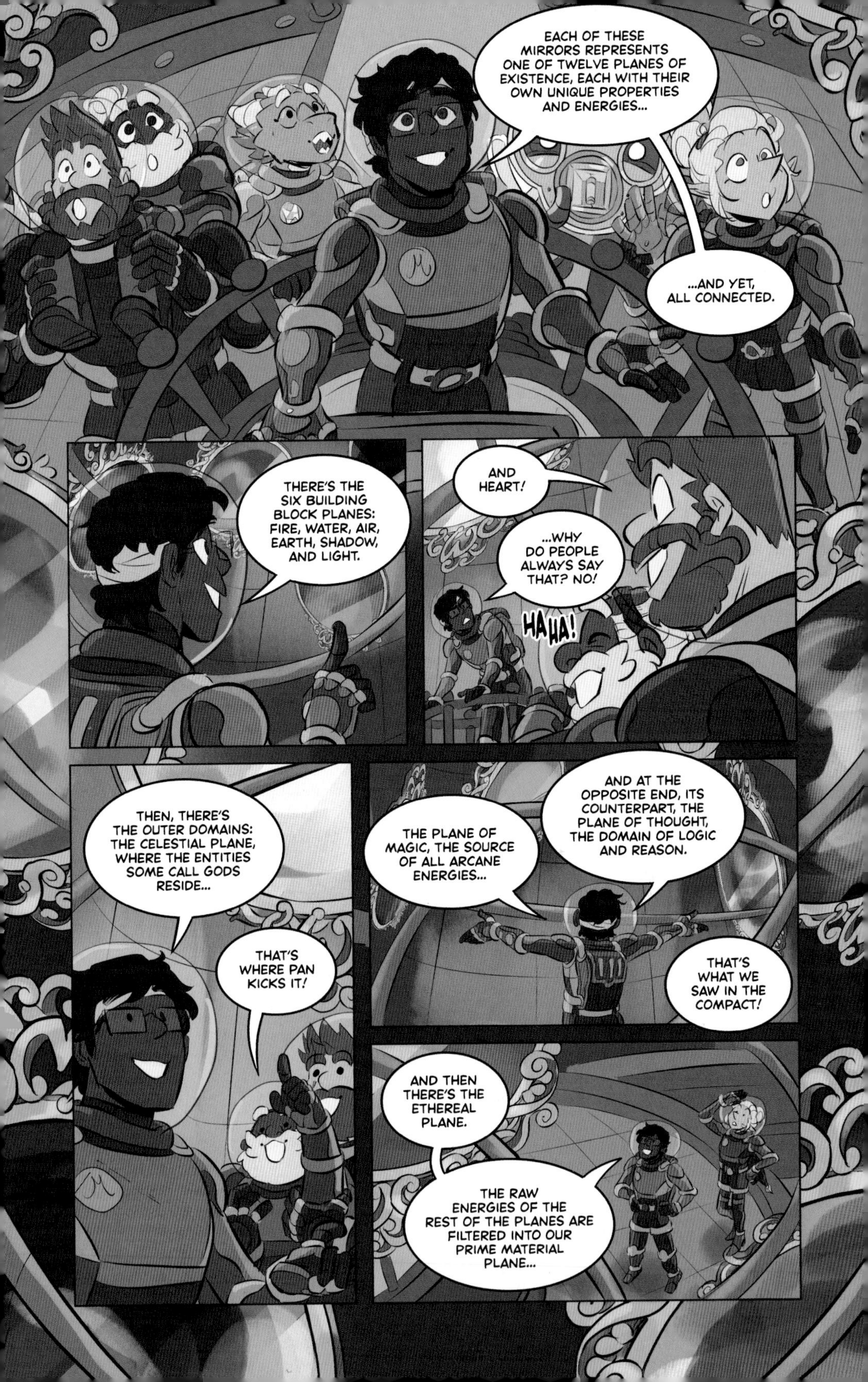
EACH OF THESE MIRRORS REPRESENTS ONE OF TWELVE PLANES OF EXISTENCE, EACH WITH THEIR OWN UNIQUE PROPERTIES AND ENERGIES...
...AND YET, ALL CONNECTED.
THERE'S THE SIX BUILDING BLOCK PLANES: FIRE, WATER, AIR, EARTH, SHADOW, AND LIGHT.
AND HEART!
...WHY DO PEOPLE ALWAYS SAY THAT? NO!
HAHA!
THEN, THERE'S THE OUTER DOMAINS: THE CELESTIAL PLANE, WHERE THE ENTITIES SOME CALL GODS RESIDE...
THAT'S WHERE PAN KICKS IT!
THE PLANE OF MAGIC, THE SOURCE OF ALL ARCANE ENERGIES...
AND AT THE OPPOSITE END, ITS COUNTERPART, THE PLANE OF THOUGHT, THE DOMAIN OF LOGIC AND REASON.
THAT'S WHAT WE SAW IN THE COMPACT!
AND THEN THERE'S THE ETHEREAL PLANE.
THE RAW ENERGIES OF THE REST OF THE PLANES ARE FILTERED INTO OUR PRIME MATERIAL PLANE...

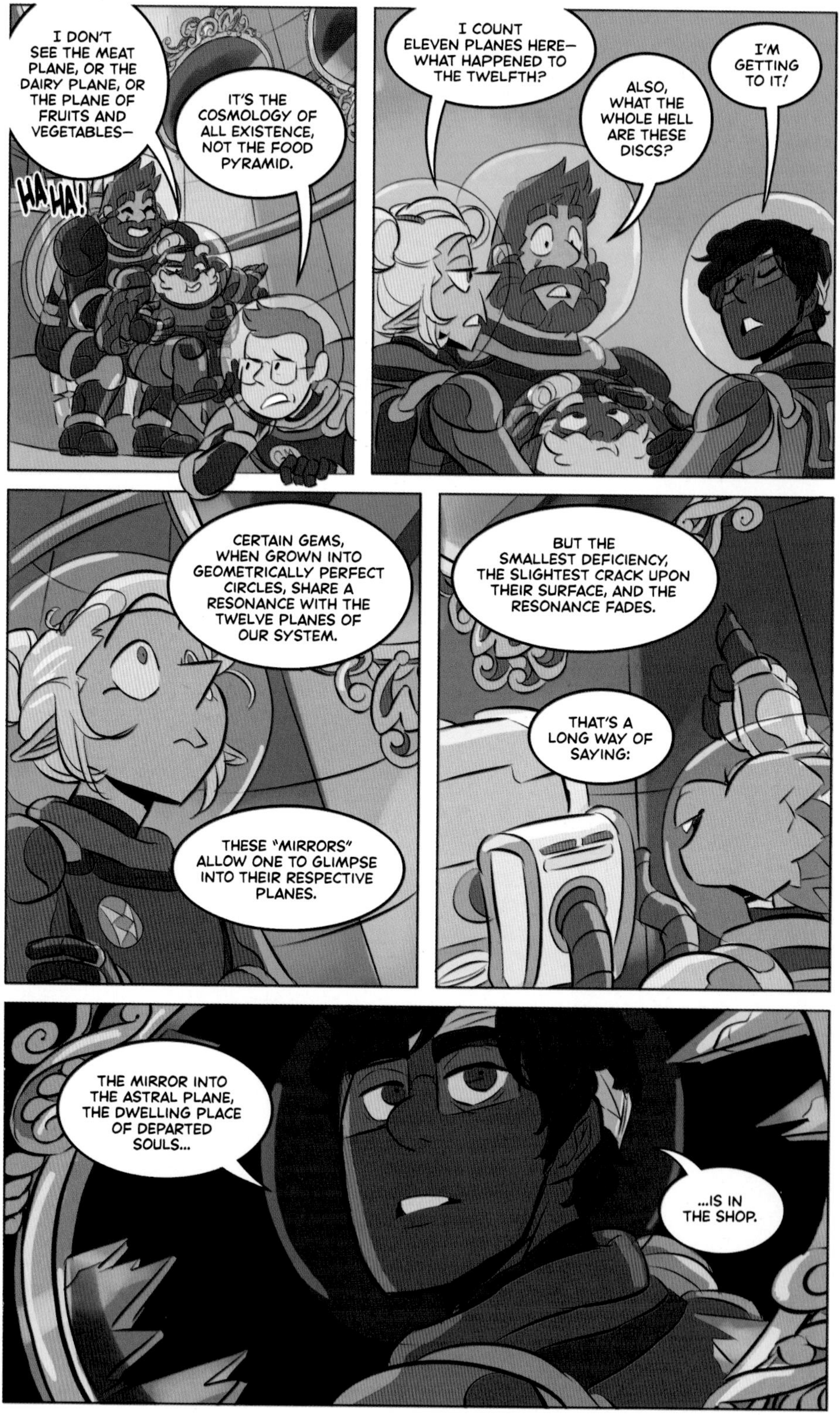
I DON'T SEE THE MEAT PLANE, OR THE DAIRY PLANE, OR THE PLANE OF FRUITS AND VEGETABLES—
HA HA!
IT'S THE COSMOLOGY OF ALL EXISTENCE, NOT THE FOOD PYRAMID.
I COUNT ELEVEN PLANES HERE—WHAT HAPPENED TO THE TWELFTH?
ALSO, WHAT THE WHOLE HELL ARE THESE DISCS?
I'M GETTING TO IT!
CERTAIN GEMS, WHEN GROWN INTO GEOMETRICALLY PERFECT CIRCLES, SHARE A RESONANCE WITH THE TWELVE PLANES OF OUR SYSTEM.
THESE "MIRRORS" ALLOW ONE TO GLIMPSE INTO THEIR RESPECTIVE PLANES.
BUT THE SMALLEST DEFICIENCY, THE SLIGHTEST CRACK UPON THEIR SURFACE, AND THE RESONANCE FADES.
THAT'S A LONG WAY OF SAYING:
THE MIRROR INTO THE ASTRAL PLANE, THE DWELLING PLACE OF DEPARTED SOULS...
...IS IN THE SHOP.

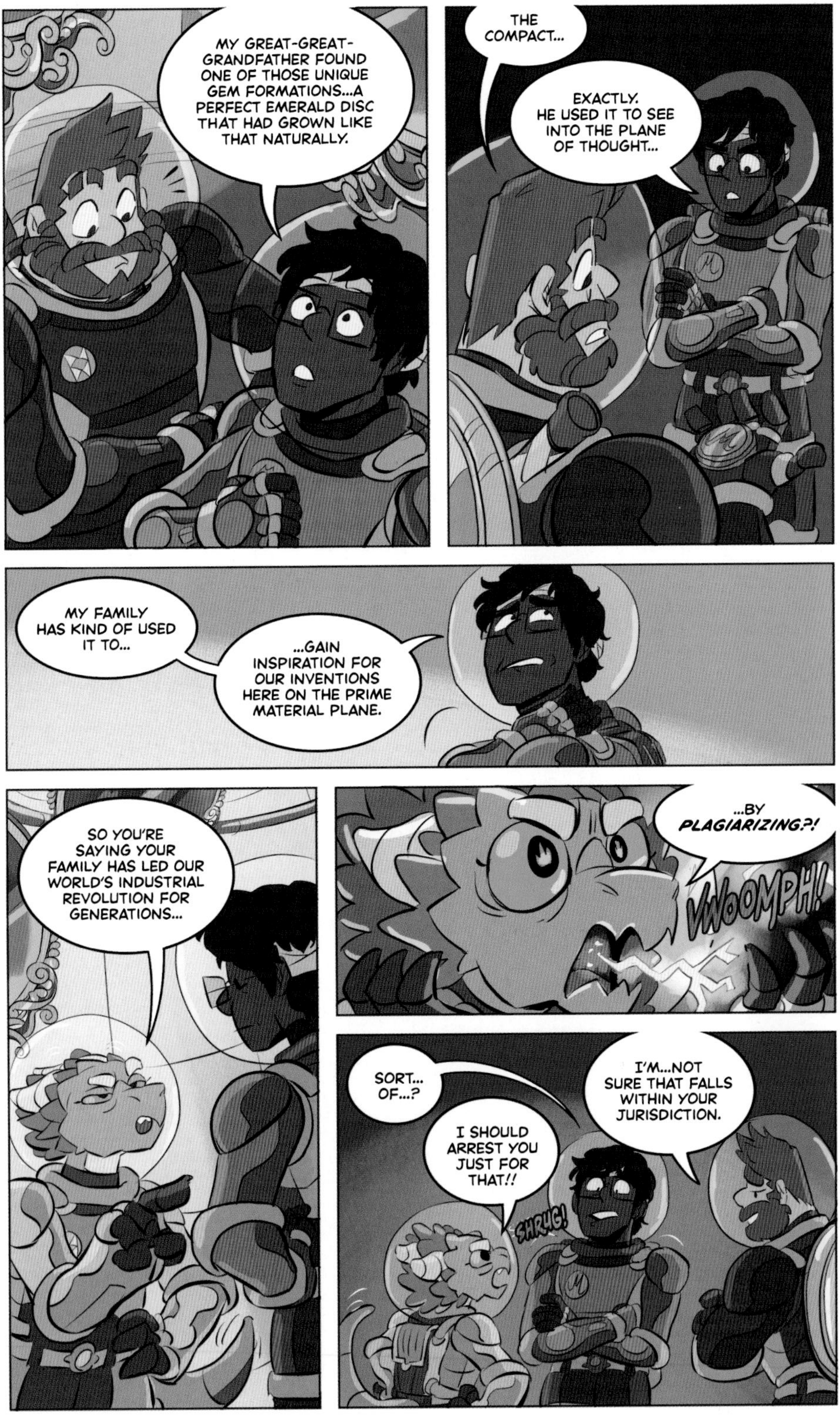
MY GREAT-GREAT-GRANDFATHER FOUND ONE OF THOSE UNIQUE GEM FORMATIONS...A PERFECT EMERALD DISC THAT HAD GROWN LIKE THAT NATURALLY.
THE COMPACT...
EXACTLY. HE USED IT TO SEE INTO THE PLANE OF THOUGHT...
MY FAMILY HAS KIND OF USED IT TO...
...GAIN INSPIRATION FOR OUR INVENTIONS HERE ON THE PRIME MATERIAL PLANE.
SO YOU'RE SAYING YOUR FAMILY HAS LED OUR WORLD'S INDUSTRIAL REVOLUTION FOR GENERATIONS...
...BY *PLAGIARIZING?!*
VWOOMPH!
SORT... OF...?
I'M...NOT SURE THAT FALLS WITHIN YOUR JURISDICTION.
I SHOULD ARREST YOU JUST FOR THAT!!
SHRUG!

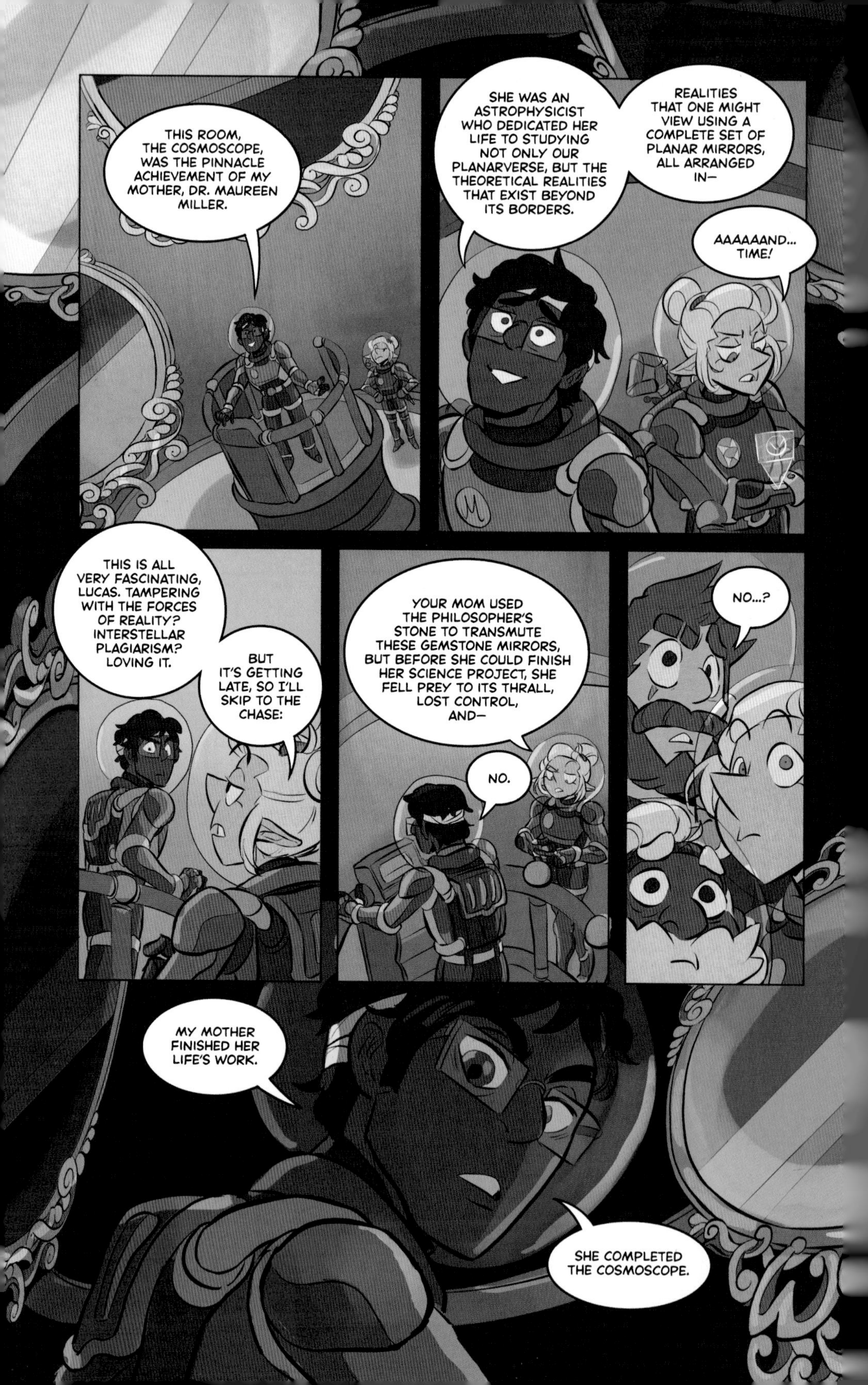
THIS ROOM, THE COSMOSCOPE, WAS THE PINNACLE ACHIEVEMENT OF MY MOTHER, DR. MAUREEN MILLER.
SHE WAS AN ASTROPHYSICIST WHO DEDICATED HER LIFE TO STUDYING NOT ONLY OUR PLANARVERSE, BUT THE THEORETICAL REALITIES THAT EXIST BEYOND ITS BORDERS.
REALITIES THAT ONE MIGHT VIEW USING A COMPLETE SET OF PLANAR MIRRORS, ALL ARRANGED IN—
AAAAAAND... TIME!
THIS IS ALL VERY FASCINATING, LUCAS. TAMPERING WITH THE FORCES OF REALITY? INTERSTELLAR PLAGIARISM? LOVING IT.
BUT IT'S GETTING LATE, SO I'LL SKIP TO THE CHASE:
YOUR MOM USED THE PHILOSOPHER'S STONE TO TRANSMUTE THESE GEMSTONE MIRRORS, BUT BEFORE SHE COULD FINISH HER SCIENCE PROJECT, SHE FELL PREY TO ITS THRALL, LOST CONTROL, AND—
NO.
NO...?
MY MOTHER FINISHED HER LIFE'S WORK.
SHE COMPLETED THE COSMOSCOPE.

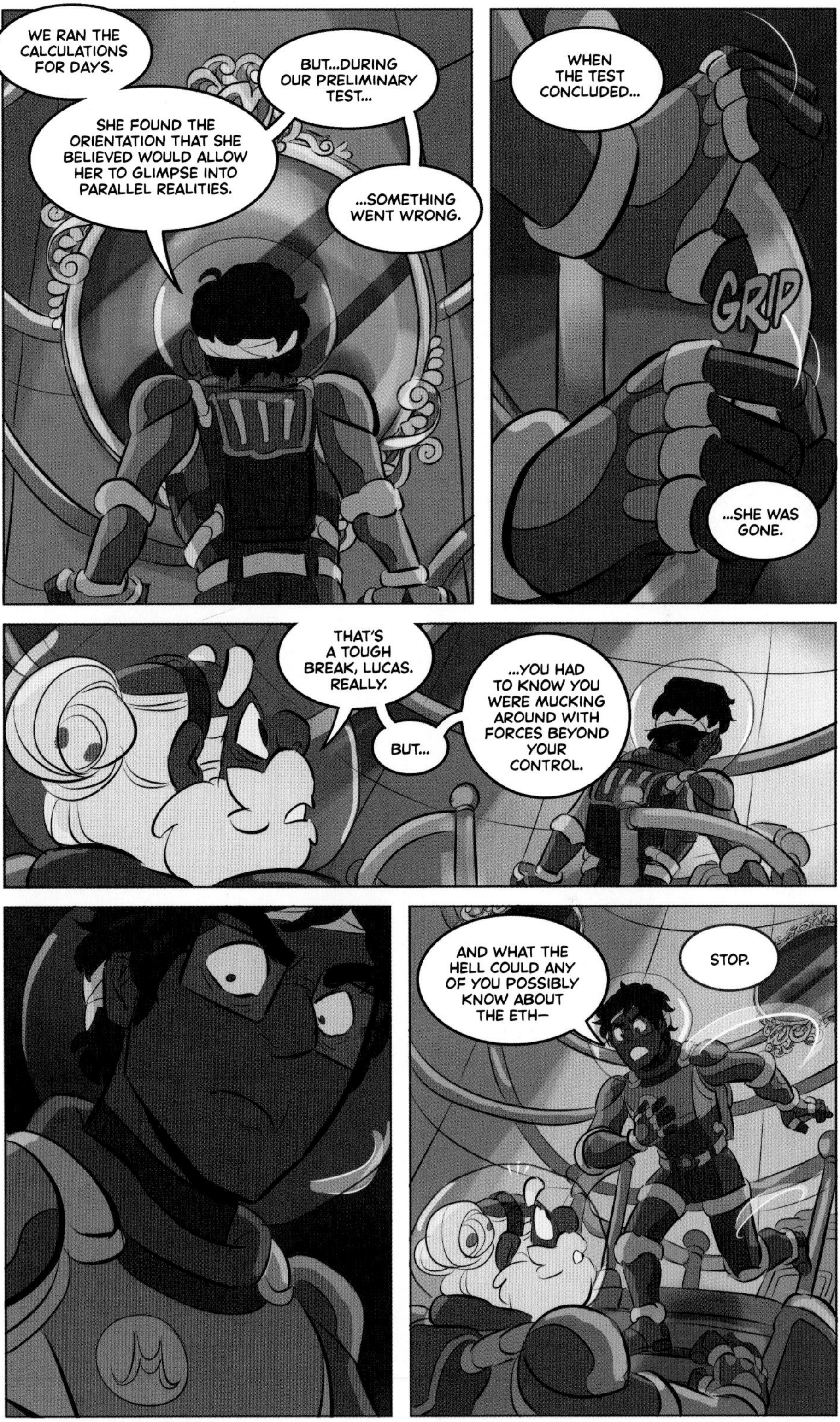
WE RAN THE CALCULATIONS FOR DAYS.
SHE FOUND THE ORIENTATION THAT SHE BELIEVED WOULD ALLOW HER TO GLIMPSE INTO PARALLEL REALITIES.
BUT...DURING OUR PRELIMINARY TEST...
...SOMETHING WENT WRONG.
WHEN THE TEST CONCLUDED...
GRIP
...SHE WAS GONE.
THAT'S A TOUGH BREAK, LUCAS. REALLY.
BUT...
...YOU HAD TO KNOW YOU WERE MUCKING AROUND WITH FORCES BEYOND YOUR CONTROL.
AND WHAT THE HELL COULD ANY OF YOU POSSIBLY KNOW ABOUT THE ETH—
STOP.

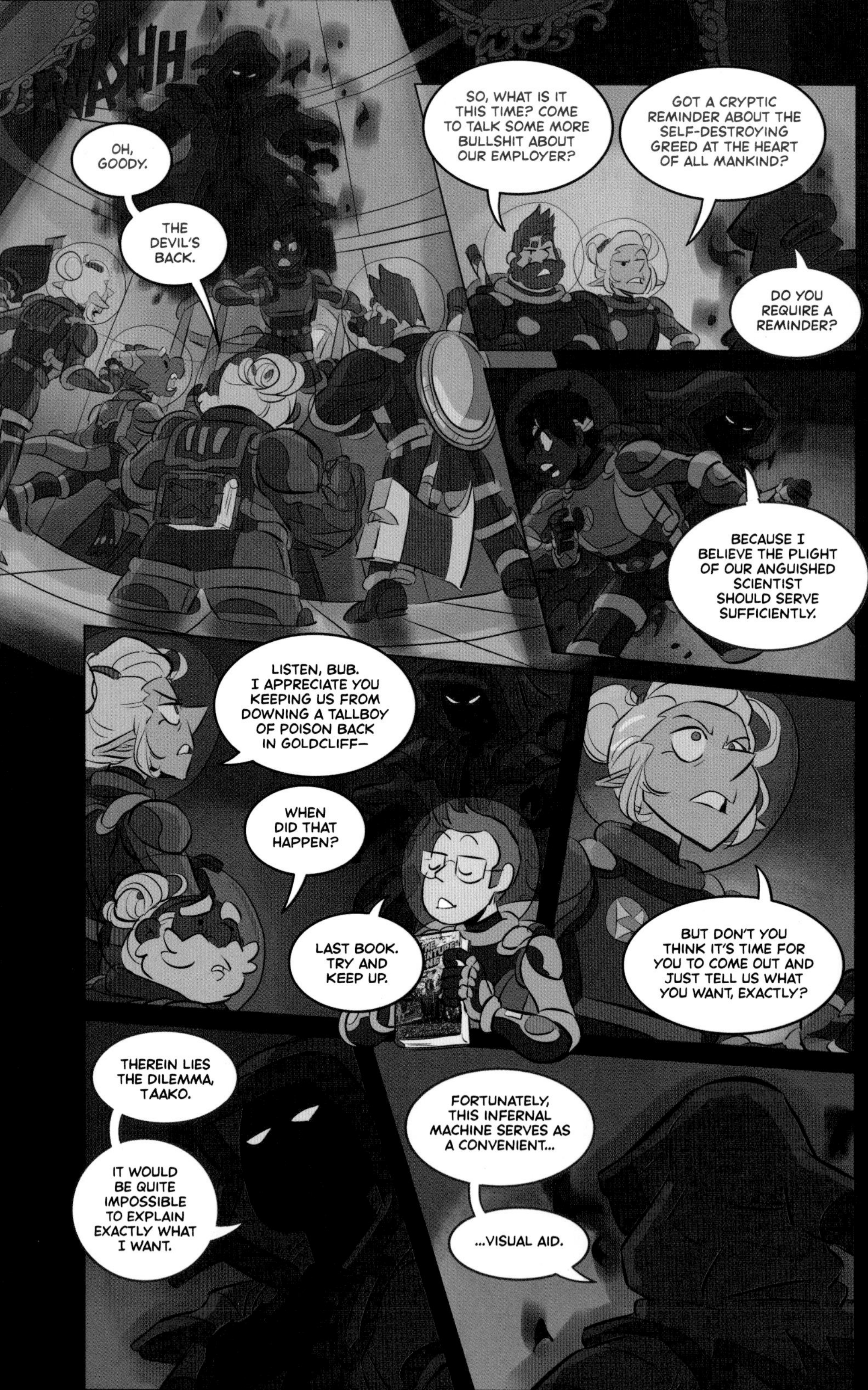

WAHH
OH, GOODY.
THE DEVIL'S BACK.
SO, WHAT IS IT THIS TIME? COME TO TALK SOME MORE BULLSHIT ABOUT OUR EMPLOYER?
GOT A CRYPTIC REMINDER ABOUT THE SELF-DESTROYING GREED AT THE HEART OF ALL MANKIND?
DO YOU REQUIRE A REMINDER?
BECAUSE I BELIEVE THE PLIGHT OF OUR ANGUISHED SCIENTIST SHOULD SERVE SUFFICIENTLY.
LISTEN, BUB. I APPRECIATE YOU KEEPING US FROM DOWNING A TALLBOY OF POISON BACK IN GOLDCLIFF—
WHEN DID THAT HAPPEN?
LAST BOOK. TRY AND KEEP UP.
BUT DON'T YOU THINK IT'S TIME FOR YOU TO COME OUT AND JUST TELL US WHAT YOU WANT, EXACTLY?
THEREIN LIES THE DILEMMA, TAAKO.
IT WOULD BE QUITE IMPOSSIBLE TO EXPLAIN EXACTLY WHAT I WANT.
FORTUNATELY, THIS INFERNAL MACHINE SERVES AS A CONVENIENT...
...VISUAL AID.

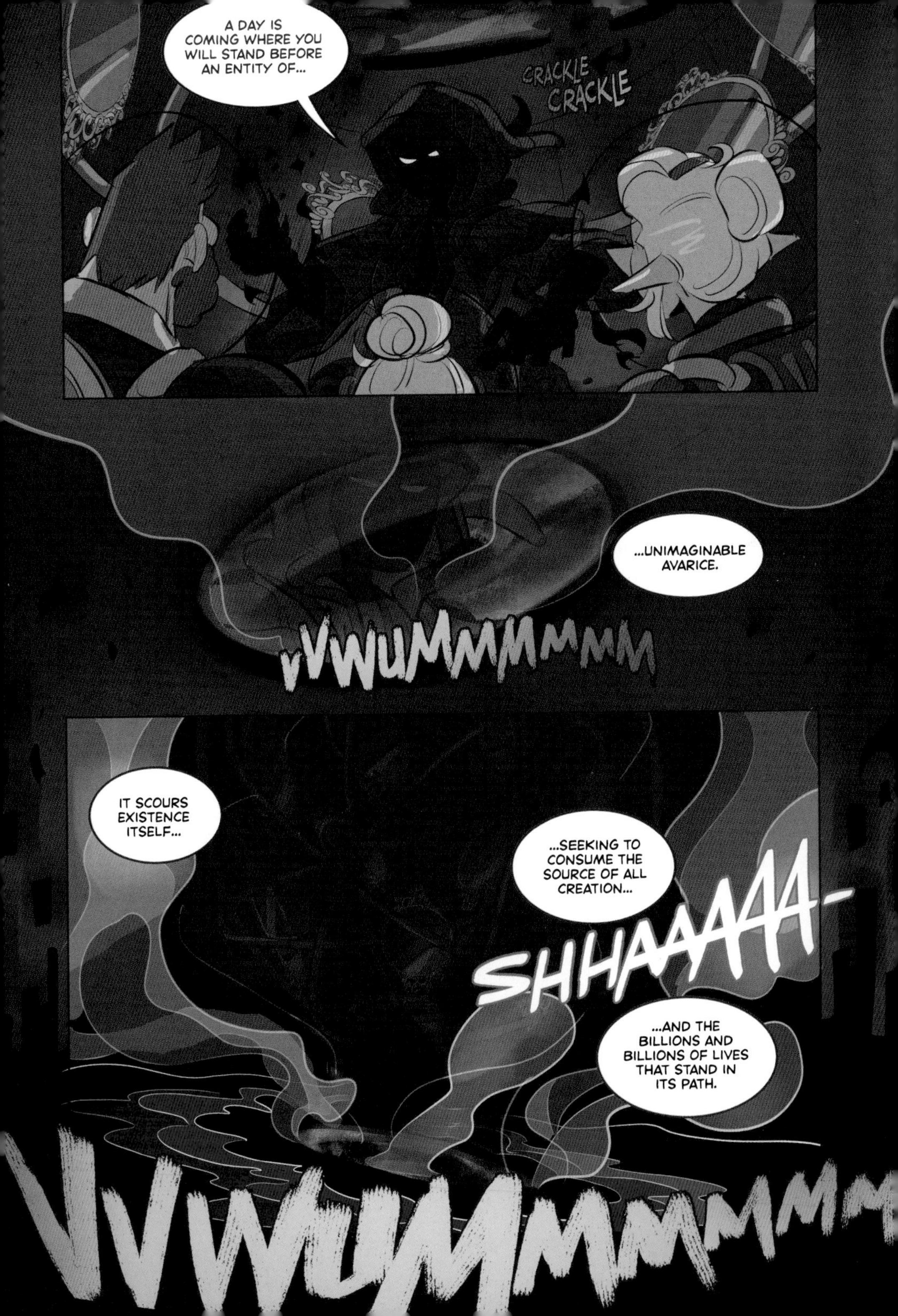
A DAY IS COMING WHERE YOU WILL STAND BEFORE AN ENTITY OF...
CRACKLE CRACKLE
...UNIMAGINABLE AVARICE.
VVWUMMMMMM
IT SCOURS EXISTENCE ITSELF...
...SEEKING TO CONSUME THE SOURCE OF ALL CREATION...
SHHAAAAA-
...AND THE BILLIONS AND BILLIONS OF LIVES THAT STAND IN ITS PATH.
VVWUMMMMMMMM

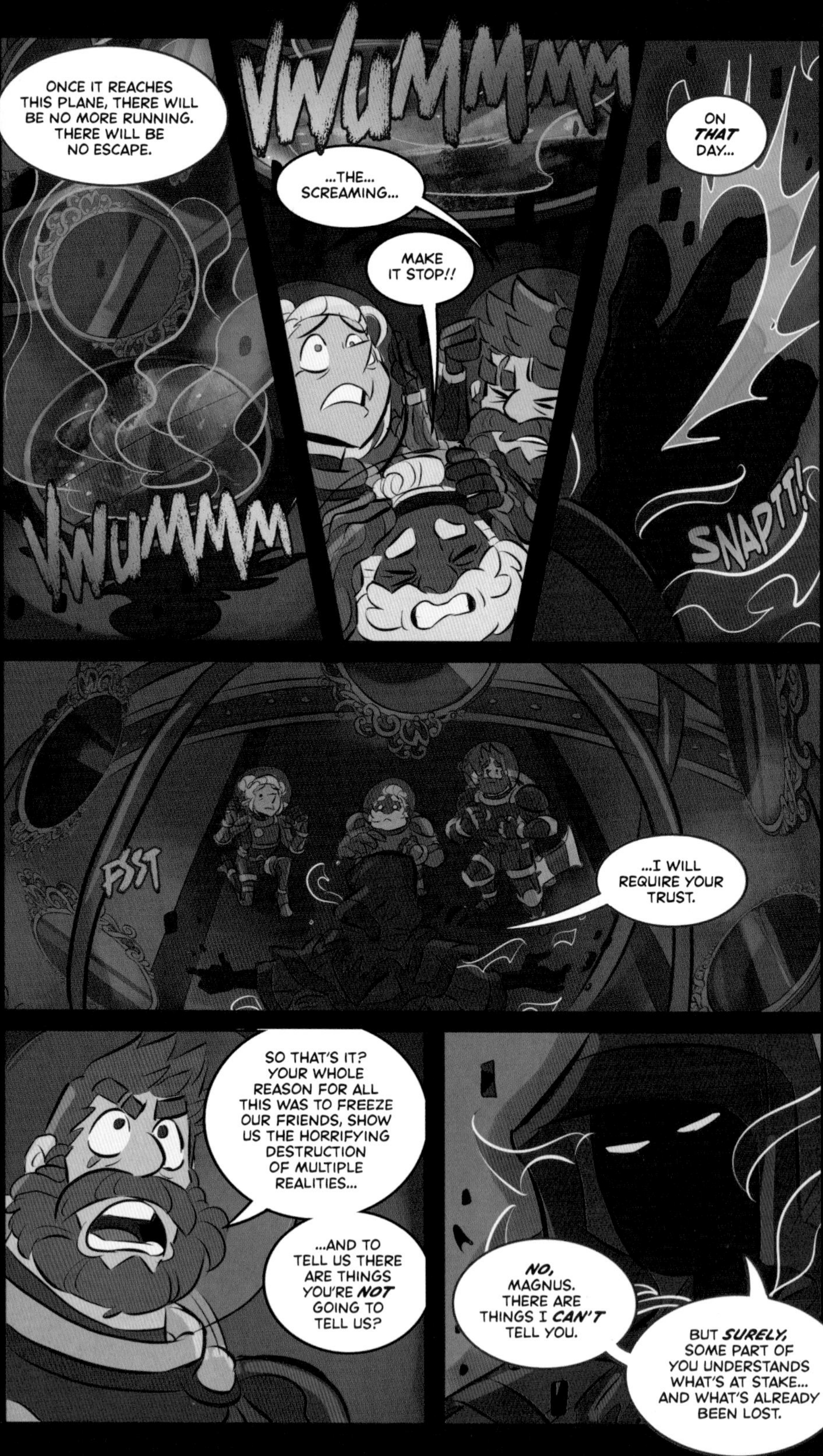
ONCE IT REACHES THIS PLANE, THERE WILL BE NO MORE RUNNING. THERE WILL BE NO ESCAPE.
VWUMMMM
VWUMMMM
...THE... SCREAMING...
MAKE IT STOP!!
ON *THAT* DAY...
SNAPTT!
FSST
...I WILL REQUIRE YOUR TRUST.
SO THAT'S IT? YOUR WHOLE REASON FOR ALL THIS WAS TO FREEZE OUR FRIENDS, SHOW US THE HORRIFYING DESTRUCTION OF MULTIPLE REALITIES...
...AND TO TELL US THERE ARE THINGS YOU'RE *NOT* GOING TO TELL US?
NO, MAGNUS. THERE ARE THINGS I *CAN'T* TELL YOU.
BUT *SURELY,* SOME PART OF YOU UNDERSTANDS WHAT'S AT STAKE... AND WHAT'S ALREADY BEEN LOST.

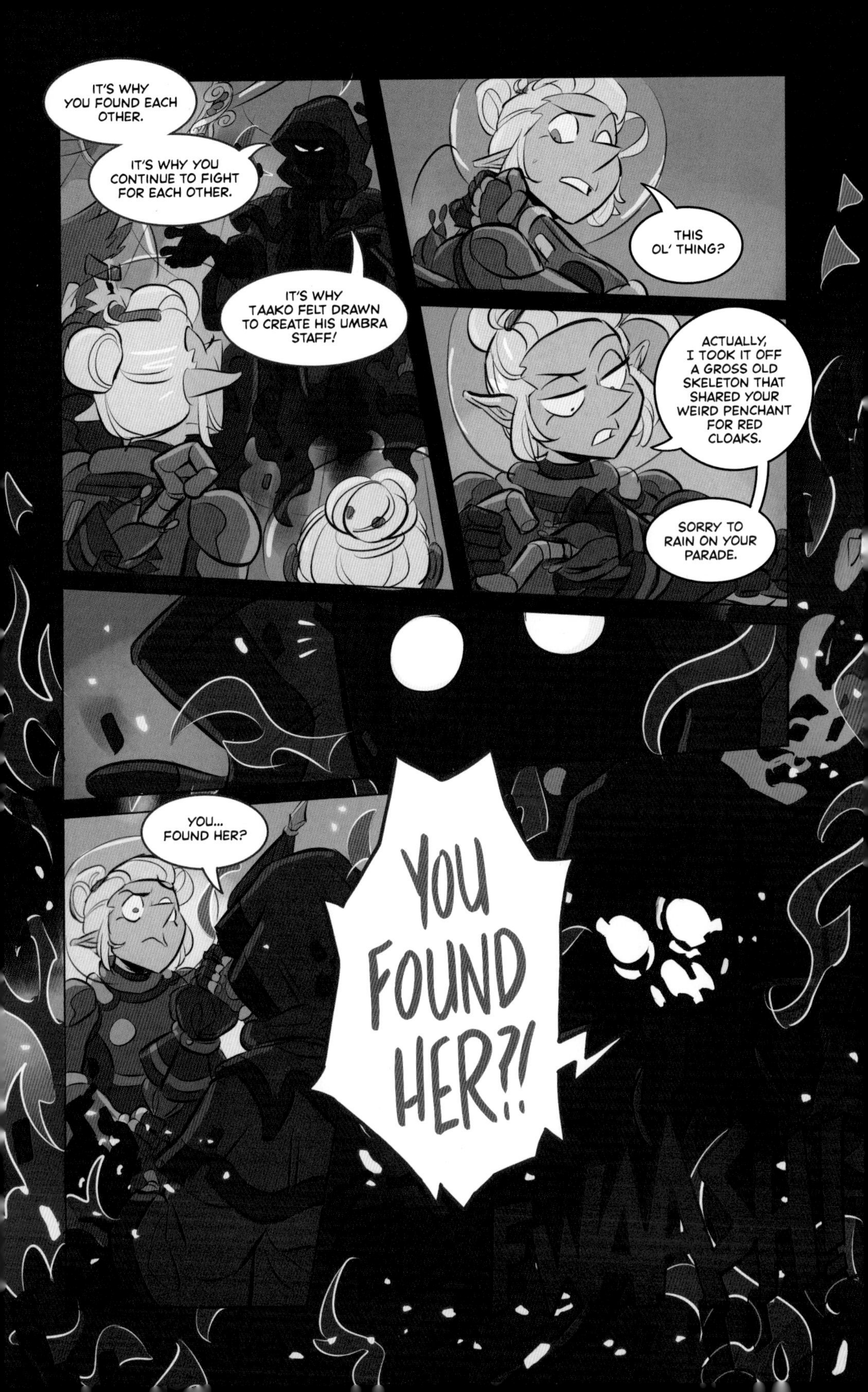
IT'S WHY YOU FOUND EACH OTHER.
IT'S WHY YOU CONTINUE TO FIGHT FOR EACH OTHER.
IT'S WHY TAAKO FELT DRAWN TO CREATE HIS UMBRA STAFF!
THIS OL' THING?
ACTUALLY, I TOOK IT OFF A GROSS OLD SKELETON THAT SHARED YOUR WEIRD PENCHANT FOR RED CLOAKS.
SORRY TO RAIN ON YOUR PARADE.
YOU... FOUND HER?
YOU FOUND HER?!

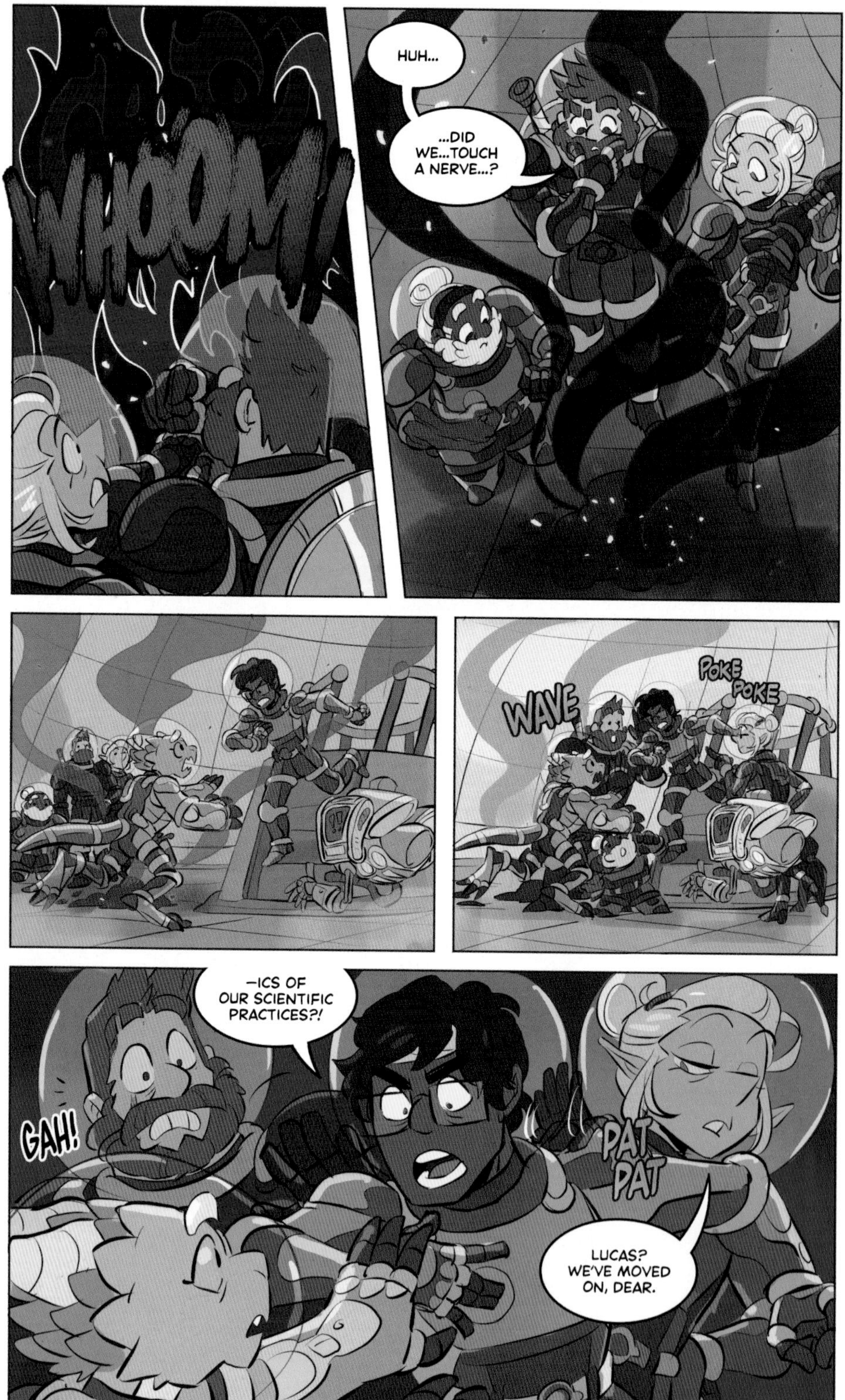
WHOOM!
HUH...
...DID WE...TOUCH A NERVE...?
WAVE
POKE POKE
—ICS OF OUR SCIENTIFIC PRACTICES?!
GAH!
PAT PAT
LUCAS? WE'VE MOVED ON, DEAR.

Chapter
6

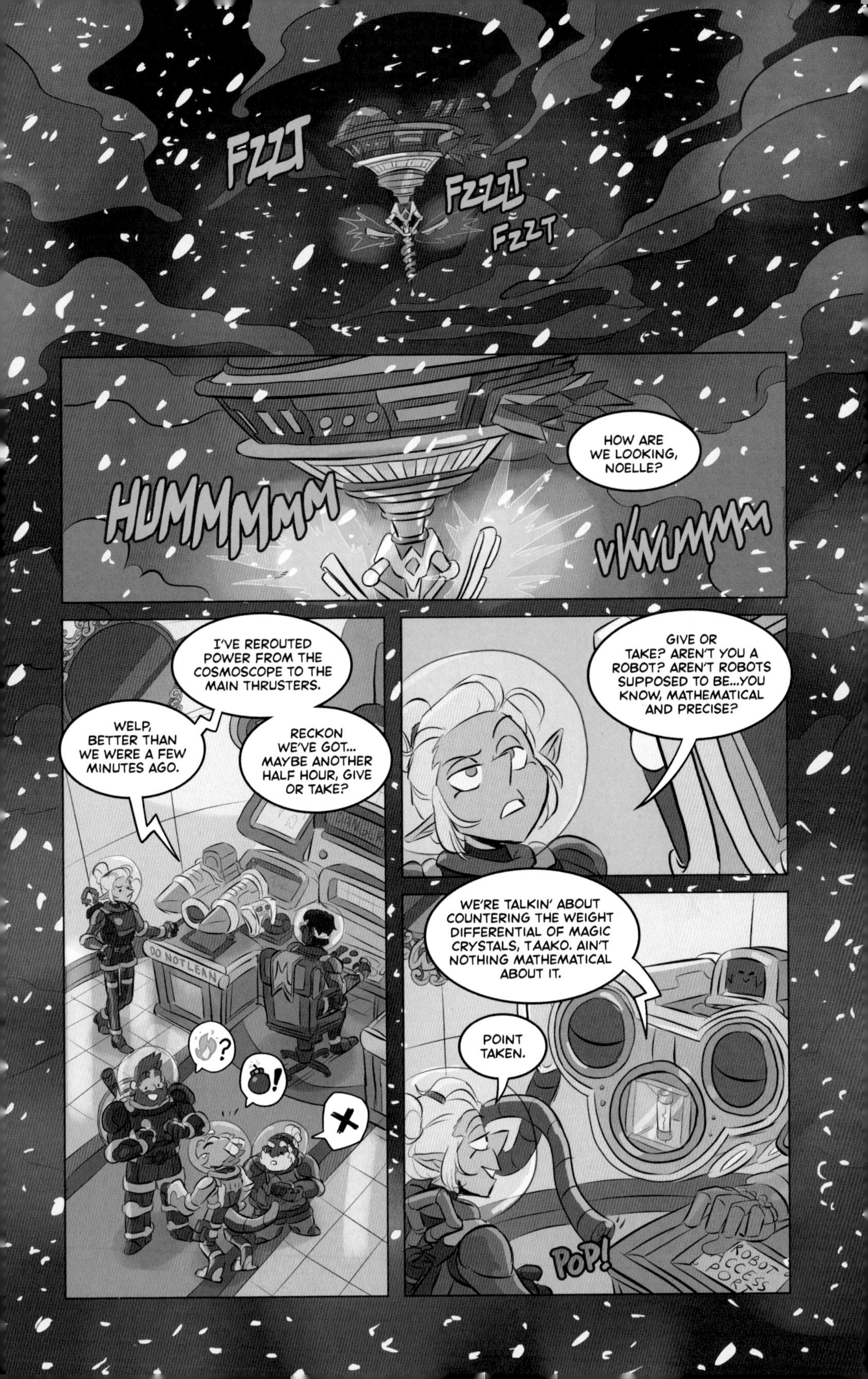
FZZT
FZZZT
FZZT
HUMMMMM
HOW ARE WE LOOKING, NOELLE?
VKVUMMM
I'VE REROUTED POWER FROM THE COSMOSCOPE TO THE MAIN THRUSTERS.
WELP, BETTER THAN WE WERE A FEW MINUTES AGO.
RECKON WE'VE GOT... MAYBE ANOTHER HALF HOUR, GIVE OR TAKE?
DO NOT LEAN
?
!
GIVE OR TAKE? AREN'T YOU A ROBOT? AREN'T ROBOTS SUPPOSED TO BE...YOU KNOW, MATHEMATICAL AND PRECISE?
WE'RE TALKIN' ABOUT COUNTERING THE WEIGHT DIFFERENTIAL OF MAGIC CRYSTALS, TAAKO. AIN'T NOTHING MATHEMATICAL ABOUT IT.
POINT TAKEN.
POP!
ROBOT CCESS PORT

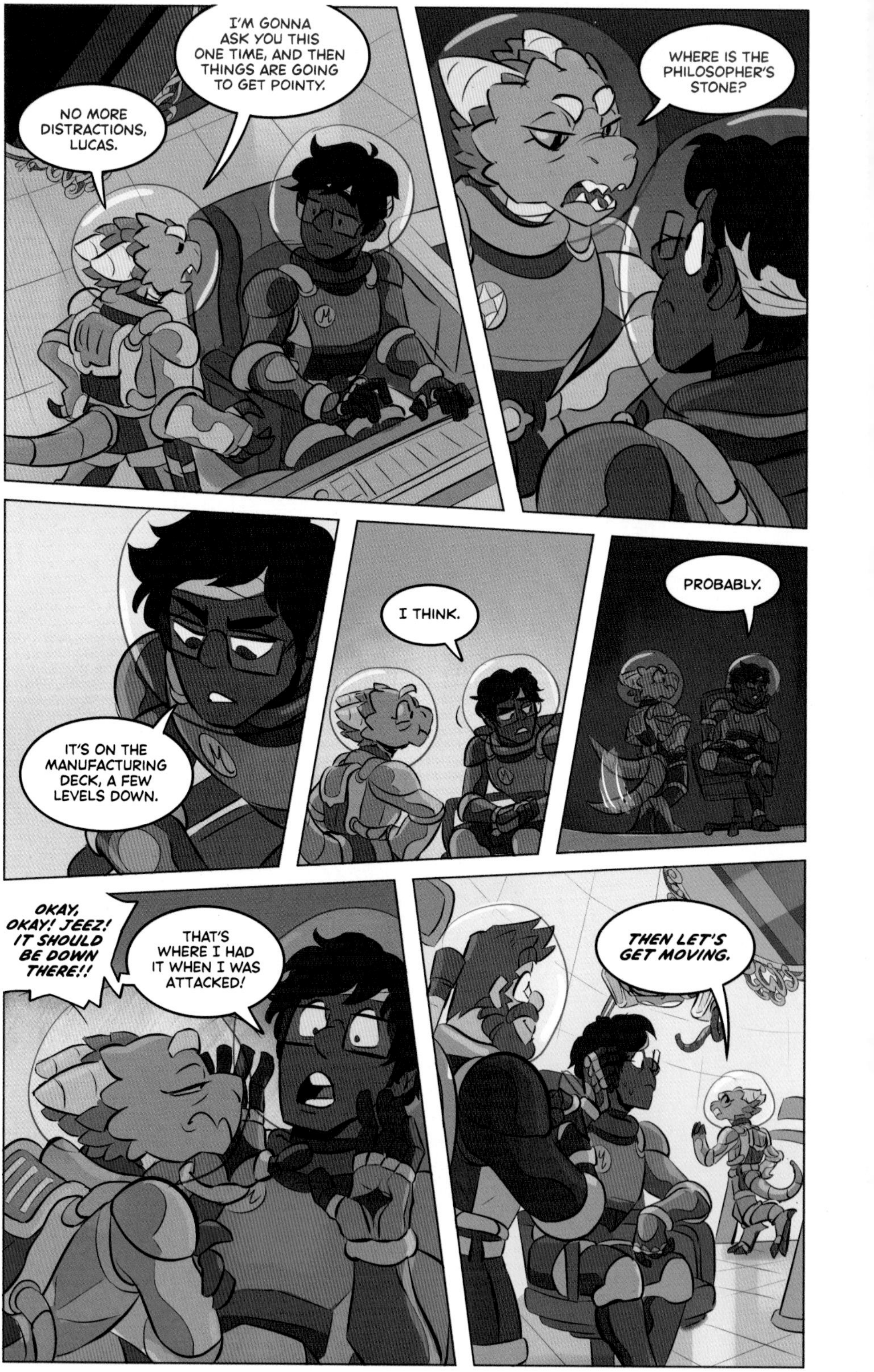
NO MORE DISTRACTIONS, LUCAS.
I'M GONNA ASK YOU THIS ONE TIME, AND THEN THINGS ARE GOING TO GET POINTY.
WHERE IS THE PHILOSOPHER'S STONE?
IT'S ON THE MANUFACTURING DECK, A FEW LEVELS DOWN.
I THINK.
PROBABLY.
OKAY, OKAY! JEEZ! IT SHOULD BE DOWN THERE!!
THAT'S WHERE I HAD IT WHEN I WAS ATTACKED!
THEN LET'S GET MOVING.

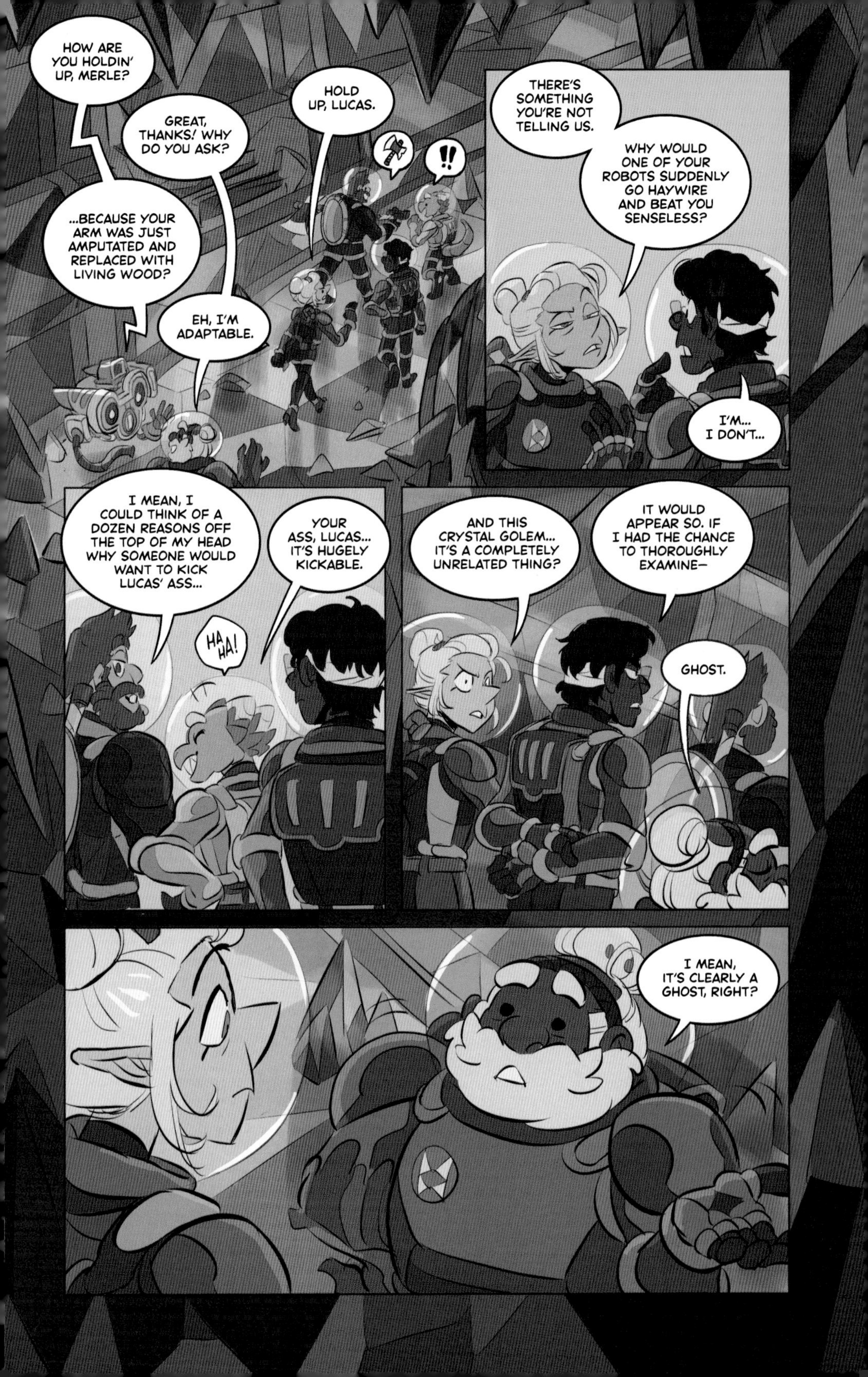

HOW ARE YOU HOLDIN' UP, MERLE?
GREAT, THANKS! WHY DO YOU ASK?
...BECAUSE YOUR ARM WAS JUST AMPUTATED AND REPLACED WITH LIVING WOOD?
EH, I'M ADAPTABLE.
HOLD UP, LUCAS.
!!
THERE'S SOMETHING YOU'RE NOT TELLING US.
WHY WOULD ONE OF YOUR ROBOTS SUDDENLY GO HAYWIRE AND BEAT YOU SENSELESS?
I'M... I DON'T...
I MEAN, I COULD THINK OF A DOZEN REASONS OFF THE TOP OF MY HEAD WHY SOMEONE WOULD WANT TO KICK LUCAS' ASS...
HA HA!
YOUR ASS, LUCAS... IT'S HUGELY KICKABLE.
AND THIS CRYSTAL GOLEM... IT'S A COMPLETELY UNRELATED THING?
IT WOULD APPEAR SO. IF I HAD THE CHANCE TO THOROUGHLY EXAMINE—
GHOST.
I MEAN, IT'S CLEARLY A GHOST, RIGHT?

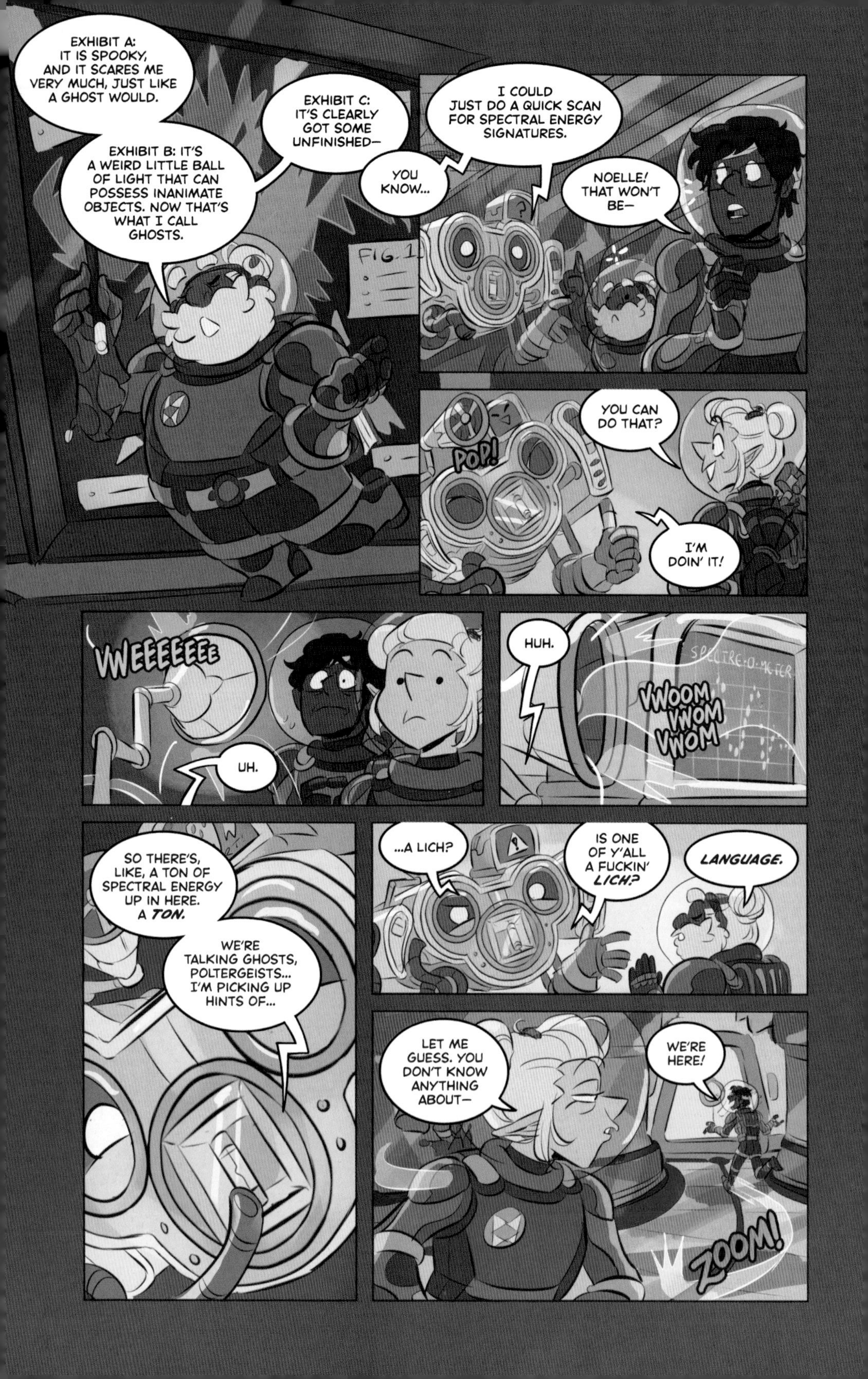
EXHIBIT A: IT IS SPOOKY, AND IT SCARES ME VERY MUCH, JUST LIKE A GHOST WOULD.
EXHIBIT B: IT'S A WEIRD LITTLE BALL OF LIGHT THAT CAN POSSESS INANIMATE OBJECTS. NOW THAT'S WHAT I CALL GHOSTS.
EXHIBIT C: IT'S CLEARLY GOT SOME UNFINISHED—
FIG. 1
YOU KNOW...
I COULD JUST DO A QUICK SCAN FOR SPECTRAL ENERGY SIGNATURES.
NOELLE! THAT WON'T BE—
POP!
YOU CAN DO THAT?
I'M DOIN' IT!
VWEEEEEEE
UH.
HUH.
SPECTRE-O-METER
VWOOM VWOM VWOM
SO THERE'S, LIKE, A TON OF SPECTRAL ENERGY UP IN HERE. A *TON.*
WE'RE TALKING GHOSTS, POLTERGEISTS... I'M PICKING UP HINTS OF...
...A LICH?
IS ONE OF Y'ALL A FUCKIN' *LICH?*
LANGUAGE.
LET ME GUESS. YOU DON'T KNOW ANYTHING ABOUT—
WE'RE HERE!
ZOOM!

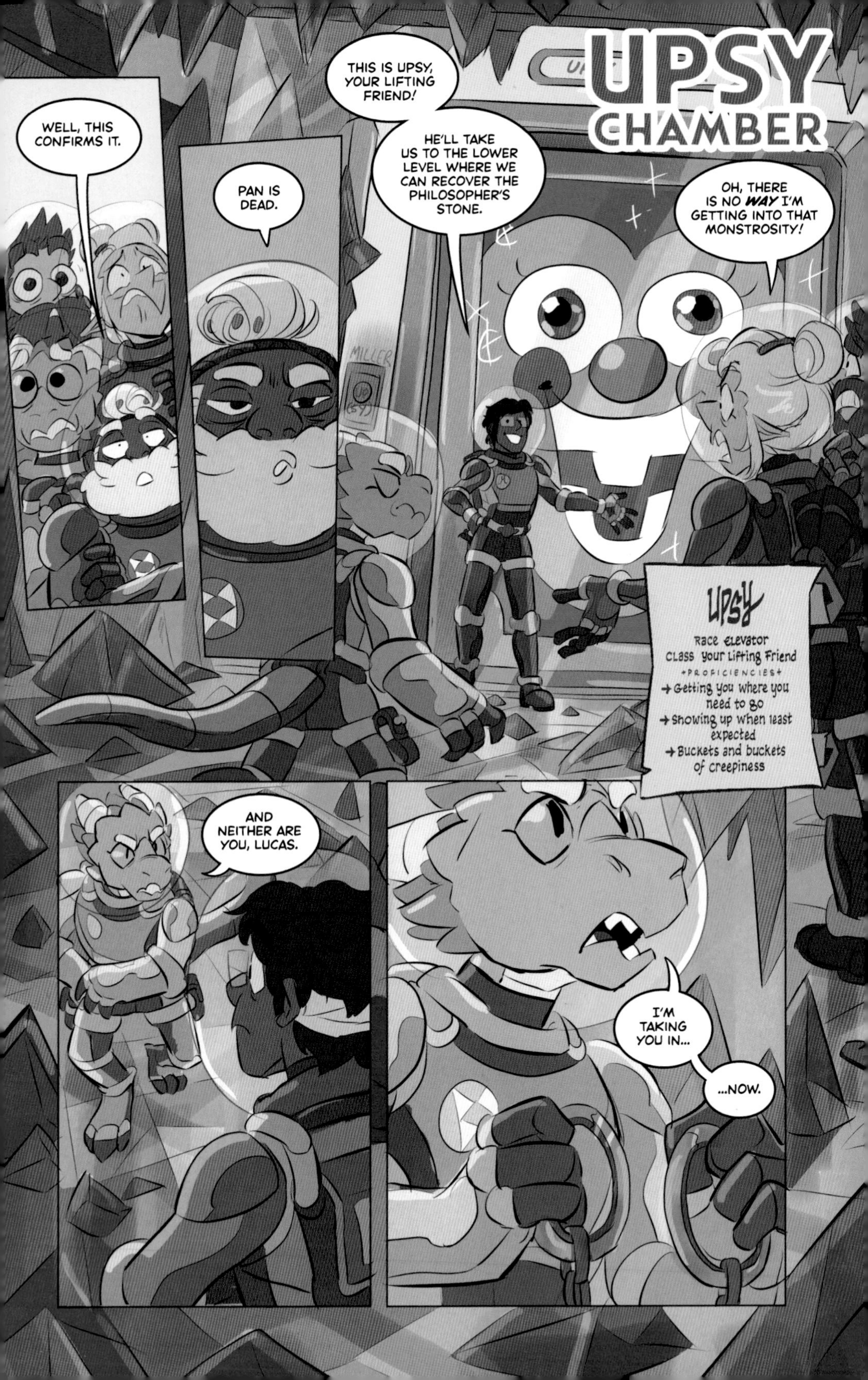
UPSY CHAMBER
WELL, THIS CONFIRMS IT.
PAN IS DEAD.
THIS IS UPSY, YOUR LIFTING FRIEND!
HE'LL TAKE US TO THE LOWER LEVEL WHERE WE CAN RECOVER THE PHILOSOPHER'S STONE.
OH, THERE IS NO *WAY* I'M GETTING INTO THAT MONSTROSITY!
MILLER
UPSY
Race Elevator
Class Your Lifting Friend
PROFICIENCIES
→ Getting you where you need to go
→ Showing up when least expected
→ Buckets and buckets of creepiness
AND NEITHER ARE YOU, LUCAS.
I'M TAKING YOU IN...
...NOW.

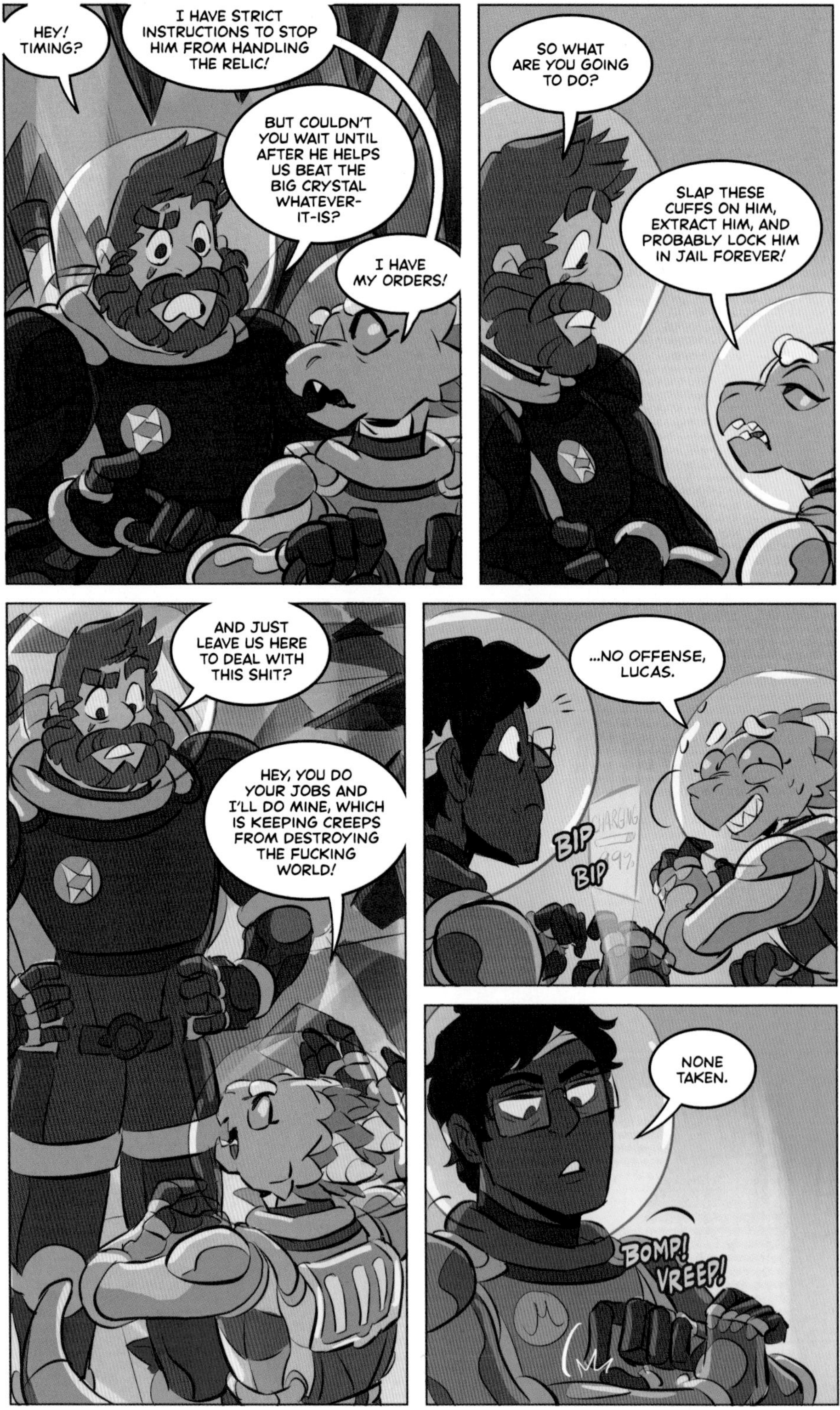
HEY! TIMING?
I HAVE STRICT INSTRUCTIONS TO STOP HIM FROM HANDLING THE RELIC!
BUT COULDN'T YOU WAIT UNTIL AFTER HE HELPS US BEAT THE BIG CRYSTAL WHATEVER-IT-IS?
I HAVE MY ORDERS!
SO WHAT ARE YOU GOING TO DO?
SLAP THESE CUFFS ON HIM, EXTRACT HIM, AND PROBABLY LOCK HIM IN JAIL FOREVER!
AND JUST LEAVE US HERE TO DEAL WITH THIS SHIT?
HEY, YOU DO YOUR JOBS AND I'LL DO MINE, WHICH IS KEEPING CREEPS FROM DESTROYING THE FUCKING WORLD!
...NO OFFENSE, LUCAS.
BIP
BIP
NONE TAKEN.
BOMP!
VREEP!

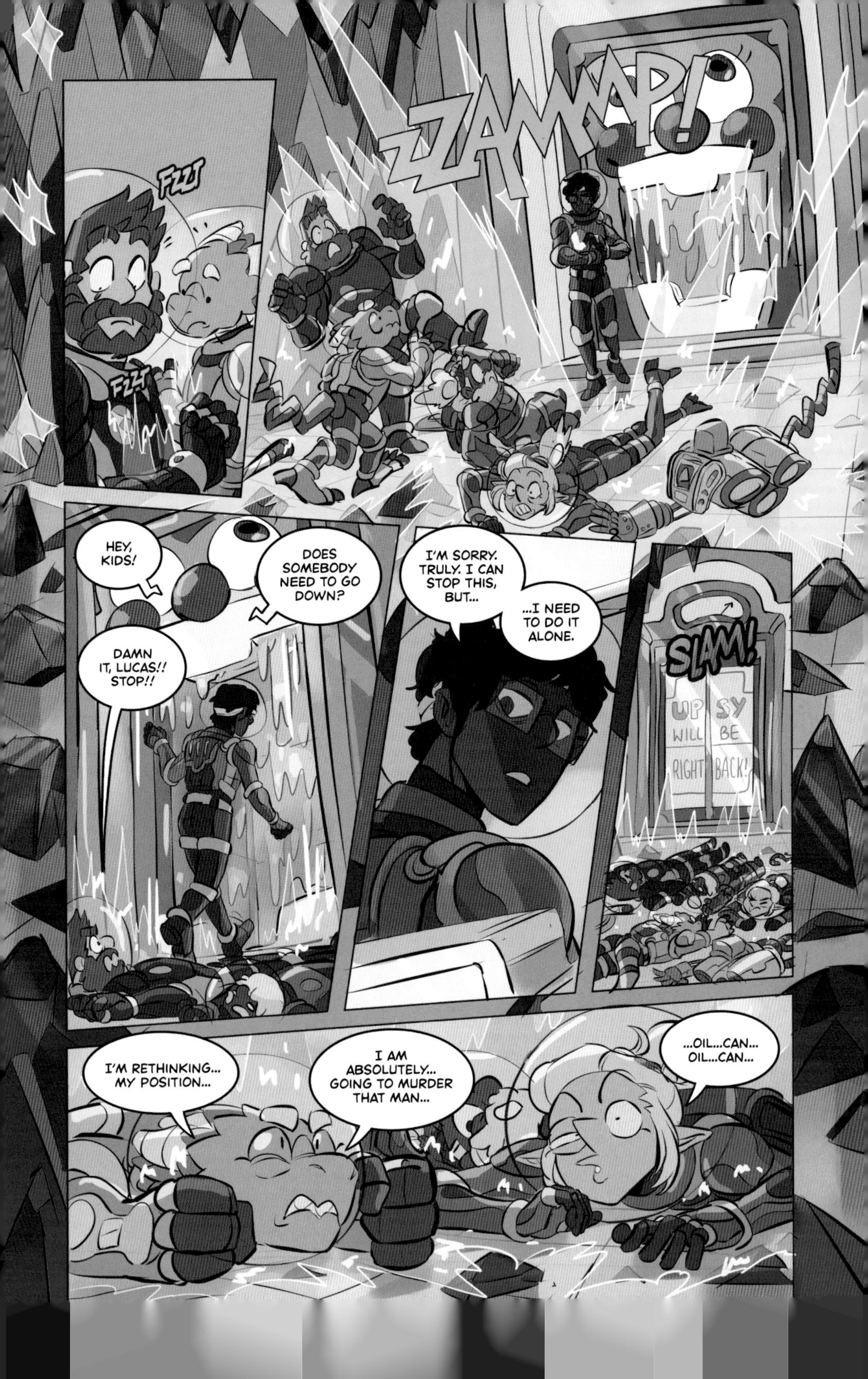
ZZAMMP!
FZZT
FZZT
HEY, KIDS!
DOES SOMEBODY NEED TO GO DOWN?
DAMN IT, LUCAS!! STOP!!
I'M SORRY. TRULY. I CAN STOP THIS, BUT...
...I NEED TO DO IT ALONE.
SLAM!
UP SY WILL BE RIGHT BACK!
I'M RETHINKING... MY POSITION...
I AM ABSOLUTELY... GOING TO MURDER THAT MAN...
...OIL...CAN... OIL...CAN...

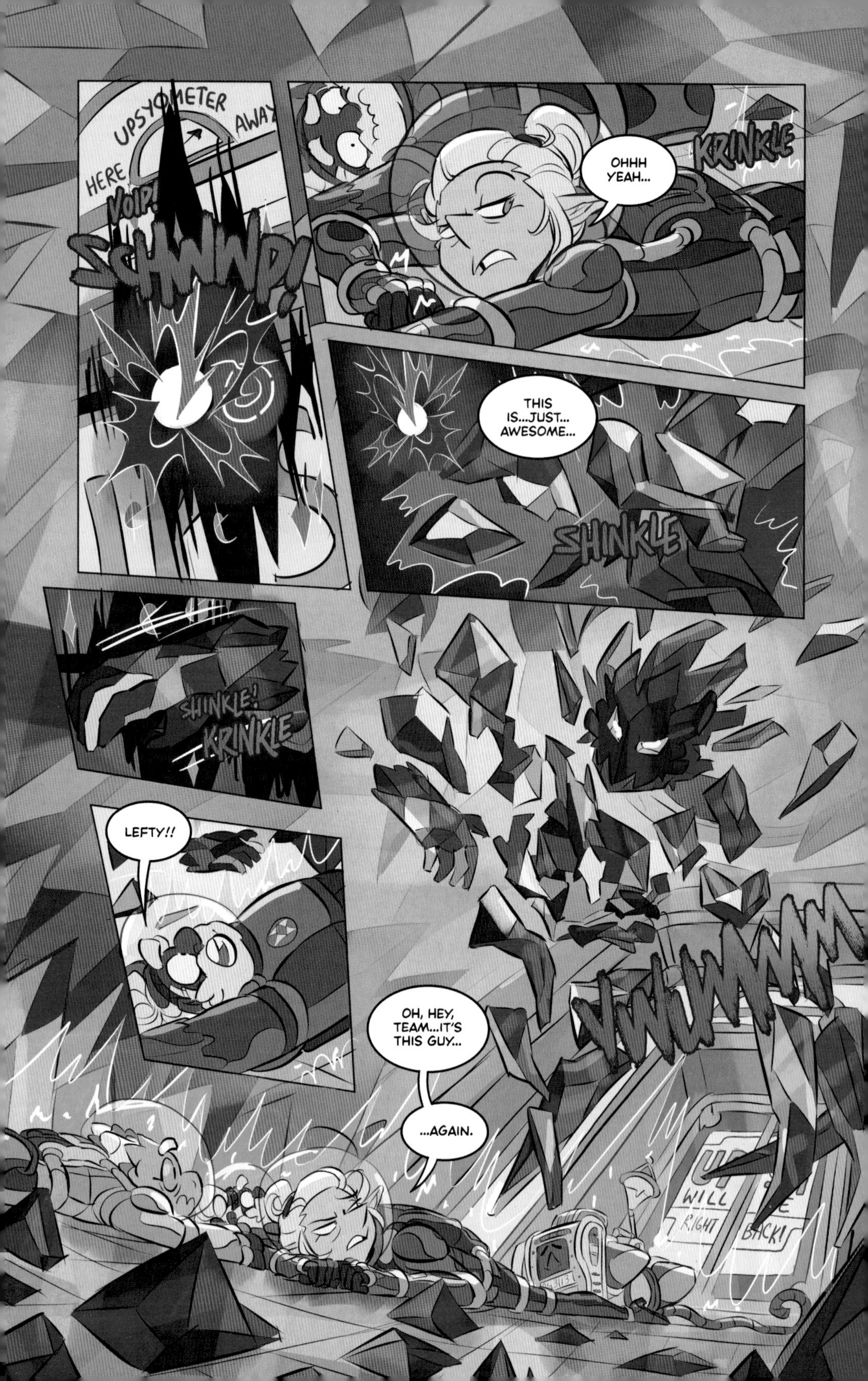
UPSYOMETER
HERE
AWAY
VOIP!
SCHWWD!
OHHH YEAH...
KRINKLE
THIS IS...JUST... AWESOME...
SHINKLE
SHINKLE!
KRINKLE
LEFTY!!
OH, HEY, TEAM...IT'S THIS GUY...
...AGAIN.
VWHUMMM
WILL
RIGHT
BACK!

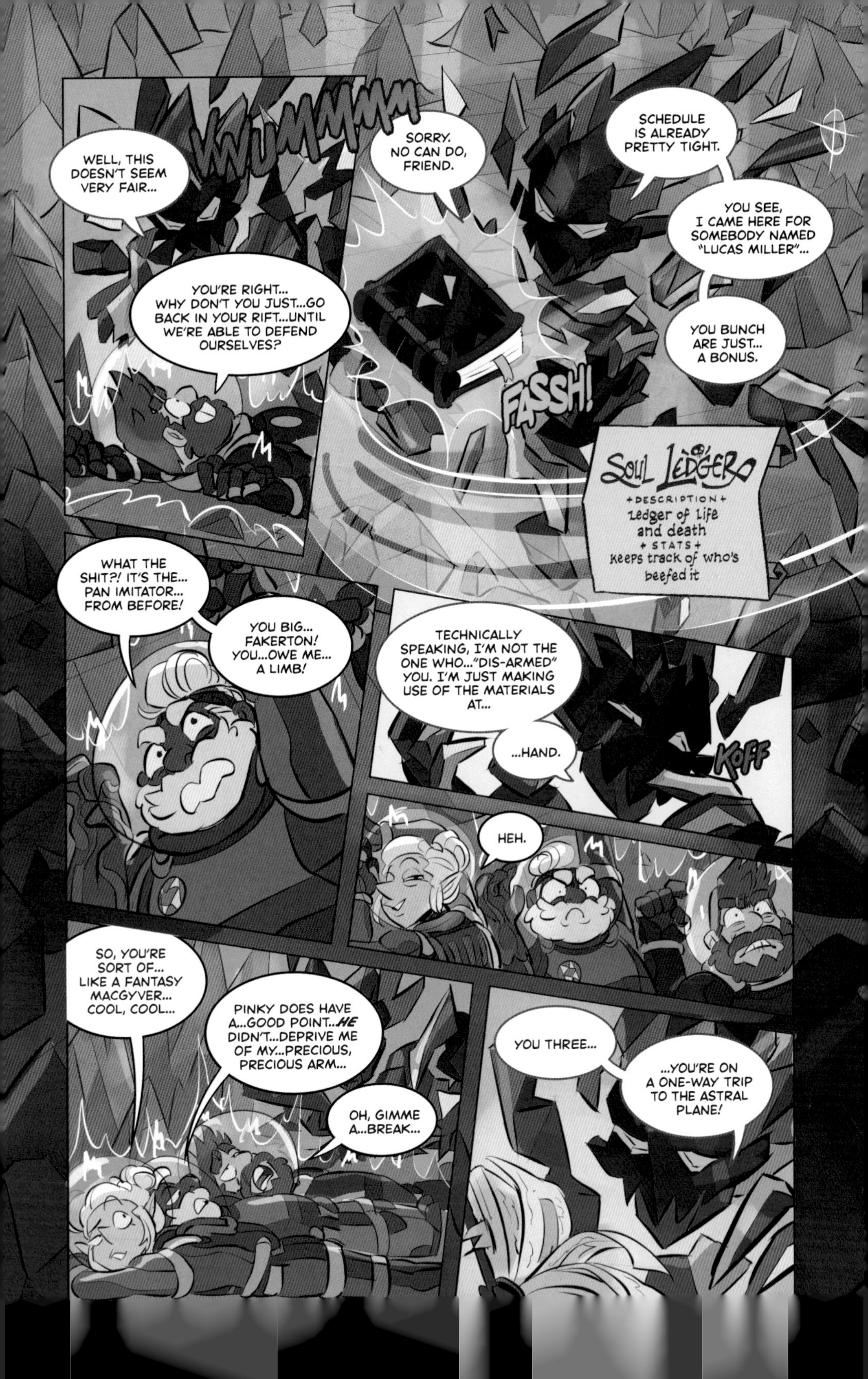
WELL, THIS DOESN'T SEEM VERY FAIR...
VWUMMMM
SORRY. NO CAN DO, FRIEND.
SCHEDULE IS ALREADY PRETTY TIGHT.
YOU SEE, I CAME HERE FOR SOMEBODY NAMED "LUCAS MILLER"...
YOU'RE RIGHT... WHY DON'T YOU JUST...GO BACK IN YOUR RIFT...UNTIL WE'RE ABLE TO DEFEND OURSELVES?
YOU BUNCH ARE JUST... A BONUS.
FASSH!
SOUL LEDGER
+DESCRIPTION+
Ledger of life and death
+STATS+
Keeps track of who's beefed it
WHAT THE SHIT?! IT'S THE... PAN IMITATOR... FROM BEFORE!
YOU BIG... FAKERTON! YOU...OWE ME... A LIMB!
TECHNICALLY SPEAKING, I'M NOT THE ONE WHO..."DIS-ARMED" YOU. I'M JUST MAKING USE OF THE MATERIALS AT...
...HAND.
KOFF
HEH.
SO, YOU'RE SORT OF... LIKE A FANTASY MACGYVER... COOL, COOL...
PINKY DOES HAVE A...GOOD POINT...HE DIDN'T...DEPRIVE ME OF MY...PRECIOUS, PRECIOUS ARM...
OH, GIMME A...BREAK...
YOU THREE...
...YOU'RE ON A ONE-WAY TRIP TO THE ASTRAL PLANE!

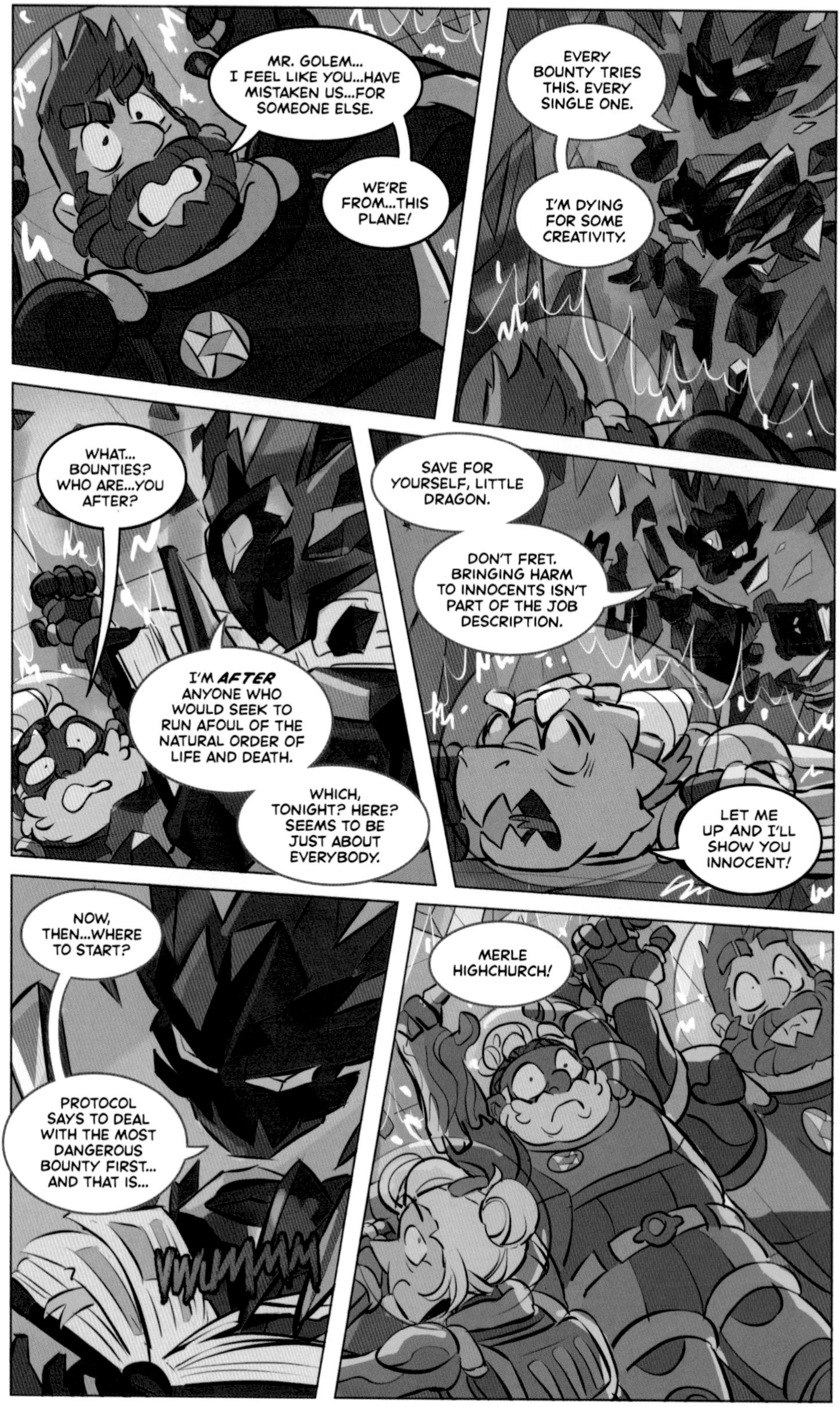
MR. GOLEM... I FEEL LIKE YOU...HAVE MISTAKEN US...FOR SOMEONE ELSE.
WE'RE FROM...THIS PLANE!
EVERY BOUNTY TRIES THIS. EVERY SINGLE ONE.
I'M DYING FOR SOME CREATIVITY.
WHAT... BOUNTIES? WHO ARE...YOU AFTER?
I'M *AFTER* ANYONE WHO WOULD SEEK TO RUN AFOUL OF THE NATURAL ORDER OF LIFE AND DEATH.
WHICH, TONIGHT? HERE? SEEMS TO BE JUST ABOUT EVERYBODY.
SAVE FOR YOURSELF, LITTLE DRAGON.
DON'T FRET. BRINGING HARM TO INNOCENTS ISN'T PART OF THE JOB DESCRIPTION.
LET ME UP AND I'LL SHOW YOU INNOCENT!
NOW, THEN...WHERE TO START?
PROTOCOL SAYS TO DEAL WITH THE MOST DANGEROUS BOUNTY FIRST... AND THAT IS...
MERLE HIGHCHURCH!

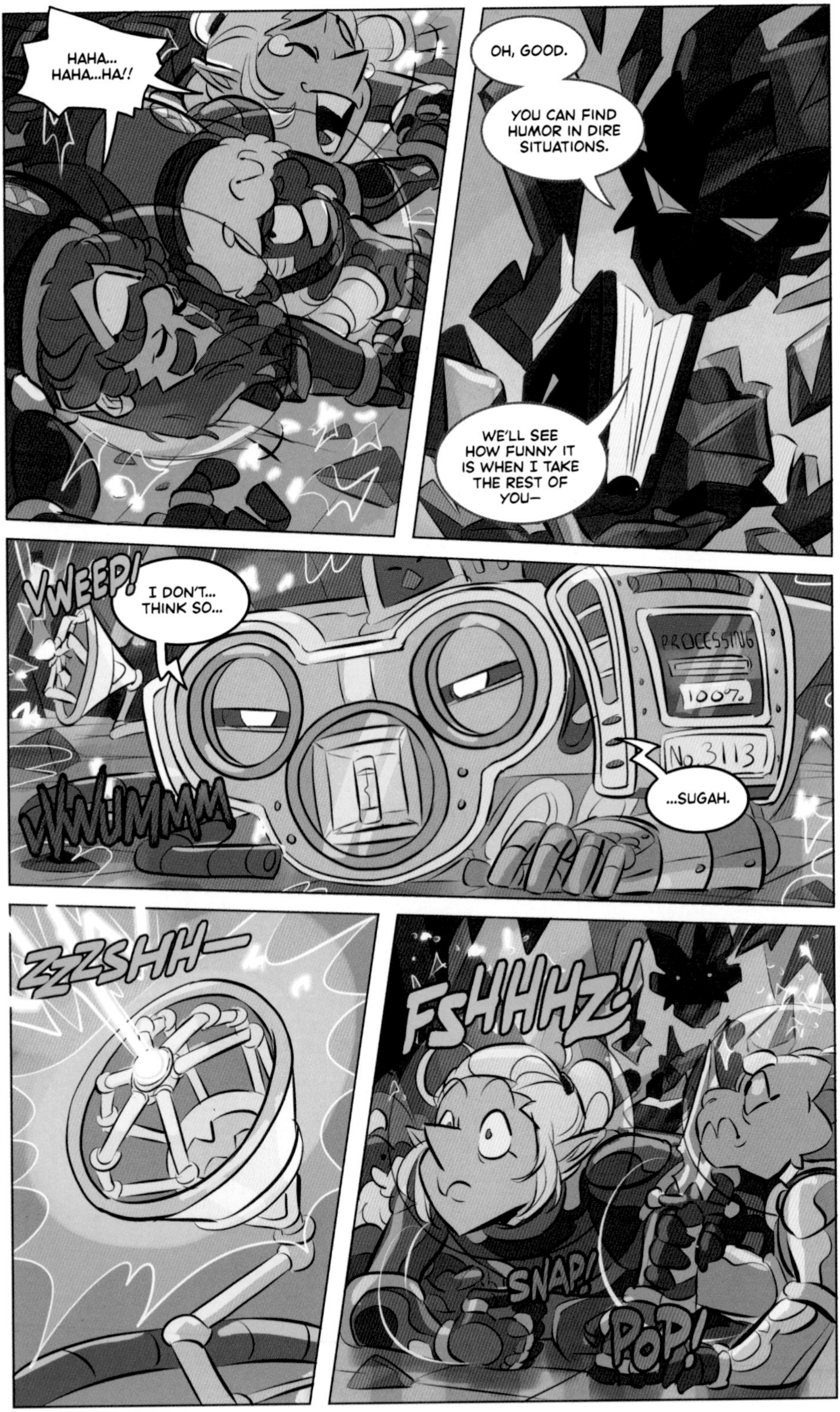
HAHA... HAHA...HA!!
OH, GOOD.
YOU CAN FIND HUMOR IN DIRE SITUATIONS.
WE'LL SEE HOW FUNNY IT IS WHEN I TAKE THE REST OF YOU—
VWEEP!
I DON'T... THINK SO...
PROCESSING
100%
No. 3113
...SUGAH.
VWUMMM
ZZZSHH—
FSHHHZ!
SNAP!
POP!

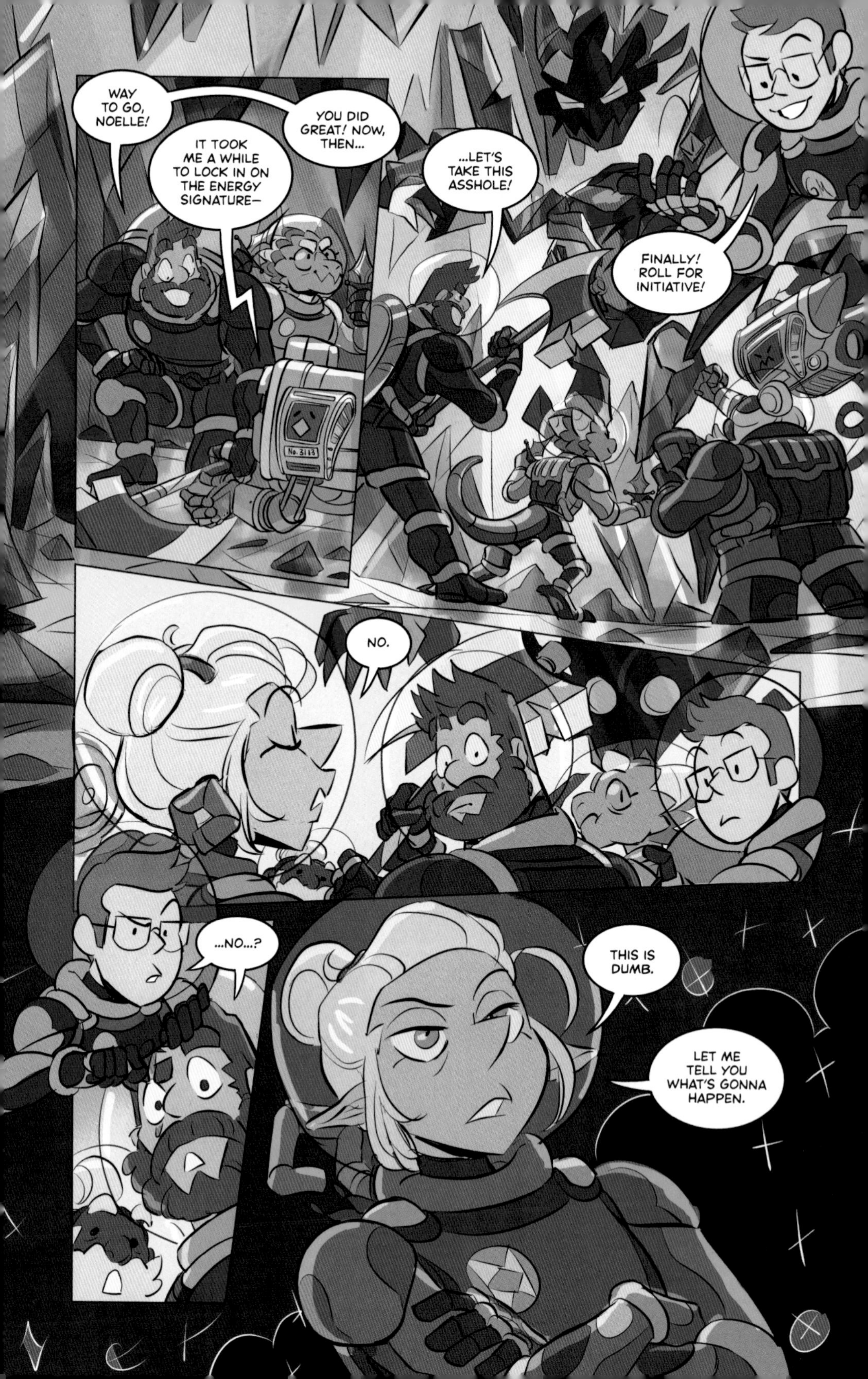
WAY TO GO, NOELLE!
IT TOOK ME A WHILE TO LOCK IN ON THE ENERGY SIGNATURE—
YOU DID GREAT! NOW, THEN...
...LET'S TAKE THIS ASSHOLE!
FINALLY! ROLL FOR INITIATIVE!
No. 3113
NO.
...NO...?
THIS IS DUMB.
LET ME TELL YOU WHAT'S GONNA HAPPEN.

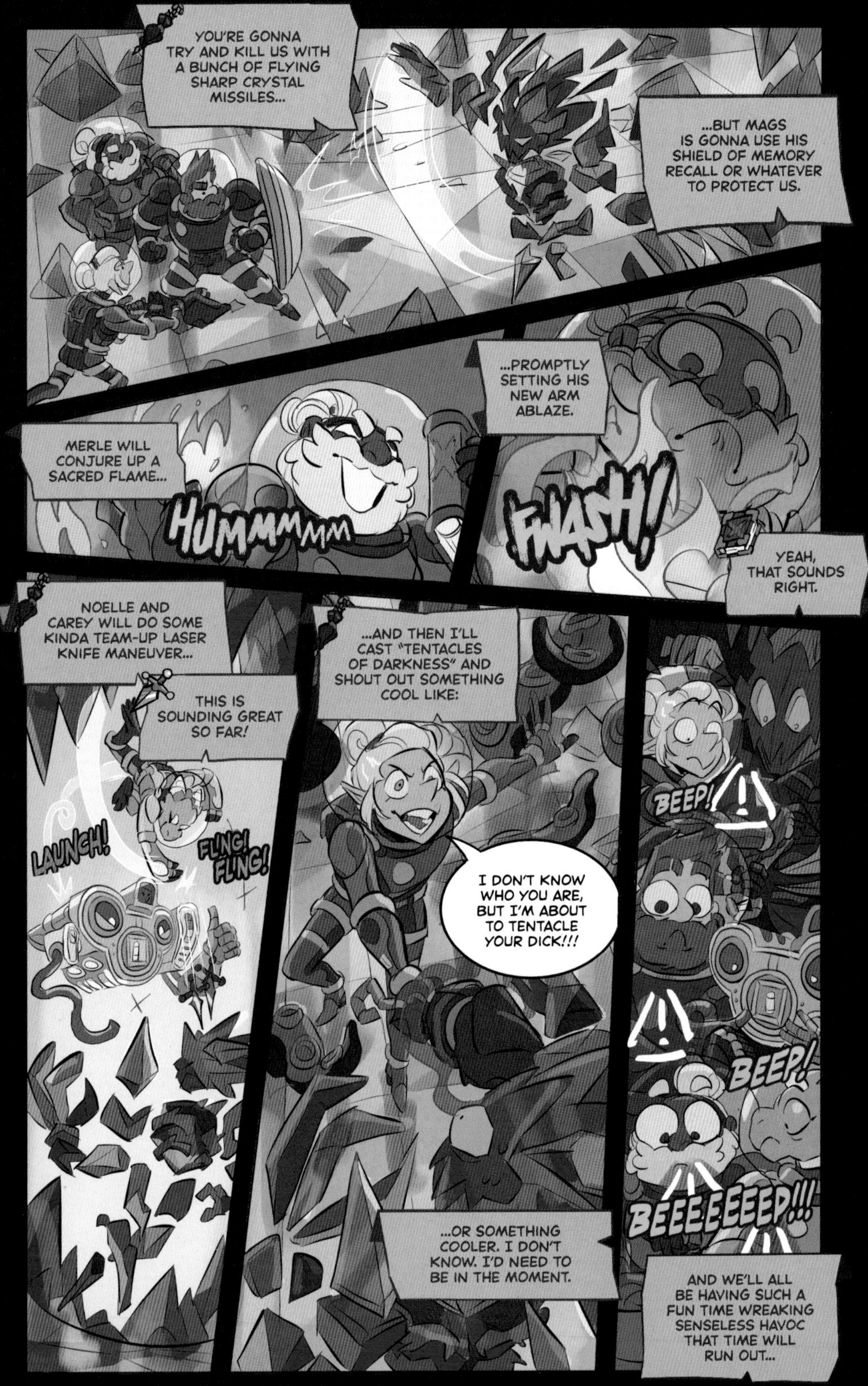
YOU'RE GONNA TRY AND KILL US WITH A BUNCH OF FLYING SHARP CRYSTAL MISSILES...
...BUT MAGS IS GONNA USE HIS SHIELD OF MEMORY RECALL OR WHATEVER TO PROTECT US.
MERLE WILL CONJURE UP A SACRED FLAME...
HUMMMMMM
...PROMPTLY SETTING HIS NEW ARM ABLAZE.
FWASH!
YEAH, THAT SOUNDS RIGHT.
NOELLE AND CAREY WILL DO SOME KINDA TEAM-UP LASER KNIFE MANEUVER...
THIS IS SOUNDING GREAT SO FAR!
LAUNCH!
FLING! FLING!
...AND THEN I'LL CAST "TENTACLES OF DARKNESS" AND SHOUT OUT SOMETHING COOL LIKE:
I DON'T KNOW WHO YOU ARE, BUT I'M ABOUT TO TENTACLE YOUR DICK!!!
...OR SOMETHING COOLER. I DON'T KNOW. I'D NEED TO BE IN THE MOMENT.
BEEP!
BEEP!
BEEEEEEEP!!!
AND WE'LL ALL BE HAVING SUCH A FUN TIME WREAKING SENSELESS HAVOC THAT TIME WILL RUN OUT...

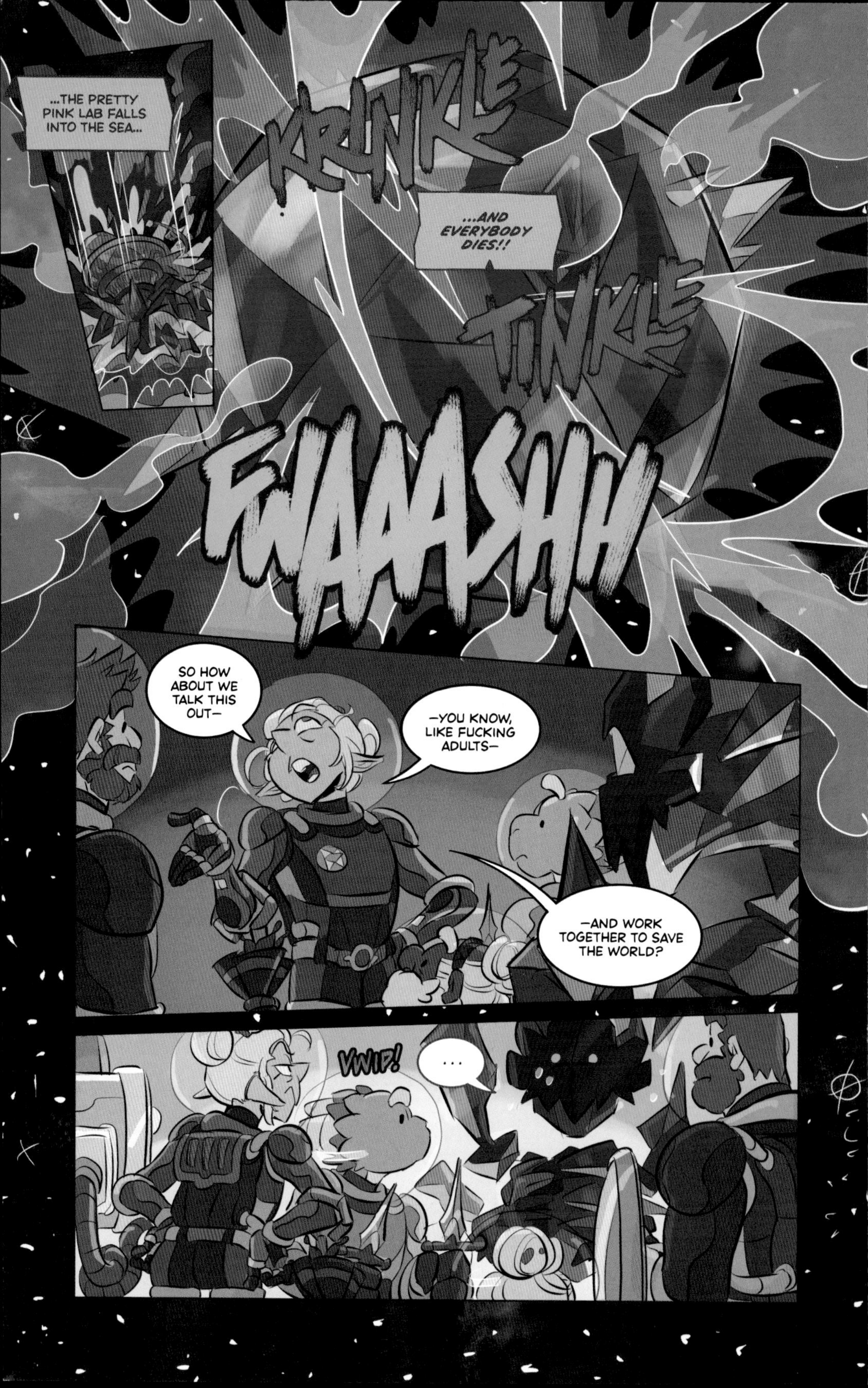
...THE PRETTY PINK LAB FALLS INTO THE SEA...
KRINKLE
...AND EVERYBODY DIES!!
TINKLE
FWAAASHH
SO HOW ABOUT WE TALK THIS OUT—
—YOU KNOW, LIKE FUCKING ADULTS—
—AND WORK TOGETHER TO SAVE THE WORLD?
VWIP!
...

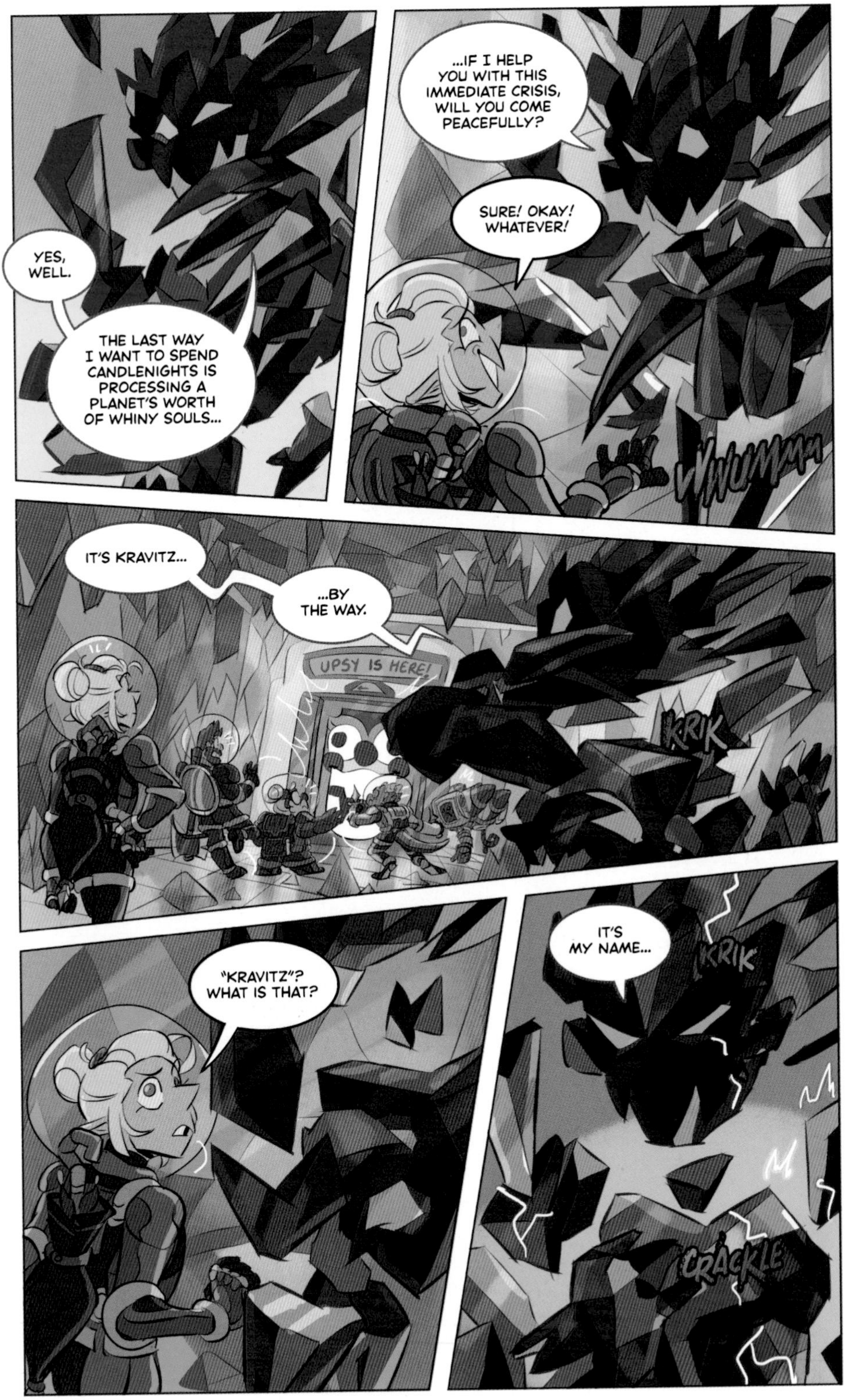
YES, WELL.
THE LAST WAY I WANT TO SPEND CANDLENIGHTS IS PROCESSING A PLANET'S WORTH OF WHINY SOULS...
...IF I HELP YOU WITH THIS IMMEDIATE CRISIS, WILL YOU COME PEACEFULLY?
SURE! OKAY! WHATEVER!
IT'S KRAVITZ...
...BY THE WAY.
UPSY IS HERE!
KRIK
"KRAVITZ"? WHAT IS THAT?
IT'S MY NAME...
KRIK
CRACKLE

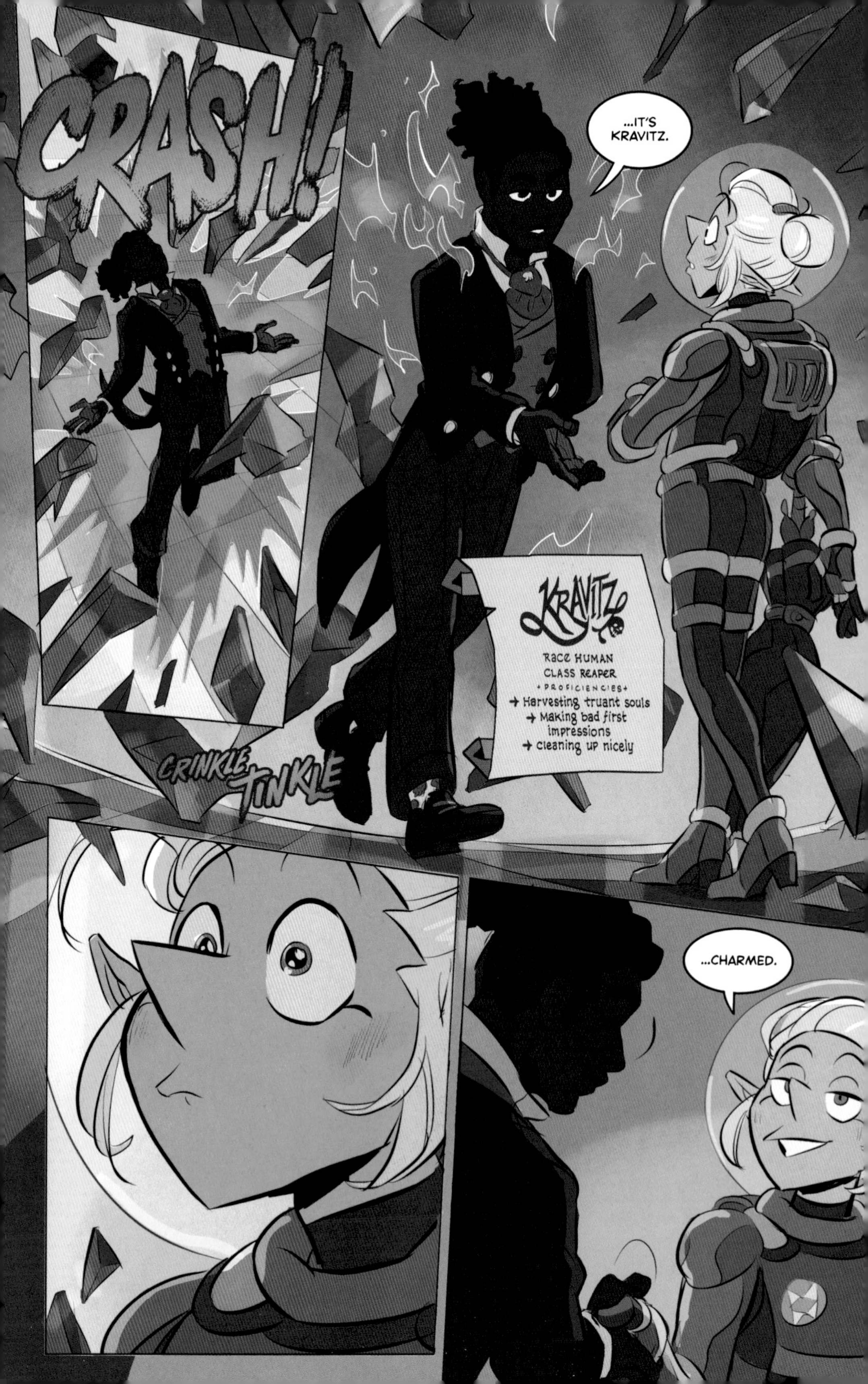
CRASH!!
...IT'S KRAVITZ.
KRAVITZ
RACE HUMAN
CLASS REAPER
+ PROFICIENCIES +
→ Harvesting truant souls
→ Making bad first impressions
→ cleaning up nicely
CRINKLE TINKLE
...CHARMED.

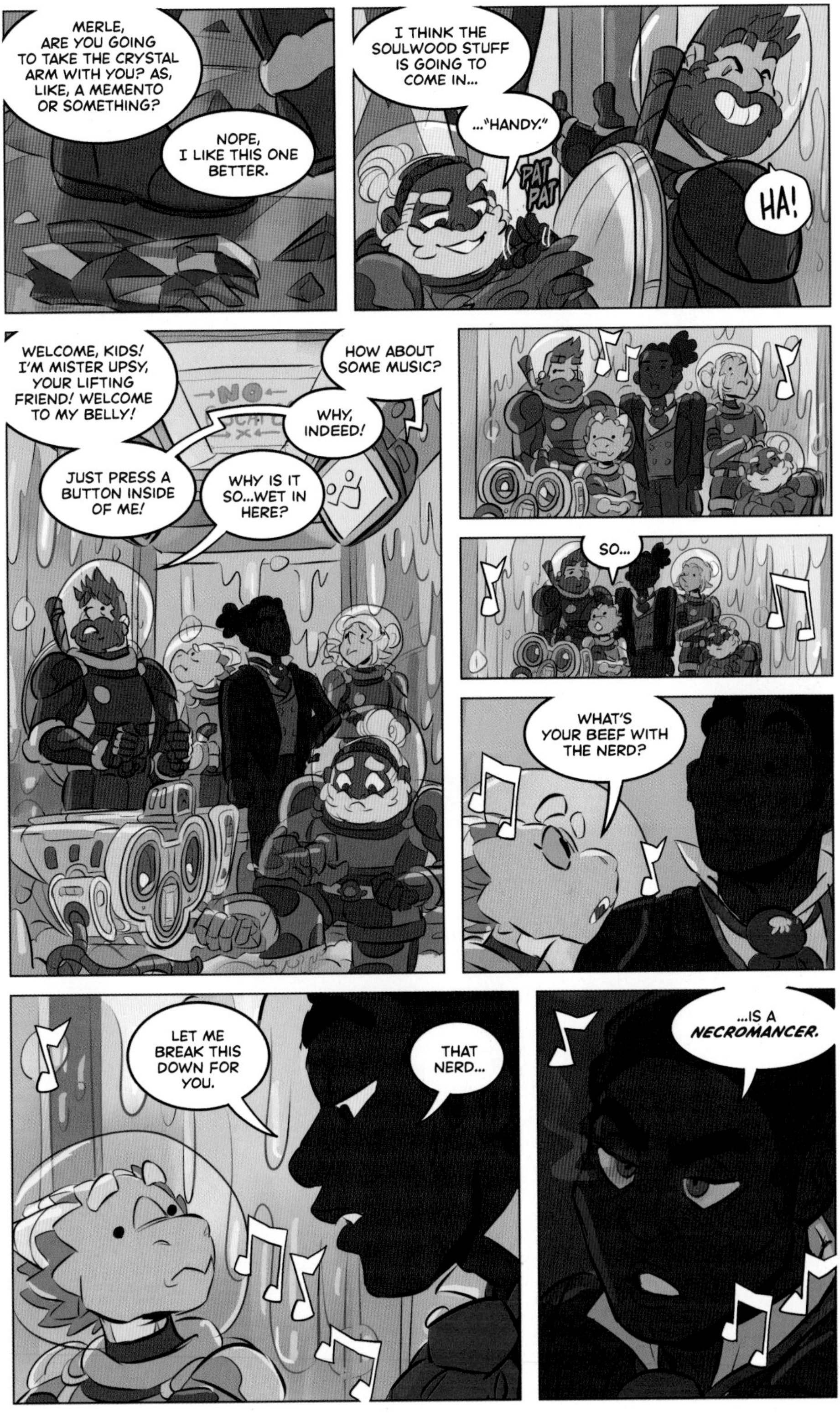
MERLE, ARE YOU GOING TO TAKE THE CRYSTAL ARM WITH YOU? AS, LIKE, A MEMENTO OR SOMETHING?
NOPE, I LIKE THIS ONE BETTER.
I THINK THE SOULWOOD STUFF IS GOING TO COME IN...
..."HANDY."
PAT PAT
HA!
WELCOME, KIDS! I'M MISTER UPSY, YOUR LIFTING FRIEND! WELCOME TO MY BELLY!
HOW ABOUT SOME MUSIC?
WHY, INDEED!
JUST PRESS A BUTTON INSIDE OF ME!
WHY IS IT SO...WET IN HERE?
NO
SO...
WHAT'S YOUR BEEF WITH THE NERD?
LET ME BREAK THIS DOWN FOR YOU.
THAT NERD...
...IS A *NECROMANCER.*

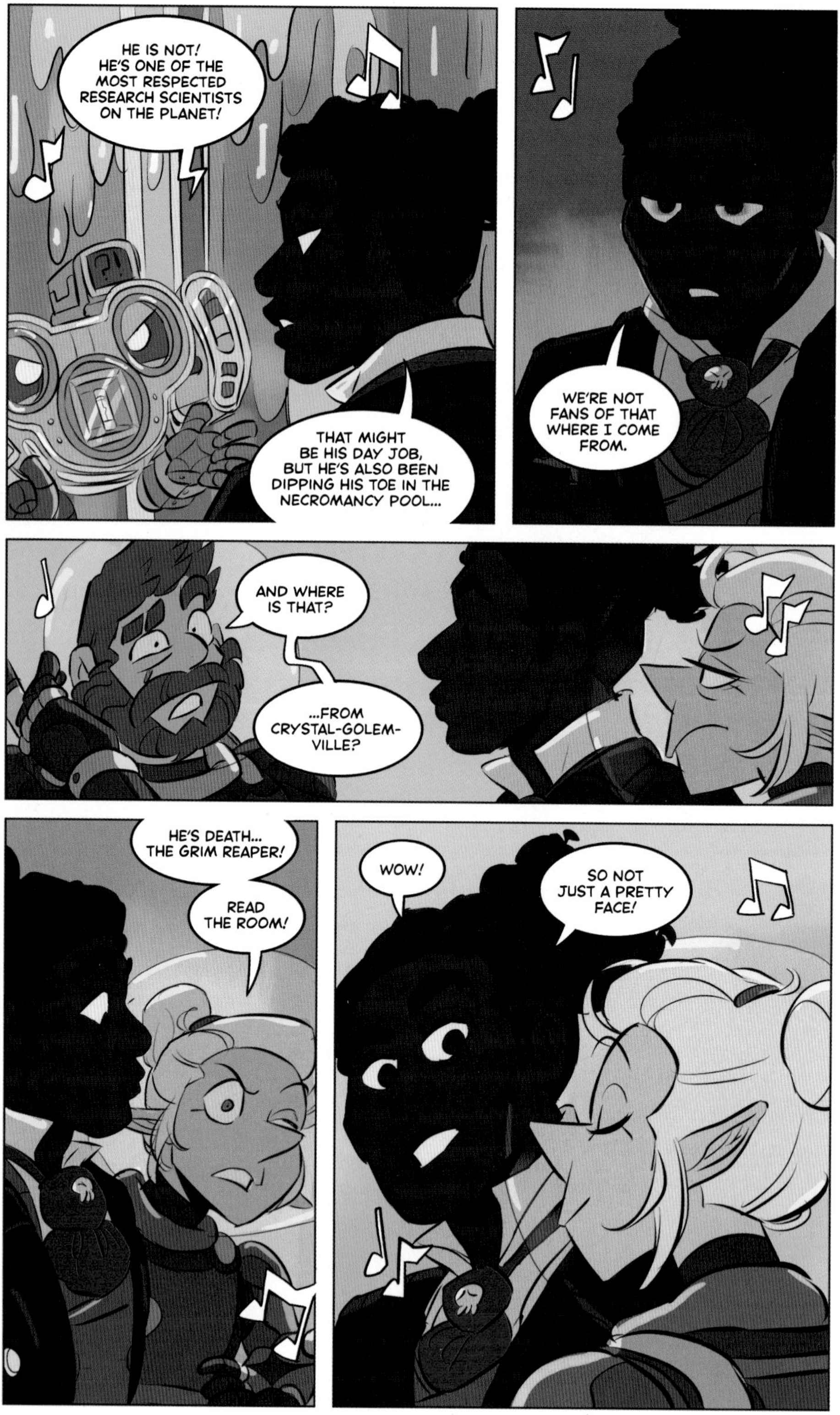
HE IS NOT! HE'S ONE OF THE MOST RESPECTED RESEARCH SCIENTISTS ON THE PLANET!
?!
THAT MIGHT BE HIS DAY JOB, BUT HE'S ALSO BEEN DIPPING HIS TOE IN THE NECROMANCY POOL...
WE'RE NOT FANS OF THAT WHERE I COME FROM.
AND WHERE IS THAT?
...FROM CRYSTAL-GOLEM-VILLE?
HE'S DEATH... THE GRIM REAPER!
READ THE ROOM!
WOW!
SO NOT JUST A PRETTY FACE!

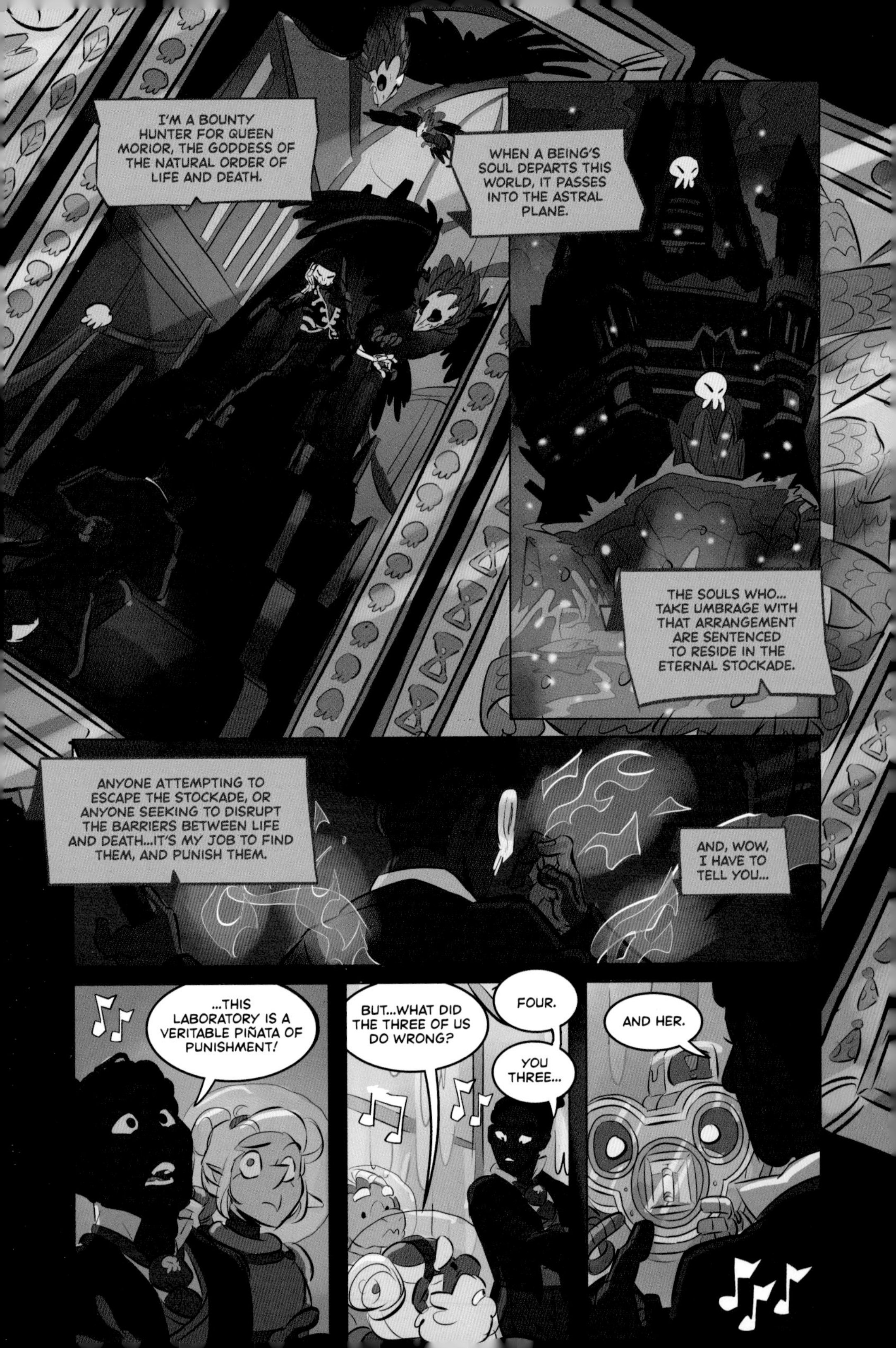
I'M A BOUNTY HUNTER FOR QUEEN MORIOR, THE GODDESS OF THE NATURAL ORDER OF LIFE AND DEATH.
WHEN A BEING'S SOUL DEPARTS THIS WORLD, IT PASSES INTO THE ASTRAL PLANE.
THE SOULS WHO... TAKE UMBRAGE WITH THAT ARRANGEMENT ARE SENTENCED TO RESIDE IN THE ETERNAL STOCKADE.
ANYONE ATTEMPTING TO ESCAPE THE STOCKADE, OR ANYONE SEEKING TO DISRUPT THE BARRIERS BETWEEN LIFE AND DEATH...IT'S MY JOB TO FIND THEM, AND PUNISH THEM.
AND, WOW, I HAVE TO TELL YOU...
...THIS LABORATORY IS A VERITABLE PIÑATA OF PUNISHMENT!
BUT...WHAT DID THE THREE OF US DO WRONG?
YOU THREE...
FOUR.
AND HER.

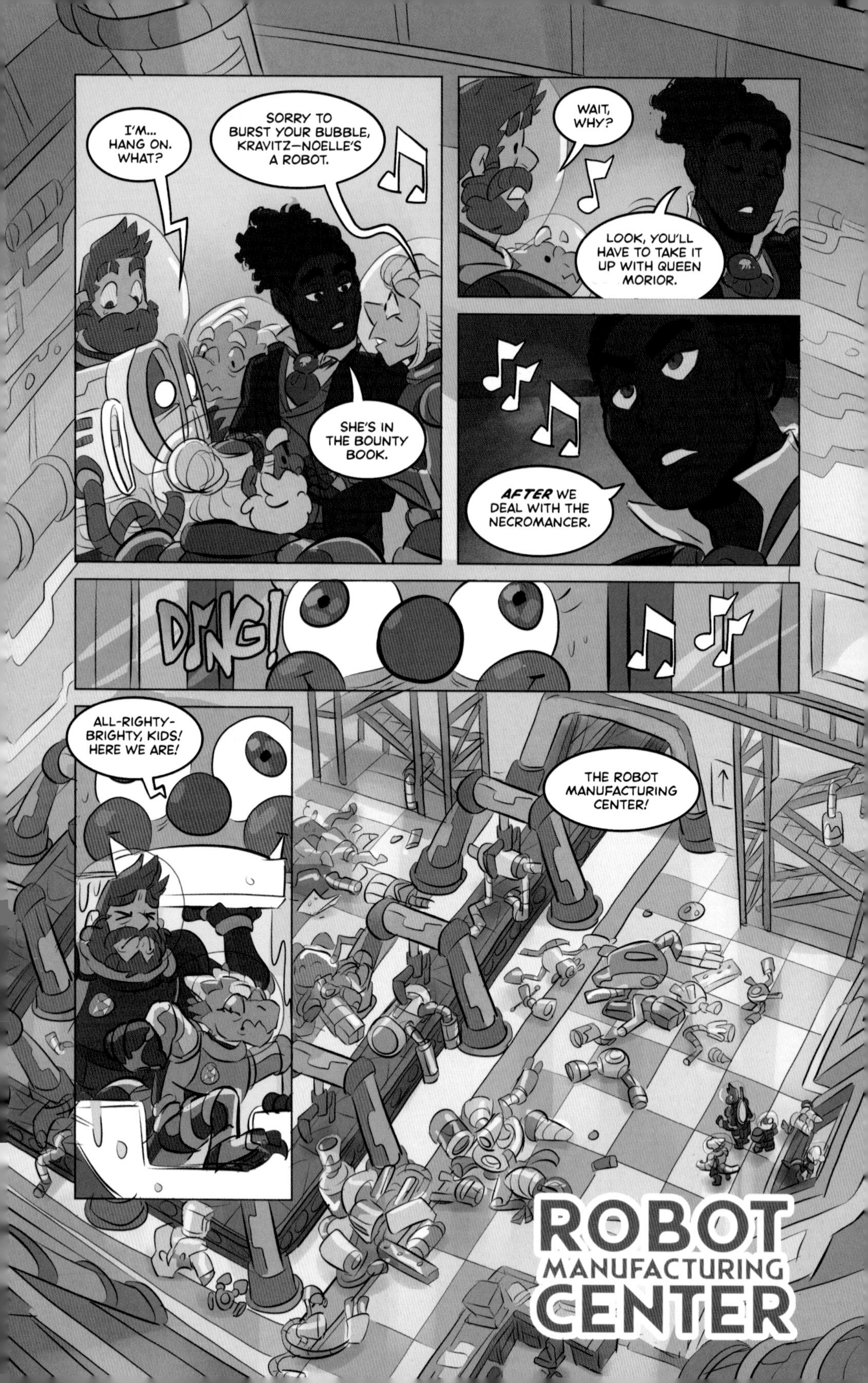
I'M... HANG ON. WHAT?
SORRY TO BURST YOUR BUBBLE, KRAVITZ—NOELLE'S A ROBOT.
SHE'S IN THE BOUNTY BOOK.
WAIT, WHY?
LOOK, YOU'LL HAVE TO TAKE IT UP WITH QUEEN MORIOR.
AFTER WE DEAL WITH THE NECROMANCER.
DING!
ALL-RIGHTY-BRIGHTY, KIDS! HERE WE ARE!
THE ROBOT MANUFACTURING CENTER!
ROBOT MANUFACTURING CENTER

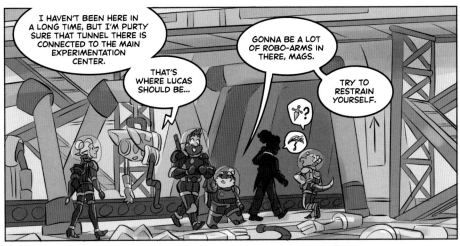

I HAVEN'T BEEN HERE IN A LONG TIME, BUT I'M PURTY SURE THAT TUNNEL THERE IS CONNECTED TO THE MAIN EXPERIMENTATION CENTER.

THAT'S WHERE LUCAS SHOULD BE...

GONNA BE A LOT OF ROBO-ARMS IN THERE, MAGS.

TRY TO RESTRAIN YOURSELF.

NOELLE?

ARE YOU...OKAY?

SOME OF THESE UNITS...

...I DON'T RECOGNIZE THEIR DESIGNS...

No. 3112

WHY WOULD LUCAS HIDE THIS FROM ME?

THE MORE... ADVANCED ONES HAVE THOSE FUSES, LIKE YOURS.

YES. LUCAS SAID THOSE ARE OUR POWER SOURCES...

I FEEL... SAD.

WHY?

I...

I DON'T KNOW...

...

WE REALLY NEED TO MOVE OUT!

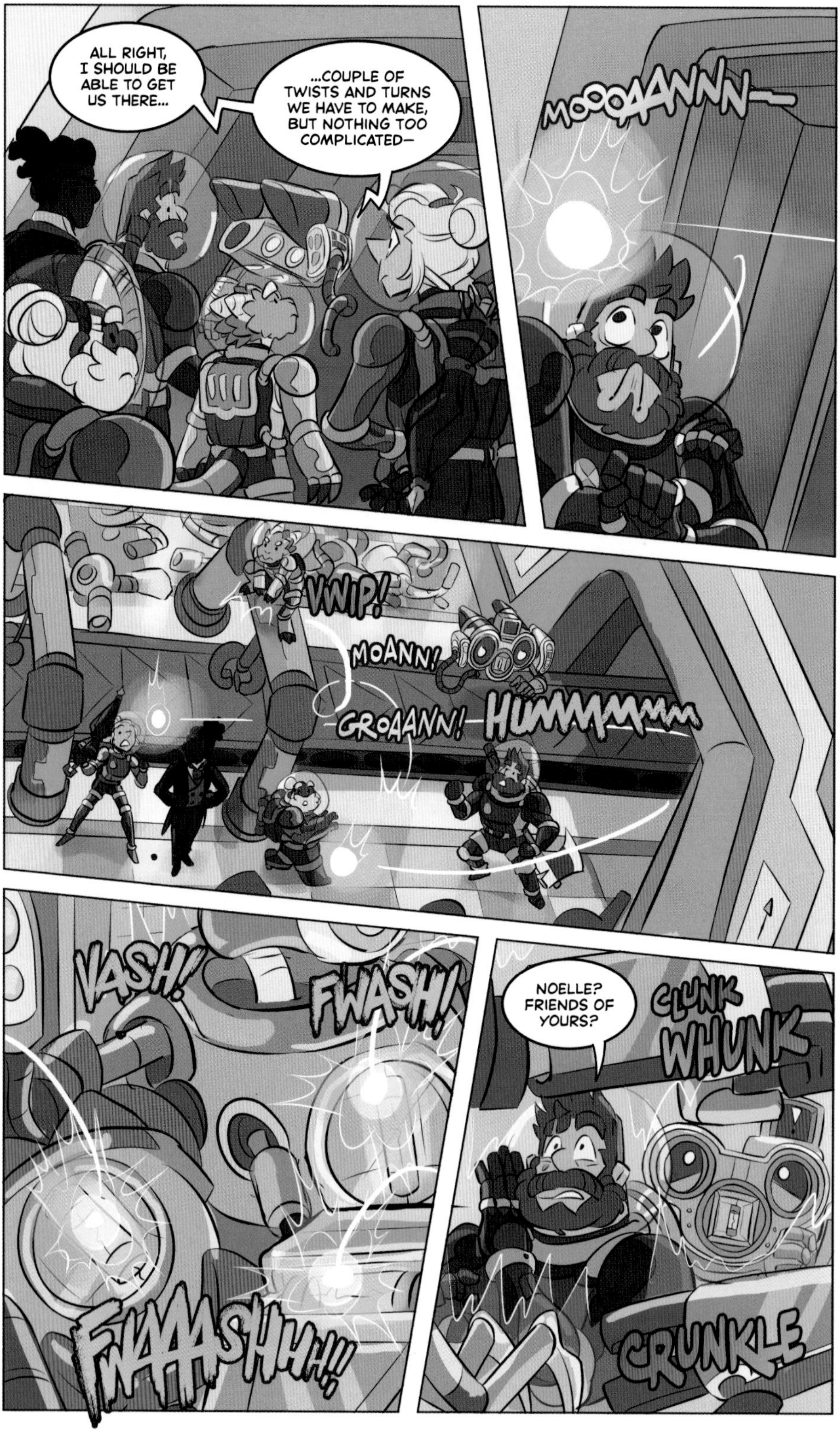
ALL RIGHT, I SHOULD BE ABLE TO GET US THERE...
...COUPLE OF TWISTS AND TURNS WE HAVE TO MAKE, BUT NOTHING TOO COMPLICATED—
MOOOAANNN—
VWIP!
MOANN!
GROAANN!
HUMMMMM
VASH!
FWASH!
FWAAASHHH!!
NOELLE? FRIENDS OF YOURS?
CLUNK
WHUNK
CRUNKLE

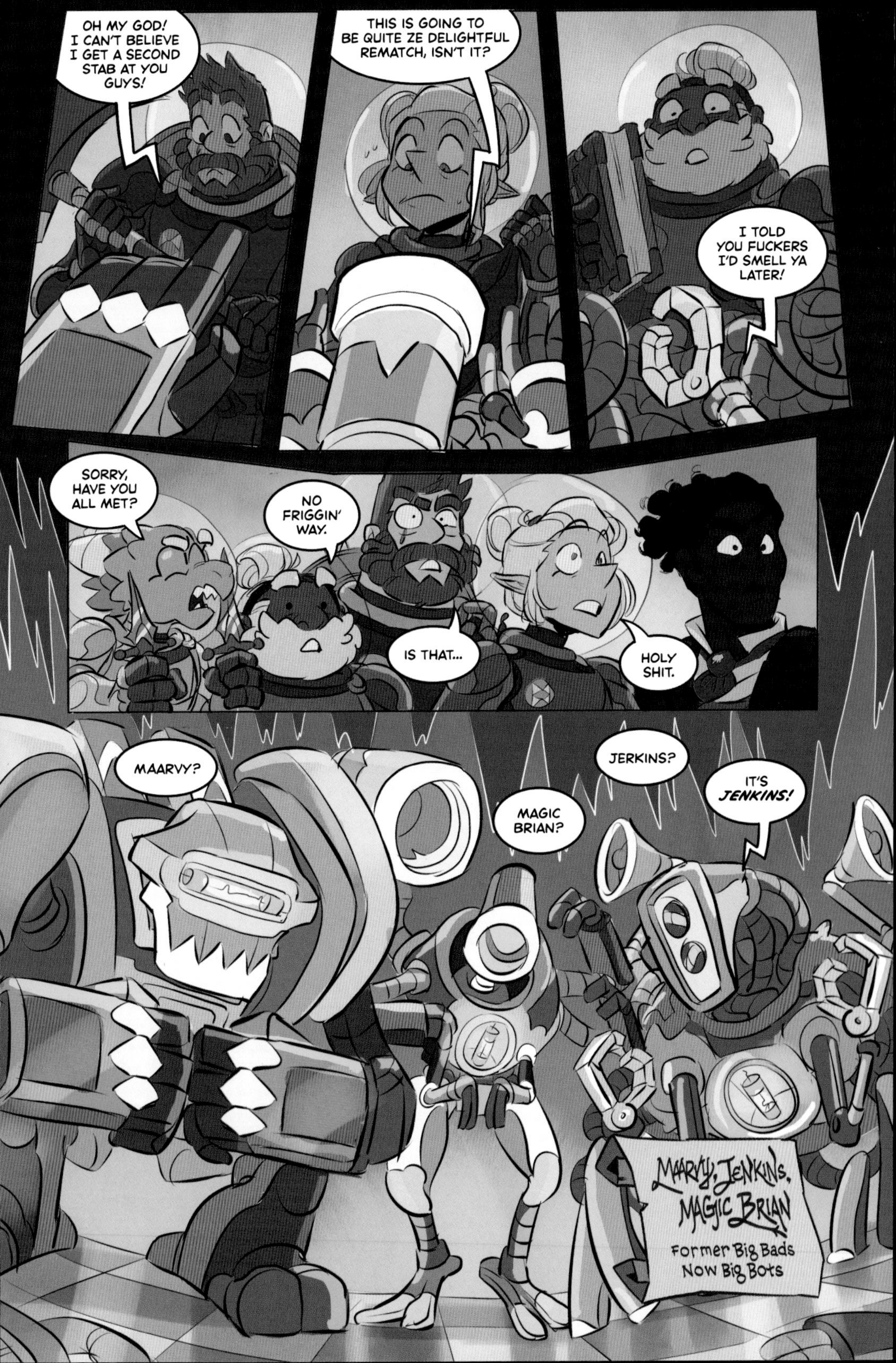
OH MY GOD! I CAN'T BELIEVE I GET A SECOND STAB AT YOU GUYS!
THIS IS GOING TO BE QUITE ZE DELIGHTFUL REMATCH, ISN'T IT?
I TOLD YOU FUCKERS I'D SMELL YA LATER!
SORRY, HAVE YOU ALL MET?
NO FRIGGIN' WAY.
IS THAT...
HOLY SHIT.
MAARVY?
MAGIC BRIAN?
JERKINS?
IT'S *JENKINS!*
MAARVY, JENKINS, MAGIC BRIAN
Former Big Bads Now Big Bots

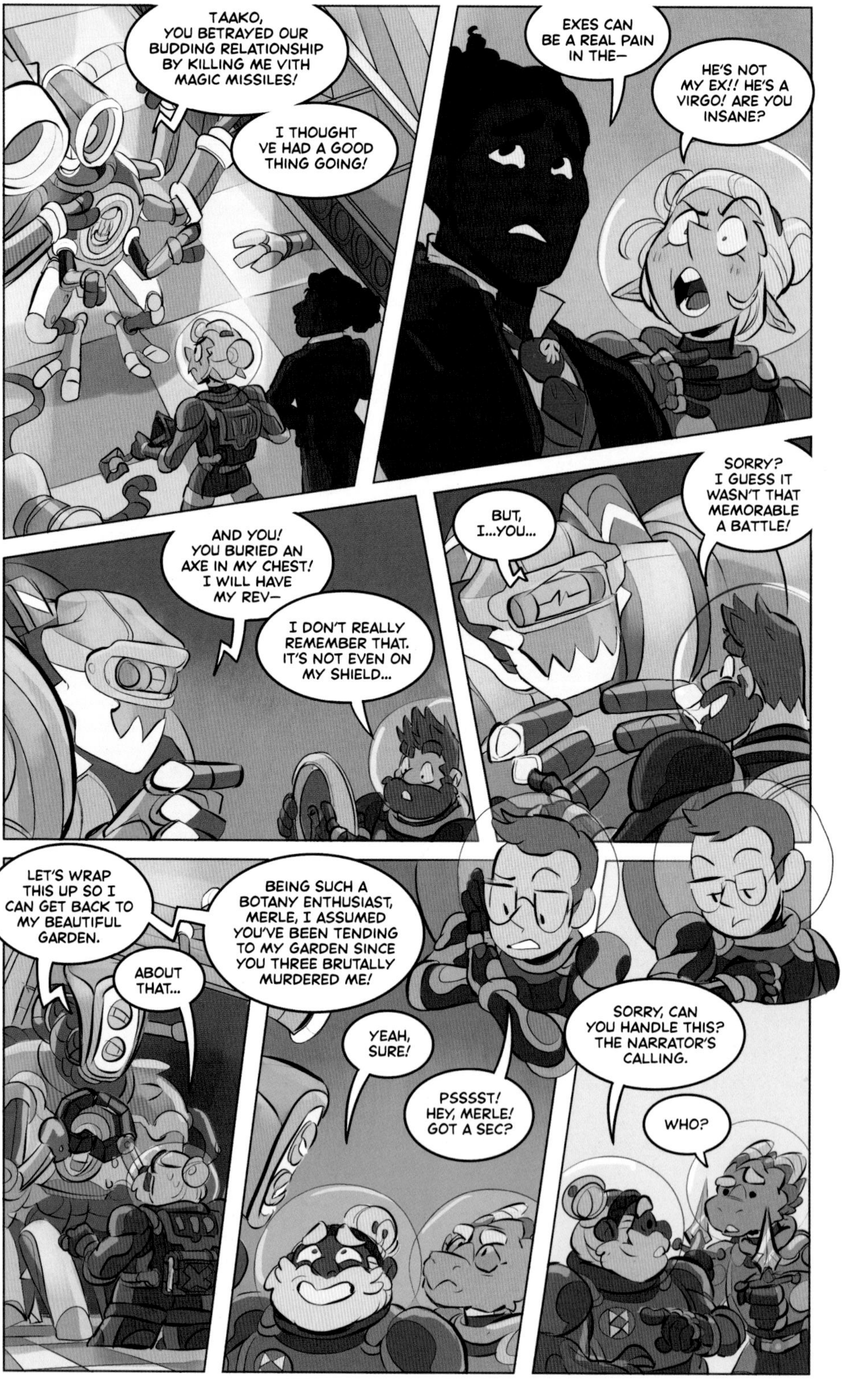
TAAKO, YOU BETRAYED OUR BUDDING RELATIONSHIP BY KILLING ME VITH MAGIC MISSILES!
I THOUGHT VE HAD A GOOD THING GOING!
EXES CAN BE A REAL PAIN IN THE—
HE'S NOT MY EX!! HE'S A VIRGO! ARE YOU INSANE?
AND YOU! YOU BURIED AN AXE IN MY CHEST! I WILL HAVE MY REV—
I DON'T REALLY REMEMBER THAT. IT'S NOT EVEN ON MY SHIELD...
BUT, I...YOU...
SORRY? I GUESS IT WASN'T THAT MEMORABLE A BATTLE!
LET'S WRAP THIS UP SO I CAN GET BACK TO MY BEAUTIFUL GARDEN.
ABOUT THAT...
BEING SUCH A BOTANY ENTHUSIAST, MERLE, I ASSUMED YOU'VE BEEN TENDING TO MY GARDEN SINCE YOU THREE BRUTALLY MURDERED ME!
YEAH, SURE!
PSSSST! HEY, MERLE! GOT A SEC?
SORRY, CAN YOU HANDLE THIS? THE NARRATOR'S CALLING.
WHO?

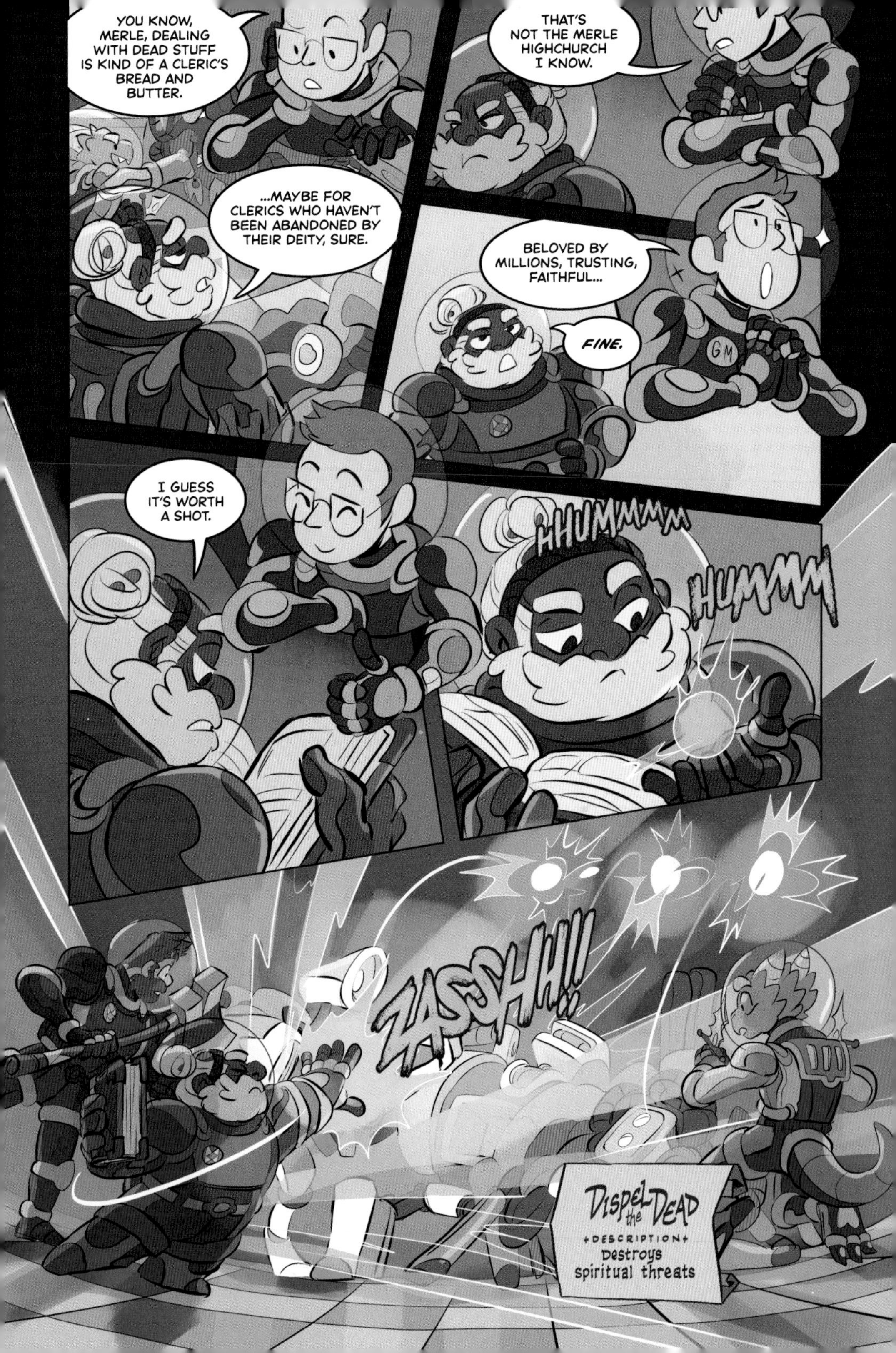
YOU KNOW, MERLE, DEALING WITH DEAD STUFF IS KIND OF A CLERIC'S BREAD AND BUTTER.
THAT'S NOT THE MERLE HIGHCHURCH I KNOW.
...MAYBE FOR CLERICS WHO HAVEN'T BEEN ABANDONED BY THEIR DEITY, SURE.
BELOVED BY MILLIONS, TRUSTING, FAITHFUL...
FINE.
I GUESS IT'S WORTH A SHOT.
HHUMMMM
HUMMM
ZASSHH!!
DISPEL the DEAD
DESCRIPTION
Destroys spiritual threats

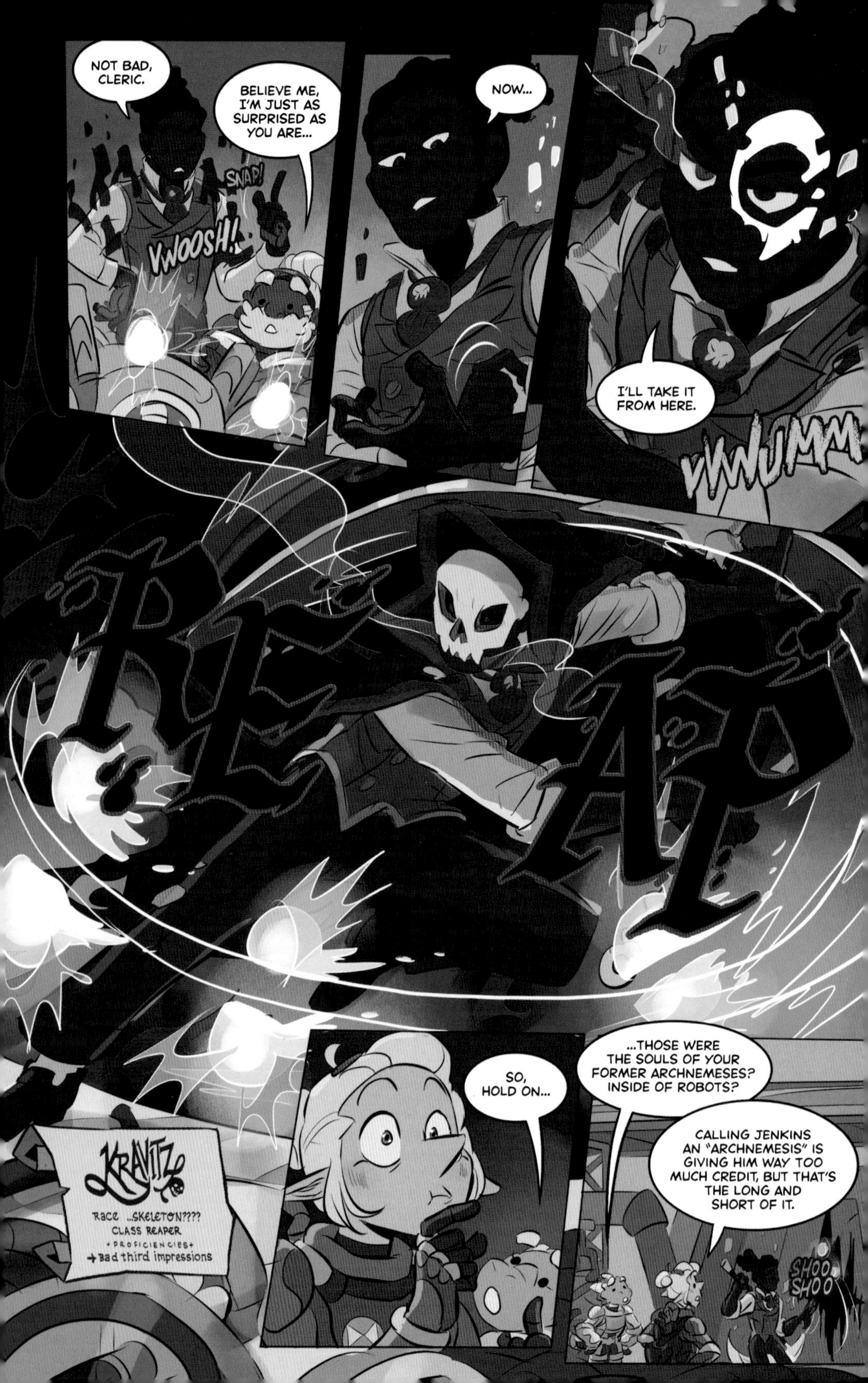
NOT BAD, CLERIC.
BELIEVE ME, I'M JUST AS SURPRISED AS YOU ARE...
SNAP!
VWOOSH!
NOW...
I'LL TAKE IT FROM HERE.
VVWUMM
REAP
KRAVITZ
Race ...SKELETON????
CLASS REAPER
PROFICIENCIES
→ Bad third impressions
SO, HOLD ON...
...THOSE WERE THE SOULS OF YOUR FORMER ARCHNEMESES? INSIDE OF ROBOTS?
CALLING JENKINS AN "ARCHNEMESIS" IS GIVING HIM WAY TOO MUCH CREDIT, BUT THAT'S THE LONG AND SHORT OF IT.
SHOO SHOO

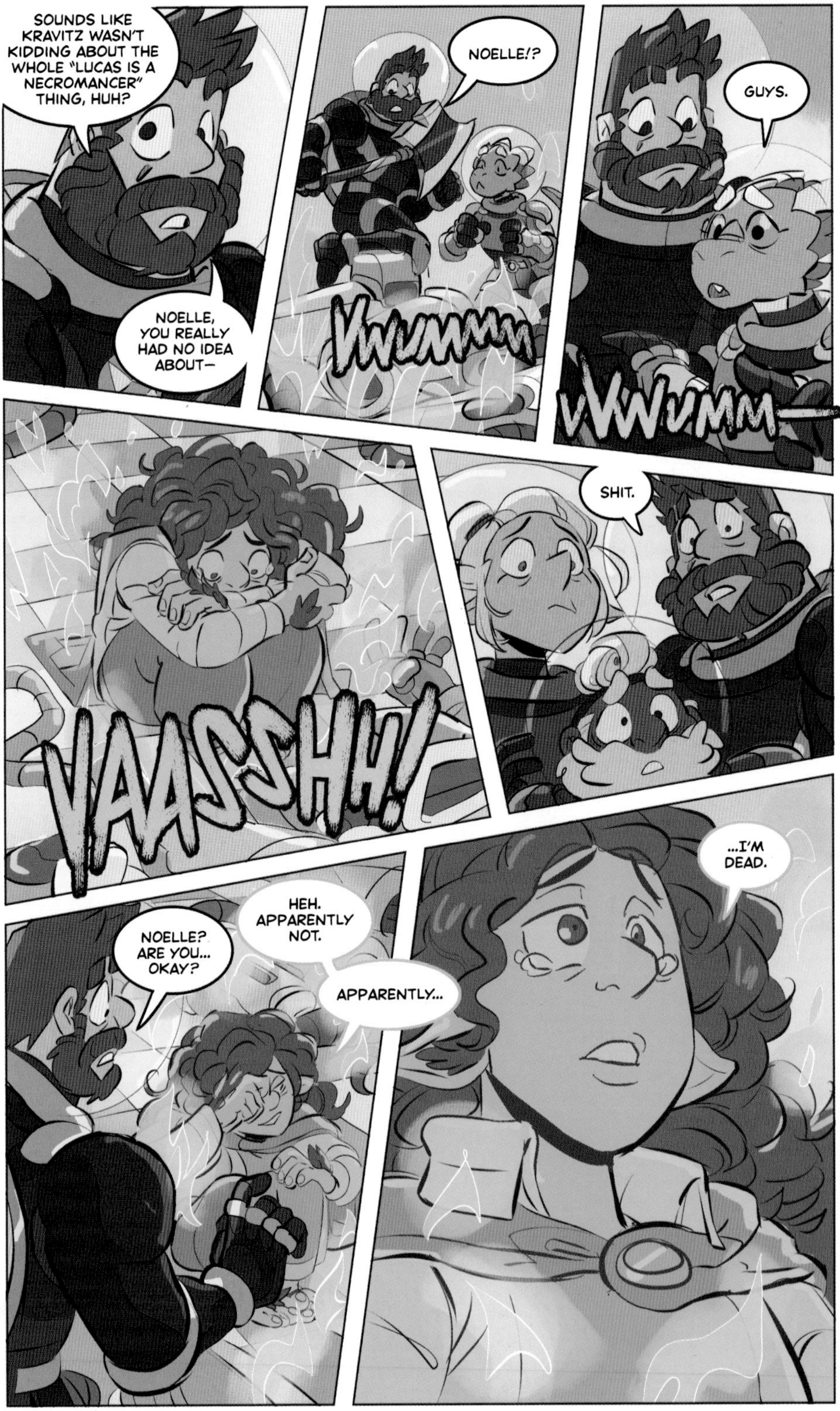
SOUNDS LIKE KRAVITZ WASN'T KIDDING ABOUT THE WHOLE "LUCAS IS A NECROMANCER" THING, HUH?
NOELLE, YOU REALLY HAD NO IDEA ABOUT—
NOELLE!?
VWUMMM
GUYS.
VWWUMM
VAASHH!
SHIT.
...I'M DEAD.
NOELLE? ARE YOU... OKAY?
HEH. APPARENTLY NOT.
APPARENTLY...

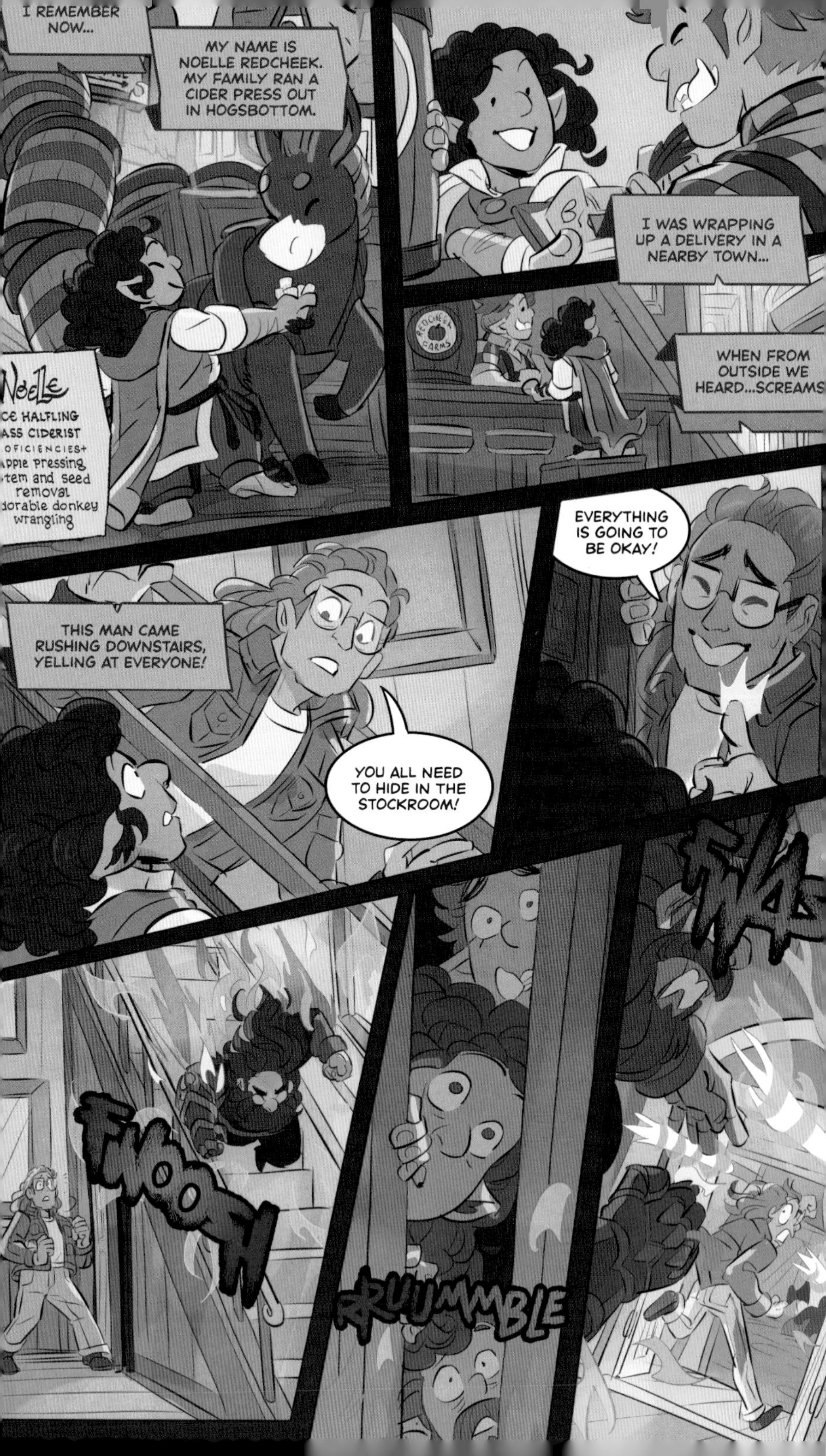
I REMEMBER NOW...
MY NAME IS NOELLE REDCHEEK. MY FAMILY RAN A CIDER PRESS OUT IN HOGSBOTTOM.
NOELLE
CE HALFLING
ASS CIDERIST
OFICIENCIES+
apple pressing
tem and seed removal
dorable donkey wrangling
I WAS WRAPPING UP A DELIVERY IN A NEARBY TOWN...
REDCHEEK FARMS
WHEN FROM OUTSIDE WE HEARD...SCREAMS
THIS MAN CAME RUSHING DOWNSTAIRS, YELLING AT EVERYONE!
YOU ALL NEED TO HIDE IN THE STOCKROOM!
EVERYTHING IS GOING TO BE OKAY!
FWA
FWOOSH
RRUUMMBLE

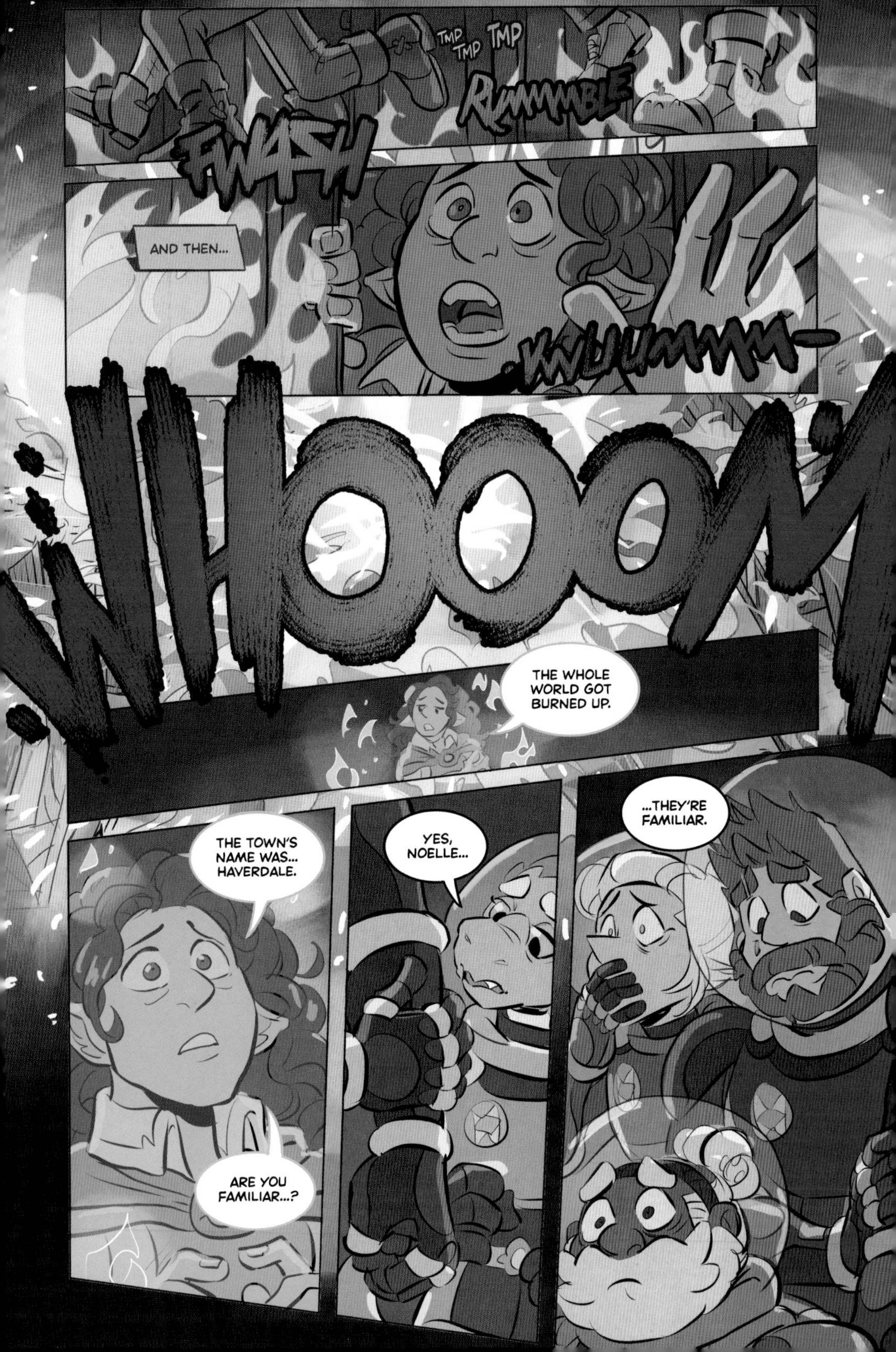
TMP TMP TMP
RUMMMBLE
FWASH
AND THEN...
-KWUUMMM-
WHOOM
THE WHOLE WORLD GOT BURNED UP.
THE TOWN'S NAME WAS... HAVERDALE.
ARE YOU FAMILIAR...?
YES, NOELLE...
...THEY'RE FAMILIAR.

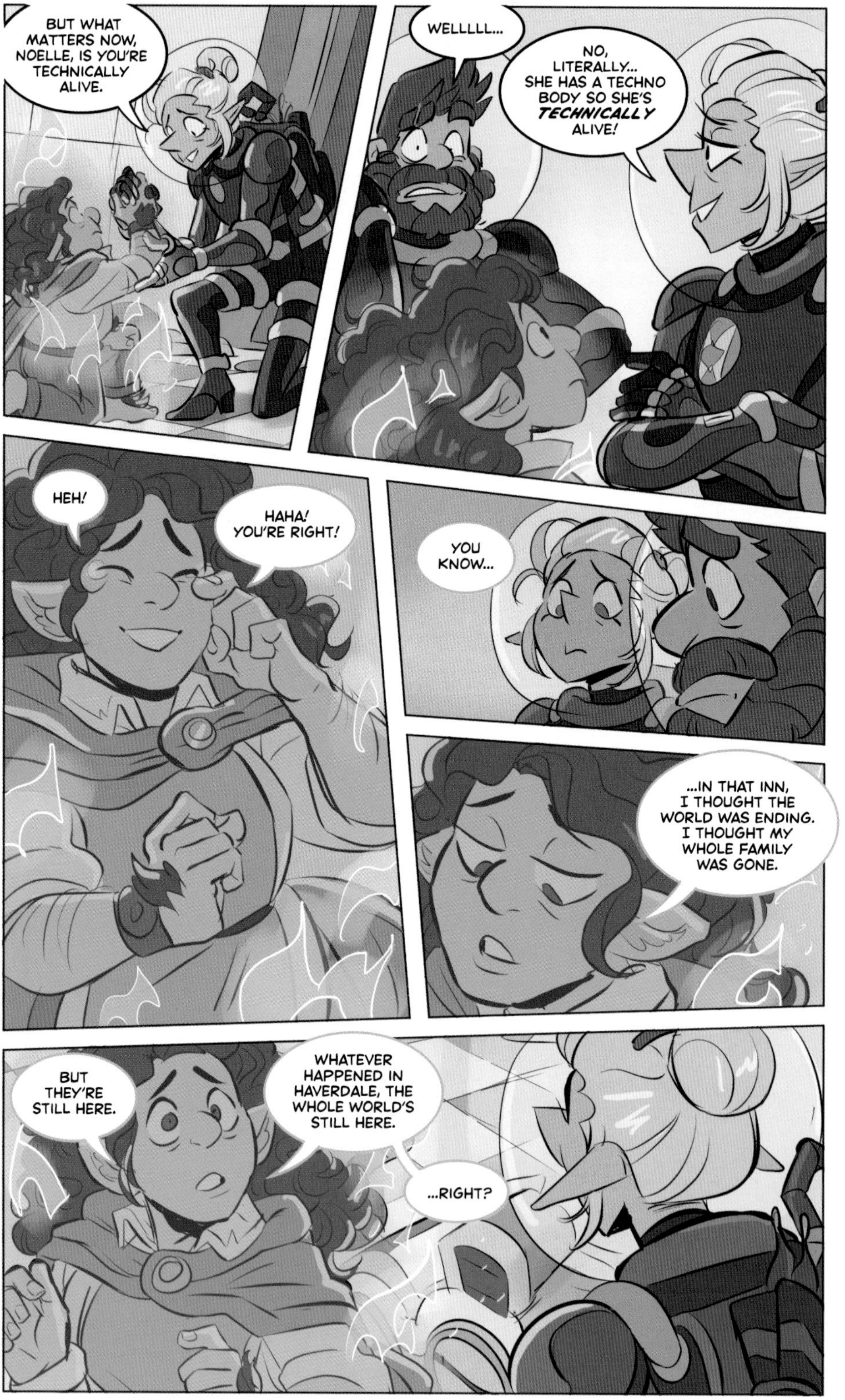

BUT WHAT MATTERS NOW, NOELLE, IS YOU'RE TECHNICALLY ALIVE.
WELLLLL...
NO, LITERALLY... SHE HAS A TECHNO BODY SO SHE'S *TECHNICALLY* ALIVE!
HEH!
HAHA! YOU'RE RIGHT!
YOU KNOW...
...IN THAT INN, I THOUGHT THE WORLD WAS ENDING. I THOUGHT MY WHOLE FAMILY WAS GONE.
BUT THEY'RE STILL HERE.
WHATEVER HAPPENED IN HAVERDALE, THE WHOLE WORLD'S STILL HERE.
...RIGHT?

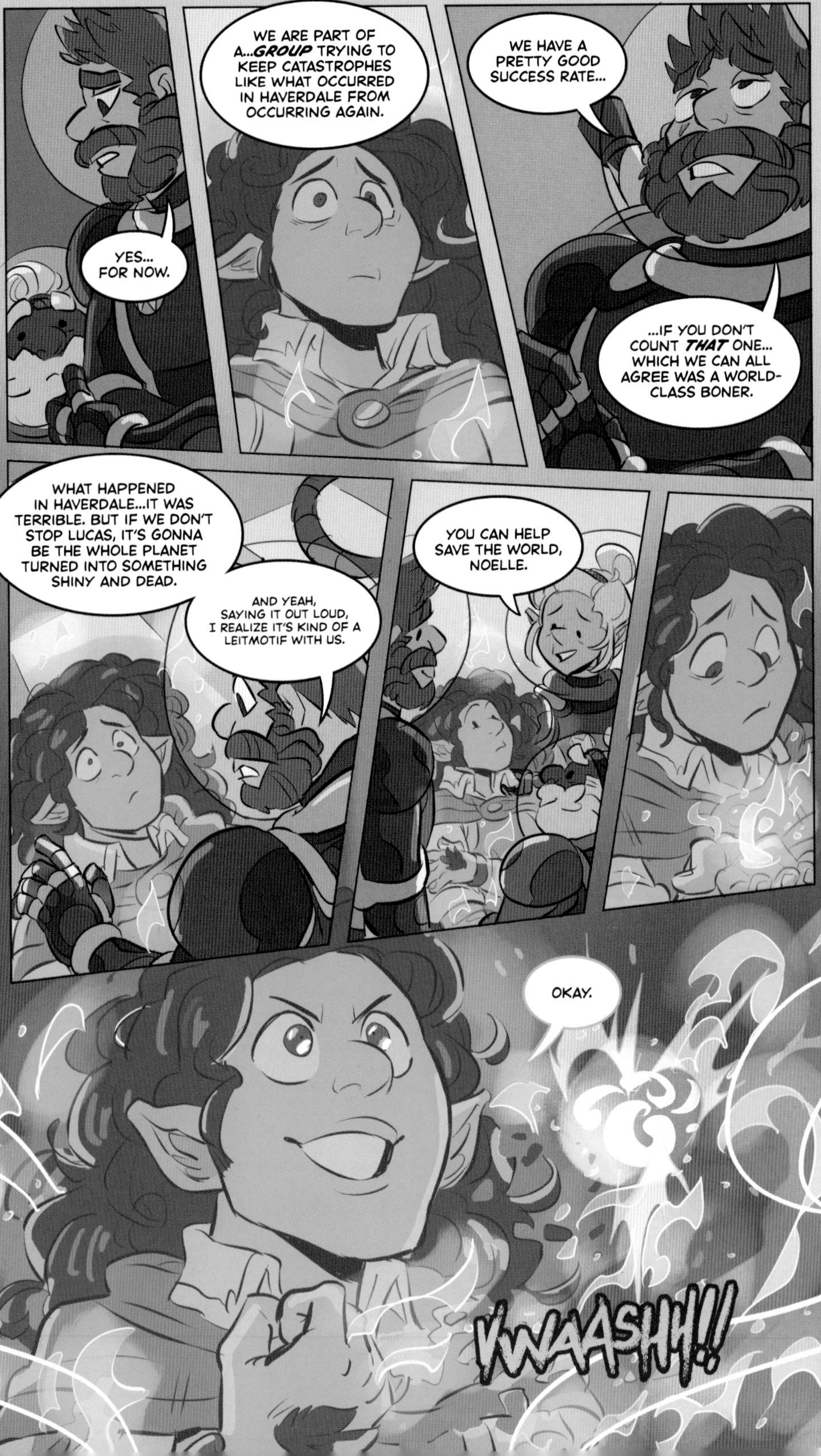
WE ARE PART OF A...GROUP TRYING TO KEEP CATASTROPHES LIKE WHAT OCCURRED IN HAVERDALE FROM OCCURRING AGAIN.
YES... FOR NOW.
WE HAVE A PRETTY GOOD SUCCESS RATE...
...IF YOU DON'T COUNT THAT ONE... WHICH WE CAN ALL AGREE WAS A WORLD-CLASS BONER.
WHAT HAPPENED IN HAVERDALE...IT WAS TERRIBLE. BUT IF WE DON'T STOP LUCAS, IT'S GONNA BE THE WHOLE PLANET TURNED INTO SOMETHING SHINY AND DEAD.
AND YEAH, SAYING IT OUT LOUD, I REALIZE IT'S KIND OF A LEITMOTIF WITH US.
YOU CAN HELP SAVE THE WORLD, NOELLE.
OKAY.
VWAASHH!!

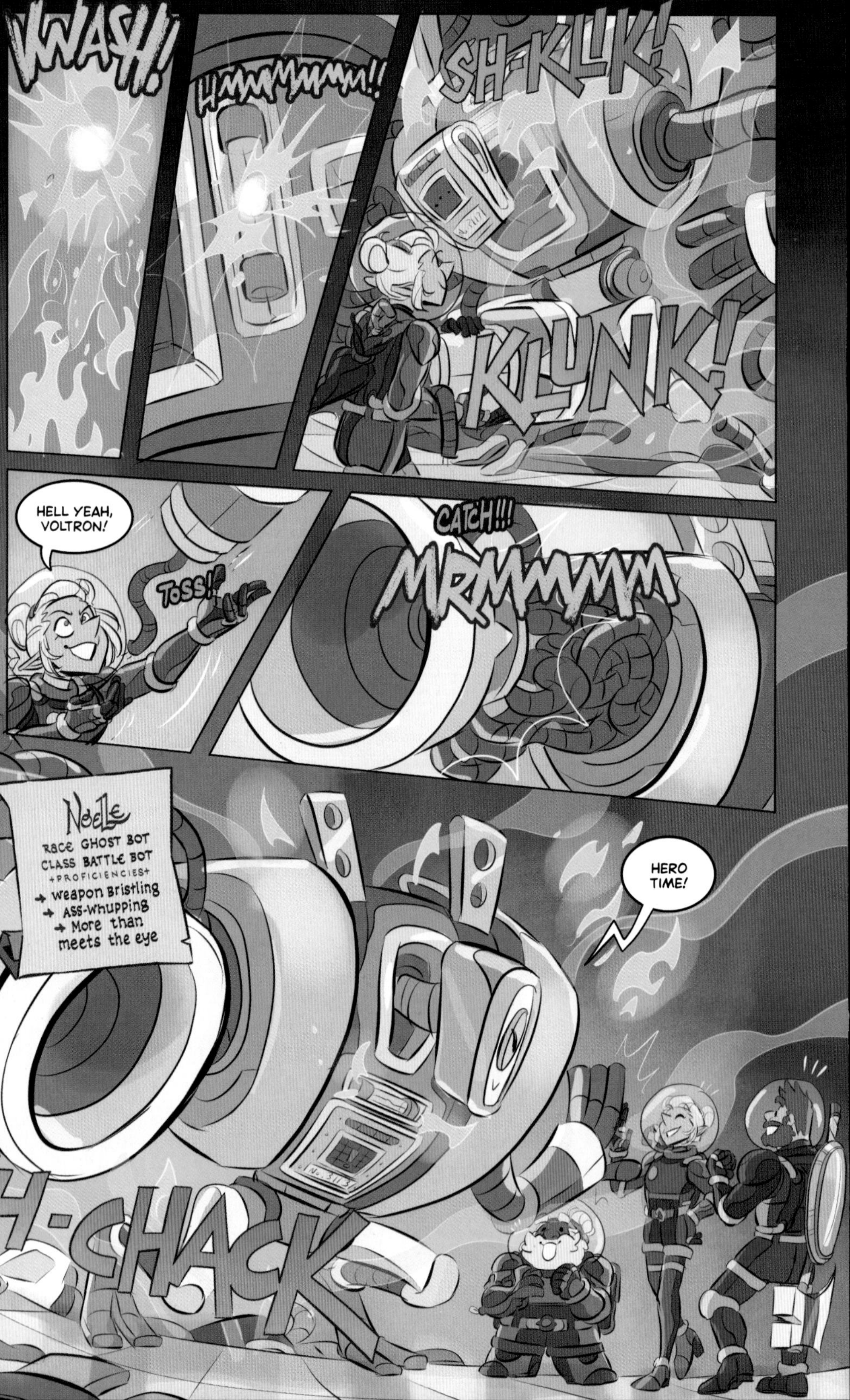
VWASH!
SH-KLIK!
KLUNK!
HELL YEAH, VOLTRON!
TOSS!
CATCH!!!
MRMMMM
NoeLLe
Race GHOST BOT
CLASS BATTLE BOT
+PROFICIENCIES+
→ Weapon Bristling
→ ASS-Whupping
→ More than meets the eye
HERO TIME!
CH-CHACK

Chapter
7

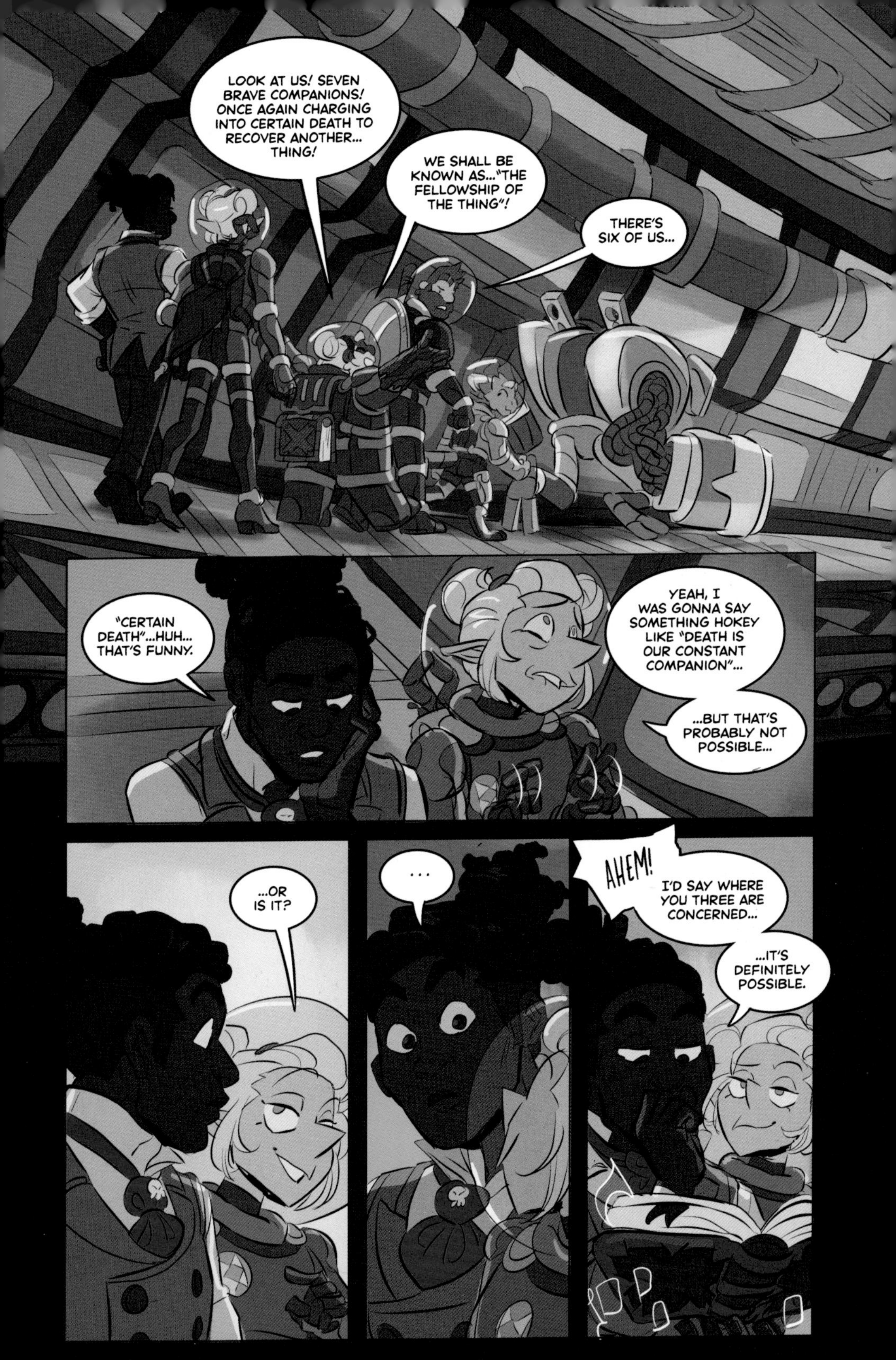
LOOK AT US! SEVEN BRAVE COMPANIONS! ONCE AGAIN CHARGING INTO CERTAIN DEATH TO RECOVER ANOTHER... THING!
WE SHALL BE KNOWN AS..."THE FELLOWSHIP OF THE THING"!
THERE'S SIX OF US...
"CERTAIN DEATH"...HUH... THAT'S FUNNY.
YEAH, I WAS GONNA SAY SOMETHING HOKEY LIKE "DEATH IS OUR CONSTANT COMPANION"...
...BUT THAT'S PROBABLY NOT POSSIBLE...
...OR IS IT?
...
AHEM!
I'D SAY WHERE YOU THREE ARE CONCERNED...
...IT'S DEFINITELY POSSIBLE.

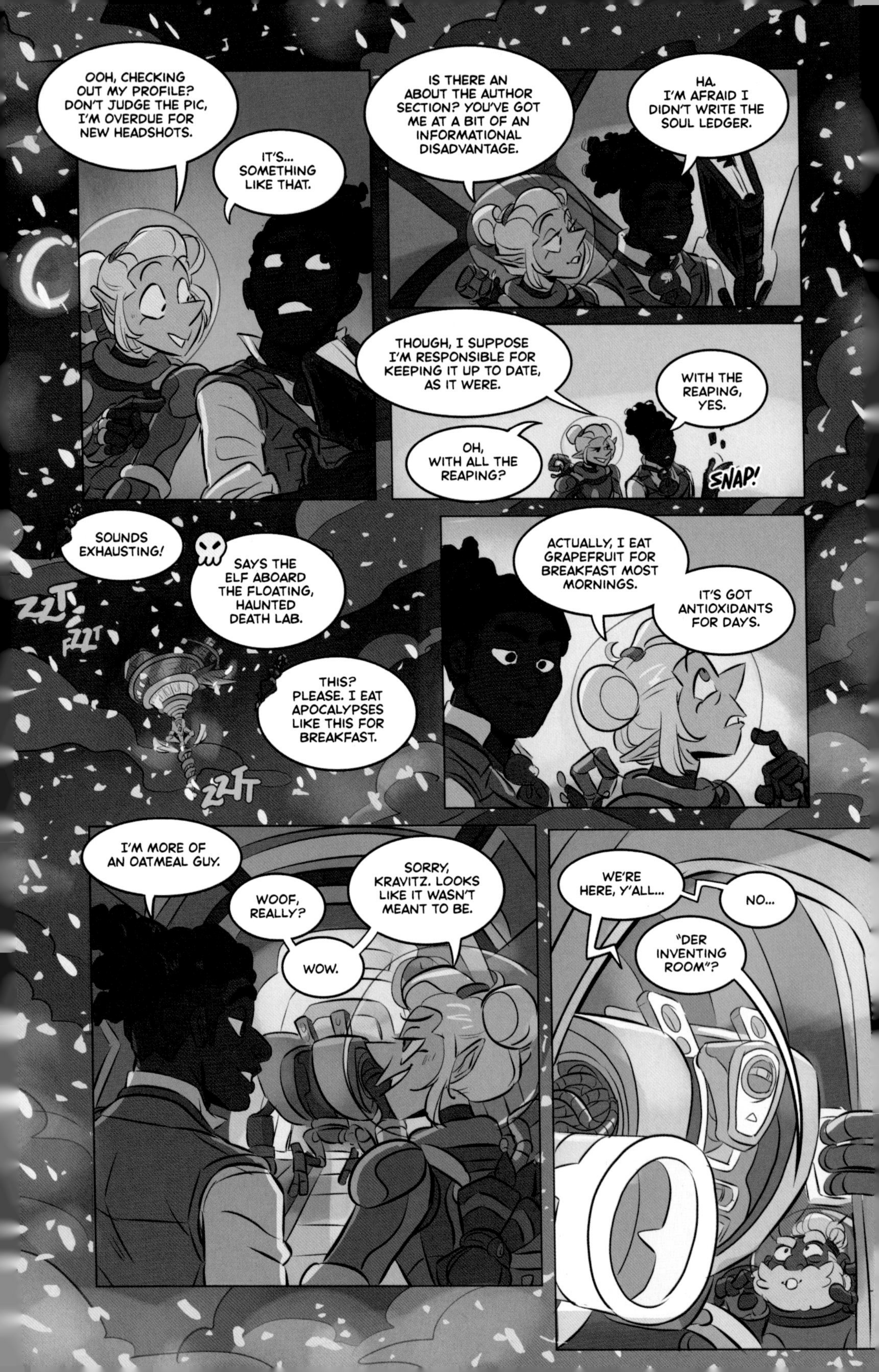
OOH, CHECKING OUT MY PROFILE? DON'T JUDGE THE PIC, I'M OVERDUE FOR NEW HEADSHOTS.
IT'S... SOMETHING LIKE THAT.
IS THERE AN ABOUT THE AUTHOR SECTION? YOU'VE GOT ME AT A BIT OF AN INFORMATIONAL DISADVANTAGE.
HA. I'M AFRAID I DIDN'T WRITE THE SOUL LEDGER.
THOUGH, I SUPPOSE I'M RESPONSIBLE FOR KEEPING IT UP TO DATE, AS IT WERE.
OH, WITH ALL THE REAPING?
WITH THE REAPING, YES.
SNAP!
SOUNDS EXHAUSTING!
SAYS THE ELF ABOARD THE FLOATING, HAUNTED DEATH LAB.
ZZT
ZZT
THIS? PLEASE. I EAT APOCALYPSES LIKE THIS FOR BREAKFAST.
ZZT
ACTUALLY, I EAT GRAPEFRUIT FOR BREAKFAST MOST MORNINGS.
IT'S GOT ANTIOXIDANTS FOR DAYS.
I'M MORE OF AN OATMEAL GUY.
WOOF, REALLY?
WOW.
SORRY, KRAVITZ. LOOKS LIKE IT WASN'T MEANT TO BE.
WE'RE HERE, Y'ALL...
NO...
"DER INVENTING ROOM"?

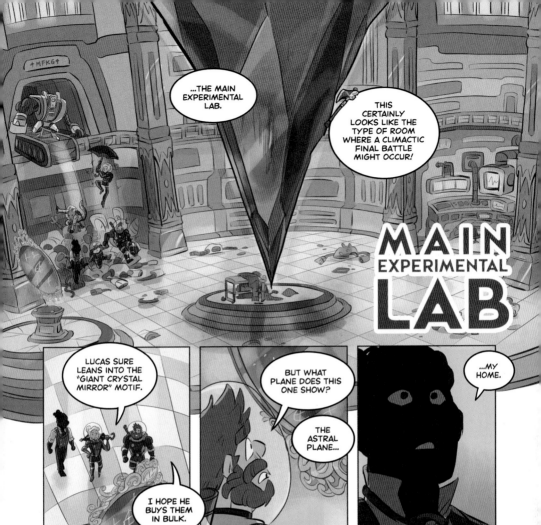

...THE MAIN EXPERIMENTAL LAB.

THIS CERTAINLY LOOKS LIKE THE TYPE OF ROOM WHERE A CLIMACTIC FINAL BATTLE MIGHT OCCUR!

MAIN EXPERIMENTAL LAB

LUCAS SURE LEANS INTO THE "GIANT CRYSTAL MIRROR" MOTIF.

I HOPE HE BUYS THEM IN BULK.

BUT WHAT PLANE DOES THIS ONE SHOW?

THE ASTRAL PLANE...

...MY HOME.

WHAT WAS HE TRYING—

WHANG!

SHIT!

WHANNGG!

SHIT!

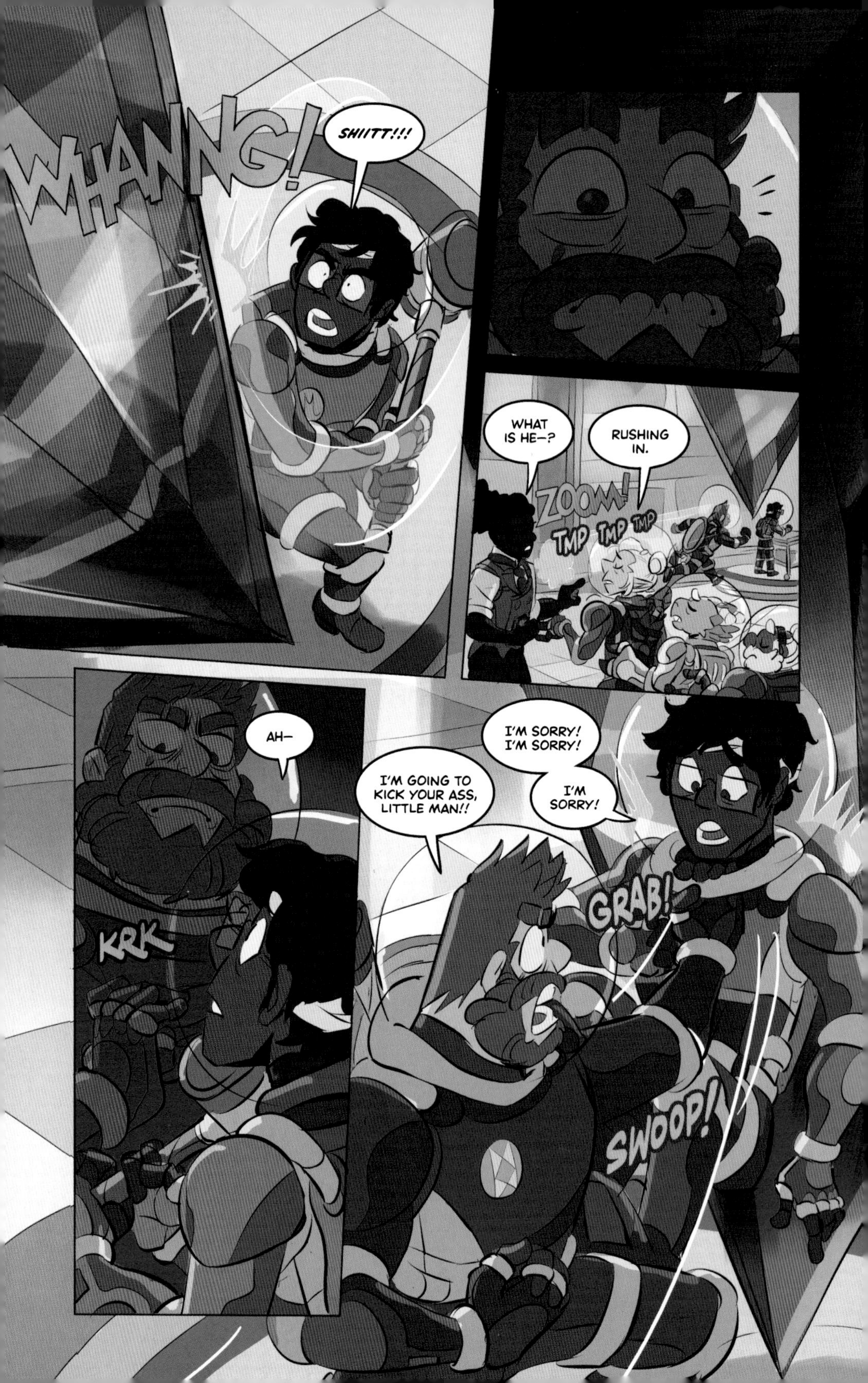
WHANNG!
SHIITT!!!
WHAT IS HE—?
RUSHING IN.
ZOOM!
TMP TMP TMP
AH—
I'M GOING TO KICK YOUR ASS, LITTLE MAN!!
I'M SORRY! I'M SORRY!
I'M SORRY!
KRK
GRAB!
SWOOP!

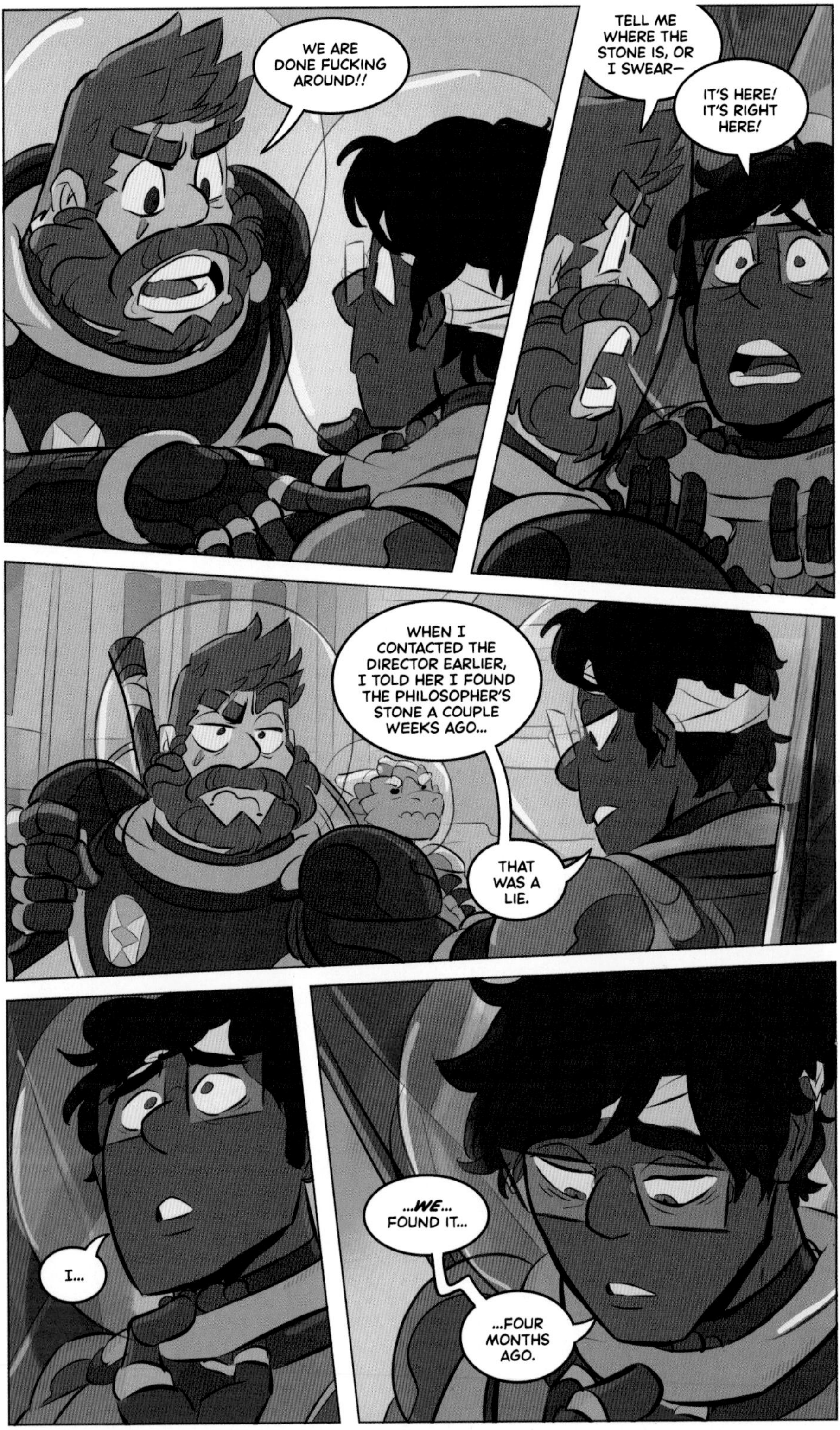
WE ARE DONE FUCKING AROUND!!
TELL ME WHERE THE STONE IS, OR I SWEAR—
IT'S HERE! IT'S RIGHT HERE!
WHEN I CONTACTED THE DIRECTOR EARLIER, I TOLD HER I FOUND THE PHILOSOPHER'S STONE A COUPLE WEEKS AGO...
THAT WAS A LIE.
I...
...*WE*... FOUND IT...
...FOUR MONTHS AGO.

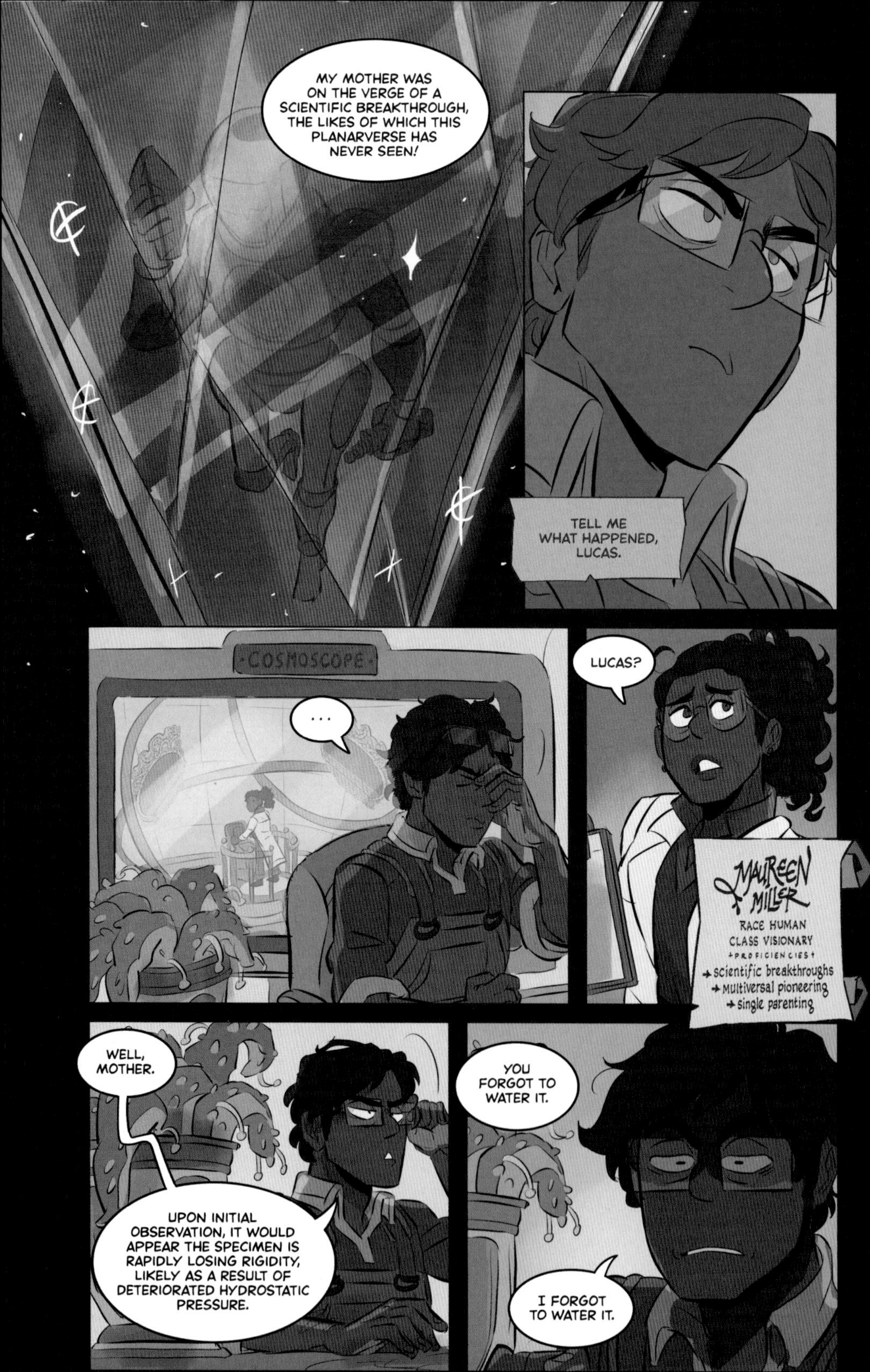
MY MOTHER WAS ON THE VERGE OF A SCIENTIFIC BREAKTHROUGH, THE LIKES OF WHICH THIS PLANARVERSE HAS NEVER SEEN!
TELL ME WHAT HAPPENED, LUCAS.
COSMOSCOPE
...
LUCAS?
MAUREEN MILLER
RACE HUMAN
CLASS VISIONARY
PROFICIENCIES
scientific breakthroughs
Multiversal pioneering
single parenting
WELL, MOTHER.
UPON INITIAL OBSERVATION, IT WOULD APPEAR THE SPECIMEN IS RAPIDLY LOSING RIGIDITY, LIKELY AS A RESULT OF DETERIORATED HYDROSTATIC PRESSURE.
YOU FORGOT TO WATER IT.
I FORGOT TO WATER IT.

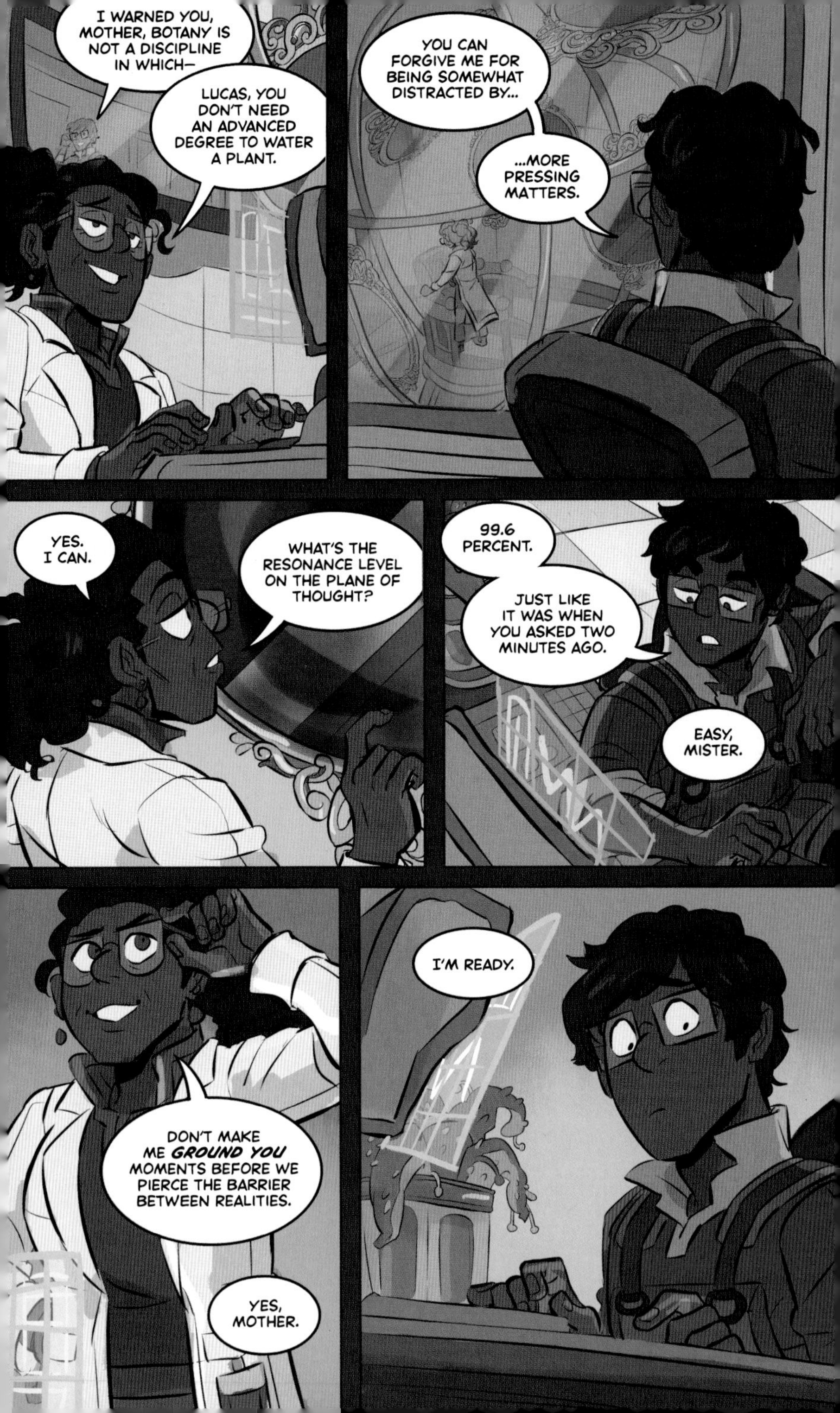
I WARNED YOU, MOTHER, BOTANY IS NOT A DISCIPLINE IN WHICH—
LUCAS, YOU DON'T NEED AN ADVANCED DEGREE TO WATER A PLANT.
YOU CAN FORGIVE ME FOR BEING SOMEWHAT DISTRACTED BY...
...MORE PRESSING MATTERS.
YES. I CAN.
WHAT'S THE RESONANCE LEVEL ON THE PLANE OF THOUGHT?
99.6 PERCENT.
JUST LIKE IT WAS WHEN YOU ASKED TWO MINUTES AGO.
EASY, MISTER.
DON'T MAKE ME ***GROUND YOU*** MOMENTS BEFORE WE PIERCE THE BARRIER BETWEEN REALITIES.
YES, MOTHER.
I'M READY.

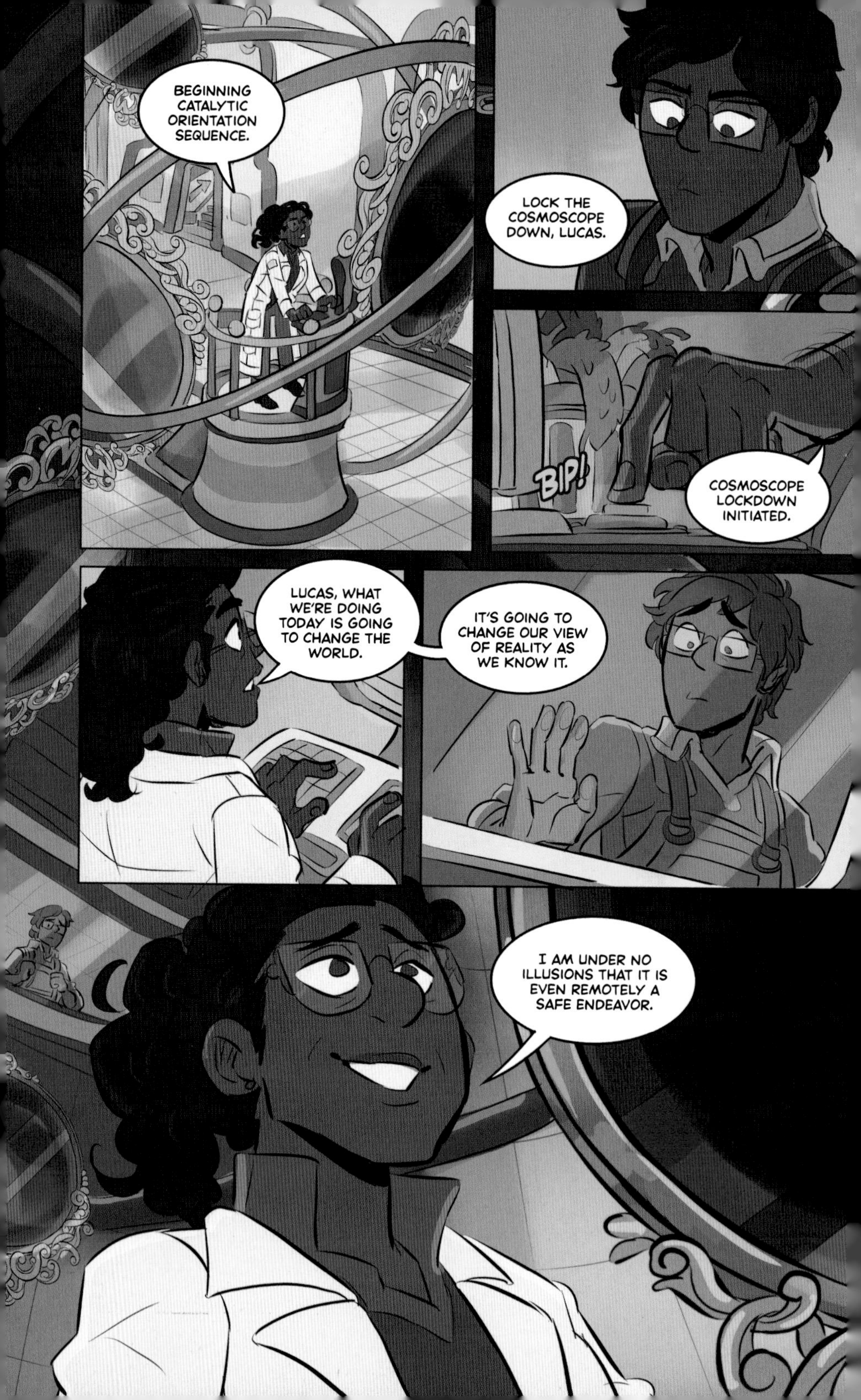
BEGINNING CATALYTIC ORIENTATION SEQUENCE.
LOCK THE COSMOSCOPE DOWN, LUCAS.
BIP!
COSMOSCOPE LOCKDOWN INITIATED.
LUCAS, WHAT WE'RE DOING TODAY IS GOING TO CHANGE THE WORLD.
IT'S GOING TO CHANGE OUR VIEW OF REALITY AS WE KNOW IT.
I AM UNDER NO ILLUSIONS THAT IT IS EVEN REMOTELY A SAFE ENDEAVOR.

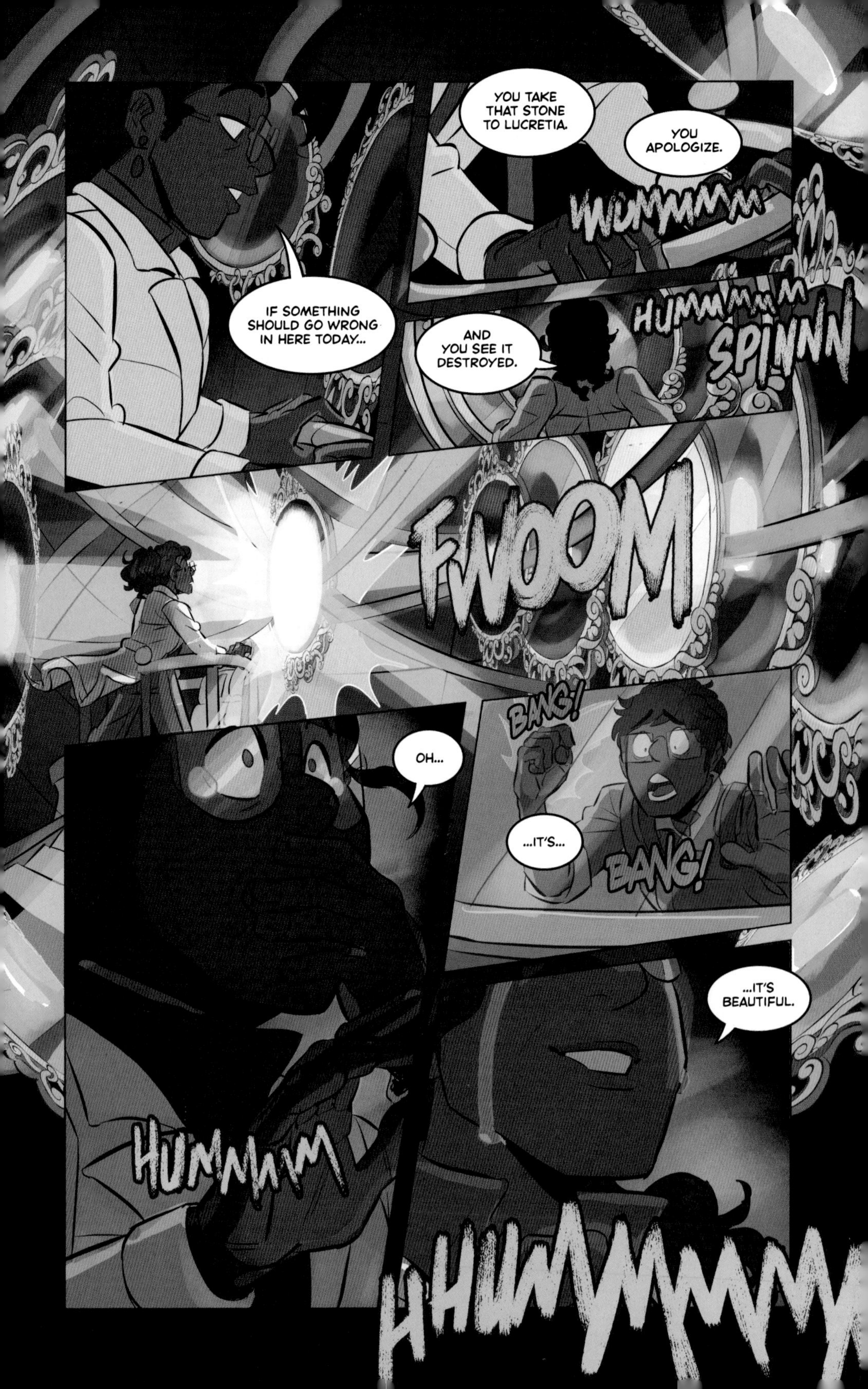
IF SOMETHING SHOULD GO WRONG IN HERE TODAY...
YOU TAKE THAT STONE TO LUCRETIA.
YOU APOLOGIZE.
WUMMMM
AND YOU SEE IT DESTROYED.
HUMMMMM
SPINNN
FWOOM
OH...
BANG!
...IT'S...
BANG!
...IT'S BEAUTIFUL.
HUMMM
HHUMMMMMM

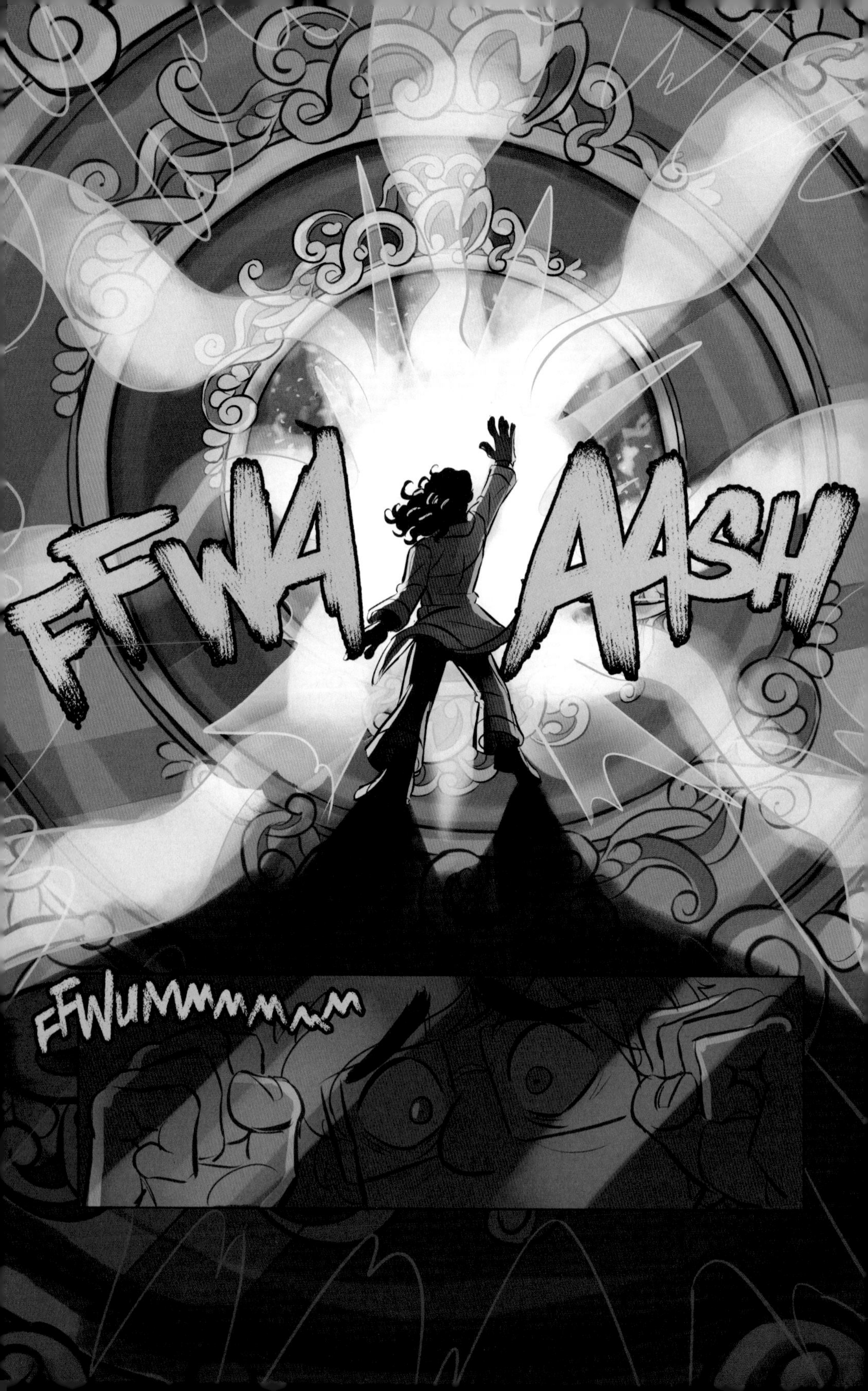
FFWAAASH
FFWUMMMMMM

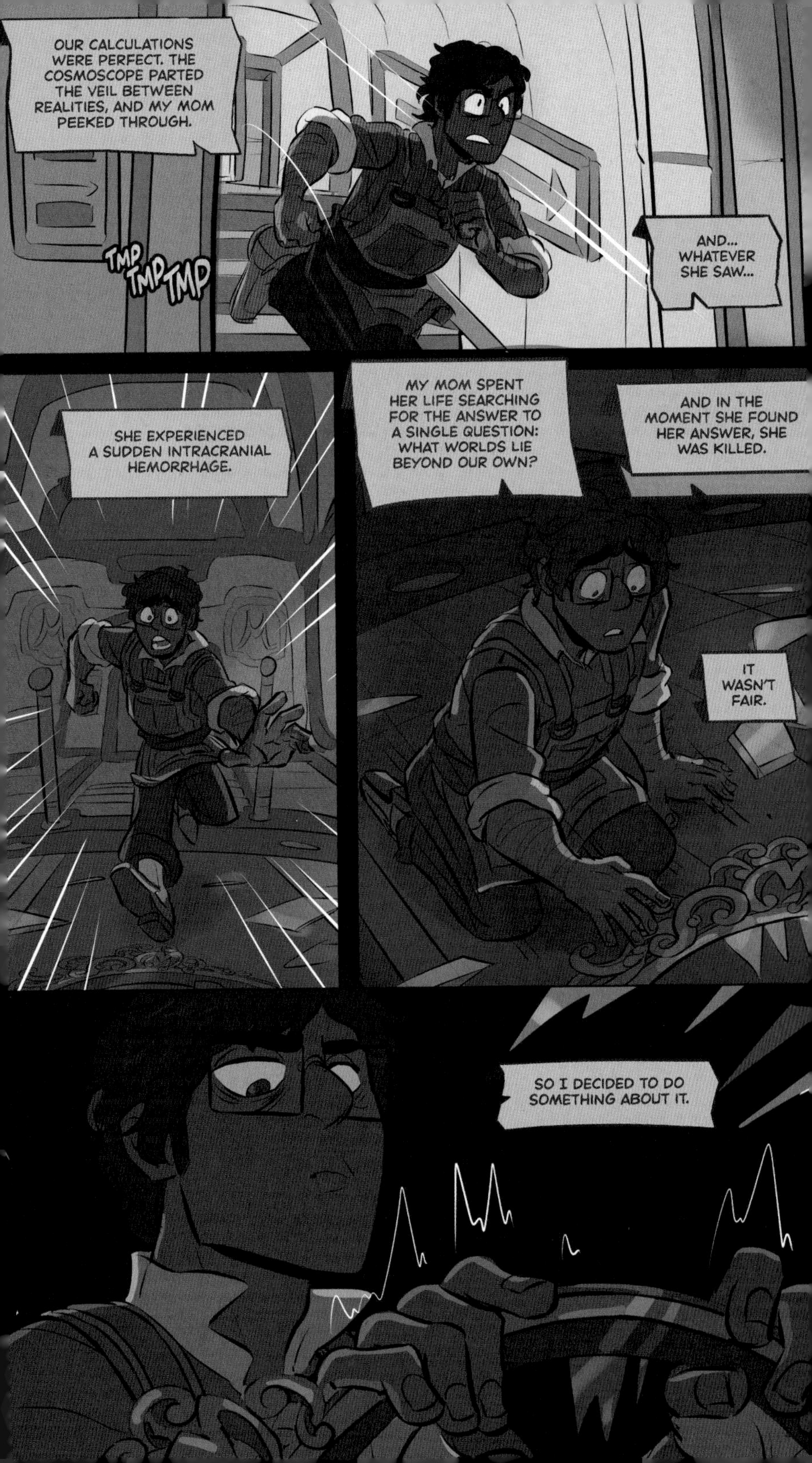
OUR CALCULATIONS WERE PERFECT. THE COSMOSCOPE PARTED THE VEIL BETWEEN REALITIES, AND MY MOM PEEKED THROUGH.
TMP TMP TMP
AND... WHATEVER SHE SAW...
SHE EXPERIENCED A SUDDEN INTRACRANIAL HEMORRHAGE.
MY MOM SPENT HER LIFE SEARCHING FOR THE ANSWER TO A SINGLE QUESTION: WHAT WORLDS LIE BEYOND OUR OWN?
AND IN THE MOMENT SHE FOUND HER ANSWER, SHE WAS KILLED.
IT WASN'T FAIR.
SO I DECIDED TO DO SOMETHING ABOUT IT.

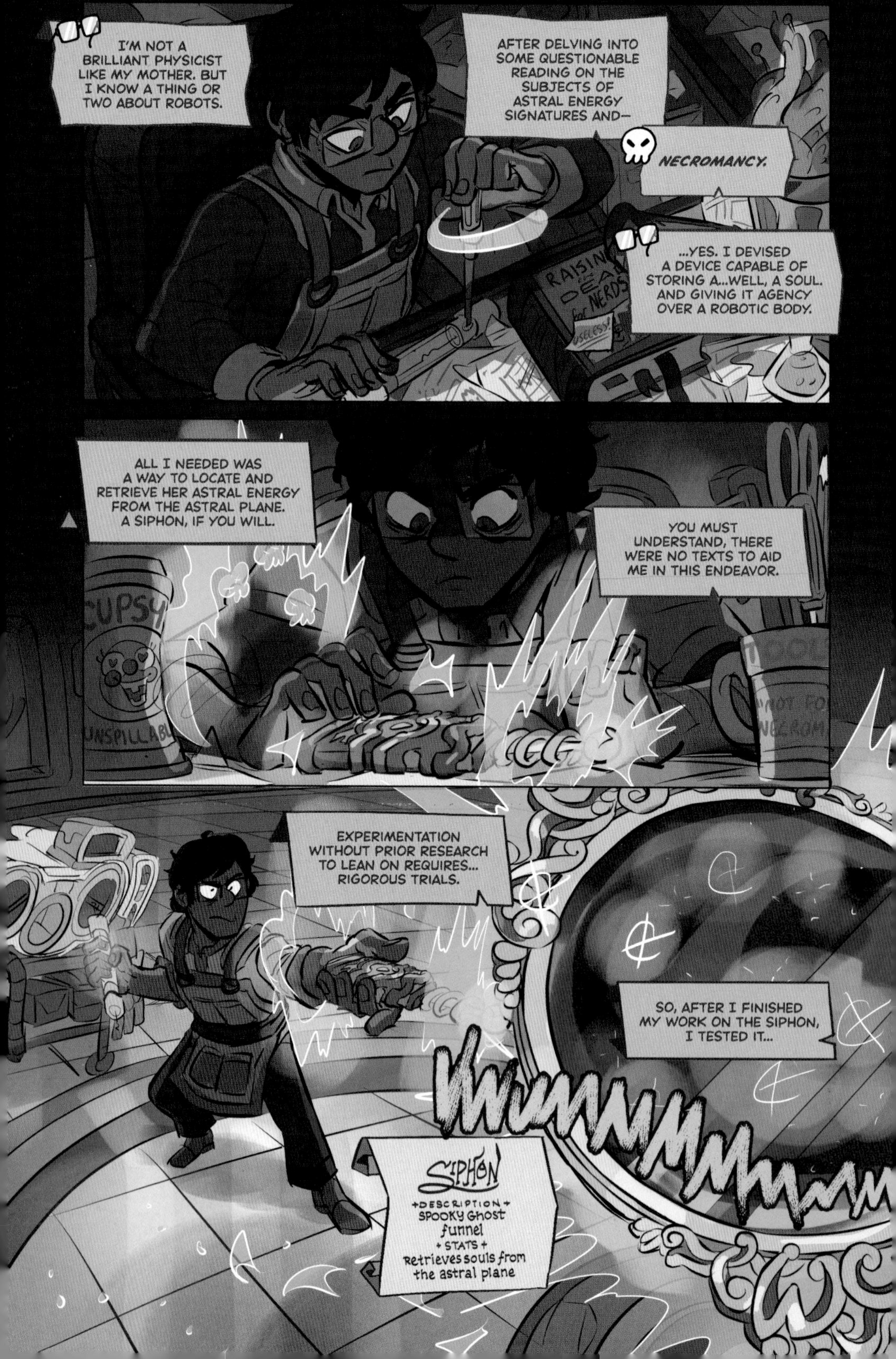
I'M NOT A BRILLIANT PHYSICIST LIKE MY MOTHER. BUT I KNOW A THING OR TWO ABOUT ROBOTS.
AFTER DELVING INTO SOME QUESTIONABLE READING ON THE SUBJECTS OF ASTRAL ENERGY SIGNATURES AND—
NECROMANCY.
...YES. I DEVISED A DEVICE CAPABLE OF STORING A...WELL, A SOUL. AND GIVING IT AGENCY OVER A ROBOTIC BODY.
USELESS!
ALL I NEEDED WAS A WAY TO LOCATE AND RETRIEVE HER ASTRAL ENERGY FROM THE ASTRAL PLANE. A SIPHON, IF YOU WILL.
YOU MUST UNDERSTAND, THERE WERE NO TEXTS TO AID ME IN THIS ENDEAVOR.
EXPERIMENTATION WITHOUT PRIOR RESEARCH TO LEAN ON REQUIRES... RIGOROUS TRIALS.
SO, AFTER I FINISHED MY WORK ON THE SIPHON, I TESTED IT...
VMMMMMMMMMM
SIPHON
DESCRIPTION
Spooky Ghost funnel
STATS
Retrieves souls from the astral plane

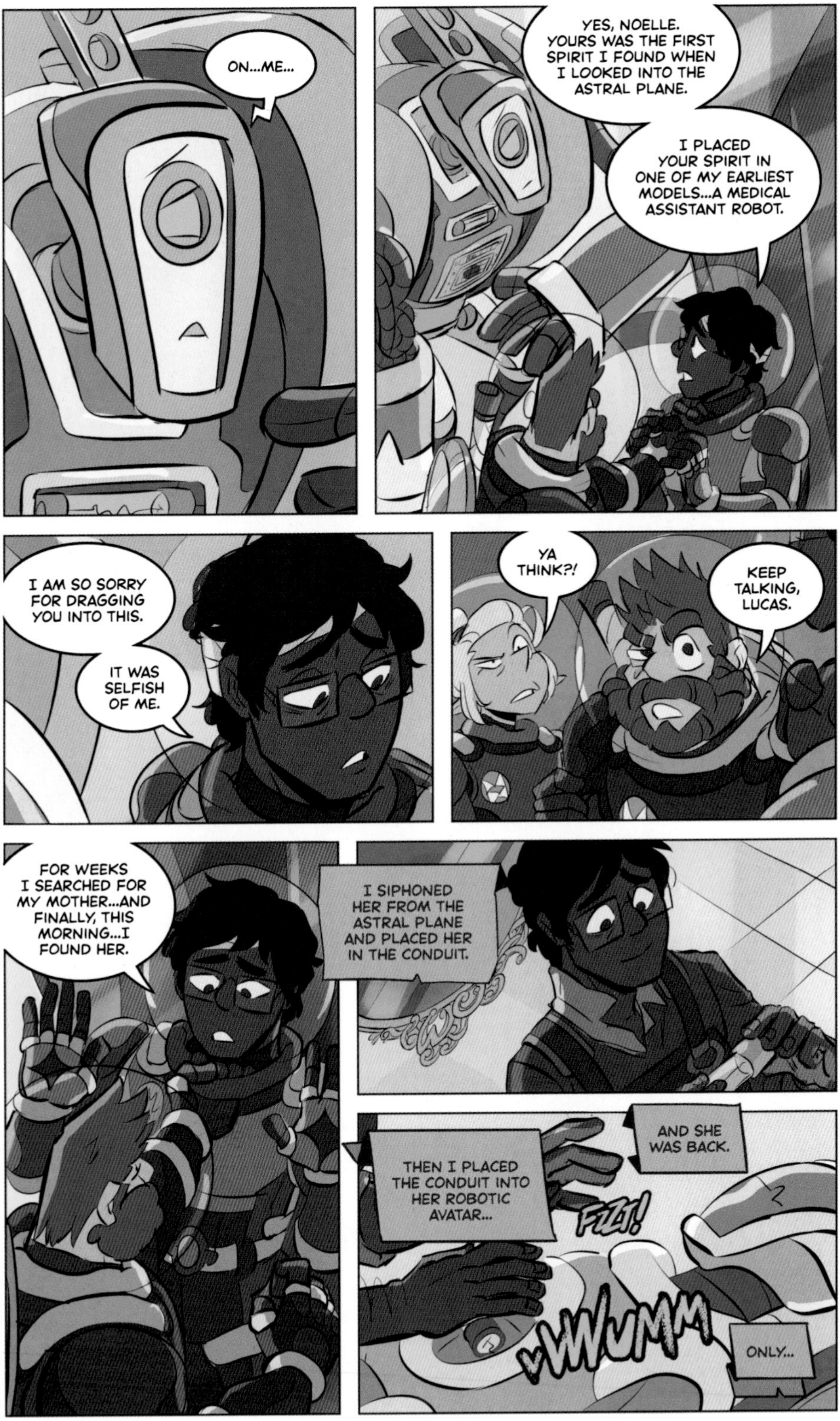
ON...ME...
YES, NOELLE. YOURS WAS THE FIRST SPIRIT I FOUND WHEN I LOOKED INTO THE ASTRAL PLANE.
I PLACED YOUR SPIRIT IN ONE OF MY EARLIEST MODELS...A MEDICAL ASSISTANT ROBOT.
I AM SO SORRY FOR DRAGGING YOU INTO THIS.
IT WAS SELFISH OF ME.
YA THINK?!
KEEP TALKING, LUCAS.
FOR WEEKS I SEARCHED FOR MY MOTHER...AND FINALLY, THIS MORNING...I FOUND HER.
I SIPHONED HER FROM THE ASTRAL PLANE AND PLACED HER IN THE CONDUIT.
THEN I PLACED THE CONDUIT INTO HER ROBOTIC AVATAR...
AND SHE WAS BACK.
FZZT!
VWUMM
ONLY...

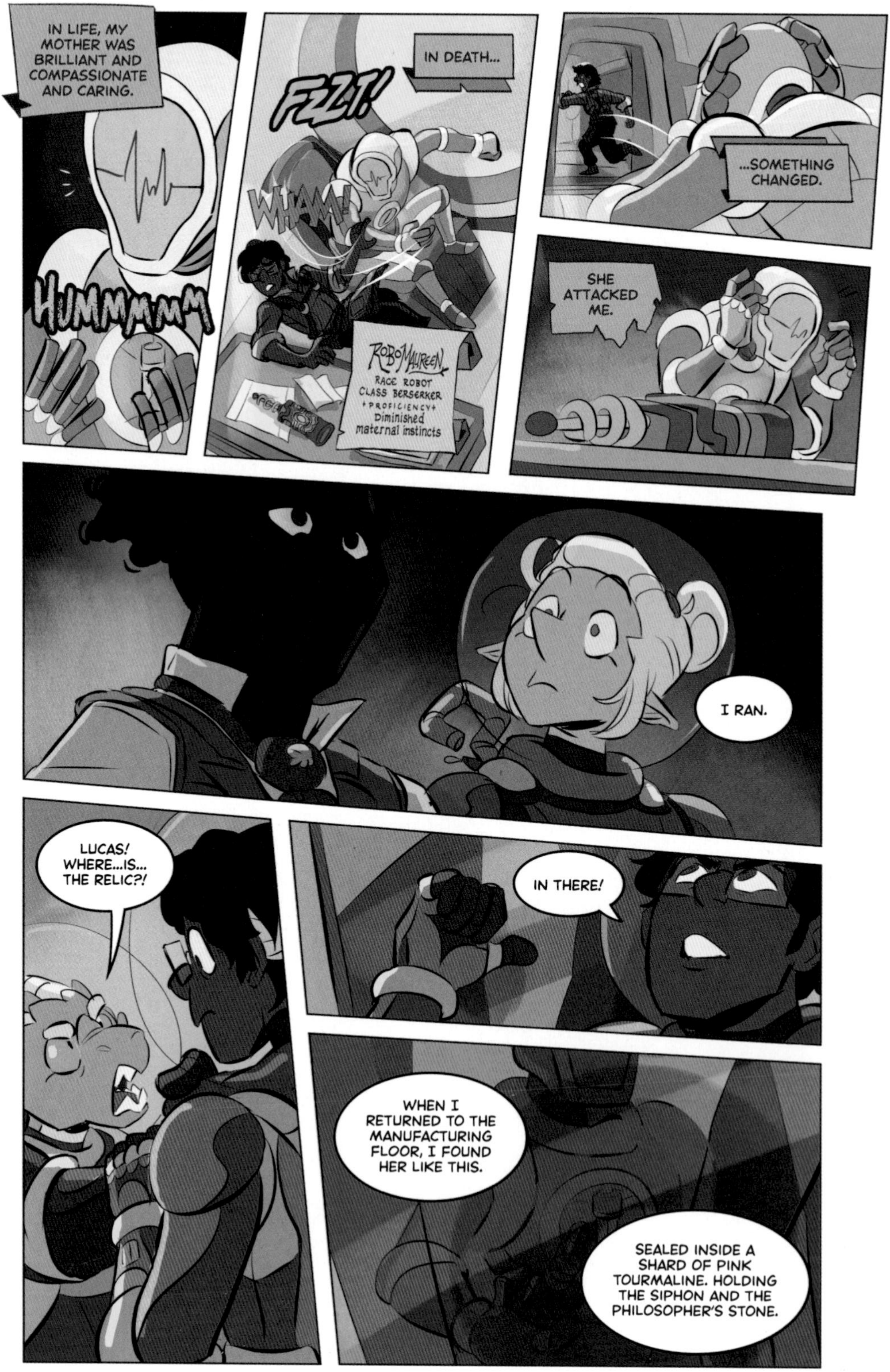
IN LIFE, MY MOTHER WAS BRILLIANT AND COMPASSIONATE AND CARING.
HUMMMMM
IN DEATH...
FZZT!
WHAM!
ROBOMAUREEN
RACE ROBOT
CLASS BERSERKER
PROFICIENCY
Diminished maternal instincts
...SOMETHING CHANGED.
SHE ATTACKED ME.
I RAN.
LUCAS! WHERE...IS... THE RELIC?!
IN THERE!
WHEN I RETURNED TO THE MANUFACTURING FLOOR, I FOUND HER LIKE THIS.
SEALED INSIDE A SHARD OF PINK TOURMALINE. HOLDING THE SIPHON AND THE PHILOSOPHER'S STONE.

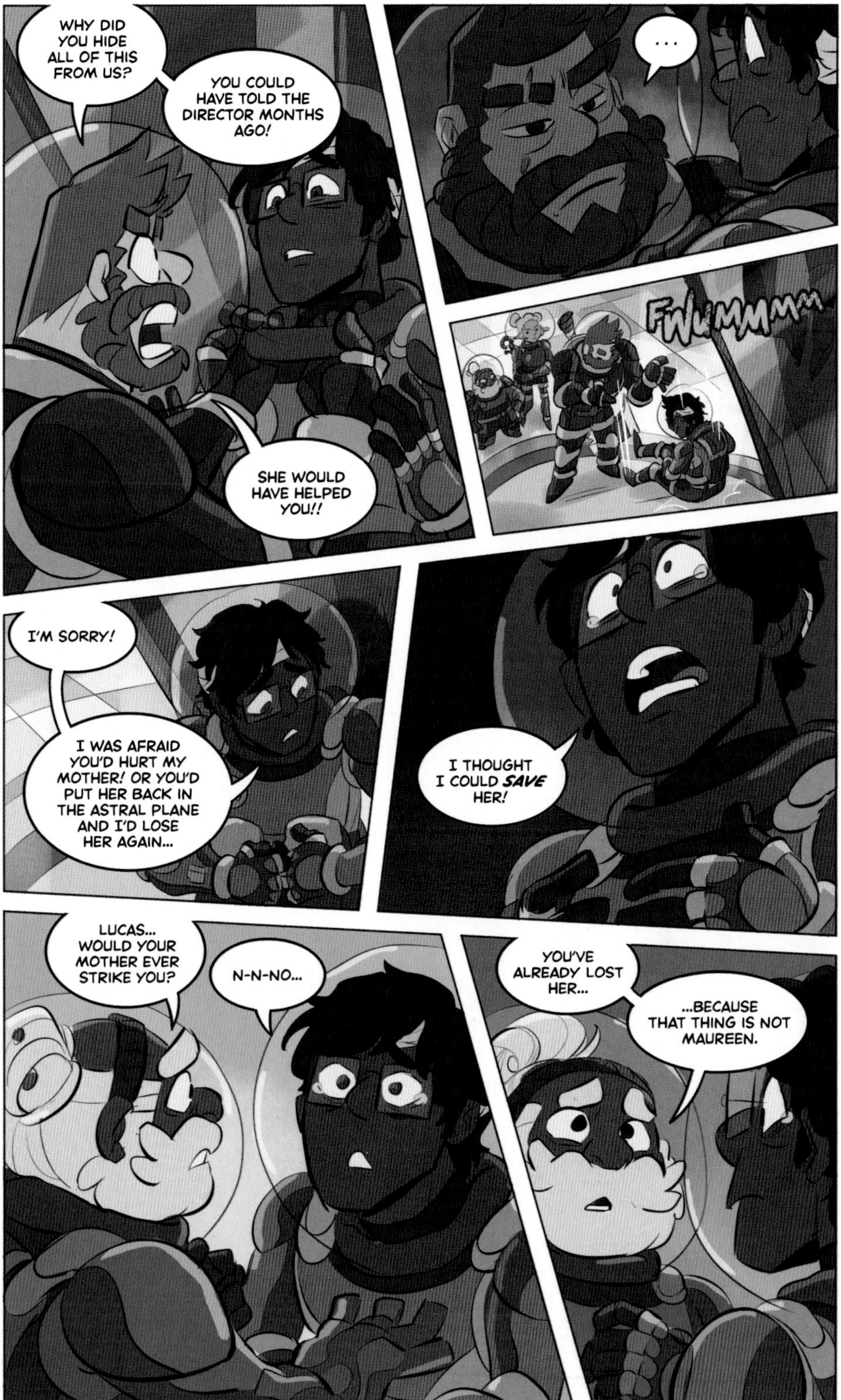
WHY DID YOU HIDE ALL OF THIS FROM US?
YOU COULD HAVE TOLD THE DIRECTOR MONTHS AGO!
SHE WOULD HAVE HELPED YOU!!
...
FWUMMMM
I'M SORRY!
I WAS AFRAID YOU'D HURT MY MOTHER! OR YOU'D PUT HER BACK IN THE ASTRAL PLANE AND I'D LOSE HER AGAIN...
I THOUGHT I COULD SAVE HER!
LUCAS... WOULD YOUR MOTHER EVER STRIKE YOU?
N-N-NO...
YOU'VE ALREADY LOST HER...
...BECAUSE THAT THING IS NOT MAUREEN.

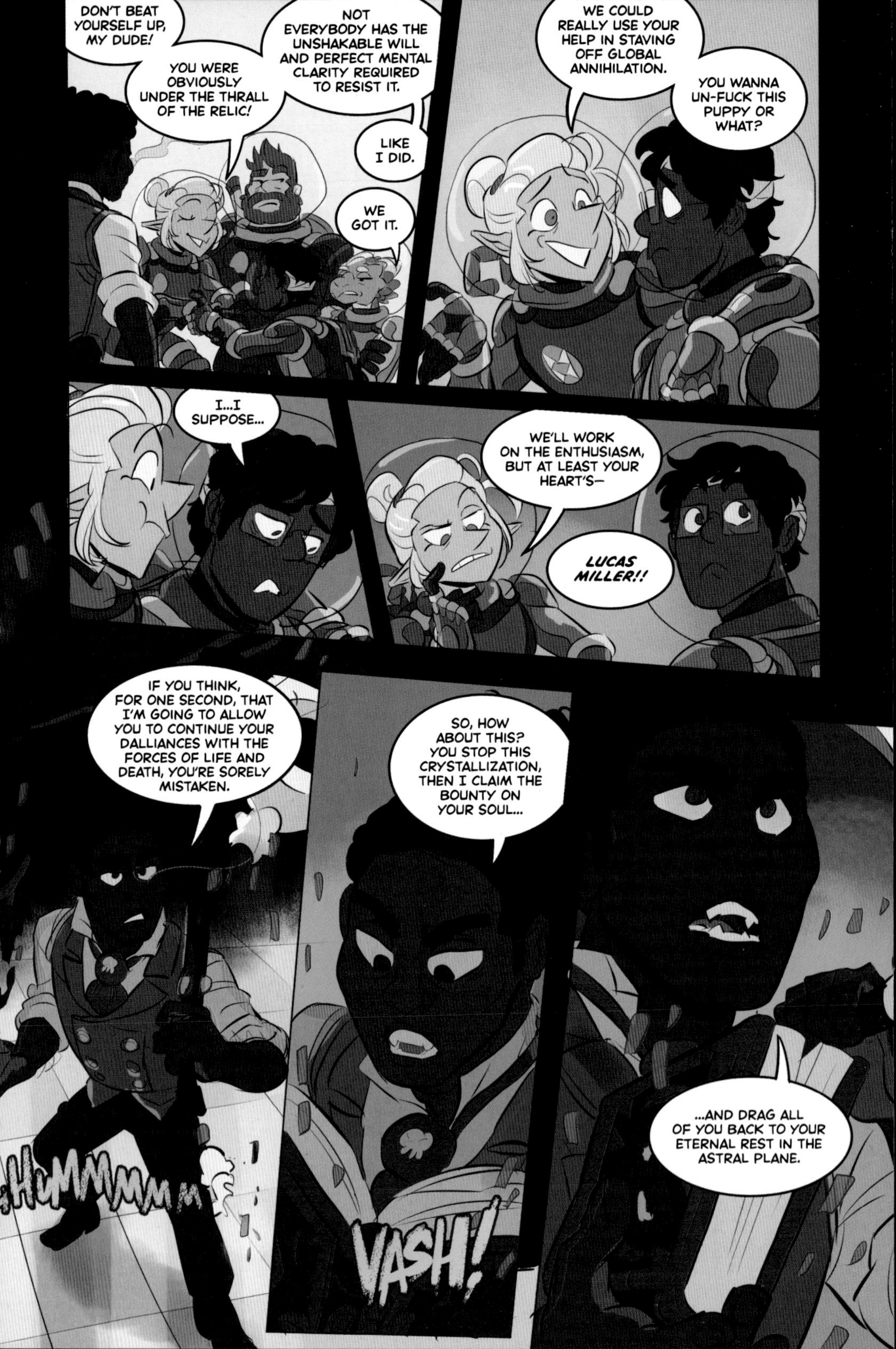
DON'T BEAT YOURSELF UP, MY DUDE!
YOU WERE OBVIOUSLY UNDER THE THRALL OF THE RELIC!
NOT EVERYBODY HAS THE UNSHAKABLE WILL AND PERFECT MENTAL CLARITY REQUIRED TO RESIST IT.
LIKE I DID.
WE GOT IT.
WE COULD REALLY USE YOUR HELP IN STAVING OFF GLOBAL ANNIHILATION.
YOU WANNA UN-FUCK THIS PUPPY OR WHAT?
I...I SUPPOSE...
WE'LL WORK ON THE ENTHUSIASM, BUT AT LEAST YOUR HEART'S—
LUCAS MILLER!!
IF YOU THINK, FOR ONE SECOND, THAT I'M GOING TO ALLOW YOU TO CONTINUE YOUR DALLIANCES WITH THE FORCES OF LIFE AND DEATH, YOU'RE SORELY MISTAKEN.
HUMMMMMM
SO, HOW ABOUT THIS? YOU STOP THIS CRYSTALLIZATION, THEN I CLAIM THE BOUNTY ON YOUR SOUL...
VASH!
...AND DRAG ALL OF YOU BACK TO YOUR ETERNAL REST IN THE ASTRAL PLANE.

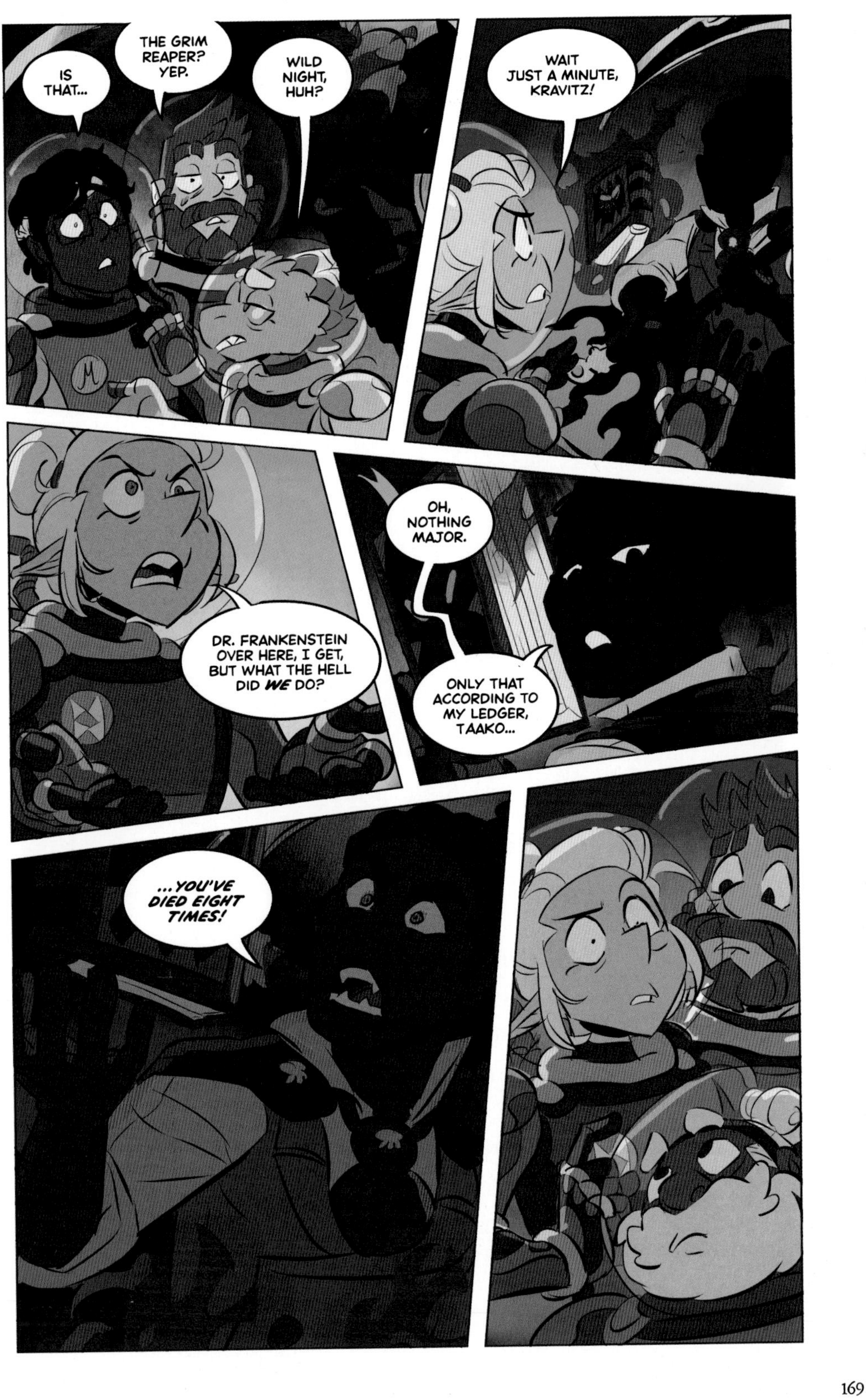
IS THAT...
THE GRIM REAPER? YEP.
WILD NIGHT, HUH?
WAIT JUST A MINUTE, KRAVITZ!
DR. FRANKENSTEIN OVER HERE, I GET, BUT WHAT THE HELL DID *WE* DO?
OH, NOTHING MAJOR.
ONLY THAT ACCORDING TO MY LEDGER, TAAKO...
...YOU'VE DIED EIGHT TIMES!

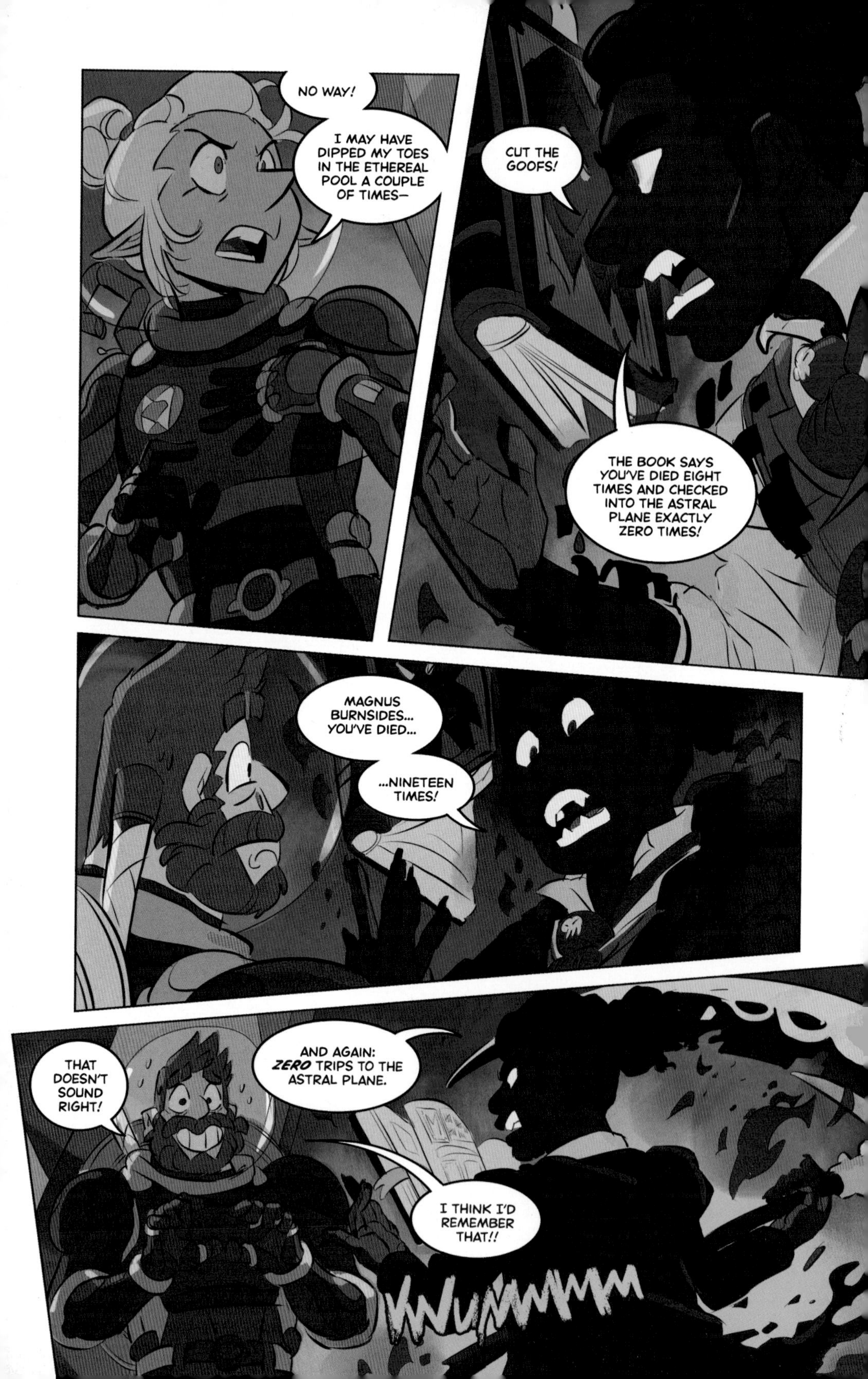
NO WAY!
I MAY HAVE DIPPED MY TOES IN THE ETHEREAL POOL A COUPLE OF TIMES—
CUT THE GOOFS!
THE BOOK SAYS YOU'VE DIED EIGHT TIMES AND CHECKED INTO THE ASTRAL PLANE EXACTLY ZERO TIMES!
MAGNUS BURNSIDES... YOU'VE DIED...
...NINETEEN TIMES!
THAT DOESN'T SOUND RIGHT!
AND AGAIN: **ZERO** TRIPS TO THE ASTRAL PLANE.
I THINK I'D REMEMBER THAT!!
WUMMMM

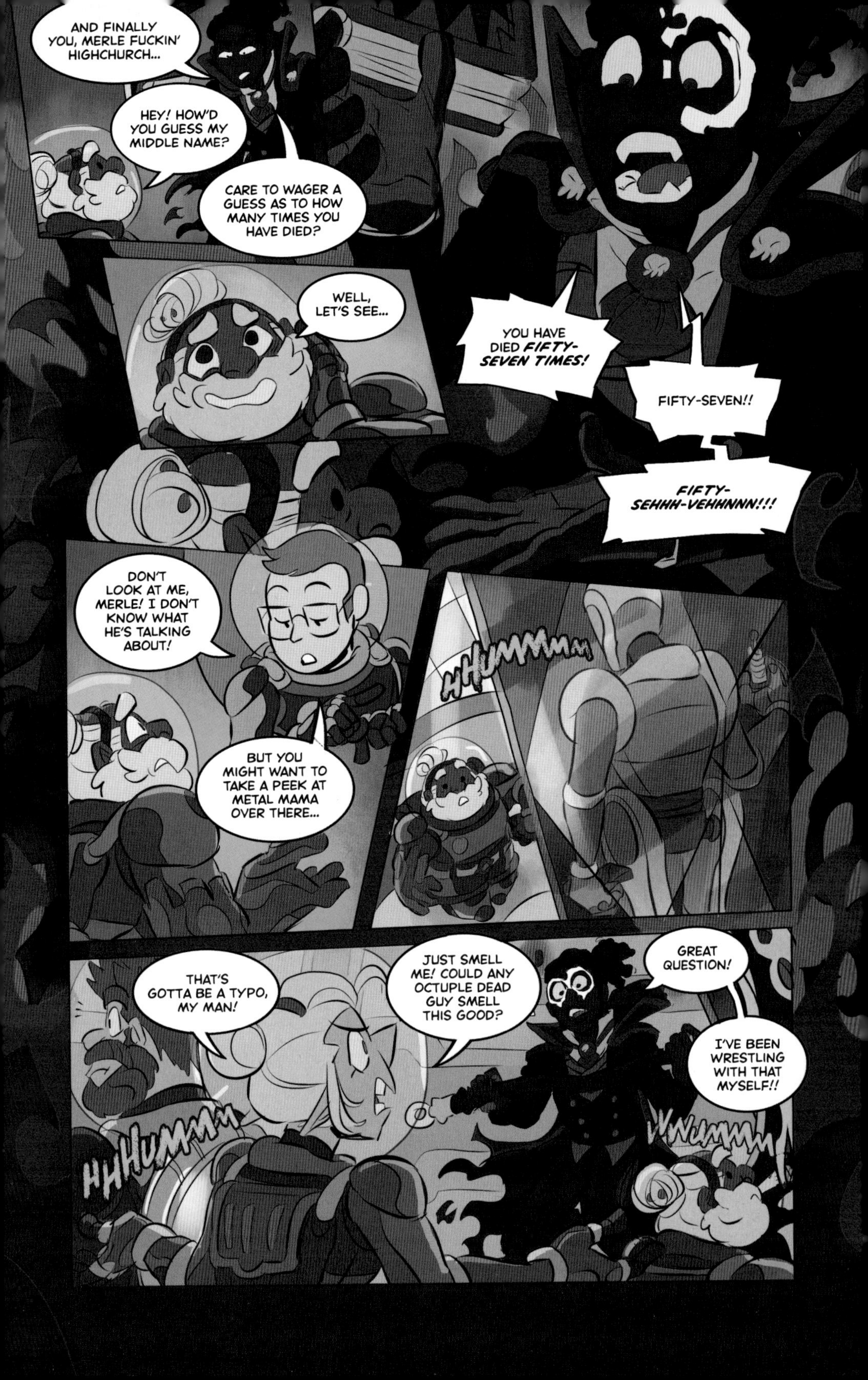
AND FINALLY YOU, MERLE FUCKIN' HIGHCHURCH...
HEY! HOW'D YOU GUESS MY MIDDLE NAME?
CARE TO WAGER A GUESS AS TO HOW MANY TIMES YOU HAVE DIED?
WELL, LET'S SEE...
YOU HAVE DIED FIFTY-SEVEN TIMES!
FIFTY-SEVEN!!
FIFTY-SEHHH-VEHHNNN!!!
DON'T LOOK AT ME, MERLE! I DON'T KNOW WHAT HE'S TALKING ABOUT!
BUT YOU MIGHT WANT TO TAKE A PEEK AT METAL MAMA OVER THERE...
HHUMMMM
THAT'S GOTTA BE A TYPO, MY MAN!
JUST SMELL ME! COULD ANY OCTUPLE DEAD GUY SMELL THIS GOOD?
GREAT QUESTION!
I'VE BEEN WRESTLING WITH THAT MYSELF!!
HHHUMMM
VWUMMMM

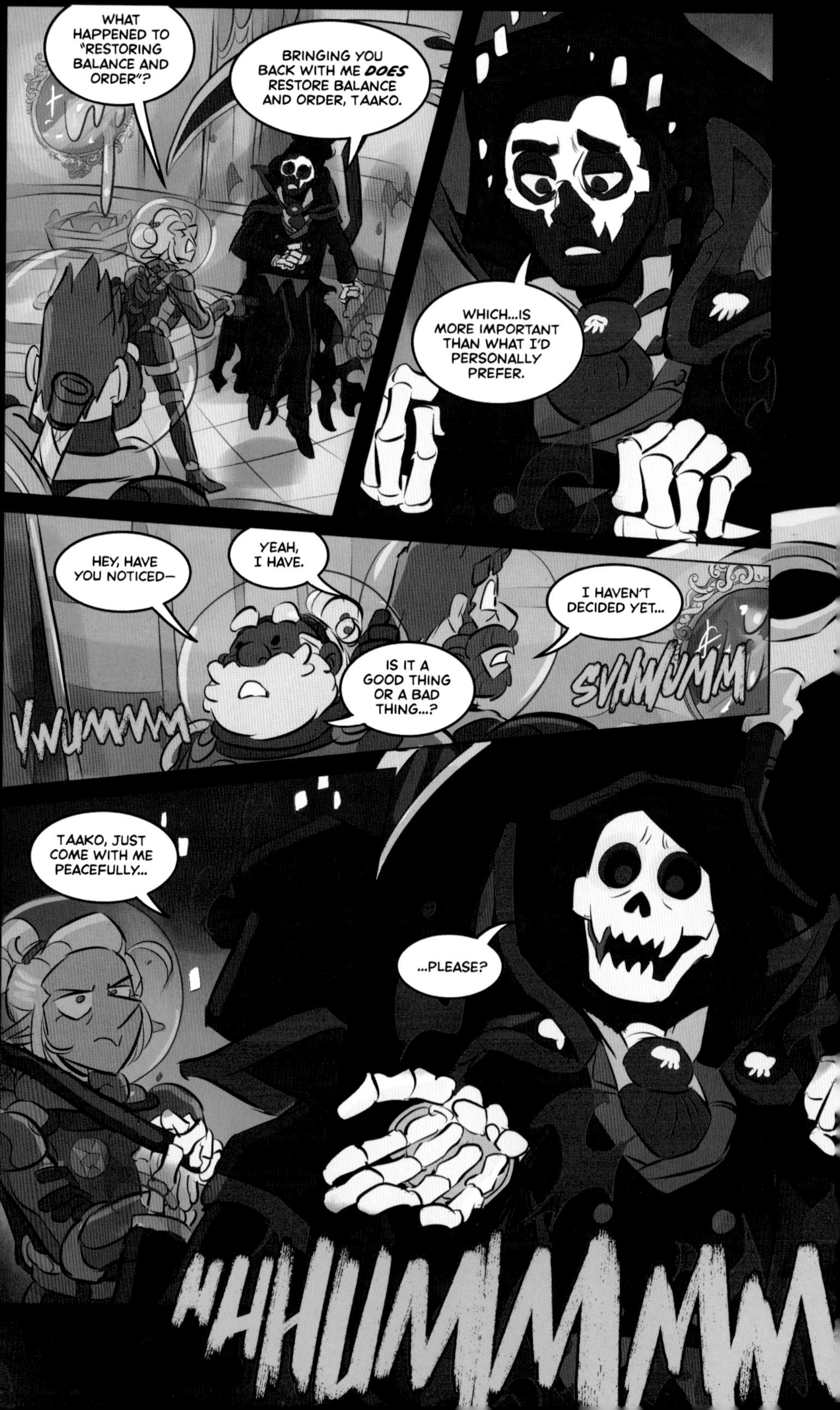
WHAT HAPPENED TO "RESTORING BALANCE AND ORDER"?
BRINGING YOU BACK WITH ME *DOES* RESTORE BALANCE AND ORDER, TAAKO.
WHICH...IS MORE IMPORTANT THAN WHAT I'D PERSONALLY PREFER.
HEY, HAVE YOU NOTICED—
YEAH, I HAVE.
I HAVEN'T DECIDED YET...
IS IT A GOOD THING OR A BAD THING...?
SVHWUMM
VWUMMM
TAAKO, JUST COME WITH ME PEACEFULLY...
...PLEASE?
HHUMMMMM

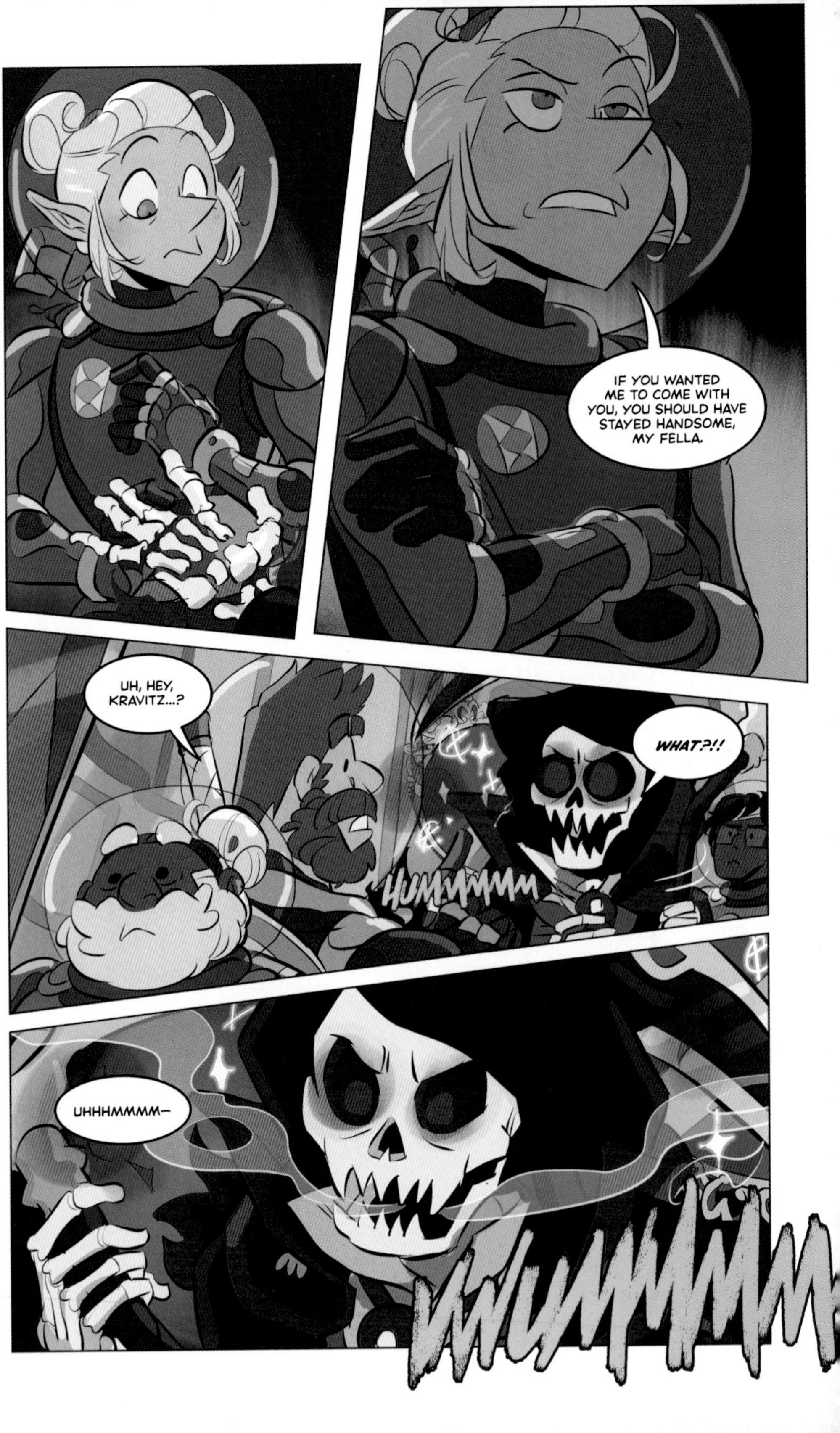
IF YOU WANTED ME TO COME WITH YOU, YOU SHOULD HAVE STAYED HANDSOME, MY FELLA.
UH, HEY, KRAVITZ...?
WHAT?!!
HUMMMMM
UHHHMMMM—
WUMMMM

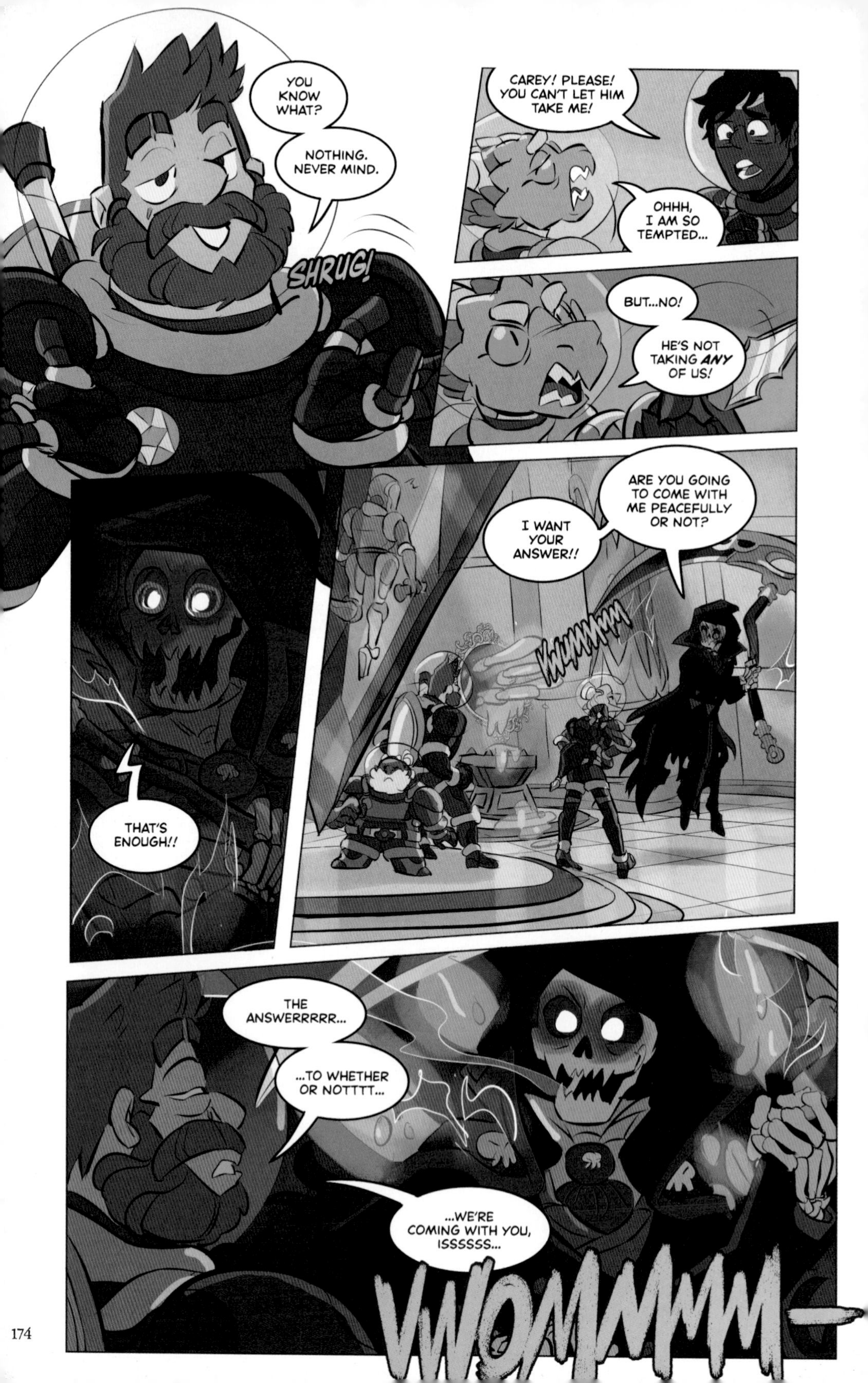
YOU KNOW WHAT?
NOTHING. NEVER MIND.
SHRUG!
CAREY! PLEASE! YOU CAN'T LET HIM TAKE ME!
OHHH, I AM SO TEMPTED...
BUT...NO!
HE'S NOT TAKING ***ANY*** OF US!
THAT'S ENOUGH!!
I WANT YOUR ANSWER!!
ARE YOU GOING TO COME WITH ME PEACEFULLY OR NOT?
VWUMMMM
THE ANSWERRRRR...
...TO WHETHER OR NOTTTT...
...WE'RE COMING WITH YOU, ISSSSSS...
VWOMMMM-

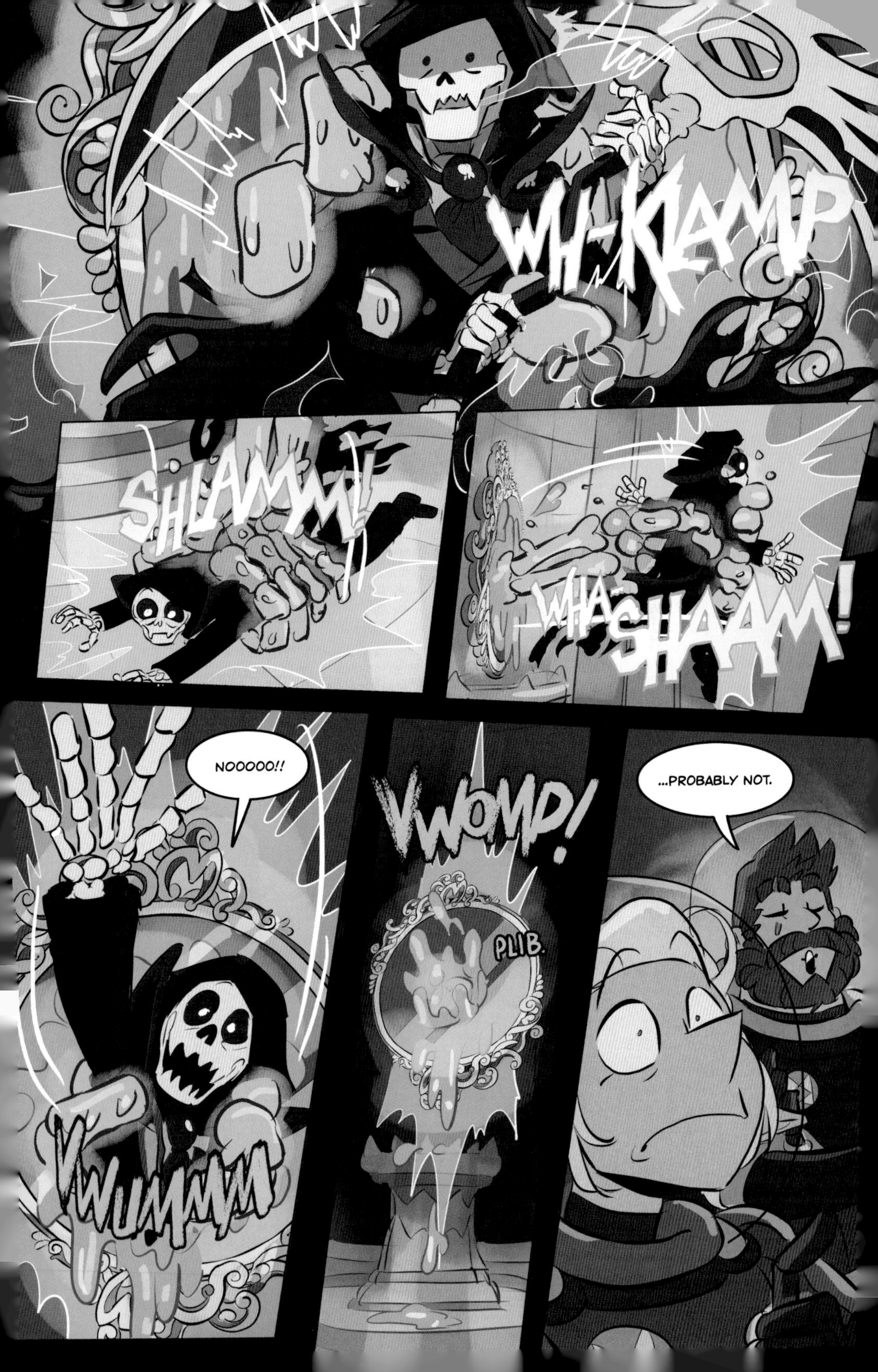
WH-KLAMP
SHLAMM!
WHA-SHAAM!
NOOOOO!!
VWUMMM
VWOMP!
PLIB.
...PROBABLY NOT.

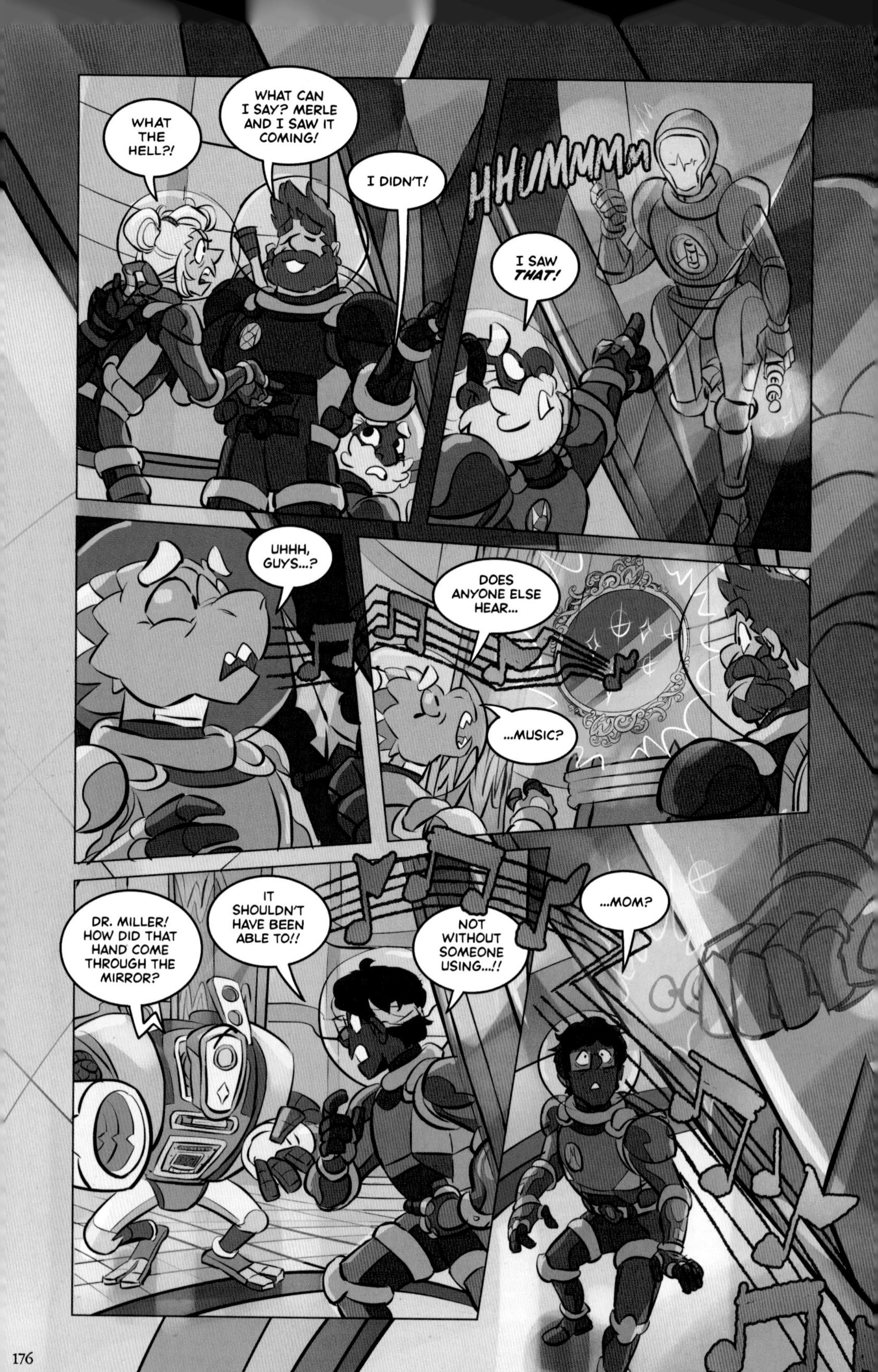
WHAT THE HELL?!
WHAT CAN I SAY? MERLE AND I SAW IT COMING!
I DIDN'T!
HHUMMMm
I SAW THAT!
UHHH, GUYS...?
DOES ANYONE ELSE HEAR...
...MUSIC?
DR. MILLER! HOW DID THAT HAND COME THROUGH THE MIRROR?
IT SHOULDN'T HAVE BEEN ABLE TO!!
NOT WITHOUT SOMEONE USING...!!
...MOM?

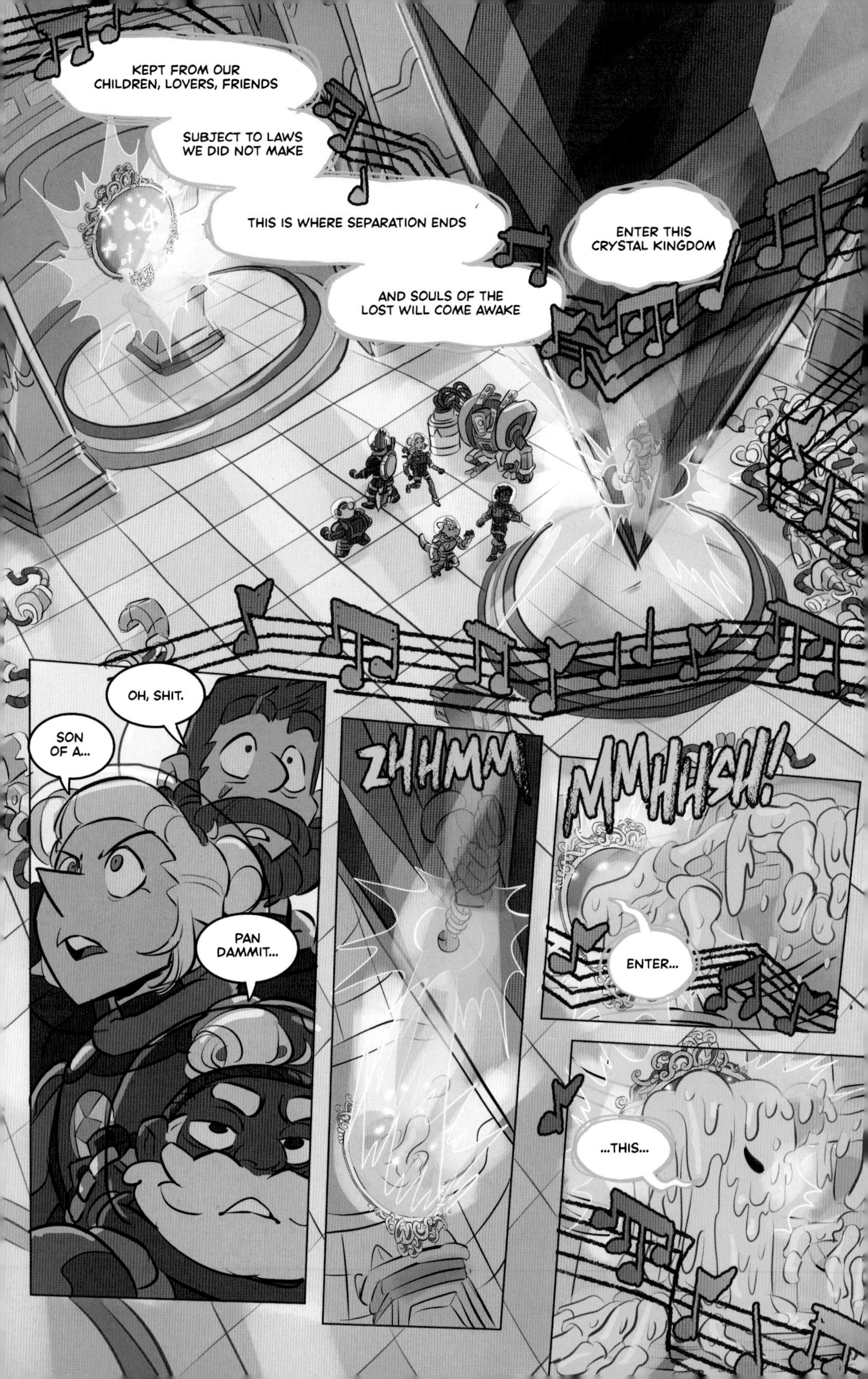
KEPT FROM OUR CHILDREN, LOVERS, FRIENDS
SUBJECT TO LAWS WE DID NOT MAKE
THIS IS WHERE SEPARATION ENDS
ENTER THIS CRYSTAL KINGDOM
AND SOULS OF THE LOST WILL COME AWAKE
OH, SHIT.
SON OF A...
PAN DAMMIT...
ZHHMM
MMHHSH!
ENTER...
...THIS...

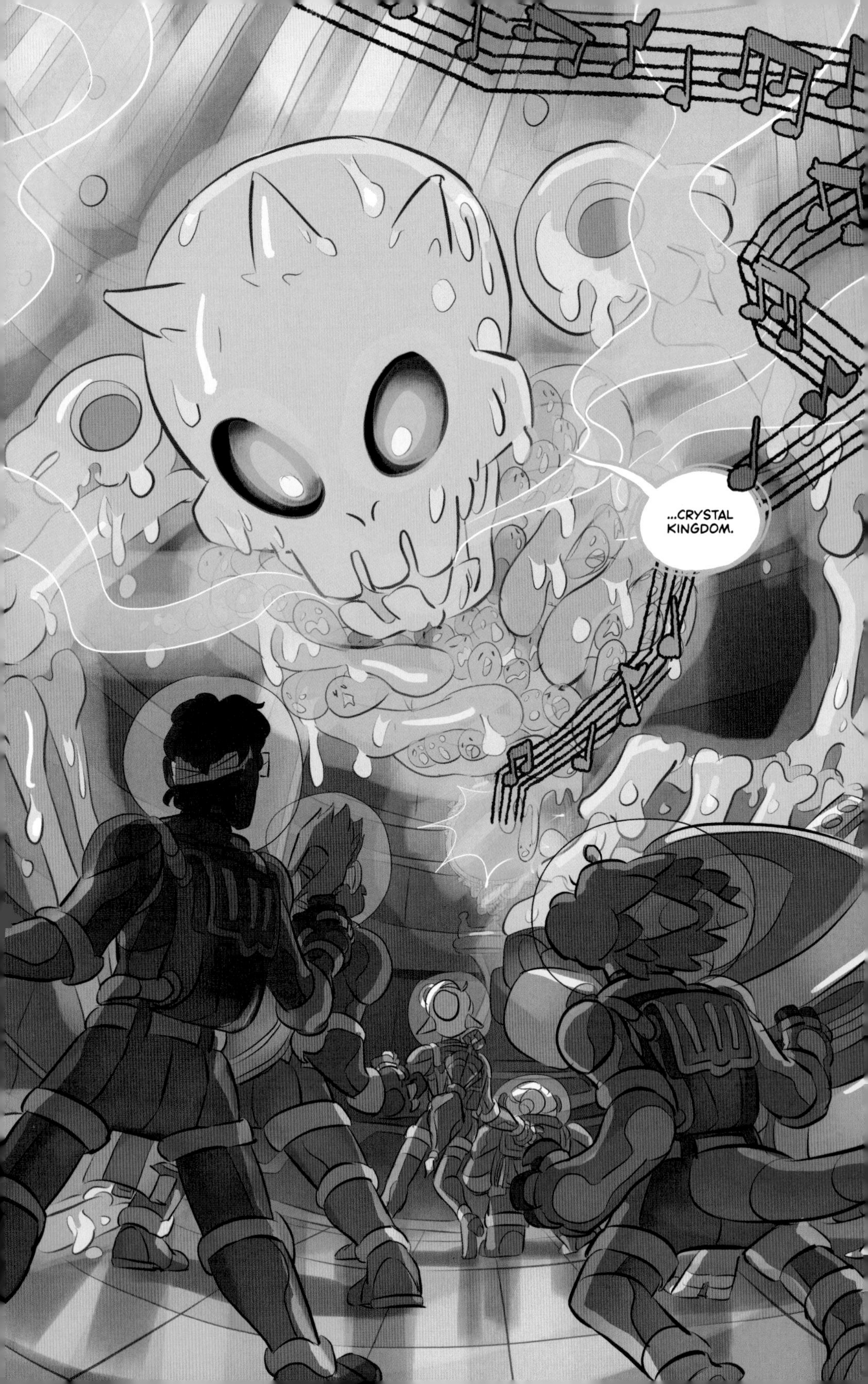
...CRYSTAL KINGDOM.

Chapter
8

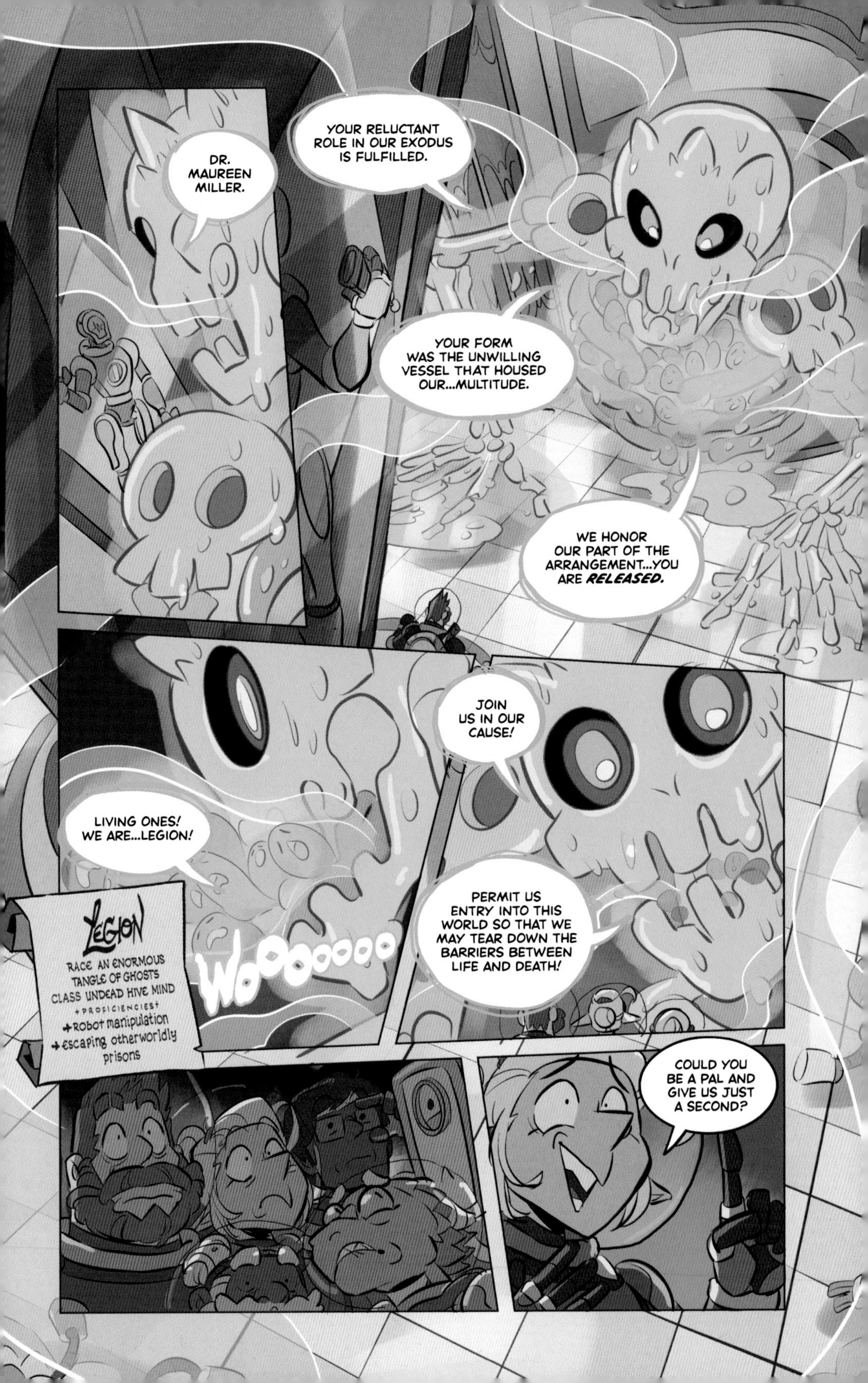

DR. MAUREEN MILLER.
YOUR RELUCTANT ROLE IN OUR EXODUS IS FULFILLED.
YOUR FORM WAS THE UNWILLING VESSEL THAT HOUSED OUR...MULTITUDE.
WE HONOR OUR PART OF THE ARRANGEMENT...YOU ARE *RELEASED.*
LIVING ONES! WE ARE...LEGION!
JOIN US IN OUR CAUSE!
LEGION
RACE AN ENORMOUS TANGLE OF GHOSTS
CLASS UNDEAD HIVE MIND
PROFICIENCIES
Robot manipulation
escaping otherworldly prisons
WOOOOOOO
PERMIT US ENTRY INTO THIS WORLD SO THAT WE MAY TEAR DOWN THE BARRIERS BETWEEN LIFE AND DEATH!
COULD YOU BE A PAL AND GIVE US JUST A SECOND?

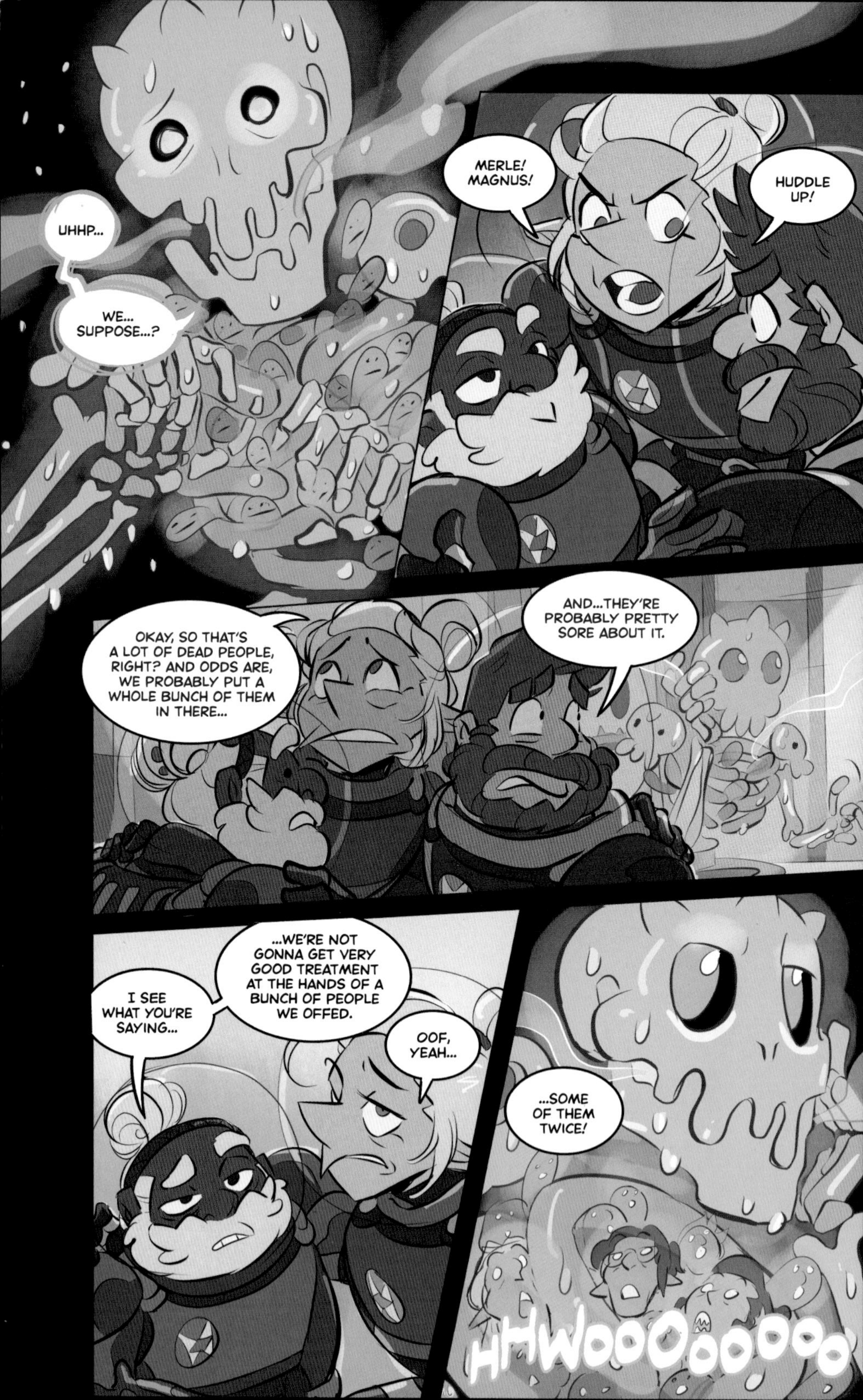
UHHP...
WE... SUPPOSE...?
MERLE! MAGNUS!
HUDDLE UP!
OKAY, SO THAT'S A LOT OF DEAD PEOPLE, RIGHT? AND ODDS ARE, WE PROBABLY PUT A WHOLE BUNCH OF THEM IN THERE...
AND...THEY'RE PROBABLY PRETTY SORE ABOUT IT.
I SEE WHAT YOU'RE SAYING...
...WE'RE NOT GONNA GET VERY GOOD TREATMENT AT THE HANDS OF A BUNCH OF PEOPLE WE OFFED.
OOF, YEAH...
...SOME OF THEM TWICE!
HHWOOOOOOOOO

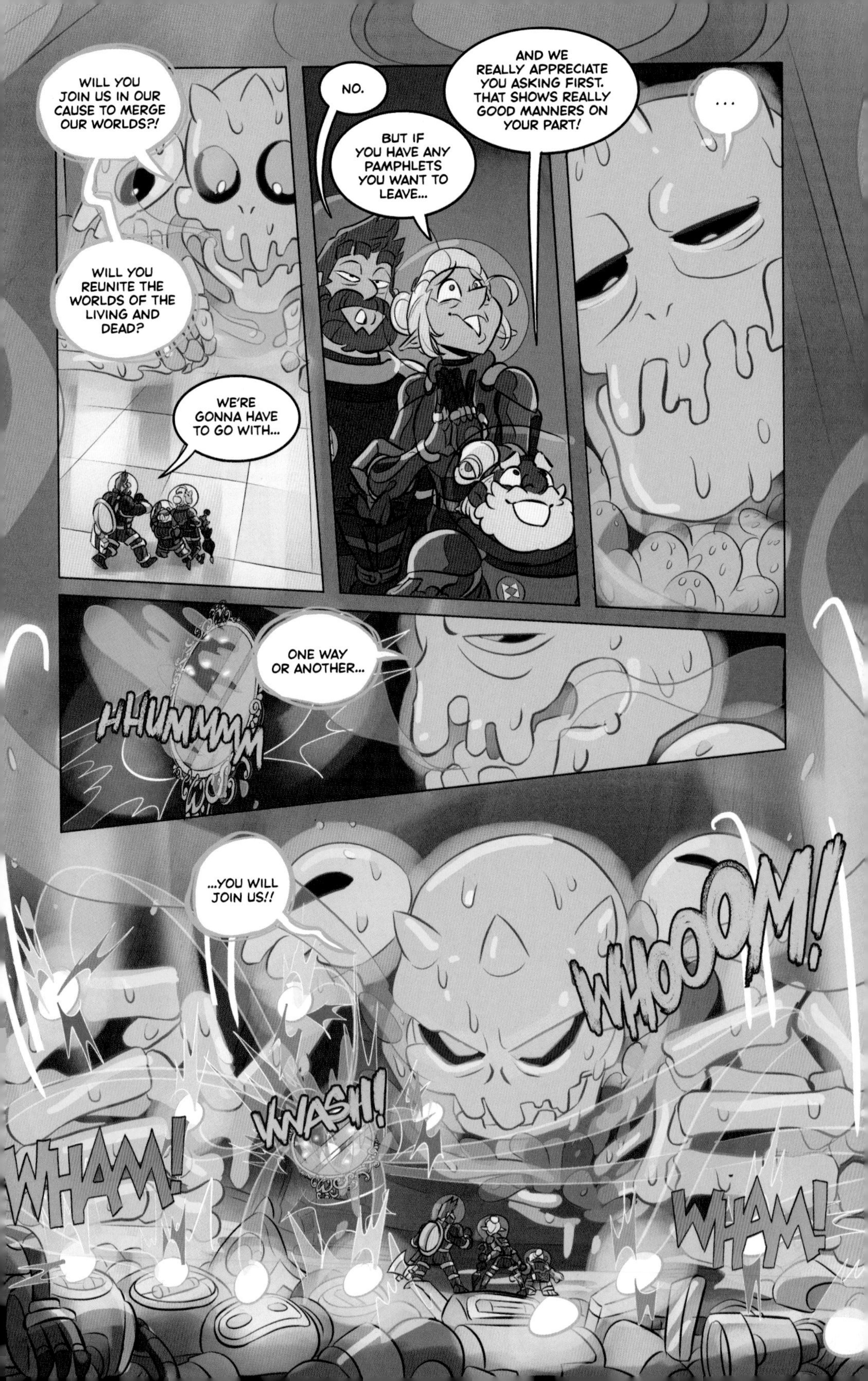
WILL YOU JOIN US IN OUR CAUSE TO MERGE OUR WORLDS?!
WILL YOU REUNITE THE WORLDS OF THE LIVING AND DEAD?
WE'RE GONNA HAVE TO GO WITH...
NO.
BUT IF YOU HAVE ANY PAMPHLETS YOU WANT TO LEAVE...
AND WE REALLY APPRECIATE YOU ASKING FIRST. THAT SHOWS REALLY GOOD MANNERS ON YOUR PART!
...
ONE WAY OR ANOTHER...
HUMMMM
...YOU WILL JOIN US!!
WHOOOOM!
WHAM!
WASH!
WHAM!

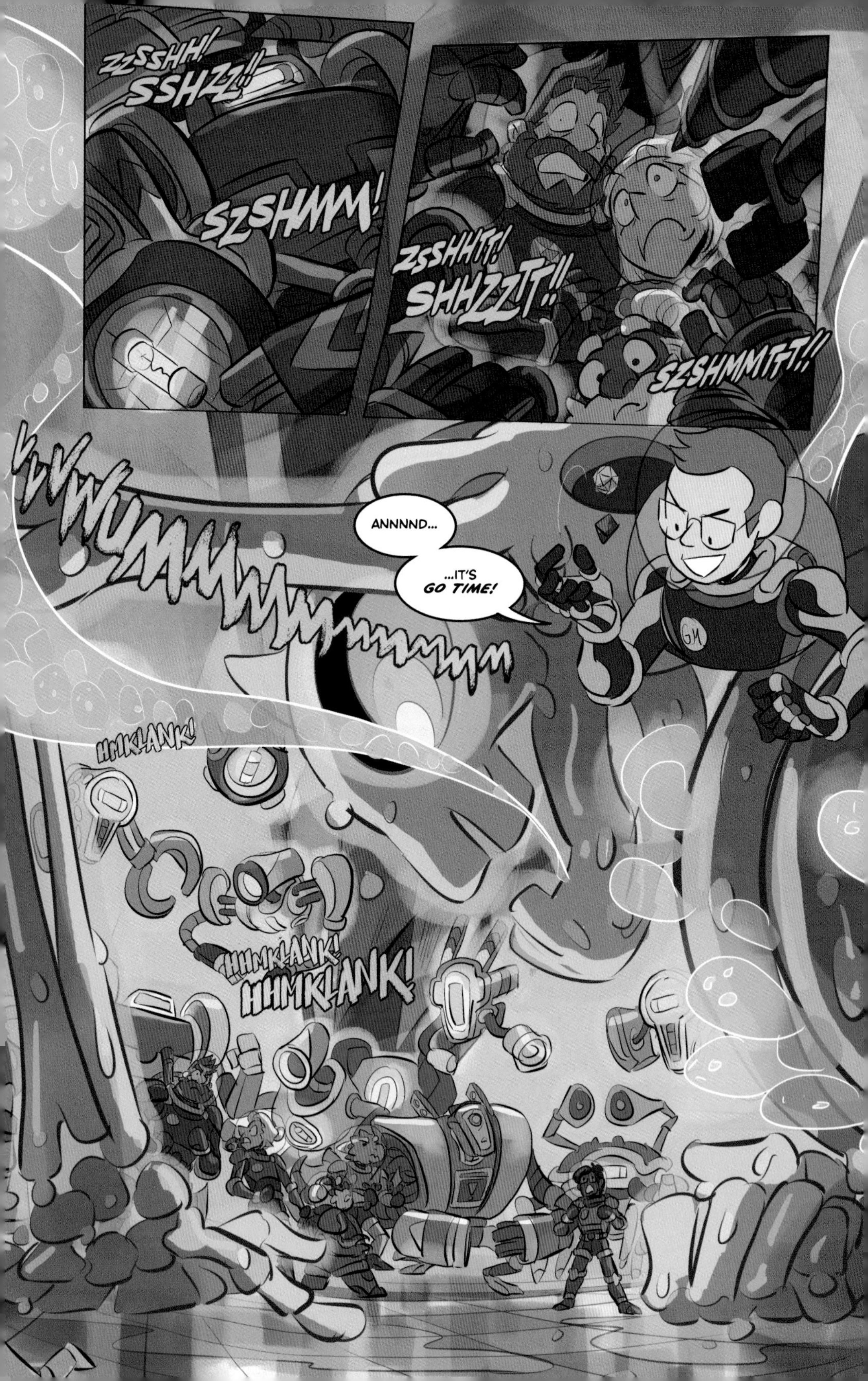
ZZSSHH!
SSHZZ!!
SZSHMM!
ZSSHHTT!
SHHZZTT!!
SZSHMMTTT!!
VVVWUMMMMMMMMMMM
ANNND...
...IT'S GO TIME!
HHMKLANK!
HHMKLANK!
HHMKLANK!

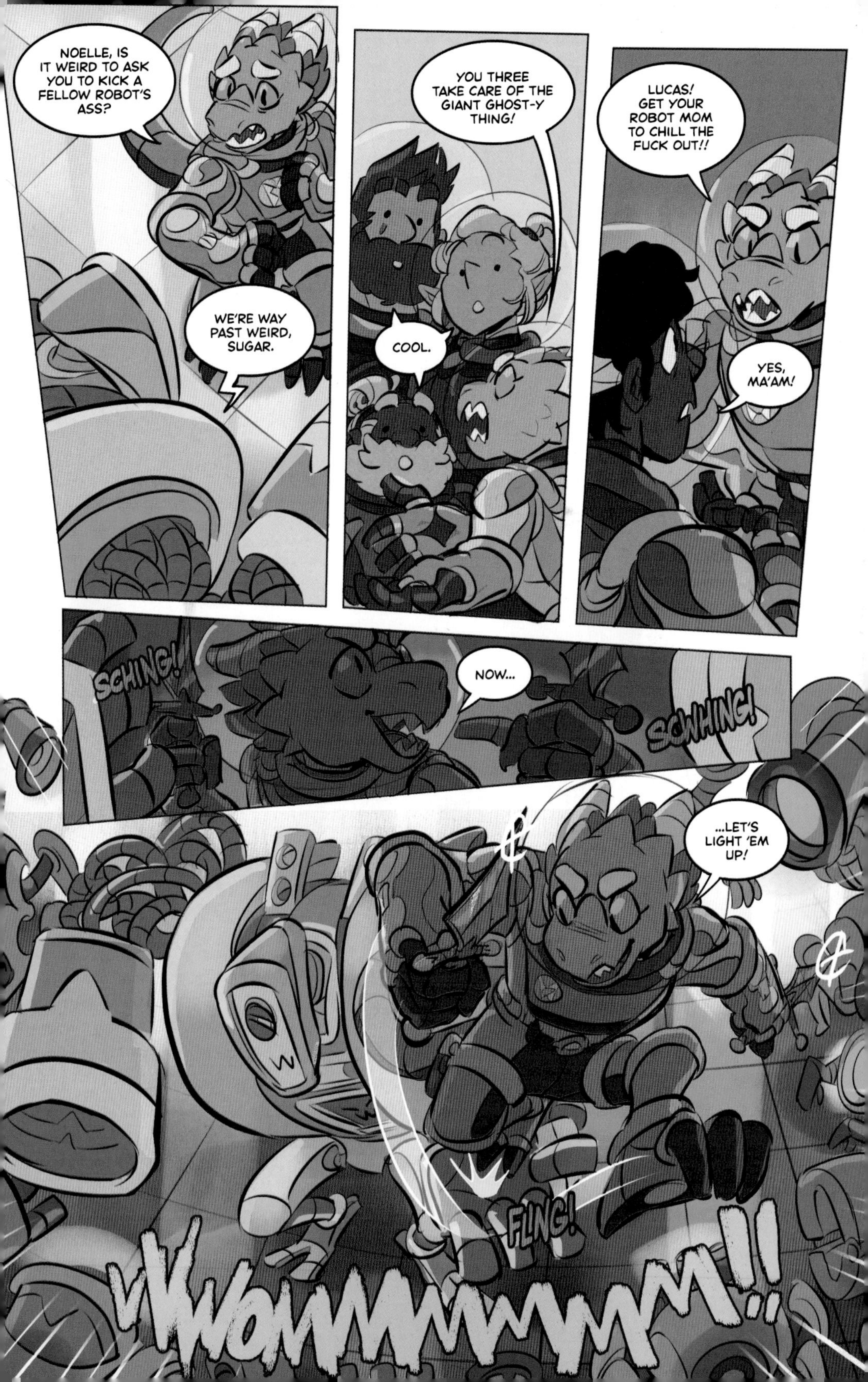
NOELLE, IS IT WEIRD TO ASK YOU TO KICK A FELLOW ROBOT'S ASS?
WE'RE WAY PAST WEIRD, SUGAR.
YOU THREE TAKE CARE OF THE GIANT GHOST-Y THING!
COOL.
LUCAS! GET YOUR ROBOT MOM TO CHILL THE FUCK OUT!!
YES, MA'AM!
SCHING!
NOW...
SCWHING!
...LET'S LIGHT 'EM UP!
FLING!
VWOMMMMM!!

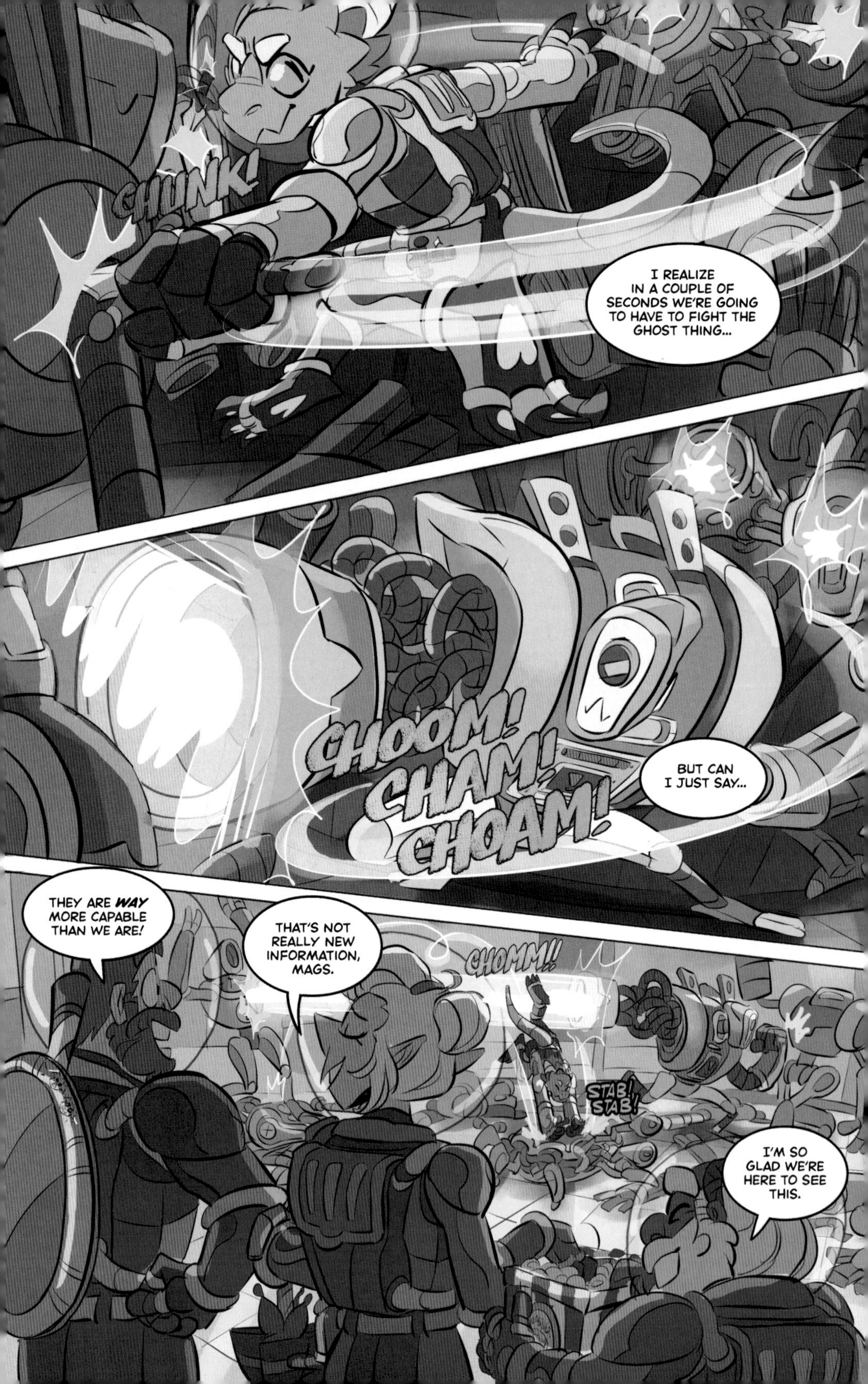
CHUNK!
I REALIZE IN A COUPLE OF SECONDS WE'RE GOING TO HAVE TO FIGHT THE GHOST THING...
CHOOM! CHAM! CHOAM!
BUT CAN I JUST SAY...
THEY ARE *WAY* MORE CAPABLE THAN WE ARE!
THAT'S NOT REALLY NEW INFORMATION, MAGS.
CHOMM!!
STAB! STAB!
I'M SO GLAD WE'RE HERE TO SEE THIS.

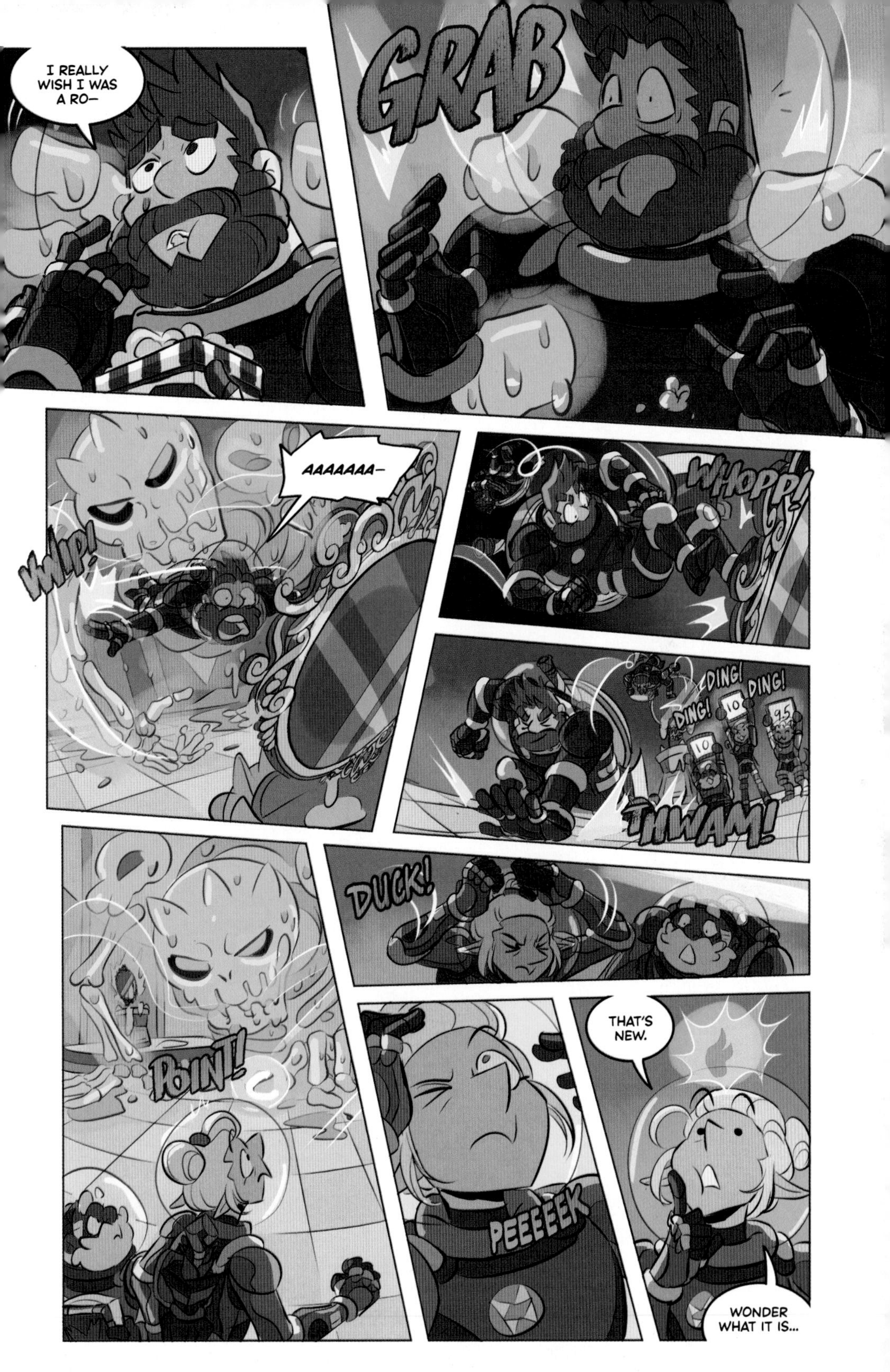

I REALLY WISH I WAS A RO—
GRAB
AAAAAAA—
WHIP!
WHOPP!
DING!
DING!
DING!
10
10
9.5
THWAM!
DUCK!
POINT!
PEEEEEK
THAT'S NEW.
WONDER WHAT IT IS...

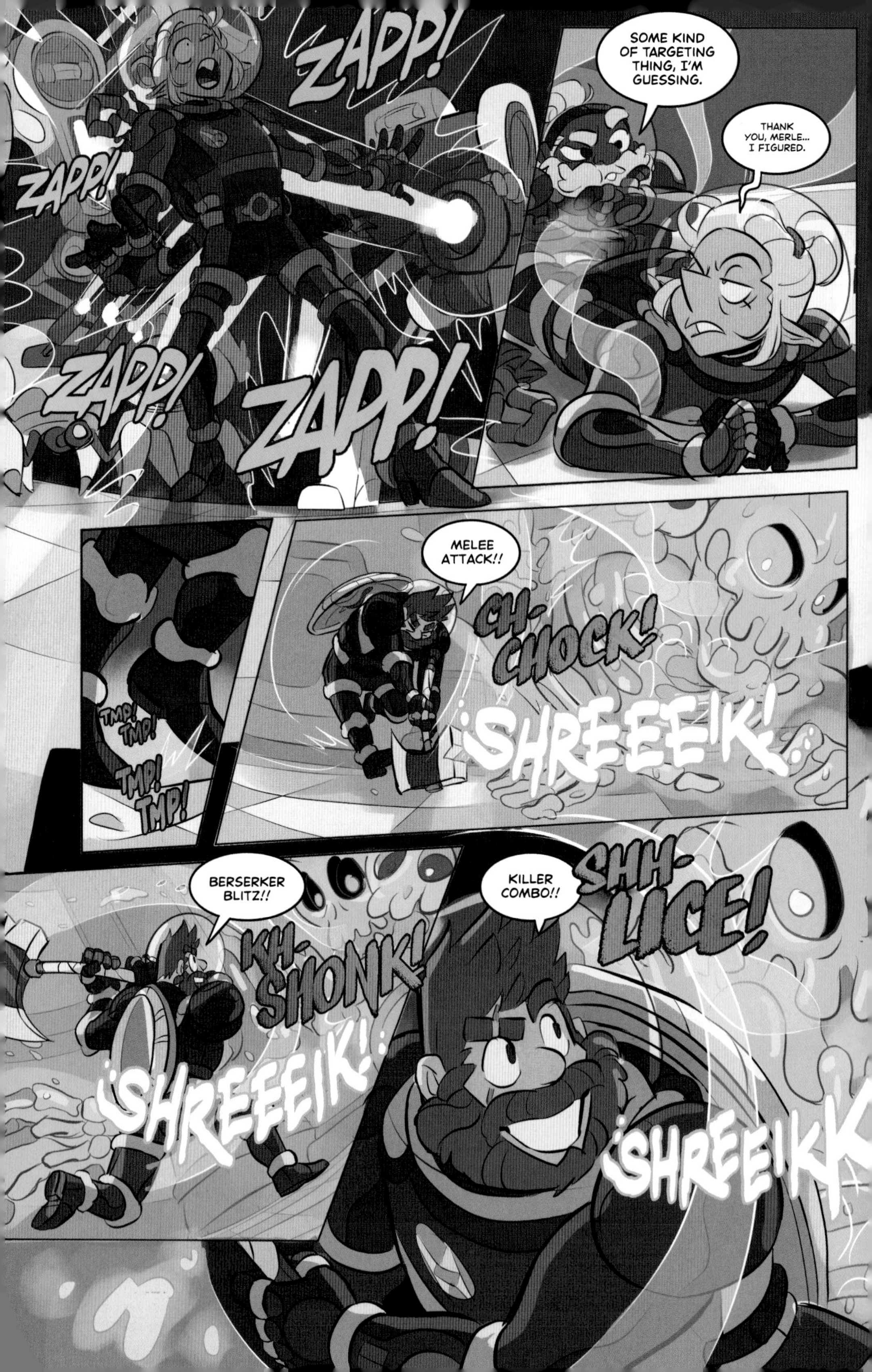

ZAPP!
ZAPP!
ZAPP!
ZAPP!
SOME KIND OF TARGETING THING, I'M GUESSING.
THANK YOU, MERLE... I FIGURED.
TMP! TMP!
TMP! TMP!
MELEE ATTACK!!
CH-CHOCK!
SHREEEIK!
BERSERKER BLITZ!!
KH-SHONK!
SHREEEIK!
KILLER COMBO!!
SHH-LICE!
SHREEIKK

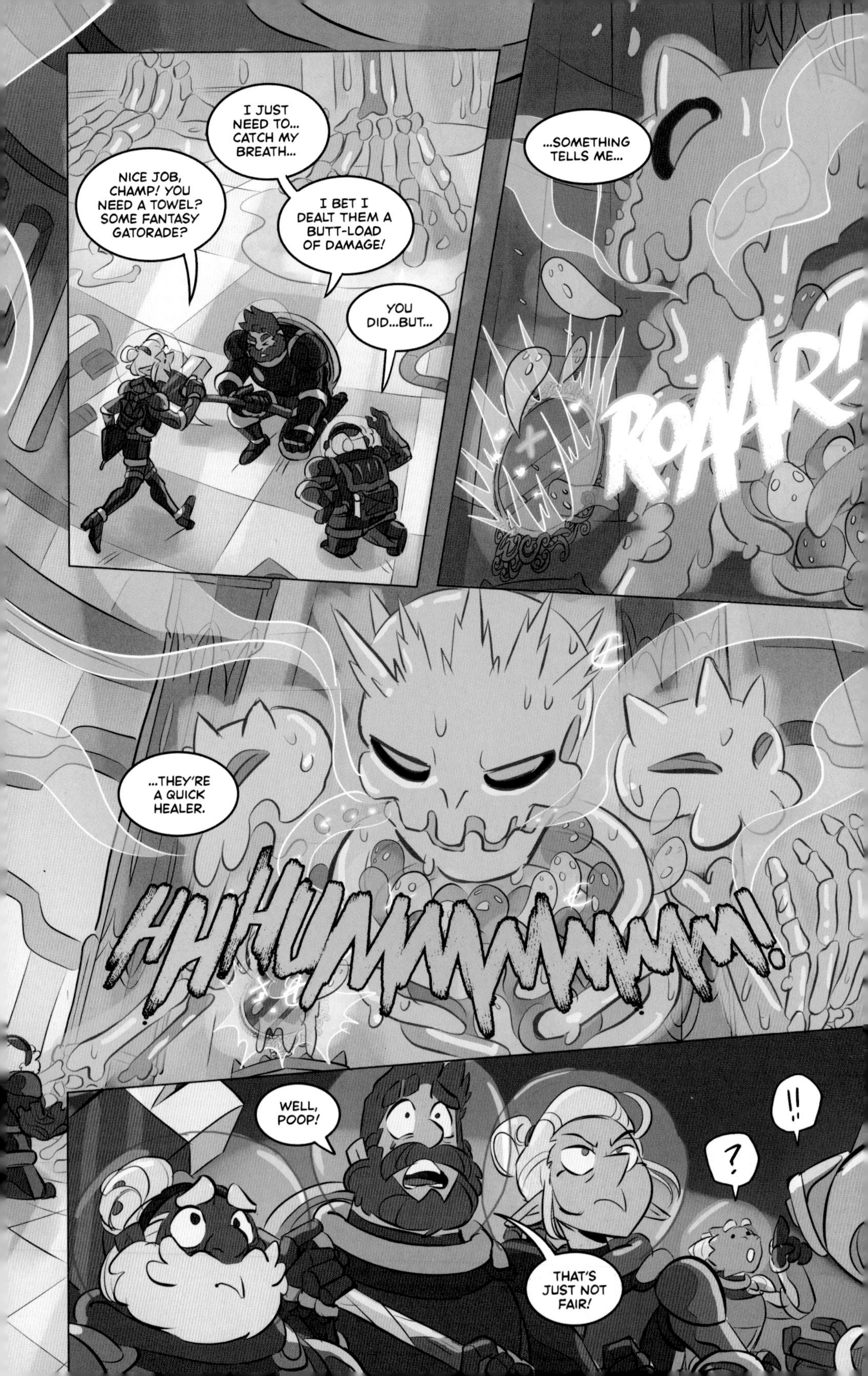
I JUST NEED TO... CATCH MY BREATH...
NICE JOB, CHAMP! YOU NEED A TOWEL? SOME FANTASY GATORADE?
I BET I DEALT THEM A BUTT-LOAD OF DAMAGE!
YOU DID...BUT...
...SOMETHING TELLS ME...
ROAAR!
...THEY'RE A QUICK HEALER.
HHHUMMMMMMM!
WELL, POOP!
!!
?
THAT'S JUST NOT FAIR!

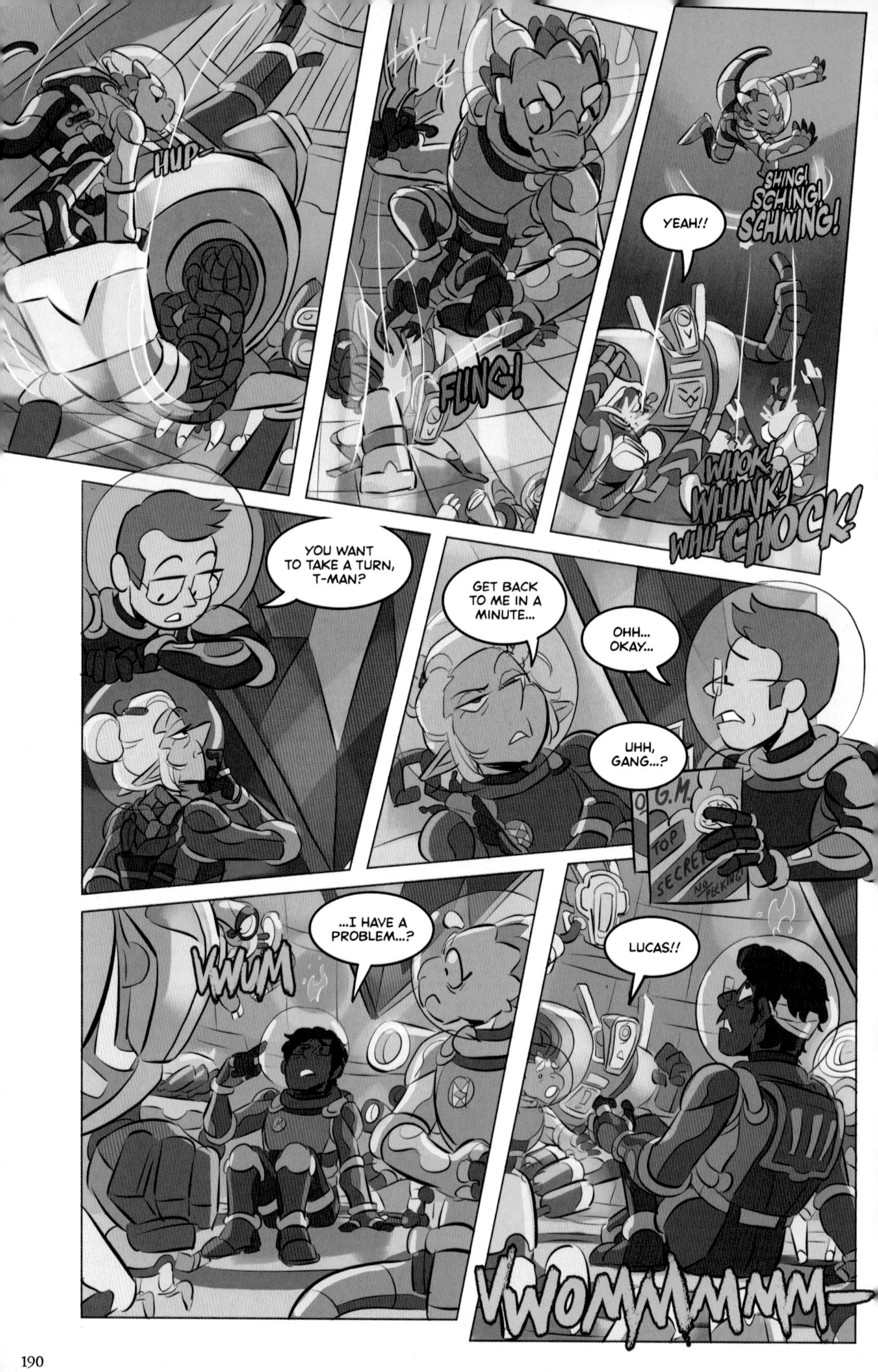
HUP-
FLING!
YEAH!!
SHING! SCHING! SCHWING!
WHOK! WHUNK! WHU-CHOCK!
YOU WANT TO TAKE A TURN, T-MAN?
GET BACK TO ME IN A MINUTE...
OHH... OKAY...
UHH, GANG...?
G.M.
TOP SECRET
NO PEEKING!
...I HAVE A PROBLEM...?
VWUM
LUCAS!!
VWOMMMMMM-

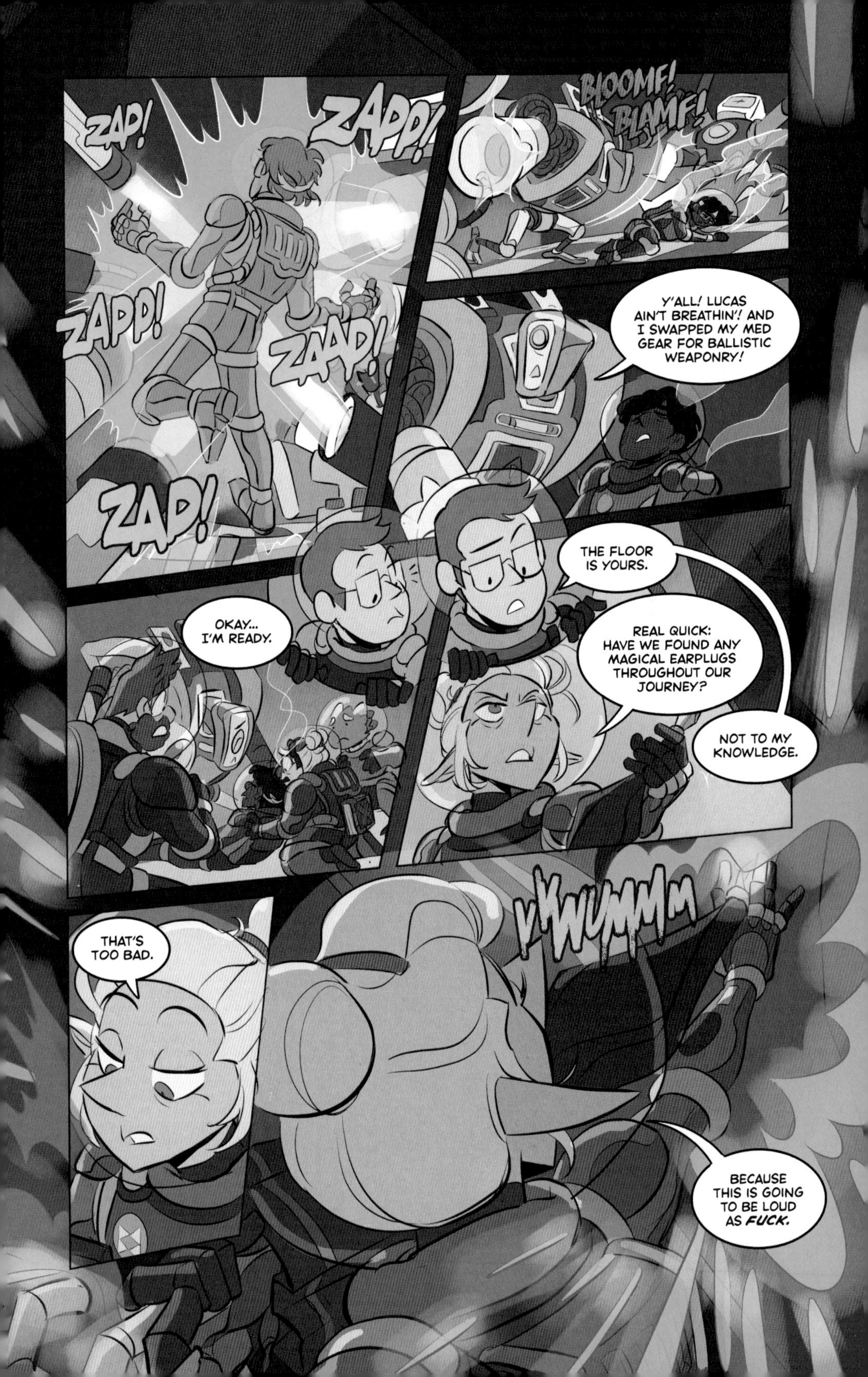
ZAP!
ZAPP!
ZAPP!
ZAAP!
ZAP!
BLOOMF!
BLAMF!
Y'ALL! LUCAS AIN'T BREATHIN'! AND I SWAPPED MY MED GEAR FOR BALLISTIC WEAPONRY!
OKAY... I'M READY.
THE FLOOR IS YOURS.
REAL QUICK: HAVE WE FOUND ANY MAGICAL EARPLUGS THROUGHOUT OUR JOURNEY?
NOT TO MY KNOWLEDGE.
VWUMMM
THAT'S TOO BAD.
BECAUSE THIS IS GOING TO BE LOUD AS ***FUCK.***

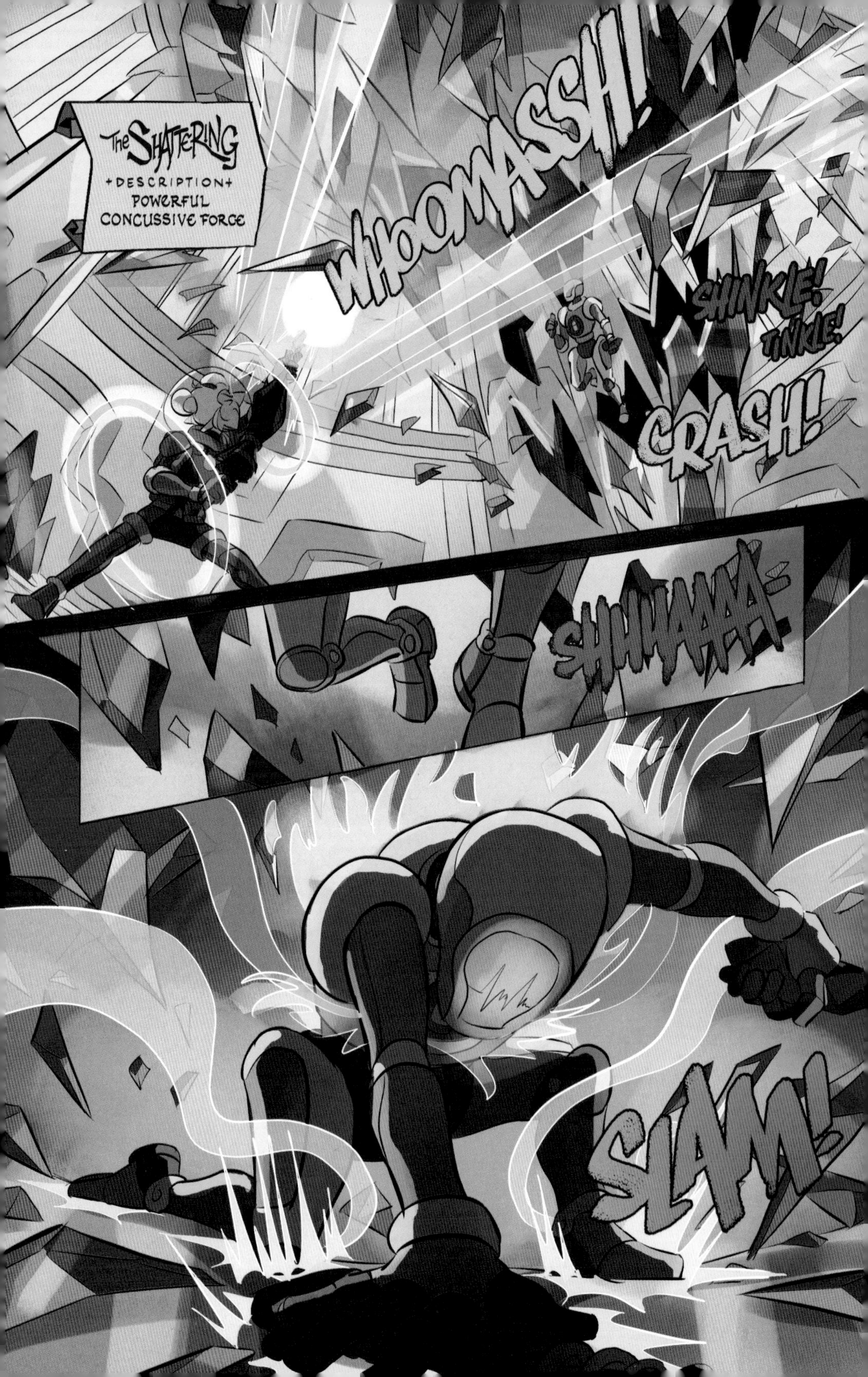

The Shattering
+DESCRIPTION+
POWERFUL CONCUSSIVE FORCE
WHOOMASSH!
SHINKLE!
TINKLE!
CRASH!
SHHHAAAAA-
SLAM!

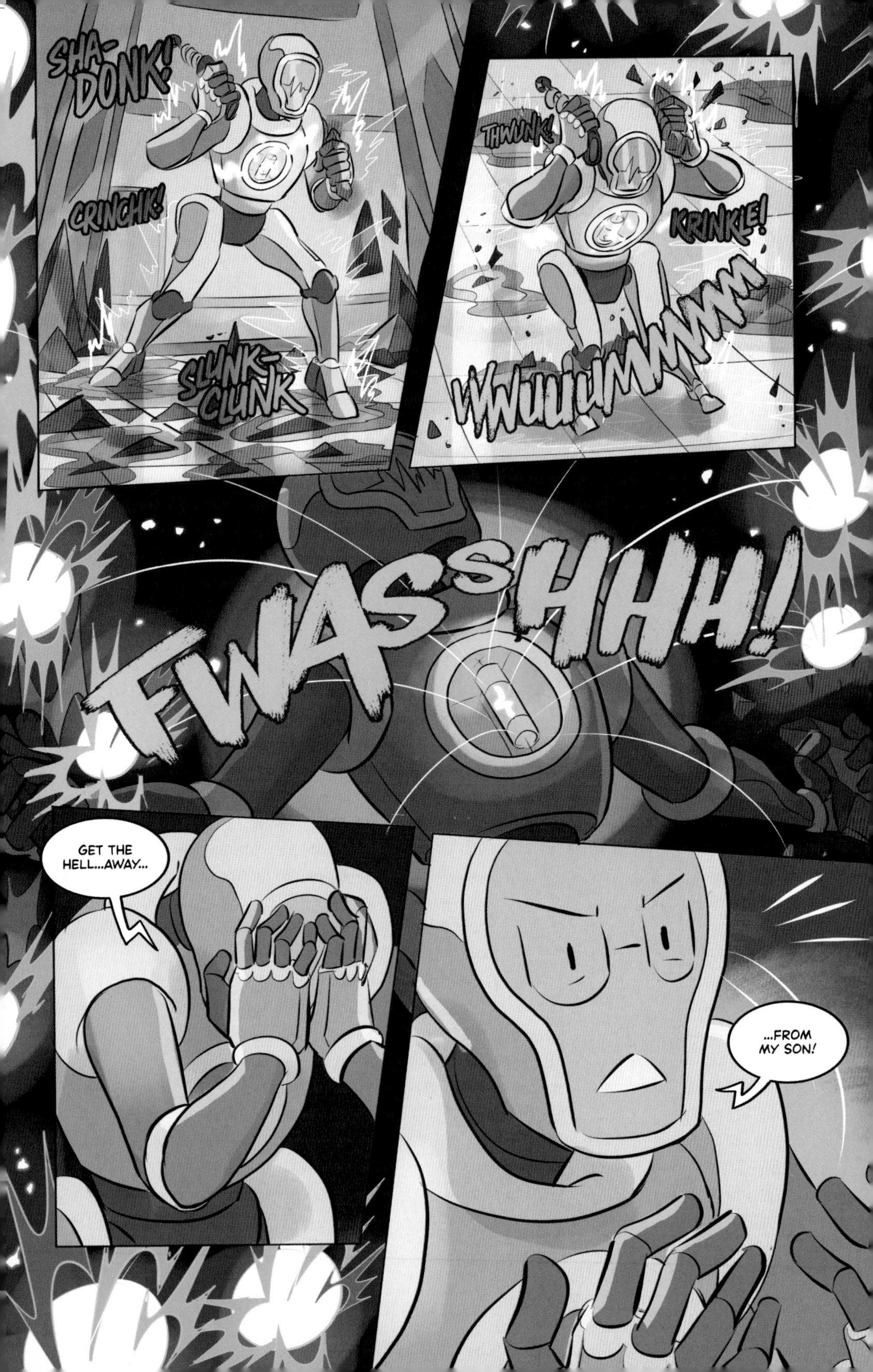
SHA-DONK!
CRINCHK!
SLUNK-CLUNK
THWUNK!
KRINKLE!
WWUUUMMMM
FWASSHHH!
GET THE HELL...AWAY...
...FROM MY SON!

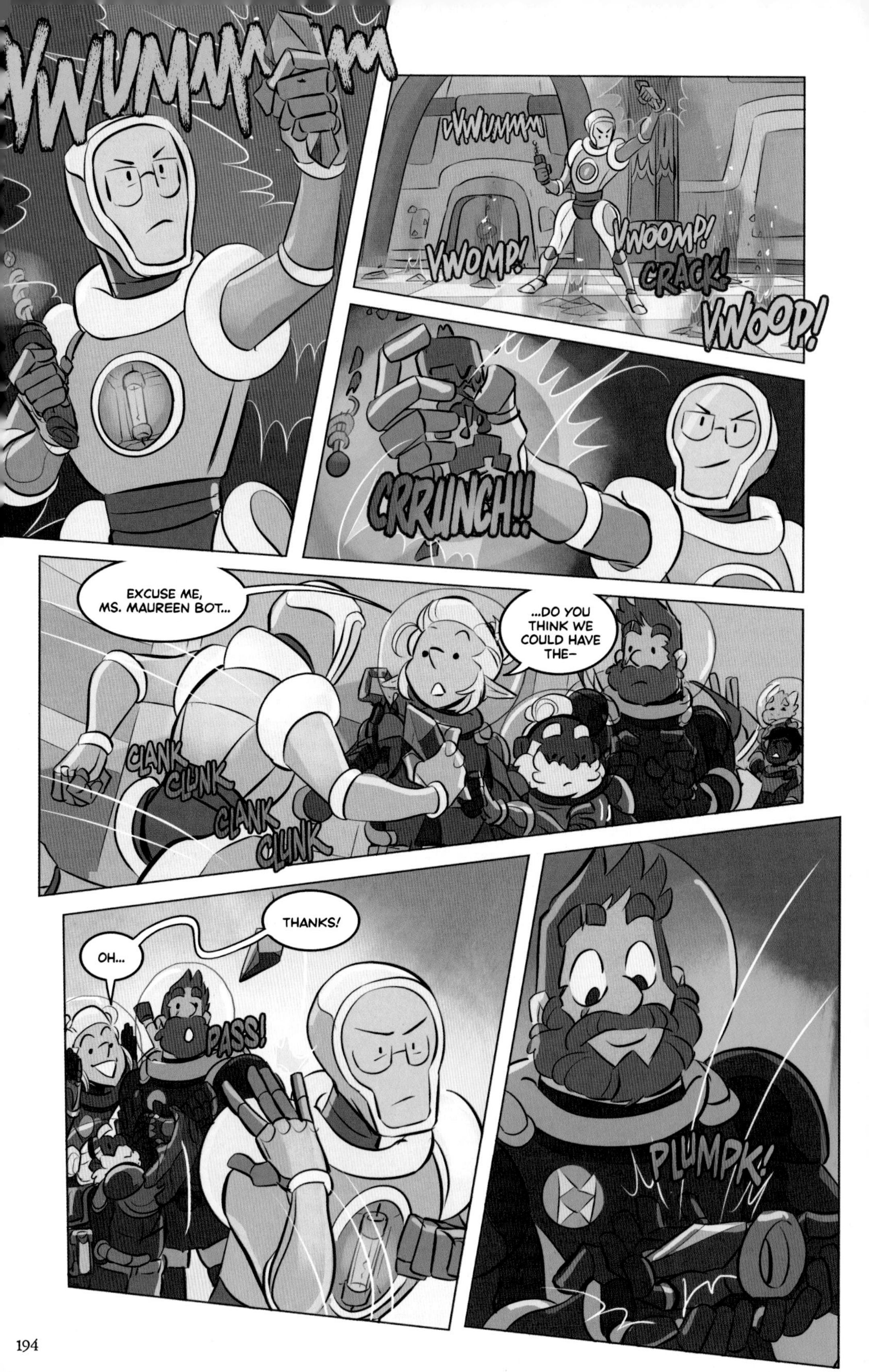
VWUMMMM
VWUMMM
VWOMP!
VWOOMP!
CRACK!
VWOOP!
CRRUNCH!!
EXCUSE ME, MS. MAUREEN BOT...
...DO YOU THINK WE COULD HAVE THE–
CLANK
CLUNK
CLANK
CLUNK
OH...
THANKS!
PASS!
PLUMPK!

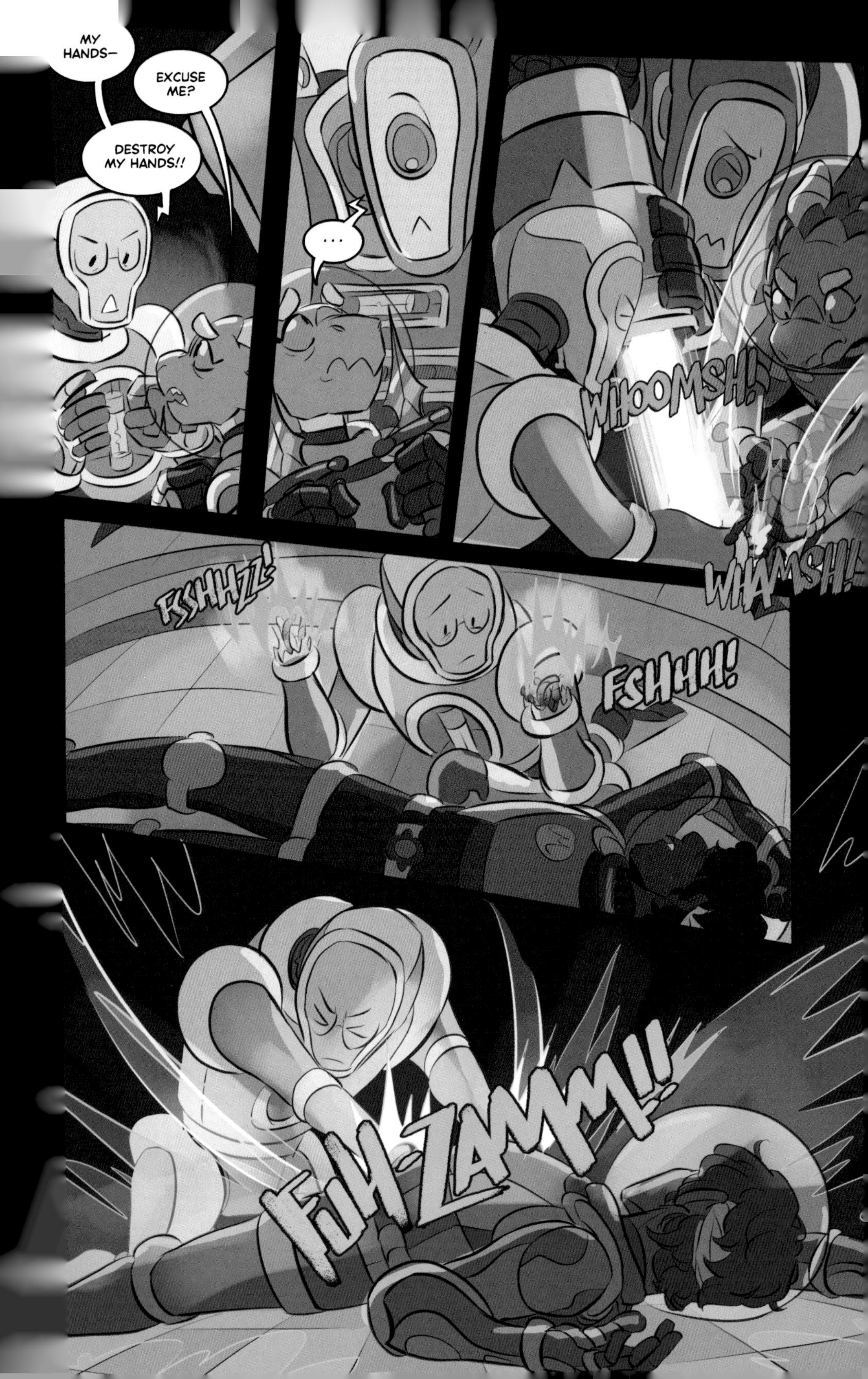
MY HANDS—
EXCUSE ME?
DESTROY MY HANDS!!
...
WHOOMSH!
WHAMSH!
FSHHZZ!
FSHHH!
FHZAMM!!

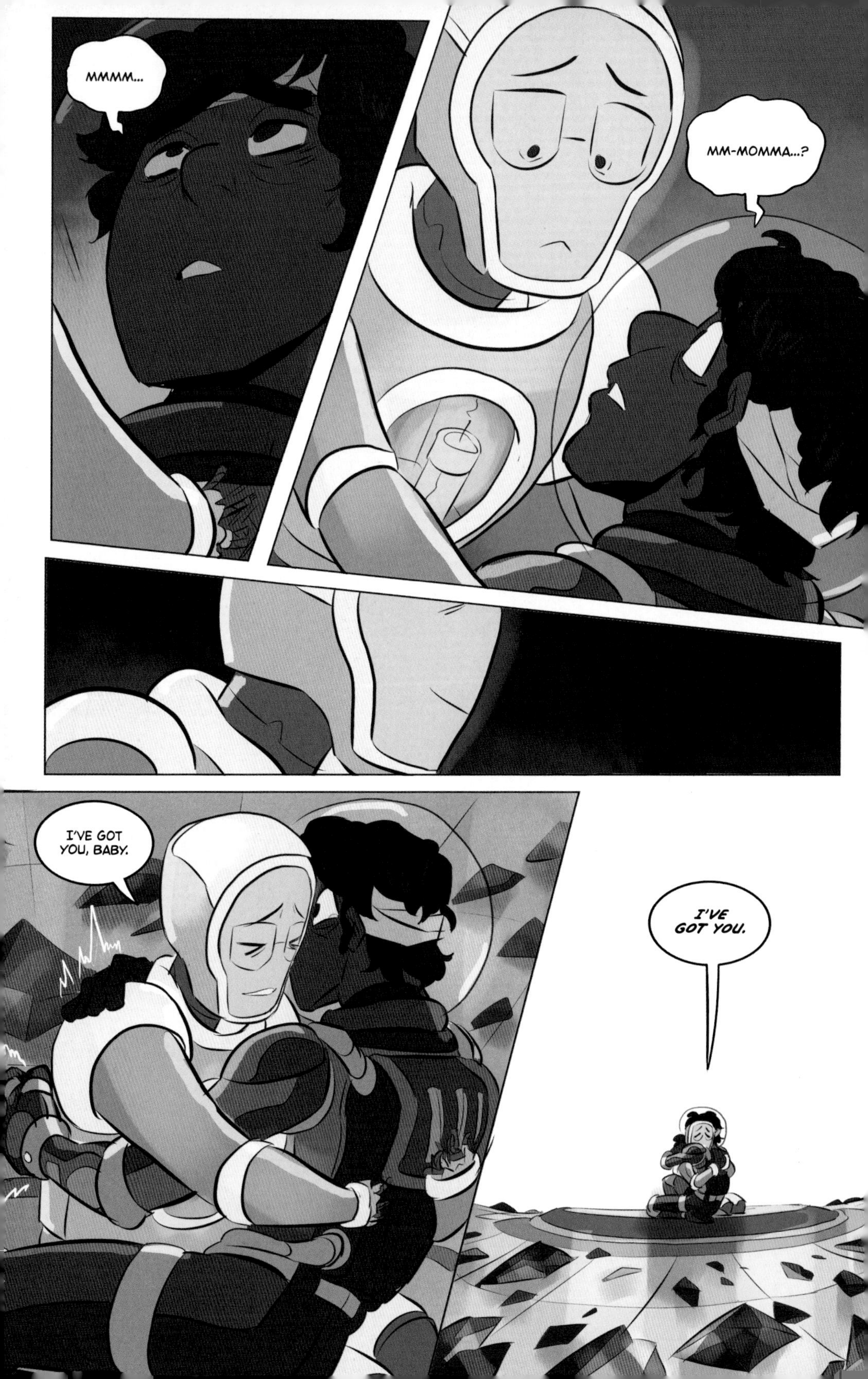
MMMM...
MM-MOMMA...?
I'VE GOT YOU, BABY.
I'VE GOT YOU.

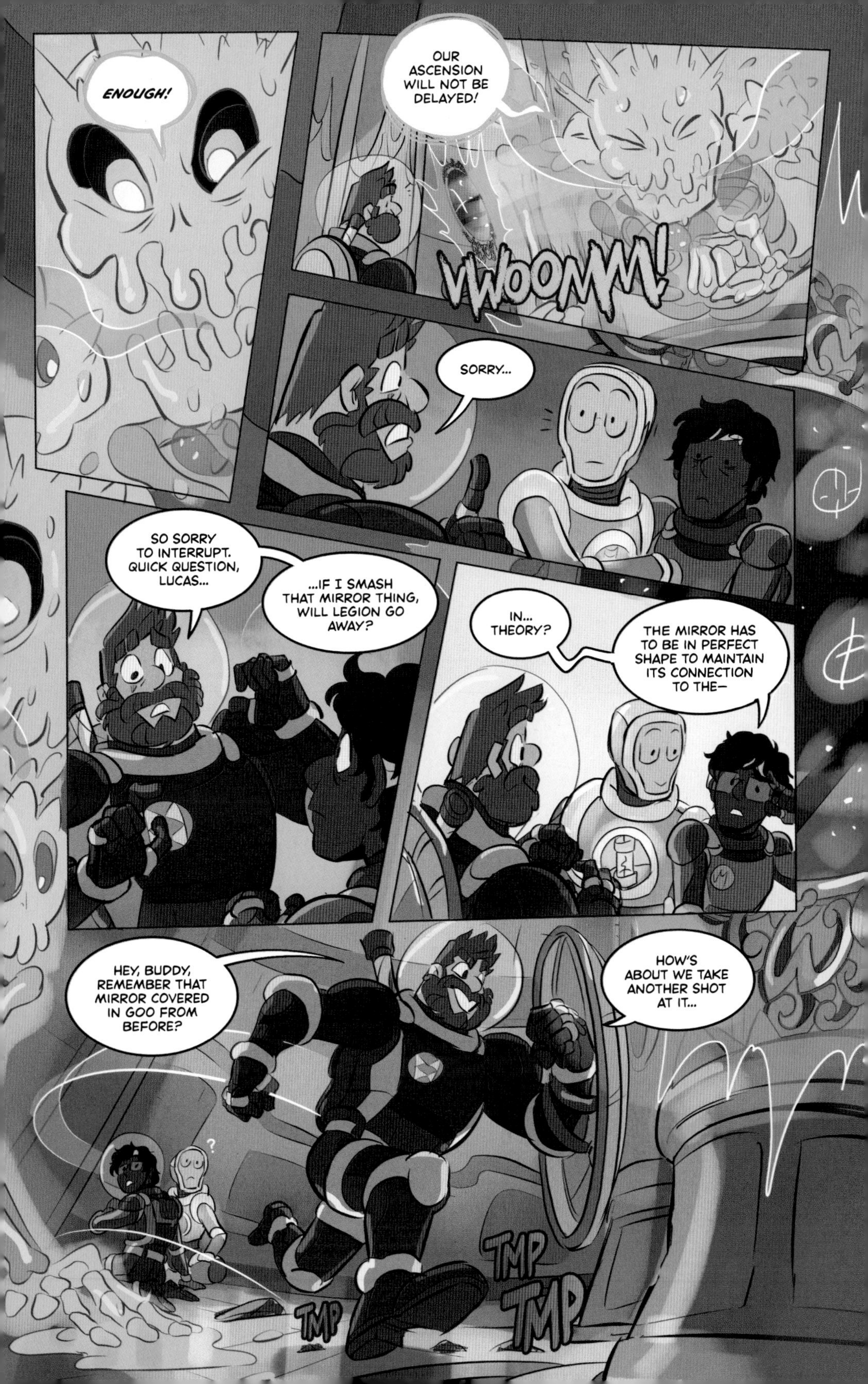
ENOUGH!
OUR ASCENSION WILL NOT BE DELAYED!
VWOOMM!
SORRY...
SO SORRY TO INTERRUPT. QUICK QUESTION, LUCAS...
...IF I SMASH THAT MIRROR THING, WILL LEGION GO AWAY?
IN... THEORY?
THE MIRROR HAS TO BE IN PERFECT SHAPE TO MAINTAIN ITS CONNECTION TO THE—
HEY, BUDDY, REMEMBER THAT MIRROR COVERED IN GOO FROM BEFORE?
HOW'S ABOUT WE TAKE ANOTHER SHOT AT IT...
?
TMP
TMP
TMP

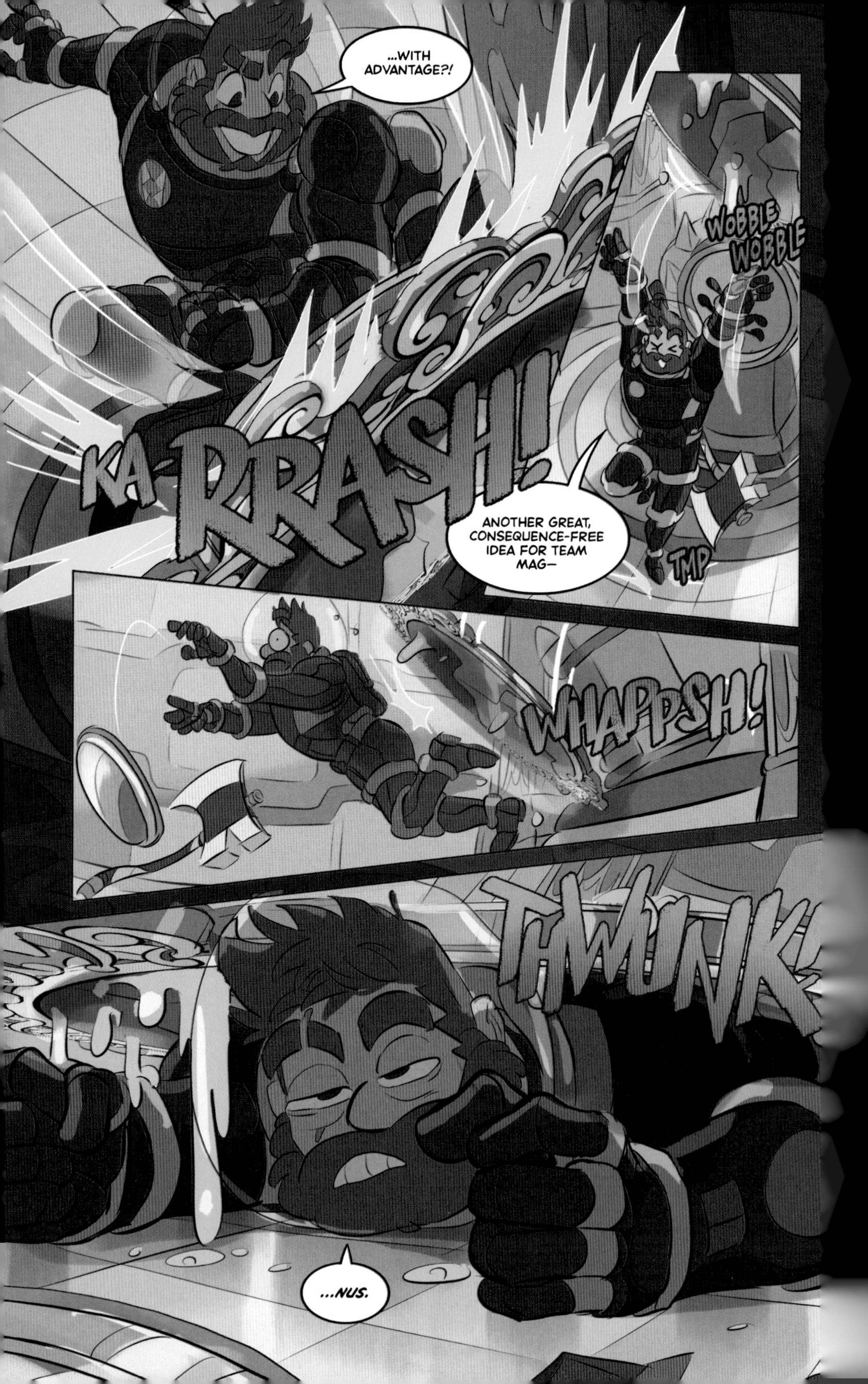
...WITH ADVANTAGE?!
WOBBLE WOBBLE
KA RRASH!
ANOTHER GREAT, CONSEQUENCE-FREE IDEA FOR TEAM MAG—
TMP
WHAPPSH!
THWUNK
...NUS.

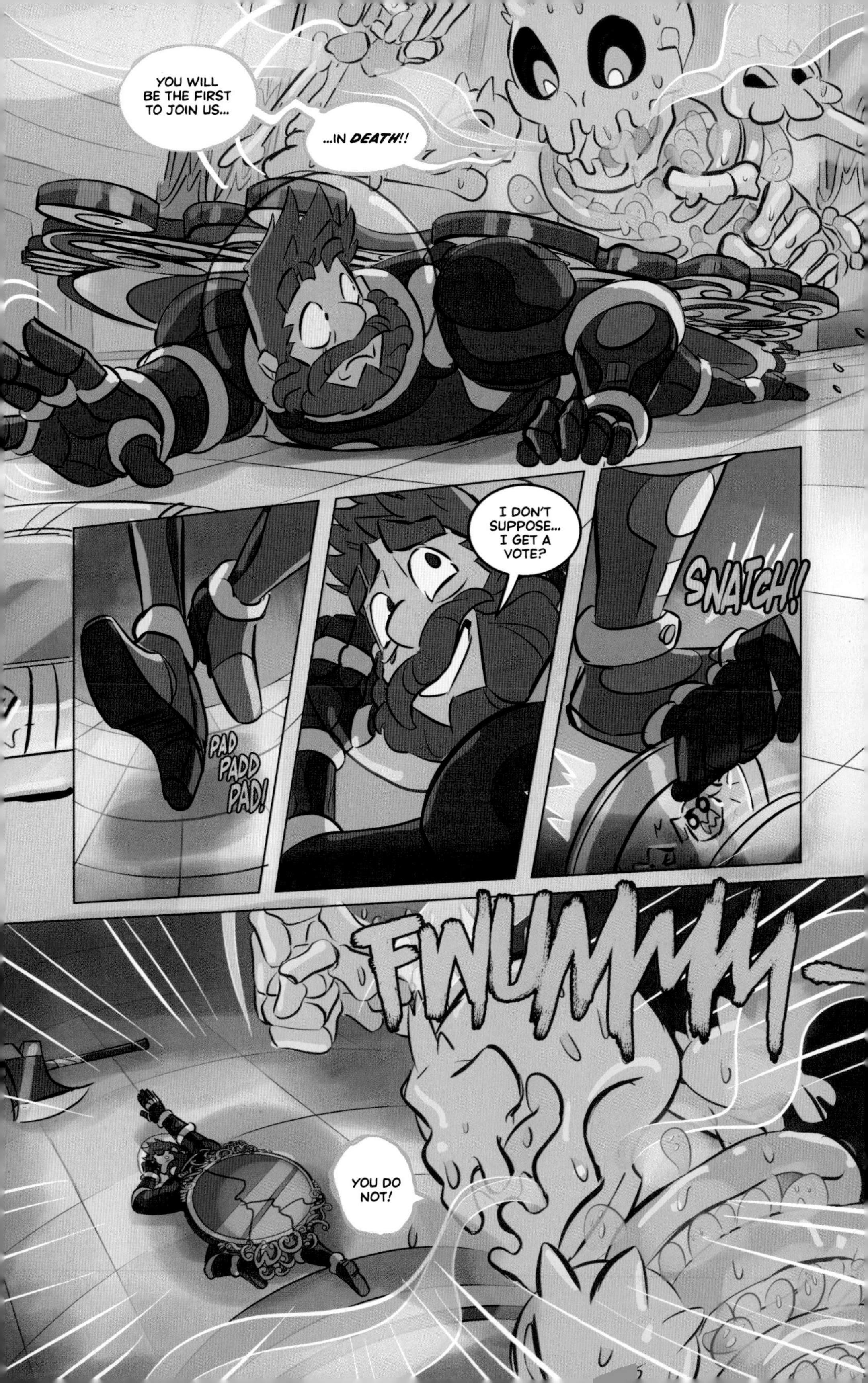

YOU WILL BE THE FIRST TO JOIN US...
...IN *DEATH*!!
PAD PADD PAD!
I DON'T SUPPOSE... I GET A VOTE?
SNATCH!!
FWUMMM
YOU DO NOT!

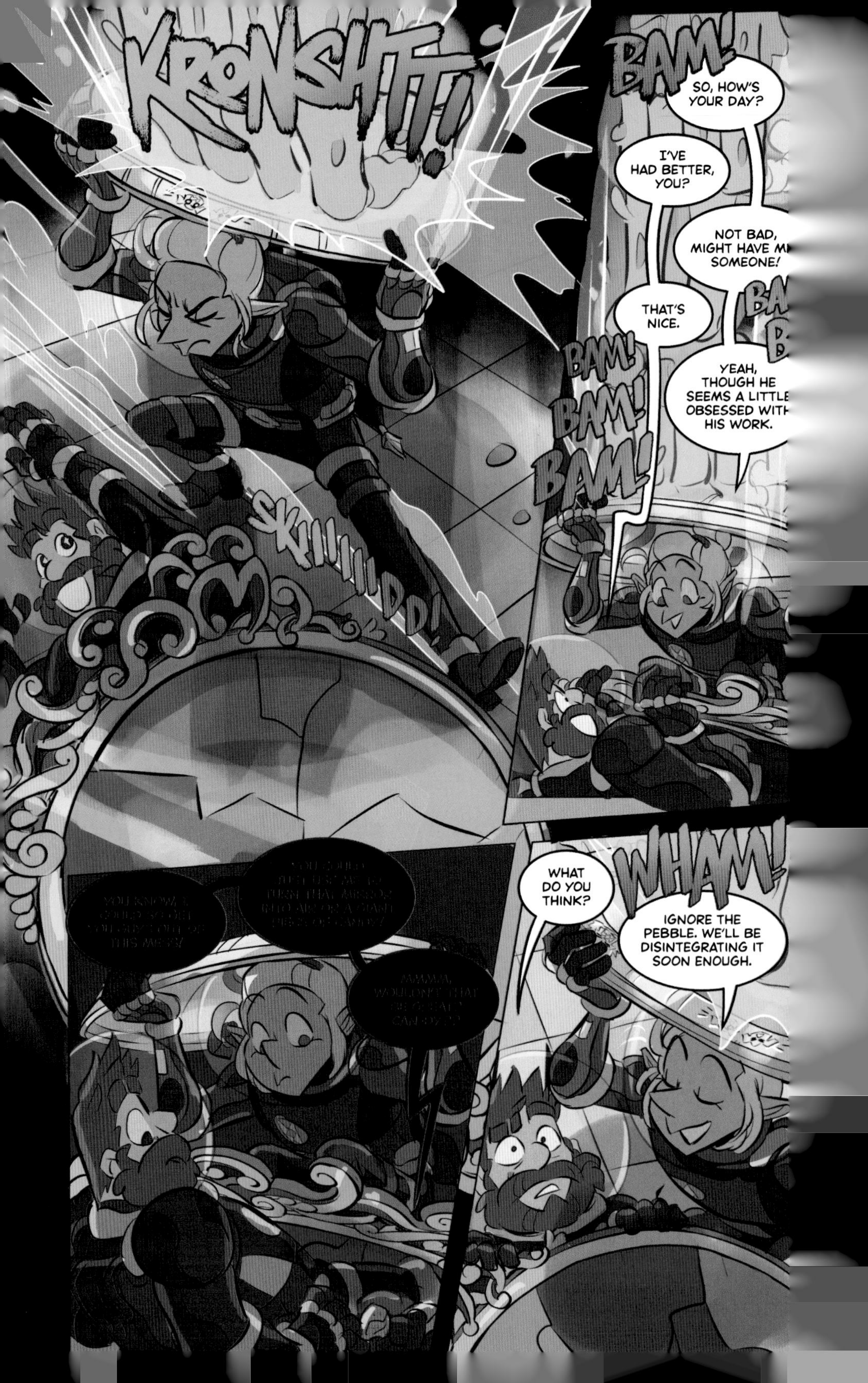

KRONSHT!!
SKIIIIIIDD!
BAM!
SO, HOW'S YOUR DAY?
I'VE HAD BETTER, YOU?
NOT BAD, MIGHT HAVE M SOMEONE!
THAT'S NICE.
BAM! BAM! BAM!
YEAH, THOUGH HE SEEMS A LITTLE OBSESSED WITH HIS WORK.
WHAT DO YOU THINK?
WHAM!
IGNORE THE PEBBLE. WE'LL BE DISINTEGRATING IT SOON ENOUGH.

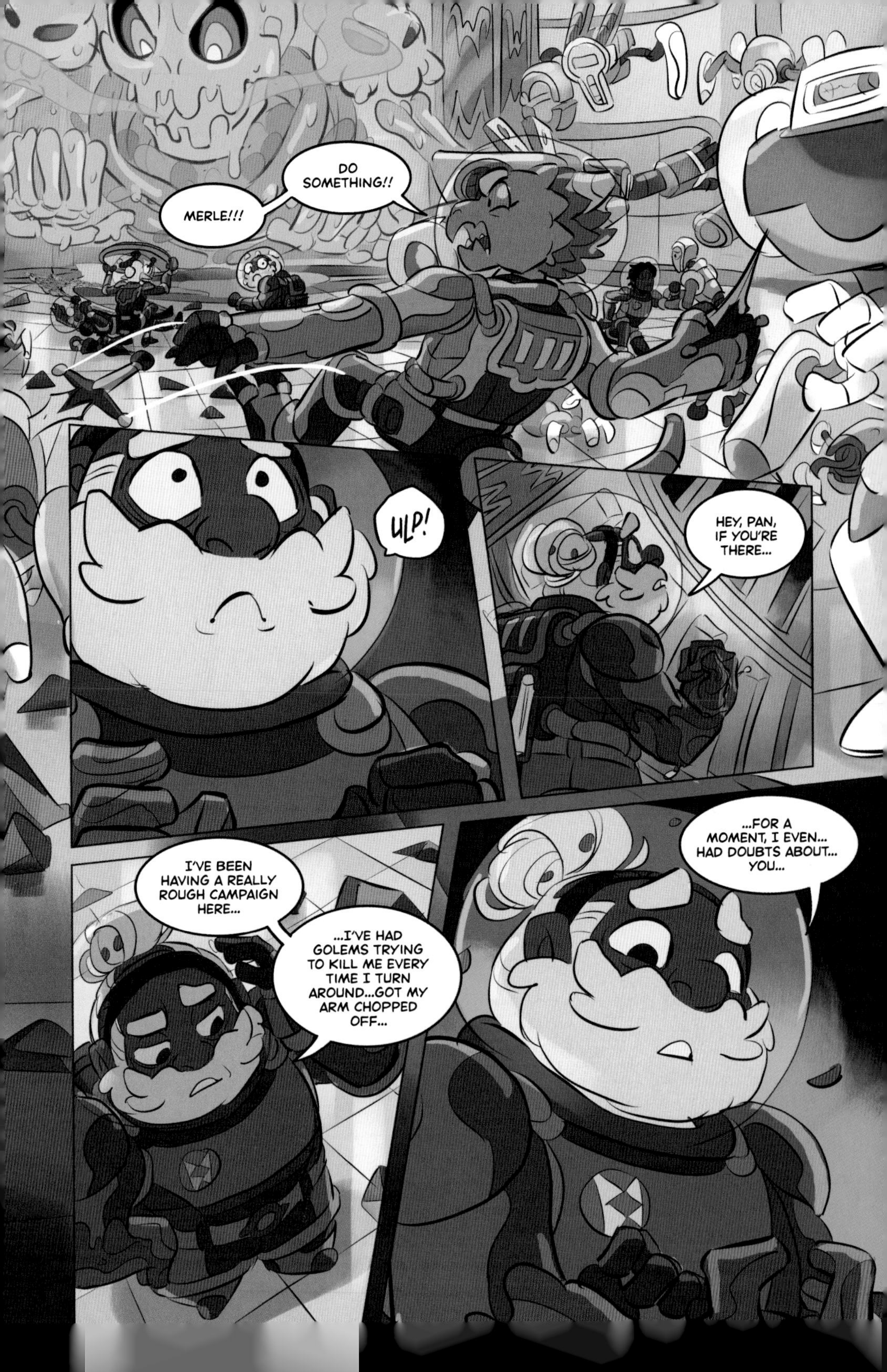
MERLE!!!
DO SOMETHING!!
ULP!
HEY, PAN, IF YOU'RE THERE...
I'VE BEEN HAVING A REALLY ROUGH CAMPAIGN HERE...
...I'VE HAD GOLEMS TRYING TO KILL ME EVERY TIME I TURN AROUND...GOT MY ARM CHOPPED OFF...
...FOR A MOMENT, I EVEN... HAD DOUBTS ABOUT... YOU...

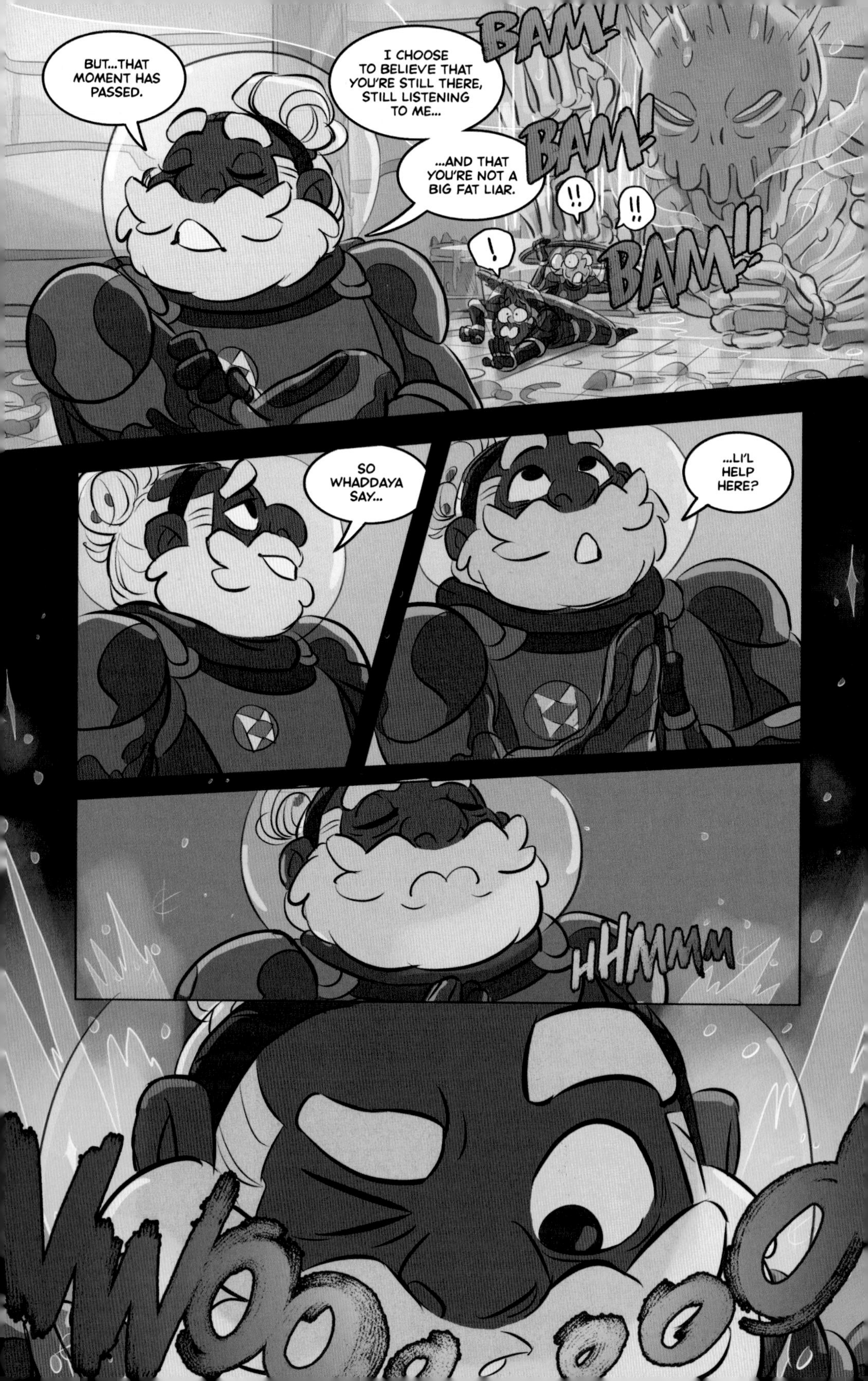
BUT...THAT MOMENT HAS PASSED.
I CHOOSE TO BELIEVE THAT YOU'RE STILL THERE, STILL LISTENING TO ME...
...AND THAT YOU'RE NOT A BIG FAT LIAR.
BAM!
BAM!
!
!!
!!
BAM!!
SO WHADDAYA SAY...
...LI'L HELP HERE?
HHMMMM
WOOOoooOOOO

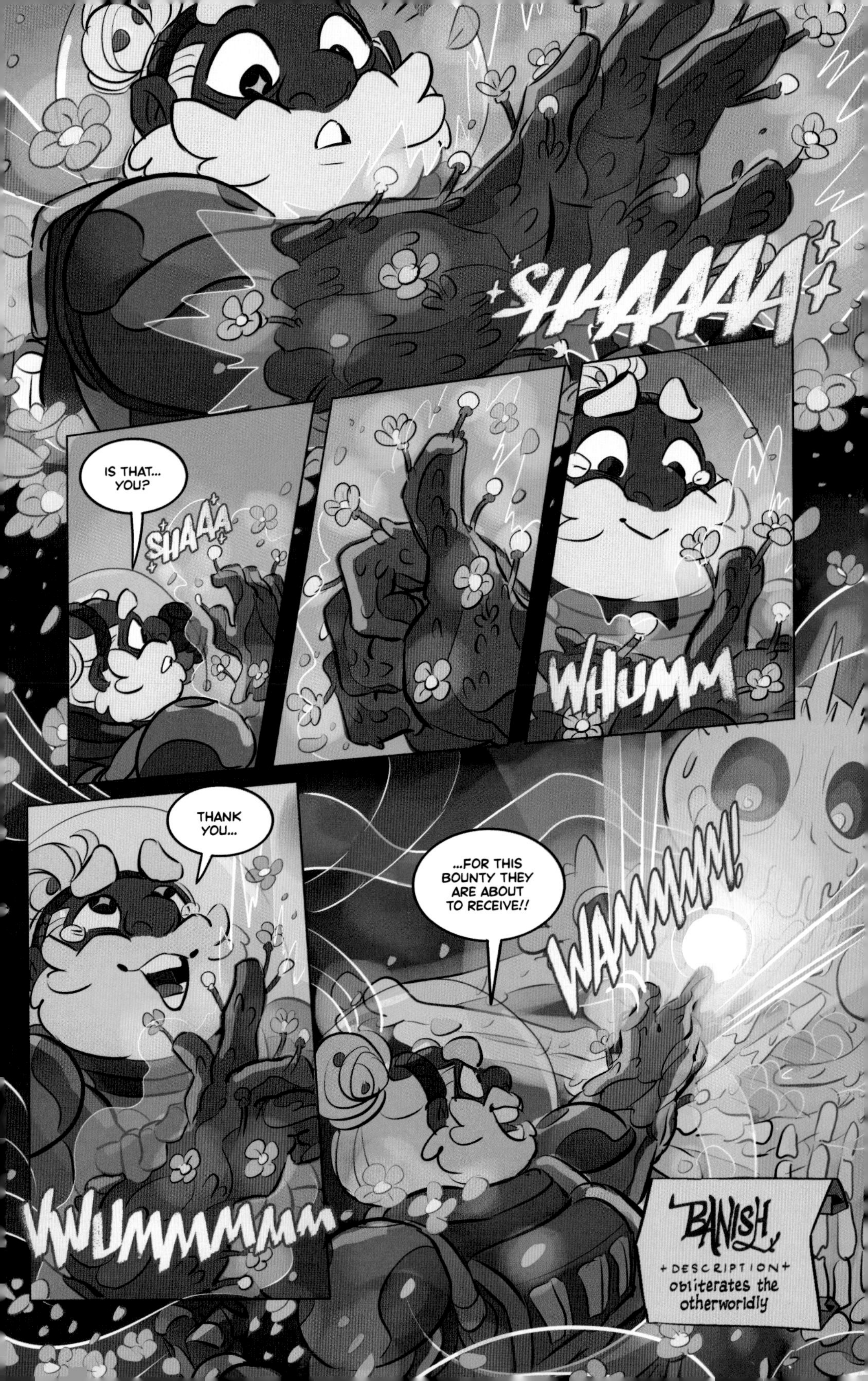
SHAAAAA
IS THAT... YOU?
SHAAA
WHUMM
THANK YOU...
VWUMMMMMM
...FOR THIS BOUNTY THEY ARE ABOUT TO RECEIVE!!
WAMMMM!
BANISH
+DESCRIPTION+
obliterates the otherworldly

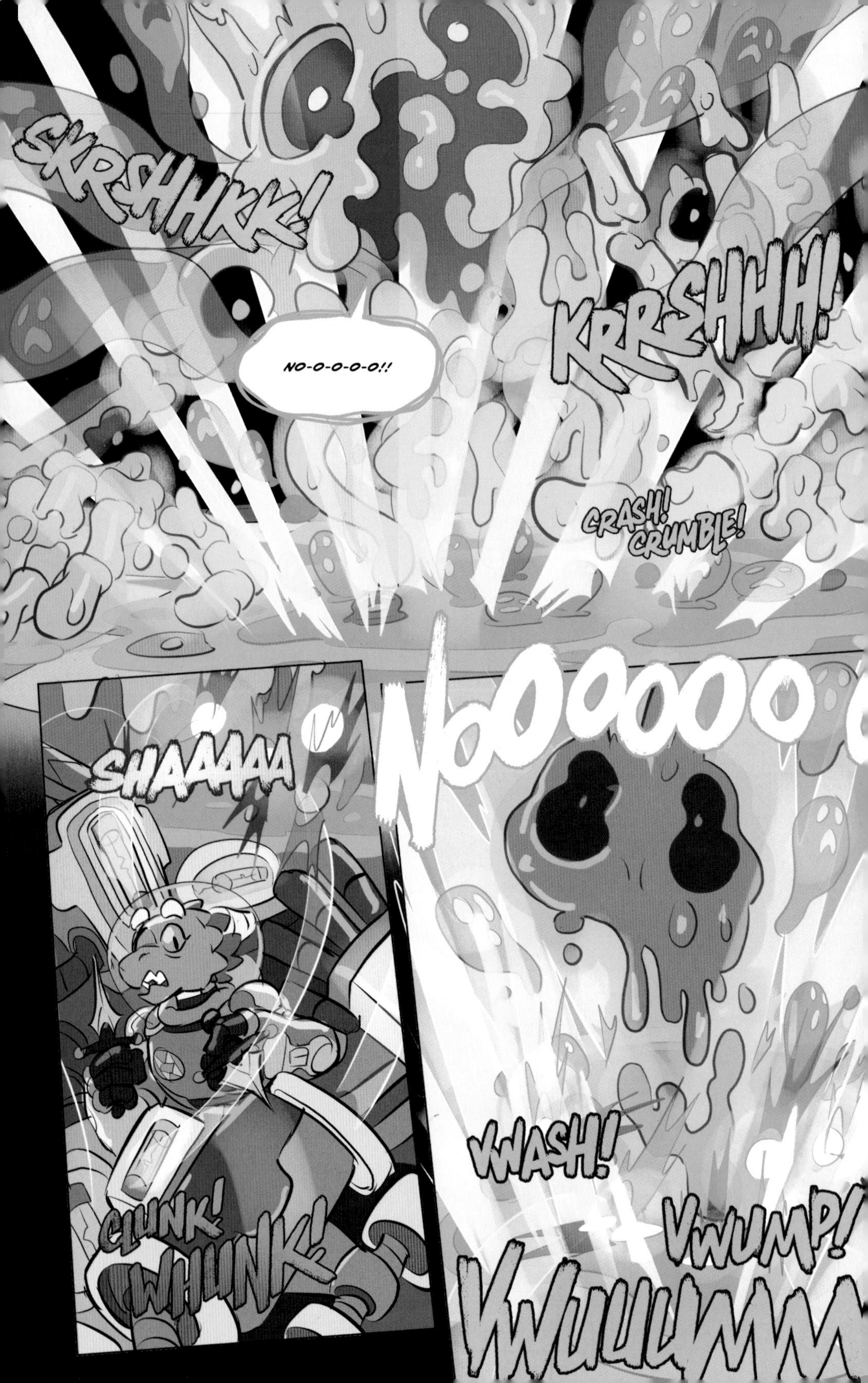
SKRSHHKK!
NO-O-O-O-O-O!!
KRRSHHH!
CRASH! CRUMBLE!
SHAAAAA
CLINK! WHUNK!
NOOOOOOO
VWASH!
VWUMP!
VWUUUMMM

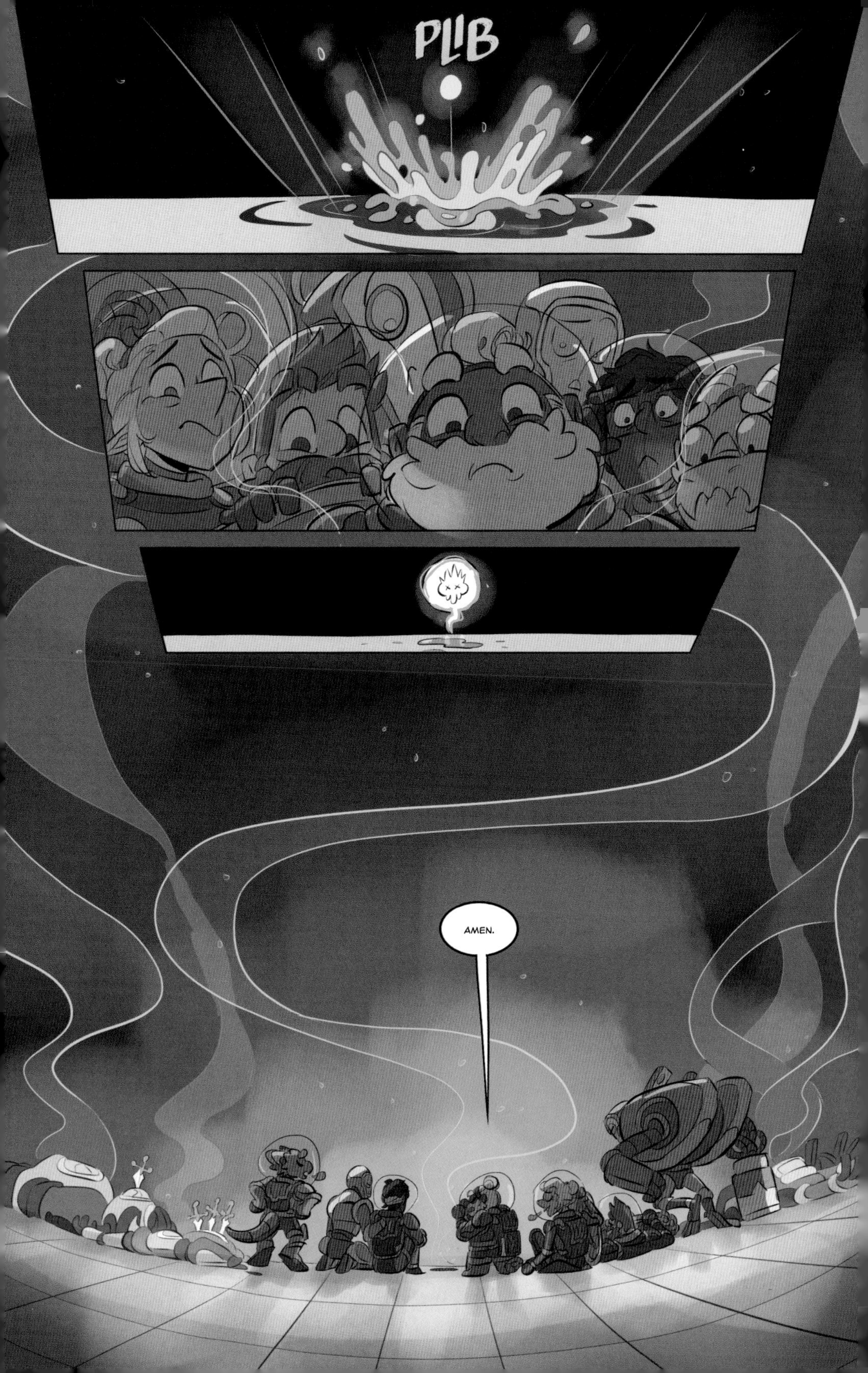
PLIB
AMEN.

Chapter

9

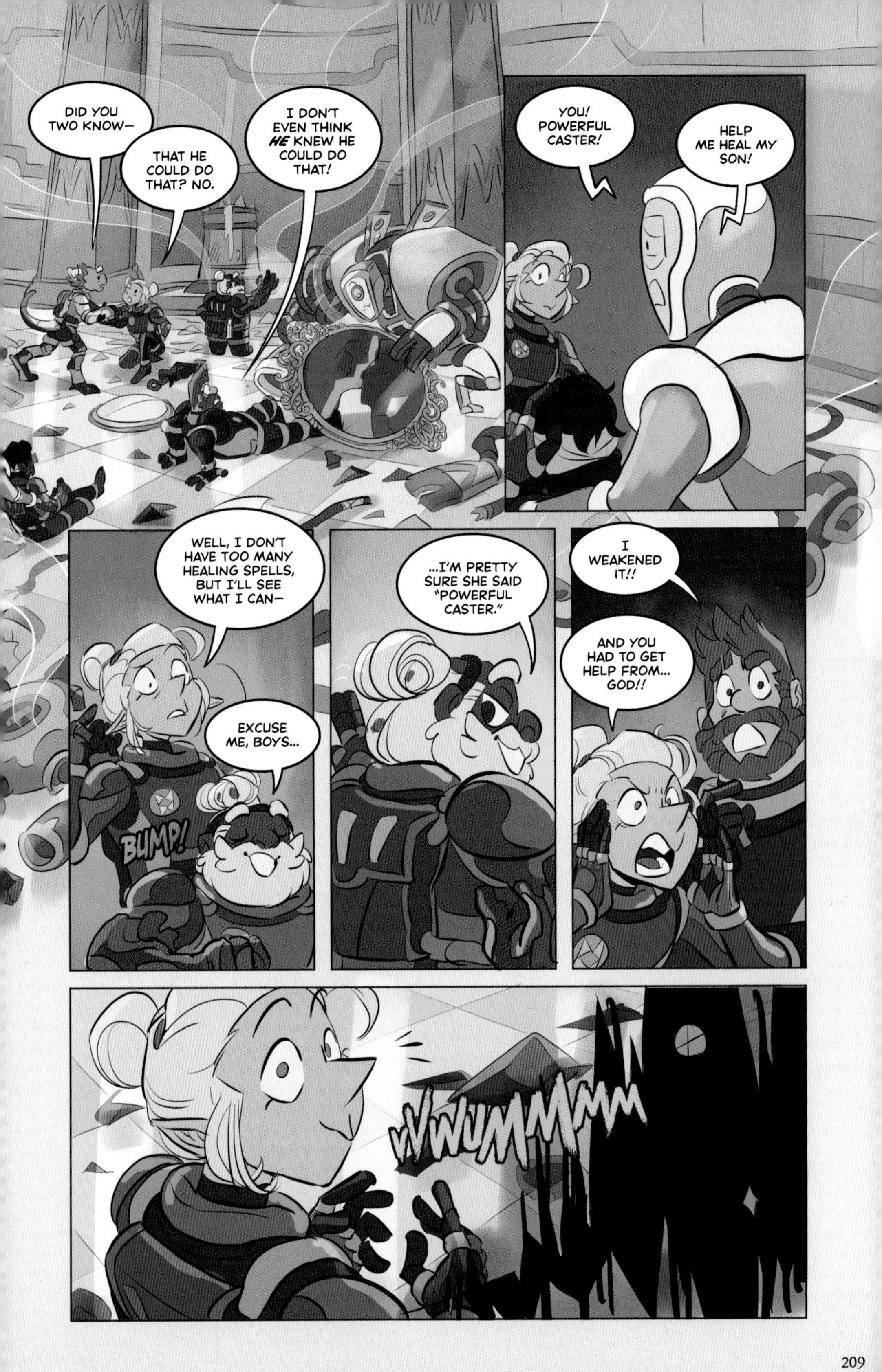
DID YOU TWO KNOW—
THAT HE COULD DO THAT? NO.
I DON'T EVEN THINK HE KNEW HE COULD DO THAT!
YOU! POWERFUL CASTER!
HELP ME HEAL MY SON!
WELL, I DON'T HAVE TOO MANY HEALING SPELLS, BUT I'LL SEE WHAT I CAN—
EXCUSE ME, BOYS...
BUMP!
...I'M PRETTY SURE SHE SAID "POWERFUL CASTER."
I WEAKENED IT!!
AND YOU HAD TO GET HELP FROM... GOD!!
VWUMMMM

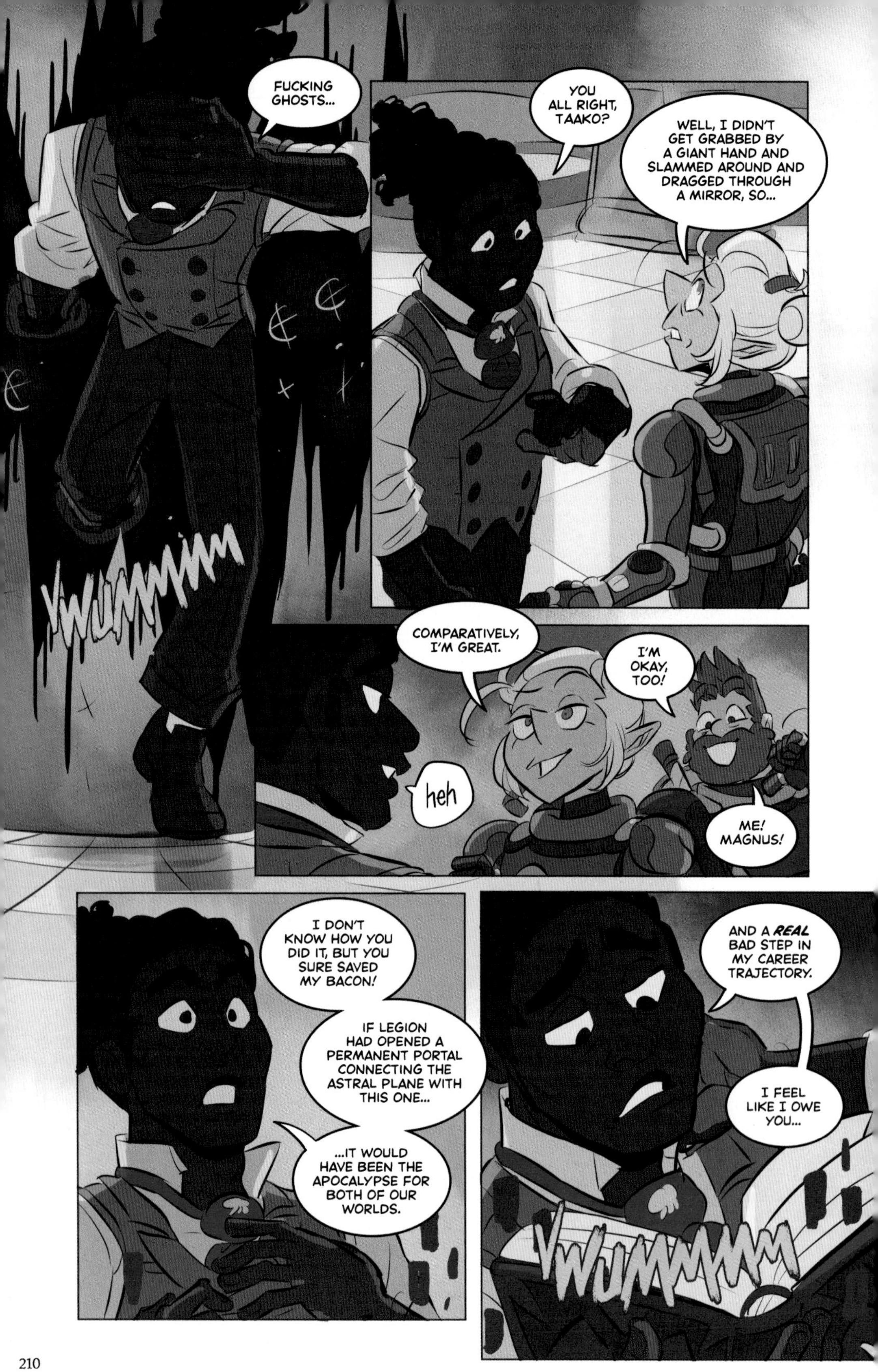
FUCKING GHOSTS...
VWUMMMM
YOU ALL RIGHT, TAAKO?
WELL, I DIDN'T GET GRABBED BY A GIANT HAND AND SLAMMED AROUND AND DRAGGED THROUGH A MIRROR, SO...
COMPARATIVELY, I'M GREAT.
I'M OKAY, TOO!
heh
ME! MAGNUS!
I DON'T KNOW HOW YOU DID IT, BUT YOU SURE SAVED MY BACON!
IF LEGION HAD OPENED A PERMANENT PORTAL CONNECTING THE ASTRAL PLANE WITH THIS ONE...
...IT WOULD HAVE BEEN THE APOCALYPSE FOR BOTH OF OUR WORLDS.
AND A *REAL* BAD STEP IN MY CAREER TRAJECTORY.
I FEEL LIKE I OWE YOU...
VWUMMMM

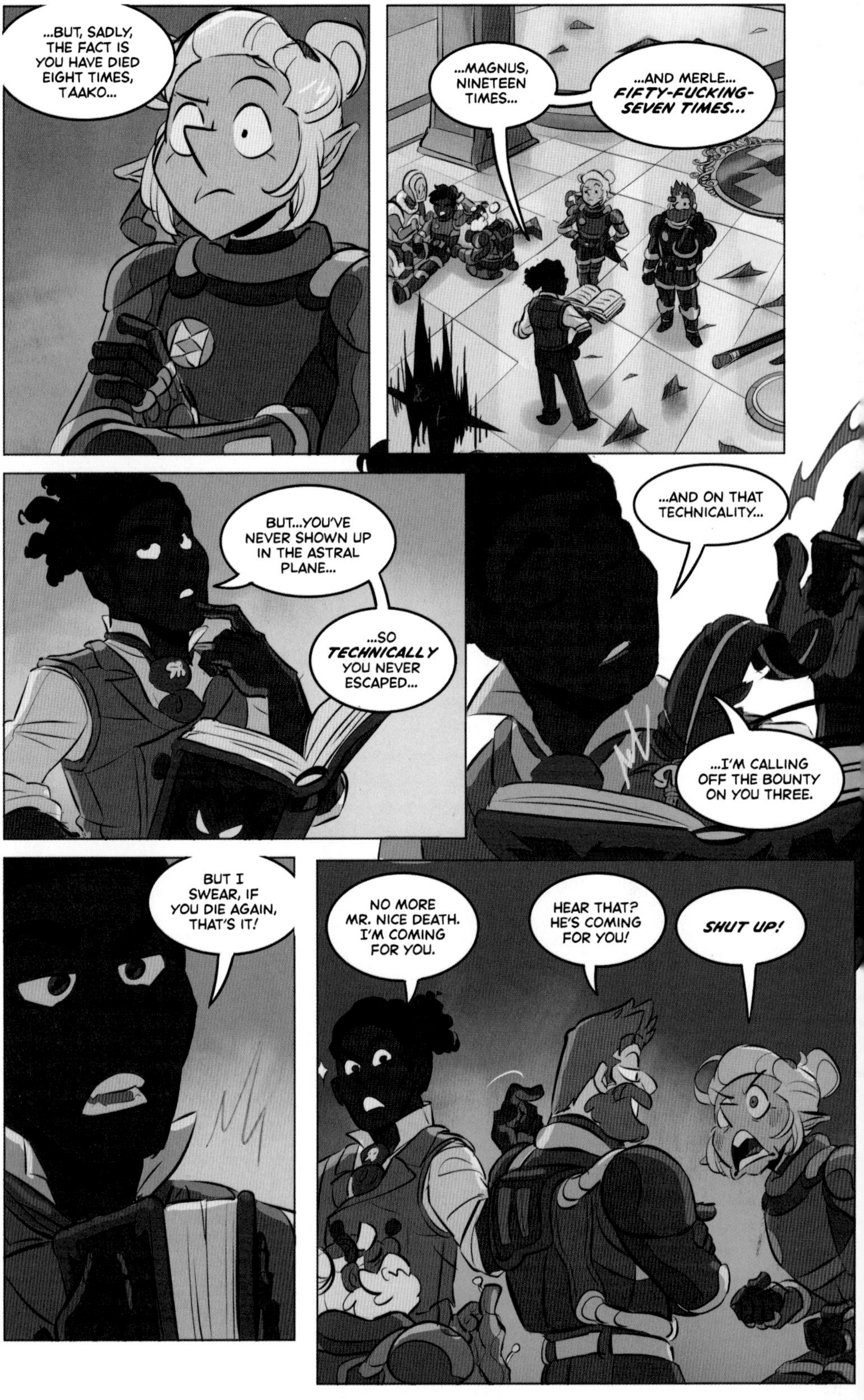
...BUT, SADLY, THE FACT IS YOU HAVE DIED EIGHT TIMES, TAAKO...
...MAGNUS, NINETEEN TIMES...
...AND MERLE... FIFTY-FUCKING-SEVEN TIMES...
BUT...YOU'VE NEVER SHOWN UP IN THE ASTRAL PLANE...
...SO TECHNICALLY YOU NEVER ESCAPED...
...AND ON THAT TECHNICALITY...
...I'M CALLING OFF THE BOUNTY ON YOU THREE.
BUT I SWEAR, IF YOU DIE AGAIN, THAT'S IT!
NO MORE MR. NICE DEATH. I'M COMING FOR YOU.
HEAR THAT? HE'S COMING FOR YOU!
SHUT UP!

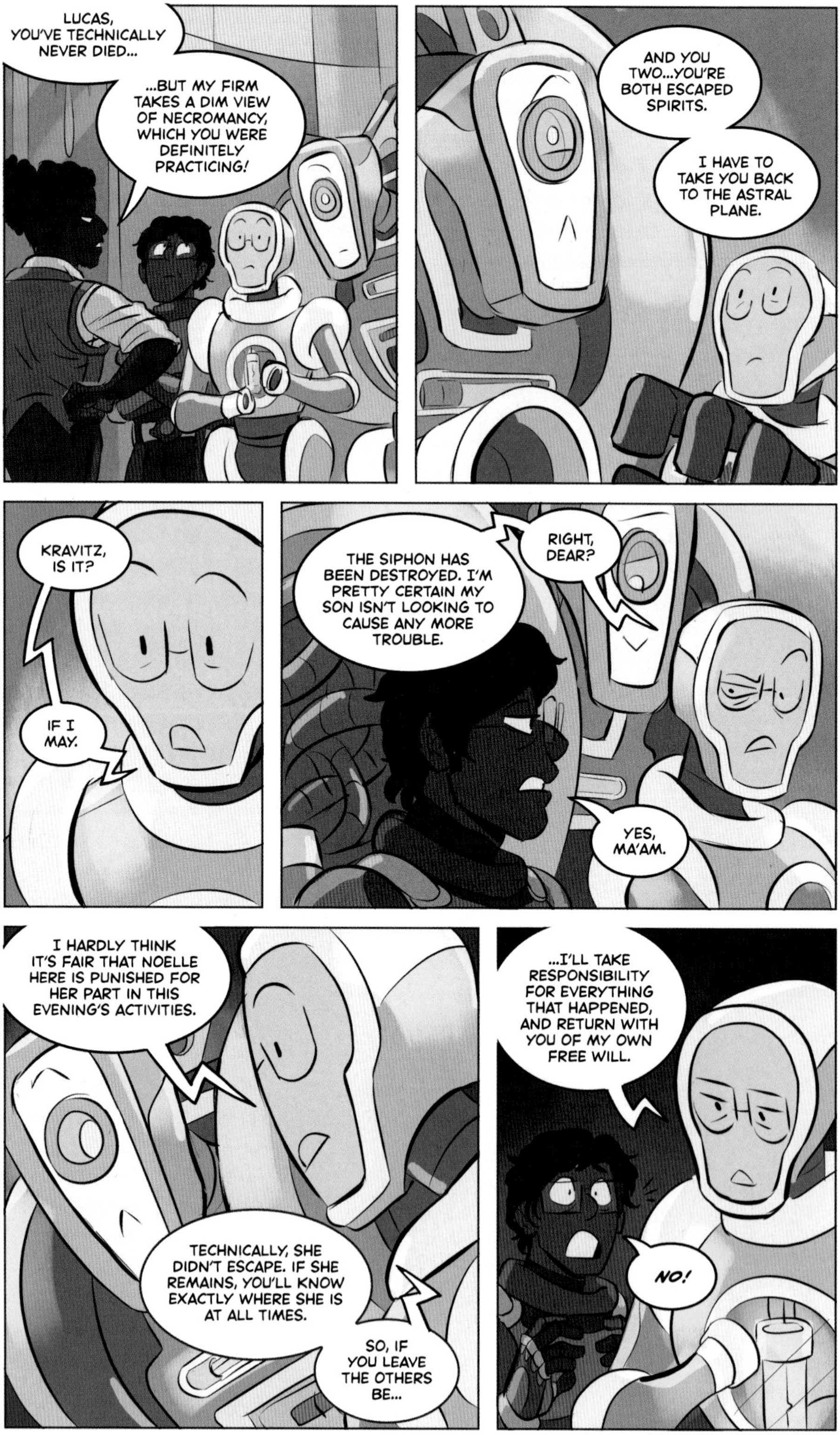
LUCAS, YOU'VE TECHNICALLY NEVER DIED...
...BUT MY FIRM TAKES A DIM VIEW OF NECROMANCY, WHICH YOU WERE DEFINITELY PRACTICING!
AND YOU TWO...YOU'RE BOTH ESCAPED SPIRITS.
I HAVE TO TAKE YOU BACK TO THE ASTRAL PLANE.
KRAVITZ, IS IT?
IF I MAY.
THE SIPHON HAS BEEN DESTROYED. I'M PRETTY CERTAIN MY SON ISN'T LOOKING TO CAUSE ANY MORE TROUBLE.
RIGHT, DEAR?
YES, MA'AM.
I HARDLY THINK IT'S FAIR THAT NOELLE HERE IS PUNISHED FOR HER PART IN THIS EVENING'S ACTIVITIES.
TECHNICALLY, SHE DIDN'T ESCAPE. IF SHE REMAINS, YOU'LL KNOW EXACTLY WHERE SHE IS AT ALL TIMES.
SO, IF YOU LEAVE THE OTHERS BE...
...I'LL TAKE RESPONSIBILITY FOR EVERYTHING THAT HAPPENED, AND RETURN WITH YOU OF MY OWN FREE WILL.
NO!

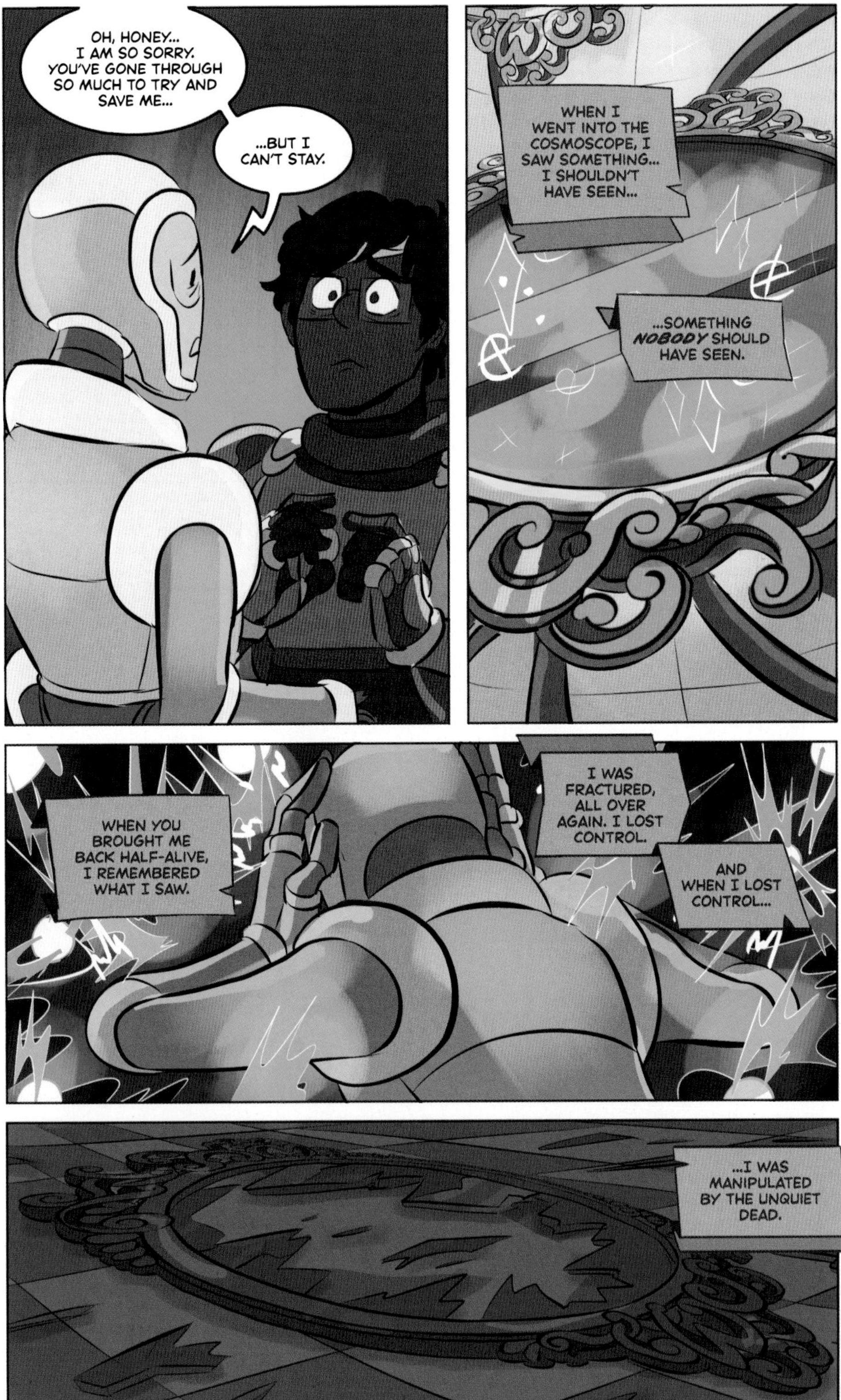
OH, HONEY... I AM SO SORRY. YOU'VE GONE THROUGH SO MUCH TO TRY AND SAVE ME...
...BUT I CAN'T STAY.
WHEN I WENT INTO THE COSMOSCOPE, I SAW SOMETHING... I SHOULDN'T HAVE SEEN...
...SOMETHING *NOBODY* SHOULD HAVE SEEN.
WHEN YOU BROUGHT ME BACK HALF-ALIVE, I REMEMBERED WHAT I SAW.
I WAS FRACTURED, ALL OVER AGAIN. I LOST CONTROL.
AND WHEN I LOST CONTROL...
...I WAS MANIPULATED BY THE UNQUIET DEAD.

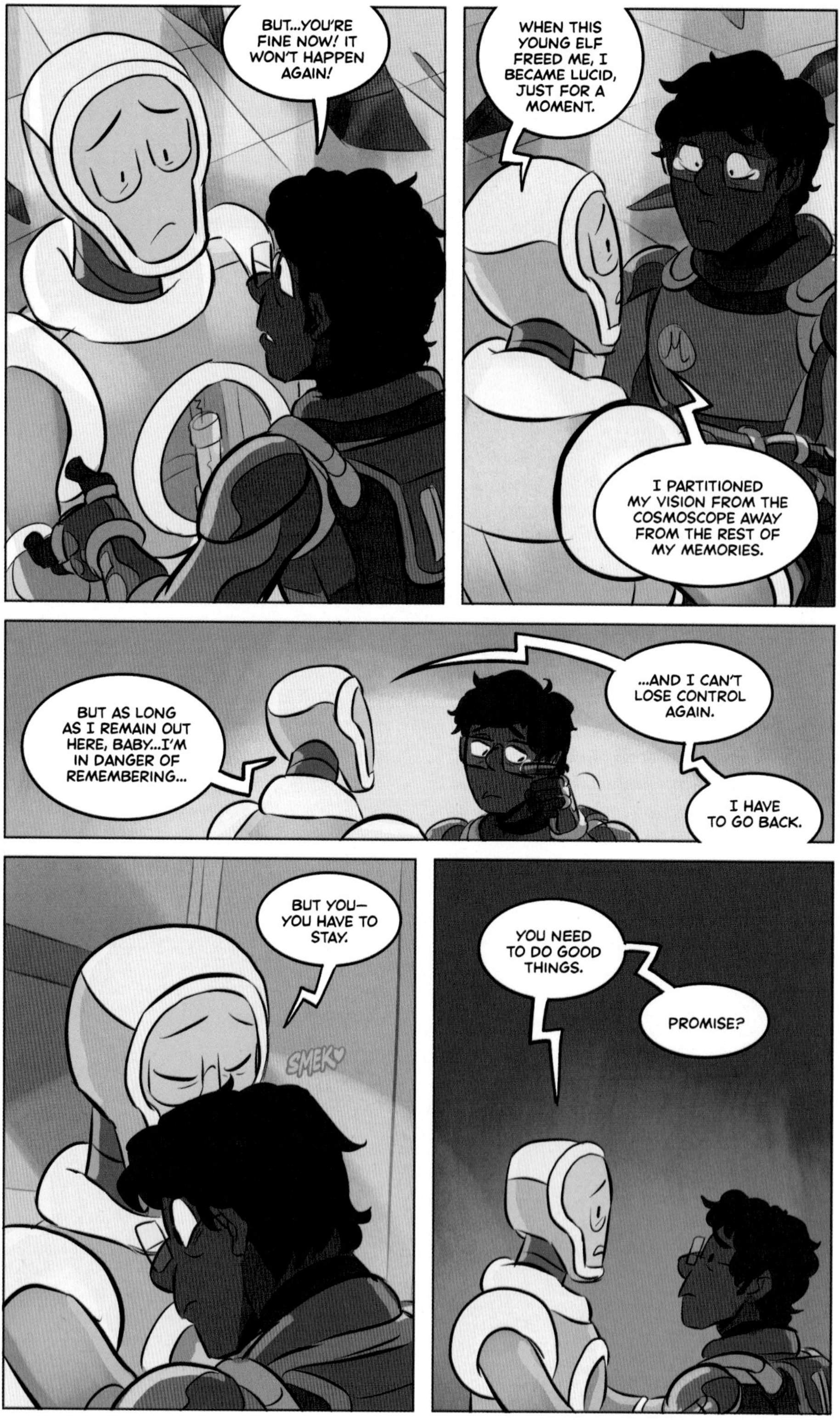
BUT...YOU'RE FINE NOW! IT WON'T HAPPEN AGAIN!
WHEN THIS YOUNG ELF FREED ME, I BECAME LUCID, JUST FOR A MOMENT.
I PARTITIONED MY VISION FROM THE COSMOSCOPE AWAY FROM THE REST OF MY MEMORIES.
BUT AS LONG AS I REMAIN OUT HERE, BABY...I'M IN DANGER OF REMEMBERING...
...AND I CAN'T LOSE CONTROL AGAIN.
I HAVE TO GO BACK.
BUT YOU— YOU HAVE TO STAY.
SMEK
YOU NEED TO DO GOOD THINGS.
PROMISE?

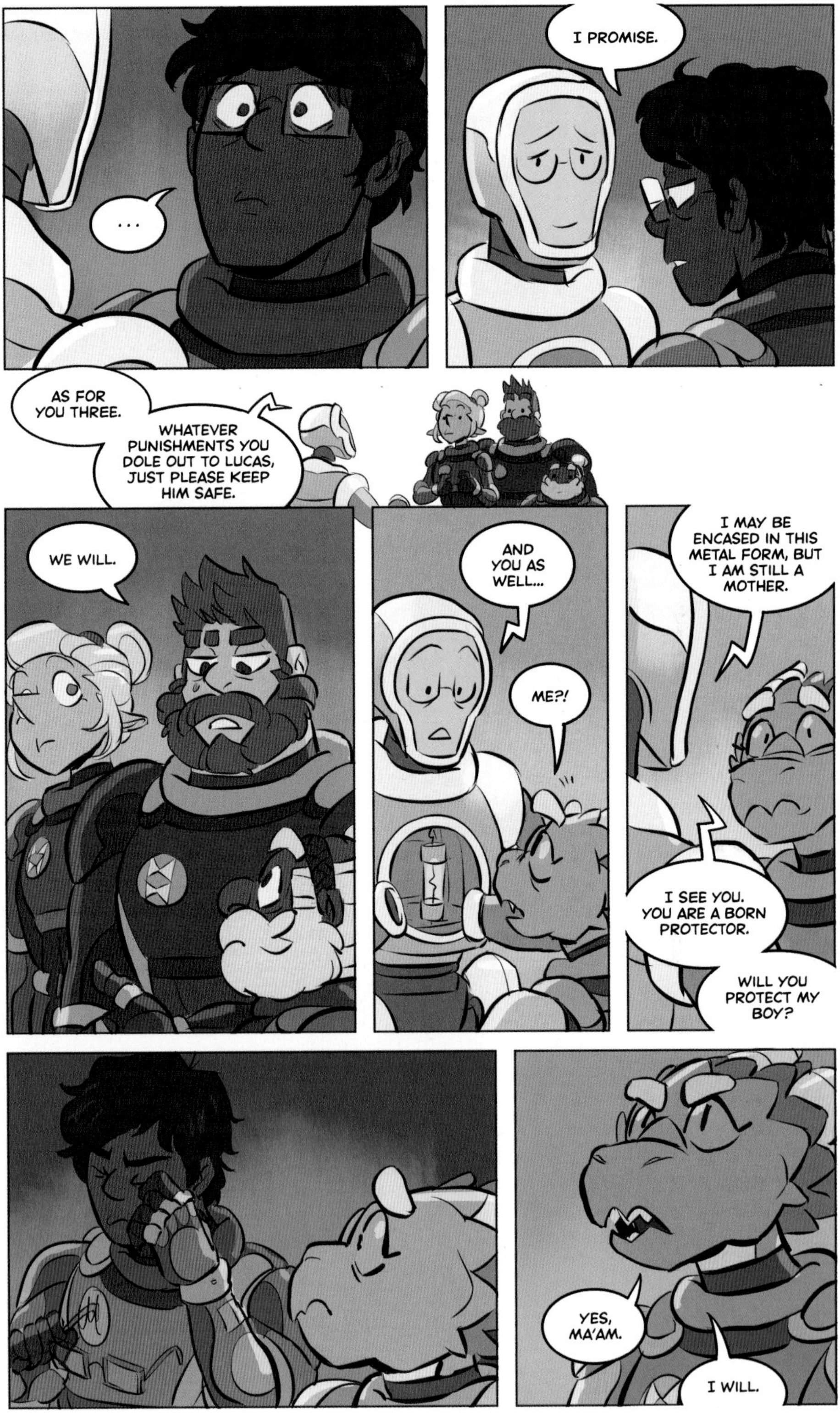
...
I PROMISE.
AS FOR YOU THREE.
WHATEVER PUNISHMENTS YOU DOLE OUT TO LUCAS, JUST PLEASE KEEP HIM SAFE.
WE WILL.
AND YOU AS WELL...
ME?!
I MAY BE ENCASED IN THIS METAL FORM, BUT I AM STILL A MOTHER.
I SEE YOU. YOU ARE A BORN PROTECTOR.
WILL YOU PROTECT MY BOY?
YES, MA'AM.
I WILL.

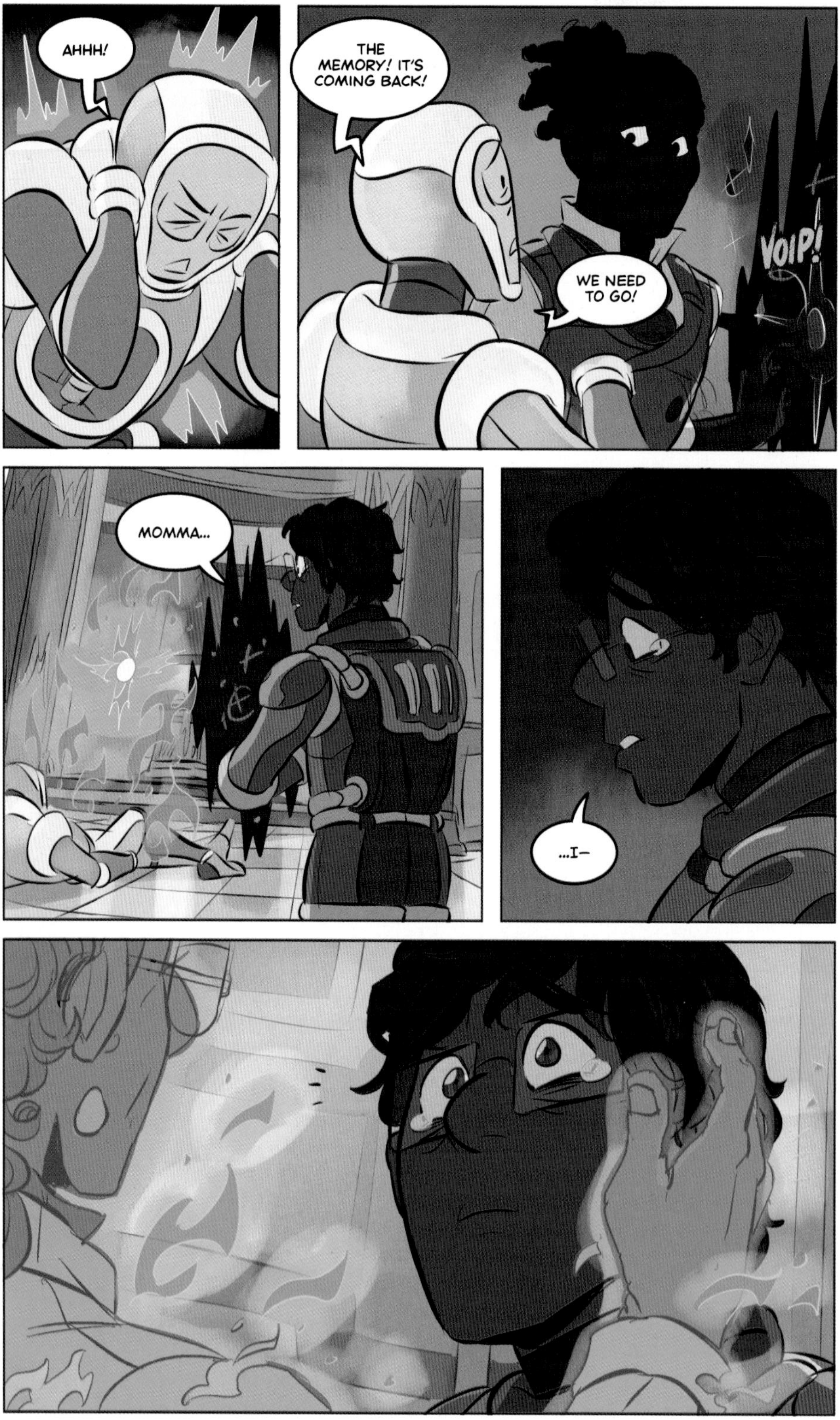
AHHH!
THE MEMORY! IT'S COMING BACK!
WE NEED TO GO!
VOIP!
MOMMA...
...I—

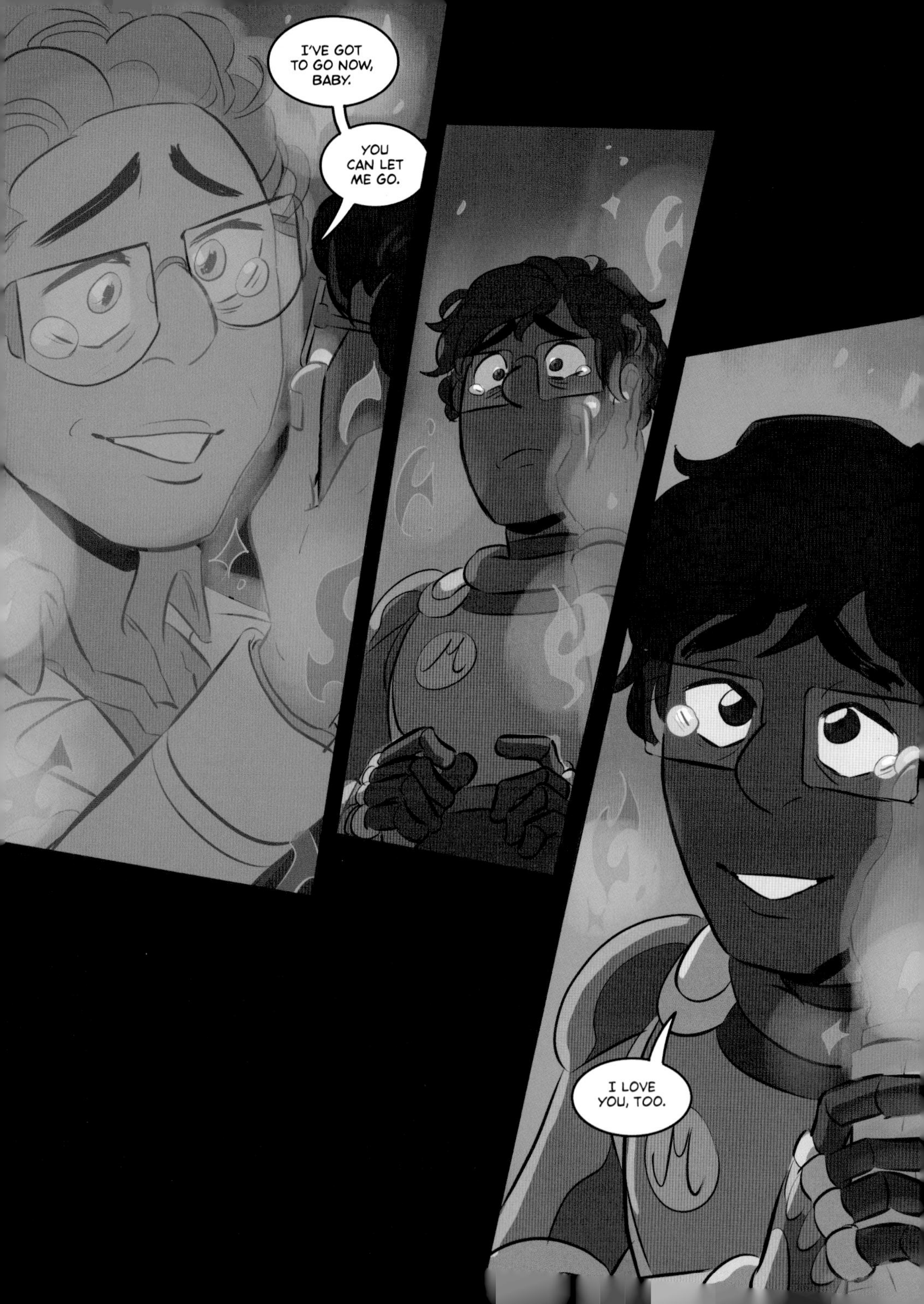
I'VE GOT TO GO NOW, BABY.
YOU CAN LET ME GO.
I LOVE YOU, TOO.

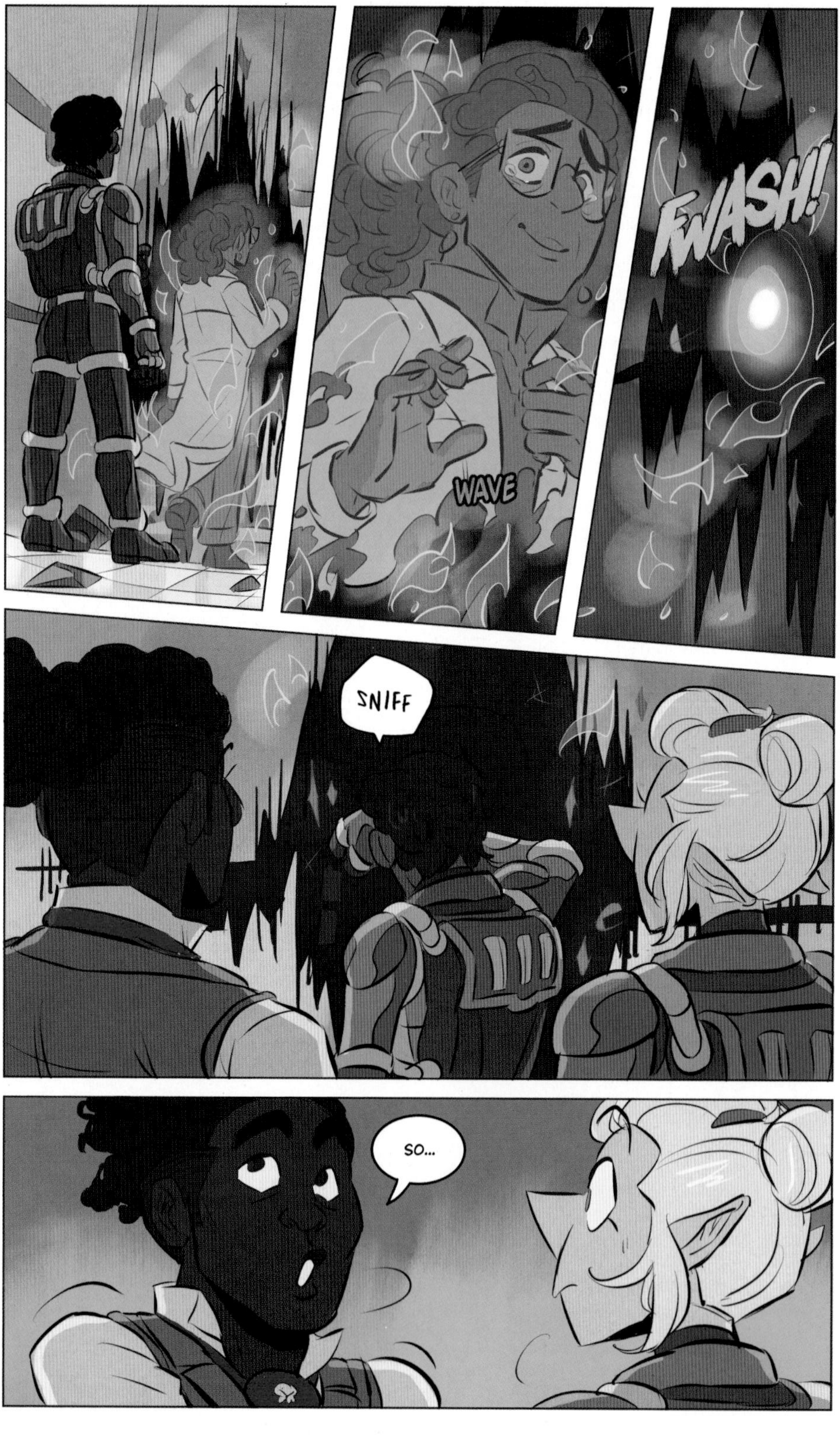
WAVE
FWASH!
SNIFF
SO...

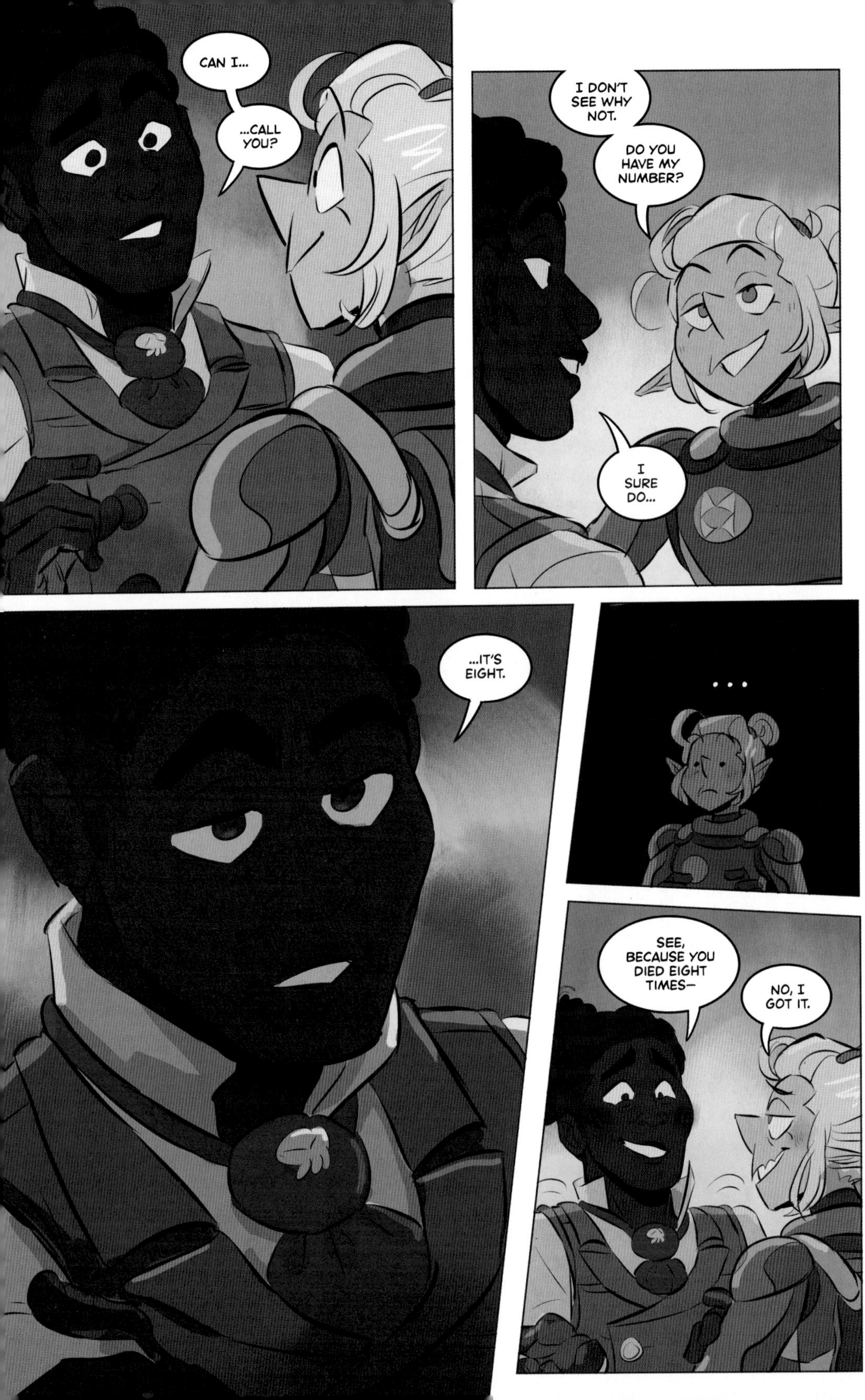
CAN I...
...CALL YOU?
I DON'T SEE WHY NOT.
DO YOU HAVE MY NUMBER?
I SURE DO...
...IT'S EIGHT.
. . .
SEE, BECAUSE YOU DIED EIGHT TIMES—
NO, I GOT IT.

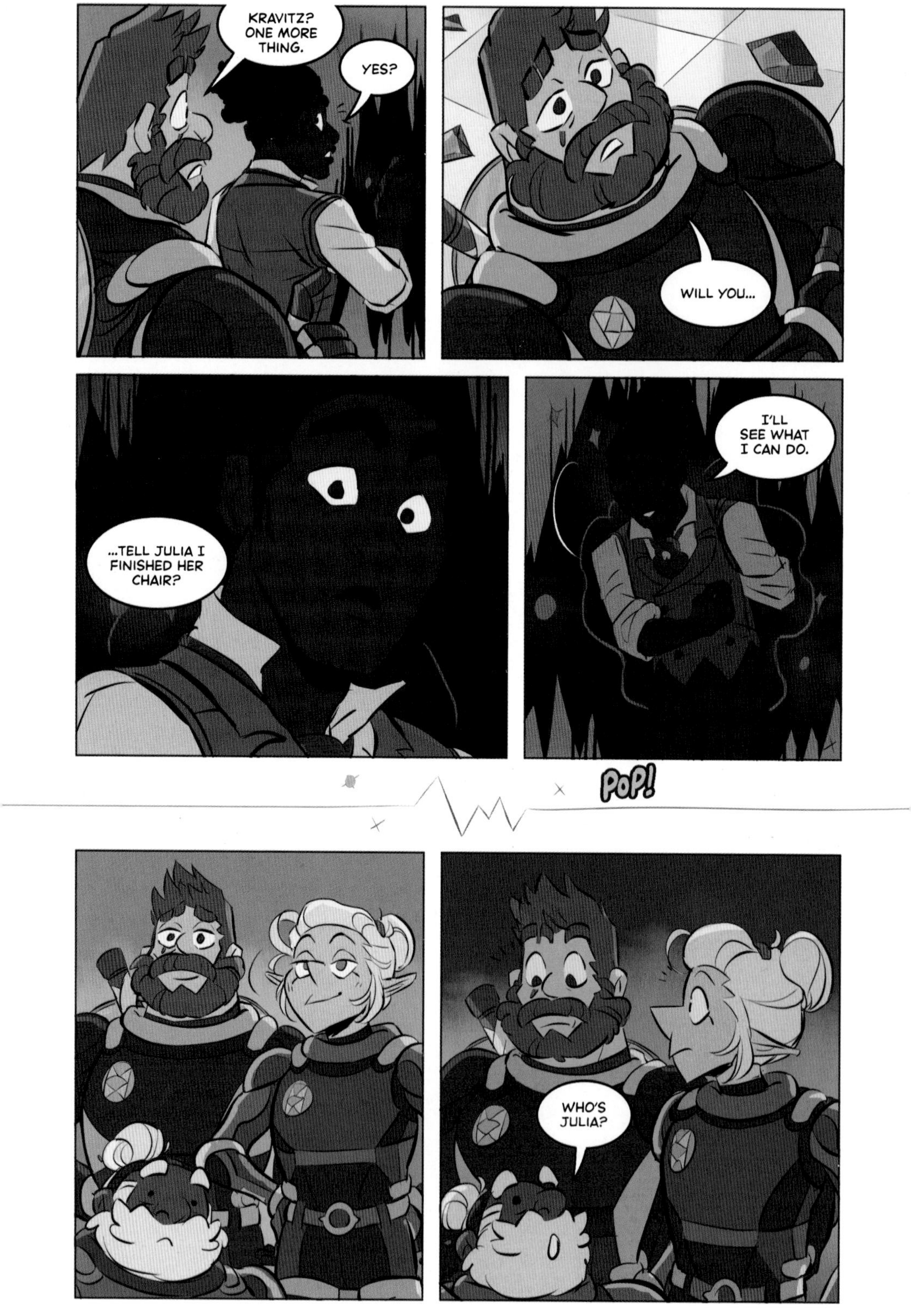
KRAVITZ? ONE MORE THING.
YES?
WILL YOU...
...TELL JULIA I FINISHED HER CHAIR?
I'LL SEE WHAT I CAN DO.
POP!
WHO'S JULIA?

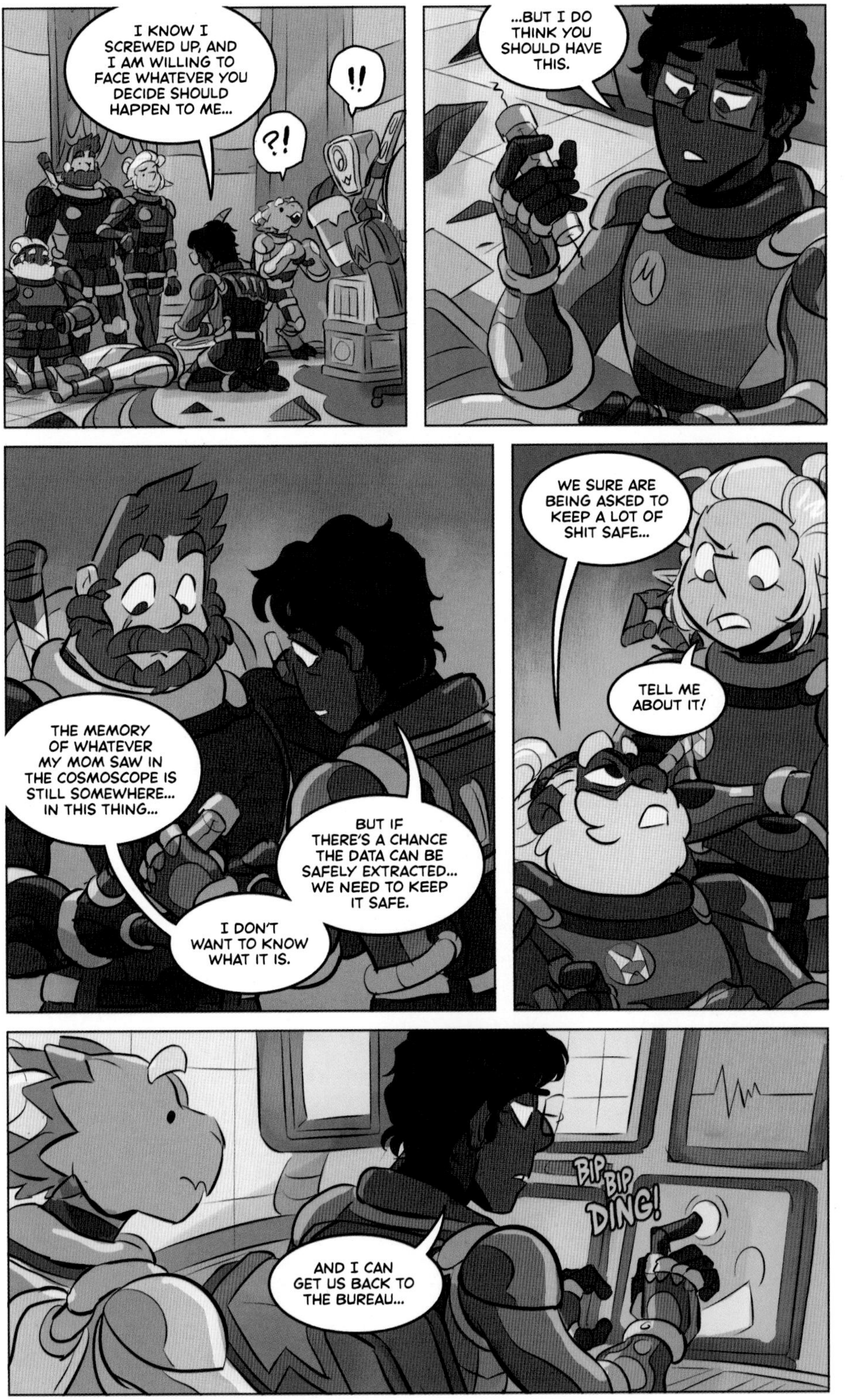
I KNOW I SCREWED UP, AND I AM WILLING TO FACE WHATEVER YOU DECIDE SHOULD HAPPEN TO ME...
!!
?!
...BUT I DO THINK YOU SHOULD HAVE THIS.
THE MEMORY OF WHATEVER MY MOM SAW IN THE COSMOSCOPE IS STILL SOMEWHERE... IN THIS THING...
I DON'T WANT TO KNOW WHAT IT IS.
BUT IF THERE'S A CHANCE THE DATA CAN BE SAFELY EXTRACTED... WE NEED TO KEEP IT SAFE.
WE SURE ARE BEING ASKED TO KEEP A LOT OF SHIT SAFE...
TELL ME ABOUT IT!
BIP BIP DING!
AND I CAN GET US BACK TO THE BUREAU...

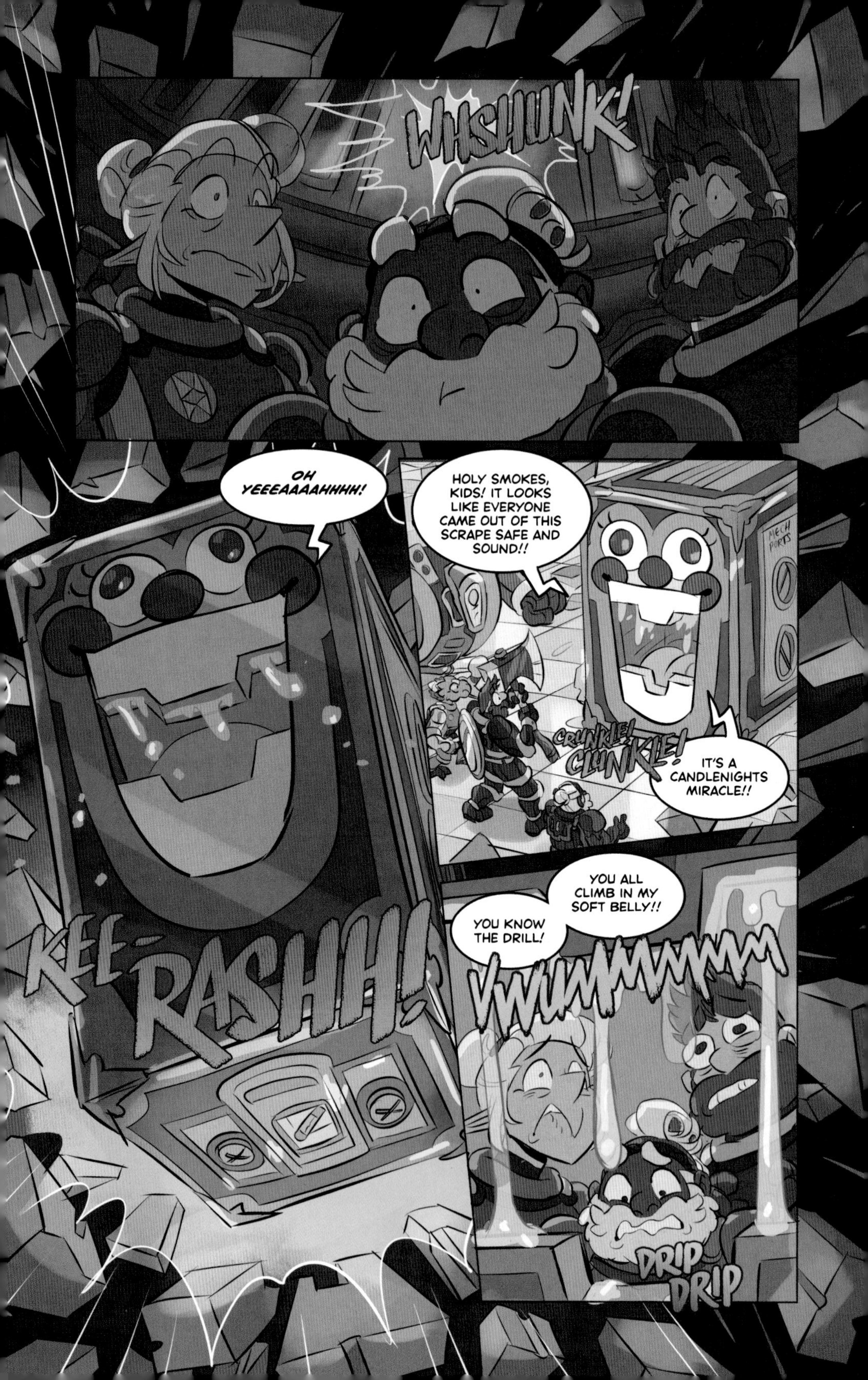
WHSHUNK!
OH YEEEAAAAHHHH!
KEE-RASHH!
HOLY SMOKES, KIDS! IT LOOKS LIKE EVERYONE CAME OUT OF THIS SCRAPE SAFE AND SOUND!!
MECH PORTS
CRUNKLE! CLUNKLE!
IT'S A CANDLENIGHTS MIRACLE!!
YOU KNOW THE DRILL!
YOU ALL CLIMB IN MY SOFT BELLY!!
VWUMMMMM
DRIP DRIP

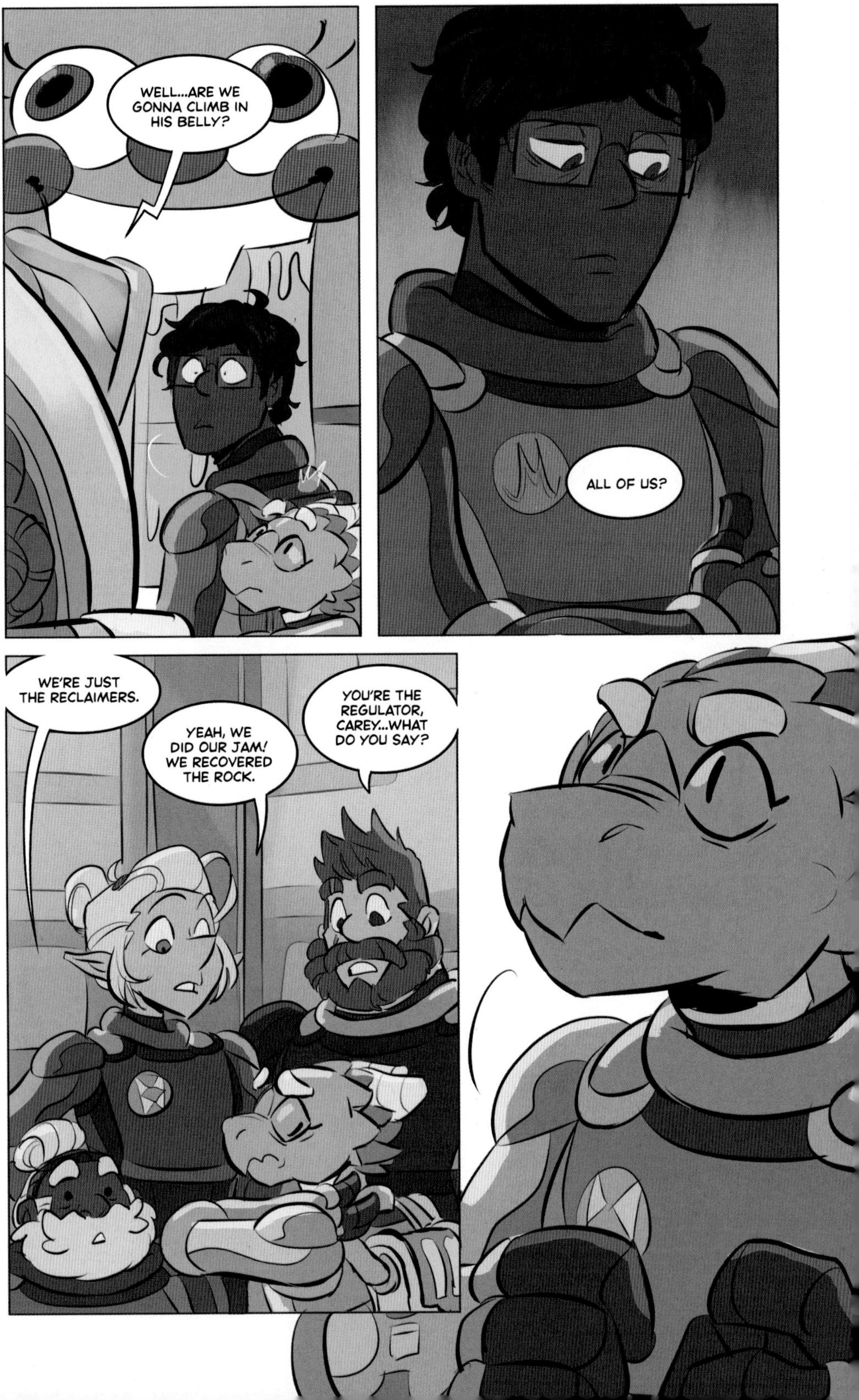
WELL...ARE WE GONNA CLIMB IN HIS BELLY?
ALL OF US?
WE'RE JUST THE RECLAIMERS.
YEAH, WE DID OUR JAM! WE RECOVERED THE ROCK.
YOU'RE THE REGULATOR, CAREY...WHAT DO YOU SAY?

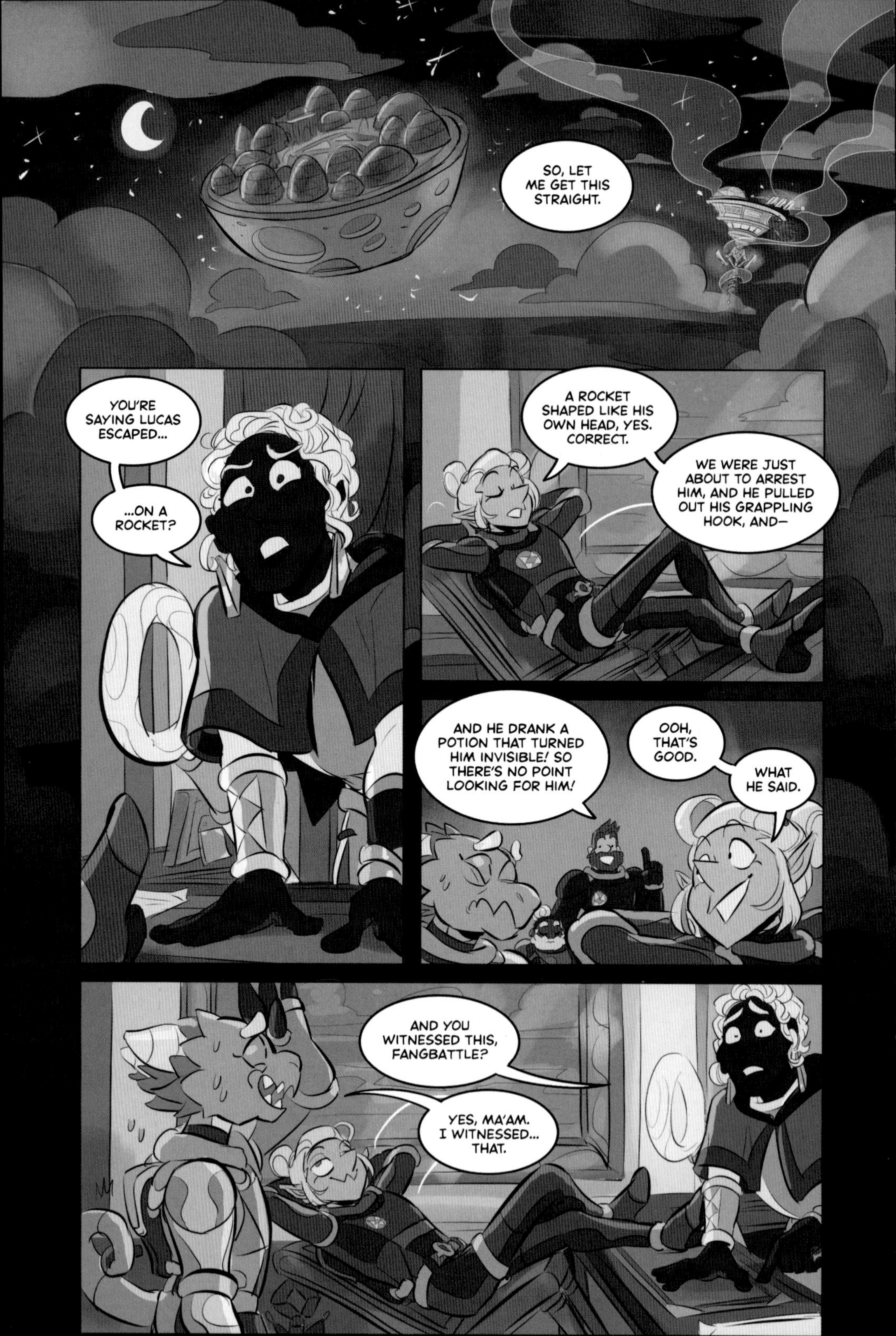
SO, LET ME GET THIS STRAIGHT.
YOU'RE SAYING LUCAS ESCAPED...
...ON A ROCKET?
A ROCKET SHAPED LIKE HIS OWN HEAD, YES. CORRECT.
WE WERE JUST ABOUT TO ARREST HIM, AND HE PULLED OUT HIS GRAPPLING HOOK, AND—
AND HE DRANK A POTION THAT TURNED HIM INVISIBLE! SO THERE'S NO POINT LOOKING FOR HIM!
OOH, THAT'S GOOD.
WHAT HE SAID.
AND YOU WITNESSED THIS, FANGBATTLE?
YES, MA'AM. I WITNESSED... THAT.

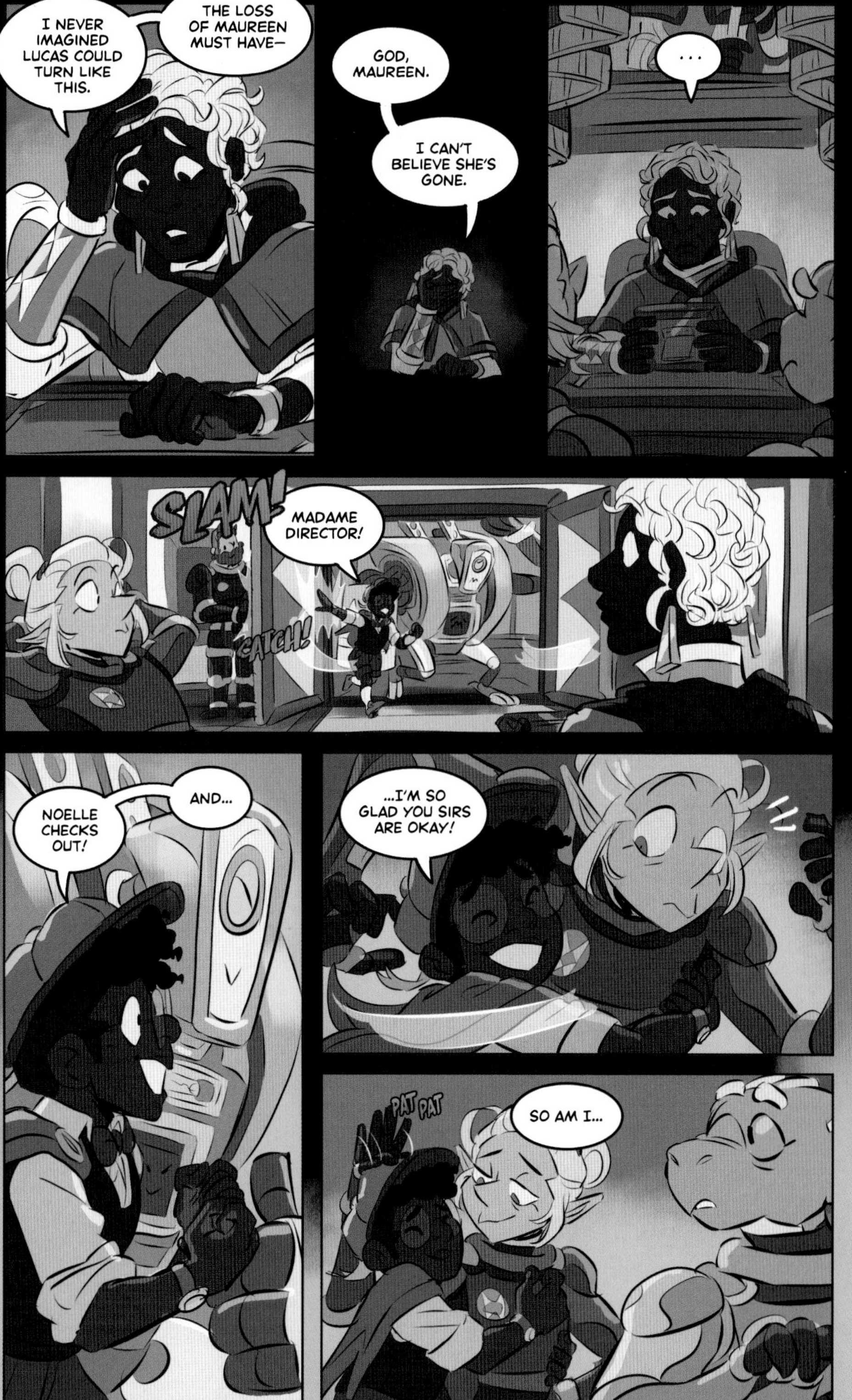
I NEVER IMAGINED LUCAS COULD TURN LIKE THIS.
THE LOSS OF MAUREEN MUST HAVE—
GOD, MAUREEN.
I CAN'T BELIEVE SHE'S GONE.
. . .
SLAM!
MADAME DIRECTOR!
CATCH!
NOELLE CHECKS OUT!
AND...
...I'M SO GLAD YOU SIRS ARE OKAY!
PAT PAT
SO AM I...

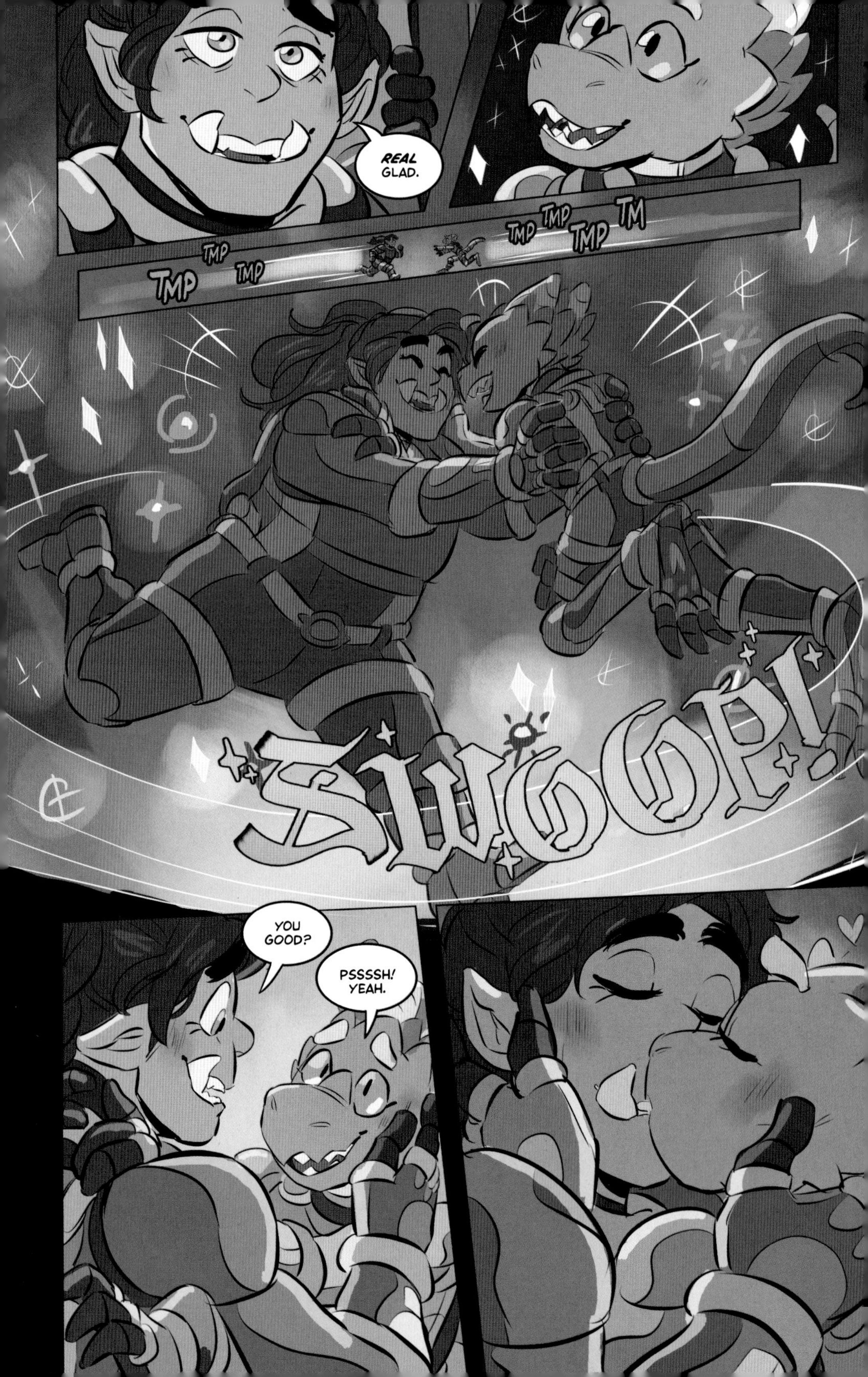
REAL GLAD.
TMP TMP TMP
TMP TMP TMP TMP TM
SWOOP!
YOU GOOD?
PSSSSH! YEAH.

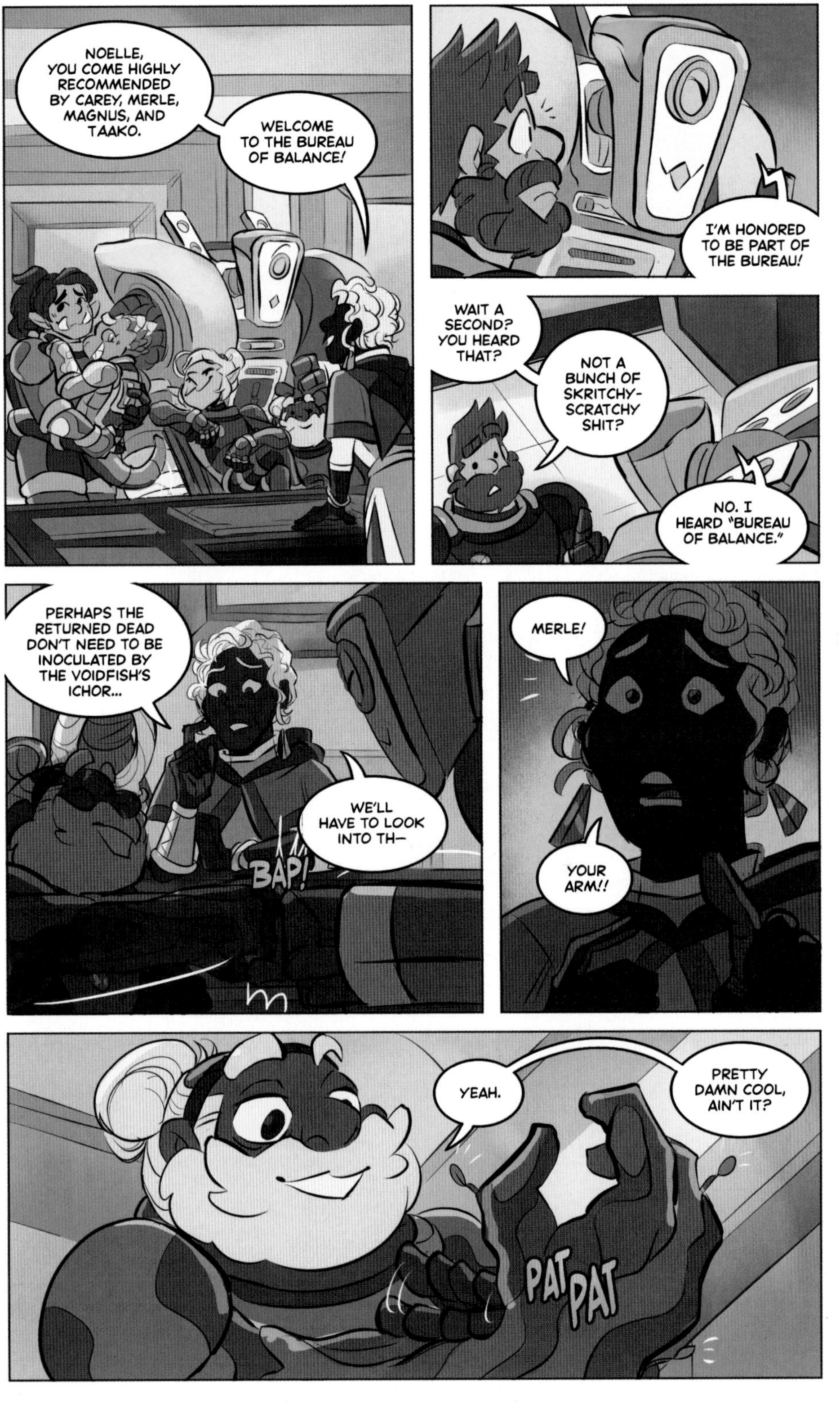
NOELLE, YOU COME HIGHLY RECOMMENDED BY CAREY, MERLE, MAGNUS, AND TAAKO.
WELCOME TO THE BUREAU OF BALANCE!
I'M HONORED TO BE PART OF THE BUREAU!
WAIT A SECOND? YOU HEARD THAT?
NOT A BUNCH OF SKRITCHY-SCRATCHY SHIT?
NO. I HEARD "BUREAU OF BALANCE."
PERHAPS THE RETURNED DEAD DON'T NEED TO BE INOCULATED BY THE VOIDFISH'S ICHOR...
WE'LL HAVE TO LOOK INTO TH—
BAP!
MERLE!
YOUR ARM!!
YEAH.
PRETTY DAMN COOL, AIN'T IT?
PAT PAT

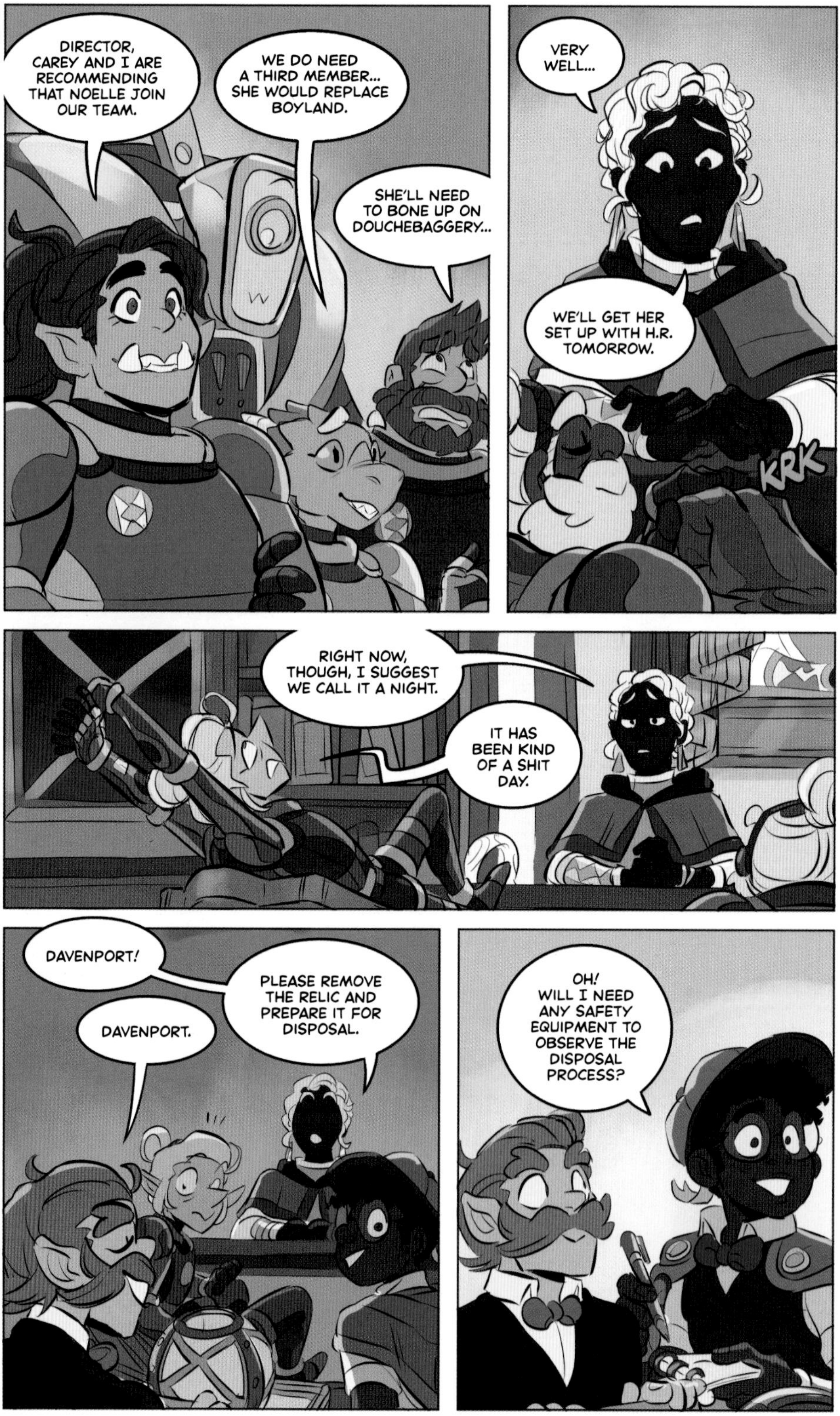
DIRECTOR, CAREY AND I ARE RECOMMENDING THAT NOELLE JOIN OUR TEAM.
WE DO NEED A THIRD MEMBER... SHE WOULD REPLACE BOYLAND.
SHE'LL NEED TO BONE UP ON DOUCHEBAGGERY...
VERY WELL...
WE'LL GET HER SET UP WITH H.R. TOMORROW.
KRK
RIGHT NOW, THOUGH, I SUGGEST WE CALL IT A NIGHT.
IT HAS BEEN KIND OF A SHIT DAY.
DAVENPORT!
DAVENPORT.
PLEASE REMOVE THE RELIC AND PREPARE IT FOR DISPOSAL.
OH! WILL I NEED ANY SAFETY EQUIPMENT TO OBSERVE THE DISPOSAL PROCESS?

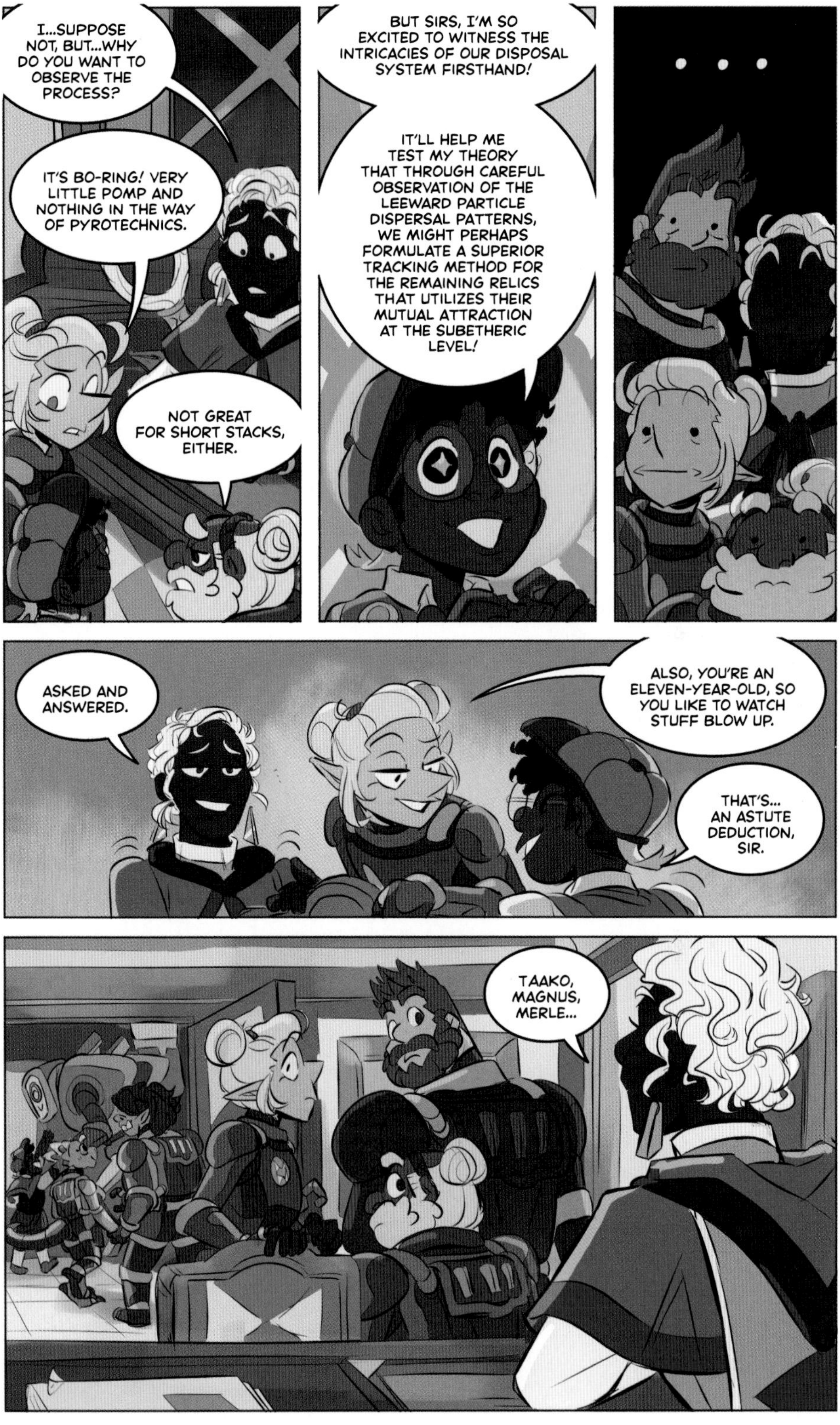
I...SUPPOSE NOT, BUT...WHY DO YOU WANT TO OBSERVE THE PROCESS?
IT'S BO-RING! VERY LITTLE POMP AND NOTHING IN THE WAY OF PYROTECHNICS.
NOT GREAT FOR SHORT STACKS, EITHER.
BUT SIRS, I'M SO EXCITED TO WITNESS THE INTRICACIES OF OUR DISPOSAL SYSTEM FIRSTHAND!
IT'LL HELP ME TEST MY THEORY THAT THROUGH CAREFUL OBSERVATION OF THE LEEWARD PARTICLE DISPERSAL PATTERNS, WE MIGHT PERHAPS FORMULATE A SUPERIOR TRACKING METHOD FOR THE REMAINING RELICS THAT UTILIZES THEIR MUTUAL ATTRACTION AT THE SUBETHERIC LEVEL!
. . .
ASKED AND ANSWERED.
ALSO, YOU'RE AN ELEVEN-YEAR-OLD, SO YOU LIKE TO WATCH STUFF BLOW UP.
THAT'S... AN ASTUTE DEDUCTION, SIR.
TAAKO, MAGNUS, MERLE...

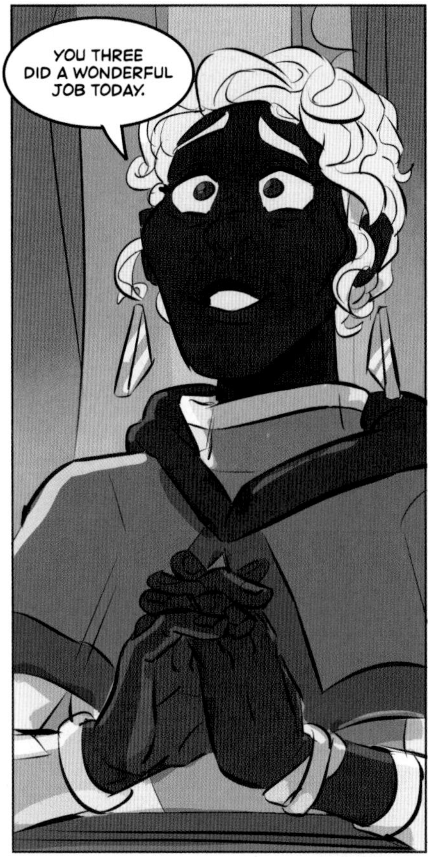
YOU THREE DID A WONDERFUL JOB TODAY.

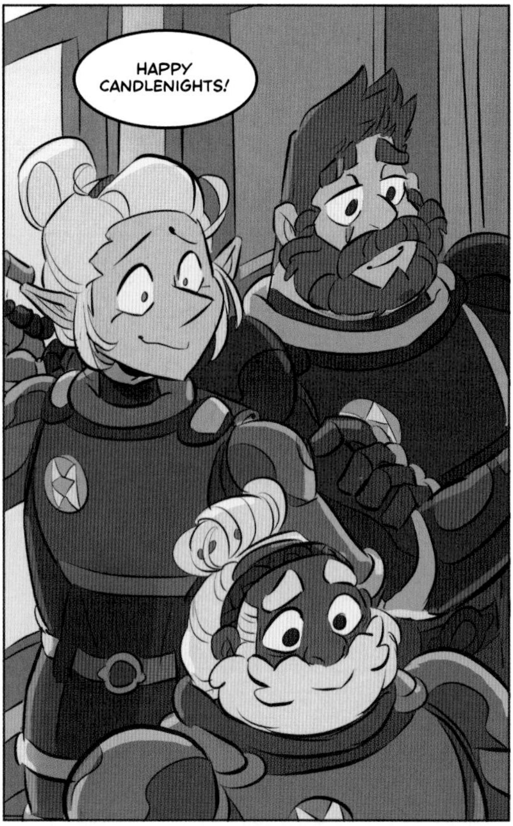
HAPPY CANDLENIGHTS!

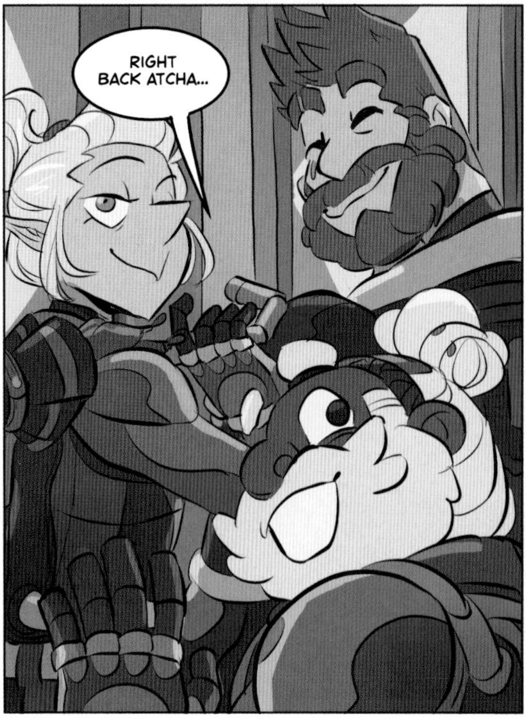
RIGHT BACK ATCHA...

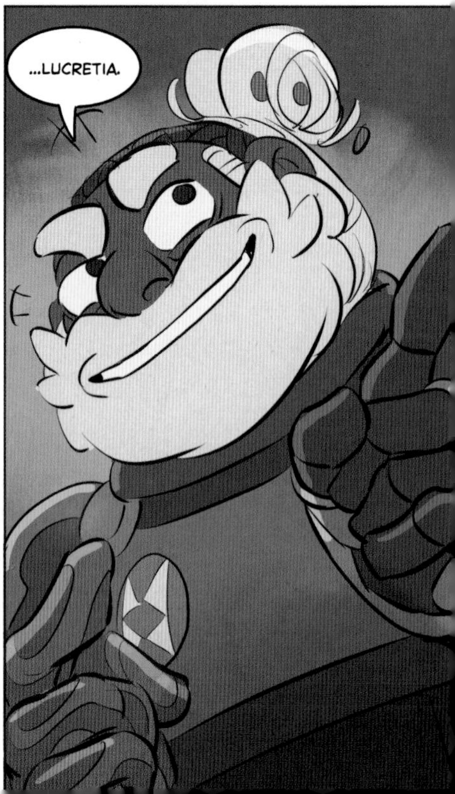
...LUCRETIA.

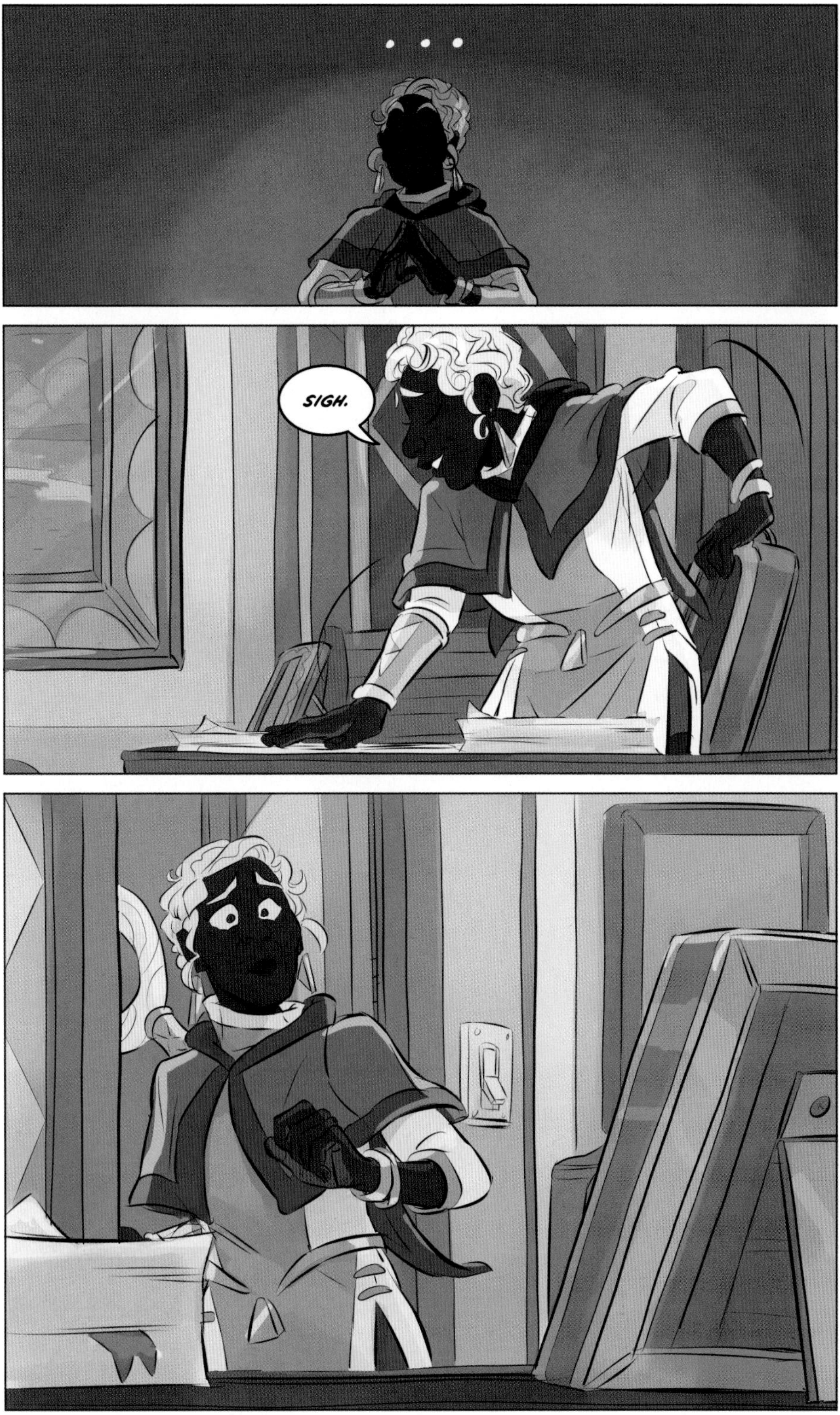
SIGH.

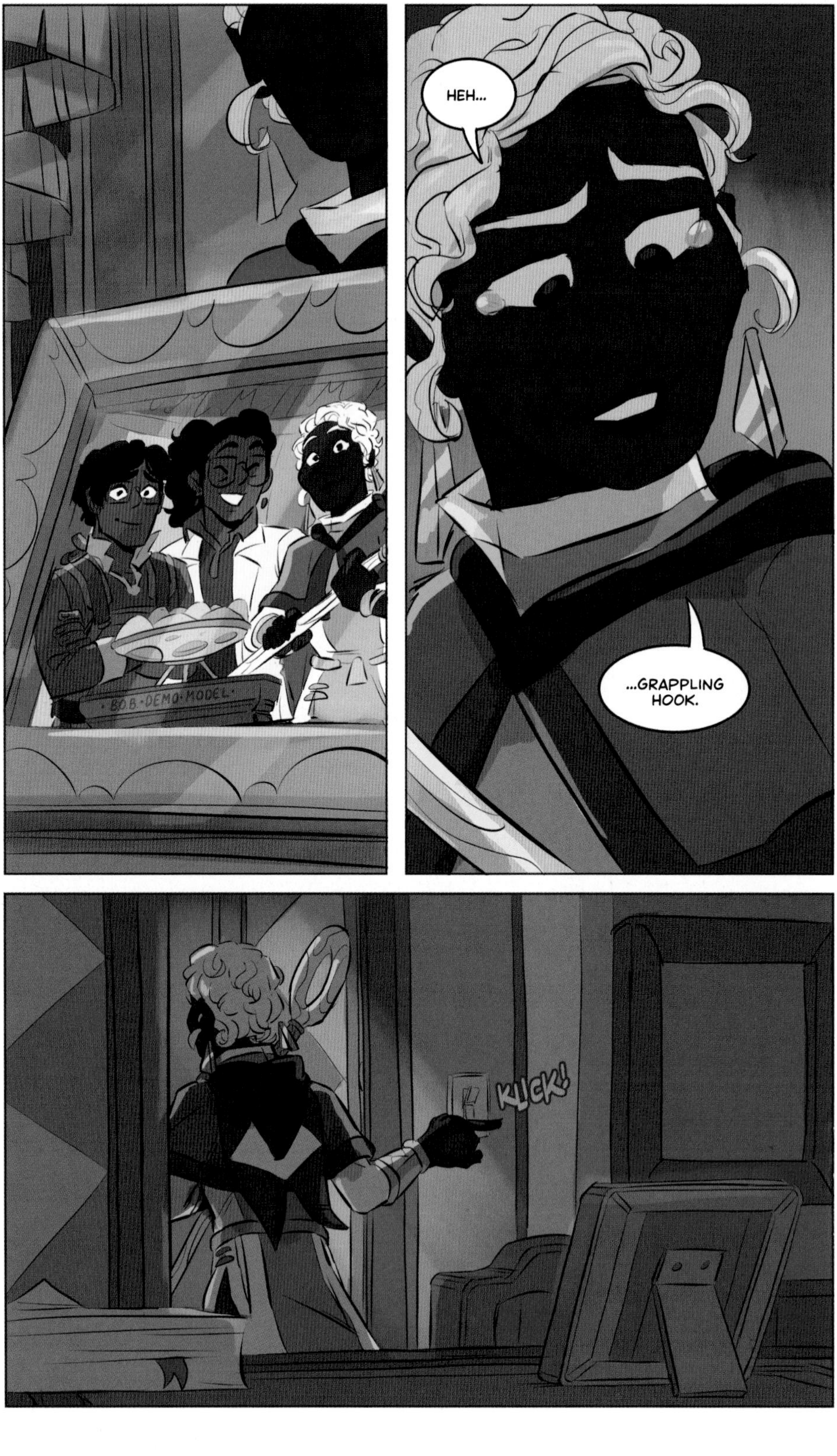
BOB·DEMO·MODEL
HEH...
...GRAPPLING HOOK.
KLICK!

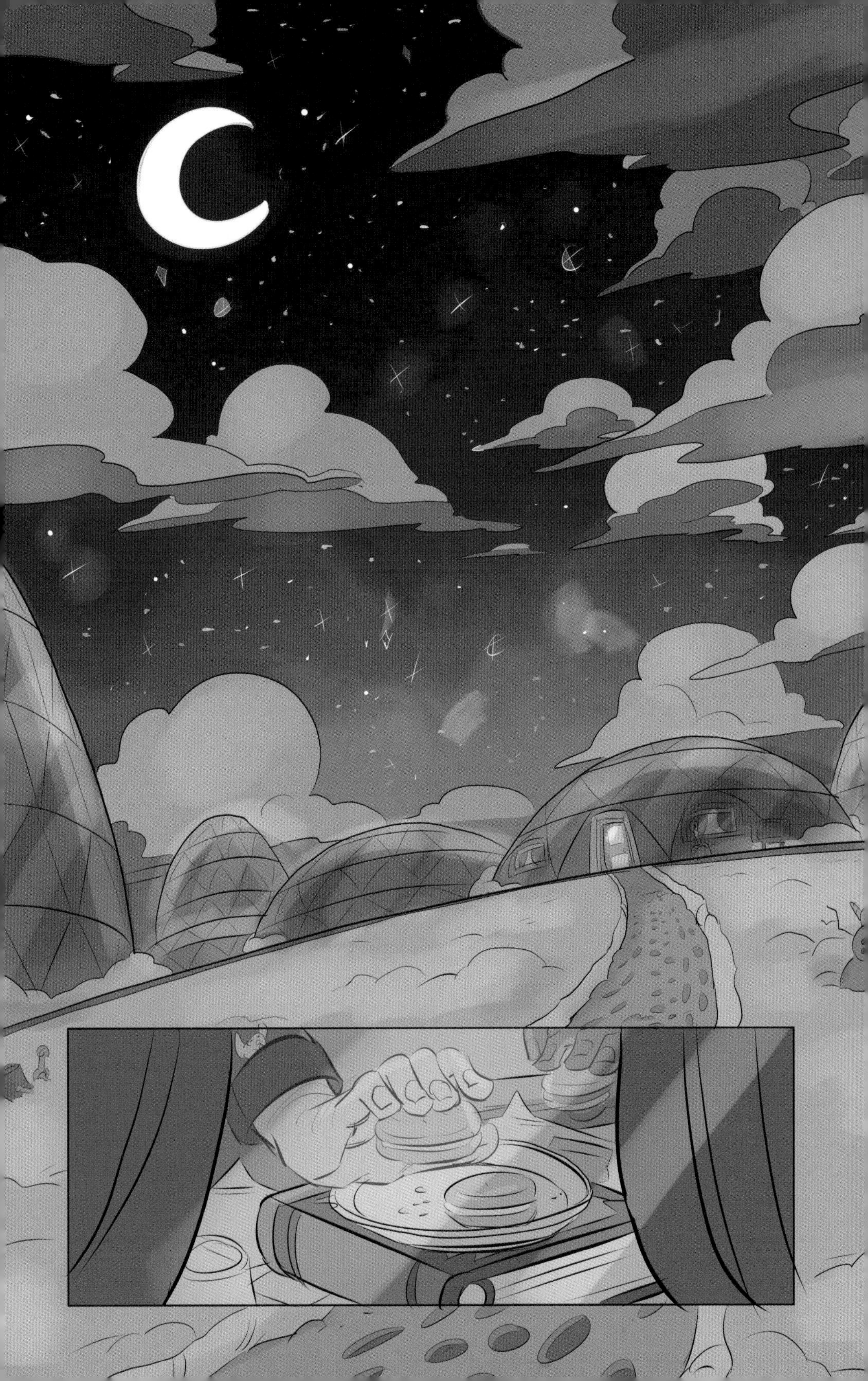

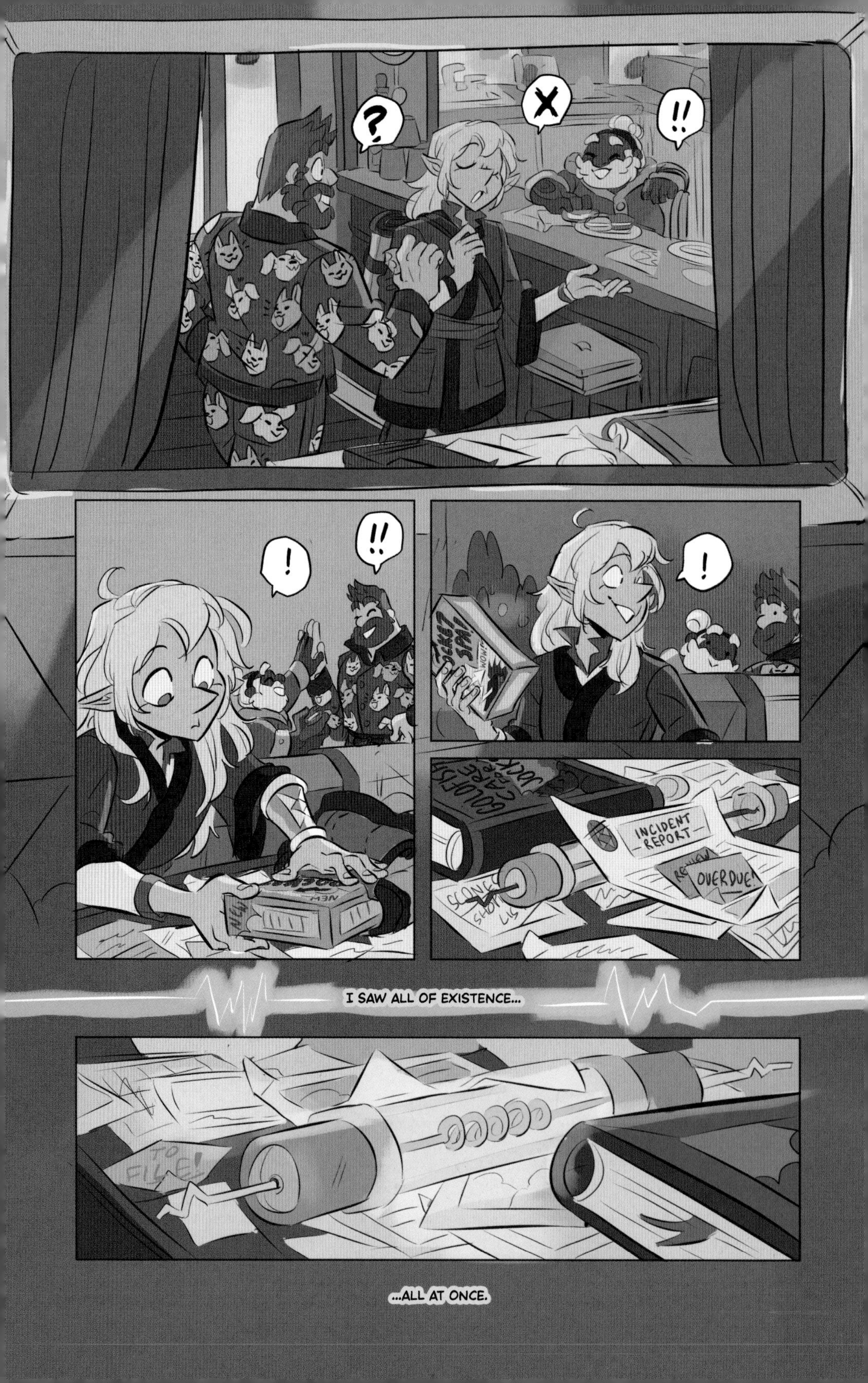
?
X
!!
!
!!
!
INCIDENT REPORT
OVERDUE!
I SAW ALL OF EXISTENCE...
TO FILE!
...ALL AT ONCE.

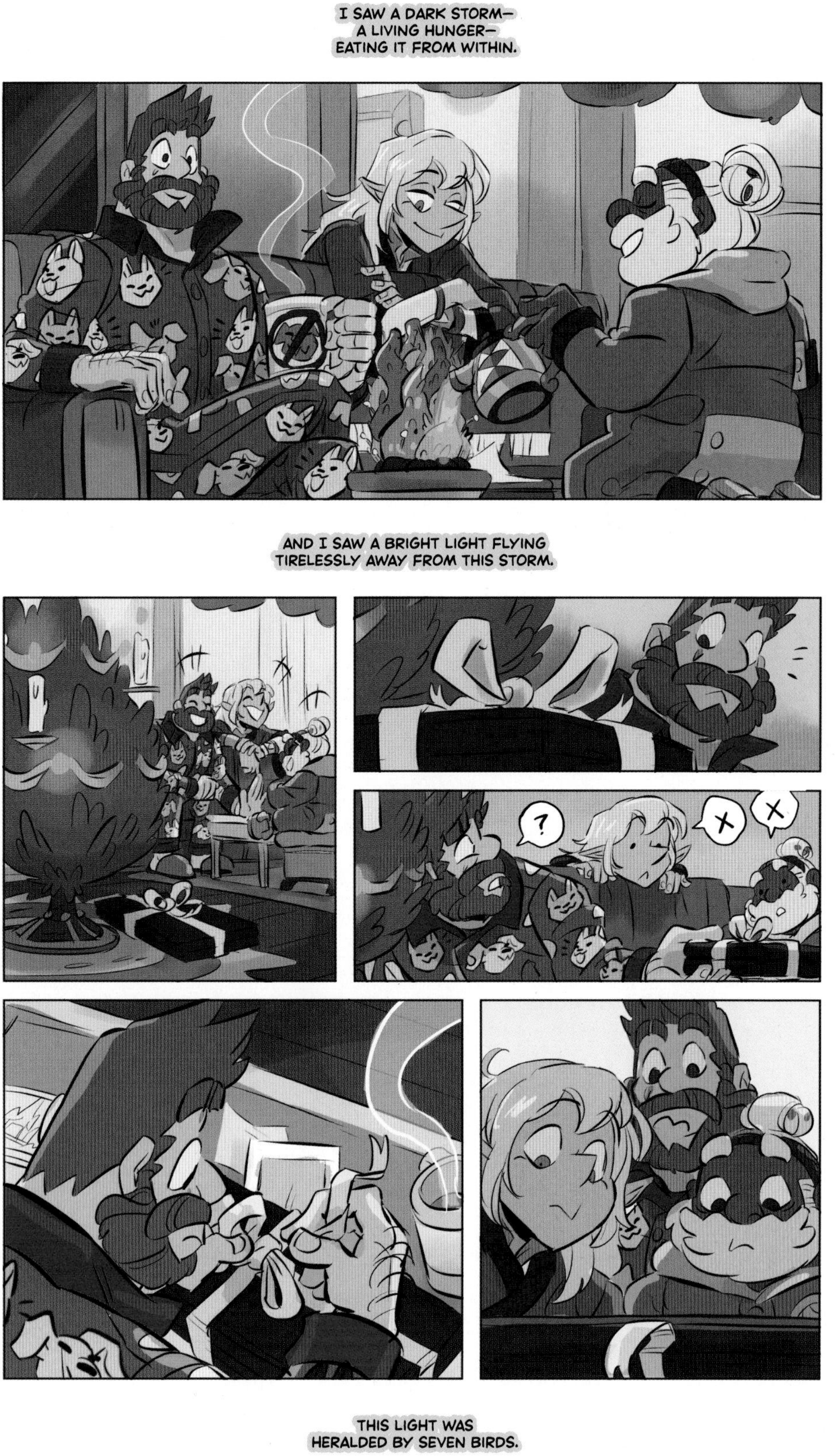
I SAW A DARK STORM—
A LIVING HUNGER—
EATING IT FROM WITHIN.
AND I SAW A BRIGHT LIGHT FLYING
TIRELESSLY AWAY FROM THIS STORM.
?
X
X
THIS LIGHT WAS
HERALDED BY SEVEN BIRDS.

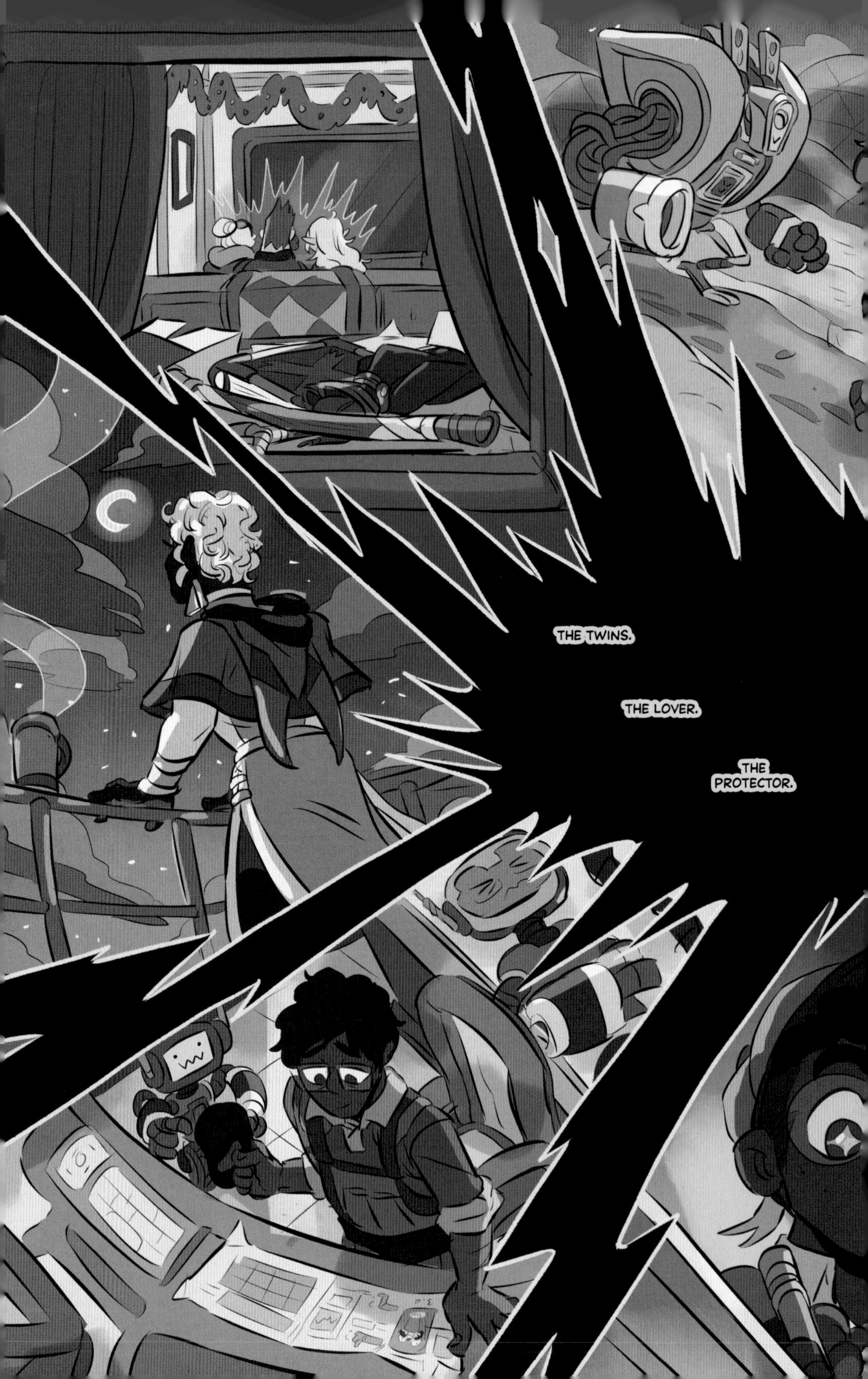
THE TWINS.
THE LOVER.
THE PROTECTOR.

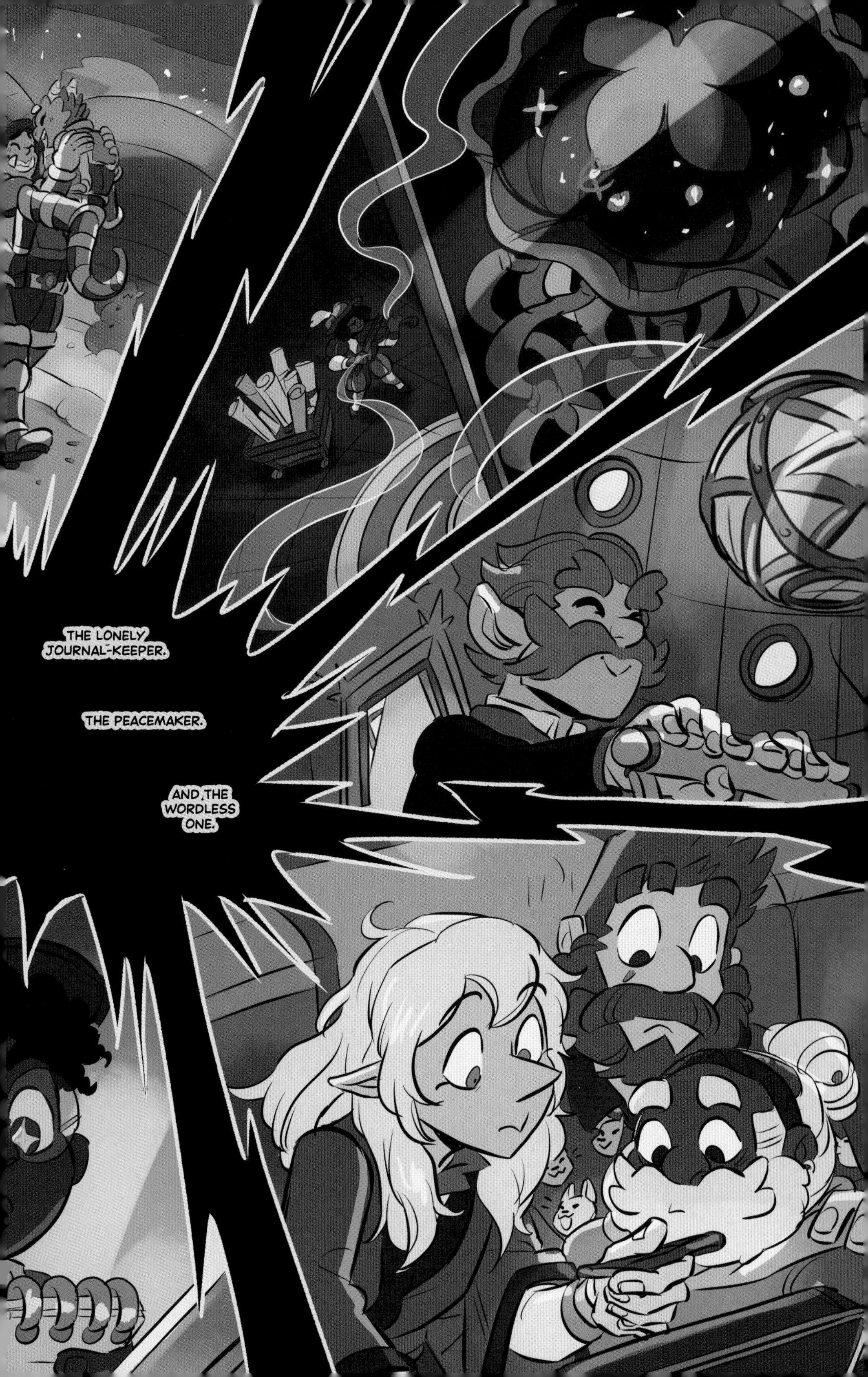
THE LONELY JOURNAL-KEEPER.
THE PEACEMAKER.
AND THE WORDLESS ONE.

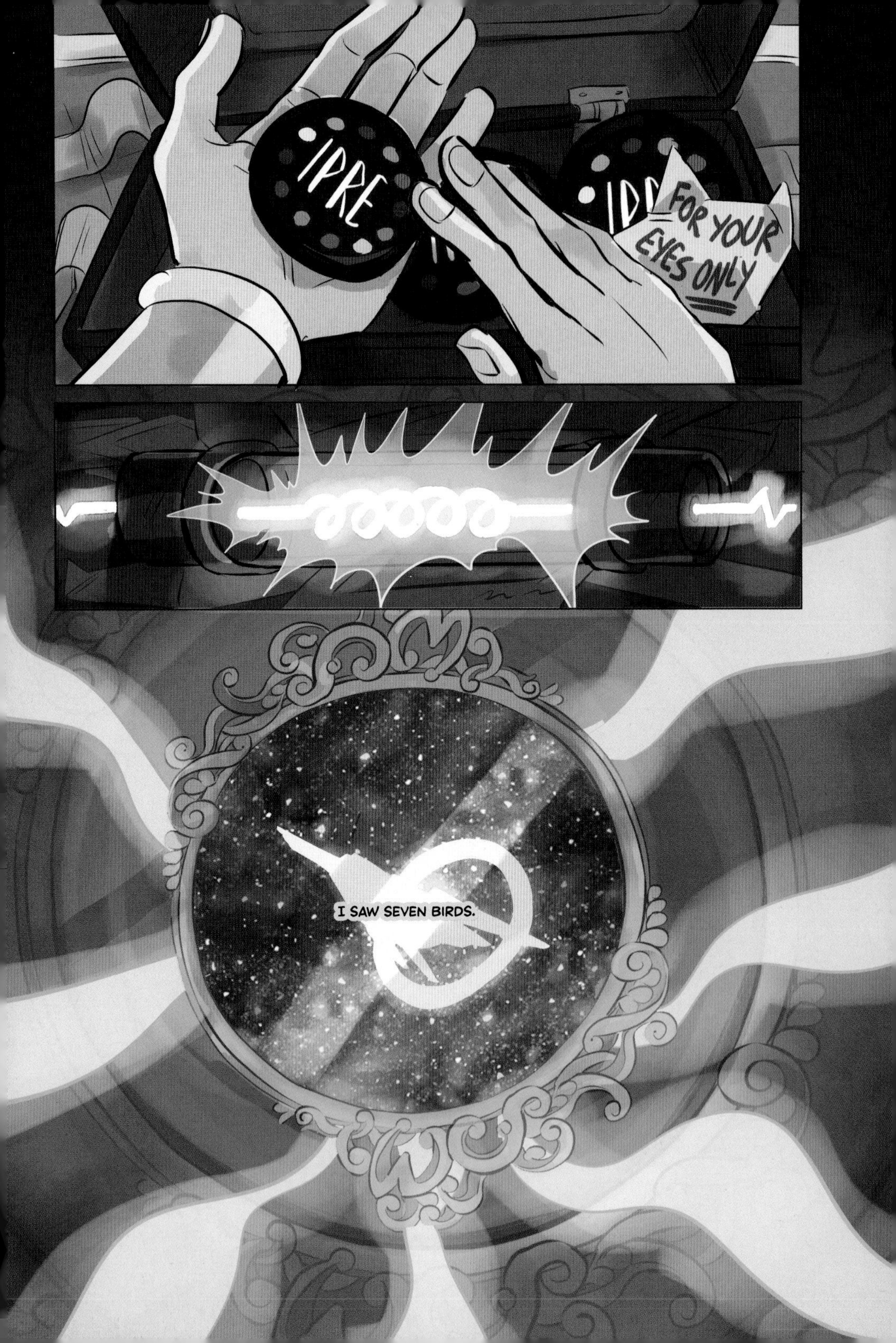
IPRE
FOR YOUR EYES ONLY
I SAW SEVEN BIRDS.

The ADVENTURE CONTINUES in

THE ADVENTURE ZONE
The Eleventh Hour

Coming Soon!

Making a Page: Script to Final

A peek into the process with artist and co-adaptor, Carey Pietsch!

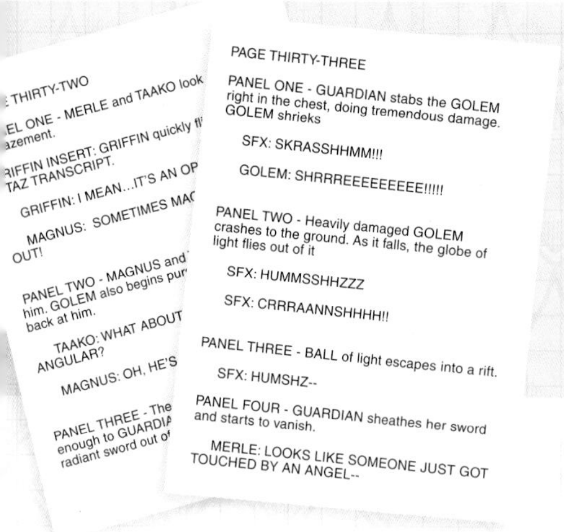
E THIRTY-TWO

EL ONE - MERLE and TAAKO look
azement.

RIFFIN INSERT: GRIFFIN quickly fl
TAZ TRANSCRIPT.

GRIFFIN: I MEAN...IT'S AN OP

MAGNUS: SOMETIMES MAG
OUT!

PANEL TWO - MAGNUS and
him. GOLEM also begins pur
back at him.

TAAKO: WHAT ABOUT
ANGULAR?

MAGNUS: OH, HE'S

PANEL THREE - The
enough to GUARDIA
radiant sword out of

PAGE THIRTY-THREE

PANEL ONE - GUARDIAN stabs the GOLEM right in the chest, doing tremendous damage. GOLEM shrieks

SFX: SKRASSHHMM!!!

GOLEM: SHRRREEEEEEEEE!!!!!

PANEL TWO - Heavily damaged GOLEM crashes to the ground. As it falls, the globe of light flies out of it

SFX: HUMMSSHHZZZ

SFX: CRRRAANNSHHHH!!

PANEL THREE - BALL of light escapes into a rift.

SFX: HUMSHZ--

PANEL FOUR - GUARDIAN sheathes her sword and starts to vanish.

MERLE: LOOKS LIKE SOMEONE JUST GOT TOUCHED BY AN ANGEL--

Scripts

By the time the script is set and I'm ready to start drawing, I'm very excited to go! At that point, we've all been talking about the outline, script, and overall story for months, and I've gone back and relistened to the relevant chunk of the podcast so the flavor we're all working to translate to the graphic novel is fresh in my mind. There's a lot of information in there—cadence, tone, music—that's a huge help in figuring out details like character acting on the page.

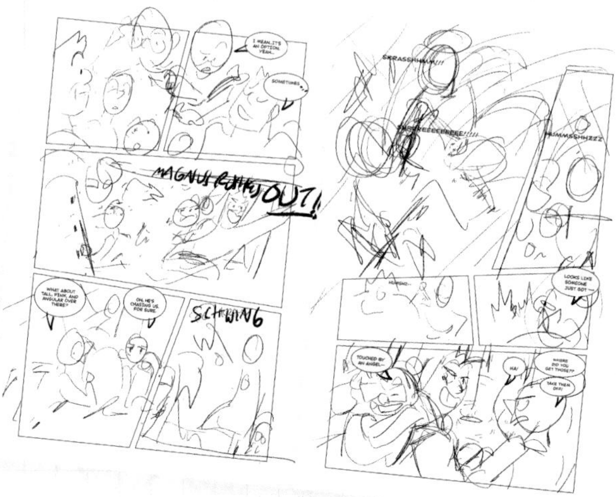
SKRASSHHMM!!
HUMMSSHHZZZ
SCHWING

Layouts

I'm usually the only person who ever sees these, so enjoy! They have a lot of really wonderful energy and are essential to the process, but they also use shorthands that are by and large illegible to anybody else.

Layouts are like an outline for the artwork! This is the point where I try to make all the biggest decisions about how to pace the action. It's also where I try to think through the composition of the page/spread as a whole as well as the general shapes of each individual panel...but I'm not fussed about little things like...uh, well, pretty much anything else quite yet.

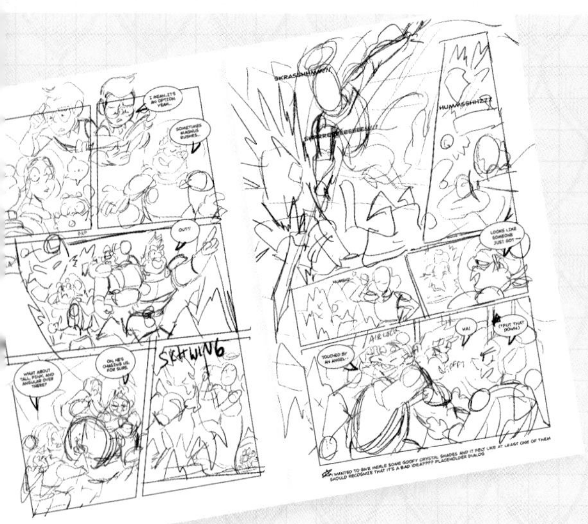
SKRASSHHMM!!
HUMMSSHHZZZ
SCHWING

Thumbnails

This is the first step I actually pass back to the rest of the team so we can all review it and talk about notes, changes, and fixes!

You can see my note calling out the balloon I added as a placeholder—I wanted to check in with the team about whether it might work to add a beat there that required more text.

This is where we're talking about big gestural actions and body language, checking whether the action is clear, if there are places where I need to add another panel or beat to flesh things out... Looking at this spread now, six months later, I wish I had given the angel a different pose in the last panel on the left-hand page to really sell a stab, not a slash... live and learn!! We'll get it next time.

Pencils

OK, NOW we're talking—this is the first place where expressions oughta be legible and we can all give it another read as a team to make sure the beat-to-beat transitions are working! This is a rare instance of using color in pencils—there were just too many lines to parse what was happening otherwise.

Inks

ONE LAST PASS on the lines to clean things up! At this stage I'm making decisions about tiny expression tweaks to really sell an emotion, plus how line weights can help emphasize volume and spatial relationships.

Once inks are done, I hand them off to our letterer, Tess Stone (one of my favorite cartoonists!)—it's always such a treat to see his final lettering on the page at the next step!

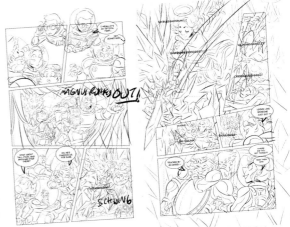

Colors

A big challenge in this book was figuring out a visual language for coloring the crystal environments & the crystal golem. I didn't want to have them competing too strongly for your attention, so there's a little more detail and layering going on with the golem—he's more important, and ideally the thing you're spending more time "reading."

And that's it!! Wow! Repeat for 217 more pages and you have a book!! I love getting to work on these pages, but my favorite part is absolutely when I finish a stage and get to send it around for all of us to talk about and polish—it's a really wonderful collaboration to get to be a part of.

Designing the Cover (Carey continues!)

Once we have a script and the artwork is well underway,
it's time to figure out what the cover will look like!

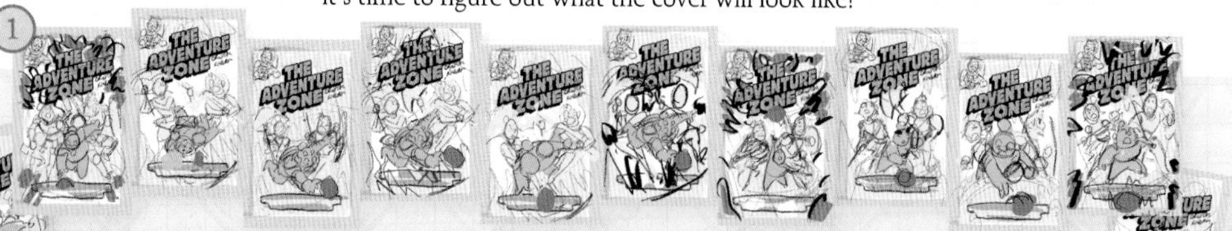
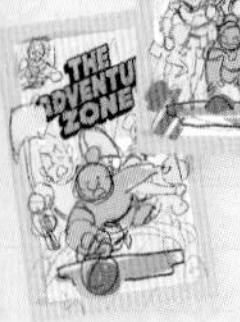
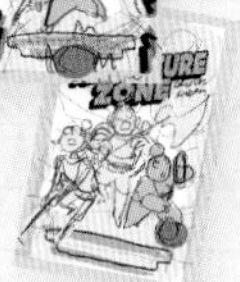

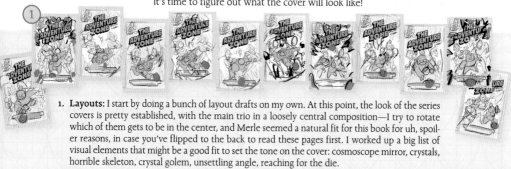

1. **Layouts:** I start by doing a bunch of layout drafts on my own. At this point, the look of the series covers is pretty established, with the main trio in a loosely central composition—I try to rotate which of them gets to be in the center, and Merle seemed a natural fit for this book for uh, spoiler reasons, in case you've flipped to the back to read these pages first. I worked up a big list of visual elements that might be a good fit to set the tone on the cover: cosmoscope mirror, crystals, horrible skeleton, crystal golem, unsettling angle, reaching for the die.

2. **Thumbnails:** After I've made a couple pages' worth of layouts and slept on it, it's time to winnow the field down to my faves, do a quick cleanup pass, and send those thumbs in! I have finally learned not to share any thumbs that I'm not genuinely excited about executing because, inevitably, someone else will think the ones I'm not into are the best options, and I will complain, and then none of us will be happy.

   So these are the three thumbnails I sent! I think they all have really strong shapes! The one we went with has the clearest Merle silhouette, but I do really like the off-balance angle of the center thumbnail... Look forward to me trying to find a way to reuse it in a future book.

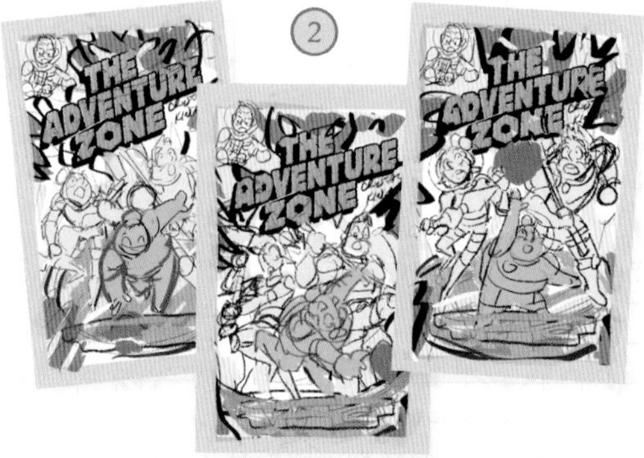

3. **Pencils with Tones:** Once we've picked a thumbnail to move forward with, I clean it up into pencils & tones to be brought to a cover meeting for (hopefully) official internal approval! The tones are a big help in making these rough drawings legible. (You can see that I still had a floating crystal golem skull as a compositional element up top at this stage. I ended up deciding that didn't work and replacing it with more crystals in inks.)

4. **Inks:** I ended up moving the characters around a tiny bit to try to eliminate some tangents with the title... thrilling stuff.

5. **Color Rough:** While I'm picking away at inks, I'm also picking away at a color rough based on my pencils! I paint this at a pretty tiny size to try to avoid overworking it; the goal is to give myself a plan that I can execute in final colors.

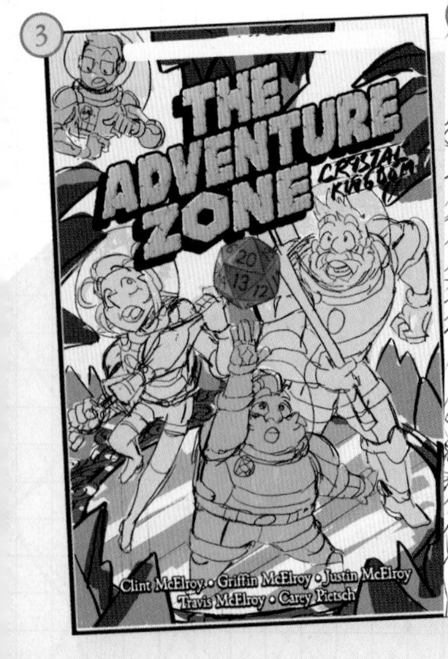
3
THE ADVENTURE ZONE
CRYSTAL KINGDOM
Clint McElroy • Griffin McElroy • Justin McElroy
Travis McElroy • Carey Pietsch
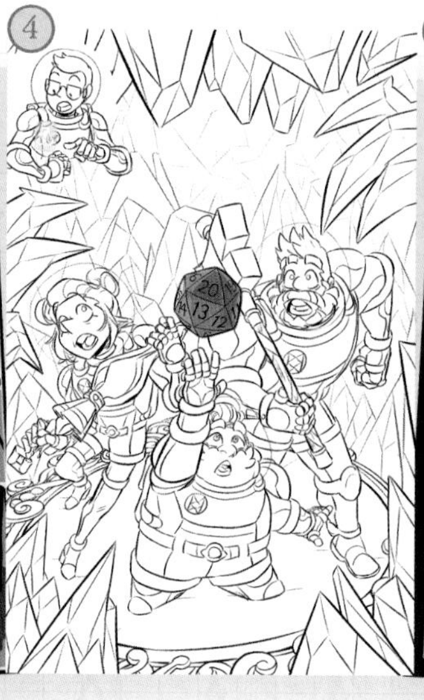
4
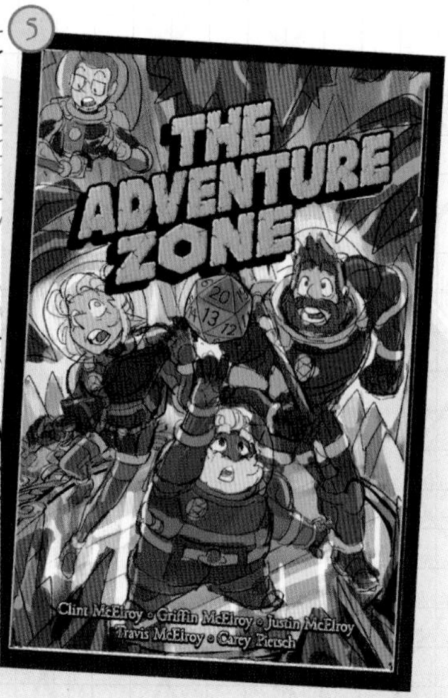
5
THE ADVENTURE ZONE
Clint McElroy • Griffin McElroy • Justin McElroy
Travis McElroy • Carey Pietsch

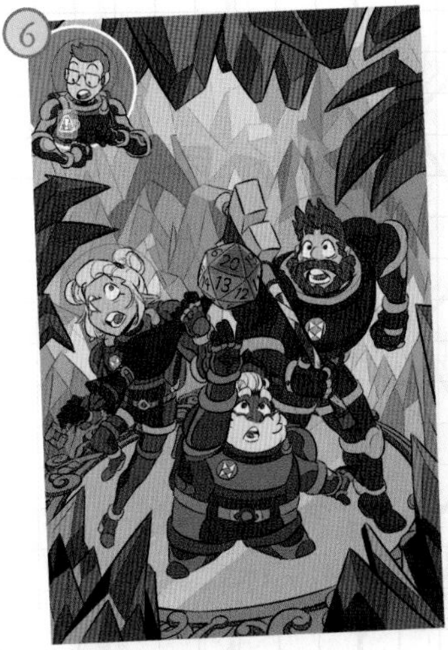
6
20
13
12
14
6

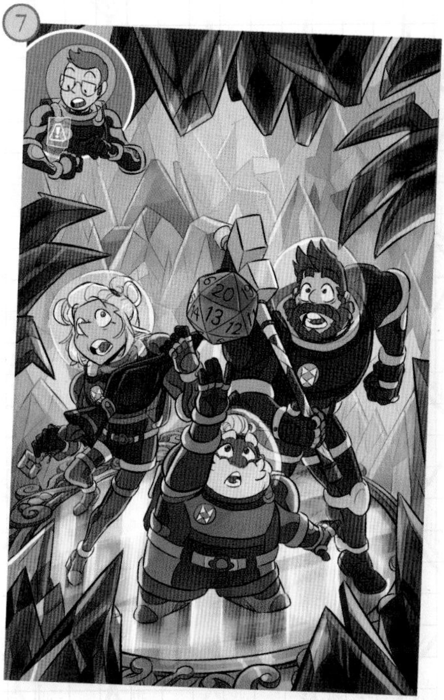
7
20
13
12
14
6

6. **Flats:** A pleasantly chill and meditative step! I really liked the flats on their own, which is a good sign. I'm big on lighting as a way to heighten drama and emotion, rather than as a literal reflection of what lighting would """"actually"""" look like, so I've been working hard to try to make palettes that work as flat colors to give me more leeway there.
7. **Finals:** Several days of off-and-on crystal painting later, here they are!! Every cover is my favorite when I finish it, and this one is no exception. Spooky tone, vague skull shape in the lighter colors of the background elements if you squint, rock candy pink crystals, a mysterious mirror... What's not to love???

Special SNEAK PEEK of rejected* covers for earlier books in the series!

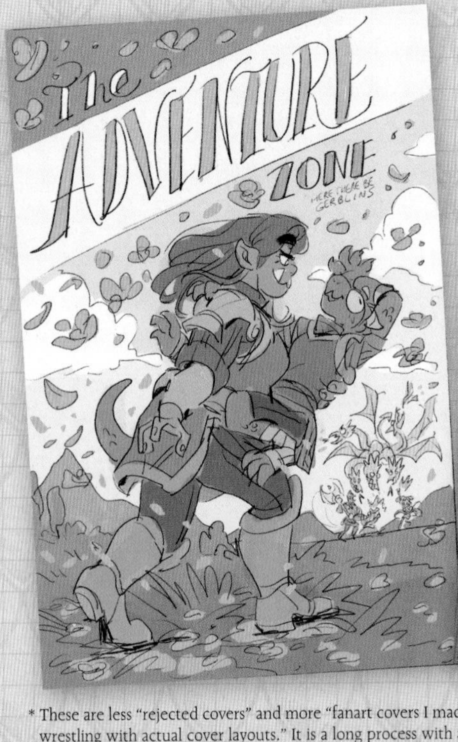
The
ADVENTURE
ZONE
HERE THERE BE GERBLINS

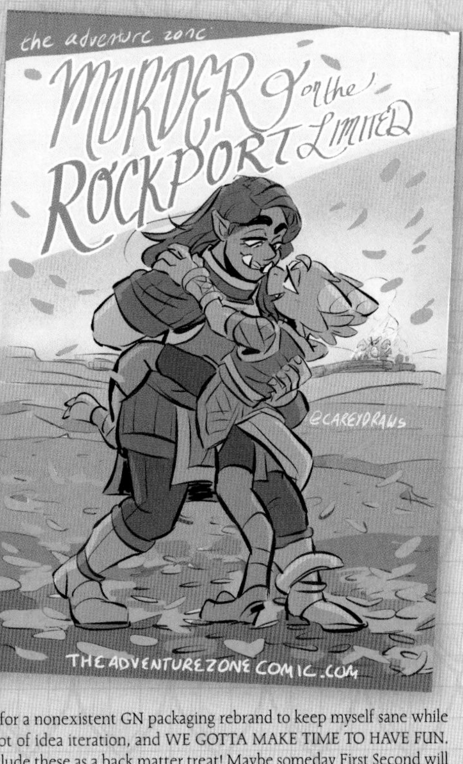
the adventure zone
MURDER on the
ROCKPORT LIMITED
@CAREYDRAWS
THEADVENTUREZONECOMIC.COM

* These are less "rejected covers" and more "fanart covers I made for a nonexistent GN packaging rebrand to keep myself sane while wrestling with actual cover layouts." It is a long process with a lot of idea iteration, and WE GOTTA MAKE TIME TO HAVE FUN. Very excited to finally be at the book where it makes sense to include these as a back matter treat! Maybe someday First Second will want to do an "Oops! All Romance Covers Edition" for the books as a super secret boxed set... I live in hope.

Visual Development (Carey concludes!)

Overall Notes on Designs: Before I dive into drawing the actual book, we all talk as a team about designs! I start out with a very loose but legible pass that I send around so we can all collectively figure out what's working and what needs tweaks and fixes. I tend to work really small at this stage, as it helps me not be precious about changes— I want to be as flexible as possible so we can land on designs that we all agree on!

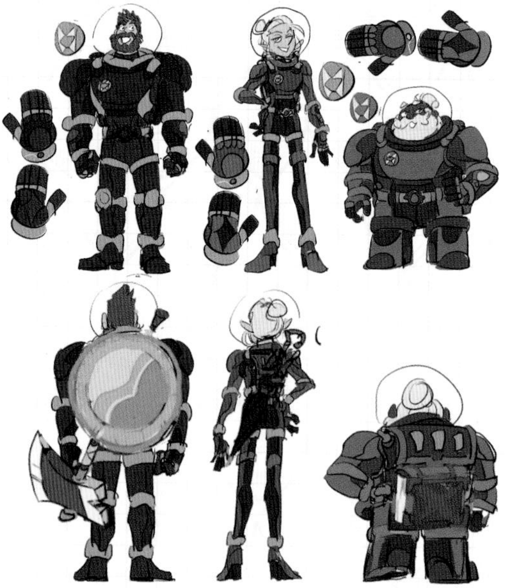

Main Trio Null Suits: I loved the all-red-null-suit-squad bit from the podcast, but it absolutely did not work on the page. RIP. All the important null suit life support is packed into the Fantasy (sci-fi) Backpack... Don't worry about it!!!

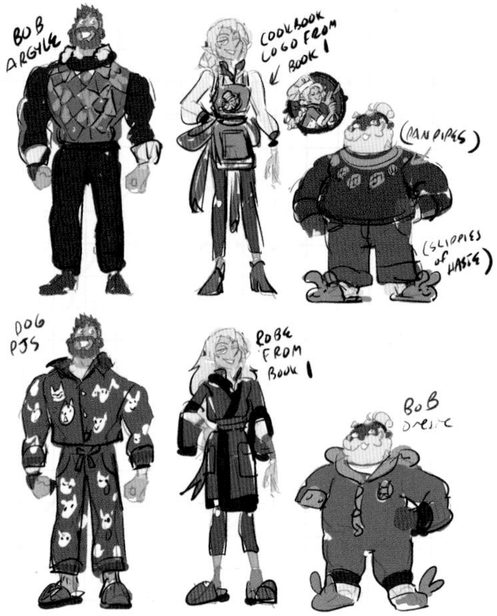
BOB ARGYLE
COOKBOOK LOGO FROM BOOK 1
(PAN PIPES)
(SLIPPIES OF HASTE)
DOG PJS
ROBE FROM BOOK 1
BOB ONESIE

Main Trio Alt Outfits: I want Merle's panpipe candlenights sweater and Magnus' dog pj's. Merle is constantly wearing his slippies of haste, and his BoB onesie is a nod to a bit from the Rockport arc in the podcast. Was Taako's book one outfit pj's all along? Maybe!!!!

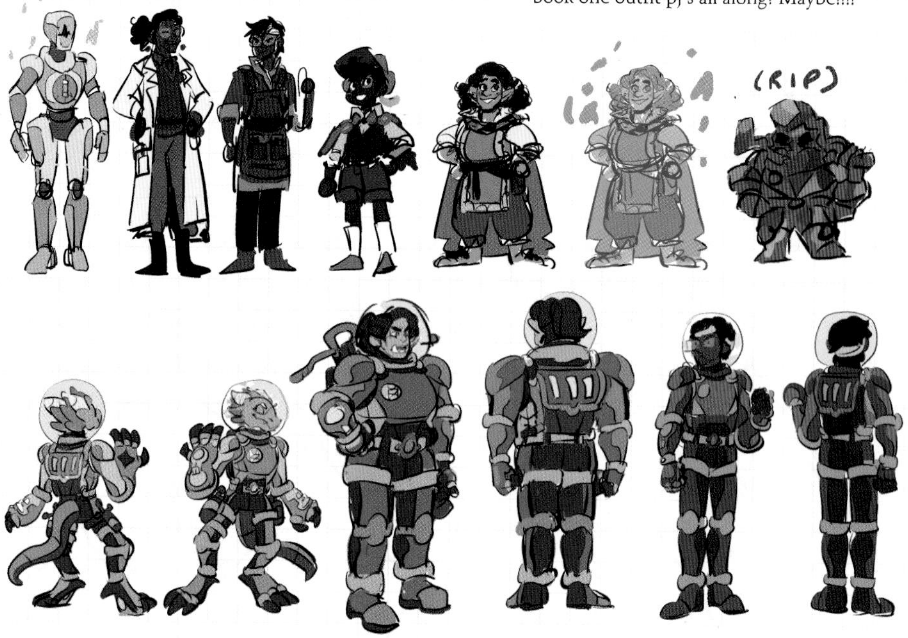
(RIP)

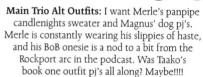

Crystal Kindgom NPCS: Shamefully, I didn't even pick a null suit color for Boyland... Sorry, Boyland, you were taken from us too soon.

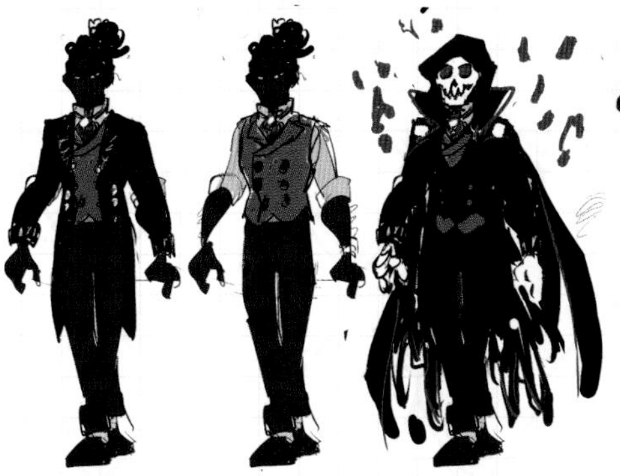

Kravitz: HE'S HERE! Very fun to come up with a multistage look for him with different levels of spookiness. Also a fun challenge to try to translate his acting between different forms, crystal golem and all!

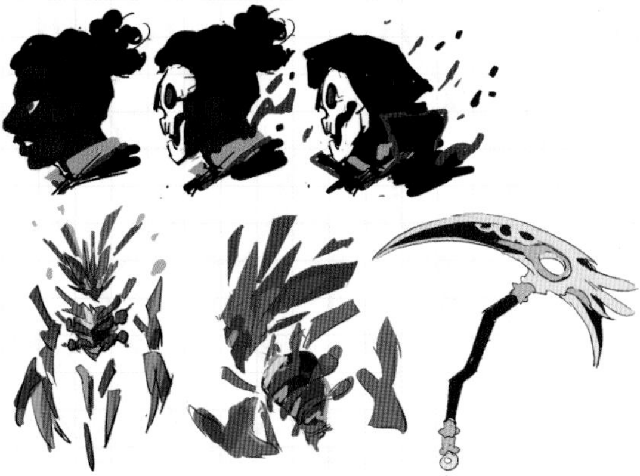

The Scythe: I think the file name for this one was "hottopicgothbird.psd"—lots of bearded vulture motifs going on with Queen Morior–adjacent designs.

Hodge-Podge: I made Hodge-Podge's design too cute and then immediately felt bad about the ending of that scene. SORRY!!

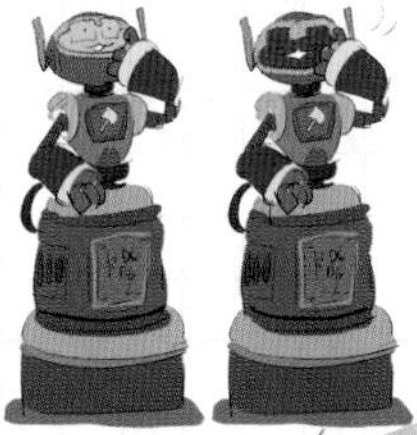

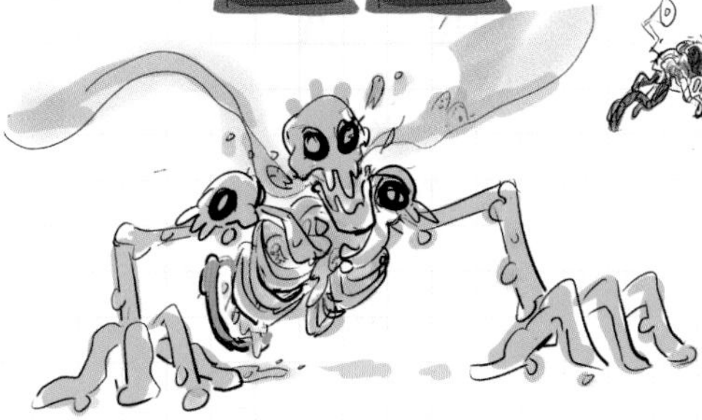

Legion: Gross, drippy, A++ would draw again.

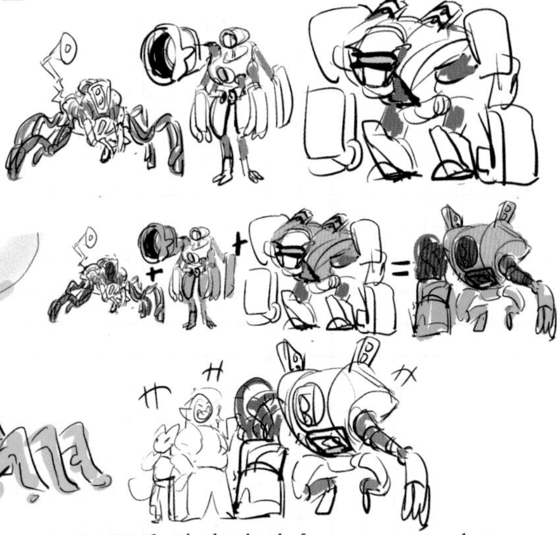

Bot Math: I had to kind of reverse engineer designs for the robot rematch trio from a final design for Big Noelle… Fun math problem!

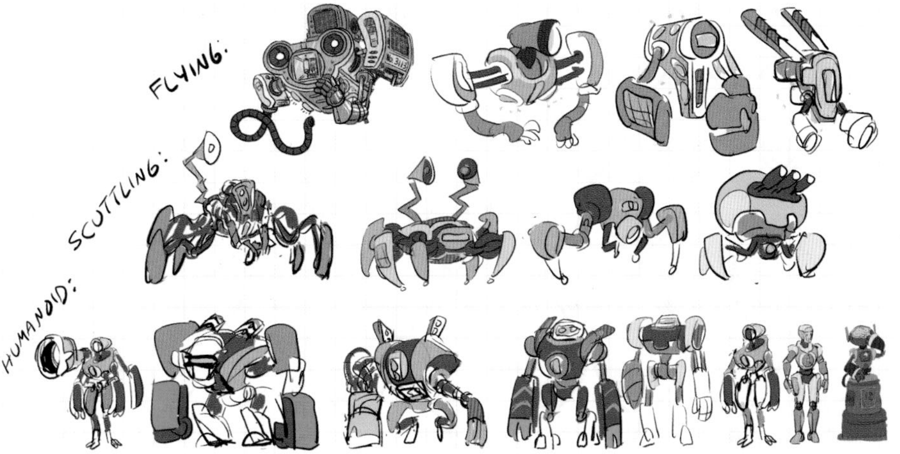
FLYING.
SCUTTLING:
HUMANOID:

Misc Bots: The central aesthetic for these was vaguely: You know those translucent iMacs that were extremely round and chunky and huggable? Like that, but also it could kill you.

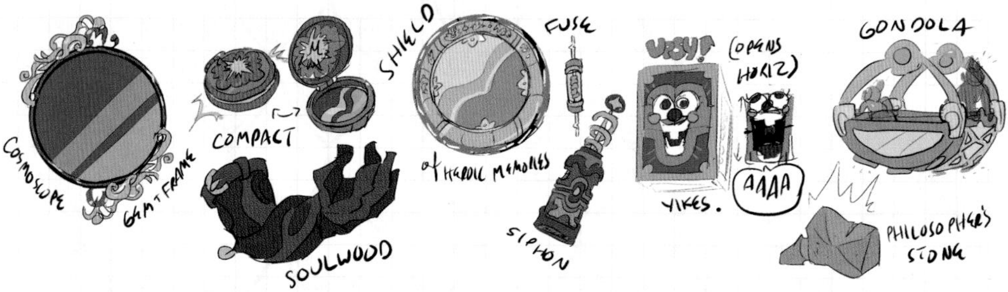
COSMOSCOPE
GEM FRAME
COMPACT
SOULWOOD
SHIELD
of HEROIC MEMORIES
FUSE
SIPHON
UPSY!
(OPENS HORIZ)
AAAA
YIKES.
GONDOLA
PHILOSOPHER'S STONE

Compact: I want this compact… I made the reflections look a little too much like the Girl Scouts logo and so I also want a cookie every time I look at it.

Siphon: The siphon is meant to visually echo Killian's MillerTech robo-animator from way back in *Gerblins*!
Upsy: Upsy is short for "upsetting…y."

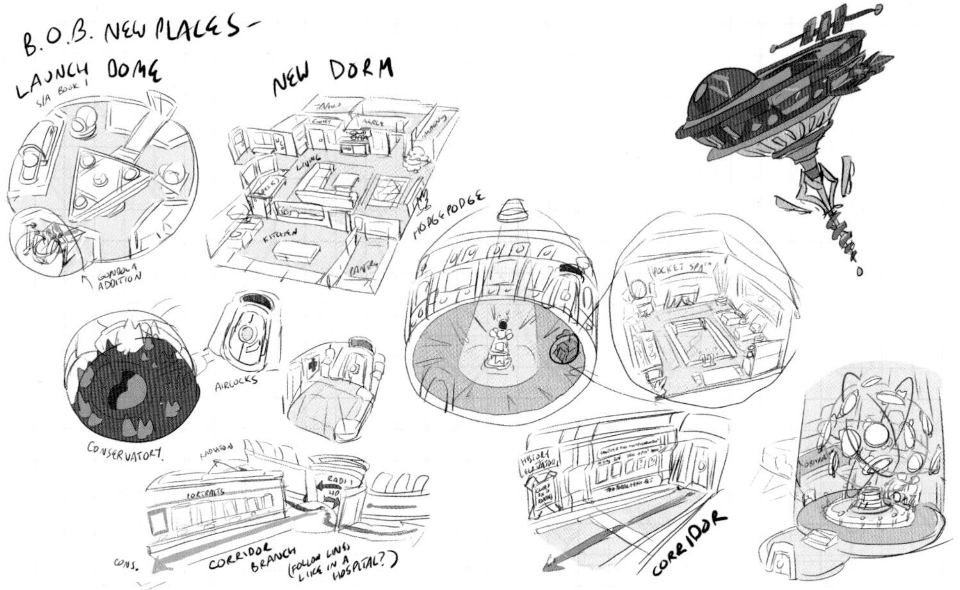
B.O.B. NEW PLACES -
LAUNCH DOME
NEW DORM
LIVING
KITCHEN
PANTRY
GONDOLA ADDITION
HODGEPODGE
POCKET SPA
CONSERVATORY
AIRLOCKS
PORTRAITS
CORRIDOR BRANCH
(FOLLOW LINES LIKE IN A HOSPITAL?)
CONS.
CORRIDOR

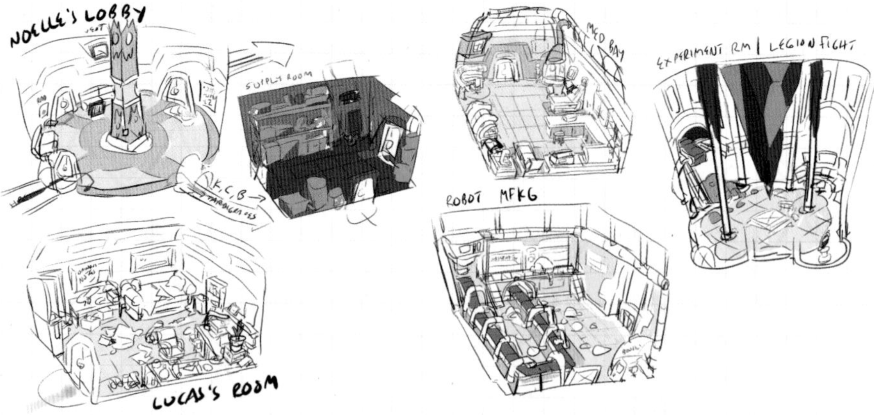
NOELLE'S LOBBY
SUPPLY ROOM
K, C, B
MED BAY
EXPERIMENT RM | LEGION FIGHT
ROBOT MFKG
LUCAS'S ROOM

Places: It's really nice to be able to talk as a team about the setting in an early stage, so we can make any changes BEFORE we get to actual book artwork. And when I get to thumbnailing, I have a much easier time mentally moving characters around while staging a scene when I can look at the space they're in—who knew! I obviously don't end up perfectly following these designs, but they're a great starting point. For instance, I gave Lucas a lofted bed while I was thumbnailing, when I realized he needed way more space for gear and tech! We also ended up tweaking the cosmoscope design a bit from its original pass to give it a little more structure with all those rails! They are attached… with fantasy MillerTech. I am begging you to please not worry about it.

Fan Art Gallery

The *Adventure Zone* has
been lucky enough to garner
a passionate and deeply
creative fandom. Many
thanks to the fan artists
who contributed pieces to
this gallery—and to all the
writers, artists, creators, and
fans of all stripes who have
made *The Adventure Zone*
what it is.

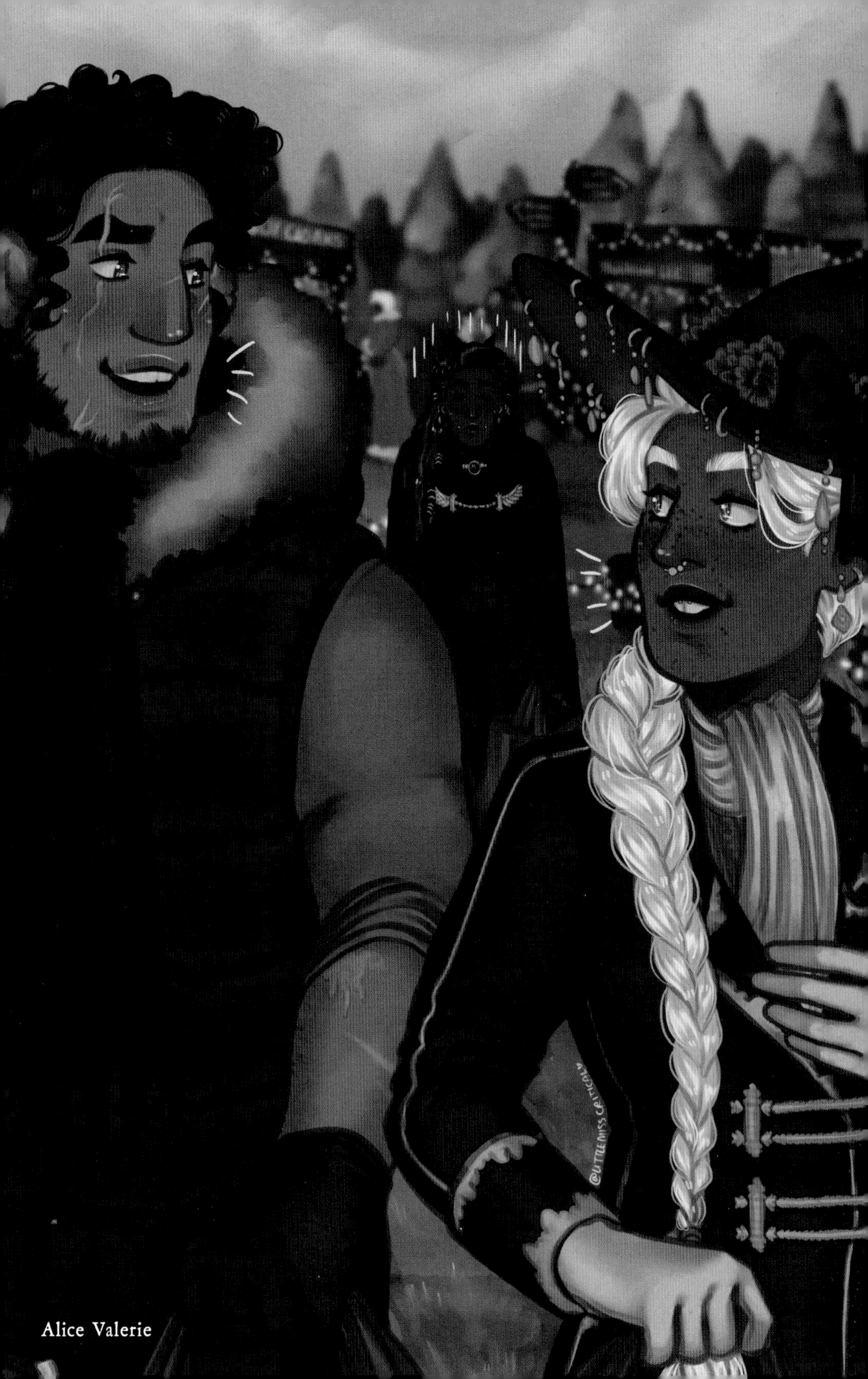
@LITTLEMISSCRITICALLY

Alice Valerie

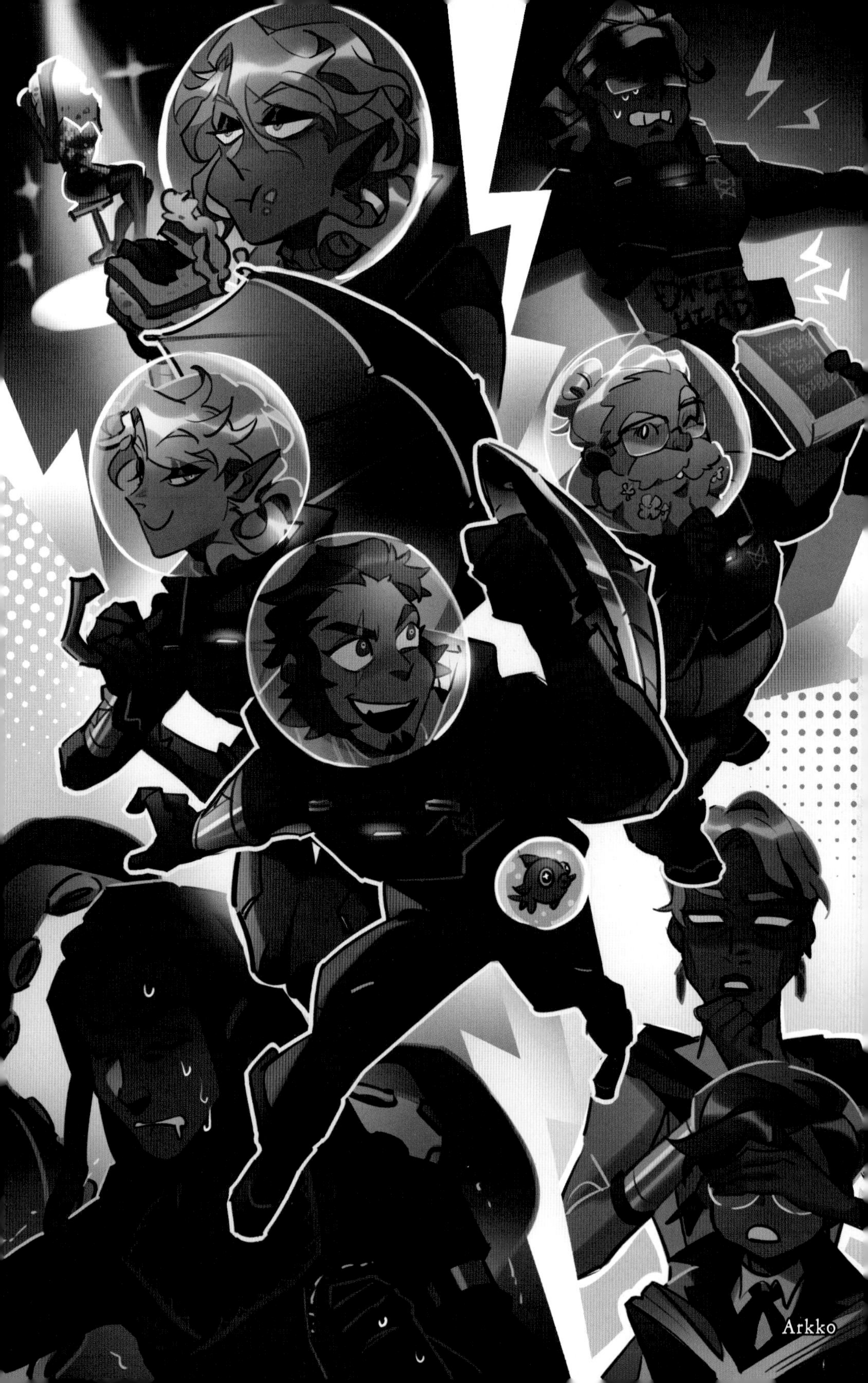
Arkko

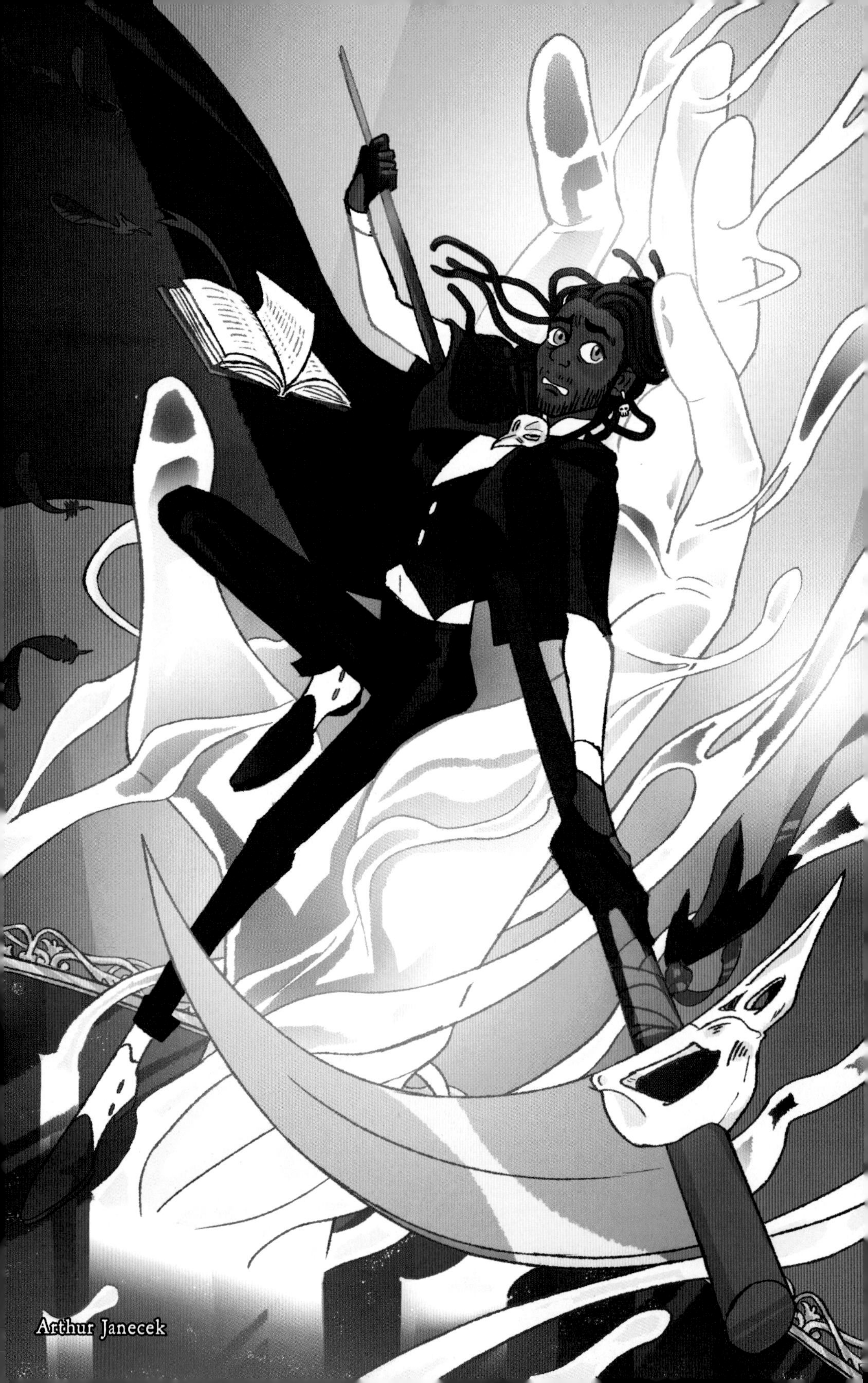
Arthur Janecek

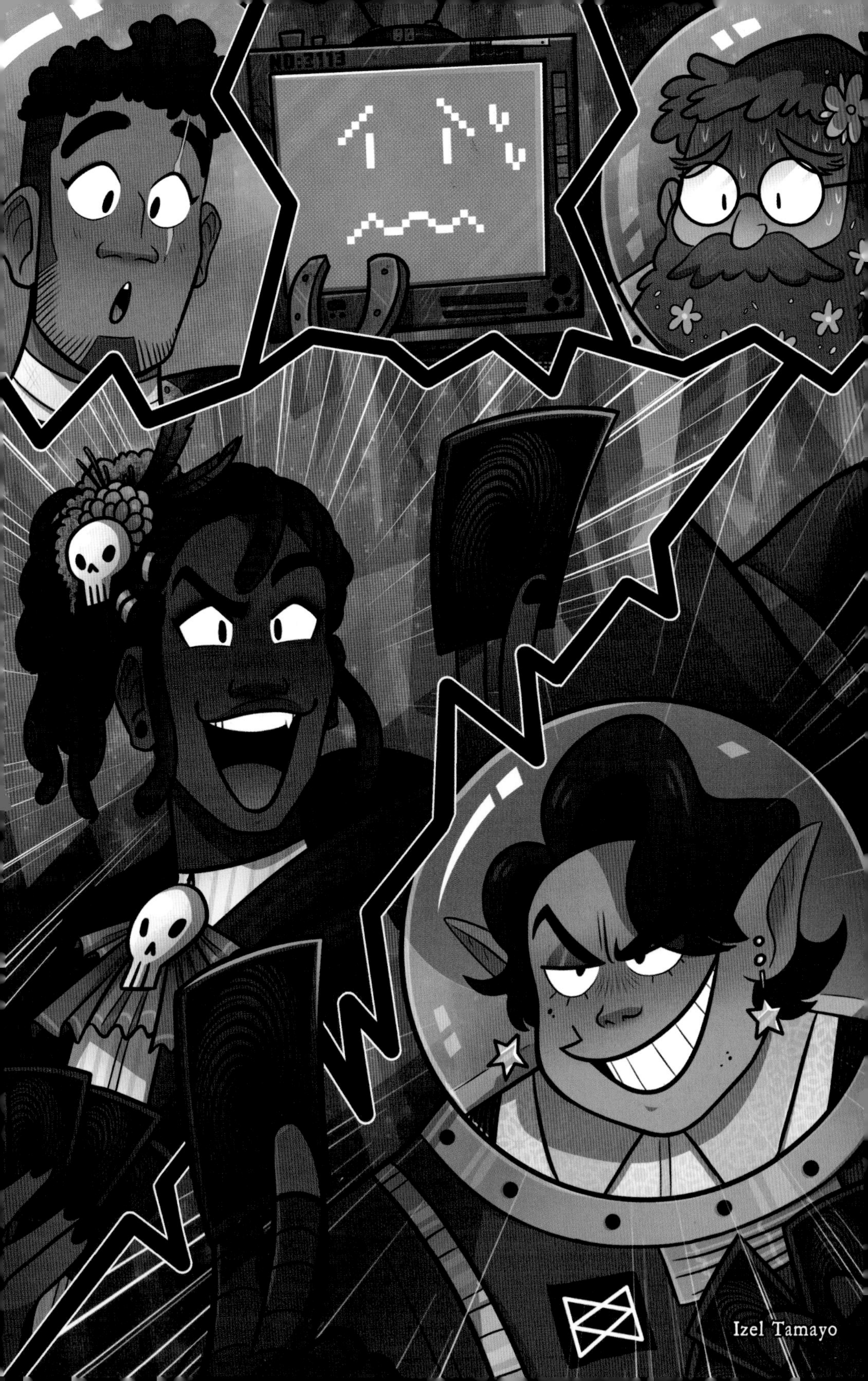
NO:3113
Izel Tamayo

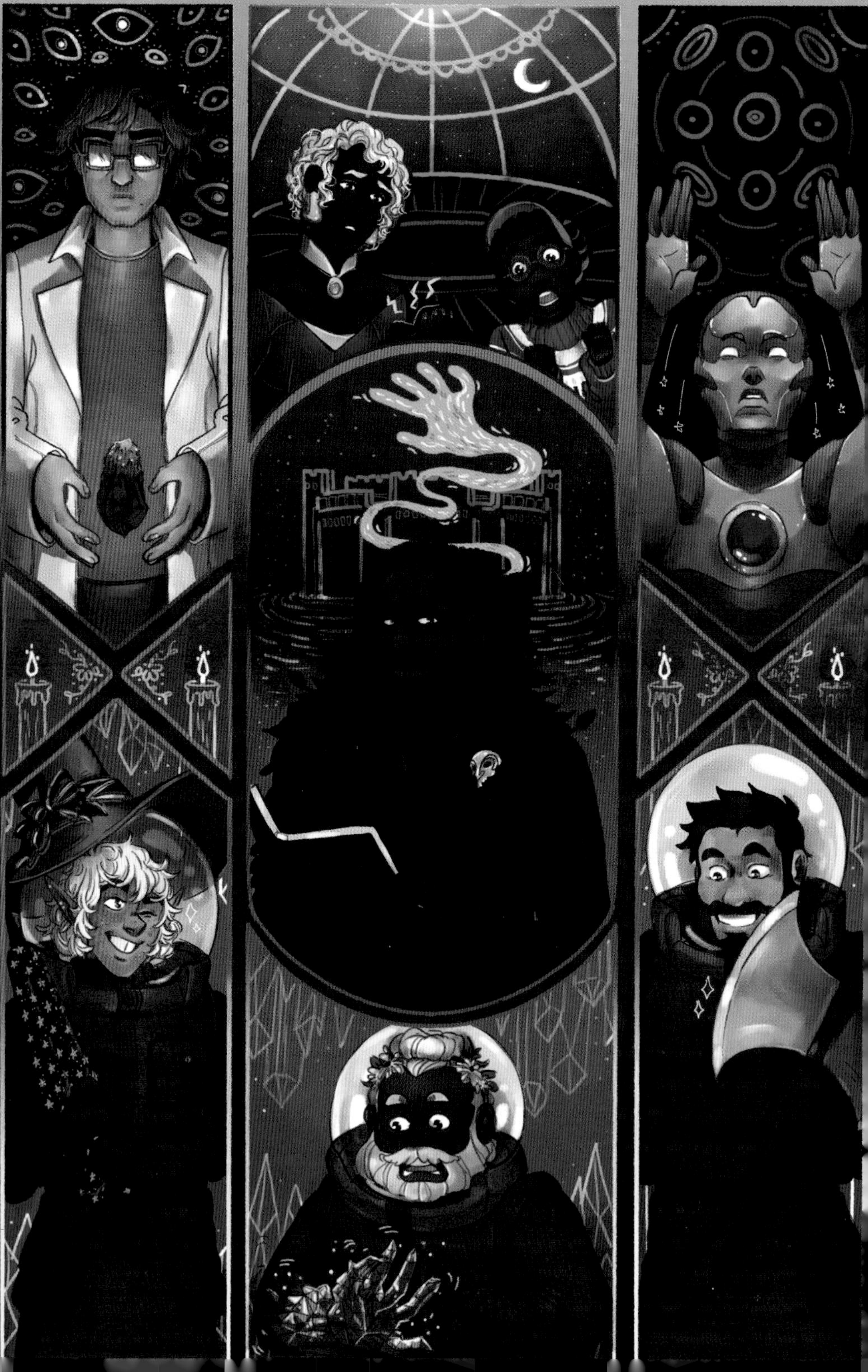

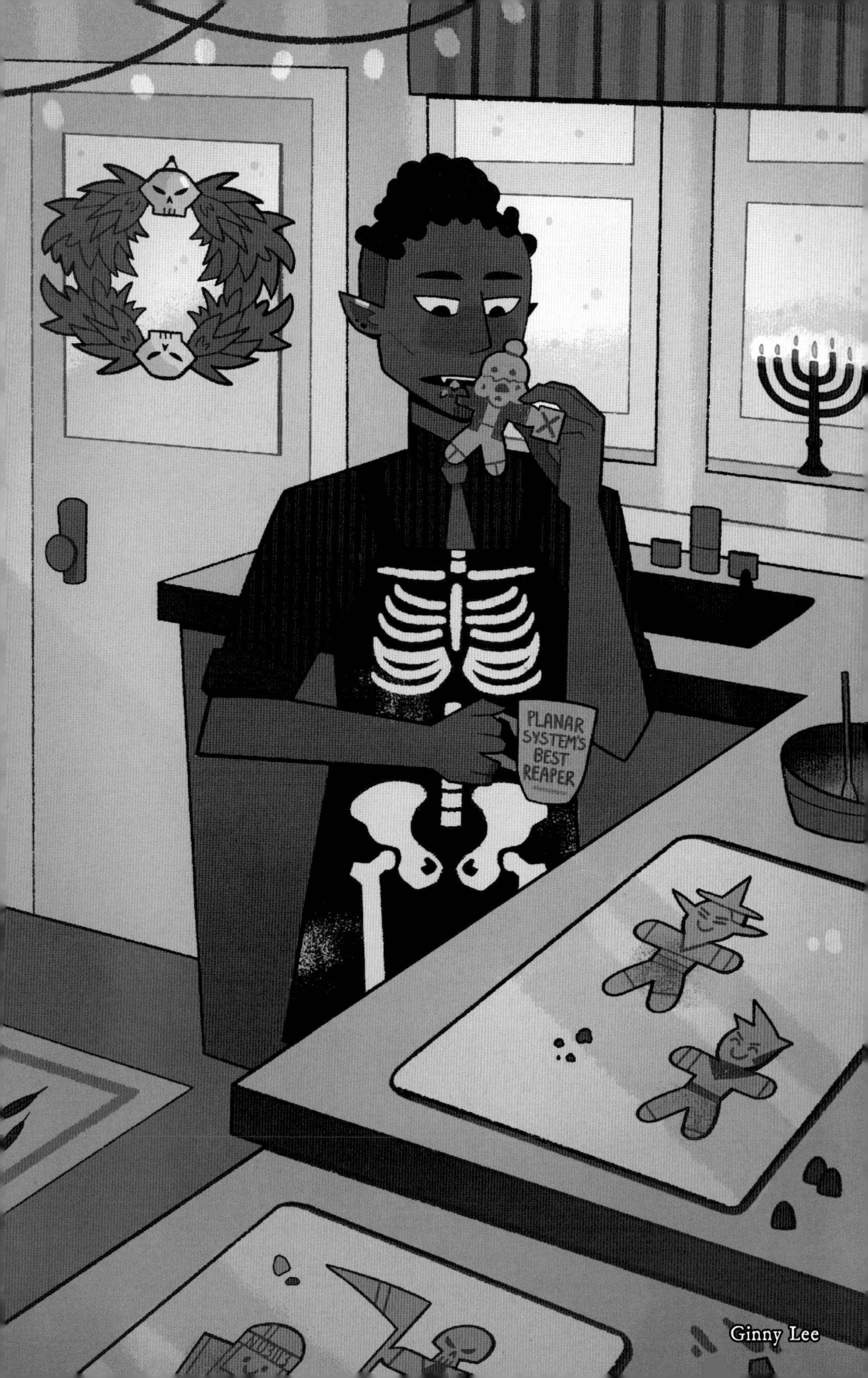
PLANAR SYSTEM'S BEST REAPER
Ginny Lee

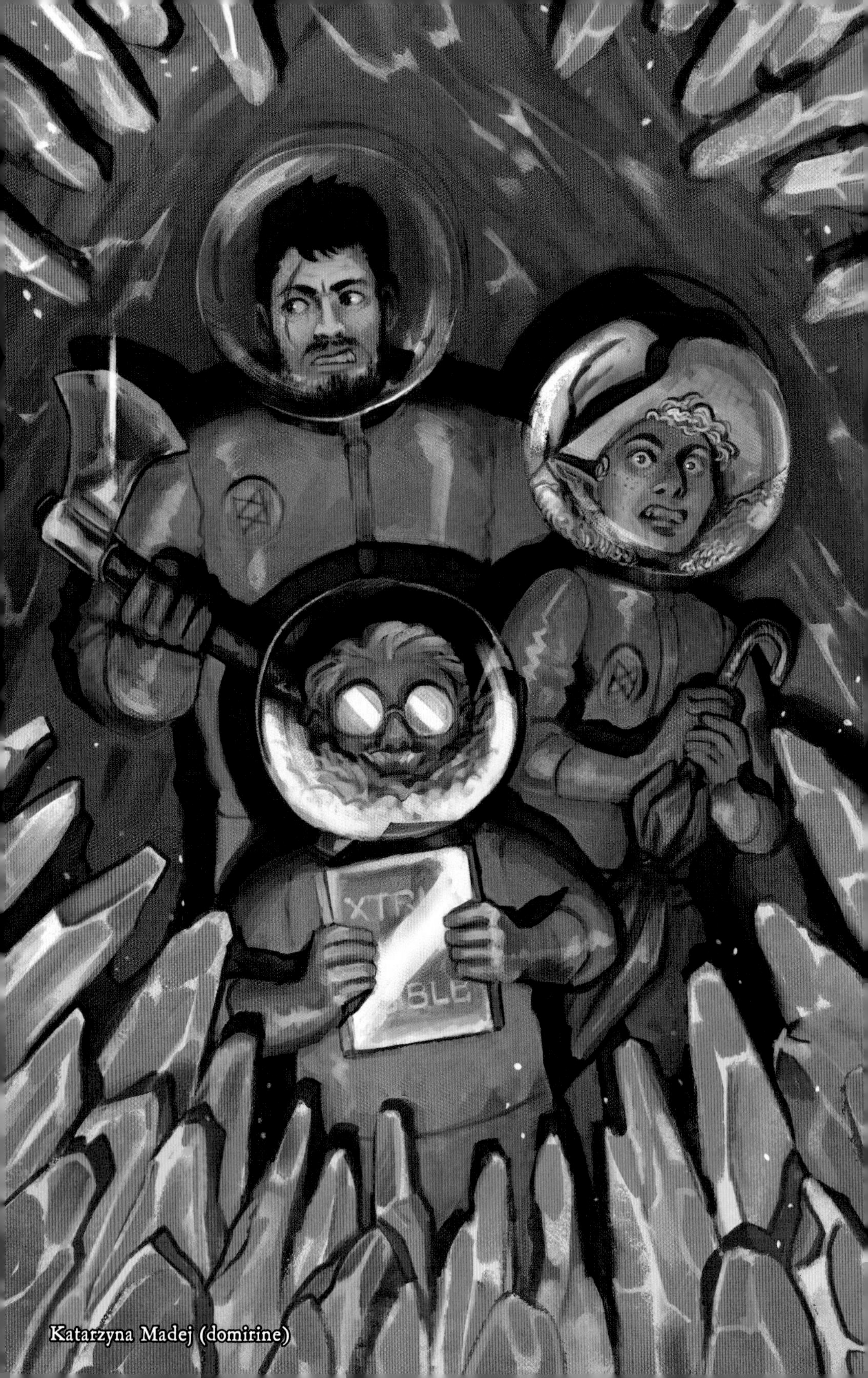

Katarzyna Madej (domirine)

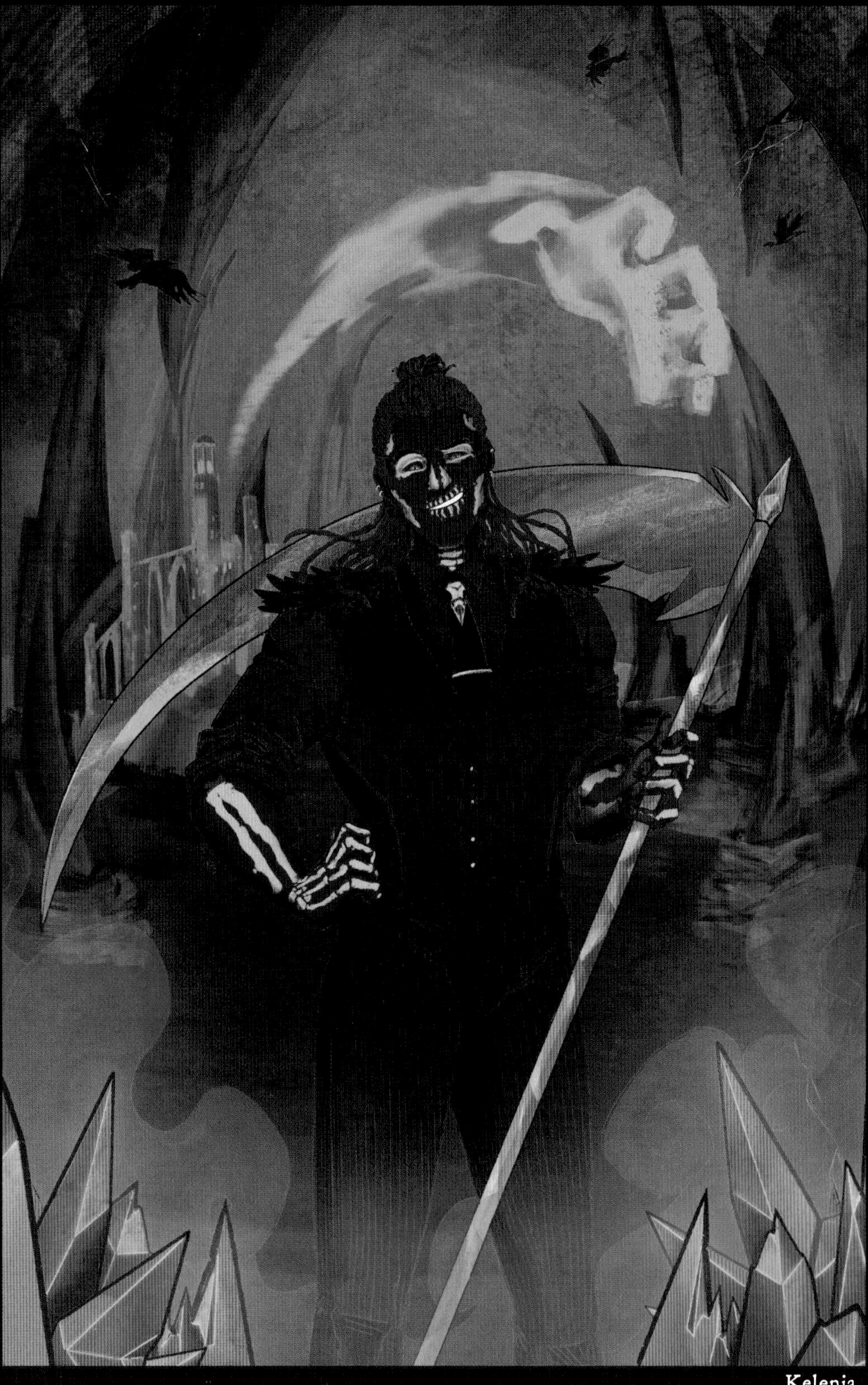

Kelenia

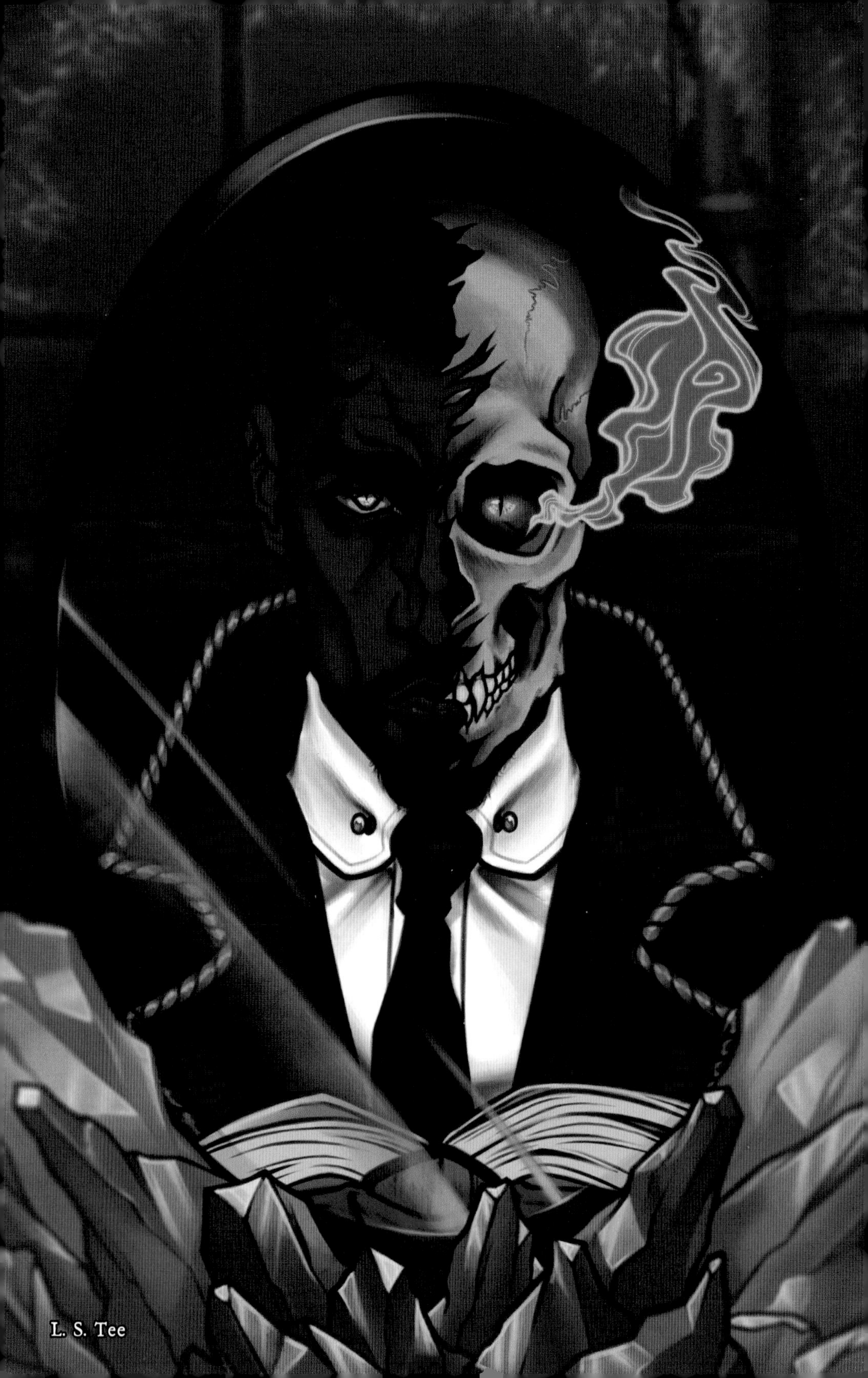
L. S. Tee

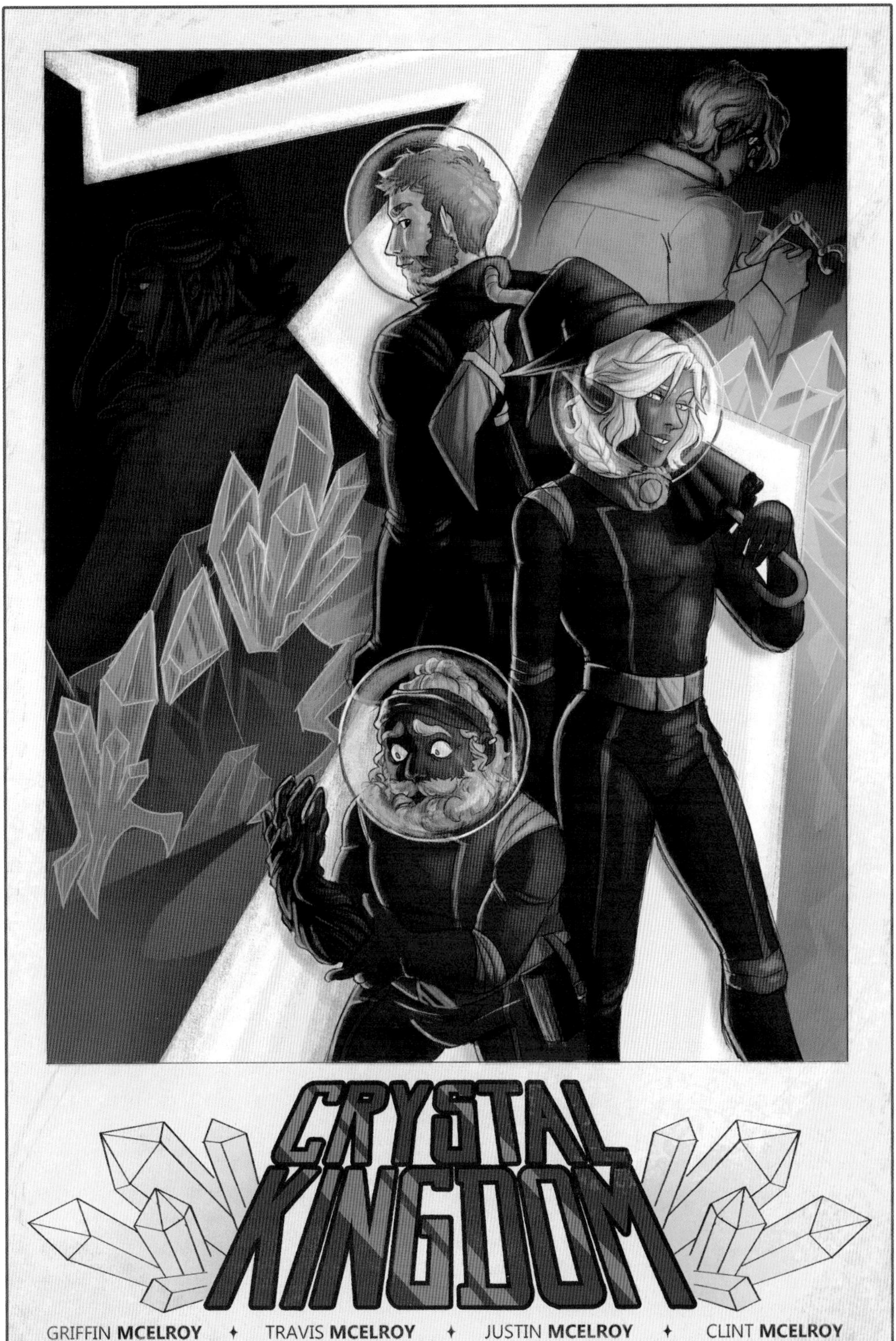
CRYSTAL KINGDOM
GRIFFIN MCELROY ✦ TRAVIS MCELROY ✦ JUSTIN MCELROY ✦ CLINT MCELROY

Michael Pounds

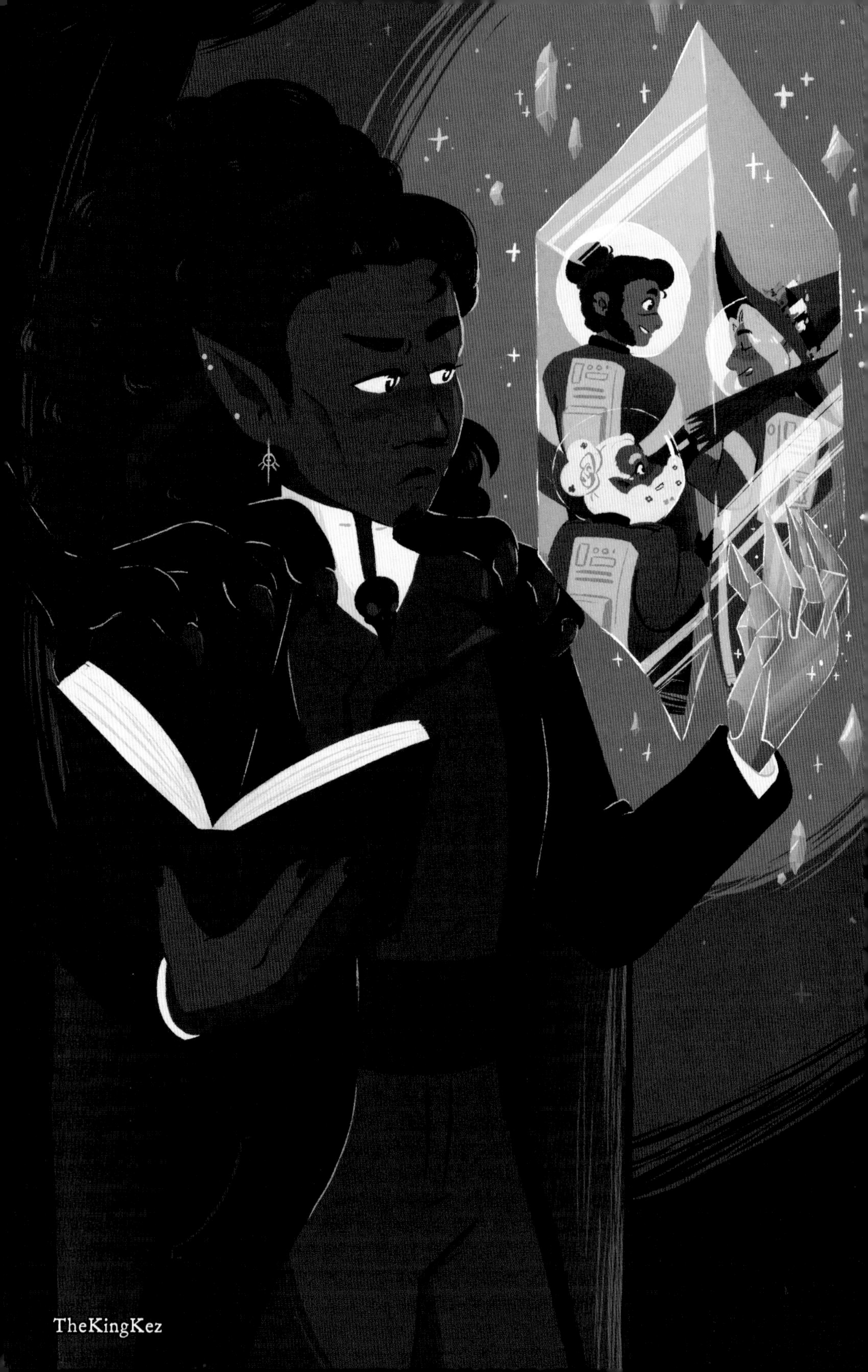
TheKingKez

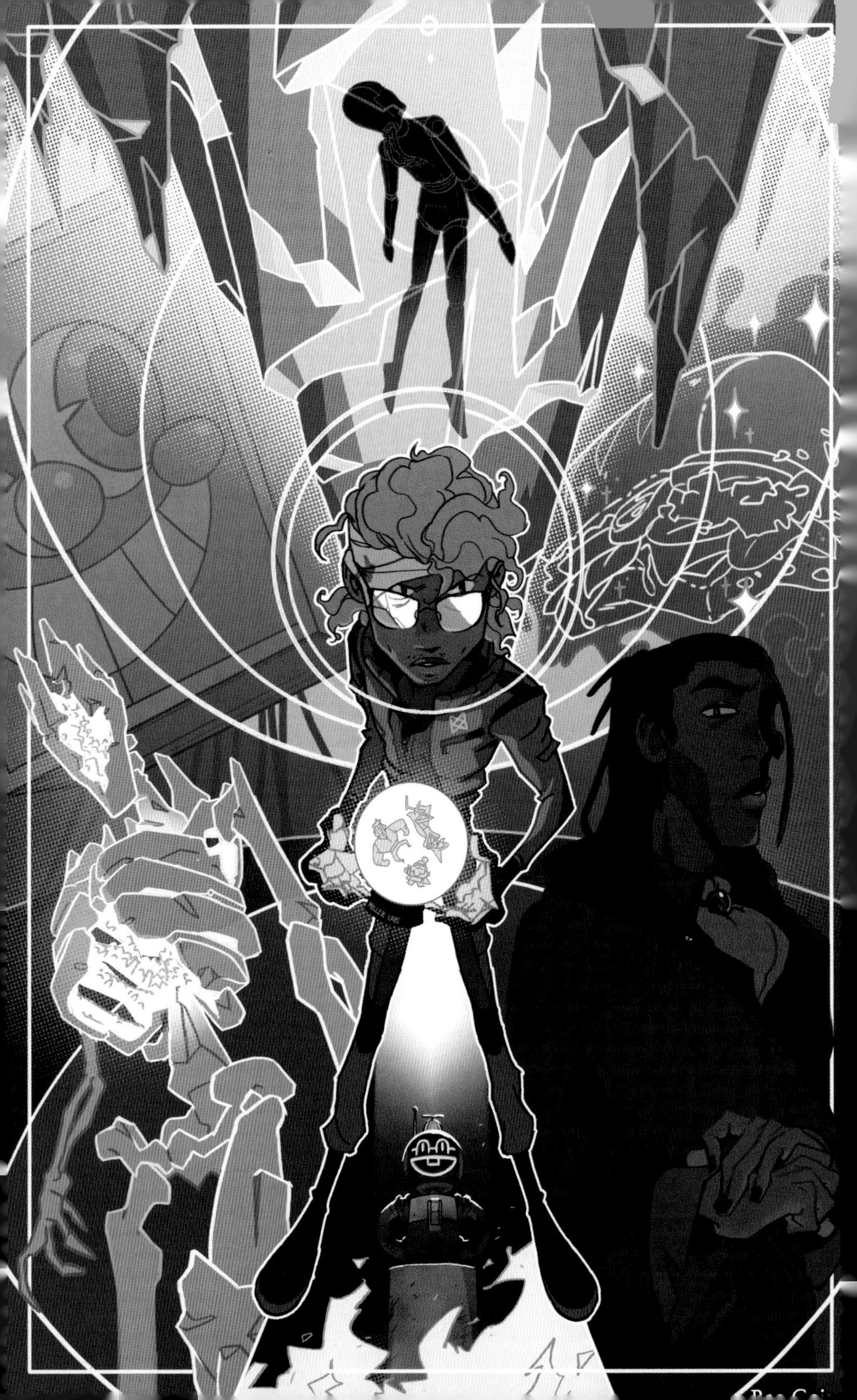
MILLER LABS

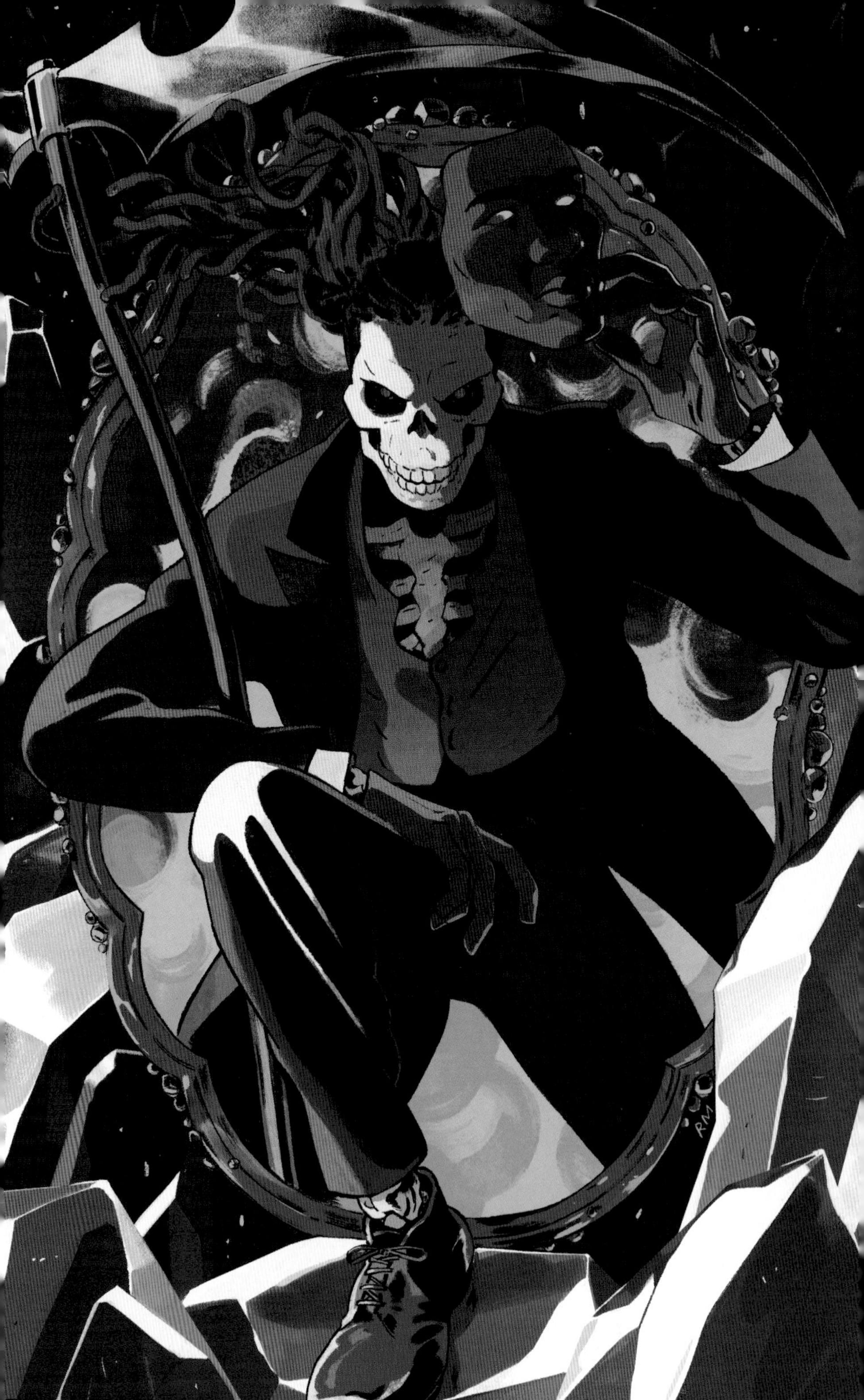
RM

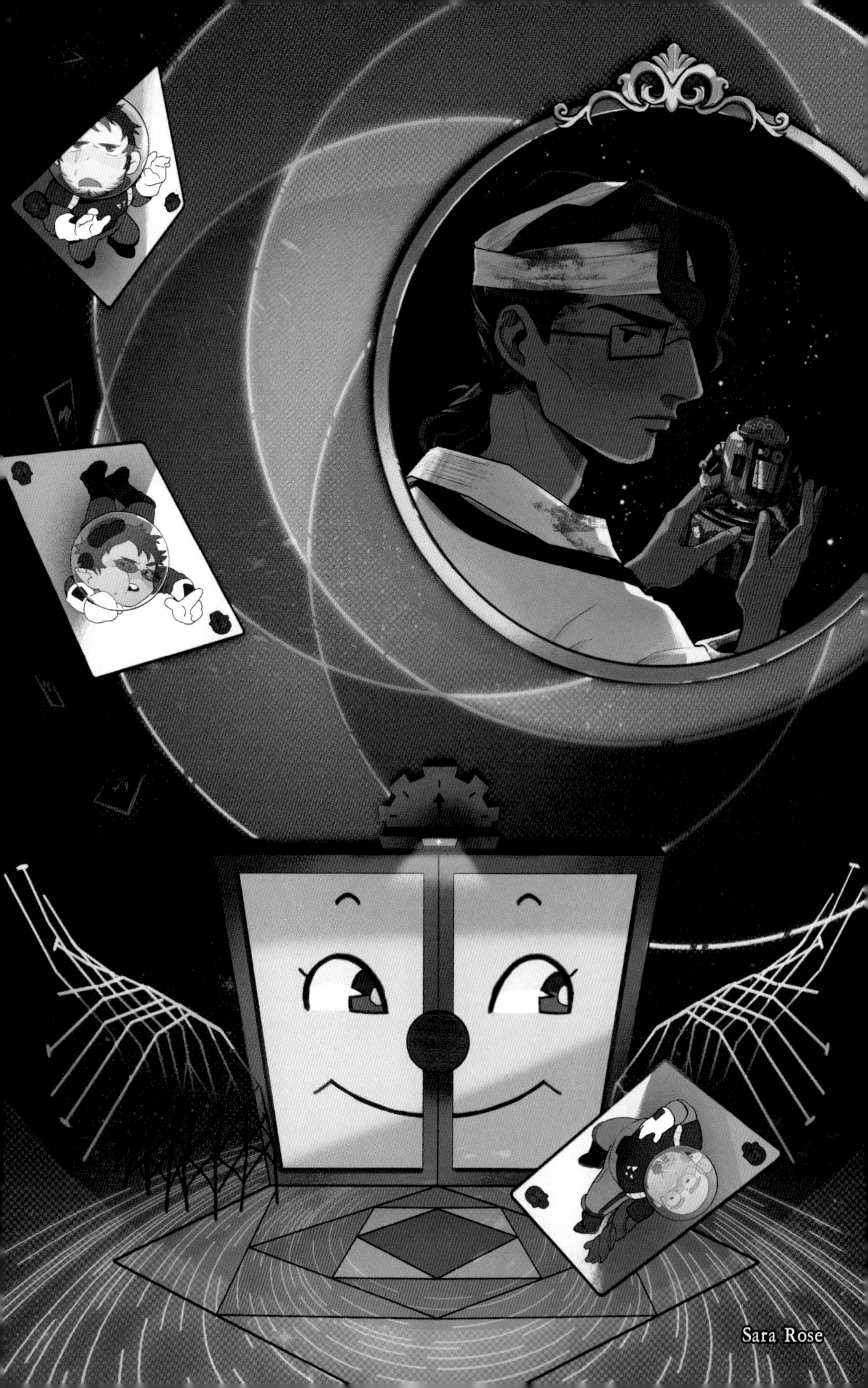
Sara Rose

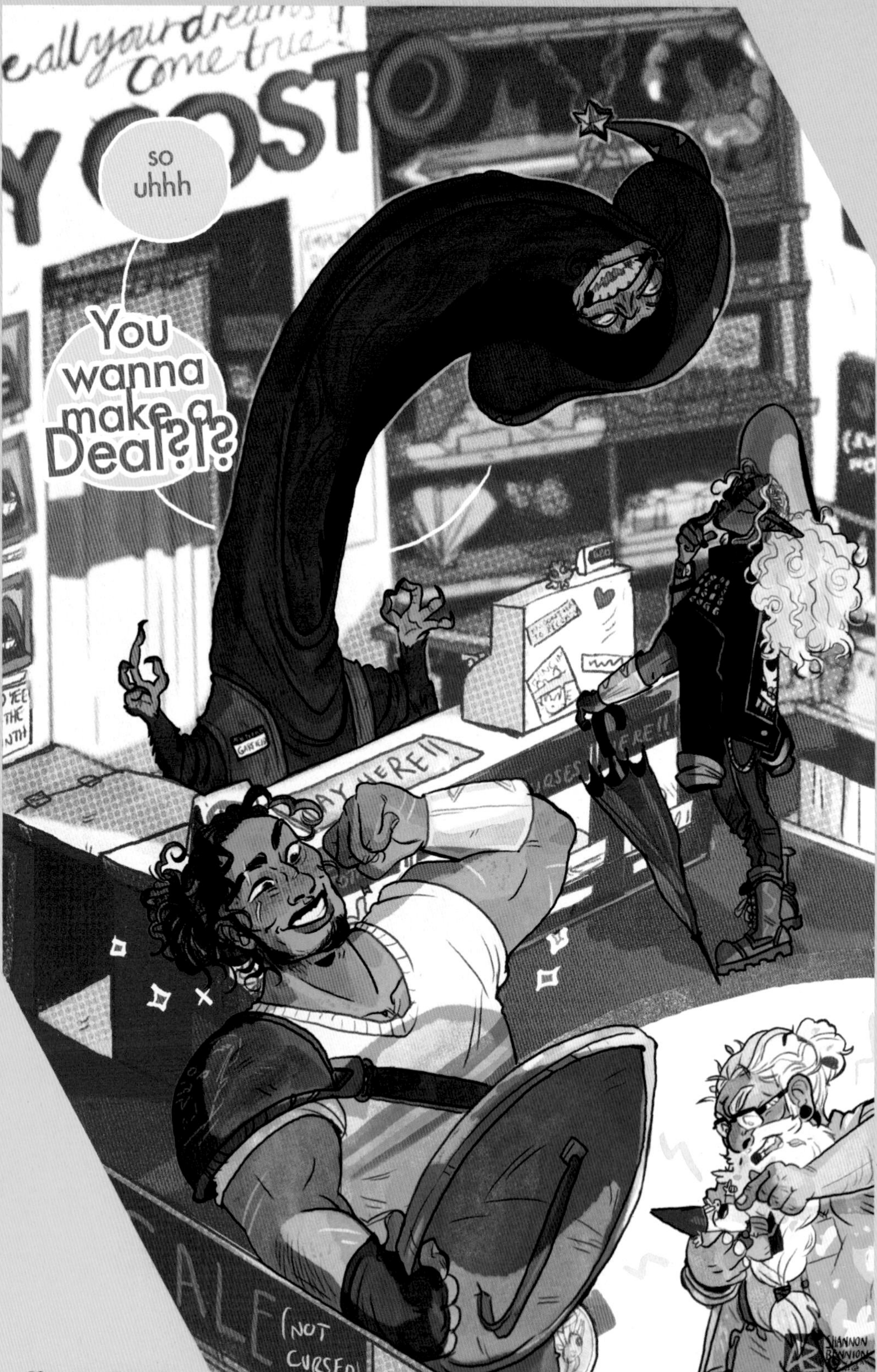
all your dreams come true!
so uhhh
You wanna make a Deal?!?
(NOT CURSED)

Shannon Bennion

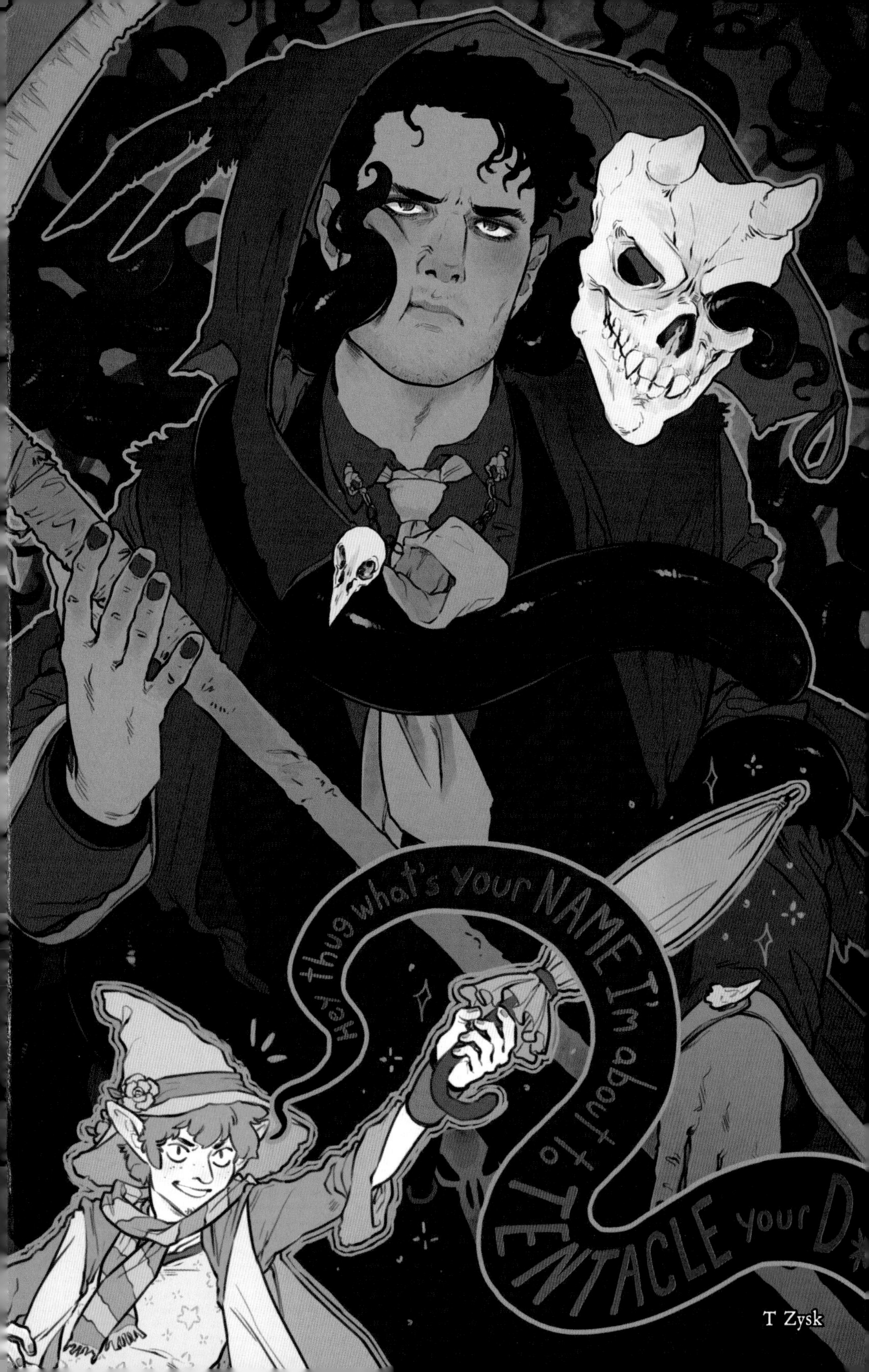
Hey thug what's your NAME I'm about to TENTACLE your D*
T Zysk

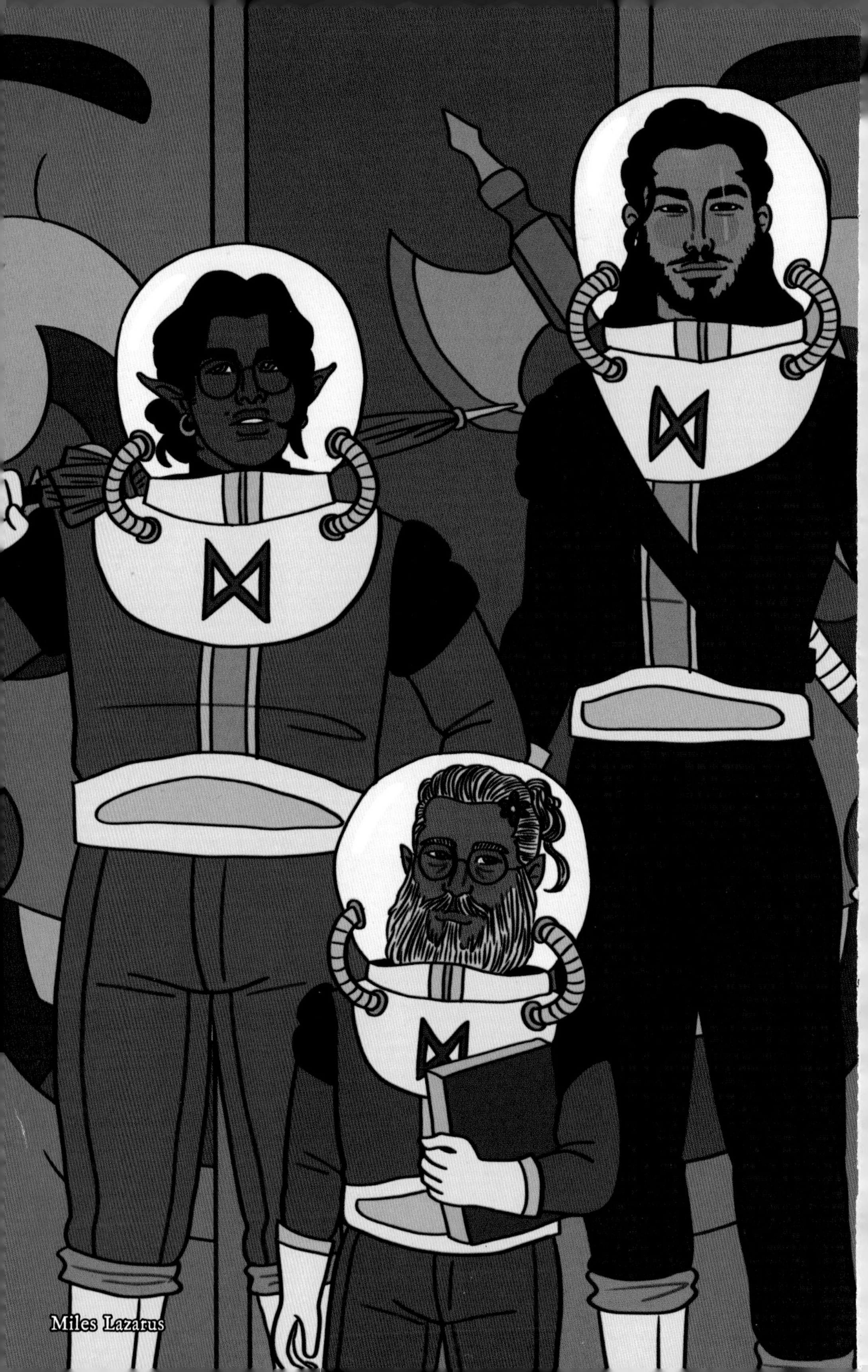
Miles Lazarus